Predicting Structured Data

ADVANCES IN NEURAL INFORMATION PROCESSING SYSTEMS

Published by The MIT Press
Neural Information Processing Series
Michael I. Jordan and Thomas Dietterich, editors

Predicting Structured Data

edited by
Gökhan Bakır
Thomas Hofmann
Bernhard Schölkopf
Alexander J. Smola
Ben Taskar
S.V. N. Vishwanathan

The MIT Press
Cambridge, Massachusetts
London, England

Printed and bound in the United States of America

Library of Congress Cataloging-in-Publication Data

Predicting Structured Data / edited by Gökhan Bakır ... [et al.].
        p.   cm.
Collected papers based on talks presented at two Neural Information Processing Systems workshops.
Includes bibliographical references and index.
ISBN 978-0-262-02617-8 (alk. paper)
1. Machine learning. 2. Computer algorithms. 3. Kernel functions.
4. Data structures (Computer science).
I. Bakır, Gökhan. II. Neural Information Processing Systems Foundation.

Q325.5.P74 2007
006.3'1 – dc22   2006047001

Contents

Series Foreword

The yearly Neural Information Processing Systems (NIPS) workshops bring together scientists with broadly varying backgrounds in statistics, mathematics, computer science, physics, electrical engineering, neuroscience, and cognitive science, unified by a common desire to develop novel computational, and statistical strategies for information processing, and to understand the mechanisms for information processing in the brain. As opposed to conferences, these workshops maintain a flexible format that both allows and encourages the presentation and discussion of work in progress, and thus serve as an incubator for the development of important new ideas in this rapidly evolving field.

The series editors, in consultation with workshop organizers and members of the NIPS foundation board, select specific workshop topics on the basis of scientific excellence, intellectual breadth, and technical impact. Collections of papers chosen and edited by the organizers of specific workshops are built around pedagogical introductory chapters, while research monographs provide comprehensive descriptions of workshop-related topics, to create a series of books that provides a timely, authoritative account of the latest developments in the exciting field of neural computation.

Michael I. Jordan and Thomas Dietterich

Preface

Machine learning develops intelligent computer systems that are able to generalize from previously seen examples. Traditionally, machine learning has mostly been involved with generalizing decisions from examples, as in the case of *classification*, or predicting a scalar number, as in the case of *regression*. Recent developments, however, have approached a wider domain where the prediction has to satisfy additional constraints, i.e., the output has *structure*.

Predicting structured data can be considered as one of the big challenges in machine learning, namely:

Learning functional dependencies between *arbitrary* input and output domains.

The current book aims at collecting and reviewing the state of the art in machine learning algorithms and machine learning theory which considers learning in this scenario. The material included in this collection covers applications as diverse as machine translation, document markup, computational biology, image restoration, and information extraction — to name just a few motivating examples.

The present book contains a number of papers based on talks presented at two Neural Information Processing Systems (NIPS) workshops on "Learning with Structured Outputs" and "Graphical Models and Kernels," along with several invited articles describing recent progress made since the workshops have taken place. We believe that it provides a timely overview of this exciting field, covering a wide range of promising methods. Structured prediction being a rather novel field, this overview cannot be comprehensive nor anticipate all future trends, but we hope it will provide a good starting point for entering this exciting area.

We would like to thank everybody who contributed toward the success of this book, in particular Karin Bierig and Bob Prior for their continuing support, assistance, and patience.

Gökhan Bakır, Thomas Hofmann, Bernhard Schölkopf,
Alexander J. Smola, Ben Taskar, S.V.N. Vishwanathan

Tübingen, Zürich, Canberra, Berkeley; September 2006

I   Introduction

1   Measuring Similarity with Kernels

1.1   Introduction

Over the last ten years, estimation and learning methods utilizing positive definite kernels have become rather popular, particularly in machine learning. Since these methods have a stronger mathematical slant than earlier machine learning methods (e.g., neural networks), there is also significant interest in the statistical and mathematical community for these methods. The present chapter aims to summarize the state of the art on a conceptual level. In doing so, we build on various sources (including Vapnik (1998); Burges (1998); Cristianini and Shawe-Taylor (2000); Herbrich (2002) and in particular Schölkopf and Smola (2002)), but we also add a fair amount of recent material which helps in unifying the exposition.

The main idea of all the described methods can be summarized in one paragraph. Traditionally, theory and algorithms of machine learning and statistics have been very well developed for the linear case. Real-world data analysis problems, on the other hand, often require nonlinear methods to detect the kind of dependences that allow successful prediction of properties of interest. By using a positive definite kernel, one can sometimes have the best of both worlds. The kernel corresponds to a dot product in a (usually high-dimensional) feature space. In this space, our estimation methods are linear, but as long as we can formulate everything in terms of kernel evaluations, we never explicitly have to work in the high-dimensional feature space.

1.2   Kernels

1.2.1   An Introductory Example

Suppose we are given empirical data

$$(x_1, y_1), \ldots, (x_n, y_n) \in \mathcal{X} \times \mathcal{Y}. \tag{1.1}$$

Here, the domain $\mathcal{X}$ is some nonempty set that the *inputs* x_i are taken from; the $y_i \in \mathcal{Y}$ are called *targets*. Here and below, $i, j = 1, \ldots, n$.

Note that we have not made any assumptions on the domain $\mathcal{X}$ other than it being a set. In order to study the problem of learning, we need additional structure. In

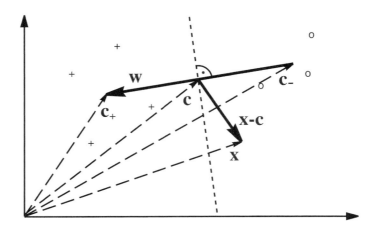

Figure 1.1 A simple geometric classification algorithm: given two classes of points (depicted by 'o' and '+'), compute their means c_+, c_- and assign a test input x to the one whose mean is closer. This can be done by looking at the dot product between $x - c$ (where $c = (c_+ + c_-)/2$) and $\mathbf{w} := c_+ - c_-$, which changes sign as the enclosed angle passes through $\pi/2$. Note that the corresponding decision boundary is a hyperplane (the dotted line) orthogonal to $\mathbf{w}$ (from Schölkopf and Smola (2002)).

learning, we want to be able to *generalize* to unseen data points. In the case of binary pattern recognition, given some new input $x \in \mathcal{X}$, we want to predict the corresponding $y \in \{\pm 1\}$. Loosely speaking, we want to choose y such that (x, y) is in some sense *similar* to the training examples. To this end, we need similarity measures in $\mathcal{X}$ and in $\{\pm 1\}$. The latter is easier, as two target values can only be identical or different.[1] For the former, we require a function

$$k : \mathcal{X} \times \mathcal{X} \to \mathbb{R}, \qquad (x, x') \mapsto k(x, x') \tag{1.2}$$

satisfying, for all $x, x' \in \mathcal{X}$,

$$k(x, x') = \langle \Phi(x), \Phi(x') \rangle , \tag{1.3}$$

where Φ maps into some dot product space $\mathcal{H}$, sometimes called the *feature space*. The similarity measure k is usually called a *kernel*, and Φ is called its *feature map*.

kernels and feature map

The advantage of using such a kernel as a similarity measure is that it allows us to construct algorithms in dot product spaces. For instance, consider the following simple classification algorithm, where $\mathcal{Y} = \{\pm 1\}$. The idea is to compute the means of the two classes in the feature space, $c_+ = \frac{1}{n_+} \sum_{\{i:y_i=+1\}} \Phi(x_i)$, and $c_- = \frac{1}{n_-} \sum_{\{i:y_i=-1\}} \Phi(x_i)$, where n_+ and n_- are the number of examples with

---

1. When $\mathcal{Y}$ has a more complex structure, things can get complicated — this is the main topic of the present book, but we completely disregard it in this introductory example.

positive and negative target values, respectively. We then assign a new point $\Phi(x)$ to the class whose mean is closer to it. This leads to

$$y = \text{sgn}(\langle \Phi(x), c_+ \rangle - \langle \Phi(x), c_- \rangle + b) \qquad (1.4)$$

with $b = \frac{1}{2}\left(\|c_-\|^2 - \|c_+\|^2\right)$. Substituting the expressions for $c_\pm$ yields

$$y = \text{sgn}\left(\frac{1}{n_+} \sum_{\{i:y_i=+1\}} \langle \Phi(x), \Phi(x_i) \rangle - \frac{1}{n_-} \sum_{\{i:y_i=-1\}} \langle \Phi(x), \Phi(x_i) \rangle + b\right). \qquad (1.5)$$

Rewritten in terms of k, this reads

$$y = \text{sgn}\left(\frac{1}{n_+} \sum_{\{i:y_i=+1\}} k(x, x_i) - \frac{1}{n_-} \sum_{\{i:y_i=-1\}} k(x, x_i) + b\right), \qquad (1.6)$$

where $b = \frac{1}{2}\left(\frac{1}{n_-^2} \sum_{\{(i,j):y_i=y_j=-1\}} k(x_i, x_j) - \frac{1}{n_+^2} \sum_{\{(i,j):y_i=y_j=+1\}} k(x_i, x_j)\right)$. This algorithm is illustrated in figure 1.1 for the case that $\mathcal{X}$ equals $\mathbb{R}^2$ and $\Phi(x) = x$.

Let us consider one well-known special case of this type of classifier. Assume that the class means have the same distance to the origin (hence $b = 0$), and that $k(., x)$ is a density for all $x' \in \mathcal{X}$. If the two classes are equally likely and were generated from two probability distributions that are correctly estimated by the Parzen windows estimators

$$p_+(x) := \frac{1}{n_+} \sum_{\{i:y_i=+1\}} k(x, x_i), \qquad p_-(x) := \frac{1}{n_-} \sum_{\{i:y_i=-1\}} k(x, x_i), \qquad (1.7)$$

then (1.6) is the Bayes decision rule.

The classifier (1.6) is quite close to the *support vector machine (SVM)* that we will discuss below. It is linear in the feature space (see (1.4)), while in the input domain, it is represented by a kernel expansion (1.6). In both cases, the decision boundary is a hyperplane in the feature space; however, the normal vectors are usually different.[2]

1.2.2 Positive Definite Kernels

We have above required that a kernel satisfy (1.3), i.e., correspond to a dot product in some dot product space. In the present section, we show that the class of kernels that can be written in the form (1.3) coincides with the class of positive definite kernels. This has far-reaching consequences. There are examples of positive definite

---

2. For (1.4), the normal vector is $w = c_+ - c_-$. As an aside, note that if we normalize the targets such that $\hat{y}_i = y_i/|\{j : y_j = y_i\}|$, in which case the $\hat{y}_i$ sum to zero, then $\|w\|^2 = \langle K, \hat{y}\hat{y}^\top \rangle_F$, where $\langle ., . \rangle_F$ is the Frobenius dot product. If the two classes have equal size, then up to a scaling factor involving $\|K\|_2$ and n, this equals the *kernel-target alignment* defined by Cristianini et al. (2002).

kernels which can be evaluated efficiently even though via (1.3) they correspond to dot products in infinite-dimensional dot product spaces. In such cases, substituting $k(x, x')$ for $\langle \Phi(x), \Phi(x') \rangle$, as we have done when going from (1.5) to (1.6), is crucial.

1.2.2.1 Prerequisites

Definition 1 (Gram Matrix) *Given a kernel k and inputs $x_1, \ldots, x_n \in \mathcal{X}$, the $n \times n$ matrix*

$$K := (k(x_i, x_j))_{ij} \tag{1.8}$$

is called the Gram matrix *(or* kernel matrix*) of k with respect to $x_1, \ldots, x_n$.*

Definition 2 (Positive Definite Matrix) *A real $n \times n$ symmetric matrix K_{ij} satisfying*

$$\sum_{i,j} c_i c_j K_{ij} \geq 0 \tag{1.9}$$

for all $c_i \in \mathbb{R}$ is called positive definite. *If for equality in (1.9) only occurs for $c_1 = \cdots = c_n = 0$, then we shall call the matrix* strictly positive definite.

Definition 3 (Positive Definite Kernel) *Let $\mathcal{X}$ be a nonempty set. A function $k : \mathcal{X} \times \mathcal{X} \to \mathbb{R}$ which for all $n \in \mathbb{N}, x_i \in \mathcal{X}$ gives rise to a positive definite Gram matrix is called a* positive definite kernel. *A function $k : \mathcal{X} \times \mathcal{X} \to \mathbb{R}$ which for all $n \in \mathbb{N}$ and distinct $x_i \in \mathcal{X}$ gives rise to a strictly positive definite Gram matrix is called a* strictly positive definite kernel.

Occasionally, we shall refer to positive definite kernels simply as a *kernels*. Note that for simplicity we have restricted ourselves to the case of real-valued kernels. However, with small changes, the below will also hold for the complex-valued case.

Since $\sum_{i,j} c_i c_j \langle \Phi(x_i), \Phi(x_j) \rangle = \left\langle \sum_i c_i \Phi(x_i), \sum_j c_j \Phi(x_j) \right\rangle \geq 0$, kernels of the form (1.3) are positive definite for any choice of Φ. In particular, if $\mathcal{X}$ is already a dot product space, we may choose Φ to be the identity. Kernels can thus be regarded as generalized dot products. While they are not generally bilinear, they share important properties with dot products, such as the Cauchy-Schwartz inequality:

Proposition 4 *If k is a positive definite kernel, and $x_1, x_2 \in \mathcal{X}$, then*

$$k(x_1, x_2)^2 \leq k(x_1, x_1) \cdot k(x_2, x_2). \tag{1.10}$$

Proof The 2×2 Gram matrix with entries $K_{ij} = k(x_i, x_j)$ is positive definite. Hence both its eigenvalues are nonnegative, and so is their product, K's determinant, i.e.,

$$0 \leq K_{11}K_{22} - K_{12}K_{21} = K_{11}K_{22} - K_{12}^2. \tag{1.11}$$

Substituting $k(x_i, x_j)$ for K_{ij}, we get the desired inequality.   ∎

1.2.2.2 Construction of the Reproducing Kernel Hilbert Space

We now define a map from $\mathcal{X}$ into the space of functions mapping $\mathcal{X}$ into $\mathbb{R}$, denoted as $\mathbb{R}^{\mathcal{X}}$, via

$$\Phi : \mathcal{X} \to \mathbb{R}^{\mathcal{X}}$$
$$x \mapsto k(.,x). \tag{1.12}$$

Here, $\Phi(x) = k(.,x)$ denotes the function that assigns the value $k(x',x)$ to $x' \in \mathcal{X}$.

We next construct a dot product space containing the images of the inputs under Φ. To this end, we first turn it into a vector space by forming linear combinations

$$f(.) = \sum_{i=1}^{n} \alpha_i k(.,x_i). \tag{1.13}$$

Here, $n \in \mathbb{N}$, $\alpha_i \in \mathbb{R}$ and $x_i \in \mathcal{X}$ are arbitrary.

Next, we define a dot product between f and another function $g(.) = \sum_{j=1}^{n'} \beta_j k(.,x'_j)$ (with $n' \in \mathbb{N}$, $\beta_j \in \mathbb{R}$ and $x'_j \in \mathcal{X}$) as

$$\langle f,g \rangle := \sum_{i=1}^{n} \sum_{j=1}^{n'} \alpha_i \beta_j k(x_i, x'_j). \tag{1.14}$$

To see that this is well-defined although it contains the expansion coefficients, note that $\langle f,g \rangle = \sum_{j=1}^{n'} \beta_j f(x'_j)$. The latter, however, does not depend on the particular expansion of f. Similarly, for g, note that $\langle f,g \rangle = \sum_{i=1}^{n} \alpha_i g(x_i)$. This also shows that $\langle \cdot, \cdot \rangle$ is bilinear. It is symmetric, as $\langle f,g \rangle = \langle g,f \rangle$. Moreover, it is positive definite, since positive definiteness of k implies that for any function f, written as (1.13), we have

$$\langle f,f \rangle = \sum_{i,j=1}^{n} \alpha_i \alpha_j k(x_i, x_j) \geq 0. \tag{1.15}$$

Next, note that given functions $f_1, \dots, f_p$, and coefficients $\gamma_1, \dots, \gamma_p \in \mathbb{R}$, we have

$$\sum_{i,j=1}^{p} \gamma_i \gamma_j \langle f_i, f_j \rangle = \left\langle \sum_{i=1}^{p} \gamma_i f_i, \sum_{j=1}^{p} \gamma_j f_j \right\rangle \geq 0. \tag{1.16}$$

Here, the left-hand equality follows from the bilinearity of $\langle \cdot, \cdot \rangle$, and the right-hand inequality from (1.15).

By (1.16), $\langle \cdot, \cdot \rangle$ is a positive definite kernel, defined on our vector space of functions. For the last step in proving that it even is a dot product, we note that by (1.14), for all functions (1.13),

$$\langle k(.,x), f \rangle = f(x), \tag{1.17}$$

and in particular

$$\langle k(.,x), k(.,x')\rangle = k(x,x'). \tag{1.18}$$

reproducing
kernel

By virtue of these properties, k is called a *reproducing kernel* (Aronszajn, 1950) .
Due to (1.17) and proposition 4, we have

$$|f(x)|^2 = |\langle k(.,x), f\rangle|^2 \le k(x,x) \cdot \langle f, f\rangle. \tag{1.19}$$

By this inequality, $\langle f, f\rangle = 0$ implies $f = 0$, which is the last property that was left
to prove in order to establish that $\langle .,.\rangle$ is a dot product.

Skipping some details, we add that one can complete the space of functions (1.13)
in the norm corresponding to the dot product, and thus get a Hilbert space H, called
a *reproducing kernel Hilbert space (RKHS)*.

reproducing
kernel Hilbert
space(RKHS)

One can define an RKHS as a Hilbert space $\mathcal{H}$ of functions on a set $\mathcal{X}$ with
the property that for all $x \in \mathcal{X}$ and $f \in \mathcal{H}$, the point evaluations $f \mapsto f(x)$ are
continuous linear functionals (in particular, all point values $f(x)$ are well-defined,
which already distinguishes RKHSs from many L_2 Hilbert spaces). From the point
evaluation functional, one can then construct the reproducing kernel using the Riesz
representation theorem. The Moore-Aronszajn theorem (Aronszajn, 1950) states
that for every positive definite kernel on $\mathcal{X} \times \mathcal{X}$, there exists a unique RKHS and
vice versa.

There is an analogue of the kernel trick for distances rather than dot products, i.e.,
dissimilarities rather than similarities. This leads to the larger class of *conditionally
positive definite kernels*. Those kernels are defined just like positive definite ones,
with the one difference being that their Gram matrices need to satisfy (1.9) only
subject to

$$\sum_{i=1}^{n} c_i = 0. \tag{1.20}$$

Interestingly, it turns out that many kernel algorithms, including SVMs and kernel
principal component analysis (PCA) (see section 1.3.2), can be applied also with
this larger class of kernels, due to their being translation invariant in feature space
(Schölkopf and Smola, 2002; Hein et al., 2005).

We conclude this section with a note on terminology. In the early years of kernel
machine learning research, it was not the notion of positive definite kernels that
was being used. Instead, researchers considered kernels satisfying the conditions of
Mercer's theorem (Mercer, 1909); see e.g. Vapnik (1998) and Cristianini and Shawe-
Taylor (2000). However, while all such kernels do satisfy (1.3), the converse is not
true. Since (1.3) is what we are interested in, positive definite kernels are thus the
right class of kernels to consider.

1.2.3   Constructing Kernels

In the following we demonstrate how to assemble new kernel functions from existing
ones using elementary operations preserving positive definiteness. The following
proposition will serve us as the main working horse:

Proposition 5 *Below, $k_1, k_2, \ldots$ are arbitrary positive definite kernels on $\mathfrak{X} \times \mathfrak{X}$,
where $\mathfrak{X}$ is a nonempty set.*
*(i) The set of positive definite kernels is a closed convex cone, i.e., (a) if $\alpha_1, \alpha_2 \geq 0$,
then $\alpha_1 k_1 + \alpha_2 k_2$ is positive definite.*
(ii) The pointwise product $k_1 k_2$ is positive definite.
*(iii) Assume that for $i = 1, 2$, k_i is a positive definite kernel on $\mathfrak{X}_i \times \mathfrak{X}_i$, where $\mathfrak{X}_i$
is a nonempty set. Then the tensor product $k_1 \otimes k_2$ and the direct sum $k_1 \oplus k_2$ are
positive definite kernels on $(\mathfrak{X}_1 \times \mathfrak{X}_2) \times (\mathfrak{X}_1 \times \mathfrak{X}_2)$.*
(iv) If $k(x, x') := \lim_{n \to \infty} k_n(x, x')$ exists for all x, x', then k is positive definite.
*(v) The function $k(x, x') := f(x)f(x')$ is a valid positive definite kernel for any
function f.*

Let us use this proposition now to construct new kernel functions.

1.2.3.1   Polynomial Kernels

From proposition 5 it is clear that homogeneous polynomial kernels $k(x, x') = \langle x, x' \rangle^p$ are positive definite for $p \in \mathbb{N}$ and $x, x' \in \mathbb{R}^d$. By direct calculation we can
derive the corresponding feature map (Poggio, 1975):

$$\langle x, x' \rangle^p = \left\langle \sum_{j=1}^{d} [x]_j, [x']_j \right\rangle^p = \sum_{j \in [d]^p} [x]_{j_1} \cdots \cdot [x]_{j_p} \cdot [x']_{j_1} \cdots \cdot [x']_{j_p} = \langle C_p(x), C_p(x') \rangle,$$

$$(1.21)$$

where C_p maps $x \in \mathbb{R}^d$ to the vector $C_p(x)$ whose entries are all possible pth-degree
ordered products of the entries of x. The polynomial kernel of degree p thus
computes a dot product in the space spanned by all monomials of degree p in
the input coordinates. Other useful kernels include the inhomogeneous polynomial,

$$k(x, x') = (\langle x, x' \rangle + c)^p \quad \text{where } p \in \mathbb{N} \text{ and } c \geq 0, \qquad (1.22)$$

which computes all monomials up to degree p.

1.2.3.2   Gaussian Kernel

Using the infinite Taylor expansion of the exponential function $e^z = \sum_{i=1}^{\infty} \frac{1}{i!} z^i$, it
follows from propostion 5(iv) that

$$e^{\gamma \langle x, x' \rangle}$$

is a kernel function for any $x, x' \in \mathcal{X}$ and $\gamma \in \mathbb{R}$. Therefore, it follows immediately that the widely used Gaussian function $e^{-\gamma||x-x'||^2}$ with $\gamma > 0$ is a valid kernel function. This can be seen as rewriting the Gaussian function as

$$e^{-\gamma||x-x'||^2} = e^{-\gamma\langle x,x\rangle}e^{2\gamma\langle x,x'\rangle}e^{-\gamma\langle x',x'\rangle},$$

and using proposition 5(ii).

We see that the Gaussian kernel corresponds to a mapping into $\mathcal{C}^\infty$, i.e. the space of continuous functions. However, the feature map is *normalized*, i.e. $||\Phi(x)||^2 = k(x,x) = 1$ for any $x \in \mathcal{X}$. Moreover, as $k(x,x') > 0$ for all $x, x' \in \mathcal{X}$, all mapped points lie inside the same orthant in feature space.

1.2.3.3   Spline Kernels

It is possible to obtain spline functions as a result of kernel expansions (Smola, 1996; Vapnik et al., 1997) simply by noting that convolution of an even number of indicator functions yields a positive kernel function. Denote by I_X the indicator (or characteristic) function on the set X, and denote by $\otimes$ the convolution operation, $(f \otimes g)(x) := \int_{\mathbb{R}^d} f(x')g(x'-x)dx'$. Then the B-spline kernels are given by

$$k(x,x') = B_{2p+1}(x-x') \text{ where } p \in \mathbb{N} \text{ with } B_{i+1} := B_i \otimes B_0. \tag{1.23}$$

Here B_0 is the characteristic function on the unit ball[3] in $\mathbb{R}^d$. From the definition of (1.23) it is obvious that for odd m we may write B_m as the inner product between functions $B_{m/2}$. Moreover, note that for even m, B_m is not a kernel.

1.2.4   The Representer Theorem

From kernels, we now move to functions that can be expressed in terms of kernel expansions. The representer theorem (Kimeldorf and Wahba, 1971; Cox and O'Sullivan, 1990) shows that solutions of a large class of optimization problems can be expressed as kernel expansions over the sample points. We present a slightly more general version of the theorem with a simple proof (Schölkopf et al., 2001). As above, $\mathcal{H}$ is the RKHS associated with the kernel k.

Theorem 6 (Representer Theorem) *Denote by* $\Omega : [0,\infty) \to \mathbb{R}$ *a strictly monotonic increasing function, by* $\mathcal{X}$ *a set, and by* $c : (\mathcal{X} \times \mathbb{R}^2)^n \to \mathbb{R} \cup \{\infty\}$ *an arbitrary loss function. Then each minimizer* $f \in \mathcal{H}$ *of the regularized risk functional*

$$c\left((x_1,y_1,f(x_1)),\ldots,(x_n,y_n,f(x_n))\right) + \Omega\left(||f||^2_{\mathcal{H}}\right) \tag{1.24}$$

---

3. Note that in $\mathbb{R}$ one typically uses $\xi_{\left[-\frac{1}{2},\frac{1}{2}\right]}$.

admits a representation of the form

$$f(x) = \sum_{i=1}^{n} \alpha_i k(x_i, x). \tag{1.25}$$

Proof We decompose any $f \in \mathcal{H}$ into a part contained in the span of the kernel functions $k(x_1, \cdot), \cdots, k(x_n, \cdot)$, and one in the orthogonal complement:

$$f(x) = f_{\|}(x) + f_{\perp}(x) = \sum_{i=1}^{n} \alpha_i k(x_i, x) + f_{\perp}(x). \tag{1.26}$$

Here $\alpha_i \in \mathbb{R}$ and $f_{\perp} \in \mathcal{H}$ with $\langle f_{\perp}, k(x_i, \cdot) \rangle_{\mathcal{H}} = 0$ for all $i \in [n] := \{1, \ldots, n\}$. By (1.17) we may write $f(x_j)$ (for all $j \in [n]$) as

$$f(x_j) = \langle f(\cdot), k(x_j, .) \rangle = \sum_{i=1}^{n} \alpha_i k(x_i, x_j) + \langle f_{\perp}(\cdot), k(x_j, .) \rangle_{\mathcal{H}} = \sum_{i=1}^{n} \alpha_i k(x_i, x_j). \tag{1.27}$$

Second, for all $f_{\perp}$,

$$\Omega(\|f\|_{\mathcal{H}}^2) = \Omega \left(\left\| \sum_{i}^{n} \alpha_i k(x_i, \cdot) \right\|_{\mathcal{H}}^2 + \|f_{\perp}\|_{\mathcal{H}}^2 \right) \geq \Omega \left(\left\| \sum_{i}^{n} \alpha_i k(x_i, \cdot) \right\|_{\mathcal{H}}^2 \right). \tag{1.28}$$

Thus for any fixed $\alpha_i \in \mathbb{R}$ the risk functional (1.24) is minimized for $f_{\perp} = 0$. Since this also has to hold for the solution, the theorem holds. ∎

Monotonicity of Ω does not prevent the regularized risk functional (1.24) from having multiple local minima. To ensure a global minimum, we would need to require convexity. If we discard the strictness of the monotonicity, then it no longer follows that each minimizer of the regularized risk admits an expansion (1.25); it still follows, however, that there is always another solution that is as good, and that *does* admit the expansion.

The significance of the representer theorem is that although we might be trying to solve an optimization problem in an infinite-dimensional space $\mathcal{H}$, containing linear combinations of kernels centered on *arbitrary* points of $\mathcal{X}$, it states that the solution lies in the span of n particular kernels — those centered on the training points. We will encounter (1.25) again further below, where it is called the *support vector expansion*. For suitable choices of loss functions, many of the α_i often equal zero.

1.3 Operating in Reproducing Kernel Hilbert Spaces

We have seen that kernels correspond to an inner product in some possibly high-dimensional feature space. Since direct computation in these spaces is computationally infeasible one might argue that sometimes the application of kernels is rather limited. However, in this section we demonstrate for some cases that direct operation in feature space is possible. Subsequently we introduce kernel PCA which can extract features corresponding to principal components in this high-dimensional feature space.

1.3.1   Direct Operations in RKHS

1.3.1.1   *Translation*

Consider the modified feature map $\tilde{\Phi}(x) = \Phi(x) + \Gamma$, with $\Gamma \in \mathcal{H}$. This feature map corresponds to a translation in feature space. The dot product $\left\langle \tilde{\Phi}(x), \tilde{\Phi}(x') \right\rangle$ yields for this case the terms

$$\langle \Phi(x), \Phi(x') \rangle + \langle \Phi(x), \Gamma \rangle + \langle \Gamma, \Phi(x') \rangle + \langle \Gamma, \Gamma \rangle,$$

which cannot always be evaluated. However, let us restrict the translation Γ to be in the span of the functions $\Phi(x_1), \cdots, \Phi(x_n) \in \mathcal{H}$ with $\{x_1, \ldots, x_n\} \in \mathcal{X}^n$. Thus if $\Gamma = \sum_{i=1}^{n} \alpha_i \Phi(x_i), \alpha_i \in \mathbb{R}$, then the dot product between translated feature maps can be evaluated in terms of the kernel functions solely. Thus we obtain for our modified feature map

$$\left\langle \tilde{\Phi}(x), \tilde{\Phi}(x') \right\rangle = k(x, x') + \sum_{i=1}^{n} \alpha_i k(x_i, x) + \sum_{i=1}^{n} \alpha_i k(x_i, x') + \sum_{i,j=1}^{n} \alpha_i \alpha_j k(x_i, x_j).$$

$$(1.29)$$

1.3.1.2   *Centering*

As a concrete application for a translation operation consider the case that we would like to *center* a set of points in the RKHS. Thus we would like to have a feature map $\tilde{\Phi}$ such that $\frac{1}{n} \sum_{i=1}^{n} \tilde{\Phi}(x_i) = 0$. Using $\tilde{\Phi}(x) = \Phi(x) + \Gamma$ with $\Gamma = -\sum_{i=1}^{n} \frac{1}{n} \Phi(x_i)$ this can be obtained immediately utilizing (1.29). The kernel matrix $\tilde{K}$ of the centered feature map $\tilde{\Phi}$ can then be expressed directly in terms of matrix operations by

$$\tilde{K}_{ij} = (K - 1_m K - K 1_m + 1_m K 1_m)_{ij},$$

where $1_m \in \mathbb{R}^{m \times m}$ is the constant matrix with all entries equal to $1/m$, and K is the kernel matrix evaluated using Φ.

1.3.1.3   *Computing Distances*

An essential tool for structured prediction is the problem of computing distances between two objects. For example, to assess the quality of a prediction we would like to measure the distance between predicted object and true object. Since kernel functions can be interpreted as dot products (see (1.3)) they provide an elegant way to measure distances between arbitrary objects. Consider two objects $x_1, x_2 \in \mathcal{X}$, such as two-word sequences or two automata. Assume we have a kernel function k on such objects; we can use their distance in the RKHS, i.e.,

$$d(x_1, x_2) = ||\Phi(x_1) - \Phi(x_2)||_{\mathcal{H}} = \sqrt{k(x_1, x_1) + k(x_2, x_2) - 2k(x_1, x_2)}.$$

Here, we have utilized the fact that the dot product in $\mathcal{H}$ can be evaluated by kernel functions and thus define the distance between the objects to be the distance between the images of the feature map Φ.

1.3.1.4 Subspace Projections

Another elementary operation which can be performed in a Hilbert space is the one-dimensional orthogonal *projection*. Given two points Ψ, Γ in the RKHS $\mathcal{H}$ we project the point Ψ to the subspace spanned by the point Γ, obtaining

$$\Psi' = \frac{\langle \Gamma, \Psi \rangle}{||\Gamma||^2} \Gamma. \tag{1.30}$$

Considering the case that Ψ and Γ are given by kernel expansions, we see immediately that any dot product with the projected point Ψ' can be expressed with kernel functions only. Using such a projection operation in RKHS, it is straightforward to define a *deflation* procedure:

$$\Psi' = \Psi - \frac{\langle \Gamma, \Psi \rangle}{||\Gamma||^2} \Gamma. \tag{1.31}$$

Using projection and deflation operations, one can perform e.g. the Gram-Schmidt orthogonalization procedure for the construction of orthogonal bases. This was used for example in information retrieval (Cristianini et al., 2001) and computer vision (Wolf and Shashua, 2003). An alternative application of deflation and subspace projection in RKHS was introduced by Rosipal and Trejo (2002) in the context of *subspace regression*.

1.3.2 Kernel Principal Component Analysis

A standard method for feature extraction is the method of principal component analysis (PCA), which aims to identify principal axes in the input. The principal axes are recovered as the eigenvectors of the empirical estimate of the covariance matrix $C_{emp} = \mathbb{E}_{emp}\left[(\mathbf{x} - \mathbb{E}_{emp}[\mathbf{x}])(\mathbf{x} - \mathbb{E}_{emp}[\mathbf{x}])^{\top}\right]$. In contrast to PCA, kernel PCA introduced by Schölkopf et al. (1998) tries to identify principal components of variables which are nonlinearly related to input variables, i.e. principal axis in some feature space $\mathcal{H}$. To this end, given some training set $(\mathbf{x}_1, \ldots, \mathbf{x}_n)$ of size n, covariance in feature space one considers the eigenvectors $\mathbf{v} \in \mathcal{H}$ of the empirical covariance operator in feature space:

$$\mathbf{C}_{emp} = \mathbb{E}_{emp}\left[(\Phi(\mathbf{x}) - \mathbb{E}_{emp}[\Phi(\mathbf{x})])(\Phi(\mathbf{x}) - \mathbb{E}_{emp}[\Phi(\mathbf{x})])^{\top}\right].$$

Although this operator and thus its eigenvectors $\mathbf{v}$ cannot be calculated directly, they can be retrieved in terms of kernel evaluations only. To see this, note that even in the case of a high-dimensional feature space $\mathcal{H}$, a finite training set $(\mathbf{x}_1, \ldots, \mathbf{x}_n)$ of size n when mapped to this feature space spans a subspace $E \subset \mathcal{H}$ whose dimension is at most n. Thus, there are at most n principal axes $(\mathbf{v}_1, \ldots, \mathbf{v}_n) \in E^n$ with nonzero eigenvalues. It can be shown that these principal axes can be expressed as linear combinations of the training points $\mathbf{v}_j = \sum_{i=1}^{N} \alpha_i^j \Phi(\mathbf{x}_i), 1 \leq j \leq n$, where the coefficients $\alpha^j \in \mathbb{R}^n$ are obtained as eigenvectors of the kernel matrix evaluated on the training set. If one retains all principal components, kernel PCA can be considered as a basis transform in E, leaving the dot product of training points invariant. To see this, let $(\mathbf{v}_1, \ldots, \mathbf{v}_n) \in E^n$ be the principal axes of $\{\Phi(\mathbf{x}_1), \ldots, \Phi(\mathbf{x}_n)\}$. The kernel PCA map $\phi_n : \mathcal{X} \to \mathbb{R}^n$ is defined coordinatewise as

$$[\phi_n]_p(\mathbf{x}) = \Phi(\mathbf{x}) \cdot \mathbf{v}_p, \quad 1 \leq p \leq n.$$

Note that by definition, for all i and j, $\Phi(\mathbf{x}_i)$ and $\Phi(\mathbf{x}_j)$ lie in E and thus

$$K(\mathbf{x}_i, \mathbf{x}_j) = \Phi(\mathbf{x}_i) \cdot \Phi(\mathbf{x}_j) = \phi_n(\mathbf{x}_i) \cdot \phi_n(\mathbf{x}_j). \tag{1.32}$$

The kernel PCA map is especially useful if one has structured data and one wants to use an algorithm which is not readily expressed in dot products.

1.4   Kernels for Structured Data

We have seen several instances of positive definite kernels, and now intend to describe some kernel functions which are particularly well suited to operate on data domains other than real vector spaces. We start with the simplest data domain: sets.

1.4.1   Set Kernels

Assume that we have given a finite alphabet Σ, i.e. a collection of symbols which we call characters. Furthermore let us denote by $\mathcal{P}(\Sigma)$ the power set of Σ. Then, we define a *set kernel* to be any valid kernel function k which takes two sets $A \in \mathcal{P}(\Sigma)$ and $B \in \mathcal{P}(\Sigma)$ as arguments. As a concrete example, consider the following kernel:

$$k(A, B) = \sum_{x \in A, \ y \in B} 1_{x=y},$$

kernels for text   where $1_{x=y}$ denotes a comparison. This kernel measures the size of the intersection of two sets and is widely used e.g. in text classification where it is referred to as the *sparse vector kernel*. Considering a text document as a set of words, the sparse vector kernel measures the similarity of text document via the number of common words. Such a kernel was used e.g. in Joachims (1998) for text categorization using SVMs.

The feature map corresponding to the set kernel can be interpreted as a *representation by its parts*. Each singleton $x_i \in \Sigma, 1 \le i \le |\Sigma|$, i.e. all sets of cardinality 1, is mapped to the vertex e_i of the unit simplex in $\mathbb{R}^{|\Sigma|}$. Each set A with $|A| > 1$ is then the average of the vertex coordinates, i.e.,

$$\Phi(A) = \sum_{x \in A} \Phi(x) = \sum_{x_i \in \Sigma, x \in A} 1_{x=x_i} e_i.$$

Set kernels are in general very efficient to evaluate as long as the alphabet is finite since the feature map yields a sparse vector in $\mathbb{R}^{|\Sigma|}$. For example, in text classification each dimension corresponds to a specific word, and a component is set to a constant whenever the related word occurs in the text. This is also known as the *bag-of-words* representation. Using an efficient sparse representation, the dot product between two such vectors can be computed quickly.

1.4.2 Rational Kernels

One of the shortcomings of set kernels in applications such as natural language applications is that any relation among the set elements such as, e.g., word order in a document, is completely ignored. However, in many applications one considers data with a more sequential nature such as word sequences in text classification, temporal utterance order in speech recognition, or chains of amino acids in protein analysis. In these cases the data are of sequential nature and can consist of variable-length sequences over some basic alphabet Σ. In the following we review kernels which were introduced to deal with such data types and which belong to the general class of *rational* kernels.

Rational kernels are in principle similarity measures over *sets* of sequences. Since sets of sequences can be compactly represented by automata, rational kernels can be considered as kernels for weighted automata. For a discussion on automata theory see e.g. Hopcroft et al. (2000). In particular, since sequences can be considered as very simple automata, rational kernels automatically implement kernels for sequences. At the heart of a rational kernel is the concept of *weighted transducers* which can be considered as a representation of a binary relation between sequences; see e.g. Mohri et al. (2002) and Cortes et al. (2004).

kernels for
automata

Definition 7 (Weighted Transducer) *Given a semiring* $K = (\mathbb{K}, \oplus, \otimes)$, *a weighted finite-state transducer (WFST)* T *over* $\mathbb{K}$ *is given by an* input *alphabet* Σ, *an output alphabet* Ω, *a finite set of* states S, *a finite set of* transitions $E \subseteq S \times (\Sigma \cup \{\epsilon\}) \times (\Omega \cup \{\epsilon\}) \times \mathbb{K} \times S$, *a set of* initial *states* $S_0 \in S$, *a set of* final *states* $S_\infty \subseteq S$, *and a weight function* $w : S \to \mathbb{K}$.

In our further discussion we restrict the output alphabet Ω to be equal to the input alphabet, i.e. $\Omega = \Sigma$. We call a sequence of transitions $h = e_1, \dots, e_n \subset E$ a *path*, where the ith transition is denoted by $\pi_i(h)$. By $\pi_0(h)$ and $\pi_\infty(h)$ we denote starting and termination states of a path h respectively. Given two sequences $x, y \in \Sigma^*$, we call a path h *successful* if it starts at an initial state, i.e. $\pi_0(h) \in S_0$, terminates in a final state, i.e. $\pi_\infty(h) \in S_\infty$, and concatenating the input and output symbols associated with the traversed transitions equals the sequences x and y. There might be more than a single successful path and we will denote the set of all successful paths depending on the pair (x, y) by $\Pi(x, y)$. Furthermore, for each transition $\pi_i[h] \in E$ we denote by $w(\pi_i[h]) \in \mathbb{K}$ the weight associated with the particular transition $\pi_i[h]$. A transducer is called *regulated* if the weight of any sequence input-output pair $(x, y) \in \Sigma^* \times \Sigma^*$ calculated by

$$[\![T]\!](x, y) := \bigoplus_{h \in \Pi(x, y)} w(\pi_0[h]) \otimes \bigotimes_{i=1}^{|h|} w(\pi_i[h]) \otimes w(\pi_\infty[h]) \tag{1.33}$$

is well-defined and in $\mathbb{K}$.

The interpretation of the weights $w(h)$ and in particular $[\![T]\!](x, y)$ depends on how they are manipulated algebraically and on the underlying semiring $\mathbb{K}$. As a concrete example for the representation of binary relations, let us consider the positive semiring $(\mathbb{K}, \oplus, \otimes, \mathbf{0}, \mathbf{1}) = (\mathbb{R}_+, +, \times, 0, 1)$ which is also called the probability or real semiring. A binary relation between two sequences $x, y \in \Sigma^*$ is e.g. the conditional probability $[\![T]\!](x, y) = P(y|x)$. Let x_i denote the ith element of the sequence x. We can calculate the conditional probability as

$$P(y|x) = \sum_{h \in \Pi(x, y)} \prod_{i=0} P(y_i | \pi_i[h], x_i) \times P(y_\infty | \pi_\infty(h), x_\infty),$$

where the sum is over all successful paths h and $w(\pi_i[h])) := P(y_i | \pi_i(h), x_i)$ denotes the probability of performing the transition $\pi_i(h)$ and observing (x_i, y_i) as input and output symbols. However, reconsidering the example with the *tropical* semiring $(\mathbb{K}, \oplus, \otimes, \mathbf{0}, \mathbf{1}) = (R \cup \{\infty, -\infty\}, \min, +, +\infty, 0)$ we obtain

$$[\![T]\!](x, y) = \max_{h \in \Pi(x, y)} \sum_{i=0} w(\pi_i[h]) + w(\pi_\infty[h]),$$

which is also known as the Viterbi approximation if the weights are negative log-probabilities, i.e. $w(\pi_\infty[h]) = -\log P(y_i | \pi_i[h], x_i)$. It is also possible to perform algebraic operations on transducers directly. Let T_1, T_2 be two weighted transducers, then a fundamental operation is *composition*.

Definition 8 (Composition) *Given two transducers* $T_1 = \{\Sigma, \Omega, S^1, E^1, S_0^1, S_\infty^1, w^1\}$ *and* $T_2 = \{\Omega, \Delta, S^2, E^2, S_0^2, S_\infty^2, w^2\}$, *the composition* $T_1 \circ T_2$ *is defined as transducer* $R = \{\Sigma, \Delta, S, E, S_0, S_\infty, w\}$ *such that*

$$S = S^1 \times S^2, \quad S_0 = S_0^1 \times S_0^2, \quad S_\infty = S_\infty^1 \times S_\infty^2$$

and each transition $e \in E$ *satisfies*

$$\forall e : (p, p') \stackrel{a:c/w}{\rightarrow} (q, q') \quad \Rightarrow \quad \exists \{p \stackrel{a:b/w_1}{\rightarrow} q, \ p' \stackrel{b:c/w_2}{\rightarrow} q'\},$$

with $w = w_1 \otimes w_2$.

For example, if the transducer T_1 models the conditional probabilities of a label given a feature observation $P(y|\phi(x))$ and another T_2 transducer models the conditional probabilities of a feature given an actual input $P(\phi(x)|x)$, then the transducer obtained by a composition $R = T_1 \circ T_2$ represents $P(y|x)$. In this sense, a composition can be interpreted as a matrix operation for transducers which is apparent if one considers the weights of the composed transducer:

$$[\![T_1 \circ T_2]\!](x, y) = \sum_{z \in \Omega} [\![T_1]\!](x, z) [\![T_2]\!](z, y).$$

Finally, let us introduce the *inverse* transducer T^{-1} that is obtained by swapping all input and output symbols on every transition of a transducer T. We are now ready to introduce the concept of rational kernels.

Definition 9 (Rational Kernel) *A kernel k over the alphabet Σ^* is called* rational *if it can be expressed as weight computation over a transducer T, i.e. $k(x, x') = \Psi([\![T]\!](x, x'))$ for some function $\Psi : \mathbb{K} \to \mathbb{R}$. The kernel is said to be defined by the pair (T, Ψ).*

kernel evaluation by transducers

Unfortunately, not any transducer gives rise to a positive definite kernel. However, from proposition 5(v) and from the definition it follows directly that any transducer $S := T \circ T^{-1}$ is a valid kernel since

$$k(x, y) = \sum_z [\![T]\!](x, z) [\![T]\!](x', z) = [\![S]\!](x, x').$$

The strength of rational kernels is their compact representation by means of transducers. This allows an easy and modular design of novel application-specific similarity measures for sequences. Let us give an example for a rational kernel.

1.4.2.1 *n-gram Kernels*

An n-gram is a block of n adjacent characters from an alphabet Σ. Hence, the number of distinct n-grams in a text is less than or equal to $|\Sigma|^n$. This shows that the space of all possible n-grams can be very high even for moderate values of n. The basic idea behind the *n-gram kernel* is to compare sequences by means of the subsequences they contain:

$$k(x, x') = \sum_{s \in \Sigma^n} \#(s \in x) \#(s \in x'), \tag{1.34}$$

where $\#(s \in x)$ denotes the number of occurrences of s in x. In this sense, the more subsequences two sequences share, the more similar they are. Vishwanathan and Smola (2004) proved that this class of kernels can be computed in $O(|x| + |x'|)$ time and memory by means of a special suited data structure allowing one to find a compact representation of all subsequences of x in only $O(|x|)$ time and space.

Furthermore, the authors show that the function $f(x) = \langle w, \Phi(x) \rangle$ can be computed in $O(|x|)$ time if preprocessing linear in the size of the expansion w is carried out. Cortes et al. (2004) showed that this kernel can be implemented by a transducer kernel by explicitly constructing a transducer that counts the number of occurrences of n symbol blocks; see e.g figure 1.2. One then can rewrite (1.34) as

$$k(x, x') = [\![T \circ T^{-1}]\!](x, x').\tag{1.35}$$

In the same manner, one can design transducers that can compute similarities incorporating various costs as, for example, for gaps and mismatches; see Cortes et al. (2004).

1.4.3 Convolution Kernels

One of the first instances of kernel functions on structured data was *convolutional kernels* introduced by Haussler (1999). The key idea is that one may take a structured object and split it up into parts. Suppose that the object $x \in \mathcal{X}$ consists of substructures $x_p \in \mathcal{X}_p$ where $1 \leq p \leq r$ and r denotes the number of overall substructures. Given then the set $\mathcal{P}(\mathcal{X})$ of all possible substructures $\bigotimes_{i=1}^{r} \mathcal{X}_i$, one can define a *relation R* between a subset of $\mathcal{P}$ and the composite object x. As an example consider the relation "part-of" between subsequences and sequences. If there are only a finite number of subsets, the relation R is called finite. Given a finite relation R, let $R^{-1}(x)$ define the set of all possible decompositions of x into its substructures: $R^{-1}(x) = \{ z \in \mathcal{P}(\mathcal{X}) : R(z, x) \}$. In this case, Haussler (1999) showed that the so-called R-convolution given as

representation by
parts

$$k(x, y) = \sum_{x' \in R^{-1}(x)} \sum_{y' \in R^{-1}(y)} \prod_{i=1}^{r} k_i(x'_i, y'_i)\tag{1.36}$$

is a valid kernel with k_i being a positive definite kernel on $\mathcal{X}_i$. The idea of decomposing a structured object into parts can be applied recursively so that one only requires to construct kernels k_i over the "atomic" parts $\mathcal{X}_i$.

Convolution kernels are very general and were successfully applied in the context of natural language processing (Collins and Duffy, 2002; Lodhi et al., 2000). However, in general the definition of R and in particular R^{-1} for a specific problem is quite difficult.

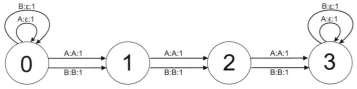

Figure 1.2 A transducer that can be used for calculation of 3-grams for a binary alphabet.

1.4.4   Kernels Based on Local Information

Sometimes it is easier to describe the local neighborhood than to construct a kernel for the overall data structure. Such a neighborhood of a data item might be defined by any item that differs only by the presence or absence of a single property. For example, when considering English words, neighbors of a word can be defined as any other word that would be obtained by misspelling. Given a set of data items, all information about neighbor relations can be represented by e.g. a *neighbor graph*. A vertex in such a neighbor graph would correspond to a data item and two vertices are connected whenever they satisfy some neighbor rule. For example, in the case of English words, a neighbor rule could be that two words are neighbors whenever their edit distance is smaller than some apriori defined threshold. Kondor and Lafferty (2002) utilize such neighbor graphs to construct global similarity measures by using a *diffusion process* analogy. To this end, the authors define a diffusion process by using the so-called *graph Laplacian*, L being a square matrix and where each entry encodes information on how to propagate the information from vertex to vertex. In particular, if A denotes the binary adjacency matrix of the neighbor graph, the graph Laplacian is given by $L = A - D$, where D is a diagonal matrix and each diagonal D_{ii} is the vertex degree of the ith data item. The resulting kernel matrix K is then obtained as the matrix exponential of βL with $\beta < 1$ being a propagation parameter:

similarities due to a diffusion process

$$K = e^{-\beta L} := \lim_{n \to \infty} \left(\mathbf{1} - \frac{\beta}{n} L \right)^n .$$

Such diffusion kernels were successfully applied to such diverse applications as text-categorization, as e.g. in Kandola et al. (2002); gene-function prediction by Vert and Kanehisa (2002); and semisupervised learning, as e.g. in Zhou et al. (2004).

Even if it is possible to define a kernel function for the whole instance space, sometimes it might be advantageous to take into account information from local structure of the data. Recall the Gaussian kernel and polynomial kernels. When applied to an image, it makes no difference whether one uses as x the image or a version of x where all locations of the pixels have been permuted. This indicates that the function space on $\mathcal{X}$ induced by k does not take advantage of the *locality* properties of the data. By taking advantage of the local structure, estimates can be improved. On biological sequences one may assign more weight to the entries of the sequence close to the location where estimates should occur, as was performed e.g. by Zien et al. (2000). In other words, one replaces $\langle x, x' \rangle$ by $x^\top \Omega x$, where $\Omega \succeq 0$ is a diagonal matrix with largest terms at the location which needs to be classified.

In contrast, for images, local interactions between image patches need to be considered. One way is to use the *pyramidal* kernel introduced in Schölkopf (1997) and DeCoste and Schölkopf (2002), which was inspired by the pyramidal cells of the brain: It takes inner products between corresponding image patches, then raises the latter to some power p_1, and finally raises their sum to another power p_2. This means that mainly short-range interactions are considered and that the long-range interactions are taken with respect to short-range groups.

1.4.5   Tree and Graph Kernels

We now discuss similarity measures on more structured objects such as trees and graphs.

1.4.5.1   *Kernels on Trees*

For trees Collins and Duffy (2002) propose a decomposition method which maps a tree x into its set of subtrees. The kernel between two trees x, x' is then computed by taking a weighted sum of all terms between both trees and is based on the convolutional kernel (see section 1.4.3). In particular, Collins and Duffy (2002) show an $O(|x| \cdot |x'|)$ algorithm to compute this expression, where $|x|$ is the number of nodes of the tree. When restricting the sum to all proper rooted subtrees it is possible to reduce the time of computation to $O(|x| + |x'|)$ time by means of a tree to sequence conversion (Vishwanathan and Smola, 2004).

1.4.5.2   *Kernels on Graphs*

A *labeled graph* G is described by a finite set of vertices V, a finite set of edges E, two sets of symbols which we denote by Σ and Ω, and two functions $\mathsf{v} : V \to \Sigma$ and $\mathsf{e} : E \to \Omega$ which assign each vertex and edge a label from the sets Σ, Ω respectively. For directed graphs, the set of edges is a subset of the Cartesian product of the ordered set of vertices with itself, i.e. $E \subseteq V \times V$ such that $(v_i, v_j) \in E$ if and only if vertex v_i is connected to vertex v_j. One might hope that a kernel for a labeled graph can be similarly constructed using some decomposition approach similar to the case of trees. Unfortunately, due to the existence of cycles, graphs cannot be as easily serialized, which prohibits, for example, the use of transducer kernels for graph comparison. A workaround is to artificially construct *walks*, i.e. eventually repetitive sequences of vertex and edge labels. Let us denote by $W(G)$ the set of all possible walks in a graph G of arbitrary length. Then, using an appropriate sequence kernel k_h, a valid kernel for two graphs G_1, G_2 would take the form

graph kernels based on paths

$$k_G(G_1, G_2) = \sum_{h \in W(G_1)} \sum_{h' \in W(G_2)} k_h(h, h'). \tag{1.37}$$

Unfortunately, this kernel can only be evaluated if the graph is acyclic since otherwise the sets $P(G_1), P(G_2)$ are not finite. However, one can restrict the set of all walks $W(G)$ to the set of all *paths* $P(G) \subset W(G)$, i.e. nonrepetitive sequences of vertex and edge labels. Borgwardt and Kriegel (2005) show that computation of this so-called *all-path kernel* is NP-complete. As an alternative, for graphs where each edge is assigned to a cost instead of a general label they propose to further restrict the set of paths. They propose to choose the subset of paths which appear in

path kernels are intractable

shortest-path
graph kernel

an all-pairs shortest-path transformed version of the original graph. Thus for each graph G_i which has to be compared, the authors build a new completely connected graph $\hat{G}_i$ of the same size. In contrast to the original graph each edge in $\hat{G}_i$ between nodes v_i and v_j corresponds to the length of the shortest path from v_i to v_j in the original graph G_i. The new kernel function between the transformed graphs is then calculated by comparing all walks of length 1, i.e.,

$$k_{\hat{G}}(G_1, G_2) = \sum_{\substack{h \in W(\hat{G}_1) \\ |h| = 1}} \sum_{\substack{h' \in W(\hat{G}_2) \\ |h'| = 1}} k_h(h, h'). \qquad (1.38)$$

Since algorithms for determining all-pairs shortest paths as, for example, Floyd-Warshall, are of cubic order and comparing all walks of length 1 is of fourth order, the all-pairs shortest-path kernel in (1.38) can be evaluated in $O(|V|^4)$ complexity.

comparing
random walks

An alternative approach proposed by Kashima et al. (2003) is to compare two graphs by measuring the similarity of the *probability distributions* of random walks on the two graphs. The authors propose to consider a walk h as a hidden variable and the kernel as a *marginalized kernel* where marginalization is over h, i.e.,

$$k_{RG}(G_1, G_2) = \mathbb{E}[k_G(G_1, G_2)] = \sum_{h \in W(G_1)} \sum_{h' \in W(G_2)} k_h(h, h')p(h|G_1)p(h|G_2),$$
$$(1.39)$$

where the conditional distributions $p(h|G_1), p(h'|G_2)$ in (1.39) for the random walk h, h' are defined as start, transition, and termination probability distribution over the vertices in V. Note that this marginalized graph kernel can be interpreted as a *randomized version* of (1.37).

By using the dot product of the two probability distributions as kernel, the induced feature space $\mathcal{H}$ is infinite-dimensional, with one dimension for every possible label sequence. Nevertheless, the authors developed an algorithm for how to calculate (1.39) explicitly with $O(|V|^6)$ complexity.

1.4.6   Kernels from Generative Models

In their quest to make density estimates directly accessible to kernel methods Jaakkola and Haussler (1999a,b) designed kernels which work directly on probability density estimates $p(x|\theta)$. Denote by

$$U_\theta(x) := \partial_\theta - \log p(x|\theta) \qquad (1.40)$$
$$I := \mathbf{E}_x \left[U_\theta(x) U_\theta^\top(x) \right] \qquad (1.41)$$

Fisher
information

the Fisher scores and the Fisher information matrix respectively. Note that for maximum likelihood estimators $\mathbf{E}_x[U_\theta(x)] = 0$ and therefore I is the covariance of $U_\theta(x)$. The Fisher kernel is defined as

$$k(x, x') := U_\theta^\top(x) I^{-1} U_\theta(x') \text{ or } k(x, x') := U_\theta^\top(x) U_\theta(x') \qquad (1.42)$$

depending on whether we study the normalized or the unnormalized kernel respectively. It is a versatile tool to reengineer existing density estimators for the purpose of discriminative estimation.

In addition to that, it has several attractive theoretical properties: Oliver et al. (2000) show that estimation using the normalized Fisher kernel corresponds to an estimation subject to a regularization on the $L_2(p(\cdot|\theta))$ norm.

Moreover, in the context of exponential families (see section 3.6 for a more detailed discussion) where $p(x|\theta) = \exp(\langle \phi(x), \theta \rangle - g(\theta))$, we have

$$k(x, x') = [\phi(x) - \partial_\theta g(\theta)] [\phi(x') - \partial_\theta g(\theta)] \qquad (1.43)$$

for the unnormalized Fisher kernel. This means that up to centering by $\partial_\theta g(\theta)$ the Fisher kernel is identical to the kernel arising from the inner product of the sufficient statistics $\phi(x)$. This is not a coincidence and is often encountered when working with nonparametric exponential families. A short description of exponential families is given further below in section 3.6. Moreover, note that the centering is immaterial, as can be seen in lemma 13.

1.5   An Example of a Structured Prediction Algorithm Using Kernels

In this section we introduce concepts for structured prediction based on kernel functions. The basic idea is based on the property that kernel methods embed any data type into a linear space and thus can be used to transform the targets to a new representation more amenable to prediction using existing technqiues. However, since one is interested in predictions of the original type one has to solve an additional *reconstruction* problem that is independent of the learning problem and therefore might be solved more easily. The first algorithm following this recipe kernel was kernel dependency estimation (KDE) introduced by Weston et al. (2002) and dependency which we discuss next.

Given n pairs of data items $D_n = \{(x_i, y_i)\}_{i=1}^n \subset \mathcal{X} \times \mathcal{Y}$ one is interested in learning a mapping $t_{\mathcal{Z}} : \mathcal{X} \to \mathcal{Y}$. As a first step in KDE one constructs a linear embedding of the targets only. For example, Weston et al. (2002) propose kernel PCA using a kernel function on $\mathcal{Y}$, i.e. $k_y(y_1, y_2) : \mathcal{Y} \times \mathcal{Y} \to \mathbb{R}$. Note that this kernel function gives rise to a feature map ϕ_y into a RKHS $\mathcal{H}_y$ and allows application of the kernel PCA map (see section 1.3.2). The new vectorial representation of the outputs can then be used to learn a map $T_{\mathcal{H}}$ from the input space $\mathcal{X}$ to the vectorial representation of the outputs, i.e. $\mathbb{R}^n$. This new learning problem using the transformed output is a standard multivariate regression problem and was solved for example in Weston et al. (2002) with kernel ridge regression using a kernel for $\mathcal{X}$.

[margin notes: kernel dependency estimation; kernel for the outputs]

Finally, for a given new input point x^* and its predicted representation $T_{\mathcal{H}}(x^*)$, one has to *reconstruct* the output element $y^* \in \mathcal{Y}$ that matches the predicted representation best, i.e.

$$y^* = \arg\min_{y \in \mathcal{Y}} \ ||\phi_y(y) - T_{\mathcal{H}}(x^*)||^2_{\mathcal{H}_y}. \tag{1.44}$$

pre-image/decoding problem

The problem (1.44) is known as the *pre-image* problem or alternatively as the *decoding* problem and has wide applications in kernel methods. , We summarize all feature maps used in KDE in figure 1.3 where we denote by $\Gamma : \mathcal{H}_y \to \mathcal{Y}$ the pre-image map which is given by (1.44). In chapter 8, we see an application of KDE to the task of string prediction where the authors design a pre-image map based on n-gram kernels.

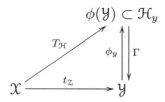

Figure 1.3   Mappings between original sets $\mathcal{X}, \mathcal{Y}$ and corresponding feature spaces $\mathcal{H}_y$ in kernel dependency estimation.

1.6   Conclusion

Kernels can be used for decorrelation of nontrivial structures between points in Euclidean space. Furthermore, they can be used to embed complex data types into linear spaces leading straightforward to distance and similarity measures among instances of arbitrary type. Finally, kernel functions *encapsulate* the data from the algorithm and thus allow use of the same algorithm on different data types without changing the implementation. Thus, whenever a learning algorithm can be expressed in kernels it can be utilized for arbitrary data types by exchanging the kernel function. This reduces the effort of using existing inference algorithms for novel application fields to introducing a novel specifically designed kernel function.

2   Discriminative Models

2.1   Introduction

In this chapter we consider the following problem: Given a set of data points $Z := \{(x_1, y_1), \ldots, (x_n, y_n)\} \subseteq \mathcal{X} \times \mathcal{Y}$ drawn from some data distribution $P(x, y)$, can we find a function $f(x) = \sigma(\langle w, x \rangle + b)$ such that $f(x) = y$ for all $(x, y) \in Z$, and $\mathbf{E}_{\mathrm{emp}}[f(x) \neq y]$ is minimized. This problem is hard because of two reasons:

- Minimization of the empirical risk with respect to (w, b) is NP-hard (Minsky and Papert, 1969). In fact, Ben-David et al. (2003) show that even approximately minimizing the empirical risk is NP-hard, not only for linear function classes but also for spheres and other simple geometrical objects. This means that even if the statistical challenges could be solved, we still would be saddled with a formidable algorithmic problem.

- The indicator function $I_{\{f(x) \neq y\}}$ is discontinuous and even small changes in f may lead to large changes in both empirical and expected risk. Properties of such functions can be captured by the VC-dimension (Vapnik and Chervonenkis, 1971), that is, the maximum number of observations which can be labeled in an arbitrary fashion by functions of the class. Necessary and sufficient conditions for estimation can be stated in these terms (Vapnik and Chervonenkis, 1991). However, much tighter bounds can be obtained by using the scale of the class, too (Alon et al., 1993; Bartlett et al., 1996; Williamson et al., 2001). In fact, there exist function classes parameterized by a scalar which have infinite VC-dimension (Vapnik, 1995).

Given the difficulty arising from minimizing the empirical risk of misclassification, we now discuss algorithms which minimize an upper bound on the empirical risk, while providing good computational properties and consistency of the estimators. A common theme underlying all such algorithms is the notion of margin maximization. In other words, these algorithms map the input data points into a high-dimensional feature space using the so-called *kernel trick* discussed in the previous chapter, and maximize the separation between data points of different classes. In this chapter, we begin by studying the perceptron algorithm and its variants. We provide a unifying exposition of common loss functions used in these algorithms. Then we move on to support vector machine (SVM) algorithms and discuss how to obtain convergence rates for large-margin algorithms.

2.2   Online Large-Margin Algorithms

2.2.1   Perceptron and Friends

Let $\mathcal{X}$ be the space of observations, and $\mathcal{Y}$ the space of labels. Let, $\{(\boldsymbol{x}_i, y_i) | \boldsymbol{x}_i \in \mathcal{X}, y_i \in \mathcal{Y}\}$ be a sequence of data points. The perceptron algorithm proposed by Rosenblatt (1962) is arguably the simplest online learning algorithm which is used to learn a separating hyperplane between two classes $\mathcal{Y} := \{\pm 1\}$. In its most basic form, it proceeds as follows. Start with the initial weight vector $w_0 = 0$. At step t, if the training example (x_t, y_t) is classified correctly, i.e., if $y_t(\langle x_t, w_t \rangle) \geq 0$, then set $w_{t+1} = w_t$; otherwise set $w_{t+1} = w_t + \eta y_t x_t$ (here, $\eta > 0$ is a learning rate). Repeat until all data points in the class are correctly classified. Novikoff's theorem shows that this procedure terminates, provided that the training set is separable with nonzero margin:

Theorem 10 (Novikoff (1962)) *Let $S = \{(x_1, y_1), \ldots, (x_n, y_n)\}$ be a dataset containing at least one data point labeled $+1$, and one data point labeled -1, and $R = \max_i \|x_i\|_2$. Assume that there exists a weight vector w^* such that $\|w^*\|_2 = 1$, and $y_i(\langle w^*, x_t \rangle) \geq \gamma$ for all i, then the number of mistakes made by the perceptron is at most $(R/\gamma)^2$.*

Collins (2002) introduced a version of the perceptron algorithm which generalizes to multiclass problems. Let, $\phi : \mathcal{X} \times \mathcal{Y} \to \mathbb{R}^d$ be a feature map which takes into account both the input as well as the labels. Then the algorithm proceeds as follows. Start with the initial weight vector $w_0 = 0$. At step t, predict with

perceptron for multiclass

$$z_t = \underset{y \in \mathcal{Y}}{\operatorname{argmax}} \langle \phi(x_t, y), w_t \rangle.$$

If $z_t = y_t$, then set $w_{t+1} = w_t$; otherwise set $w_{t+1} = w_t + \eta(\phi(x_t, y_t) - \phi(x_t, z_t))$. As before, $\eta > 0$ is a learning rate. A theorem analogous to the Novikoff theorem exists for this modified perceptron algorithm:

Theorem 11 (Collins (2002)) *Let $S = \{(x_1, y_1), \ldots, (x_n, y_n)\}$ be a nontrivial dataset, and $R = \max_i \max_y \|\phi(x_i, y_i) - \phi(x_i, y)\|_2$. Assume that there exists a weight vector w^* such that $\|w^*\|_2 = 1$, and $\min_{y \neq y_t} \langle w^*, \phi(x_t, y_t) \rangle - \langle w^*, \phi(x_t, y) \rangle \geq \gamma$ for all t, then the number of mistakes made by the modified perceptron is at most $(R/\gamma)^2$.*

In fact, a modified version of the above theorem also holds for the case when the data are not separable.

We now proceed to derive a general framework for online learning using large-margin algorithms and show that the above two perceptron algorithms can be viewed as special cases.

2.2.2 General Online Large-Margin Algorithms

regularized risk

As before, let $\mathcal{X}$ be the space of observations, and $\mathcal{Y}$ the space of labels. Given a sequence $\{(\boldsymbol{x}_i, y_i) | \boldsymbol{x}_i \in \mathcal{X}, y_i \in \mathcal{Y}\}$ of examples and a loss function $l : \mathcal{X} \times \mathcal{Y} \times \mathcal{H} \to \mathbb{R}$, large-margin online algorithms aim to minimize the regularized risk

$$J(f) = \frac{1}{m} \sum_{i=1}^{m} l(x_i, y_i, f) + \frac{\lambda}{2} \|f\|_{\mathcal{H}}^2,$$

derivatives in $\mathcal{H}$

where $\mathcal{H}$ is a reproducing kernel Hilbert space (RKHS) of functions on $\mathcal{X}$. Its defining kernel satisfies the reproducing property i.e., $\langle f, k(x, \cdot) \rangle_{\mathcal{H}} = f(x)$ for all $f \in \mathcal{H}$. Let $\phi : \mathcal{X} \to \mathcal{H}$ be the corresponding feature map of the kernel $k(\cdot, \cdot)$; then we predict the label of $x \in \mathcal{X}$ as $\operatorname{sgn}(\langle w, \phi(x) \rangle)$. Finally, we make the assumption that l only depends on f via its evaluations at $f(x_i)$ and that l is piecewise differentiable.

By the reproducing property of $\mathcal{H}$ we can compute derivatives of the evaluation functional. That is,

$$g := \partial_f f(x) = \partial_f \langle f, k(x, \cdot) \rangle_{\mathcal{H}} = k(x, \cdot).$$

Since l depends on f only via its evaluations we can see that $\partial_f l(x, y, f) \in \mathcal{H}$. Using the stochastic approximation of $J(f)$,

$$J_t(f) := l(x_t, y_t, f) + \frac{\lambda}{2} \|f\|_{\mathcal{H}}^2$$

and setting

$$g_t := \partial_f J_t(f_t) = \partial_f l(x_t, y_t, f_t) + \lambda f_t,$$

we obtain the following simple update rule:

$$f_{t+1} \leftarrow f_t - \eta_t g_t,$$

where η_t is the step size at time t. This algorithm, also known as NORMA (Kivinen et al., 2004), is summarized in algorithm 2.1.

Algorithm 2.1 Online learning

---

1. Initialize $f_0 = 0$
2. **Repeat**
   - (a) Draw data sample (x_t, y_t)
   - (b) Predict $f_t(x_t)$ and incur loss $l(x_t, y_t, f_t)$
   - (c) Update $f_{t+1} \leftarrow f_t - \eta_t g_t$

Observe that, so far, our discussion of the online update algorithm is independent of the particular loss function used. In other words, to apply our method to a new setting we simply need to compute the corresponding loss function and its gradient. We discuss particular examples of loss functions and their gradients in section 2.4. But, before that, we turn our attention to the perceptron algorithms discussed above.

In order to derive the perceptron as a special case, set $\mathcal{H} = \mathbb{R}^d$ with the Euclidean dot product, $\eta_t = \eta$, and the loss function

$$l(x, y, f) = \max(0, -y \langle x, f \rangle).$$

It is easy to check that

$$g = \partial_f l(x, y, f) = \begin{cases} 0 \text{ if } y \langle x, f \rangle \geq 0 \\ -yx \text{ otherwise,} \end{cases}$$

and hence algorithm 2.1 reduced to the perceptron algorithm.

As for the modified perceptron algorithm, just set $\mathcal{H} = \mathbb{R}^d$ with the Euclidean dot product, $\eta_t = \eta$, and the loss function

$$l(x, y, f) = \max(0, \max_{\tilde{y} \neq y} \langle \phi(x, \tilde{y}), f \rangle - \langle \phi(x, y), f \rangle).$$

Observe that the feature map ϕ now depends on both x and y. This and other extensions to multiclass algorithms will be discussed in more detail in section 2.4. But for now it suffices to observe that

$$g = \partial_f l(x, y, f) = \begin{cases} 0 \text{ if } \langle \phi(x, y), f \rangle \geq \max_{\tilde{y} \neq y} \langle \phi(x, \tilde{y}), f \rangle \\ \max_{\tilde{y} \neq y} \{\phi(x, \tilde{y}) - \phi(x, y)\} \text{ otherwise,} \end{cases}$$

and we recover the modified perceptron algorithm from algorithm 2.1.

2.3   Support Vector Estimation

Until now we concentrated on online learning algorithms. Now we turn our attention to batch algorithms which predict with a hypothesis that is computed after seeing all data points.

2.3.1   Support Vector Classification

Assume that $Z := \{(x_1, y_1), \ldots, (x_n, y_n)\} \subseteq \mathcal{X} \times \mathcal{Y}$ is separable, i.e. there exists a linear function $f(x)$ such that $\operatorname{sgn} y f(x) = 1$ on Z. In this case, the task of finding a large-margin separating hyperplane can be viewed as one of solving (Vapnik and Lerner, 1963)

maximally
separating
hyperplane

$$\underset{w,b}{\text{minimize}} \ \tfrac{1}{2} \|w\|^2 \text{ subject to } \ y_i (\langle w, x \rangle + b) \geq 1. \tag{2.1}$$

Note that $\|w\|^{-1} f(x_i)$ is the distance of the point x_i to the hyperplane $H(w, b) := \{x | \langle w, x \rangle + b = 0\}$. The condition $y_i f(x_i) \geq 1$ implies that the margin of separation is at least $2 \|w\|^{-1}$. The bound becomes exact if equality is attained for some $y_i = 1$ and $y_j = -1$. Consequently minimizing $\|w\|$ subject to the constraints maximizes the margin of separation. Eq. (2.1) is a quadratic program which can be solved efficiently (Luenberger, 1984; Fletcher, 1989; Boyd and Vandenberghe, 2004; Nocedal and Wright, 1999).

Mangasarian (1965) devised a similar optimization scheme using $\|w\|_1$ instead of $\|w\|_2$ in the objective function of (2.1). The result is a *linear* program. In general, one may show (Smola et al., 2000) that minimizing the ℓ_p norm of w leads to the maximizing of the margin of separation in the ℓ_q norm where $\frac{1}{p} + \frac{1}{q} = 1$. The ℓ_1 norm leads to sparse approximation schemes (see also Chen et al. (1999)), whereas the ℓ_2 norm can be extended to Hilbert spaces and kernels.

nonseparable problem

To deal with nonseparable problems, i.e. cases when (2.1) is infeasible, we need to relax the constraints of the optimization problem. Bennett and Mangasarian (1992) and Cortes and Vapnik (1995) impose a linear penalty on the violation of the large-margin constraints to obtain:

$$\underset{w, b, \xi}{\text{minimize}} \ \frac{1}{2} \|w\|^2 + C \sum_{i=1}^{n} \xi_i \ \text{subject to} \ y_i \left(\langle w, x_i \rangle + b \right) \geq 1 - \xi_i \ \text{and} \ \xi_i \geq 0. \quad (2.2)$$

Eq.(2.2) is a quadratic program which is always feasible (e.g. $w, b = 0$ and $\xi_i = 1$ satisfy the constraints). $C > 0$ is a regularization constant trading off the violation of the constraints vs. maximizing the overall margin.

Lagrange function

Whenever the dimensionality of $\mathcal{X}$ exceeds n, direct optimization of (2.2) is computationally inefficient. This is particularly true if we map from $\mathcal{X}$ into an RKHS. To address these problems one may solve the problem in dual space as follows. The Lagrange function of (2.2) is given by

$$L(w, b, \xi, \alpha, \eta) = \frac{1}{2} \|w\|^2 + C \sum_{i=1}^{n} \xi_i + \sum_{i=1}^{n} \alpha_i \left(1 - \xi_i - y_i \left(\langle w, x_i \rangle + b \right) \right) - \sum_{i=1}^{n} \eta_i \xi_i,$$

where $\alpha_i, \eta_i \geq 0$ for all $i \in [n]$. To compute the dual of L we need to identify the first-order conditions in w, b. They are given by

$$\partial_w L = w - \sum_{i=1}^{n} \alpha_i y_i x_i = 0, \quad \partial_b L = -\sum_{i=1}^{n} \alpha_i y_i = 0 \ \text{and} \ \partial_{\xi_i} L = C - \alpha_i + \eta_i = 0. \quad (2.3)$$

This translates into $w = \sum_{i=1}^{n} \alpha_i y_i x_i$, the linear constraint $\sum_{i=1}^{n} \alpha_i y_i = 0$, and the box-constraint $\alpha_i \in [0, C]$ arising from $\eta_i \geq 0$. Substituting (2.3) into L yields the

dual problem

Wolfe dual (Wolfe, 1961):

$$\underset{\alpha}{\text{minimize}} \ \frac{1}{2} \alpha^\top Q \alpha - \alpha^\top 1 \ \text{subject to} \ \alpha^\top y = 0 \ \text{and} \ \alpha_i \in [0, C]. \quad (2.4)$$

$Q \in \mathbb{R}^{n \times n}$ is the matrix of inner products $Q_{ij} := y_i y_j \langle x_i, x_j \rangle$. Clearly this can be extended to feature maps and kernels easily via $K_{ij} := y_i y_j \langle \Phi(x_i), \Phi(x_j) \rangle = y_i y_j k(x_i, x_j)$. Note that w lies in the span of the x_i. This is an instance of the representer theorem (see section 1.2.4). The Karush-Kuhn-Tucker (KKT) conditions (Karush, 1939; Kuhn and Tucker, 1951; Boser et al., 1992; Cortes and Vapnik, 1995) require that at optimality $\alpha_i(y_i f(x_i) - 1) = 0$. This means that only those x_i may appear in the expansion (2.3) for which $y_i f(x_i) \leq 1$, as otherwise $\alpha_i = 0$. The x_i are commonly referred to as support vectors, (SVs).

Note that $\sum_{i=1}^n \xi_i$ is an upper bound on the empirical risk, as $y_i f(x_i) \leq 0$ implies $\xi_i \geq 1$ (see also lemma 12). The number of misclassified points x_i itself depends on the configuration of the data and the value of C. The result of Ben-David et al. (2003) suggests that finding even an approximate minimum classification error solution is difficult. That said, it is possible to modify (2.2) such that a desired target number of observations violates $y_i f(x_i) \geq \rho$ for some $\rho \in \mathbb{R}$ by making the threshold itself a variable of the optimization problem (Schölkopf et al., 2000). This leads to the following optimization problem (ν-SV classification):

ν-SV classification

$$\underset{w,b,\xi}{\text{minimize}} \ \tfrac{1}{2} \|w\|^2 + \sum_{i=1}^n \xi_i - n\nu\rho \ \text{subject to} \ y_i \left(\langle w, x_i \rangle + b \right) \geq \rho - \xi_i \ \text{and} \ \xi_i \geq 0.$$

(2.5)

The dual of (2.5) is essentially identical to (2.4) with the exception of an additional constraint:

$$\underset{\alpha}{\text{minimize}} \ \tfrac{1}{2} \alpha^\top Q \alpha \ \text{subject to} \ \alpha^\top y = 0 \ \text{and} \ \alpha^\top 1 = n\nu \ \text{and} \ \alpha_i \in [0,1]. \quad (2.6)$$

One can show that for every C there exists a ν such that the solution of (2.6) is a multiple of the solution of (2.4). Schölkopf et al. (2000) prove that solving (2.6) for which $\rho > 0$ satisfies:

1. ν is an upper bound on the fraction of margin errors.

2. ν is a lower bound on the fraction of SVs.

Moreover, under mild conditions with probability 1, asymptotically, ν equals both the fraction of SVs and the fraction of errors.

This statement implies that whenever the data are sufficiently well separable (that is, $\rho > 0$), ν-SV classification finds a solution with a fraction of at most ν margin errors. Also note that for $\nu = 1$, all $\alpha_i = 1$, that is, f becomes an affine copy of the Parzen windows classifier (1.6).

2.3.2 Estimating the Support of a Density

We now extend the notion of linear separation to that of estimating the support of a density (Schölkopf et al., 2001; Tax and Duin, 1999). Denote by $X = \{x_1, \ldots, x_n\} \subseteq \mathcal{X}$ the sample drawn i.i.d. from $\Pr(x)$. Let $\mathcal{C}$ be a class of measurable subsets of $\mathcal{X}$

and let λ be a real-valued function defined on $\mathcal{C}$. The *quantile function* (Einmal and Mason, 1992) with respect to $(\mathrm{Pr}, \lambda, \mathcal{C})$ is defined as

$$U(\mu) = \inf \{\lambda(C) | \mathrm{Pr}(C) \geq \mu, C \in \mathcal{C}\} \text{ where } \mu \in (0, 1].$$

We denote by $C_\lambda(\mu)$ and $C_\lambda^m(\mu)$ the (not necessarily unique) $C \in \mathcal{C}$ that attain the infimum (when it is achievable) on $\mathrm{Pr}(x)$ and on the empirical measure given by X respectively. A common choice of λ is the Lebesgue measure, in which case $C_\lambda(\mu)$ is the minimum volume set $C \in \mathcal{C}$ that contains at least a fraction μ of the probability mass.

Support estimation requires us to find some $C_\lambda^m(\mu)$ such that $|\mathrm{Pr}(C_\lambda^m(\mu)) - \mu|$ is small. This is where the complexity tradeoff enters: On the one hand, we want to use a rich class $\mathcal{C}$ to capture all possible distributions; on the other hand large classes lead to large deviations between μ and $\mathrm{Pr}(C_\lambda^m(\mu))$. Therefore, we have to consider classes of sets which are suitably restricted. This can be achieved using an SVM regularizer.

In the case where $\mu < 1$, it seems the first work was reported in Sager (1979) and Hartigan (1987), in which $\mathcal{X} = \mathbb{R}^2$, with $\mathcal{C}$ being the class of closed convex sets in $\mathcal{X}$. Nolan (1991) considered higher dimensions, with $\mathcal{C}$ being the class of ellipsoids. Tsybakov (1997) studied an estimator based on piecewise polynomial approximation of $C_\lambda(\mu)$ and showed it attains the asymptotically minimax rate for certain classes of densities. Polonik (1997) studied the estimation of $C_\lambda(\mu)$ by $C_\lambda^m(\mu)$. He derived asymptotic rates of convergence in terms of various measures of richness of $\mathcal{C}$. More information on minimum volume estimators can be found in that work, and in Schölkopf et al. (2001).

learning the support SV support estimation[1] relates to previous work as follows: set $\lambda(C_w) = \|w\|^2$, where $C_w = \{x | f_w(x) \geq \rho\}$, and (w, ρ) are respectively a weight vector and an offset with $f_w(x) = \langle w, x \rangle$. Stated as a convex optimization problem we want to separate the data from the origin with maximum margin via:

$$\underset{w, \xi, \rho}{\text{minimize}} \ \tfrac{1}{2} \|w\|^2 + \sum_{i=1}^n \xi_i - n\nu\rho \text{ subject to } \langle w, x_i \rangle \geq \rho - \xi_i \text{ and } \xi_i \geq 0. \quad (2.7)$$

Here, $\nu \in (0, 1]$ plays the same role as in (2.5), controlling the number of observations x_i for which $f(x_i) \leq \rho$. Since nonzero slack variables ξ_i are penalized in the objective function, if w and ρ solve this problem, then the decision function $f(x)$ will attain or exceed ρ for at least $1 - \nu$ instances x_i contained in X while the regularization term $\|w\|$ will still be small. The dual of (2.7) yields:

$$\underset{\alpha}{\text{minimize}} \ \tfrac{1}{2} \alpha^\top K \alpha \text{ subject to } \alpha^\top 1 = \nu n \text{ and } \alpha_i \in [0, 1]. \quad (2.8)$$

To compare (2.8) to a Parzen windows estimator assume that k is such that it can be normalized as a density in input space, such as a Gaussian. Using $\nu = 1$ in (2.8)

---

1. Note that this is also known as one-class SVM.

the constraints automatically imply $\alpha_i = 1$. Thus f reduces to a Parzen windows estimate of the underlying density. For $\nu < 1$, the equality constraint (2.8) still ensures that f is a thresholded density, now depending only on a *subset* of X — those which are important for the decision $f(x) \leq \rho$ to be taken.

2.4   Margin-Based Loss Functions

In the previous sections we implicitly assumed that $\mathcal{Y} = \{\pm 1\}$. But many estimation problems cannot be easily written as binary classification problems. We need to make three key changes in order to tackle these problems. First, in a departure from tradition, but keeping in line with Collins (2002), Altun et al. (2004b), Tsochantaridis et al. (2004), and Cai and Hofmann (2004), we need to let our kernel depend on the labels as well as the observations. In other words, we minimize a regularized risk

$$J(f) = \frac{1}{m} \sum_{i=1}^{m} l(x_i, y_i, f) + \frac{\lambda}{2} \|f\|_{\mathcal{H}}^2, \tag{2.9}$$

where $\mathcal{H}$ is a reproducing kernel Hilbert space (RKHS) of functions on both $\mathcal{X} \times \mathcal{Y}$. Its defining kernel is denoted by $k : (\mathcal{X} \times \mathcal{Y})^2 \to \mathbb{R}$, and the corresponding feature map by $\phi : \mathcal{X} \times \mathcal{Y} \to \mathcal{H}$. Second, we predict the label of $x \in \mathcal{X}$ as

$$\operatorname*{argmax}_{y \in \mathcal{Y}} f(x, y) = \operatorname*{argmax}_{y \in \mathcal{Y}} \langle w, \phi(x, y) \rangle,$$

and finally we need to modify the loss function in order to deal with structured output spaces. While the online variants minimize a stochastic approximation of the above risk, the batch algorithms predict with the best hypothesis after observing the whole dataset.

Also, observe that the perceptron algorithms did not enforce a margin constraint as a part of their loss. In other words, they simply required that the data points be well classified. On the other hand, large-margin classifiers not only require a point to be well classified but also enforce a margin constraint on the loss function.

In this section, we discuss some commonly used loss functions and put them in perspective. Later, we specialize the general recipe described above to multicategory classification, ranking, and ordinal regression. Since the online update depends on it, we will state the gradient of all loss functions we present below, and give their kernel expansion coefficients.

2.4.0.1 Loss Functions on Unstructured Ouput Domains

Binary classification uses the hinge or soft-margin loss (Bennett and Mangasarian, 1992; Cortes and Vapnik, 1995),

$$l(x, y, f) = \max(0, \rho - yf(x)), \tag{2.10}$$

where $\rho > 0$, and $\mathcal{H}$ is defined on $\mathcal{X}$ alone. We have

$$\partial_f l(x, y, f) = \begin{cases} 0 & \text{if } yf(x) \geq \rho \\ -yk(x, \cdot) & \text{otherwise} \end{cases} . \tag{2.11}$$

Multiclass classification employs a definition of the margin arising from log-likelihood ratios (Crammer and Singer, 2000). This leads to

$$l(x, y, f) = \max(0, \rho + \max_{\tilde{y} \neq y} f(x, \tilde{y}) - f(x, y)) \tag{2.12}$$

$$\partial_f l(x, y, f) = \begin{cases} 0 & \text{if } f(x, y) \geq \rho + f(x, y^*) \\ k((x, y^*), \cdot) - k((x, y), \cdot) & \text{otherwise} \end{cases} . \tag{2.13}$$

Here we defined $\rho > 0$, and y^* to be the maximizer of the $\max_{\tilde{y} \neq y}$ operation. If several y^* exist we pick one of them arbitrarily, e.g. by dictionary order.

Logistic regression works by minimizing the negative log-likelihood. This loss function is used in Gaussian process classification (MacKay, 1998). For binary classification this yields

$$l(x, y, f) = \log(1 + \exp(-yf(x))) \tag{2.14}$$

$$\partial_f l(x, y, f) = -yk(x, \cdot) \frac{1}{1 + \exp(yf(x))}. \tag{2.15}$$

Again the RKHS $\mathcal{H}$ is defined on $\mathcal{X}$ only.

Multiclass logistic regression works similarly to the example above. The only difference is that the log-likelihood arises from a conditionally multinomial model (MacKay, 1998). This means that

$$l(x, y, f) = -f(x, y) + \log \sum_{\tilde{y} \in \mathcal{Y}} \exp f(x, \tilde{y}) \tag{2.16}$$

$$\partial_f l(x, y, f) = \sum_{\tilde{y} \in \mathcal{Y}} k((x, \tilde{y}), \cdot)[p(\tilde{y}|x, f) - \delta_{y, \tilde{y}}], \tag{2.17}$$

where we used $\quad p(y|x, f) = \dfrac{e^{f(x,y)}}{\sum_{\tilde{y} \in \mathcal{Y}} e^{f(x, \tilde{y})}}. \tag{2.18}$

Novelty detection uses a trimmed version of the log-likelihood as a loss function. In practice this means that labels are ignored and the one-class margin needs to exceed 1 (Schölkopf et al., 2001). This leads to

$$l(x, y, f) = \max(0, \rho - f(x)) \tag{2.19}$$

$$\partial_f l(x, y, f) = \begin{cases} 0 \text{ if } f(x) \geq \rho \\ -k(x, \cdot) \text{ otherwise} \end{cases}. \tag{2.20}$$

2.4.0.2 *Loss Functions on Structured Label Domains*

class hierarchies

In many applications the output domain has an inherent structure. For example, document categorization deals with the problem of assigning a set of documents to a set of predefined topic hierarchies or taxonomies. Consider a typical taxonomy shown in figure 2.1 which is based on a subset of the open directory project.[2] If a document describing CDROMs is classified under hard disk drives (HDD), intuitively the loss should be smaller than when the same document is classified under Cables. Roughly speaking, the value of the loss function should depend on the length of the shortest path connecting the actual label to the predicted label, i.e., the loss function should respect the structure of the output space (Tsochantaridis et al., 2004).

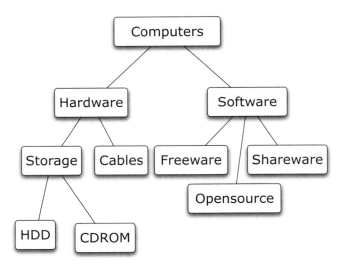

Figure 2.1   A taxonomy based on the open directory project.

To formalize our intuition, we need to introduce some notation. A weighted graph $G = (V, E)$ is defined by a set of nodes V and edges $E \subseteq V \times V$, such that each

---

2. http://www.dmoz.org/.

edge $(v_i, v_j) \in E$ is assigned a nonnegative weight $w(v_i, v_j) \in \mathbb{R}^+$. A path from $v_1 \in V$ to $v_n \in V$ is a sequence of nodes $v_1 v_2 \ldots v_n$ such that $(v_i, v_{i+1}) \in E$. The weight of a path is the sum of the weights on the edges. For an undirected graph, $(v_i, v_j) \in E \implies (v_j, v_i) \in E \wedge w(v_i, v_j) = w(v_j, v_i)$.

A graph is said to be connected if every pair of nodes in the graph is connected by a path. In the sequel we will deal exclusively with connected graphs, and let $\Delta_G(v_i, v_j)$ denote the weight of the shortest (i.e., minimum weight) path from v_i to v_j. If the output labels are nodes in a graph G, the following loss function takes the structure of G into account:

$$l(x, y, f) = \max\{0, \max_{\tilde{y} \neq y}[\Delta_G(\tilde{y}, y) + f(x, \tilde{y})] - f(x, y)\}. \tag{2.21}$$

This loss requires that the output labels $\tilde{y}$ which are "far away" from the actual label y (on the graph) must be classified with a larger margin while nearby labels are allowed to be classified with a smaller margin. More general notions of distance, including kernels on the nodes of the graph, can also be used here instead of the shortest path $\Delta_G(\tilde{y}, y)$.

Analogous to (2.17), by defining y^* to be the maximizer of the $\max_{\tilde{y} \neq y}$ operation we can write the gradient of the loss as

$$\partial_f l(x, y, f) = \begin{cases} 0 \text{ if } f(x, y) \geq \Delta_G(y, y^*) + f(x, y^*) \\ k((x, y^*), \cdot) - k((x, y), \cdot) \text{ otherwise} \end{cases}. \tag{2.22}$$

The multiclass loss (2.12) is a special case of graph-based loss (2.21): consider a simple two-level tree in which each label is a child of the root node, and every edge has a weight of $\frac{\rho}{2}$. In this graph, any two labels $y \neq \tilde{y}$ will have $\Delta_G(y, \tilde{y}) = \rho$, and thus (2.21) reduces to (2.12). In the sequel, we will use $\Delta(y, \tilde{y})$ (without the subscript G) to denote the desired margin of separation between y and $\tilde{y}$.

2.4.1 Multicategory Classification, Ranking, and Ordinal Regression

Key to deriving convex optimization problems using the generalized risk function (2.9) for various common tasks is the following lemma:

Lemma 12 *Let $f : \mathcal{X} \times \mathcal{Y} \to \mathbb{R}$ and assume that $\Delta(y, \tilde{y}) \geq 0$ with $\Delta(y, y) = 0$. Moreover let $\xi \geq 0$ such that $f(x, y) - f(x, \tilde{y}) \geq \Delta(y, \tilde{y}) - \xi$ for all $\tilde{y} \in \mathcal{Y}$. In this case $\xi \geq \Delta(y, \mathrm{argmax}_{\tilde{y} \in \mathcal{Y}} f(x, \tilde{y}))$.*

Proof Denote by $y^* := \mathrm{argmax}_{\tilde{y} \in \mathcal{Y}} f(x, \tilde{y})$. By assumption we have $\xi \geq \Delta(y, y^*) + f(x, y^*) - f(x, y)$. Since $f(x, y^*) \geq f(x, \tilde{y})$ for all $\tilde{y} \in \mathcal{Y}$ the inequality holds. ∎

The construction of the estimator was suggested in Taskar et al. (2004b) and Tsochantaridis et al. (2004), and a special instance of the above lemma is given by Joachims (2005). We now can derive the following optimization problem from (2.9) (Tsochantaridis et al., 2004):

$$\underset{w,\xi}{\text{minimize}} \; \frac{1}{2} \|w\|^2 + C \sum_{i=1}^{n} \xi_i \qquad (2.23a)$$

$$\text{s.t. } \langle w, \phi(x_i, y_i) - \phi(x_i, y) \rangle \geq \Delta(y_i, y) - \xi_i \text{ for all } y \in \mathcal{Y}. \qquad (2.23b)$$

This is a convex optimization problem which can be solved efficiently if the constraints can be evaluated without high computational cost. One typically employs column-generation methods (Hettich and Kortanek, 1993; Rätsch, 2001; Bennett et al., 2000; Tsochantaridis et al., 2004; Fletcher, 1989) which identify one violated constraint at a time to find an approximate minimum of the optimization problem.

To describe the flexibility of the framework set out by (2.23) we give several examples of its application.

■ Binary classification can be recovered by setting $\Phi(x, y) = y\Phi(x)$, in which case the constraint of (2.23) reduces to $2y_i \langle \Phi(x_i), w \rangle \geq 1 - \xi_i$. Ignoring constant offsets and a scaling factor of 2, this is exactly the standard SVM optimization problem.

■ Multicategory classification problems (Crammer and Singer, 2000; Collins, 2002; Allwein et al., 2000; Rätsch et al., 2002a) can be encoded via $\mathcal{Y} = [N]$, where N is the number of classes, $[N] := \{1, \dots N\}$, and $\Delta(y, y') = 1 - \delta_{y,y'}$. In other words, the loss is 1 whenever we predict the wrong class and is 0 for correct classification. Corresponding kernels are typically chosen to be $\delta_{y,y'} k(x, x')$.

■ We can deal with joint labeling problems by setting $\mathcal{Y} = \{\pm 1\}^n$. In other words, the error measure does not depend on a single observation but on an entire set of labels. Joachims (2005) shows that the so-called F_1 score (van Rijsbergen, 1979) used in document retrieval and the area under the receiver operating characteristic (ROC) curve (Bamber, 1975; Gribskov and Robinson, 1996) fall into this category of problems. Moreover, Joachims (2005) derives an $O(n^2)$ method for evaluating the inequality constraint over $\mathcal{Y}$.

■ Multilabel estimation problems deal with the situation where we want to find the best subset of labels $\mathcal{Y} \subseteq 2^{[N]}$ which correspond to some observation x. The problem is described in Elisseeff and Weston (2001), where the authors devise a ranking scheme such that $f(x, i) > f(x, j)$ if label $i \in y$ and $j \notin y$. It is a special case of a general ranking approach described next.

Note that (2.23) is invariant under translations $\phi(x, y) \leftarrow \phi(x, y) + \phi_0$ where ϕ_0 is constant, as $\phi(x_i, y_i) - \phi(x_i, y)$ remains unchanged. In practice this means that transformations $k(x, y, x', y') \leftarrow k(x, y, x', y') + \langle \phi_0, \phi(x, y) \rangle + \langle \phi_0, \phi(x', y') \rangle + \|\phi_0\|^2$ do not affect the outcome of the estimation process. Since ϕ_0 was arbitrary, we have the following lemma:

Lemma 13 *Let $\mathcal{H}$ be an RKHS on $\mathcal{X} \times \mathcal{Y}$ with kernel k. Moreover, let $g \in \mathcal{H}$. Then the function $k(x, y, x', y') + f(x, y) + f(x', y') + \|g\|^2_{\mathcal{H}}$ is a kernel and it yields the same estimates as k.*

We need a slight extension to deal with general ranking problems. Denote by $\mathcal{Y} = \mathcal{G}[N]$ the set of all directed graphs on N vertices which do not contain loops of less than three nodes. Here an edge $(i, j) \in y$ indicates that i is preferred to j with respect to the observation x. Our goal is to find some function $f : \mathcal{X} \times [N] \to \mathbb{R}$ which imposes a total order on $[N]$ (for a given x) by virtue of the function values $f(x, i)$ such that the total order and y are in good agreement.

More specifically, Dekel et al. (2003), Crammer (2005), and Crammer and Singer (2005) propose a decomposition algorithm $\mathcal{A}$ for the graphs y such that the estimation error is given by the number of subgraphs of y which are in disagreement with the total order imposed by f. As an example, multiclass classification can be viewed as a graph y where the correct label i is at the root of a directed graph and all incorrect labels are its children. Multilabel classification can be seen as a bipartite graph where the correct labels only contain outgoing arcs and the incorrect labels only incoming ones.

This setting leads to a form similar to (2.23) except for the fact that we now have constraints over each subgraph $G \in \mathcal{A}(y)$. We solve

$$\underset{w, \xi}{\text{minimize}} \; \frac{1}{2} \|w\|^2 + C \sum_{i=1}^{n} |\mathcal{A}(y_i)|^{-1} \sum_{G \in \mathcal{A}(y_i)} \xi_{iG}$$

subject to $\langle w, \Phi(x_i, u) - \Phi(x_i, v) \rangle \geq 1 - \xi_{iG}$ and $\xi_{iG} \geq 0$ for all $(u, v) \in G \in \mathcal{A}(y_i)$.

That is, we test for all $(u, v) \in G$ whether the ranking imposed by the subgraph $G \in y_i$ is satisfied.

Finally, ordinal regression problems which perform ranking not over labels y but rather over observations x were studied by Herbrich et al. (2000) and Chapelle and Harchaoui (2005) in the context of ordinal regression and conjoint analysis respectively. In ordinal regression x is preferred to x' if $f(x) > f(x')$ and hence one minimizes an optimization problem akin to (2.23), with constraint $\langle w, \Phi(x_i) - \Phi(x_j) \rangle \geq 1 - \xi_{ij}$. In conjoint analysis the same operation is carried out for $\Phi(x, u)$, where u is the user under consideration. Similar models were also studied by Basilico and Hofmann (2004).

2.5 Margins and Uniform Convergence Bounds

So far we motivated the algorithms by means of practicality and the fact that $0 - 1$ loss functions yield hard-to-control estimators. We now follow up on the analysis by providing uniform convergence bounds for large-margin classifiers. We focus on the case of scalar-valued functions applied to classification for two reasons: The derivation is well established and it can be presented in a concise fashion. Secondly, the derivation of corresponding bounds for the vectorial case is by and large still an open problem. Preliminary results exist, such as the bounds by Collins (2002) for the case of perceptrons; Taskar et al. (2004b), who derive capacity bounds in terms of covering numbers by an explicit covering construction; and Bartlett and

Mendelson (2002), who give Gaussian average bounds for vectorial functions. We believe that the scaling behavior of these bounds in the number of classes $|\mathcal{Y}|$ is currently not optimal, when applied to the problems of type (2.23).

Our analysis is based on the following ideas: firstly the $0 - 1$ loss is upper-bounded by some function $\psi(yf(x))$ which can be minimized, such as the soft-margin function $\max(0, 1 - yf(x))$ of the previous section. Secondly we prove that the empirical average of the ψ-loss is concentrated close to its expectation. This will be achieved by means of Rademacher averages. Thirdly we show that under rather general conditions the minimization of the ψ-loss is consistent with the minimization of the expected risk. Finally, we combine these bounds to obtain rates of convergence which only depend on the Rademacher average and the approximation properties of the function class under consideration.

concentration

2.5.1   Margins and Empirical Risk

Unless stated otherwise $\mathbf{E}[\cdot]$ denotes the expectation with respect to all random variables of the argument. Subscripts, such as $\mathbf{E}_X[\cdot]$, indicate that the expectation is taken over X. We will omit them wherever obvious. Finally we will refer to $\mathbf{E}_{\mathrm{emp}}[\cdot]$ as the empirical average with respect to an n-sample.

While the sign of $yf(x)$ can be used to assess the accuracy of a binary classifier we saw that for algorithmic reasons one rather optimizes a (smooth function of) $yf(x)$ directly. In the following we assume that the binary loss $\chi(\xi) = \frac{1}{2}(1 - \mathrm{sgn}\,\xi)$ is majorized by some function $\psi(\xi) \geq \chi(\xi)$, e.g. via the construction of lemma 12. Consequently $\mathbf{E}\left[\chi(yf(x))\right] \leq \mathbf{E}\left[\psi(yf(x))\right]$ and likewise $\mathbf{E}_{\mathrm{emp}}\left[\chi(yf(x))\right] \leq \mathbf{E}_{\mathrm{emp}}\left[\psi(yf(x))\right]$. The hope is (as will be shown in section 2.5.3) that minimizing the upper bound leads to consistent estimators.

There is a long-standing tradition of minimizing $yf(x)$ rather than the number of misclassifications. $yf(x)$ is known as "margin" (based on the geometrical reasoning) in the context of SVMs (Vapnik and Lerner, 1963; Mangasarian, 1965), as "stability" in the context of neural networks (Krauth and Mézard, 1987; Ruján, 1993), and as the "edge" in the context of arcing (Breiman, 1999). One may show (Makovoz, 1996; Barron, 1993; Herbrich and Williamson, 2002) that functions f in an RKHS achieving a large margin can be approximated by another function f' achieving almost the same empirical error using a much smaller number of kernel functions.

Note that by default, uniform convergence bounds are expressed in terms of minimization of the empirical risk average with respect to a *fixed* function class $\mathcal{F}$, e.g. Vapnik and Chervonenkis (1971). This is very much unlike what is done in practice: in SVM (2.23) the sum of empirical risk and a regularizer is minimized. However, one may check that minimizing $\mathbf{E}_{\mathrm{emp}}\left[\psi(yf(x))\right]$ subject to $\|w\|^2 \leq W$ is equivalent to minimizing $\mathbf{E}_{\mathrm{emp}}\left[\psi(yf(x))\right] + \lambda \|w\|^2$ for suitably chosen values of λ. The equivalence is immediate by using Lagrange multipliers. For numerical reasons, however, the second formulation is much more convenient (Tikhonov, 1963; Morozov, 1984), as it acts as a regularizer. Finally, for the design of adaptive estimators, so-called luckiness results exist, which provide risk bounds in a data-dependent fashion (Shawe-Taylor et al., 1998; Herbrich and Williamson, 2002).

2.5.2 Uniform Convergence and Rademacher Averages

The next step is to bound the deviation $\mathbf{E}_{\text{emp}}[\psi(yf(x))] - \mathbf{E}[\psi(yf(x))]$ by means of Rademacher averages. For details see Boucheron et al. (2005), Mendelson (2003), Bartlett et al. (2002), and Koltchinskii (2001). Denote by $g : \mathcal{X}^n \to \mathbb{R}$ a function of n variables and let $c > 0$ such that $|g(x_1, \ldots, x_n) - g(x_1, \ldots, x_{i-1}, x_i', x_{i+1}, \ldots, x_n)| \leq c$ for all $x_1, \ldots, x_n, x_i' \in \mathcal{X}$ and for all $i \in [n]$, then (McDiarmid, 1989)

$$\Pr\left\{ \mathbf{E}\left[g(x_1, \ldots, x_n)\right] - g(x_1, \ldots, x_n) > \epsilon \right\} \leq \exp\left(-2\epsilon^2/nc^2\right). \tag{2.24}$$

Assume that $f(x) \in [0, B]$ for all $f \in \mathcal{F}$ and let $g(x_1, \ldots, x_n) := \sup_{f \in \mathcal{F}} |\mathbf{E}_{\text{emp}}[f(x)] - \mathbf{E}[f(x)]|$. Then it follows that $c \leq \frac{B}{n}$. Solving (2.24) for g we obtain that with probability at least $1 - \delta$,

$$\sup_{f \in \mathcal{F}} \mathbf{E}[f(x)] - \mathbf{E}_{\text{emp}}[f(x)] \leq \mathbf{E}\left[\sup_{f \in \mathcal{F}} \mathbf{E}[f(x)] - \mathbf{E}_{\text{emp}}[f(x)] \right] + B\sqrt{-\frac{\log \delta}{2n}}. \tag{2.25}$$

This means that with high probability the largest deviation between the sample average and its expectation is concentrated around its mean and within an $O(n^{-\frac{1}{2}})$ term. The expectation can be bounded by a classical symmetrization argument (Vapnik and Chervonenkis, 1971) as follows:

$$\begin{aligned}
&\mathbf{E}_X\left[\sup_{f \in \mathcal{F}} \mathbf{E}[f(x')] - \mathbf{E}_{\text{emp}}[f(x)] \right] \leq \mathbf{E}_{X,X'}\left[\sup_{f \in \mathcal{F}} \mathbf{E}_{\text{emp}}[f(x')] - \mathbf{E}_{\text{emp}}[f(x)] \right] \\
= \;&\mathbf{E}_{X,X',\sigma}\left[\sup_{f \in \mathcal{F}} \mathbf{E}_{\text{emp}}[\sigma f(x')] - \mathbf{E}_{\text{emp}}[\sigma f(x)] \right] \leq 2\mathbf{E}_{X,\sigma}\left[\sup_{f \in \mathcal{F}} \mathbf{E}_{\text{emp}}[\sigma f(x)] \right].
\end{aligned}$$

The first inequality follows from the convexity of the argument of the expectation; the second equality follows from the fact that x_i and x_i' are drawn i.i.d. from the same distribution; hence we may swap terms. Here σ_i are independent ± 1-valued zero-mean Rademacher random variables. The final term $\mathbf{E}_{X,\sigma}\left[\sup_{f \in \mathcal{F}} \mathbf{E}_{\text{emp}}[\sigma f(x)]\right] := R_n[\mathcal{F}]$ is referred as the *Rademacher average* (Mendelson, 2002; Bartlett and Mendelson, 2002; Koltchinskii, 2001) of $\mathcal{F}$ w.r.t. sample size n.

Radermacher
averages for
linear functions

For linear function classes $R_n[\mathcal{F}]$ takes on a particularly nice form. We begin with $\mathcal{F} := \{f | f(x) = \langle x, w \rangle \text{ and } \|w\| \leq 1\}$. It follows that $\sup_{\|w\| \leq 1} \sum_{i=1}^n \sigma_i \langle w, x_i \rangle = \|\sum_{i=1}^n \sigma_i x_i\|$. Hence

$$nR_n[\mathcal{F}] = \mathbf{E}_{X,\sigma}\|\sum_{i=1}^n \sigma_i x_i\|$$

$$\leq \mathbf{E}_X\left[\mathbf{E}_\sigma\left[\left\|\sum_{i=1}^n \sigma_i x_i\right\|^2\right]\right]^{\frac{1}{2}}$$

$$= \mathbf{E}_X\left[\sum_{i=1}^n \|x_i\|^2\right]^{\frac{1}{2}} \leq \sqrt{n\mathbf{E}\left[\|x\|^2\right]}. \tag{2.26}$$

Here the first inequality is a consequence of Jensen's inequality, the second equality follows from the fact that σ_i are i.i.d. zero-mean random variables, and the last step again is a result of Jensen's inequality. Corresponding tight lower bounds by a factor of $1/\sqrt{2}$ exist and they are a result of the Khintchine-Kahane inequality (Kahane, 1968).

Note that (2.26) allows us to bound $R_n[\mathcal{F}] \leq n^{-\frac{1}{2}}r$ where r is the average length of the sample. An extension to kernel functions is straightforward: by design of the inner product we have $r = \sqrt{\mathbf{E}_x[k(x,x)]}$. Note that this bound is *independent* of the dimensionality of the data but rather only depends on the expected length of the data. Moreover r is the trace of the integral operator with kernel $k(x, x')$ and probability measure on $\mathcal{X}$.

Since we are computing $\mathbf{E}_{\text{emp}}[\psi(yf(x))]$ we are interested in the Rademacher complexity of $\psi \circ \mathcal{F}$. Bartlett and Mendelson (2002) show that $R_n[\psi \circ \mathcal{F}] \leq LR_n[\mathcal{F}]$ for any Lipschitz continuous function ψ with Lipschitz constant L and with $\psi(0) = 0$. Secondly, for $\{yb \text{ where } |b| \leq B\}$ the Rademacher average can be bounded by $B\sqrt{2\log 2/n}$, as follows from (Boucheron et al., 2005, eq. (4)). This takes care of the offset b. For sums of function classes $\mathcal{F}$ and $\mathcal{G}$ we have $R_n[\mathcal{F} + \mathcal{G}] \leq R_n[\mathcal{F}] + R_n[\mathcal{G}]$. This means that for linear functions with $\|w\| \leq W$, $|b| \leq B$, and ψ Lipschitz continuous with constant L, we have $R_n \leq \frac{L}{\sqrt{n}}(Wr + B\sqrt{2\log 2})$.

2.5.3 Upper Bounds and Convex Functions

We briefly discuss consistency of minimization of the surrogate loss function $\psi : \mathbb{R} \to [0, \infty)$ about which assume that it is convex and that $\psi \geq \chi$ (Jordan et al., 2003; Zhang, 2004). Examples of such functions are the soft-margin loss $\max(0, 1 - \gamma\xi)$, which we discussed in section 2.3, and the boosting loss $e^{-\xi}$, which is commonly used in AdaBoost (Schapire et al., 1998; Rätsch et al., 2001).

Denote by f_χ^* the minimizer of the expected risk and let f_ψ^* be the minimizer of $\mathbf{E}\left[\psi(yf(x))\right]$ with respect to f. Then, under rather general conditions on ψ (Zhang, 2004), for all f the following inequality holds:

$$\mathbf{E}\left[\chi(yf(x))\right] - \mathbf{E}\left[\chi(yf_\chi^*(x))\right] \leq c\left(\mathbf{E}\left[\psi(yf(x))\right] - \mathbf{E}\left[\psi(yf_\psi^*(x))\right]\right)^s. \quad (2.27)$$

In particular we have $c = 4$ and $s = 1$ for soft-margin loss, whereas for boosting and logistic regression $c = \sqrt{8}$ and $s = \frac{1}{2}$. Note that (2.27) implies that the minimizer of the ψ loss is consistent, i.e. $\mathbf{E}\left[\chi(yf_\psi(x))\right] = \mathbf{E}\left[\chi(yf_\chi(x))\right]$.

2.5.4 Rates of Convergence

We now have all tools at our disposal to obtain rates of convergence to the minimizer of the expected risk which depend only on the complexity of the function class and its approximation properties in terms of the ψ-loss. Denote by $f_{\psi,\mathcal{F}}^*$ the minimizer of $\mathbf{E}\left[\psi(yf(x))\right]$ restricted to $\mathcal{F}$, let $f_{\psi,\mathcal{F}}^n$ be the minimizer of the empirical ψ-risk, and let $\delta(\mathcal{F}, \psi) := \mathbf{E}\left[yf_{\psi,\mathcal{F}}^*(x)\right] - \mathbf{E}\left[yf_\psi^*(x)\right]$ be the approximation error due to the restriction of f to $\mathcal{F}$. Then a simple telescope sum yields

$$\begin{aligned}\mathbf{E}\left[\chi(yf_{\psi,\mathcal{F}}^n)\right] \leq & \mathbf{E}\left[\chi(yf_\chi^*)\right] + 4\left[\mathbf{E}\left[\psi(yf_{\psi,\mathcal{F}}^n)\right] - \mathbf{E}_{\text{emp}}\left[\psi(yf_{\psi,\mathcal{F}}^n)\right]\right] \\ & + 4\left[\mathbf{E}_{\text{emp}}\left[\psi(yf_{\psi,\mathcal{F}}^*)\right] - \mathbf{E}\left[\psi(yf_{\psi,\mathcal{F}}^*)\right]\right] + \delta(\mathcal{F}, \psi) \\ \leq & \mathbf{E}\left[\chi(yf_\chi^*)\right] + \delta(\mathcal{F}, \psi) + 4\frac{RW\gamma}{\sqrt{n}}\left[\sqrt{-2\log\delta} + r/R + \sqrt{8\log 2}\right].\end{aligned}$$
$$(2.28)$$

Here γ is the effective margin of the soft-margin loss $\max(0, 1 - \gamma yf(x))$, W is an upper bound on $\|w\|$, $R \geq \|x\|$, r is the average radius, as defined in the previous section, and we assumed that b is bounded by the largest value of $\langle w, x \rangle$. A similar reasoning for logistic and exponential loss is given in Boucheron et al. (2005).

Note that we get an $O(1/\sqrt{n})$ rate of convergence regardless of the dimensionality of x. Moreover, note that the rate is dominated by $RW\gamma$, that is, the classical radius-margin bound (Vapnik, 1995). Here R is the radius of an enclosing sphere for the data and $1/(W\gamma)$ is an upper bound on the radius of the data — the soft-margin loss becomes active only for $yf(x) \leq \gamma$.

2.5.5 Localization and Noise Conditions

In many cases it is possible to obtain better rates of convergence than $O(1/\sqrt{n})$ by exploiting information about the magnitude of the error of misclassification and about the variance of f on $\mathcal{X}$. Such bounds use Bernstein-type inequalities and they lead to localized Rademacher averages (Bartlett et al., 2002; Mendelson, 2003; Boucheron et al., 2005).

Basically the slow $O(1/\sqrt{n})$ rates arise whenever the region around the Bayes optimal decision boundary is large. In this case, determining this region produces the slow rate, whereas the well-determined region could be estimated at an $O(1/n)$ rate.

Tsybakov's noise condition (Tsybakov, 2003) requires that there exist $\beta, \gamma \geq 0$ such that

$$\Pr\left\{\left|\Pr\left\{y = 1|x\right\} - \tfrac{1}{2}\right| \leq t\right\} \leq \beta t^{\gamma} \text{ for all } t \geq 0. \tag{2.29}$$

Note that for $\gamma = \infty$ the condition implies that there exists some s such that $\left|\Pr\left\{y = 1|x\right\} - \tfrac{1}{2}\right| \geq s > 0$ almost surely. This is also known as Massart's noise condition.

The key benefit of (2.29) is that it implies a relationship between variance and expected value of classification loss. More specifically, for $\alpha = \frac{\gamma}{1+\gamma}$ and $g : \mathcal{X} \to \mathcal{Y}$ we have

$$\mathbf{E}\left[\left[\{g(x) \neq y\} - \{g^*(x) \neq y\}\right]^2\right] \leq c\left[\mathbf{E}\left[\{g(x) \neq y\} - \{g^*(x) \neq y\}\right]\right]^{\alpha}. \tag{2.30}$$

Here $g^*(x) := \operatorname{argmax}_y \Pr(y|x)$ denotes the Bayes optimal classifier. This is sufficient to obtain faster rates for finite sets of classifiers. For more complex function classes localization is used. See, e.g., Boucheron et al. (2005) and Bartlett et al. (2002) for more details.

2.6 Conclusion

In this chapter we reviewed some online and batch discriminative models. In particular, we focused on methods employing the kernel trick in conjunction with a large margin loss. We showed how these algorithms can naturally be extended to structured output spaces. We also showed how various loss functions used in the literature are related. Furthermore, we showed statistical properties of the estimators, as, e.g., convergence rates using Rademacher averages and related concepts.

3 Modeling Structure via Graphical Models

3.1 Introduction

Graphical models combine probability theory and graph theory in order to address one of the key objectives in designing and fitting probabilistic models, which is to capture dependencies among relevant random variables, both on a qualitative as well as quantitative level. The *qualitative* aspects of a model specify, loosely speaking, which variables depend on each other directly and which ones do not. Understanding such independencies is crucial in complex domains, since it allows breaking down the overall modeling or inference problem into smaller modules, often leading to concise model representations and efficient inference algorithms. The language of graphs provides a suitable formalism for dealing with dependency structures. While the power of qualitative modeling is to exclude and simplify dependencies, it is as important to *quantify* the existing dependencies and to provide ways to interface models to data via a suitable inference calculus; this is where the power of probability theory comes in.

Although the focus of this chapter is on graphical models, we also briefly review models that capture recursive dependency structure in syntactic natural language constructions.

3.2 Conditional Independence

In defining probabilistic models, *conditional independence* is a concept of fundamental importance that also underpins the theory of graphical models. If one wants to model domains with a potentially large number of variables among which complex dependencies exist, as is typical in many real-world applications, everything may depend on everything else and it is crucial to make appropriate assumptions about the ways variables *do not* depend on each other.

types of
independence

Statistical independence is the strongest such assumption: given two random variables X and Y with joint distribution $p(X, Y)$, X and Y are independent, if $p(X, Y) = p(X)\, p(Y)$. We will use the convenient notation $X \perp\!\!\!\perp Y$ to indicate independence of X and Y. The above condition on the joint distribution is equivalent to the condition $p(X|Y) = p(X)$, where the conditional probability distribution is given by $p(X|Y) = p(X, Y)/p(Y)$. However, complete independence is often too restrictive and uninteresting in that we can effectively model independent variables separately.

Conditional independence is a more differentiated and useful concept. Two random variables X and Y are conditionally independent given a third random variable Z, denoted by $X \perp\!\!\!\perp Y | Z$, if $p(X, Y | Z) = p(X | Z) \, p(Y | Z)$, which is equivalent to the formulation $p(X | Y, Z) = p(X | Z)$. The latter expresses a key fact about conditional independence: it allows discarding variables from the conditioning set in the presence of others. In short, if $X \perp\!\!\!\perp Y | Z$, then knowing Z renders Y irrelevant for predicting X.

There are many ways in which one or more conditional independence statements imply others. The following proposition is related to the concept of a *graphoid* (see Lauritzen (1996) for more detail).

Proposition 14 *For random variables $X, Y, Z,$ and W and arbitrary functions g of X, the following implications hold:*

$$X \perp\!\!\!\perp Y | Z \iff Y \perp\!\!\!\perp X | Z \tag{3.1a}$$

$$X \perp\!\!\!\perp Y | Z \implies X' \perp\!\!\!\perp Y | Z, \quad X' = g(X) \tag{3.1b}$$

$$X \perp\!\!\!\perp Y | Z \implies X \perp\!\!\!\perp Y | (Z, X'), \quad X' = g(X) \tag{3.1c}$$

$$X \perp\!\!\!\perp Y | Z \text{ and } X \perp\!\!\!\perp W | (Y, Z) \implies X \perp\!\!\!\perp (Y, W) | Z \tag{3.1d}$$

For distributions with full support we also have that

$$X \perp\!\!\!\perp Y | (Z, W) \text{ and } X \perp\!\!\!\perp W | (Z, Y) \implies X \perp\!\!\!\perp (Y, W) | Z \tag{3.1e}$$

(Note: As a special case one may define g such that $X' \subseteq X$.)

3.3 Markov Networks

3.3.1 Conditional Independence Graphs

In large domains, dealing with many conditional independence statements can become quite complex and may even lead to inconsistencies. Independence graphs – also known as Markov networks or Markov random fields (MRFs) – are a very elegant formalism to express and represent a large set of conditional independencies in a concise and consistent manner.

Definition 15 (Markov Network) *Given random variables $V = \{X_1, \ldots, X_m\}$ an independence graph (or Markov network) of V is an undirected graph $\mathcal{G} = (V, E)$, representing the following set of conditional independencies: $\{X_i, X_j\} \notin E$ if and only if $X_i \perp\!\!\!\perp X_j | V - \{X_i, X_j\}$ for all $X_i, X_j \in V$.*

Definition 16 (Independence Map) *A Markov network $\mathcal{G}$ is an* independence map *(I-map) for a probability distribution p, if all pairwise Markov assumptions*

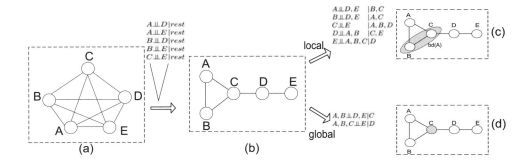

Figure 3.1   Simple example illustrating the concept of conditional independence.

represented by $\mathcal{G}$ hold under p. $\mathcal{G}$ is a minimal I-map, if there is no $\mathcal{G}' \subsetneq \mathcal{G}$ which is an I-map of p.

Notice that the construction of a Markov network given a set of pairwise independencies is trivial, since it just amounts to eliminating all edges corresponding to conditionally independent pairs from the complete graph. Obviously, for each set of pairwise independencies, there is a unique corresponding Markov network which is a minimal I-map. Figure 3.1 shows an illustrative example: Starting from a complete graph (a), the list of pairwise conditional independence statements specifies edges to be eliminated, resulting in the graph (b).

3.3.2   Pairwise, Local, and Global Markov Properties

The above definition is based on the *pairwise Markov* property of a graph and only deals with special types of conditional independencies. However, one can ask whether it is possible to read off additional or strengthened conditional independencies from a Markov network. Clearly, as witnessed by the identities in (3.1), a given set of conditional independence statements may imply many more conditional independencies. But how can such statements be derived in a systematic way from the graph representation? One way to interpret an undirected graph in terms of conditional independencies is in terms of the so-called *local Markov* property:

$$X \perp\!\!\!\perp \overline{bd}(X) | bd(X), \tag{3.2}$$

where $bd(X)$ denotes the boundary (neighbors) of X, $bd(X) = \{X' : (X, X') \in E\}$ and $\overline{bd}(X) = V - (bd(X) \cup \{X\})$ refers to the remaining nodes. $bd(X)$ is also called the *Markov blanket* of X. Thus the local Markov property simply states that given its Markov blanket, a random variable is rendered independent of the rest of the variables. It can be shown that this interpretation of a Markov network graph is in fact valid and equivalent to the interpretation of a graph in terms of pairwise Markov properties. We show here one direction of this equivalence:

Proposition 17 *The local Markov property of a graph implies the pairwise Markov properties.*

Proof Note that if $(X, Y) \notin E$ and $X \neq Y$, then $Y \in \overline{bd}(X)$. Now by assumption we know that $X \perp\!\!\!\perp \overline{bd}(X)|bd(X)$. The claim follows from property (3.1b) since $\{Y\} \subseteq \overline{bd}(X)$. ∎

Returning to the example in figure 3.1, this results in a list of additional independence statements (c), such as A being independent of D, E given its immediate neighbors B, C.

Finally, by virtue of the separation theorem (cf. Whittaker (1990)) one can also show the equivalence between the above definition and one that is based on global separation properties of the graph, called the *global Markov* property: for disjoint subsets $A, B, C \subseteq V$, where C separates A from B in $\mathcal{G}$ one has that $A \perp\!\!\!\perp B|C$. Separation in an undirected graph means that every path between nodes in A and B contains at least one node in C. An example is shown in figure 3.1 (d): C separates A, B from D, E, in fact removing C effectively cuts the graph into the subgraphs $A - B$ and $D - E$. Here we show first one direction of this equivalence:

Proposition 18 *The global Markov property of a graph implies the local Markov property.*

Proof Every path from X to a node $Y \in \overline{bd}(X)$ has to pass through $bd(X)$. Hence $bd(X)$ separates X from $\overline{bd}(X)$ and by assumption $X \perp\!\!\!\perp \overline{bd}(X)|bd(X)$. ∎

To complete the above proofs, we show the more involved result that the pairwise Markov property implies the global Markov property. This completes a circle of three implications, which together establish the equivalence of all three Markov properties.

Proposition 19 *For distributions with full support, the pairwise Markov property of a graph implies the global Markov property.*

Proof (i) *Given disjoint variables sets A, B, C with $V = A \cup B \cup C$ such that C separates A from B in $\mathcal{G}$. Performing reverse induction on the cardinality of C we show that $A \perp\!\!\!\perp B|C$ is implied by the pairwise Markov properties of $\mathcal{G}$. First consider the case of singleton sets $A = \{X\}$ and $B = \{Y\}$, i.e. $|C| = n - 2$. If C separates A and B, then $(X, Y) \notin E$ and the result follows directly from the pairwise Markov property $X \perp\!\!\!\perp Y|V - \{X, Y\}$. Now consider w.l.o.g. $|A| \geq 2$, so that $A = A_1 \cup A_2$, for some A_1, A_2 with $|A_1|, |A_2| \geq 1$. If C separates A and B, then $C \cup A_1$ separates A_2 from B and by the induction hypothesis $A_1 \perp\!\!\!\perp B|(C, A_2)$. By exchanging A_1 and A_2 one also obtains $A_2 \perp\!\!\!\perp B|(C, A_1)$. Applying (3.1e) finishes this part of the proof. (ii) The second case of $A \cup B \cup C \subsetneq V$ also uses reverse induction over the size of C, leading to the same base case: pick $\alpha \in V - (A \cup B \cup C)$. If C separates A and B, so does $C \cup \{\alpha\}$, hence by induction hypothesis we get $A \perp\!\!\!\perp B|(C, \alpha)$. Note further that either $C \cup A$ separates α from B or $C \cup B$ separates A from α. W.l.o.g. assume* *the former, which implies* $\alpha \perp\!\!\!\perp B | (C, A)$. *From (3.1e) we get* $(A, \alpha) \perp\!\!\!\perp B | C$ *and from (3.1b) we can derive that* $A \perp\!\!\!\perp B | C$. ■

3.3.3 Factorization Theorem

Another result that is even more important in our context is the following factorization result (Hammersley and Clifford, 1971; Besag, 1974; Winkler, 1995) that shows how conditional independencies imply a decomposition of the joint distribution into a product of simpler functions. Denote by $\mathcal{C}(\mathcal{G})$ the cliques of $\mathcal{G}$, i.e. the maximal complete subgraphs. We will think of $c \in \mathcal{C}(\mathcal{G})$ in terms of index sets $c \subseteq \{1, \ldots, m\}$ and will write $X_c = \{X_i : i \in c\}$.

Theorem 20 (Hammersley-Clifford) *Given random variables* $\{X_1, \ldots, X_m\}$ *with independence graph* $\mathcal{G}$. *Any probability density (or probability mass) function with full support factorizes over* $\mathcal{C}(\mathcal{G})$ *as follows:*

$$p(X_1 \ldots, X_n) = \prod_{c \in \mathcal{C}(\mathcal{G})} \psi_c(X_c) = \exp\left[\sum_{c \in \mathcal{C}(\mathcal{G})} f_c(X_c).\right] \tag{3.3}$$

The positive functions $\psi_c = \exp[f_c]$ are also called potential functions. This shows how a model that obeys the conditional independence statements encoded in an independence graph naturally decomposes into local models over (typically overlapping) subsets of random variables, namely the maximal cliques of the graphs. Coming back to the example graph in figure 3.1, $\mathcal{G}$ has three maximal cliques, (A, B, C), (C, D), and (D, E), so that the Hammersley-Clifford theorem tells us that there have to be positive functions ψ_1, ψ_2, ψ_3 such that $p(A, B, C, D, E) = \psi_1(A, B, C)\psi_2(C, D)\psi_3(D, E)$.

implications of Hammersley-Clifford theorem

This factorization has two main implications: First, the specification of the joint distribution involves simpler, local functions that are defined over subsets of variables, namely the cliques of the graph. This has advantages for representing and assessing/estimating probability distributions. Second, the above factorization can be exploited for efficient inference, for instance, the junction tree algorithm, which performs computations by passing and processing of messages between cliques (cf. section 3.5).

3.4 Bayesian Networks

3.4.1 Markov Properties in Directed Graphs

Bayesian networks represent conditional independence properties in terms of a *directed acyclic graph* (DAG). We introduce some terminology: The *parents* or parent set $pa(X)$ of a node X in a DAG $\mathcal{G}$ is the set of immediate predecessors of X. The *descendants* $dc(X)$ of a node X are all nodes Y which can be reached from X

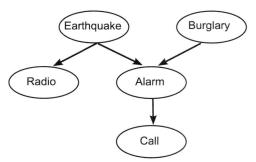

Earthquake $\perp\!\!\!\perp$ Burglary

Burglary $\perp\!\!\!\perp$ Earthquake |Radio

Radio $\perp\!\!\!\perp$ Burglary, Alarm, Call|Earthquake

Alarm $\perp\!\!\!\perp$ Radio—Burglary, Earthquake

Call $\perp\!\!\!\perp$ Radio, Burglary, Earthquake|Alarm

Figure 3.2 Earthquake and burglary network.

by a directed path. The remaining nodes are called *nondescendants ndc(X)*. The Bayesian network semantics interprets a DAG by making the following conditional independence assumptions:

Definition 21 (Bayesian Network) *A Bayesian network for a set of variables* $V = \{X_1, \ldots, X_m\}$ *is a directed acyclic graph* $\mathcal{G} = (V, E)$ *representing the conditional independence statements that each* $X \in V$ *is independent of its nondescendants given its parents, i.e.* $X \perp\!\!\!\perp ndc(X)|pa(X)$.

Definition 22 (Independence Map) *A Bayesian network* $\mathcal{G}$ *is an* independence map *(I-map) for a probability distribution p, if the conditional independencies* $X \perp\!\!\!\perp ndc(X)|pa(X)$ *hold for every* $X \in V$. $\mathcal{G}$ *is a minimal I-map, if there is no* $\mathcal{G}' \subsetneq \mathcal{G}$ *which is an I-map of p.*

In the following we will assume (without loss of generality) that the ordering of the variables $X_1, \ldots, X_m$ is consistent with the partial order induced by the DAG, so that $i < j$ implies that $X_j \notin pa(X_i)$.

To illustrate the Bayesian networks semantics, let us look at a simple example, the so-called burglar network shown in figure 3.2 (left). The conditional independence statements are listed in figure 3.2 (right). For instance, whether or not the alarm went off does not depend on whether a call was received, if we know about the presence/absence of an earthquake and burglary.

There are again two questions one should ask: First, how can a probability distribution that obeys these conditional independencies be factored into a product of simpler functions? Second, which other conditional independence statements are implied by the set of statements that define the Bayesian network semantics?

3.4.2　Factorization Theorem

In order to address the first question, we prove:

Proposition 23 *Let $\mathcal{G} = (V, E)$ be a Bayesian network over $V = \{X_1, \ldots, X_m\}$. Then every probability distribution which has $\mathcal{G}$ as an I-map factors as follows:*

$$p(X_1, \ldots, X_m) = \prod_{i=1}^{m} p(X_i | pa(X_i)). \tag{3.4}$$

Proof Let us start by applying the product (or chain) rule to express the joint probability distribution as the product,

$$p(X_1, \ldots, X_m) = p(X_1)p(X_2|X_1) \ldots p(X_m|X_1, \ldots X_{m-1}) = \prod_{i=1}^{m} p(X_i | X_{1:i-1}).$$

By assumption on the ordering $pa(X_i) \subseteq \{X_1, \ldots, X_{i-1}\} = X_{1:i-1}$ and $X_{1:i-1} - pa(X_i) \subseteq ndc(X_i)$, hence the conditional independence $X_i \perp\!\!\!\perp ndc(X_i)|pa(X_i)$ together with eq. (3.1b) implies $p(X_i|X_{1:i-1}) = p(X_i|pa(X_i))$. Applying this to every node results in the claimed factorization ∎

Proposition 23 shows that the joint probability distribution can be written as a product of "local" conditional probabilities over each variable X that only depend on the parents $pa(X)$ as specified by the DAG. It is also possible to show that the converse holds, i.e. the above factorization implies the conditional independence statements in definition 21.

Proposition 24 *Assume that a probability distribution over $\{X_1, \ldots, X_m\}$ factors as in eq. (3.4) with respect to a DAG $\mathcal{G}$. Then $\mathcal{G}$ is an I-map.*

Proof

$$p(X, pa(X), ndc(X)) = \sum_{dc(X)} \prod_{i=1}^{m} p(X_i | pa(X_i))$$

$$= p(X|pa(X)) \left[\prod_{\substack{X' \in pa(X) \\ \cup ndc(X)}} p(X'|pa(X')) \right] \cdot \sum_{dc(X)} \left[\prod_{X' \in dc(X)} p(X'|pa(X')) \right]$$

$$= p(X|pa(X)) \cdot p(pa(X), ndc(X))$$

Here the fact that the above sum over $dc(X)$ reduces to 1 can be seen by rearranging

$$\sum_{dc(X)} \left[\prod_{X' \in dc(X)} p(X'|pa(X')) \right] = \sum_{X_{i_1}} p(X_{i_1}|pa(X_{i_1})) \cdots \sum_{X_{i_r}} p(X_{i_r}|pa(X_{i_r})),$$

where $dc(X) = \{X_{i_1}, \ldots X_{i_r}\}$ and $i_1 > i_2 \cdots > i_r$. Moreover

$$\prod_{X' \in pa(X) \cup ndc(X)} p(X'|pa(X')) = p(pa(X), ndc(X))$$

follows from the fact that for every node $X' \in pa(X) \cup ndc(X)$, $pa(X') \in pa(X) \cup ndc(X)$. ∎

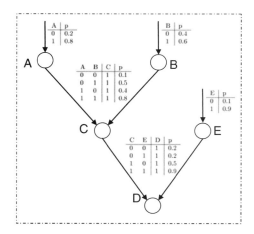

Figure 3.3 Example of a Bayesian network with five nodes.

Because of this equivalence, one often defines Bayesian networks over the factorization in (3.4), which can be done (blindly) without even thinking about the concept of conditional independence.

In the case of finite random variables the conditional distributions can be represented as multidimensional tables, called conditional probability tables (CPTs), but other functional forms are also quite common, e.g. linear or logistic regression models or the noisy-OR model for binary random variables (Pearl, 1988). Figure 3.3 shows a simple Bayesian network over a set of binary variables along with the CPTs. Note that the table sizes depend on the number of parent configurations and a reasonably small number of parents per node is required in order to guarantee a compact representation.[1]

advantages of Bayesian networks

There are many situations where it is quite natural to use the Bayesian network semantics to specify models. For instance, whenever the data-generating process can be modeled as an iterative process of generating the outcome of some variable X based on a subset of previously generated outcomes $pa(X)$, Bayesian networks are the most natural representation. Another situation is one where a causal relationship between variables may be known (or assumed) and directly encoded in the graph structure. However, the general issue of causal models goes beyond Bayesian networks (Pearl, 2000).

In addition to the fact that Bayesian networks are often highly interpretable and may thereby offer advantages for interfacing with human experts, they also have a "technical" advantage that is important in the context of learning: the proper normalization of the local conditional probabilities in the factorization of (3.4). Whereas the normalization of potential functions in the Markov network

---

1. Note that since $p(X = 0|pa(X)) = 1 - p(X = 1|pa(X))$, we have omitted some redundant entries in the CPTs of figure 3.3.

representation of (3.3) depends on the product as a whole, the normalization can be performed independently in Bayesian networks for each factor $p(X|pa(X))$. This is crucial for parameter estimation as well as structure learning. See Heckerman (1999) for more details on learning in Bayesian networks.

In comparing the factorization in (3.4) with the one in (3.3), we see that – modulo the technical issue of nonmaximal cliques – it is possible to convert a Bayesian network to a Markov network, by dropping the directionality of the edges and by adding – whenever necessary – edges between nodes that are coparents, i.e. nodes that have a common child node in the Bayesian network. This procedure of "marrying" coparents is also known as *moralization*. An example is provided in figure 3.3 (B).

3.4.3   d-Separation

While the factorization of the joint distribution can be read off directly from a Bayesian network, stating the implied conditional statements requires a bit more thought. Ideally, one would like to have a simple procedure based on global graph-separation properties (as in the case of the global Markov property) that would allow deciding whether a certain conditional independence statement is or is not implied by the Bayesian network. This leads to the concept of d-separation. In this context it is important to identify the so-called *v*-structures or colliders in a DAG. A *collider* on a path is a node in which edges meet head-to-head, for instance B is collider in the graph $A \rightarrow B \leftarrow C$.

Definition 25 (Collider) *Given a DAG* $\mathcal{G} = (V, E)$ *and an undirected path* $\pi = X_{\pi(0)}, X_{\pi(1)}, \ldots, X_{\pi(l)}$ *of length* l. *The set of colliders of* π *is defined as follows:*

$$coll(\pi) = \{X | \exists 0 < t < l : X = X_{\pi(t)} \land (X_{\pi(t-1)}, X) \in E \land (X_{\pi(t+1)}, X) \in E\}.$$

Intuitively, the variables in a Bayesian network are coupled through active paths that propagate dependencies. The following definition turns out to be appropriate to capture this intuition.

Definition 26 (Active Path) *Given a DAG* $\mathcal{G} = (V, E)$, *an undirected path* π *is active with respect to a conditioning set* $C \subseteq V$, *if*

$$(coll(\pi) \cup dc(coll(\pi))) \cap C \neq \emptyset \quad and \quad (\pi - coll(\pi)) \cap C = \emptyset.$$

A path that is not active is called nonactive or blocked.

This means a path is rendered active by conditioning on a collider or one or more of its descendants and by not conditioning on any of the noncollider nodes. The different cases are sketched in figure 3.4

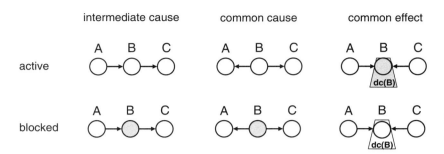

Figure 3.4   Active and blocking paths.

Definition 27 (d-Separation) *For disjoint sets of variables* $A, B, C \subseteq V = \{X_1, \ldots, X_n\}$ *A is d-separated from B given C, if all paths from A to B are blocked given C.*

The notion of d-separation is indeed the one that allows identifying inferred independency statements in Bayesian networks:

Proposition 28 *Given a Bayesian network with DAG* $\mathcal{G} = (V, E)$. *For disjoint nonempty sets* $A, B, C \subset V$ $A \perp\!\!\!\perp B | C$ *if and only if* C *d-separates* A *from* B *in* $\mathcal{G}$.

Finally, one may ask which one of the above representations – Markov networks or Bayesian networks – is more powerful. The answer is neither, since there are Markov networks that have no equivalent formulation as Bayesian networks and vice versa. Without going into depth, we show simple examples in figure 3.5. Hence, in converting a Bayesian network to a Markov network and vice versa we will often only be able to represent a (strict) subset of the conditional independencies represented in the original graph.

3.5   Inference Algorithms

The most common type of inference problem is the conditional probability query: computing probabilities of assignments to unobserved variables of interest given observations for a subset of the variables. The first set is called the query set X_Q and the second set the evidence set X_E for which we have observed evidence x_E. We are then interested in computing $p(X_Q | X_E = x_E)$.

Often one is also interested in finding the most probable configuration of the unobserved variables given the observed ones, $X_Q = V - X_E$, a problem that is known as most probable explanation (MPE), although many authors also refer to

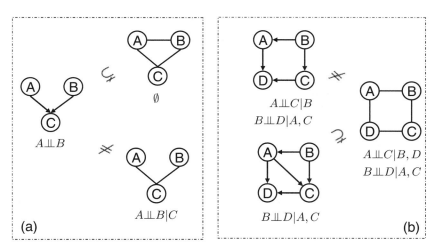

Figure 3.5   Markov networks and Bayes networks.

it as maximum a posteriori (or simply MAP), $x_Q^* = \mathrm{argmax}_{x_Q}\, p(X_Q = x_Q | X_E = x_E)$.[2]

inference is hard

In general, inference in directed and undirected graphical models is computationally hard even if the model is specified compactly (cf. Cowell et al. (1999)).

Theorem 29 *The following problems are NP-complete:*

- *Given a graphical model defining a distribution $p(\cdot)$ over a set of variables $X_1, \ldots, X_n$, a variable $X \in V$, and a value x of X, decide whether $p(X = x) > 0$.*
- *Given a graphical model defining a distribution $p(\cdot)$ over a set of variables $X_1, \ldots, X_n$, and a threshold θ, decide whether there exists an assignment $\mathbf{x}$ such that $p(\mathbf{x}) > \theta$.*

However, there are several special classes of networks for which efficient inference algorithms exist. Most notable examples are linear-chain networks, like hidden Markov models and Kalman filters, for which inference algorithms are well-known (Viterbi and forward-backward).

3.5.1   Decomposable Graphs and Junction Trees

One of the standard algorithms for inference in general Markov networks is the cluster tree or junction tree algorithm (cf. Jensen et al. (1990); Dawid (1992)). The algorithm works on a data structure that is known as a *junction tree*, which

---

2. More broadly, MAP queries ask for the most probable configuration of a *subset* of unobserved variables $X_Q \subseteq V - X_E$. Then $x_Q^* = \mathrm{argmax}_{x_Q} \sum_{x_H} p(X_Q = x_Q, X_H = x_H | X_E = x_E)$, where the set of variables $X_H = V - X_E - X_V$ must be summed out.

is a special type of tree defined over the cliques of the graph fulfilling the *running intersection* property.

Definition 30 (Junction Tree) *A **junction tree** for a graph $\mathcal{G}$ is a tree $\mathcal{T} = (\mathcal{C}(\mathcal{G}), E)$ over the cliques of the graph, with the following property: for all pairs of cliques $c, c' \in \mathcal{C}$ and every clique $d \in \mathcal{C}$ on the (unique) path from c to c' in $\mathcal{T}$ one has that $c \cap c' \subseteq d$, i.e. all variables contained in both c and c' are also contained in every clique on the path connecting the two.*

In order for a junction tree to exist, the underlying graph needs to be decomposable.

Definition 31 (Decomposable) *A graph $\mathcal{G}$ is **decomposable** (or chordal) if any cycle with four or more nodes contains at least one chord.*

The standard procedure for obtaining a junction tree is to first triangulate $\mathcal{G}$, hence enforcing decomposability, and then to apply a maximum spanning tree algorithm to the weighted clique graph $(\mathcal{C}(\mathcal{G}), W)$ with edge weights $W_{cd} = |c \cap d|$ (cf. Shibata (1988), Jensen and Jensen (1994)). Once this data structure is constructed, inference can be performed by local message passing between neighboring cliques in the junction tree. Finding an optimal triangulation, e.g. one that needs the minimum number of fill-in edges or that leads to the smallest maximum clique size, is a hard problem in itself, but reasonable heuristics and constant factor approximations exist (Shoikhet and Geiger, 1997; Becker and Geiger, 2001).

3.5.2   Junction Tree Algorithm

Assume now a junction tree $\mathcal{T}$ for a Markov network $\mathcal{G}$ has been constructed. Denote by X_H the unobserved nodes and by X_E the observed nodes, $V = X_H \cup X_E$. Introduce separators $S = C \cap C'$ for all cliques that are neighbors in $\mathcal{T}$. The sum product algorithm maintains a representation

$$p(X_H, X_E = x_E) = \frac{1}{Z} \frac{\prod_C \phi_C(X_C)}{\prod_S \psi_S(X_S)} \tag{3.5}$$

where we initially set all $\psi_S = 1$. Evidence is absorbed on the level of the clique potential functions ϕ_C by fixing all variables in $C \cap X_E$ at their observed values. We aim at a representation in which $\phi_C(X_C) = p(X_C|X_E)$ and $\psi_S(X_S) = p(X_S|X_E)$ correspond to the (conditional) marginals on the cliques and separator sets, respectively. This requires in particular that marginals for variables occurring in several cliques need to be consistent. Such global consistency can be accomplished by local message passing. Let us first look how at how one may obtain local consistency between pairs of cliques C, D with separator S. We first compute a message that C passes to D as follows:

$$\text{message (1) generation} \quad \psi_S^* \equiv \sum_{X_C - X_S} \phi_C, \tag{3.6a}$$

$$\text{message (1) absorption} \quad \phi_D^* \equiv \frac{\psi_S^*}{\psi_S} \phi_D . \tag{3.6b}$$

Note how this leaves the representation in (3.5) invariant. Now we compute a similar message that D sends back to C

$$\text{message (2) generation} \quad \psi_S^{**} = \sum_{X_D - X_S} \phi_D, \tag{3.7a}$$

$$\text{message (2) absorption} \quad \phi_C^* = \frac{\psi_S^{**}}{\psi_S^*} \phi_C \tag{3.7b}$$

The marginals are now consistent, since

$$\sum_{X_C - X_S} \phi_C^* = \sum_{X_C - X_S} \frac{\psi_S^{**}}{\psi_S^*} \phi_C = \frac{\psi_S^{**}}{\psi_S^*} \sum_{X_C - X_S} \phi_C = \frac{\psi_S^{**}}{\psi_S^*} \psi_S^* = \sum_{X_D - X_S} \phi_D^* . \tag{3.8}$$

This message scheme can be easily extended to a clique tree by fixing a suitable message propagation order, for instance, by picking an arbitrary clique as the root of the tree and by first propagating messages (1) inward from the leaves to the root and then messages (2) outward again from the root to the leaves. One can show, that the fact that the clique tree is a junction tree ensures that all clique potentials are consistent.

3.5.3   Approximate Inference

In many realistic problems, the size of the largest clique of the triangulated graph is too large to perform the junction tree algorithm. However, a similar message-passing scheme has been used widely to perform approximate inference on untriangulated graphs. Instead of passing messages from leaves to root and back in a tree, neighboring cliques pass messages to each other synchronously in a general graph. Although this scheme, called loopy belief propagation (Pearl, 1988), is only guaranteed to converge to the correct marginal probabilities for trees, empirical results (Murphy et al., 1999) show that it often converges in general networks, and when it does, the marginals are a good approximation to the correct posteriors.

Approximate inference algorithms broadly divide into deterministic (e.g., variational methods) and sampling (e.g., Markov chain Monte Carlo methods) based schemes. It is beyond the scope of this chapter to review the wide range of available techniques. We refer the interested reader to several recent surveys (Jordan et al., 1998; Wainwright and Jordan, 2003; Neal, 1993; Doucet et al., 2001).

3.6   Exponential Families

3.6.1   Definition

Another perspective of looking at factorization properties of probability distributions is provided by *exponential families* (Barndorff-Nielsen, 1978), which can be defined as follows:

$$p(\mathbf{x}; \mathbf{w}) = \exp\left[\langle \mathbf{w}, \Phi(\mathbf{x}) \rangle - g(\mathbf{w}) + h(\mathbf{x})\right], \quad \text{where} \tag{3.9}$$

$$g(\mathbf{w}) \equiv \log \int_{\mathcal{X}} \exp\left[\langle \mathbf{w}, \Phi(\mathbf{x}) \rangle + h(\mathbf{x})\right] d\mathbf{x}. \tag{3.10}$$

Here, $\mathbf{w}$ are the canonical parameters, Φ are the sufficient statistics, g is the log-partition (or cummulant-generating) function, and h is an arbitrary, fixed function, which we will omit in the sequel for ease of presentation (it can be absorbed by changing the underlying measure).

3.6.2   Basic Properties

Exponential families have the characteristic property that the dimensionality of the sufficient statistics remains constant, if joint distribution over i.i.d. samples are considered, i.e. for an n sample $S = \{\mathbf{x}_1, \ldots, \mathbf{x}_n\}$,

$$p(S; \mathbf{w}) = \exp\left[\sum_{i=1}^{n} \langle \mathbf{w}, \Phi(\mathbf{x}_i) \rangle - ng(\mathbf{w})\right] = \exp\left[\langle \mathbf{w}, \Phi(S) \rangle - ng(\mathbf{w})\right], \tag{3.11}$$

advantages

which is also in exponential form, the sufficient statistics being $\Phi(S) \equiv \sum_{i=1}^{n} \Phi(\mathbf{x}_i)$. Among other things this implies that in many cases statistical inference about the unknown parameters $\mathbf{w}$ will only depend on the sufficient statistics, a fact that is also stressed by the Rao-Blackwell theorem. It is well-known that much of the structure of exponential models can be derived from the log partition function $g(\mathbf{w})$, in particular (cf. Lauritzen (1996)),

$$\nabla_{\mathbf{w}} g(\mathbf{w}) = \mathbf{E}[\Phi(\mathbf{x})], \quad \text{and} \quad \nabla_{\mathbf{w}}^2 g(\mathbf{w}) = \mathbf{V}[\Phi(\mathbf{x})], \tag{3.12}$$

where the expectation $\mathbf{E}[\cdot]$ and the variance $\mathbf{V}[\cdot]$ are computed with respect to $p(\mathbf{x}; \mathbf{w})$. Another trait that makes exponential families very convenient to work with from a computational point of view is that the maximum likelihood estimates for $\mathbf{w}$ can be computed in closed form using the expected sufficient statistics $\mathbf{E}[\Phi(\mathbf{x})]$ (DeGroot, 1970; Hastie et al., 2001). More precisely the maximum likelihood equations are given by

$$\nabla_{\mathbf{w}} \log p(S; \mathbf{w}) = \Phi(S) - n\nabla g(\mathbf{w}) = \Phi(S) - n \int_{\mathcal{X}} \Phi(\mathbf{x}) p(\mathbf{x}; \mathbf{w}) d\mathbf{x} \stackrel{!}{=} 0, \tag{3.13}$$

which leads to the simple and concise condition $\mathbf{E}[\Phi(\mathbf{x})] = \Phi(S) = \mathbf{E}_S[\Phi(\mathbf{x})]$, where the latter denotes the sample average of the sufficient statistics.

3.6.3 Exponential Families for Markov Networks

Exponential families can be related to Markov networks by taking the factorization theorem as the starting point. From (3.3) we know that any (full support) probability distribution that fulfills the Markov properties encoded in a conditional dependency graph can be written in the form

$$\log p(\mathbf{x}) = \sum_{c \in \mathcal{C}(\mathcal{G})} f_c(\mathbf{x}_c), \tag{3.14}$$

with suitable functions f_c. Now, if we do not treat these functions as given, but rather define a family of distributions by assuming that each f_c can be written as a simple linear expansion using basis function f_{cr}, $r = 1, \ldots, R_c$ (modulo proper normalization), we arrive at the following model:

$$\log p(\mathbf{x}; \mathbf{w}) = \sum_{c \in \mathcal{C}(\mathcal{G})} \sum_{r=1}^{R_c} w_{cr} f_{cr}(\mathbf{x}_c) - g(\mathbf{w}). \tag{3.15}$$

In the case of random variables with finite sample spaces, the functions f_{cr} may, for instance, correspond to indicator functions for the R_c possible clique configurations. More generally, we can think of every potential function as being a member of a suitably defined exponential family. By joining all functions in a single vector-valued statistic, we can see that (3.15) corresponds to an exponential family.

3.7 Probabilistic Context-Free Grammars

In this section, we consider important dependency structures that are not naturally handled by the graphical model formalism. Context-free grammars (CFGs) are one of the primary formalisms for modeling syntactic constructions (Manning and Schütze, 1999). Recently, the CFGs have also been used to capture RNA secondary structure (Durbin et al., 1998). In natural language grammars (see example in figure 3.6), the nonterminal symbols (labels of internal nodes) typically correspond to syntactic categories such as noun phrase (NP), verbal phrase (VP), or prepositional phrase (PP), and part-of-speech tags like nouns (N), verbs (V), determiners (Det), and prepositions (P). The terminal symbols (leaves) are the words of the sentence.

3.7.1   Representation

For simplicity, we restrict our attention to grammars in Chomsky normal form (CNF), where all rules in the grammar are of the form: $A \to B\ C$ and $A \to D$, where $A, B,$ and C are nonterminal symbols, and D is a terminal symbol.

Definition 32 (CFG) *A CFG $\mathcal{G}$ consists of*

- *set of nonterminal symbols, $\mathcal{N}$;*
- *designated start symbol, S;*
- *set of terminal symbols, $\mathcal{T}$;*
- *set of productions, $\mathcal{P} = \{A \to \lambda\}$, divided into*
    - *binary productions, $\mathcal{P}_B = \{A \to B\ C : A, B, C \in \mathcal{N}\}$ and*
    - *unary productions, $\mathcal{P}_U = \{A \to D : A \in \mathcal{N}, D \in \mathcal{T}\}$.*

Consider a very simple grammar:

- $\mathcal{N} = \{S, NP, VP, PP, N, V, Det, P\}$.
- $\mathcal{T} = \{The, the, cat, dog, tree, chased, from\}$.
- $\mathcal{P}_B = \{S \to NP\ VP, NP \to Det\ N, NP \to NP\ PP, VP \to V\ NP, VP \to VP\ PP, PP \to P\ NP\}$.
- $\mathcal{P}_U = \{Det \to The, Det \to the, N \to cat, N \to dog, N \to tree, V \to chased, P \to from\}$.

example

A grammar generates a sentence by starting with the symbol S and applying the productions in $\mathcal{P}$ to rewrite nonterminal symbols. For example, we can generate *The dog chased the cat* by starting with $S \to NP\ VP$, rewriting the NP as $NP \to Det\ N$ with $Det \to The$ and $N \to dog$, then rewriting the VP as $VP \to V\ NP$ with $V \to chased$, again using $NP \to Det\ N$, but now with $Det \to the$ and $N \to cat$. We can represent such derivations using parse trees as in the bottom left of figure 3.6.

The simple grammar above can generate sentences of arbitrary length, since it has several recursive productions. It can also generate the same sentence several ways. In general, there are exponentially many parse trees that produce a sentence of length. Consider the sentence: *The dog chased the cat from the tree.* The likely analysis of the sentence is that the dog chased the cat away from the tree. A less likely but possible alternative is that the dog chased the cat who lives in the tree. Our grammar allows both interpretations, with the difference being in the analysis of the top-level VP as seen in figure 3.6.

So far we have considered the set of legal strings (as well as corresponding parse trees) that a grammar can generate. To capture which sentences are likely and which are not, we can define a joint probability distribution over the space of parse trees and sentences. A probabilistic (or stochastic) CFG (PCFG) defines such a

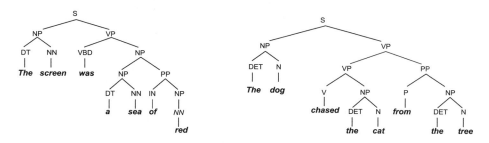

Figure 3.6 Examples of parse trees.

distribution $p(t)$ over trees by assigning a probability to each production and such that the sum of probabilities of all productions starting with each symbol is 1:

$$\sum_{\lambda:A\to\lambda\in\mathcal{P}} p(A \to \lambda \mid A) = 1, \quad \forall A \in \mathcal{N}.$$

The probability of a given tree (including the sentence) is simply the product of probabilities of the productions used in the tree.

$$p(t) = \prod_{A\to\lambda\in t} p(A \to \lambda \mid A).$$

A PCFG induces a probability distribution over the yields of trees, sequences of terminals $\mathcal{T}^*$. The probability of a sequence s is the sum of the probabilities of trees that yield it, $T(s)$:

$$p(s) = \sum_{t\in T(s)} p(t).$$

Conversely, a PCFG defines the most likely tree for a given sentence:

$$t^*(s) = \operatorname*{argmax}_{t\in T(s)} p(t).$$

Next, we review an efficient algorithm for PCFG inference.

3.7.2 Inference

We can use the Cocke-Younger-Kasami (CKY) dynamic programming algorithm to compute the most likely parse tree in $\mathcal{O}(n^3)$ time (Younger, 1967; Manning and Schütze, 1999). The input to the algorithm is a sequence $s_1, ..., s_n$ of terminal symbols. The algorithm recursively fills out an array $\pi(i, j, A)$ representing highest probability of any subtree starting with the symbol A yielding $s_i, ..., s_j$. When the array is completed, the probability of the most likely parse tree spanning the entire sequence will be stored in $\pi(1, n, S)$.

Base step: for $i = 1, \ldots, n$, set

$$\pi(i, i, A) = p(A \to s_i | A), \quad \forall A \in \mathcal{N}.$$

Recursive step: for $d = 1, \ldots, n-1$, for $i = 1, \ldots, n-d$, set $j = i + d$ and

$$\pi(i, j, A) = \max_{\substack{A \to B\,C \in \mathcal{P}_B \\ i \leq k < j}} \{p(A \to B\,C \mid A) * \pi(i, k, B) * \pi(k+1, j, C)\}, \quad \forall A \in \mathcal{N}.$$

Using the argmax's of the max's in the computation of π, we can backtrace the most likely tree itself. We assume that ties are broken in a predetermined way, say according to a lexicographic order of the symbols. A similar dynamic program can be used to compute the probability of a sequence $p(s)$, where the max operation above is replaced with a sum.

3.8 Structured Prediction

We now turn to using structured models for prediction tasks. In contrast to standard supervised learning problems such as classification and regression, which involve simple scalar outputs, structured prediction deals with structured or compound response variables, including structures such as sequences, strings, trees, lattices, or graphs. Here, we will focus in particular on the supervised setting of learning mappings between arbitrary input spaces $\mathcal{X}$ and discrete output spaces $\mathcal{Y}$, based on a sample of input-output pairs $\{(\mathbf{x}_i, \mathbf{y}_i) : i = 1 \ldots, n\}$, a scenario that is called *structured classification*. In the simplest case, we will be dealing with fixed-length vector-valued outputs $\mathbf{y} = (y_1, \ldots, y_L) \in \mathcal{Y} \subseteq \mathcal{Y}_1 \times \ldots \times \mathcal{Y}_L$, where each $\mathcal{Y}_j$ is a finite set. This setting is also referred to as *collective classification*, since a prediction is made collectively for all L response variables y_j. In some cases, the range of allowed outputs may also depend on the input, i.e. $\mathcal{Y} = \mathcal{Y}(\mathbf{x})$. More complex problems may involve outputs such as strings, trees, or graphs.

The crucial question is: Why would one want to make predictions jointly instead of simply predicting each output independently? The key benefit is that it allows taking interdependencies between outputs into account, in addition to the statistical dependencies that exist between inputs and outputs. These interdependencies may be expressible beforehand in the form of constraints that restrict the set of admissible outputs $\mathcal{Y}$, or take the more malleable form of statistical correlations between the different output variables.

The range of prediction problems these broad definitions encompass is immense, arising in fields as diverse as natural language analysis, machine vision, and computational biology, to name just a few. For concreteness consider the task of handwriting recognition. Figure 3.7 shows an example of a handwritten word brace. Distinguishing between the second letter and fourth letter (r and c) *in isolation* is far from trivial, but in the context of the surrounding letters that together form a

Figure 3.7 Handwritten word recognition: sample from (Kassel, 1995) dataset.

word, this task is much less error-prone for humans and should be for computers as well. In word recognition, each $\mathcal{Y}_j$ is the alphabet, while $\mathcal{Y}$ corresponds to the dictionary of words. The dictionary might a priori exclude certain character sequences; for instance, the letter q may never be follows by z in English. In addition to "hard" constraints, the output variables may also be highly correlated, for instance, due to phonetic regularities that make certain letter combinations more or less likely.

3.8.1   Conditional Models

An important distinction in using probabilistic models for prediction tasks is between *generative* and *conditional models*. In the generative case, one aims at modeling the joint distribution over a domain of interest, without a priori committing to a fixed split of the variables into input $\mathbf{x}$ and output $\mathbf{y}$. For example, PCFGs define a joint model over trees and sentences. Yet, in many applications it is typically known which variables are considered inputs and outputs, respectively, in which case conditional (or discriminative) modeling based on the conditional distribution $p(\mathbf{y}|\mathbf{x})$ may be advantageous.

In principle, one could derive a conditional model for $\mathbf{y}$ given $\mathbf{x}$ from a generative model over $(\mathbf{x}, \mathbf{y})$ by conditioning on the input $\mathbf{x}$, $p(\mathbf{y}|\mathbf{x}) = p(\mathbf{x}, \mathbf{y})/p(\mathbf{x})$, where $p(\mathbf{x}) = \sum_{\mathbf{y} \in \mathcal{Y}} p(\mathbf{x}, \mathbf{y})$. However, it is often more advantageous to directly learn conditional models. One reason is that generative models often require making strong simplifying assumptions, e.g. (conditional) independence assumptions, which may be overly restrictive for a specific problem of predicting $\mathbf{y}$ from $\mathbf{x}$. Another reason is that by fitting a joint distribution $p(\mathbf{x}, \mathbf{y})$, we may be tuning the approximation away from the optimal conditional distribution $p(\mathbf{y}|\mathbf{x})$, which we use to make the predictions. Given sufficient data, the conditional model will aim at learning the best approximation to $p(\mathbf{y}|\mathbf{x})$ possible, while the generative model $p(\mathbf{x}, \mathbf{y})$ will not necessarily do so.

3.8.2   Linear Models for Structured Prediction

The class of structured models $\mathcal{H}$ we consider generalizes the notion of linear discriminant functions utilized in the context of classification, e.g. in perceptron and support vector machine (SVM) classification. Instead of using feature maps defined over the input space alone, we assume here that an appropriate *joint feature map* $\Phi : \mathcal{X} \times \mathcal{Y} \to \mathbb{R}^m$ is available. Given such a vector-valued function Φ, we can

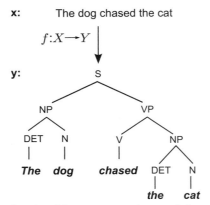

Figure 3.8   Illustration of natural language parsing model.

compatibility
function

then define $\mathcal{H}$ to be the set of linear functions f, parametrized by a weight vector $\mathbf{w}$,

$$f(\mathbf{x}, \mathbf{y}) = \langle \mathbf{w}, \Phi(\mathbf{x}, \mathbf{y}) \rangle . \qquad (3.16)$$

We also refer to f as a *compatibility function* between inputs and outputs. A compatibility function implicitly defines a mapping F from inputs to outputs (up to tie-breaking) via

$$F(\mathbf{x}) = \operatorname*{argmax}_{\mathbf{y} \in \mathcal{Y}} f(\mathbf{x}, \mathbf{y}) . \qquad (3.17)$$

This formulation is very general; clearly, for many choices of Φ and $\mathcal{Y}$, finding the optimal $\mathbf{y}$ for a given $\mathbf{x}$ may be intractable. However, as we will see, there are many models where the optimization problem in (3.17) can be solved in polynomial time.

To illustrate the concept of a joint feature map, consider the problem of natural language parsing with CFGs illustrated in figure 3.8. We can choose Φ such that the linear model in (3.16) becomes isomorphic to a PCFG (cf. Manning and Schütze (1999)). A valid parse tree $\mathbf{y} \in \mathcal{Y}(\mathbf{x})$ for a sentence $\mathbf{x}$ is one that has the designated start symbol as the root and the words in the sentence as the leaves. Each node of the parse tree corresponds to a production q_j with associated weight w_j, from which a score is computed by adding up all weights w_j. This score can thus be written as a linear function in $\Phi(\mathbf{x}, \mathbf{y})$, where each feature ϕ_j corresponds to the number of times production q_j has been used in the parse tree. $F(\mathbf{x})$ can be efficiently computed by finding the structure $\mathbf{y} \in \mathcal{Y}(\mathbf{x})$ that maximize f via the CKY algorithm (Manning and Schütze, 1999).

A very generic way of designing joint feature maps is to independently specify feature maps over inputs and outputs, Φ^x and Φ^y, respectively, and to combine them via the Kronecker (or tensor) product $\Phi(\mathbf{x}, \mathbf{y}) = \Phi^x(\mathbf{x}) \otimes \Phi^y(\mathbf{y})$. Every joint feature will thus be a multiplicative combination of some input and some output feature, corresponding to a simple logical conjunction in the case of Boolean features. For such tensor product feature maps inner products factorize nicely, $\langle \Phi(\mathbf{x}, \mathbf{y}), \Phi(\hat{\mathbf{x}}, \hat{\mathbf{y}}) \rangle = \langle \Phi^x(\mathbf{x}), \Phi^x(\hat{\mathbf{x}}) \rangle \langle \Phi^y(\mathbf{y}), \Phi^y(\hat{\mathbf{y}}) \rangle$, which often is advantageous in the context of kernel-based learning algorithms.

3.8.3 Generalized Linear Models

To link this back to the previous paragraphs on exponential families and linear models for structured prediction, one may define

$$p(\mathbf{y}|\mathbf{x}; \mathbf{w}) = \exp\left[f(\mathbf{x}, \mathbf{y}) - g(\mathbf{x}, \mathbf{w})\right], \quad g(\mathbf{x}, \mathbf{w}) \equiv \log \sum_{\mathbf{y} \in \mathcal{Y}} \exp\left[f(\mathbf{x}, \mathbf{y})\right] . \quad (3.18)$$

Since $f(\mathbf{x}, \mathbf{y}) = \langle \mathbf{w}, \Phi(\mathbf{x}, \mathbf{y}) \rangle$, the conditional distributions parameterized by $\mathbf{w}$ form an *exponential family* with sufficient statistics $\Phi_{\mathbf{x}}(\mathbf{y}) \equiv \Phi(\mathbf{x}, \mathbf{y})$ for every $\mathbf{x}$. We refer to this as a *conditional exponential family*.

Probabilistic semantics are certainly not necessary for a good predictive model if we are simply interested in the optimal prediction (the argmax in (3.17)). As we discussed in the previous chapter, SVMs, which do not represent a conditional distribution, typically perform as well or better than probabilistic models in many applications (Vapnik, 1995; Cristianini and Shawe-Taylor, 2000).

In general, we can often achieve higher accuracy models when we do not learn a normalized distribution over the outputs, but concentrate on the margin or decision boundary, the difference between the optimal $\mathbf{y}$, and the rest. We can still rely on the representation and inference tools familiar from probabilistic models for the construction of and prediction in unnormalized models, but largely dispense with the probabilistic interpretation when needed. Essentially, we use the term model very broadly, to include any scheme that assigns scores to the output space $\mathcal{Y}$ and has a procedure for finding the optimal scoring $\mathbf{y}$.

3.9 Conclusion

The graphical model formalism is currently the predominant framework for representing structured probability distributions across a wide variety of fields, including computer vision and robotics, computational biology and linguistics, signal processing, and decision analysis. A large proportion of active research is concerned with developing and analyzing efficient algorithms for approximate inference and learning in graphical models, bringing together tools from convex optimization and graph-theoretic algorithms as well as stochastic simulation. Among the several themes in this collection is the lifting and adaptation of recent methodologies for problems of classification and regression to graphical models. The questions raised by such efforts exhibit a rich interplay between the statistical and the computational aspects of structured prediction.

II Structured Prediction Based on Discriminative Models

4   Joint Kernel Maps

Jason Weston, Gökhan Bakır, Olivier Bousquet, Tobias Mann, William Stafford Noble, and Bernhard Schölkopf

We develop a methodology for solving high-dimensional estimation problems between pairs of arbitrary data types as a regression problem. This is achieved by mapping the objects into a continuous or discrete space using joint kernels. The resulting algorithm is an extension of the large-margin classification-based structured output algorithms to the regression case, and includes all standard support vector machine (SVM)-type optimization problems as special cases. Joint kernels allow us to explicitly specify a priori known input-output and output-output correlations for each output dimension. We provide examples of such kernels and empirical results on mass spectrometry prediction and a problem of image transformation.

4.1   Introduction

A standard concern in predicting output data that are nonvectorial is to represent the structural dependencies between output variables in a form amenable to prediction. Consider, for example, predicting a binary sequence where the nth bit depends on a subset of other output bits. A learning algorithm has to take into account the structure of the output while learning to yield an accurate prediction model. One approach to incorporate such constraints into the learning process is to pose each output variable as a single output dimension and to encode the dependency as an output-output correlation. This will be one of the main concerns of this chapter.

Our framework, which extends (Weston et al., 2005), is based on a multivariate regression setting where we use kernels to map the data into a single *joint* feature space using *joint kernels* (Tsochantaridis et al., 2004), a way of implicitly embedding data by only requiring the computation of dot products in the embedding space. Using such joint kernels on inputs and outputs simultanously we are able to encode any prior knowledge on possible correlations into our learning algorithm.

chapter
organization

This chapter is organized as follows. In the following section we start with the basic setting of linear regression and discuss how to incorporate correlation into the problem of learning linear maps. We will show that our formulation is very general, and is in fact a generalization of classification-based structured output algorithms to the regression case. It includes all standard SVM-type optimization problems as special cases: binary (Boser et al., 1992), multiclass (Weston and Watkins, 1998), and regression (Vapnik, 1995).

Subsequently we extend our formulation to use joint kernels on both input and output variables simultaneously, which leads to the development of a structured output learning algorithm for the continuous output variable case. We show how this is related to the existing discrete structured output learning case (Tsochantaridis et al., 2004). Finally we put our framework to use on two problems: predicting peptides given an observed mass spectrum, posed as a prediction problem from a spectrum to a string; and solving an image transformation problem between related pairs of images where the output is high-dimensional, but local dependencies are known: given images of people with a plain expression, we predict how they will look when they are smiling.

4.2   Incorporating Correlations into Linear Regression

We begin with the problem of linear regression. Given a training set of input-output pairs $\{(\mathbf{x}_1, \mathbf{y}_1), .., (\mathbf{x}_m, \mathbf{y}_m)\}$ identically and independently sampled from a distribution P over the product space $\mathcal{X} \times \mathcal{Y}$, we wish to find a function W that maps from $\mathcal{X}$ into $\mathcal{Y}$ such that

$$\int_{\mathcal{X} \times \mathcal{Y}} \|\mathbf{y} - W\mathbf{x}\|_{\mathcal{Y}}^2 \mathrm{dP}(\mathbf{x}, \mathbf{y})$$

is minimized. Here, we assume $\mathcal{X}$ and $\mathcal{Y}$ are vector spaces; later we will consider them to be any objects, and use kernels to embed them in a vector space. This is a classical learning problem that has been widely studied when $\mathcal{X} = \mathbb{R}^p$, $\mathcal{Y} = \mathbb{R}^q$, and q is small with the most prominent example being least squares regression.

exploiting correlation

When the output dimension becomes very high, to learn effectively, one must take into account (i) correlation between output variables, (ii) correlation between input variables, and (iii) correlation between input *and* output variables.

Known input correlations can be exploited with weight sharing (choosing a regularizer that treats these features similarly) or in nonlinear methods by lowering the amount of regularization on nonlinear features that are a function of correlated features, as has been exploited e.g. in digit recognition (Vapnik, 1998).

A classical approach for incorporating output correlations is to adopt the cost function

$$\frac{1}{m} \sum_{s,t}^{\dim(\mathcal{Y})} \sum_{i=1}^{m} [W\mathbf{x}_i - \mathbf{y}_i]_s [W\mathbf{x}_i - \mathbf{y}_i]_t \sigma_{st},$$

where $[\mathbf{z}]_s$ denotes the sth component of vector $\mathbf{z}$ and $\Sigma = (\sigma_{ij}) \in \mathbb{R}^{\dim(\mathcal{Y}) \times \dim(\mathcal{Y})}$ is a reweighting of the error metric. That is, we replace the Euclidean distance by an arbitrary quadratic form, hence off-diagonal elements of Σ incorporate the correlations.

In contrast, if prior knowledge exists on input-output correlations as well, one could choose to introduce a regularization functional $\Omega : \mathcal{X}^{\mathcal{Y}} \to \mathbb{R}_+$ instead of altering the used error metric. Then, a classical approach to minimization scheme could be adopted that minimizes

encoding correlation into the regularizer

$$\frac{1}{m} \sum_{i=1}^{m} \|W\mathbf{x}_i - \mathbf{y}_i\|^2 + \Omega[W].$$

For instance, we propose

$$\Omega[W] = \sum_{i,j=1}^{\dim(\mathcal{X})} \sum_{s,t=1}^{\dim(\mathcal{Y})} W_{is} W_{jt} S_{ijst}, \tag{4.1}$$

where the tensor S_{ijst} encodes the correlation between parameters W_{is} and W_{jt}. For example, suppose one is learning a mapping between two images of equal and large dimension, where it is known that the top left corner of the input image is correlated to the top left-hand corner of the output image. This knowledge can be encoded into S. The challenge is to rewrite such an optimization problem in the general case so that (i) it can be solved in a dual form to make it tractable for high dimension and (ii) it can be generalized with kernels to also solve nonlinear problems. We will see that regularization schemes based on (4.1) will allow us to achieve this goal.

We now show how to encode such prior knowledge by defining appropriate joint kernel functions and subsequent minimization in dual variables, building on work such as kernel dependency estimation (KDE)(see section 1.5) and work presented in Tsochantaridis et al. (2004). The subsequent algorithm will solve much more than linear regression: it will generalize nonlinear SVMs for classification *and* regression, and will also be able to deal with structured outputs such as strings, trees, and graphs via kernels (Haussler, 1999; Watkins, 1999; Tsochantaridis et al., 2004). This will be an extension of previous work on structured outputs, as our method will be able to deal with both the discrete and continuous output variable cases, whereas only the discrete case was addressed before.

4.3 Linear Maps and Kernel Methods : Generalizing Support Vector Machines

In the following section we describe an algorithm which contains all standard support vector algorithms as special cases. We start by considering a linear map W. We will make predictions on data using the equation

$$\mathbf{y}(\mathbf{x}) = \text{argmin}_{\mathbf{y} \in \mathcal{Y}} \|W\mathbf{x} - \mathbf{y}\|^2 = W\mathbf{x}.$$

We consider an ε-insensitive loss approach, as in support vector regression (SVR) (Vapnik (1998)). We choose the W that minimizes

$$\|\mathrm{W}\|^2_{FRO},\qquad(4.2)$$

using the Frobenius norm, subject to

$$\|\mathrm{W}\mathbf{x}_i - \mathbf{y}\|^2 \geq \|\mathrm{W}\mathbf{x}_i - \mathbf{y}_i\|^2 + \varepsilon^2/2,\quad \forall i, \{\forall \mathbf{y} \in \mathcal{Y} : \|\mathbf{y}_i - \mathbf{y}\| \geq \varepsilon\}.\qquad(4.3)$$

Note that the constraints can also be written as $\forall i \{\forall \mathbf{y} \in \mathcal{Y} : \|\mathbf{y}_i - \mathbf{y}\| \geq \varepsilon\}$: $2(\mathbf{y}_i - \mathbf{y})^\top W x_i \geq \varepsilon^2/2 + \|\mathbf{y}_i\|^2 - \|\mathbf{y}\|^2$. Let us postpone the technical difficulty that this formulation has possibly infinitely many constraints for later (see section 4.4.1). We now show how this algorithm generalizes both support vector classification and regression:

4.3.1   Support Vector Regression

For $\mathbf{y} \in \mathbb{R}$ one obtains SVR (Vapnik, 1998) without threshold, and for $\mathbf{y} \in \mathbb{R}^q$ one obtains vector-valued ε-insensitive SVR (Pérez-Cruz et al., 2002). We rewrite (4.3) as $\min_{\mathbf{y} \in C_\epsilon(\mathbf{y}_i)} \|\mathbf{W}\mathbf{x}_i - \mathbf{y}\|^2 \geq \|\mathbf{W}\mathbf{x}_i - \mathbf{y}_i\|^2 + \epsilon^2/2$ where $C_\epsilon(\mathbf{y}_i)$ is the complement of the open ball of radius ϵ centered at $\mathbf{y}_i$. If $\mathbf{W}\mathbf{x}_i$ is not in the latter ball, the value of this minimum is zero and the problem does not have any solution. On the other hand, if $\mathbf{W}\mathbf{x}_i$ is in the ball, then this minimum is not zero and can be computed directly. Its value is attained for the following $\mathbf{y}$:

$$\mathbf{y} = \mathbf{y}_i + \frac{\mathbf{W}\mathbf{x}_i - \mathbf{y}_i}{\|\mathbf{W}\mathbf{x}_i - \mathbf{y}_i\|}\epsilon.$$

The value of the minimum is then $(\epsilon - \|\mathbf{W}\mathbf{x}_i - \mathbf{y}_i\|)^2$. We then have the constraint $(\epsilon - \|\mathbf{W}\mathbf{x}_i - \mathbf{y}_i\|)^2 \geq \|\mathbf{W}\mathbf{x}_i - \mathbf{y}_i\|^2 + \epsilon^2/2$ which gives, after some algebra, $\|\mathbf{W}\mathbf{x}_i - \mathbf{y}_i\| \leq \epsilon/4$. Disregarding the scaling, this is the same as the usual SVR constraints.

4.3.2   Support Vector Classification

For $y \in \{\pm 1\}$ and $0 \leq \varepsilon < 2$ we obtain two-class SVMs (Vapnik, 1998) (W is a $1 \times p$ matrix). Expanding the constraint (4.3) for each i gives $-2y\mathrm{W}x_i + 2y_i\mathrm{W}x_i \geq \varepsilon^2/2$. For $y, y_i \in \{\pm 1\}, \|y_i - y\| \geq \varepsilon$ only occurs for $y = -y_i$, in which case we have $y_i\mathrm{W}x_i \geq \varepsilon^2/8$, the usual SVM constraints, disregarding scaling and threshold b.

4.3.3   Multiclass Support Vector Machines

Similarly, for $\mathbf{y} \in \{0,1\}^q$, where the c_ith entry is 1 when example i is in class c_i, and 0 otherwise, and $0 \leq \varepsilon < \sqrt{2}$, we can obtain multiclass SVMs (Weston and Watkins, 1998). As $\|\mathbf{y}\| = 1$ we have the constraints $\mathbf{y}_i^\top W\mathbf{x}_i - \mathbf{y}^\top \mathrm{W}\mathbf{x}_i \geq \varepsilon^2/4$ where the q rows of $\mathrm{W} = \left(\ \mathbf{w}_1^\top \ldots \mathbf{w}_q^\top \ \right)^\top$ correspond to the q hyperplanes of multiclass SVMs (W is a $q \times p$ matrix). Because only one constraint is switched on at one time due to the zeros in $\mathbf{y}$ we have to minimize $\|W\|_{\text{FRO}} = \sum_i \|\mathbf{w}_i\|^2$ subject to $\forall i, \ \mathbf{w}_{c_i}\mathbf{x}_i - \mathbf{w}_j\mathbf{x}_i \geq \varepsilon^2/4, \ \forall j \in \{1, \ldots, q\} \setminus c_i$ which is the same as in Weston and Watkins (1998), again disregarding scaling and thresholds.

4.3.4 Structured Output Case

Let us now restrict ourselves slightly to the situation where the outputs are normalized so $\forall \mathbf{y} \in \mathcal{Y} : \|\mathbf{y}\| = 1$. (Obviously this is only useful in the multidimensional case.) Hence, we rewrite our optimization problem as: minimize

$$\|W\|_{FRO}^2 \tag{4.4}$$

subject to

$$\forall i, \{\forall \mathbf{y} \in \mathcal{Y} : \|\mathbf{y}_i - \mathbf{y}\| \geq \varepsilon\} : \ \mathbf{y}_i^\top W \mathbf{x}_i - \mathbf{y}^\top W \mathbf{x}_i \geq \varepsilon^2/4. \tag{4.5}$$

We can regard $F(\mathbf{x}, \mathbf{y}) = \mathbf{y}^\top W \mathbf{x}$ as a function that returns the degree of fit between $\mathbf{x}$ and $\mathbf{y}$. The output on a test point can now be written

$$\mathbf{y}(\mathbf{x}) = \operatorname{argmin}_{\mathbf{y} \in \mathcal{Y}} \|W \mathbf{x} - \mathbf{y}\|^2$$
$$= \operatorname{argmax}_{\mathbf{y} \in \mathcal{Y}} \mathbf{y}^\top W \mathbf{x} = \frac{W\mathbf{x}}{\|W\mathbf{x}\|}. \tag{4.6}$$

because, by Cauchy-Schwarz, the function $\operatorname{argmax}_{\mathbf{y}} \mathbf{y}^\top W \mathbf{x}$ is maximal if $\frac{\mathbf{y}}{\|\mathbf{y}\|}$ is parallel to $W\mathbf{x}$.

With this optimization problem for the case of discrete $\mathcal{Y}$ and $\varepsilon \to 0$, we obtain the SVM for interdependent and structured output spaces (SVM-ISOS) of Tsochantaridis et al. (2004). In practice, one could relax the restriction upon the normalization of $\mathbf{y}$ during training because separability could still be obtained. However, if one is dealing with continuous outputs without this restriction, then the pre-image given by $\operatorname{argmax}_{\mathbf{y} \in \mathcal{Y}} \mathbf{y}^\top W \mathbf{x}$ would not be well defined. This is the reason why in the work of Tsochantaridis et al. (2004) normalization was not an issue, as only the discrete output case was considered.[1]

normalization of the outputs

We now show how to develop our method for joint kernels.

4.4 Joint Kernel Maps

We can rewrite the last optimization problem by considering the matrix W as a vector $\mathbf{w}$ of dimension $\dim(\mathcal{X})\dim(\mathcal{Y})$, and choosing the feature map

$$[\Phi_{\mathcal{X}\mathcal{Y}}(\mathbf{x}, \mathbf{y})]_{ij} = (\mathbf{x}\mathbf{y}^\top)_{ij}, \quad i = 1, \ldots, \dim(\mathcal{Y}), \quad j = 1, \ldots, \dim(\mathcal{X}), \tag{4.7}$$

---

1. In practice, in our experiments with joint kernels, we normalize the joint kernel itself, not the outputs, because the output in this case is not easily accessible.

where the dimensions are indexed by i and j. The optimization problem then consists of minimizing[2]

$$\|\mathbf{w}\|^2 \tag{4.8}$$

subject to

$$\langle \mathbf{w}, \Phi_{xy}(\mathbf{x}_i, \mathbf{y}_i) - \Phi_{xy}(\mathbf{x}_i, \mathbf{y}) \rangle \geq \varepsilon^2/2, \tag{4.9}$$

$$\forall i, \{\forall \mathbf{y} \in \mathcal{Y} : \|\mathbf{y}_i - \mathbf{y}\| \geq \varepsilon\}.$$

However, we are free to choose a mapping other than the one given above in (4.7), as we shall see later. (Indeed, choosing a mapping which incorporates prior knowledge is the whole point of using this approach.) We call Φ_{xy} the *joint kernel map* (JKM), and

$$J((\mathbf{x}, \mathbf{y}), (\hat{\mathbf{x}}, \hat{\mathbf{y}})) = \Phi_{xy}(\mathbf{x}, \mathbf{y})^\top \Phi_{xy}(\hat{\mathbf{x}}, \hat{\mathbf{y}})$$

the *joint kernel*. This relates our method to the work of Collins and Duffy (2002), Hofmann et al. (2002), and chapter 5 of this book.

dual problem

Constructing the corresponding dual problem we obtain: maximize[3]

$$\frac{\varepsilon^2}{4} \sum_{i,\mathbf{y}:\|\mathbf{y}_i-\mathbf{y}\|\geq\varepsilon} \alpha_{i\mathbf{y}} - (1/2) \sum_{\substack{i,\mathbf{y}\,:\,\|\mathbf{y}_i-\mathbf{y}\|\geq\varepsilon \\ j,\hat{\mathbf{y}}\,:\,\|\mathbf{y}_j-\hat{\mathbf{y}}\|\geq\varepsilon}} \alpha_{i\mathbf{y}}\,\alpha_{j\hat{\mathbf{y}}} \langle \Phi_{xy}(\mathbf{x}_i, \mathbf{y}_i)$$

$$-\Phi_{xy}(\mathbf{x}_i, \mathbf{y}), \Phi_{xy}(\mathbf{x}_j, \mathbf{y}_j) - \Phi_{xy}(\mathbf{x}_j, \hat{\mathbf{y}}) \rangle$$

---

2. Note that we could also simplify the optimization problem further by splitting the constraints: i.e. minimize $\|\mathbf{w}\|^2$ subject to

$$\forall i : \langle \mathbf{w}, \Phi_{xy}(\mathbf{x}_i, \mathbf{y}_i) \rangle + b \geq \varepsilon^2/8$$

$$\{\forall \mathbf{y} \in \mathcal{Y} : \|\mathbf{y}_i - \mathbf{y}\| \geq \varepsilon\} : \quad \langle \mathbf{w}, \Phi_{xy}(\mathbf{x}_i, \mathbf{y}) \rangle + b \leq -\varepsilon^2/8.$$

If this problem is linearly separable, then its solution $\mathbf{w}$ is also a feasible solution of (4.8)-(4.9).

3. Note that with infinitely many constraints, standard duality does not apply for our optimization problem. However, for the purposes of the present chapter, we are not concerned with this. For practical purposes, we may assume that for any $\epsilon > 0$, our data domain has a finite ϵ-cover (e.g., our domain could be a compact subset of $\mathbb{R}^n$). Since on a computer implementation, a constraint can only be enforced up to machine precision, we can thus imagine choosing a sufficiently small ϵ, which reduces our setting to one with a finite number of constraints. Furthermore, we find experimentally that the number of active constraints is small and scales sublinearly with the number of examples or output dimension (see figure 4.1).

subject to

$$\alpha_{i\mathbf{y}} \geq 0, \quad i = 1, \ldots, m, \{\forall \mathbf{y} \in \mathcal{Y} : \|\mathbf{y}_i - \mathbf{y}\| \geq \varepsilon\}.$$

The objective can be rewritten with kernels:

$$\frac{\varepsilon^2}{4} \sum_{i,\mathbf{y}:\|\mathbf{y}_i-\mathbf{y}\|\geq\varepsilon} \alpha_{i\mathbf{y}} - (1/2) \sum_{\substack{i,\mathbf{y}\,:\,\|\mathbf{y}_i-\mathbf{y}\|\geq\varepsilon \\ j,\hat{\mathbf{y}}\,:\,\|\mathbf{y}_i-\hat{\mathbf{y}}\}|\geq\varepsilon}} \alpha_{i\mathbf{y}}\alpha_{j\hat{\mathbf{y}}}[J((\mathbf{x}_i,\mathbf{y}_i),(\mathbf{x}_j,\mathbf{y}_j))$$

linear joint kernel

$$-J((\mathbf{x}_i,\mathbf{y}_i),(\mathbf{x}_j,\hat{\mathbf{y}})) - J((\mathbf{x}_i,\mathbf{y}),(\mathbf{x}_j,\mathbf{y}_j)) + J((\mathbf{x}_i,\mathbf{y}),(\mathbf{x}_j,\hat{\mathbf{y}}))].$$

The standard linear map therefore implies $J((\mathbf{x}_i,\mathbf{y}_i),(\mathbf{x}_j,\mathbf{y}_j)) = \langle\mathbf{x}_i,\mathbf{x}_j\rangle\langle\mathbf{y}_i,\mathbf{y}_j\rangle = K(\mathbf{x}_i,\mathbf{x}_j)L(\mathbf{y}_i,\mathbf{y}_j)$, where $K(\mathbf{x}_i,\mathbf{x}_j) = \langle\mathbf{x}_i,\mathbf{x}_j\rangle$ and $L(\mathbf{y}_i,\mathbf{y}_j) = \langle\mathbf{y}_i,\mathbf{y}_j\rangle$ are kernel maps for input and output respectively.

Now

$$\mathbf{w} = \sum_{i,\mathbf{y}:\|\mathbf{y}_i-\mathbf{y}\|\geq\varepsilon} \alpha_{i\mathbf{y}}[\Phi_{\mathcal{X}\mathcal{Y}}(\mathbf{x}_i,\mathbf{y}_i) - \Phi_{\mathcal{X}\mathcal{Y}}(\mathbf{x}_i,\mathbf{y})].$$

For certain joint kernels (that are linear in the outputs) we can compute the matrix W explicitly to calculate the mapping (in the equation above we see the vectorized version of this matrix). However, for general nonlinear mappings of the output (or input) we must solve the pre-image problem (cf. (4.6)):

$$\mathbf{y}(\mathbf{x}^*) = \underset{\mathbf{y}^*\in\mathcal{Y}}{\mathrm{argmax}}\langle W, \Phi_{\mathcal{X}\mathcal{Y}}(\mathbf{x}^*,\mathbf{y}^*)\rangle$$

$$= \underset{\mathbf{y}^*\in\mathcal{Y}}{\mathrm{argmax}} \sum_{i,\mathbf{y}:\|\mathbf{y}_i-\mathbf{y}\|\geq\varepsilon} \alpha_{i\mathbf{y}} J((\mathbf{x}_i,\mathbf{y}_i),(\mathbf{x}^*,\mathbf{y}^*)) - \alpha_{i\mathbf{y}} J((\mathbf{x}_i,\mathbf{y}),(\mathbf{x}^*,\mathbf{y}^*)).$$

In the next section we discuss joint kernels, and consider several examples that do not require one to solve the general pre-image problem. First, let us discuss related work, and practical implementation considerations.

4.4.1 Optimization

So far we simply ignored the fact that the discussed optimization problems above have infinite constraints of the form:

$$\{\forall \mathbf{y} \in \mathcal{Y} : \|\mathbf{y}_i - \mathbf{y}\| \geq \varepsilon\} : \quad 2(\mathbf{y}_i - \mathbf{y})^\top W x_i \geq \varepsilon^2/2 + \|\mathbf{y}_i\|^2 - \|\mathbf{y}\|^2,$$

semi-infinite program

for each training pair $(\mathbf{x}_i, \mathbf{y}_i)$. Optimization problems of this form are called semi-infinite programs (SIPs). Duality theorems exist that are in spirit similar to weak and strong duality theorems for the finite case. For a detailed discussion see Hettich and Kortanek (1993) and Shapiro (2005). In practice SIPs are treated by two possible strategies: discretization and greedy search. Discretization corresponds to quantizing the set of constraints regarding a particular threshold and solving the new finite program. However, due to its relevance we will focus more on the greedy strategy. The greedy strategy is an iterative procedure to solve SIPs and corresponds to a bilevel program where one tries to identify repeatedly the *most violating constraint* in the set. Thus, one replaces the set of infinite constraints by a single one,

$$2(\mathbf{y}_i - \mathbf{y}^*)^\top W x_i \geq \varepsilon^2/2 + \|\mathbf{y}_i\|^2 - \|\mathbf{y}^*\|^2,$$

where the single $\mathbf{y}^*$ is found by a new optimization subproblem. In our case, we could identify $\mathbf{y}^*$ by the program

$$\mathbf{y}^* = \operatorname*{argmax}_{\mathbf{y} \in \mathcal{Y}} \quad \|\mathbf{y}_i\|^2 - \|\mathbf{y}\|^2 - 2(\mathbf{y}_i - \mathbf{y})^\top W x_i$$

subject to

$$\|\mathbf{y}_i - \mathbf{y}\| \geq \varepsilon.$$

Due to the nonconvex nature of this problem one usually applies some form of approximations such as to restrict the possible set of candidates $\mathbf{y}$ to all patterns in the training set. A method for the SVM for interdependent and structured output spaces (ISOS) along these lines was developed in Tsochantaridis et al. (2004) and can be analogously implemented for JKMs by using an iterative scheme: add the most violating example to the working set and reoptimize, repeating until completion. One can then show that on each iteration the objective function strictly improves and is guaranteed to terminate if the problem is separable.

This strategy is mostly feasible since one assumes that the solution violates only a finite set of constraints. In fact, using the Lagrangian approach as above we found out that the solution tends to be very sparse (see figure 4.1). In the current approach, we used the following simple approximation: For each example i compute $\mathbf{y} = W\mathbf{x}_i$. We require $\|W\mathbf{x}_i - \mathbf{y}_i\| \leq \varepsilon/4$ (see section 4.3). So, if $\|\mathbf{y} - \mathbf{y}_i\| > \varepsilon/4$, one of the constraints from (4.9) is violated. We thus add $\mathbf{y}$ to our list of active constraints, and reoptimize. We repeat this until there are no more violations. In practice, in our experiments we also start with ε large, and decrease it upon separability, similar to the procedure in Tsochantaridis et al. (2004), mixing solution strategies ideas from discretization and greedy optimization.

(margin: greedy strategy)

4.4.2 Related Algorithms

The idea of learning maps by embedding both input and output spaces using kernels was first employed in the KDE algorithm (Weston et al., 2002), where the kernels were defined separately. This allowed correlations to be encoded between output features, nonlinear loss functions to be defined, and for outputs to be structured objects such as strings and trees (Haussler, 1999; Watkins, 1999; Tsochantaridis et al., 2004) (however, one must then solve an often difficult pre-image problem). The method first decorrelates the outputs via performing a kernel principal component analysis (kernel PCA). Kernel PCA (Schölkopf et al., 1998) yields principal components $v_l \in \mathbb{R}^q, l = 1 \ldots n$ and corresponding variances λ_l. Henceforth the output labels $\{y_i\}_{i=1}^m$ are projected to the column vectors v_l to retrieve the m principal coordinates $z_i \in \mathbb{R}^n$. This projection results in the new estimation task

$$\underset{W \in \mathbb{R}^{n \times p}}{\arg\min} \sum_{i=1}^m \|z_i - W x_i\|^2.$$

KDE, for example, performs a ridge regression on each component $z_{ij}, 1 \le j \le n$ to overcome overfitting. Predictions for a new point $x^\star$ are made via predicting first the principal coordinates $z^\star = W x^\star$, and then using the principal components:

$$y^\star = V z^\star.$$

Here $V \in \mathbb{R}^{q \times n}$ consists of the n principal components v_l. In the case where $n = q$ the prediction performance will only depend on the basic regression used for estimating $z^\star$ since V acts as a basis transformation.

If one assumes that the main variation in the output is according to signal and the small variances according to noise, then it is reasonable to take the first n principal components corresponding to the largest variance λ_l. Alternatively, instead of cutting off, it is also possible to *shrink* the directions according to their variance.

Compared to the current work and work such as SVM-ISOS (Tsochantaridis et al., 2004), KDE has the advantage during training of not requiring the computation of pre-images. On the other hand, it requires an expensive matrix inversion step, and does not give sparse solutions. The inability to use joint kernels in KDE means that prior knowledge cannot be so easily encoded into the algorithm. In our experiments (see section 4.6) the difference between using this prior knowledge or not in real applications can be large, at least for small sample size.

We note that Cortes et al. (2005) and chapter 8 of this book also deal with the structured output regression case. In particular, their use of regularization to incorporate the same kind of prior knowledge as in joint kernels is similar to that described in section 4.2.

vector-valued kernel functions

Micchelli and Pontil (2003) also provide a method of using kernels to deal with high-dimensional output regression problems using vector-valued kernel functions. One defines a prediction function as follows:

$$f(\mathbf{x}) = \sum_{i=1}^m K(\mathbf{x}_i, \mathbf{x}) \mathbf{c}_i,$$

where $K(\mathbf{x}_i, \mathbf{x}_j)$ is a q by q matrix which in position $K_{s,t}$ encodes the similarity between training points i and j with respect to outputs s and t (for a discussion of how this relates to standard kernel machines, cf. Hein and Bousquet (2004)). The weights $\mathbf{c}_i$ are hence q by 1 vectors. Although at first sight this approach seems very complicated in terms of defining kernels, there are some natural examples where known correlation across outputs can be encoded. However, simply minimizing $\sum_i \|\mathbf{y}_i - f(\mathbf{x}_i)\|^2$ yields a large, nonsparse optimization problem with qm variables.

Considering once again classification problems, the current work also turns out to have strong relations with the work of Collins and Duffy (2002) who employed a ranking perceptron algorithm and a specific joint kernel on the natural language problem of parsing (outputting a parse tree). In this case, the difficult pre-image problem was avoided by only selecting among n candidate parse trees. The algorithm they used is thus similar to the one given in footnote 2, except in their case not all possible negative constraints are enforced, but only $n-1$ per example. Using the multiclass SVM formulation of Vapnik (1998) and Weston and Watkins (1998),

$$f(\mathbf{x}_i, \mathbf{y}_i) > f(\mathbf{x}_i, \mathbf{y}), \quad \forall \{\mathbf{y} \in \mathcal{Y} \setminus \mathbf{y}_i\}, \tag{4.10}$$

and considering $\mathcal{Y}$ as some large set, e.g. of structured objects, one arrives at the formulation of SVM-ISOS (Tsochantaridis et al., 2004). Essentially, this is a special case of our algorithm, where the output is structured (discrete $\mathcal{Y}$) and $\varepsilon = 0$.[4] The authors apply the algorithm to problems of label sequence learning, named entity recognition, and others. Our work complements this last one in helping to understand the role of joint kernels in learning problems where one can supply prior knowledge by way of the similarity measure. Taskar et al. (2004b) provide a similar formulation to Tsochantaridis et al. (2004) but with a probabilistic interpretation. Finally, both Tsochantaridis et al. (2004) and Taskar et al. (2004b) have generalized the constraints of type (4.10) to be able to quantify how good a prediction is relative to the correct output. One way of doing this is by defining a loss function of choice on $L(\mathbf{y}, \mathbf{y}_i)$ and enforcing a margin on each constraint equal to this loss. See chapter 5 for detailed discussion.

4.5   Joint Kernels

As discussed before, a joint kernel is a nonlinear similarity measure between input-output pairs, i.e.,

$$J((\mathbf{x}, \mathbf{y}), (\mathbf{x}', \mathbf{y}')),$$

where $(\mathbf{x}, \mathbf{y})$ and $(\mathbf{x}', \mathbf{y}')$ are labeled training examples,[5]

$$J((\mathbf{x}, \mathbf{y}), (\mathbf{x}', \mathbf{y}')) = \langle \Phi_{\mathcal{XY}}(\mathbf{x}, \mathbf{y}), \Phi_{\mathcal{XY}}(\mathbf{x}', \mathbf{y}') \rangle,$$

---

4. Ignoring the normalization conditions on the output which come from our original derivation, as discussed previously.

5. Note there is nothing stopping us considering not just pairs here but also kernels on n-tuples, e.g., of the form $(\mathbf{x}, \mathbf{y}, \mathbf{z})$.

where $\Phi_{\mathcal{X}\mathcal{Y}}$ is a map into a dot product space. All functions $J((\mathbf{x},\mathbf{y}),(\mathbf{x}',\mathbf{y}'))$ that take this form are positive definite, and all positive definite kernels $J((\mathbf{x},\mathbf{y}),(\mathbf{x}',\mathbf{y}'))$ can be written in this form. This follows directly from the corresponding statements for kernels $k(\mathbf{x},\mathbf{x}')$ (see, for example, Schölkopf and Smola (2002)). The point of a joint kernel is to describe the similarity between input-output pairs by mapping pairs into a joint space. A joint kernel can encode more than just information about inputs or outputs independent of each other: it can also encode known dependencies/correlations between inputs and outputs. Joint kernels have already begun to be studied (Hofmann et al., 2002; Tsochantaridis et al., 2004); however, so far only discrete output spaces and structured outputs (such as sequences) were considered. One of the problems with joint kernels is that only for a subset of possible kernels can one compute the pre-image easily. In Tsochantaridis et al. (2004) kernels on sequences are chosen that are amenable to dynamic programming. Although some methods for speeding up pre-image computations exist (Schölkopf and Smola, 2002; Kwok and Tsang, 2004; Bakır et al., 2004), this remains a difficult problem. In the following we describe some kernels which avoid complex pre-image problems.

4.5.1 Tensor Product Kernels

kernels with simple pre-images

A kernel that does not encode any correlations can be obtained by using the product

$$J_{\text{LINEAR}}((\mathbf{x},\mathbf{y}),(\mathbf{x}',\mathbf{y}')) = K(\mathbf{x},\mathbf{x}')L(\mathbf{y},\mathbf{y}') = \langle\Phi_{\mathcal{X}}(\mathbf{x}),\Phi_{\mathcal{X}}(\mathbf{x}')\rangle\langle\Phi_{\mathcal{Y}}(\mathbf{y}),\Phi_{\mathcal{Y}}(\mathbf{y}')\rangle,$$

where K and L are respectively kernels on the inputs and outputs. If K and L are positive definite, then J will be, too; moreover, the associated feature space is known to be the tensor product of the individual feature spaces.

An interesting special case is when L is a linear kernel. In that case

$$\mathrm{W}_{\text{LINEAR}} = \sum_{i,\mathbf{y}:\|\mathbf{y}_i-\mathbf{y}\|\geq\varepsilon} \alpha_{i\mathbf{y}}\Phi_{\mathcal{X}}(\mathbf{x}_i)\mathbf{y}_i^\top - \alpha_{i\mathbf{y}}\Phi_{\mathcal{X}}(\mathbf{x}_i)\mathbf{y}^\top.$$

When $\dim(\mathcal{X})$ or $\dim(\mathcal{Y})$ are very large it can be more efficient to avoid the calculation of W and calculate a test prediction directly:

$$\mathrm{W}_{\text{LINEAR}}\mathbf{x} = \sum_{i,\mathbf{y}:\|\mathbf{y}_i-\mathbf{y}\|\geq\varepsilon} \alpha_{i\mathbf{y}}K(\mathbf{x}_i,\mathbf{x})\mathbf{y}_i^\top - \alpha_{i\mathbf{y}}K(\mathbf{x}_i,\mathbf{x})\mathbf{y}^\top.$$

Hence we avoid difficult pre-image problems in this case.

4.5.2 Diagonal Regularization

Consider the case where $\dim(\mathcal{X}) = \dim(\mathcal{Y})$, and it is known that one is looking for a linear map where the true matrix W is close to the identity map. Slightly more generally, one may know that the nth dimension of the input is correlated with the nth dimension of the output. Instances of such problems include decoding mass spectrometry (mapping from observed to theoretical spectra) and image mapping problems (deblurring, morphing, etc.). This correlation can be directly encoded:

$$J_{\text{DIAG}}((\mathbf{x}, \mathbf{y}), (\mathbf{x}', \mathbf{y}')) = (1 - \lambda)K(\mathbf{x}, \mathbf{x}')\langle \mathbf{y}, \mathbf{y}' \rangle + \lambda \Big[\sum_{k=1}^{q} x_k x_k' y_k y_k' \Big], \tag{4.11}$$

where λ controls the amount of encoded correlation. If λ is large, then the nth dimension in the input is presumed highly correlated with the nth dimension in the output, and the similarity measure is dominated by these relationships. Algorithms that minimize the Frobenius norm choose these dimensions as relevant, because this regularizer gives these features larger weights. Furthermore, the solution is still linear (does not require a pre-image) because we can write

$$W_{\text{DIAG}}\mathbf{x} = (1 - \lambda)W_{\text{LINEAR}}\mathbf{x} + \lambda \sum_{i, \mathbf{y}: \|\mathbf{y}_i - \mathbf{y}\| \geq \varepsilon} \alpha_{i\mathbf{y}}[\text{DIAG}(\mathbf{x}_i \mathbf{y}_i^\top) - \text{DIAG}(\mathbf{x}_i \mathbf{y}^\top)]\mathbf{x},$$

where $D = \text{DIAG}(M)$ is a diagonal matrix with $D_{ii} = M_{ii}$.

4.5.3   Patchwise Correlation

The natural generalization of the previous kernel is when you know that the nth dimension of the output is strongly correlated with a known set of dimensions in the input; e.g., for mappings between images, one could know that a region in the output image is strongly correlated with a region in the input image. This knowledge can be encoded with the kernel

$$J_{\text{PATCH}}((\mathbf{x}, \mathbf{y}), (\mathbf{x}', \mathbf{y}')) = (1 - \lambda)K(\mathbf{x}, \mathbf{x}')\langle \mathbf{y}, \mathbf{y}' \rangle + \lambda \sum_{k=1}^{|\mathcal{P}|} \Big[\sum_{p \in \mathcal{P}_k} \mathbf{x}_p \mathbf{x}_p' \sum_{p \in \mathcal{P}_k} \mathbf{y}_p \mathbf{y}_p' \Big],$$

where $\mathcal{P}$ is the set of known correlated patches. This encodes patch correlation between dimensions in $\mathbf{x}$, between dimensions in $\mathbf{y}$, and correlation between input and output, i.e. between $\mathbf{x}$ and $\mathbf{y}$.[6] The evaluation on a test example can be expressed as:

$$W_{\text{PATCH}}\mathbf{x} = (1 - \lambda)W_{\text{LINEAR}}\mathbf{x} + \lambda \sum_{i, \mathbf{y}: \|\mathbf{y}_i - \mathbf{y}\| \geq \varepsilon} \alpha_{i\mathbf{y}}[\sum_{k=1}^{|\mathcal{P}|} P_k(\mathbf{x}_i \mathbf{y}_i^\top) - \sum_{k=1}^{|\mathcal{P}|} P_k(\mathbf{x}_i \mathbf{y}^\top)]\mathbf{x},$$

where $P = P_k(M)$ is a matrix such that $P_{ij} = M_{ij}$ if $i \in \mathcal{P}_k$ or $j \in \mathcal{P}_k$ (if i or j is in the kth patch), or $P_{ij} = 0$, otherwise.

---

6. One can introduce a weighting function over the patches, corresponding to the assumption that the closer the pixels are, the more reliable is their correlation (cf. Schölkopf and Smola (2002), Eq. (13.21)).

4.6 Experiments

As said before, the JKM algorithm reduces to support vector classification and regression for particular $\mathcal{Y}$. We therefore only test our algorithm on regression problems of multiple outputs, and show how employing joint kernels can benefit in this case.

4.6.1 Artificial Problem: The Identity Map

learning the identity

We performed a first experiment on toy data to demonstrate the potential of the approach. We chose a very simple problem: the input is $x_i \in R^p$, each dimension drawn independently from a normal distribution of mean 0, standard deviation 1. The output is the same as the input, $y_i = x_i$, i.e. the task is to learn the identity map.

Table 4.1 Mean-squared error for different joint kernels encoding the identity map (first three rows) compared to ridge regression (RR) and k-NN. Incorporating prior knowledge in the joint kernel approach ($\lambda > 0$) improves generalization performance

$\dim(\mathcal{X}) = \dim(\mathcal{Y})$	20	30	50	75	100
$\mathrm{JKM_{DIAG}}$ ($\lambda = 1$)	0.00	0.00	0.01	0.02	0.02
$\mathrm{JKM_{DIAG}}$ ($\lambda = 0.5$)	0.03	0.14	0.34	0.50	0.62
$\mathrm{JKM_{DIAG}}$ ($\lambda = 0$)	0.06	0.40	0.78	1.00	1.14
RR (best γ)	0.06	0.43	0.82	1.07	1.21
k-NN (best k)	0.92	1.09	1.27	1.40	1.47

We compared k-nearest neighbor and ridge regression with our approach. For the former (k-NN and RR) we chose the best possible parameters; for the latter (JKM) we show the results for the identity-map regularizing joint kernel (4.11) for $\lambda = 0$, $\frac{1}{2}$, and 1, with $\varepsilon = \frac{0.5}{\sqrt{p}}$. For $\lambda = 0$ the set of possible linear maps is free; for $\lambda = 1$ only linear maps that are diagonal matrices are considered.

The mean-squared error for $p = 20, \ldots, 100$ features are given in table 4.1, with 20 examples for training and 100 for testing, averaged over 20 runs. A Wilcoxon signed ranked test confirms that the two kernels with $\gamma > 0$ outperform the other techniques. Further experiments adding noise to the dataset (not shown) yielded similar conclusions. Figure 4.1 shows the number of active constraints (support vectors) for varying output dimensions with training size 20 (left) and varying training set sizes with output dimension 20 (right). The solutions are relatively sparse (consider that dual ridge regression (Saunders et al., 1998) uses pm variables for p outputs and m examples). Note that larger values of λ (where the capacity of the set of functions is lower) have less active constraints.

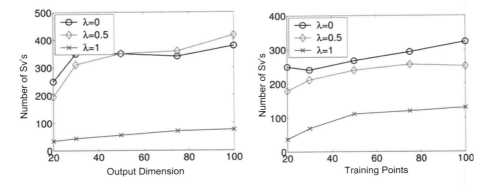

Figure 4.1 Number of active constraints (support vectors) on artificial data for varying output dimension (*left*) and training set size (*right*).

4.6.2 Mass Spectrometry: Prediction of Peptides

An important application of protein mass spectrometry (MS) is to identify proteins in a complex mixture, e.g. blood taken from a patient. In this technique, proteins are ionized and transferred to the gas phase. Their mass-to-charge ratio can be measured by directing them to an ion detector using an electric field, and this measurement can be used to infer protein identity. In practice, the protein is first dissolved into peptides using an enzyme. These peptides are of varying lengths up to about 20 amino acids. The peptides are run through an MS device, further fragmented, and subjected to a second MS analysis. The final result is one spectrum per peptide, in which the x-axis is the mass-to-charge ratio (m/z) and the y-axis reflects the abundance of subpeptides with the given m/z. This spectrum thus contains information about the peptide sequence, and can be used to identify the protein from which the peptide was cleaved.

The problem is, given such a spectrum, to infer the peptide that generated it. Hence the problem is to map from a spectrum to a string. We used a dataset taken from (Keller et al., 2002) with a training set of 290 spectra, and a test set of 1277 spectra.

Table 4.2 Test error (mean rank of true peptides) on the mass spectrometry problem

	JKM–PATCH ($\lambda = 0.95$)	JKM–LINEAR ($\lambda = 0$)	RR (best γ)	k-NN (best k)
Test error	10.98 ± 0.50	40.7 ± 0.96	29.6 ± 0.78	49.7 ± 1.28

INPUT   OUTPUT   JKM$_{PATCH}$ JKM$_{LINEAR}$ RR (best γ) k-NN (best k)

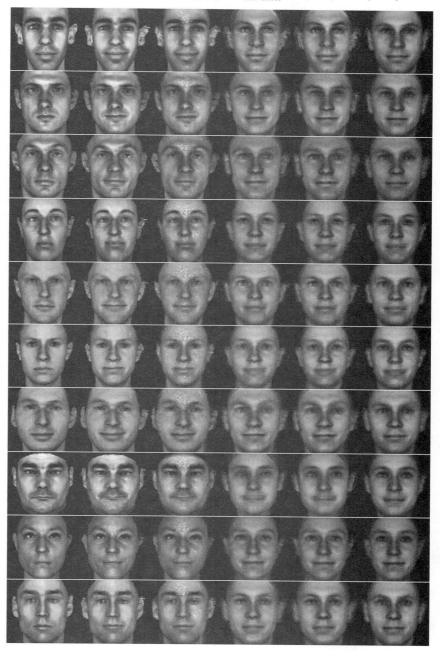

Figure 4.2   Prediction of smiling face given plain expression by joint kernel maps (patch and linear) and ridge regression and k-NN. The large dimensionality means there are many solutions with low empirical error; RR (after choosing the optimal regularization constant) selects one that uses many (irrelevant) inputs due to its regularizer $||w||^2$ which favors nonsparse solutions. Only the patch-kernel joint kernel map is successful, as the choice of (joint) kernel limits the possible choice of functions to ones which are close to the identity map.

As stated before, JKM generalizes to the case of nonvectorial outputs via the (joint) kernel trick, effectively defining an embedding space via the joint map. For each peptide in our database the peaks that could be observed in a mass spectrum are known, and are represented as 1000-dimensional vectors. Similarly, the input (the observed spectra) is a vector of the same length. We therefore use the diagonal regularization kernel (4.11) to encode the prior knowledge that the input vector is a noisy variant of the output vector. The quality of a given predictor is inversely proportional to the rank assigned to the true peptide in the ranked output. We use this rank as our performance metric. Here, $\mathcal{Y}$ is the set of known spectra in the database, $|\mathcal{Y}| = 1567$, and $\varepsilon = 0$. As shown in table 4.2, the diagonal kernel outperforms conventional regression techniques (RR and k-NN) even when using their best choice of hyperparameters chosen using the testing set. This preliminary result gives us a hint at the improvement one can get from both encoding information about the known classes in the output space and via encoding knowledge about the map. Note that using existing kernels such as the string kernels used by Tsochantaridis et al. (2004) to represent the outputs would be unlikely to improve this result, because then the joint representation with the inputs would not be possible. We aim to more deeply explore this application in future work.

4.6.3   Image Mapping: Learning to Smile

We consider the problem of mapping from the image of a face with a plain expression to an image of the same person smiling using images from the Max Planck Institute (MPI) face database (Blanz and Vetter, 1999). We use 20 examples for training, and 50 for testing. The images are $156 \times 176 = 27456$ pixels. We selected a small number of training examples because in this setting the weakness of existing methods was further exposed.

We applied a joint kernel mapping using the tensor product (linear) kernel ($\epsilon = 0.05$) and the patchwise kernel with $\gamma = 0.95, \epsilon = 0.1$ and patches of size 10×10 which overlap by 5 pixels. Training took 344 and 525 steps of adding a single violating example for the linear and patch kernels, resulting in 150 and 162 support vectors, respectively. Again, we compared with conventional regression techniques, choosing their best possible hyperparameters. A naive employment of RR on this task fails, outputting a kind of "average" face image, independent of the input (see figure 4.2). The large dimensionality means there are many solutions with low empirical error; RR (after choosing the optimal regularization constant) selects one that uses many (irrelevant) inputs due to its regularizer. Similarly, k-NN cannot solve this problem well for small sample size. See figure 4.2 for example images, and table 4.3 for mean-squared error rates comparing all these methods. By way of comparison, the baseline of simply predicting the input image as the output (the plain expression) gives a test error of 0.1823 ± 0.003. The complete test set can be viewed at the supplementary website.

Table 4.3 Test error on the smiling problem of the MPI face database

	JKM–PATCH ($\varepsilon = 0.1$)	JKM–LINEAR ($\varepsilon = 0.05$)	RR (best γ)	k-NN (best k)
Test error	0.142	0.227	0.222	0.244
Test error	±0.002	±0.006	±0.006	±0.006

4.7 Conclusions

In this work we presented a general method of supervised learning via joint kernel mappings, and showed how such kernels can encode certain regularization properties which reflect prior knowledge in mappings. While the experiments shown here used only simple types of joint kernels taking advantage of patchwise information, these examples are only an instantiation of our approach, to show its validity and to bring insight into why and how joint kernels are useful. Joint kernels are mainly useful in cases where their pre-image is easily computable and are extendable to complex outputs such as strings, trees, and graphs. Indeed, we believe the gain of joint kernel methods is in employing such complex structured outputs that go beyond standard classification and regression such as in parsing, machine translation, and other applications. In those cases the difference between coding prior knowledge into a joint kernel and using two separate kernels for input and output could potentially be large, at least in the small sample size case. Although first studies in some of these areas have been completed (Collins and Duffy, 2002; Tsochantaridis et al., 2004), no study that we know of has yet directly compared this benefit.

Future work should also address issues of training efficiency, pre-images for more complex nonlinear and structured kernels.

Acknowledgments

We thank Christian Wallraven for providing the MPI face data. We thank André Elisseeff, Jan Eichorn, Olivier Chapelle, Arthur Gretton, Massimiliano Pontil, and Thomas Hofmann for useful discussions.

5   Support Vector Machine Learning for Interdependent and Structured Output Spaces

Yasemin Altun, Thomas Hofmann, and Ioannis Tsochantaridis

5.1   Introduction

Supervised learning, one of the most important areas of machine learning, is the general problem of learning a function that predicts the best value for a response variable y for an observation x by making use of a sample of input-output pairs. Traditionally, in classification, the values that y can take are *simple*, in the sense that they can be characterized by an arbitrary identifier. However, in many real-world applications the outputs are often complex, in that either there are dependencies between classes (e.g. taxonomies used in document classification), or the classes are objects that have some internal structure such that they describe a configuration over interdependent components (e. g. sequences, parse trees). For such problems, which are commonly called *structured output prediction* problems, standard multiclass approaches render ineffective, since the size of the output space is very large (e.g. the set of label sequences scale exponentially with the length of the input sequence). More importantly, it is crucial to capture the common properties that are shared by the set of classes in order to generalize across classes as well as to generalize across input patterns.

In this chapter, we approach the structured output prediction problems by generalizing a multiclass support vector machine (SVM) formulation by Crammer and Singer (2001) to the broad problem of learning for interdependent and structured outputs. To that extent, we specify discriminant functions that exploit the dependencies and structure of outputs. This framework enables generalization across classes and prediction of classes that may not have been observed in the training set. We provide the details of this framework for three important special cases, namely hierarchical classification, label sequence learning, and weighted context-free grammar learning.

The standard 0-1 cost function is not adequate to capture the differences between classes in interdependent and structured output spaces. More sophisticated cost functions such as Hamming loss and F_1 score are common in practice, for example for sequence and parse trees. We generalize the separation margin notion for structured outputs and device max-margin formulations that directly incorporate the cost functions that the classifier is evaluated on. These formulations result in a potentially prohibitive, more specifically exponential, number of constraints. However, exploiting the sparsity and the (de-)coupling of these constraints, we present a cutting-plane algorithm that is guaranteed to satisfy the exponential number of constraints up to an ϵ-precision without evaluating them explicitly.

We empirically evaluate our approach in document classification as an instance of hierarchical classification, named entity recognition as an instance of label-sequence learning, and natural language parsing as an instance of learning weighted context-free grammars. Experimental results show that our framework is advantageous over the more standard approaches in terms of the cost function on which the classifiers are evaluated.

5.2   A Framework for Structured/Interdependent Output Learning

We are interested in the task of inferring a *complex* label $\mathbf{y} \in \mathcal{Y}$ for a (possibly structured) observation $\mathbf{x} \in \mathcal{X}$. Given a sample of input-output pairs $S = \{(\mathbf{x}_1, \mathbf{y}_1), \dots, (\mathbf{x}_n, \mathbf{y}_n)\}$ generated from an unknown distribution P, the goal is to learn a mapping $f : \mathcal{X} \to \mathcal{Y}$ between input spaces $\mathcal{X}$ and interdependent/structured output spaces $\mathcal{Y}$. Hence, it is a generalization of the supervised classification problem where values of the random variables are predicted not only with respect to observations but also with respect to the values of other related random variables.

The prediction function f is evaluated according to a cost function $\triangle : \mathcal{Y} \times \mathcal{Y} \to \Re$, which measures the similarity between two labels. We focus on cost functions where $\triangle(\mathbf{y}, \mathbf{y}) = 0$ and $\triangle(\mathbf{y}, \mathbf{y}') \geq 0, \mathbf{y} \neq \mathbf{y}'$. For example, 0-1 loss, Hamming loss, and $1 - F_1$ loss are the canonical cost functions of multiclass classification, label sequence learning, and parsing, respectively. The goal of learning a function that minimizes the cost over the unknown P is commonly approximated by learning a function that minimizes the empirical cost

$$\mathcal{R}_S^{\triangle}(f) = \frac{1}{n} \sum_{i=1}^{n} \triangle(\mathbf{y}_i, f(\mathbf{x}_i)). \tag{5.1}$$

In general, minimizing this cost on the sample is NP-complete. Following the usual practice in machine learning, we investigate optimizing surrogate functions of the empirical cost.

In structured and interdependent output prediction, two factors make it essential to generalize across sets of labels as well as to generalize across input patterns. First, in most cases, the very large size of the label sets renders any learning that is independent over class labels intractable. More importantly, capturing common properties shared by sets of labels enables us to use data points across classes, and even generalize to class labels that are not observed in the sample but likely to occur as the label of a new observation. Therefore, the standard approach of multiclass classification, i.e. learning a function $F_y : \mathcal{X} \to \Re$ for each class independently and inferring the label of an observation by maximizing $F_y(\mathbf{x})$ over all labels, is not appropriate for this setting. We define a *discriminant function* $F : \mathcal{X} \times \mathcal{Y} \to \Re$ over the joint input-output space where $F(\mathbf{x}, \mathbf{y})$ can be interpreted as measuring the compatibility of $\mathbf{x}$ and $\mathbf{y}$. Each such function F induces a mapping f,

$F(\mathbf{x}, \mathbf{y})$ measures compatibility

$$f(\mathbf{x}) = \underset{\mathbf{y} \in \mathcal{Y}}{\operatorname{argmax}} \, F(\mathbf{x}, \mathbf{y}; \mathbf{w}), \tag{5.2}$$

where $\mathbf{w}$ denotes a parameter vector and ties are broken arbitrarily. We restrict the space of F to linear functions over some feature representation Ψ, which is defined on the joint input-output space

$$F(\mathbf{x}, \mathbf{y}; \mathbf{w}) = \langle \mathbf{w}, \Psi(\mathbf{x}, \mathbf{y}) \rangle.$$

Ψ is chosen with respect to the dependency structure of $\mathbf{y}$ and $\mathbf{x}$ and commonalities within $\mathbf{y}$'s in order to enable generalization across labels. Before we present several interesting special cases, we need some definitions. We define the canonical (binary) representation of outputs $y \in \mathcal{Y} = \{1, \ldots, k\}$ by unit vectors

$$\Lambda^c(y) \equiv (\delta(y, 1), \delta(y, 2), \ldots, \delta(y, k))' \in \{0, 1\}^k,$$

so that $\langle \Lambda^c(y), \Lambda^c(y') \rangle = \delta(y, y')$. Let the tensor product $\otimes$ and the concatenation $\odot$ be defined as

$$\otimes : \Re^d \times \Re^k \to \Re^{dk}, \quad [\mathbf{a} \otimes \mathbf{b}]_{i+(j-1)d} \equiv [\mathbf{a}]_i [\mathbf{b}]_j,$$
$$\odot : \Re^d \times \Re^k \to \Re^{d+k}, \quad \mathbf{a} \odot \mathbf{b} \equiv (\mathbf{a}', \mathbf{b}')'.$$

The following proposition states that feature representations derived from $\odot$ and $\otimes$ operations, such as all the joint feature maps Ψ defined in this chapter, are induced by valid kernels.

Proposition 33 *Let Φ and $\bar{\Phi}$ be feature representations induced by kernels $k, \bar{k}$ over $X \times X, \bar{X} \times \bar{X}$ respectively (i. e. $k(a, \bar{a}) = \langle \Phi(a), \Phi(\bar{a}) \rangle$). Then, for any $a, \bar{a} \in X, b, \bar{b} \in \bar{X}$, $\Phi \otimes \bar{\Phi}$ and $\Phi \odot \bar{\Phi}$ are induced by kernels $k_\otimes, k_\odot$ where*

$$k_\otimes((a, b), (\bar{a}, \bar{b})) = k(a, \bar{a})\bar{k}(b, \bar{b}), \tag{5.3}$$
$$k_\odot((a, b), (\bar{a}, \bar{b})) = k(a, \bar{a}) + \bar{k}(b, \bar{b}). \tag{5.4}$$

concatenation and tensor product lead to valid kernels

Proof   The claims follow from the definitions of $\odot$ and $\otimes$ operations and from the fact that sums and pointwise products of two kernels are also kernels (Schölkopf and Smola, 2002). ∎

For the rest of this section, we assume the existence of an arbitrary feature representation of the inputs, $\Phi(\mathbf{x}) \in \Re^d$, and a kernel function k that induces Φ.

It is easy to see that multiclass classification is a special case of our framework where $\mathcal{Y} = \{1, \ldots, k\}$. Let the weight vector $\mathbf{w}$ be a concatenation of all $\mathbf{w}_r$, with $\mathbf{w}_r$ being a weight vector associated with the rth class, $\mathbf{w} = \mathbf{w}_1 \odot \cdots \odot \mathbf{w}_k$. Defining the joint feature map is given by $\Psi(\mathbf{x}, y) \equiv \Phi(\mathbf{x}) \otimes \Lambda^c(y)$, resulting in the familiar multiclass discriminant function $F(\mathbf{x}, y; \mathbf{w}) = \langle \mathbf{w}_y, \Phi(\mathbf{x}) \rangle$.

Let us now examine more interesting special cases.

5.2.1   Hierarchical Classification

In many applications, such as document classification and word sense disambiguation, taxonomies and hierarchies are natural ways to organize classes of objects. These problems are instances of interdependent output spaces where the feature representation is defined as follows: Let a taxonomy be a set of elements $\mathcal{Z} \supseteq \mathcal{Y}$ equipped with a partial order $\prec$, which can be by a tree or a lattice, and let $\beta_{(y,z)} \in \Re$ be a measure of similarity with respect to the partial order $\prec$. We generalize the canonical representation of outputs to $\Lambda(y) \in \Re^p$, such that for all $z \in \mathcal{Z}$

$$\lambda_z(y) = \begin{cases} \beta_{(y,z)} & \text{if } y \prec z \text{ or } y = z \\ 0 & \text{otherwise} \end{cases}.$$

Then, defining the joint input-output feature map via the tensor product,

$$\Psi(\mathbf{x}, y) = \Phi(\mathbf{x}) \otimes \Lambda(y),$$

effectively introduces a weight vector $\mathbf{w}_z$ for all $z \in \mathcal{Z}$, i.e. for every node in the hierarchy. A simple derivation shows that the weight vector of a class is a linear combination of its processors' weights, and the discriminant is given by

$$F(\mathbf{x}, y; \mathbf{w}) = \sum_{z : y \prec z \text{ or } z = y} \beta(y, z) \langle \mathbf{w}_z, \Phi(\mathbf{x}) \rangle.$$

sharing features in taxonomies

Thus, the features λ_z are shared by all successor classes of z and the joint feature representation enables *generalization across classes*. Figure 5.1 shows an example of the joint feature map Ψ of the second class for a given hierarchy. It follows immediately from (5.3) of proposition 33 that the inner product of the joint feature map decomposes into kernels over input and output spaces

$$\langle \Psi(\mathbf{x}, y), \Psi(\mathbf{x}', y') \rangle = \langle \Lambda(y), \Lambda(y') \rangle \, k(\mathbf{x}, \mathbf{x}').$$

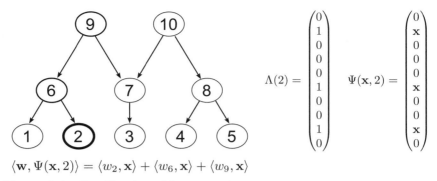

$$\langle \mathbf{w}, \Psi(\mathbf{x}, 2) \rangle = \langle w_2, \mathbf{x} \rangle + \langle w_6, \mathbf{x} \rangle + \langle w_9, \mathbf{x} \rangle$$

Figure 5.1   Classification with taxonomies.

5.2.2   Label Sequence Learning

Label sequence learning is the task of predicting a sequence of labels $\mathbf{y} = (y^1, \ldots, y^l)$ for a given observation sequence $\mathbf{x} = (\mathbf{x}^1, \ldots, \mathbf{x}^l)$. Applications of this problem are ubiquitous in many domains such as computational biology, information retrieval, natural language processing, and speech recognition. We denote by $l_\mathbf{x}$ the length of an observation sequence, by Σ the set of possible labels for each individual variable y^t, and by $\mathcal{Y}(\mathbf{x})$ the set of label sequences for $\mathbf{x}$. Then, $\mathcal{Y}(\mathbf{x}) = \Sigma^{l_\mathbf{x}}$.

In order to encode the dependencies of the observation-label sequences which are commonly realized as a Markov chain, we define Ψ to include interactions between input features and labels $(\Phi(\mathbf{x}^t) \otimes \Lambda^c(y^t))$, as well as interactions between neighboring label variables $(\Lambda^c(y^t) \otimes \Lambda^c(y^{t+1}))$ for every position t. Then, using the stationary property, our joint feature map is a sum over all positions,

encoding
neighbor
correlation

$$\Psi(\mathbf{x}, \mathbf{y}) = \left[\sum_{t=1}^{l_\mathbf{x}} \Phi(\mathbf{x}^t) \otimes \Lambda^c(y^t) \right] \odot \left[\eta \sum_{t=1}^{l_\mathbf{x}-1} \Lambda^c(y^t) \otimes \Lambda^c(y^{t+1}) \right], \qquad (5.5)$$

where $\eta \geq 0$ is a scalar balancing the two types of contributions. Clearly, this representation can be generalized by including higher-order interdependencies of labels (e. g. $\Lambda^c(y^t) \otimes \Lambda^c(y^{t+1}) \otimes \Lambda^c(y^{t+2})$), by including input features from a window centered at the current position (e. g. replacing $\Phi(\mathbf{x}^t)$ with $\Phi(\mathbf{x}^{t-r}, \ldots, \mathbf{x}^t, \ldots, \mathbf{x}^{t+r})$), or by combining higher-order output features with input features (e. g. $\sum_t \Phi(\mathbf{x}^t) \otimes \Lambda^c(y^t) \otimes \Lambda^c(y^{t+1})$). The important constraint on designing the feature map is the efficient computation of the discriminant function, which in the case of (5.5) is given by

efficiency

$$F(\mathbf{x}, \mathbf{y}; \mathbf{w}) = \left\langle \mathbf{w}_{ol}, \sum_{t=1}^{l_\mathbf{x}} \Phi(\mathbf{x}^t) \otimes \Lambda^c(y^t) \right\rangle + \eta \left\langle \mathbf{w}_{ll}, \sum_{t=1}^{l_\mathbf{x}-1} \Lambda^c(y^t) \otimes \Lambda^c(y^{t+1}) \right\rangle,$$
$$(5.6)$$

where $\mathbf{w} = \mathbf{w}_{ol} \odot \mathbf{w}_{ll}$ is the concatenation of weights of the two dependency types.

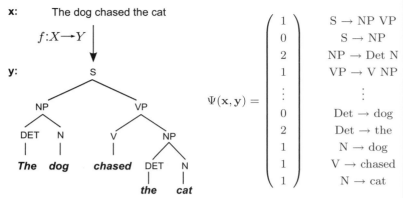

Figure 5.2 Natural language parsing.

As indicated in proposition 33, the inner product of the joint feature map decomposes into kernels over input and output spaces,

$$\langle \Psi(\mathbf{x}, \mathbf{y}), \Psi(\mathbf{x}', \mathbf{y}') \rangle = \sum_{t=1}^{l_{\mathbf{x}}} \sum_{s=1}^{l_{\mathbf{x}'}} \delta(y^t, \bar{y}^s) k(\mathbf{x}^t, \bar{\mathbf{x}}^s) + \eta^2 \sum_{t=1}^{l_{\mathbf{x}}-1} \sum_{s=1}^{l_{\mathbf{x}'}-1} \delta(y^t, \bar{y}^s)\delta(y^{t+1}, y^{s+1}),$$

(5.7)

where we used the equality $\langle \Lambda^c(\sigma), \Lambda^c(\bar{\sigma}) \rangle = \delta(\sigma, \bar{\sigma})$.

5.2.3 Weighted Context-Free Grammars

Parsing is the task of predicting a labeled tree $\mathbf{y}$ that is a particular configuration of grammar rules generating a given sequence $\mathbf{x} = (x^1, ..., x^l)$. Let us consider a context-free grammar in Chomsky normal form. The rules of this grammar are of the form $\sigma \to \sigma'\sigma''$, or $\sigma \to x$, where $\sigma, \sigma', \sigma'' \in \Sigma$ are nonterminals, and $x \in T$ are terminals. Similar to the sequence case, we define the joint feature map $\Psi(x, y)$ to contain features representing interdependencies between labels of the nodes of the tree (e.g. $\psi_{\sigma \to \sigma'\sigma''}$ via $\Lambda^c(y^{rs}) \otimes \Lambda^c(y^{rt}) \otimes \Lambda^c(y^{(t+1)s})$) and features representing the dependence of labels to observations (e.g. $\psi_{\sigma \to \tau}$ via $\Phi^c(x^t) \otimes \Lambda^c(y^t)$). Here y^{rs} denotes the label of the root of a subtree spanning from x^r to x^s. This definition leads to equations similar to (5.5), (5.6), and (5.7). Extensions to this representation are possible, for example by defining higher-order features that can be induced using kernel functions over subtrees (Collins and Duffy, 2002).

5.3 A Maximum-Margin Formulation

We propose a maximum-margin approach for the problem of learning in structured and interdependent output spaces. We first generalize the multiclass separation margin of Crammer and Singer (2001), where the margin of an instance $(\mathbf{x}, \mathbf{y})$ with respect to $\mathbf{w}$ is given by

$$\gamma(\mathbf{x}, \mathbf{y}; \mathbf{w}) = F(\mathbf{x}, \mathbf{y}; \mathbf{w}) - \max_{\mathbf{y}' \in \mathcal{Y} \backslash \mathbf{y}} F(\mathbf{x}, \mathbf{y}'; \mathbf{w}).$$

Then, the maximum-margin problem can be defined as finding the weight vector $\mathbf{w}$ that maximizes the minimum margin of the sample, $\min_i \gamma(\mathbf{x}^i, \mathbf{y}^i)$. If the data are separable ($\gamma > 0$), there exist multiple solutions to this problem, since the margin can be made arbitrarily large by scaling $\mathbf{w}$. This can be resolved by fixing either the norm of $\mathbf{w}$ (e.g. $\|\mathbf{w}\| = 1$) or the margin (e.g. $\min_i \gamma(\mathbf{x}^i, \mathbf{y}^i) \geq 1$). Following the latter, we have a constraint optimization problem:

$$\text{SVM}_0: \quad \min_{\mathbf{w}} \ \frac{1}{2} \|\mathbf{w}\|^2$$
$$\text{s.t. } F(\mathbf{x}_i, \mathbf{y}_i; \mathbf{w}) - \max_{\mathbf{y} \in \mathcal{Y} \backslash \mathbf{y}_i} F(\mathbf{x}_i, \mathbf{y}; \mathbf{w}) \geq 1, \quad \forall i.$$

In order to accommodate for margin violations, we generalize this formulation by introducing linear penalties that are scaled according to the cost incurred by misclassification. Intuitively, violating a margin constraint involving a $\mathbf{y} \neq \mathbf{y}_i$ with high loss $\triangle(\mathbf{y}_i, \mathbf{y})$ should be penalized more severely than a violation involving an output value with smaller loss. This can be accomplished by multiplying the margin violation, given by $(1 - \langle \mathbf{w}, \delta \Psi_i(\mathbf{y}) \rangle)$ where $\delta \Psi_i(\mathbf{y}) = \Psi(\mathbf{x}_i, \mathbf{y}_i) - \Psi(\mathbf{x}_i, \mathbf{y})$), by the cost

$$\text{SVM}_1^{\triangle s}: \quad \min_{\mathbf{w}, \boldsymbol{\xi}} \ \frac{1}{2} \langle \mathbf{w}, \mathbf{w} \rangle + \frac{C}{n} \sum_{i=1}^n \xi_i \tag{5.9a}$$
$$\text{s.t. } \max_{\mathbf{y} \in \mathcal{Y} \backslash \mathbf{y}_i} [\triangle(\mathbf{y}_i, \mathbf{y})(1 - \langle \mathbf{w}, \delta \Psi_i(\mathbf{y}) \rangle)] \geq 1 - \xi_i \quad \forall i. \tag{5.9b}$$

Here $C > 0$ is a constant controlling the tradeoff between the loss and the regularizer. Note that $\text{SVM}_1^{\triangle s}$ can also be stated without constraints via a hinge loss function,

$$\text{SVM}_1^{\triangle s}: \quad \min_{\mathbf{w}} \frac{1}{2} \|\mathbf{w}\|^2 + \frac{C}{n} \sum_{i=1}^n \max_{\mathbf{y} \in \mathcal{Y} \backslash \mathbf{y}_i} [\triangle(\mathbf{y}_i, \mathbf{y})(1 - \langle \mathbf{w}, \delta \Psi_i(\mathbf{y}) \rangle)_+], \tag{5.10}$$

where $(a)_+ = \max(0, a)$ denotes the hinge loss. It is easy to show that $\text{SVM}_1^{\triangle s}$ is a surrogate of the empirical cost (5.1).

Proposition 34 *Let $\mathbf{w}^*$ be the optimal solution to $SVM_1^{\triangle s}$. Then, the empirical risk $\mathcal{R}_s^{\triangle}(\mathbf{w}^*)$ is upper-bounded by $\frac{1}{n} \sum_{i=1}^n \max_{\mathbf{y} \neq \mathbf{y}^i} [\triangle(\mathbf{y}_i, \mathbf{y})(1 - \langle \mathbf{w}^*, \delta \Psi_i(\mathbf{y}) \rangle)_+].$*

Proof If $f(\mathbf{x}_i; \mathbf{w}^*) = \mathbf{y}_i$ then $\triangle(\mathbf{y}_i, f(\mathbf{x}_i; \mathbf{w})) = 0$ and the bound holds trivially. If $\hat{\mathbf{y}} \equiv f(\mathbf{x}_i; \mathbf{w}^*) \neq \mathbf{y}_i$, then $\max_{\mathbf{y} \neq \mathbf{y}^i} [\triangle(\mathbf{y}_i, \mathbf{y})(1 - \langle \mathbf{w}^*, \delta \Psi_i(\mathbf{y}) \rangle)_+] \geq \triangle(\mathbf{y}_i, \mathbf{y})$, because $\langle \mathbf{w}^*, \delta \Psi_i(\mathbf{y}) \rangle < 0$. Since the bound holds for every training instance, it also holds for the average. ∎

A similar optimization problem can be given by the squared hinge loss, or equivalently by the squared penalties on the slack variable This loss, which we denote by $\mathrm{SVM}_2^{\triangle s}$, is also an upper bound on the empirical cost $\mathcal{R}_S^{\triangle}(\mathbf{w})$.

5.3.1 Optimizing the Primal Problem

By specifying the class of discriminant functions F to be the reproducing kernel Hilbert space (RKHS) associated with the kernel k, where $k((\mathbf{x}, \mathbf{y}), (\bar{\mathbf{x}}, \bar{\mathbf{y}})) = \langle \Psi(\mathbf{x}, \mathbf{y}), \Psi(\bar{\mathbf{x}}, \bar{\mathbf{y}}) \rangle$, it is easy to show that $\mathrm{SVM}_1^{\triangle s}$ (5.10) is an instance of a more general optimization problem given by

$$F^* = \underset{F \in \mathcal{H}}{\operatorname{argmin}} \ \sum_{i=1}^{n} \mathcal{L}(x^i, y^i, F) + \lambda \|F\|_{\mathcal{H}}^2,$$

where $\mathcal{L}$ is a convex loss function. The well-known representer theorem (Kimeldorf and Wahba, 1971) states that the solution F^* lies in the span of data points, in this case $(\mathbf{x}_i, \mathbf{y})$ for all $\mathbf{x}_i \in S$ and $\mathbf{y} \in \mathcal{Y}(\mathbf{x})$. Under fairly mild conditions, one can show that this space can be further reduced to the span of the substructures of the data points, via a straightforward variant of the representer theorem which was also presented in Lafferty et al. (2004) and Altun et al. (2006). Let $\mathcal{C}(\mathbf{x}, \mathbf{y})$ be the set of assignments of all subcomponents of $(\mathbf{x}, \mathbf{y})$. For example, if $(\mathbf{x}, \mathbf{y})$ corresponds to a Markov random field, $\mathcal{C}(\mathbf{x}, \mathbf{y})$ is given by the clique assignments. Furthermore, let $\mathcal{C}(S) = \cup_{\mathbf{x} \in S, \mathbf{y} \in \mathcal{Y}(\mathbf{x})} \mathcal{C}(\mathbf{x}, \mathbf{y})$. If the discriminant $F(\mathbf{x}, \mathbf{y})$ decomposes into a function h defined over the subcomponents of $(\mathbf{x}, \mathbf{y})$ and the loss $\mathcal{L}$ is local in the sense that $\mathcal{L}(\mathbf{x}, \mathbf{y}, F)$ is determined by the values of h over the set $\mathcal{C}(\mathbf{x})$, F^* can be represented over $\mathcal{C}(S)$.

decomposition of
$F(\mathbf{x}, \mathbf{y})$

Theorem 35 *For any local loss function $\mathcal{L}$ and any sample S, there exist some weights $\alpha_c, \forall c \in \mathcal{C}(S)$ such that F^* admits a representation of the form*

$$F^*(\mathbf{x}, \mathbf{y}; \alpha) = \sum_{c \in \mathcal{C}(\mathbf{x}, \mathbf{y})} h^*(c; \alpha),$$

$$h^*(c; \alpha) = \sum_{c' \in \mathcal{C}(S)} \alpha_c \tilde{k}(c, c),$$

where the kernel function $\tilde{k}$ is defined so that $h(c) = \left\langle h, \tilde{k}(c, .) \right\rangle$.

Note that since all joint feature maps $\Psi(\mathbf{x}, \mathbf{y})$ considered in section 5.2 decompose into subcomponents of $(\mathbf{x}, \mathbf{y})$, the corresponding F and the margin losses, $\mathrm{SVM}_1^{\triangle s}$ and $\mathrm{SVM}_2^{\triangle s}$, satisfy the conditions in theorem 35. Then, we can reformalize $\mathrm{SVM}_1^{\triangle s}$ as an optimization problem over α:

primal problem

$$\min_{\alpha, \xi_i(\alpha)} \frac{1}{2} \sum_{c, c' \in \mathcal{C}(S)} \alpha_c \alpha_{c'} k(c, c') + \frac{C}{n} \sum_{i=1}^{n} \xi_i(\alpha)$$

$$\text{s.t.} \max_{\mathbf{y} \in \mathcal{Y} \setminus \mathbf{y}_i} \left[\triangle(\mathbf{y}_i, \mathbf{y})(1 + F(\mathbf{x}_i, \mathbf{y}; \alpha) - F(\mathbf{x}_i, \mathbf{y}_i; \alpha)) \right] \geq 1 - \xi_i(\alpha) \quad \forall i. \qquad (5.11)$$

This gives a convex program over the vectors indexed by $\mathcal{C}(S)$, which scales polynomially in terms of the size of the output variables. Every one of the nonlinear inequalities (5.11) implicitly represents exponentially many linear constraints given by

$$\forall i, \forall \mathbf{y} \in \mathcal{Y} \setminus \mathbf{y}_i : \quad \triangle(\mathbf{y}_i, \mathbf{y})(1 + F(\mathbf{x}_i, \mathbf{y}; \alpha) - F(\mathbf{x}_i, \mathbf{y}_i; \alpha)) \geq 1 - \xi_i(\alpha). \qquad (5.12)$$

If one can perform the max operation in (5.11) via a polynomial time dynamic programming (DP) algorithm, then there exist a polynomial number of constraints that satisfy (5.12). Each such constraint involves a cost variable C, which is coupled within instances $\mathbf{x}_i$ and upper-bounded by ξ_i. The resulting optimization problem, which is closely related to the factored primal of Taskar et al. (2004b), is a polynomial-sized quadratic program (QP) with polynomial number of highly coupled constraints. Unfortunately, this coupling prohibits the use of decomposition methods such as sequential minimal optimization (Platt, 1999) and may render the optimization intractable for large datasets. In the next section, we present a method for optimizing the dual problem which benefits the decomposition methods.

5.3.2 Dual Problem

Using the standard Lagrangian techniques, i.e., introducing a Lagrange parameter $\alpha_{(i\mathbf{y})}$ enforcing the margin constraint for label $\mathbf{y} \neq \mathbf{y}_i$ and input $\mathbf{x}_i$, writing out the Lagrangian, differentiating it with respect to the primal parameters $\mathbf{w}$ and ξ, and substituting the optimality equations of the primals into the Lagrangian results, in a dual QP. Let $k((\mathbf{x}_i, \mathbf{y}), (\mathbf{x}_j, \bar{\mathbf{y}})) = \langle \delta \Psi_i(\mathbf{y}), \delta \Psi_j(\bar{\mathbf{y}}) \rangle$ denote the kernel function.[1] Then, the QP of $\mathrm{SVM}_1^{\triangle s}$ and $\mathrm{SVM}_2^{\triangle s}$ is given in the following proposition.

---

1. Note that k can be computed from the inner products involving values of Ψ due to the linearity of the inner product, and is a valid kernel.

dual problem

Proposition 36 *The dual problem to $SVM_1^{\triangle s}$ and $SVM_2^{\triangle s}$ is given by the program*

$$\boldsymbol{\alpha}^* = \underset{\boldsymbol{\alpha}}{\operatorname{argmax}} -\frac{1}{2} \sum_{i,j} \sum_{\mathbf{y} \neq \mathbf{y}_i, \bar{\mathbf{y}} \neq \mathbf{y}_j} \alpha_{(i\mathbf{y})} \alpha_{(j\bar{\mathbf{y}})} k((\mathbf{x}_i, \mathbf{y}), (\mathbf{x}_j, \bar{\mathbf{y}})) + \sum_i \sum_{\mathbf{y} \neq \mathbf{y}_i} \alpha_{(i\mathbf{y})}, \quad (5.13)$$

$$s.\ t.\ \boldsymbol{\alpha} \geq 0,$$

where $SVM_1^{\triangle s}$ has additional box constraints

$$\sum_{\mathbf{y} \neq \mathbf{y}_i} \frac{\alpha_{(i\mathbf{y})}}{\triangle(\mathbf{y}_i, \mathbf{y})} \leq \frac{C}{n}, \quad \forall i = 1, \ldots, n$$

and $SVM_2^{\triangle s}$ has a modified kernel function

$$k((\mathbf{x}_i, \mathbf{y}), (\mathbf{x}_j, \bar{\mathbf{y}})) = \langle \delta \Psi_i(\mathbf{y}), \delta \Psi_j(\bar{\mathbf{y}}) \rangle + \frac{n \delta_{ij}}{C \sqrt{\triangle(\mathbf{y}_i, \mathbf{y})} \sqrt{\triangle(\mathbf{y}_j, \bar{\mathbf{y}})}}. \quad (5.14)$$

The optimality equation of $\mathbf{w}$ is given by

$$\mathbf{w}^* = \sum_j \sum_{\mathbf{y}} \alpha_{(j\mathbf{y})}^t \delta \Psi_j(\mathbf{y}). \quad (5.15)$$

5.4   Cutting-Plane Algorithm

The main computational challenge in optimizing (5.13) is posed by the extremely large number of variables $(n|\mathcal{Y}| - n)$. If $\mathcal{Y}$ is a product space, its cardinality grows exponentially in the size of $\mathbf{y}$, for instance in sequences of length l, $|\mathcal{Y}| = |\Sigma|^l$, rendering the optimization of (5.13) by standard quadratic programming solvers intractable. The max-margin problem in structured-output prediction has two properties that can be exploited for efficient optimization. First, we expect only a very small fraction of the constraints (and therefore a small number of parameters) to be active, due to the hinge loss but more importantly due to the overlap of information among classes represented via the joint feature map. The analysis of sparsity is presented in section 5.4.2. Secondly, the constraint matrix is (at least) block diagonal (diagonal for the $SVM_2^{\triangle s}$ variant), resulting in dual variables to be coupled only within a block of variables associated with the same training instance.

efficient
implementation

We propose a general cutting-plane algorithm (Kelley, 1960) for cost-sensitive SVMs. This algorithm exploits the above-mentioned properties of the maximum-margin problem, so that only a small number of constraints are examined explicitly and a small-size QP is solved at each iteration of the algorithm. In a nutshell, the algorithm starts with no constraints (which corresponds to the most relaxed version of the primal) and iteration adds constraints via a variable selection approach in the dual formulation leading to tighter relaxations.

Pseudocode of the algorithm is depicted in algorithm 5.1. The algorithm maintains working sets S_i for each instance to keep track of the selected constraints which

---

Algorithm 5.1 Cost-sensitive support vector machines ($\text{SVM}_1^{\triangle s}$ and $\text{SVM}_2^{\triangle s}$)

1:   input: $(\mathbf{x}_1, \mathbf{y}_1), \ldots, (\mathbf{x}_n, \mathbf{y}_n)$, C, ϵ

2:   output: $\boldsymbol{\alpha}$

3:   $S_i \leftarrow \emptyset$ for all $i = 1, \ldots, n$

4:   **repeat**

5:     **for** $i = 1, \ldots, n$ **do**

6:       $H(\mathbf{y}) \equiv \begin{cases} (1 - \langle \delta\Psi_i(\mathbf{y}), \mathbf{w} \rangle) \, \triangle(\mathbf{y}_i, \mathbf{y}) & (\text{SVM}_1^{\triangle s}) \\ (1 - \langle \delta\Psi_i(\mathbf{y}), \mathbf{w} \rangle) \, \sqrt{\triangle(\mathbf{y}_i, \mathbf{y})} & (\text{SVM}_2^{\triangle s}) \end{cases}$

       where $\mathbf{w} \equiv \sum_j \sum_{\mathbf{y}' \in S_j} \alpha_{(j\mathbf{y}')} \delta\Psi_j(\mathbf{y}')$.

7:     compute $\hat{\mathbf{y}} = \arg\max_{\mathbf{y} \in \mathcal{Y}} H(\mathbf{y})$

8:     compute $\xi_i = \max\{0, \max_{\mathbf{y} \in S_i} H(\mathbf{y})\}$

9:     **if** $H(\hat{\mathbf{y}}) > \xi_i + \epsilon$ **then**

10:       $S_i \leftarrow S_i \cup \{\hat{\mathbf{y}}\}$

10a: /* Variant (a): perform full optimization */

       $\alpha_S \leftarrow$ optimize the dual of $\text{SVM}_1^{\triangle s}$ or $\text{SVM}_2^{\triangle s}$ over S, $S = \cup_i S_i$

10b: /* Variant (b): perform subspace ascent */

       $\alpha_{S_i} \leftarrow$ optimize the dual of $\text{SVM}_1^{\triangle s}$ or $\text{SVM}_2^{\triangle s}$ over S_i

13:     **end if**

14:    **end for**

15:   **until** no S_i has changed during iteration

---

define the current relaxation. Iterating through the training examples $(\mathbf{x}_i, \mathbf{y}_i)$, the algorithm finds the (potentially) "most violated" constraint of $\mathbf{x}_i$, involving some output value $\hat{\mathbf{y}}$. If the scaled margin violation of this constraint exceeds the current value of ξ_i by more than ϵ, the dual variable corresponding to $\hat{\mathbf{y}}$ is added to the working set, leading to the cutoff of the current primal solution from the feasible set (see figure 5.3). Once a constraint has been added, the QP is solved with respect to S or S_i (leading to smaller QP problems) depending on the ratio of the complexity of the constraint selection in step 7 and the complexity of solving the relaxed QP. Since at each iteration only one constraint is added, it is possible to initialize the QP solver to the current solution, which greatly reduces the runtime. If $\hat{\mathbf{y}}$ satisfies the soft-margin constraint up to ϵ precision, it implies that the rest of constraints are approximately satisfied as well and no further improvement is necessary for $\mathbf{x}_i$.

Due to the generality of the algorithm, by implementing the feature mapping $\Psi(\mathbf{x}, \mathbf{y})$ (either explicit or via a joint kernel function), the cost function $\triangle(\mathbf{y}, \mathbf{y}')$, and the maximization in step 7 accordingly, one achieves a max-margin classifier for all the special cases considered in section 5.2 as well as others such as string-to-string matching.

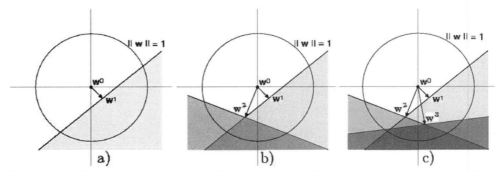

Figure 5.3 Cutting-plane algorithm. Successive steps of the cutting-plane algorithm. In the first step no constraints have been added (*no shading*); $\mathbf{w}^0 = 0$ is the current solution. a) Second step: the (potentially) most violated constraint has been added. It cuts off the current solution $\mathbf{w}^0$ from the feasible region (*shaded*). b) Third step: one more violated constraint is added, and the new solution is computed. c) Fourth step: the process is repeated until there are no more violating constraints.

5.4.1 Finding Most Violated Constraint

We now describe efficient algorithms to compute the maximization in step 7 of algorithm 5.1. Note that the crucial computation involves finding

$$\underset{\mathbf{y} \neq \mathbf{y}_i}{\operatorname{argmax}} \triangle(\mathbf{y}, \mathbf{y}^i) F(\mathbf{x}_i, \mathbf{y}), \qquad (5.16)$$

since the other terms computed by simple operations. There exist well-known DP algorithms for finding $\operatorname{argmax}_{\mathbf{y}} F(\mathbf{x}, \mathbf{y})$ for various dependency structures, such as the Viterbi algorithm for sequences and the Cocke-Younger-Kasami (CKY) algorithm for parsing (Manning and Schütze, 1999). When $\triangle$ is 0/1 loss, (5.16) can be found by modifying these algorithms to find the n-best labeling of an observation, for $n = 2$ (Schwarz and Chow, 1990). In cases where $\triangle(\mathbf{y}_i, \cdot)$ only takes on a finite number of values, a generic strategy is a two-stage approach, where one first computes the maximum over those $\mathbf{y}$ for which the cost $\triangle(\mathbf{y}_i, \mathbf{y})$ is constant, and then maximizes over the finite number of levels. However, this strategy can scale the computational complexity by the size of $\mathbf{y}$ (e.g. when the cost is the Hamming loss). We now present the recursion rules of a simple modification of the DP algorithms to compute (5.16) for Hamming loss and $1 - F_1$ score. The resulting algorithms are as efficient as the original DP algorithm (up to a small constant). This approach can easily be generalized to any cost function that decomposes into factors that are linear in the cost of subcomponents of $\mathbf{y}$.

Note that the Hamming loss is given by $\triangle(\mathbf{y}, \bar{\mathbf{y}}) = \sum_{t=1}^{T} \bar{\delta}(y^t, \bar{y}^t)$, where y^t denotes the tth component of $\mathbf{y}$ (e.g. tth position in a sequence of length T) and $\bar{\delta}(a, b)$ equals 0 if $a = b$ and 1 otherwise. Let $c(t, \sigma, \sigma'; \mathbf{w})$ be the local contribution of assigning σ to the tth component with respect to $\mathbf{w}$ given the previous variable assignments σ'. Suppressing the dependence on $\mathbf{y}^i$ and $\mathbf{w}$, the recursive rules are

pre-images via
dynamic
programming

given by

$$S_t(\sigma) = \max_{\sigma'} \left(S_{t-1}(\sigma') + \bar{\delta}(y_i^t, \sigma) F_{t-1}(\sigma') + c(t, \sigma, \sigma')[D_{t-1}(\sigma') + \bar{\delta}(y_i^t, \sigma)] \right)$$

$$A_t(\sigma) = \underset{\sigma'}{\operatorname{argmax}} \left(T_{t-1}(\sigma') + \bar{\delta}(y_i^t, \sigma) F_{t-1}(\sigma') + c(t, \sigma, \sigma')[D_{t-1}(\sigma') + \bar{\delta}(y_i^t, \sigma)] \right)$$

$$D_t(\sigma) = D_{t-1}(A_t(\sigma)) + \bar{\delta}(y_i^t, \sigma)$$

$$F_t(\sigma) = F_{t-1}(A_t(\sigma)) + c(t, \sigma, A_t(\sigma)).$$

where all the variables at $t = 0$ is 0. Then, the best labeling is achieved by reconstructing the path from A via $\operatorname{argmax}_\sigma S_T(\sigma)$ in reverse direction.

Note that the F_1 score, which is the harmonic mean of precision and recall, is given by $\triangle(\mathbf{y}, \bar{\mathbf{y}}) = 2a/(p + o)$, where a is the number of correctly predicted subcomponents, p is the number of predicted subcomponents, and o is the number of correct subcomponents. Define $\hat{c}$ such that $\hat{c}(t, \sigma, \sigma') = 1$ if labeling the tth component with σ increases the number of predicted components given previous labeling σ' and 0 otherwise. Then the recursive rules are given by

$$R_t(\sigma) = \max_{\sigma'} \left[R_{t-1}(\sigma') + c(t, \sigma, \sigma') \left(1 - 2\frac{D_t(\sigma)}{N_t(\sigma) + o} \right) + 2\frac{F_{t-1}(\sigma')}{N_t(\sigma) + o} V \right]$$

$$A_t(\sigma) = \underset{\sigma'}{\operatorname{argmax}} \left[R_{t-1}(\sigma') + c(t, \sigma, \sigma') \left(1 - 2\frac{D_t(\sigma)}{N_t(\sigma) + o} \right) + 2\frac{F_{t-1}(\sigma')}{N_t(\sigma) + o} V \right]$$

$$D_t(\sigma) = D_{t-1}(A_t(\sigma)) + \delta(y_i^t, \sigma)$$

$$F_t(\sigma) = F_{t-1}(A_t(\sigma)) + c(t, \sigma, A_t(\sigma))$$

$$N_t(\sigma) = N_{t-1}(A_t(\sigma)) + \hat{c}(t, \sigma, A_t(\sigma)).$$

where $V = \frac{D_{t-1}(\sigma')\hat{c}(t,\sigma,\sigma')}{N_{t-1}(\sigma')+o} - \delta(\sigma, y_i^t)$. The best labeling is achieved by reconstructing the path from A via $\operatorname{argmax}_\sigma R_T(\sigma)$ in the reverse direction.

5.4.2   Analysis

We now show that algorithm 5.1 computes arbitrary close approximations to SVMs by evaluating only a polynomial number of constraints so that the exponentially many constraints are guaranteed to be satisfied up to an ϵ-precision without explicit evaluation. We start by providing lower bounds of the improvements in $\text{SVM}_2^{\triangle s}$ and $\text{SVM}_1^{\triangle s}$ at each iteration of algorithm 5.1. The proof can be found in the appendix.

Proposition 37 *Let $\triangle_i \equiv \max_{\mathbf{y}} \{\triangle(\mathbf{y}_i, \mathbf{y})\}$ and $R_i \equiv \max_{\mathbf{y}} \{\|\delta\Psi_i(\mathbf{y})\|\}$. The dual objective improves by at least*

$$\frac{1}{2} \frac{\epsilon^2}{\triangle_i R_i^2 + \frac{n}{C}} \quad \text{and} \quad \min \left\{ \frac{C\epsilon}{2n}, \frac{\epsilon^2}{8\triangle_i^2 R_i^2} \right\} \tag{5.19}$$

in step 10 of algorithm 5.1 for $\text{SVM}_2^{\triangle s}$ and $\text{SVM}_1^{\triangle s}$ respectively.

Theorem 38 *With $\bar{R} = \max_i R_i$, $\bar{\triangle} = \max_i \triangle_i$ and for a given $\epsilon > 0$, algorithm 5.1 terminates after incrementally adding at most*

$$\max\left\{\frac{2n\bar{\triangle}}{\epsilon}, \frac{8C\bar{\ell}^3\bar{R}^2}{\epsilon^2}\right\}, \quad and \quad \frac{C\bar{\ell}^2\bar{R}^2 + n\bar{\triangle}}{\epsilon^2} \tag{5.20}$$

constraints to the working set S for the $SVM_1^{\triangle s}$ and $SVM_2^{\triangle s}$ respectively.

Proof   With $S = \emptyset$ the optimal value of the dual is 0. In each iteration a constraint $(i\mathbf{y})$ is added that is violated by at least ϵ, provided such a constraint exists. After solving the S-relaxed QP in step 10, the objective will increase by at least the amounts suggested by proposition 37. Hence after t constraints, the dual objective will be at least t times these amounts. The result follows from the fact that the dual objective is upper-bounded by the minimum of the primal, which in turn can be bounded by $C\bar{\triangle}$ and $\frac{1}{2}C\bar{\triangle}$ for $SVM_1^{\triangle s}$ and $SVM_2^{\triangle s}$ respectively.   ■

To make the bounds more concrete, let us now examine how R is bounded for the special cases studied in section 5.2. For hierarchical classification, we define $r_i \equiv \|\Phi(\mathbf{x}_i)\|$ and $S \equiv \max_{\mathbf{y} \in \mathcal{Y}} \|\Lambda(y)\|$. Using proposition 33 and simple derivation, we can show that $\|\Psi(\mathbf{x}_i, y) - \Psi(\mathbf{x}_i, y')\|^2$ is upper-bounded by

$$2\langle\Psi(\mathbf{x}_i, y), \Psi(\mathbf{x}_i, y)\rangle = 2\|\Phi(\mathbf{x}_i)\|^2\|\Lambda(y)\|^2 \leq 2r_i^2 S^2. \tag{5.21}$$

For label sequence learning, we define $r_i \equiv \max_t \|\Phi(\mathbf{x}_i^t)\|$ and $l = \max_i l_{\mathbf{x}_i}$. Then $\|\Psi(\mathbf{x}_i, \mathbf{y}) - \Psi(\mathbf{x}_i, \mathbf{y}')\|^2$ is upper-bounded by

$$2\|\sum_t \Phi(\mathbf{x}_i^t) \otimes \Lambda^c(y^t)\|^2 + \eta^2\|\sum_t \Lambda^c(y^t) \otimes \Lambda^c(y^{t+1})\|^2 \leq 2l^2(R_i^2 + \eta^2). \tag{5.22}$$

In parsing, a sequence $\mathbf{x}$ of length l has $l - 1$ internal and l preterminal nodes. Thus, $\|\Psi(\mathbf{x}, \mathbf{y})\|_1 = 2l - 1$. Then, $\|\Psi(\mathbf{x}, \mathbf{y}) - \Psi(\mathbf{x}, \mathbf{y}')\|_2 \leq \sqrt{4l^2 + 4(l-1)^2} < 2\sqrt{2}l$.

5.5   Alternative Margin Formulations

In addition to the margin approaches of $SVM_1^{\triangle s}$ and $SVM_2^{\triangle s}$, a second way to incorporate the cost function into the optimization problem is to rescale the margin as proposed by Taskar et al. (2004b) for the special case of the Hamming loss,

$$SVM_1^{\triangle m}: \qquad \min_{\mathbf{w}} \frac{1}{2}\|\mathbf{w}\|^2 + \frac{C}{n}\sum_{i=1}^{n} \max_{\mathbf{y} \in \mathcal{Y} \backslash \mathbf{y}_i} (\triangle(\mathbf{y}_i, \mathbf{y}) - \langle\mathbf{w}, \delta\Psi_i(\mathbf{y})\rangle)_+.$$

$SVM_2^{\triangle m}$ can be defined similarly with the squared hinge loss. Both $SVM_1^{\triangle m}$ and $SVM_2^{\triangle m}$ are upper bounds on $\mathcal{R}_S^{\triangle}(\mathbf{w}^*)$. Dynamic programming algorithms similar to ones in section 5.4.1 can be given to compute

$$\max_{\mathbf{y} \in \mathcal{Y} \backslash \mathbf{y}_i} (\triangle(\mathbf{y}_i, \mathbf{y}) - \langle\mathbf{w}, \delta\Psi_i(\mathbf{y})\rangle), \tag{5.23}$$

Table 5.1   Results on the WIPO-alpha corpus. "flt" is a standard (flat) SVM multiclass model, "tax" the hierarchical architecture. "0/1" denotes training based on the classification loss, "$\triangle$" refers to training based on the tree loss

	flt 0/1	tax 0/1	flt $\triangle$	tax $\triangle$	
4 training instances per class (3-fold x-val)					
acc	28.32	28.32	27.47	29.74	+5.01 %
$\triangle$-loss	1.36	1.32	1.30	1.21	+12.40 %
2 training instances per class(5-fold x-val)					
acc	20.20	20.46	20.20	21.73	+7.57 %
$\triangle$-loss	1.54	1.51	1.39	1.33	+13.67 %

and algorithm 5.1 can be used for these formulations simply by changing line 6. An advantage of $\mathrm{SVM}_1^{\triangle s}$ over $\mathrm{SVM}_1^{\triangle m}$ is its scaling invariance.

Proposition 39 *Suppose $\triangle' \equiv \eta\triangle$ with $\eta > 0$, i.e. $\triangle'$ is a scaled version of the original loss $\triangle$. Then the optimal weight vector $\mathbf{w}^*$ for $SVM_1^{\triangle' s}$ is also optimal for $SVM_1^{\triangle s}$ and vice versa, if we rescale $C' = C/\eta$.*

Proof   If $\mathbf{w}$ is fixed in $SVM_1^{\triangle s}$ and $SVM_1^{\triangle' s}$, then the optimal values for ξ_i^* in each of the problems are related to one another by a scale change of η. By scaling C with the inverse of η, this effectively cancels. ∎

This is not the case for $\mathrm{SVM}_1^{\triangle m}$. One needs, for example, to rescale the feature map Ψ by a corresponding scale factor as well, which seems to indicate that one has to calibrate the scaling of the loss and the scaling of the feature map more carefully in the $\mathrm{SVM}_1^{\triangle m}$ formulation.

More importantly, $\mathrm{SVM}_1^{\triangle m}$ can potentially give significant weight to output values $\mathbf{y} \in \mathcal{Y}$ that are not even close to being confusable with the target values $\mathbf{y}_i$, i. e. $F(\mathbf{x}_i, \mathbf{y}_i) - F(\mathbf{x}_i, \mathbf{y})$ might be large but smaller than $\triangle(\mathbf{y}_i, \mathbf{y})$. $\mathrm{SVM}_1^{\triangle m}$, on the other hand, only depends on $\mathbf{y}$ for which $F(\mathbf{x}_i, \mathbf{y}_i) - F(\mathbf{x}_i, \mathbf{y}) \leq 1$, i. e. outputs only receive a relatively high discriminant score.

5.6   Experiments

We present experiments on hierarchical classification, label sequence learning, and parsing, reported in Tsochantaridis et al. (2005).

5.6.1   Hierarchical Classification

Experiments were performed using a 1710-document subsample of the World Intellectual Property Organization (WIPO)-alpha document collection. The title and

Table 5.2   Results of various algorithms on the named entity recognition task

Method	HMM	CRF	Perceptron	SVM
Error	9.36	5.17	5.94	5.08

Table 5.3   Results of various joint kernel SVM formulations on NER

	SVM_2	$\mathrm{SVM}_2^{\triangle s}$	$\mathrm{SVM}_2^{\triangle m}$
Test Err	5.1 ± 0.6	5.1 ± 0.8	5.1 ± 0.7
Const	2824 ± 106	2626 ± 225	2628 ± 119

claim tags were indexed. Document parsing, tokenization, and term normalization have been performed with the MindServer retrieval engine.[2] The cost function $\triangle$ is the height of the first common ancestor of the arguments y, y' in the taxonomy. Results in table 5.1 show that the proposed hierarchical SVM learning architecture improves the performance over the standard multiclass SVM in terms of classification accuracy as well as in terms of the tree loss.

5.6.2   Label Sequence Learning

We performed experiments on a named entity recognition (NER) problem using fivefold crossvalidation on a 300-sentence subcorpus of the Spanish newswire article corpus provided by CoNLL2002. The label set consists of nonname and the beginning and continuation of person names, organizations, locations, and miscellaneous names, resulting in a total of nine different labels, i.e. $|\Sigma| = 9$. The joint feature map $\Psi(\mathbf{x}, \mathbf{y})$ is the histogram of label-label interactions plus a set of features describing the observation-label interactions. For both perceptron and SVM, a second-degree polynomial kernel was used. No special tuning was performed, and C was set to 1 and ϵ to 0.01. The cost function $\triangle$ is given by the Hamming distance. Results given in table 5.2 for the zero-one loss, where we compare the generative hidden Markov model (HMM) with conditional random fields (CRF) (Lafferty et al., 2001), perceptron (Collins, 2002), and the joint kernel SVM algorithm. All discriminative learning methods substantially outperform the standard HMM. In addition, the SVM performs slightly better than the perceptron and CRFs, demonstrating the benefit of a large-margin approach. Table 5.3 shows that all joint kernel SVM formulations perform comparably, probably due to the fact that the vast majority of the support label sequences end up having Hamming distance 1 to the correct label sequence. Note that for loss equal to 1 all SVM formulations are equivalent.

Table 5.4 Results for learning a weighted context-free grammar on the Penn Treebank

	PCFG	SVM$_2$	SVM$_2^{\triangle s}$	SVM$_2^{\triangle m}$
Test Acc	55.2	58.9	58.9	58.3
Test F_1	86.0	86.2	88.5	88.4
Const	N/A	7494	8043	7117

5.6.2.1 Parsing

Experiments were performed on a subset of the Penn Treebank corpus, where the 4098 sentences of length at most 10 from sections F2-21 were used as the training set, and the 163 sentences of length at most 10 from F22 were used as the test set. The feature representation include the grammar rules observed in the training data. The cost function is given by $\triangle(\mathbf{y}, \mathbf{y}^i) = 1 - F_1(\mathbf{y}_i, \mathbf{y})$. All results are for $C = 1$ and $\epsilon = 0.01$. All values of C between 10^{-1} to 10^2 gave comparable prediction performance.

The results are given in table 5.4. For the zero-one loss (i.e. predicting the complete tree correctly), the generative PCFG model using the maximum likelihood estimate (MLE) achieves better accuracy than the max-margin approaches. However, optimizing the SVM for the F_1-loss outperforms PCFG significantly in terms of F_1-scores. Table 5.4 also shows that the total number of constraints added to the working set is small, roughly twice the number of training examples in all cases.

5.7 Conclusions

We presented a maximum-margin approach to learn functional dependencies for interdependent and structured output spaces. The key idea is to model the problem as a (kernelized) linear discriminant function over a joint feature space of inputs and outputs. We showed that this framework is applicable to a wide range of problems, in particular hierarchical classification, label sequence learning, and parsing. We presented an efficient algorithm with polynomial time convergence. This algorithm combines the advantages of maximum-margin classifiers and kernels with the efficiency of dynamic programming algorithms. Experimental evaluation shows the competitiveness of our method.

5.8 Proof of Proposition 37

2. http://www.recommind.com.

Lemma 40 *For a symmetric, positive semidefinite matrix, $\boldsymbol{J}$, let*

$$\boldsymbol{\Theta}(\boldsymbol{\alpha}) = -\tfrac{1}{2}\boldsymbol{\alpha}'\boldsymbol{J}\boldsymbol{\alpha} + \langle \mathbf{h}, \boldsymbol{\alpha} \rangle \tag{5.24}$$

be concave in $\boldsymbol{\alpha}$ and bounded from above. Assume $\langle \nabla\boldsymbol{\Theta}(\boldsymbol{\alpha}^t), \boldsymbol{\eta} \rangle > 0$ for a solution $\boldsymbol{\alpha}^t$ and an optimization direction $\boldsymbol{\eta}$. Let $\beta \leq D$ for some $D > 0$. Then the improvement of the objective along $\boldsymbol{\eta}$ starting from $\boldsymbol{\alpha}^t$ $\delta\boldsymbol{\Theta}(\beta) \equiv \max_{0 < \beta \leq D}\{\boldsymbol{\Theta}(\boldsymbol{\alpha}^t + \beta\boldsymbol{\eta})\} - \boldsymbol{\Theta}(\boldsymbol{\alpha}^t)$ is bounded by

$$\frac{1}{2}\min\left\{D, \frac{\langle \nabla\boldsymbol{\Theta}(\boldsymbol{\alpha}^t), \boldsymbol{\eta} \rangle}{\boldsymbol{\eta}'\boldsymbol{J}\boldsymbol{\eta}}\right\} \langle \nabla\boldsymbol{\Theta}(\boldsymbol{\alpha}^t), \boldsymbol{\eta} \rangle. \tag{5.25}$$

For special cases where $\boldsymbol{\eta} = \boldsymbol{e}_r$ and where $\boldsymbol{\eta} = \boldsymbol{e}_r, \beta < D = \infty$, (5.25) is equivalent to

$$\frac{1}{2}\min\left\{D, \frac{\frac{\partial\boldsymbol{\Theta}}{\partial\alpha_r}(\boldsymbol{\alpha}^t)}{J_{rr}}\right\} \frac{\partial\boldsymbol{\Theta}}{\partial\alpha_r}(\boldsymbol{\alpha}^t) \quad and \quad \frac{1}{2J_{rr}}\left(\frac{\partial\boldsymbol{\Theta}}{\partial\alpha_r}(\boldsymbol{\alpha}^t)\right)^2. \tag{5.26}$$

Proof   Writing out $\delta\boldsymbol{\Theta}(\beta^*) = \beta \langle \nabla\boldsymbol{\Theta}(\boldsymbol{\alpha}^t), \boldsymbol{\eta} \rangle - \frac{\beta^2}{2}\boldsymbol{\eta}'\boldsymbol{J}\boldsymbol{\eta}$, solving for β to maximize $\delta\boldsymbol{\Theta}(\beta^*)$ yields $\beta^* = \langle \nabla\boldsymbol{\Theta}(\boldsymbol{\alpha}^t), \boldsymbol{\eta} \rangle/(\boldsymbol{\eta}'\boldsymbol{J}\boldsymbol{\eta})$. Substituting this value in $\delta\boldsymbol{\Theta}(\beta^*)$ gives the bound on improvement with unconstraint β,

$$\delta\boldsymbol{\Theta}(\beta^*) = \langle \nabla\boldsymbol{\Theta}(\boldsymbol{\alpha}^t), \boldsymbol{\eta} \rangle^2/(2\boldsymbol{\eta}'\boldsymbol{J}\boldsymbol{\eta}) > 0. \tag{5.27}$$

If $D < \beta^*$, i.e. $\langle \nabla\boldsymbol{\Theta}(\boldsymbol{\alpha}^t), \boldsymbol{\eta} \rangle/(\boldsymbol{\eta}'\boldsymbol{J}\boldsymbol{\eta}) > D$, due to the concavity of $\boldsymbol{\Theta}$, $\beta = D$ and

$$\delta\boldsymbol{\Theta}(D) = D\left(\langle \nabla\boldsymbol{\Theta}(\boldsymbol{\alpha}^t), \boldsymbol{\eta} \rangle - \frac{D}{2}\boldsymbol{\eta}'\boldsymbol{J}\boldsymbol{\eta}\right). \tag{5.28}$$

Combining the two cases yields (5.25). When $\boldsymbol{\eta} = \boldsymbol{e}_r$, $\langle \nabla\boldsymbol{\Theta}, \boldsymbol{\eta} \rangle = \frac{\partial\boldsymbol{\Theta}}{\partial\alpha_r}$ and $\boldsymbol{\eta}'\boldsymbol{J}\boldsymbol{\eta} = J_{rr}$, which yields the first term in (5.26). The second term is achieved by substituting ∞ for D. ∎

Proof of Proposition 37.   We first prove the bound for $\mathrm{SVM}_2^{\triangle s}$. Using (5.15), (5.14), $\xi_i^* = \sum_{\mathbf{y} \neq \mathbf{y}_i} \frac{n\alpha_{(i\mathbf{y})}^t}{C\sqrt{\triangle(\mathbf{y}_i, \mathbf{y})}}$ given by the optimality equations for the primal variables and the condition of step 10, namely $\sqrt{\triangle(\mathbf{y}_i, \hat{\mathbf{y}})}\,(1 - \langle \mathbf{w}^*, \delta\Psi_i(\hat{\mathbf{y}}) \rangle) > \xi_i^* + \epsilon$ yields $\frac{\partial\boldsymbol{\Theta}}{\partial\alpha_{(i\hat{\mathbf{y}})}}(\boldsymbol{\alpha}^t) \geq \frac{\epsilon}{\sqrt{\triangle(\mathbf{y}_i, \hat{\mathbf{y}})}}$. Inserting this and $J_{rr} = \|\delta\Psi_i(\hat{\mathbf{y}})\|^2 + \frac{n}{C\triangle(\mathbf{y}_i, \mathbf{y})}$ in the second term of (5.26) yields the first term of (5.19).

For $\mathrm{SVM}_1^{\triangle s}$, consider two cases:

Case I:

If the working set does not contain an element $(i\mathbf{y})$, $S_i = 0$, then we can optimize over $\alpha_{(i\hat{\mathbf{y}})}$ such that $\alpha_{(i\hat{\mathbf{y}})} \leq \triangle(\mathbf{y}_i, \hat{\mathbf{y}})\frac{C}{n} = D$. Then, via the condition of step 10 and $\xi_i^* \geq 0$, $\frac{\partial\boldsymbol{\Theta}}{\partial\alpha_{(i\hat{\mathbf{y}})}}(\boldsymbol{\alpha}^t) = 1 - \langle \mathbf{w}^*, \delta\Psi_i(\hat{\mathbf{y}}) \rangle > \frac{\xi_i^* + \epsilon}{\triangle(\mathbf{y}_i, \hat{\mathbf{y}})} \geq \frac{\epsilon}{\triangle(\mathbf{y}_i, \hat{\mathbf{y}})}$. Substituting this and $J_{(i\hat{\mathbf{y}})(i\hat{\mathbf{y}})} \leq R_i^2$ in the first term of (5.26) yields

$$\delta\boldsymbol{\Theta} \geq \min\left\{\frac{C\epsilon}{2n}, \frac{\epsilon^2}{2R_i^2\triangle(\mathbf{y}_i, \hat{\mathbf{y}})^2}\right\}. \tag{5.29}$$

Case II:

If $S_i \neq \emptyset$, optimization is performed over $\alpha_{(i\hat{\mathbf{y}})}$ and $\alpha_{(i\mathbf{y})}, \forall \mathbf{y} \in S_i$. We need to upper-bound $\boldsymbol{\eta}' \boldsymbol{J} \boldsymbol{\eta}$ and lower-bound $\langle \nabla \boldsymbol{\Theta}(\boldsymbol{\alpha}^t), \boldsymbol{\eta} \rangle$. Without losing any generality let $\eta_{(i\hat{\mathbf{y}})} = 1$ and $\eta_{(i\mathbf{y})} = -\frac{\alpha_{(i\mathbf{y})}}{\triangle(\mathbf{y}_i, \hat{\mathbf{y}})} \frac{n}{C} \leq 0$ for $(i\mathbf{y}) \in S_i$. Then $\boldsymbol{\alpha}^t + \beta \boldsymbol{\eta} \geq 0$ since $\beta \leq \frac{C}{n} \triangle(\mathbf{y}_i, \hat{\mathbf{y}})$.

In order to bound $\langle \nabla \boldsymbol{\Theta}(\boldsymbol{\alpha}^t), \boldsymbol{\eta} \rangle$, notice that for $\delta \geq \epsilon > 0$,

$$\triangle(\mathbf{y}_i, \hat{\mathbf{y}}) \left(1 - \langle \mathbf{w}^*, \delta \Psi_i(\hat{\mathbf{y}}) \rangle \right) = \xi_i^* + \delta, \tag{5.30a}$$

$$\triangle(\mathbf{y}_i, \mathbf{y}) \left(1 - \langle \mathbf{w}^*, \delta \Psi_i(\mathbf{y}) \rangle \right) = \xi_i^*, \quad \mathbf{y} \in S_i \tag{5.30b}$$

Then via $\langle \nabla \boldsymbol{\Theta}(\boldsymbol{\alpha}^t), \boldsymbol{\eta} \rangle = \sum_{\mathbf{y}} \eta_{(i\mathbf{y})} \left(1 - \langle \mathbf{w}^*, \delta \Psi_i(\mathbf{y}) \rangle \right)$, we get

$$\langle \nabla \boldsymbol{\Theta}(\boldsymbol{\alpha}^t), \boldsymbol{\eta} \rangle = \frac{\xi_i^*}{\triangle(\mathbf{y}_i, \hat{\mathbf{y}})} \left(1 - \frac{n}{C} \sum_{\mathbf{y}} \frac{\alpha_{(i\mathbf{y})}}{\triangle(\mathbf{y}_i, \mathbf{y})} \right) + \frac{\delta}{\triangle(\mathbf{y}_i, \hat{\mathbf{y}})} \geq \frac{\epsilon}{\triangle(\mathbf{y}_i, \hat{\mathbf{y}})}. \tag{5.31}$$

Using $\sum_{\mathbf{y} \neq \hat{\mathbf{y}}} \alpha_{(i\mathbf{y})}^t \leq \triangle_i \sum_{\mathbf{y} \neq \hat{\mathbf{y}}} \frac{\alpha_{(i\mathbf{y})}^t}{\triangle(\mathbf{y}_i, \mathbf{y})} \leq \frac{C \triangle_i}{n}$, we bound $\boldsymbol{\eta}' \boldsymbol{J} \boldsymbol{\eta}$ as

$$\boldsymbol{\eta}' \boldsymbol{J} \boldsymbol{\eta} = J_{(i\hat{\mathbf{y}})(i\hat{\mathbf{y}})} - 2 \frac{n}{C} \sum_{\mathbf{y} \neq \hat{\mathbf{y}}} \frac{\alpha_{(i\mathbf{y})}^t J_{(i\hat{\mathbf{y}})(i\mathbf{y})}}{\triangle(\mathbf{y}_i, \hat{\mathbf{y}})} + \frac{n^2}{C^2} \sum_{\mathbf{y} \neq \hat{\mathbf{y}}} \sum_{\mathbf{y}' \neq \hat{\mathbf{y}}} \frac{\alpha_{(i\mathbf{y})}^t \alpha_{(i\mathbf{y}')}^t J_{(i\mathbf{y})(i\mathbf{y}')}}{\triangle(\mathbf{y}_i, \hat{\mathbf{y}}) \triangle(\mathbf{y}_i, \hat{\mathbf{y}})} \tag{5.32a}$$

$$\leq R_i^2 + 2 \frac{n R_i^2}{C \triangle(\mathbf{y}_i, \hat{\mathbf{y}})} \sum_{\mathbf{y} \neq \hat{\mathbf{y}}} \alpha_{(i\mathbf{y})}^t + \frac{n^2 R_i^2}{C^2 \triangle(\mathbf{y}_i, \hat{\mathbf{y}})^2} \sum_{\mathbf{y} \neq \hat{\mathbf{y}}} \sum_{\mathbf{y}' \neq \hat{\mathbf{y}}} \alpha_{(i\mathbf{y})}^t \alpha_{(i\mathbf{y}')}^t \tag{5.32b}$$

$$\leq R_i^2 + 2 \frac{R_i^2 \triangle_i}{\triangle(\mathbf{y}_i, \hat{\mathbf{y}})} + \frac{R_i^2 \triangle_i^2}{\triangle(\mathbf{y}_i, \hat{\mathbf{y}})^2} \leq \frac{4 R_i^2 \triangle_i^2}{\triangle(\mathbf{y}_i, \hat{\mathbf{y}})^2}. \tag{5.32c}$$

Substituting (5.31) and (5.32c) into (5.25) yields

$$\min \left\{ \frac{C\epsilon}{2n}, \frac{\epsilon^2}{8 R_i^2 \triangle_i^2} \right\}. \tag{5.33}$$

Combining (5.29) and (5.33) yields the second term of (5.19). ∎

6   Efficient Algorithms for Max-Margin Structured Classification

Juho Rousu, Craig Saunders, Sandor Szedmak, and John Shawe-Taylor

We present a general and efficient optimization methodology for max-margin structured classification tasks. The efficiency of the method relies on the interplay of several techniques: formulation of the structured support vector machine (SVM) or max-margin Markov problem as an optimization problem; marginalization of the dual of the optimization; partial decomposition via a gradient formulation; and finally tight coupling of a maximum likelihood inference algorithm into the optimization algorithm, as opposed to using inference as a working set maintenance mechanism only. The tight coupling also allows fast approximate inference to be used effectively in the learning.

The generality of the method follows from the fact that changing the output structure in essence only changes the inference algorithm, that is, the method can to a large extent be used in a "plug and play" fashion.

6.1   Introduction

Structured classification methods based on the conditional random field (CRF) model (Lafferty et al., 2001) are proving themselves in various application fields. Recently, techniques inspired by SVMs for learning the parameters of CRFs (Taskar et al., 2004b; Tsochantaridis et al., 2004; Lafferty et al., 2004) or related graphical models (Altun et al., 2003b; Bartlett et al., 2004) have emerged.

In this chapter, we present a general and efficient approach for max-margin learning of CRF parameters when the CRF takes the form of a hypergraph. The method benefits from many of the above works and also from the related research on exponential families and their inference methods (Wainwright and Jordan, 2003; Wainwright et al., 2003).

The main contribution of this chapter is to show that the max-margin optimization relying on the marginal dual formulation (c.f. Taskar et al. 2004b) can be made efficient without simplifying the problem or settling for approximations. Key ingredients are feature and loss representations that adhere to the hypergraph structure, a partial decomposition via gradient-based optimization, and, finally, tight coupling of the inference algorithm to conditional gradient optimization, which avoids an explicit description of the constraints.

6.1.1   Outline of the Chapter

The structure of this chapter is the following. In section 6.2 we present the classification framework, review loss functions, and derive a quadratic optimization problem for finding the maximum-margin model parameters. In section 6.3 we present an efficient learning algorithm relying on a decomposition of the problem into single training example subproblems, and then conducting iterative conditional gradient ascent in marginal dual variable subspaces corresponding to single training examples. We show that search directions of the conditional gradient method can be efficiently found by solving an inference problem on the hypergraph. We demonstrate the algorithm's behavior in section 6.4 in a hierarchical classification task. We conclude the chapter with a discussion in section 6.5.

6.1.2   Notation

For a Cartesian product $S = S_1 \times \cdots \times S_k$ of sets, and $p = \{p_1, \ldots, p_l\} \subset \{1, \ldots, k\}$ an index set, we use the shorthand $S_p = S_{p_1} \times \cdots \times S_{p_l}$ to denote the restriction of S to the index set p. Similarly, we use $s = (s_1, \ldots, s_k) \in S$ and $s_p = (s_{p_1}, \ldots, s_{p_l})$ to denote the members of the set and their restrictions to p, respectively. When p is clear from the context, we sometimes drop the subscripts and write s instead of s_p.

In this chapter we need to refer extensively to vectors with a nested block structure; for example a marginal dual vector $\mu = (\mu_i)_{i=1}^m$, where $\mu_i = (\mu_{ie})_{e \in E}$ (E will be a set of hyperedges introduced below with $\mathcal{Y}_e$ the set of values over the hyperedge node e) and $\mu_{ie} = (\mu_{ie}(\mathbf{u}))_{\mathbf{u} \in \mathcal{Y}_e}$. To denote individual items in these vectors we may use multi-indices $\mu(i, e, \mathbf{u}) = \mu_i(e, \mathbf{u}) = \mu_{ie}(\mathbf{u})$. With no confusion we sometimes transpose the vectors so that $\mu_e = (\mu_{ie})_{i=1}^m$; the subscript will make clear which vector is meant.

For matrices with nested block structure similar conventions are used (figure 6.1): the notation $K = (K_{ii'})_{i,i'=1}^m$, $K_{ii'} = (K_{ie,i'e'})_{e,e' \in E}$ and

$$K_{ie,i'e'} = (K_{ie,i'e'}(\mathbf{u}, \mathbf{u}'))_{\mathbf{u} \in \mathcal{Y}_e, \mathbf{u}' \in \mathcal{Y}_{e'}}$$

is used to refer to the blocks, and multi-indices

$$K(i, e, \mathbf{u}; i', e', \mathbf{u}') = K_{ii'}(e, \mathbf{u}; e', \mathbf{u}') = K_{ie,i'e'}(\mathbf{u}, \mathbf{u}')$$

are used to access the individual items. Furthermore, different permutations will be used, $K_{ee'} = (K_{ie,ie'})_{i=1}^m$, that will again be clear from the context. For

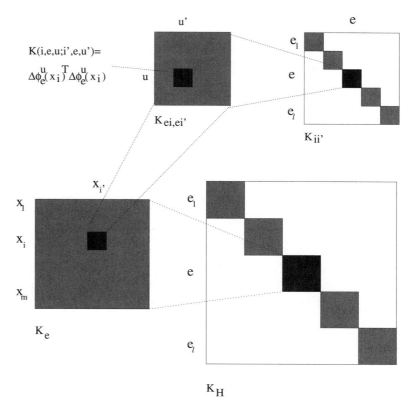

Figure 6.1 Illustration of the nested block structure of the kernels applied in this chapter. The kernel block $K_{ie,i'e'}$ (*top, left*) occurs as a block both in the $K_{ii'}$ kernel (*top, right*) and the edge-kernel K_e (*bottom, left*). The full marginalized kernel K_H (*bottom, right*) is composed of K_e blocks on the diagonal. Gray color indicates potentially nonzero values.

diagonal blocks the double subscript is sometimes replaced with a single one: $K_i = K_{ii}, K_e = K_{ee}$.

When referring to elements of the training set, when no confusion arises we sometimes use the shorthand i in place of $\mathbf{x}_i$ or $\mathbf{y}_i$, e.g. $\alpha(i, \mathbf{y})$ instead of $\alpha(\mathbf{x}_i, \mathbf{y})$, and $\ell_e(i, \mathbf{u}_e)$ in place of $\ell_e(y_{ie}, \mathbf{u}_e)$.

6.2 Structured Classification Model

In this chapter we use the CRF model for structured classification. We first briefly introduce the setting.

multi- and microlabels

We consider data from a domain $\mathcal{X} \times \mathcal{Y}$ where $\mathcal{X}$ is a set and $\mathcal{Y} = \mathcal{Y}_1 \times \cdots \times \mathcal{Y}_k$ is a Cartesian product of finite sets $\mathcal{Y}_j = \{1, \ldots, |\mathcal{Y}_j|\}, j = 1, \ldots, k$. A vector $\mathbf{y} = (y_1, \ldots, y_k) \in \mathcal{Y}$ is called the *multilabel* and the components y_j are called *microlabels*.

We assume that a training set $\{(\mathbf{x}_i, \mathbf{y}_i)\}_{i=1}^{m} \subset \mathcal{X} \times \mathcal{Y}$ has been given, consisting of training examples $(\mathbf{x}_i, \mathbf{y}_i)$ of a training pattern $\mathbf{x}_i$ and multilabel $\mathbf{y}_i$. A pair $(\mathbf{x}, \mathbf{y})$, where $\mathbf{x}_i$ is a training pattern and $\mathbf{y} \in \mathcal{Y}$ is arbitrary, is called a *pseudoexample* in order to denote the fact that the output may or may not have been generated by the distribution generating the training examples.

The multilabels conform to a given fixed hypergraph structure $H = (V, E)$ that consists of nodes $V = \{1, \ldots, k\}$ and hyperedges $E = \{e_1, \ldots, e_r\}$, with $e_h \subset V$ for $h = 1, \ldots, r$. For some or all nodes $v \in V$, the singleton hyperedge $\{v\}$ may be contained in E. The existence of a hyperedge $e = \{v_1, \ldots, v_l\} \in E$ indicates that there is a potential statistical dependency between the microlabels $y_{v_1}, \ldots, y_{v_l}$.

In the CRF defined on H, the probability of a multilabel $\mathbf{y}$ given a training pattern $\mathbf{x}$ is determined by the product of hyperedge potentials

$$P(\mathbf{y}|\mathbf{x}, \mathbf{w}) = \frac{1}{Z(\mathbf{x}, \mathbf{w})} \prod_{e \in E} \varphi_e(\mathbf{x}, \mathbf{y}_e, \mathbf{w}),$$

where $Z(\mathbf{x}, \mathbf{w}) = \sum_{\mathbf{u} \in \mathcal{Y}} \prod_{e \in E} \varphi(\mathbf{x}, \mathbf{u}_e, \mathbf{w})$ is the normalization factor also referred to as the partition function. We concentrate on the case where the potentials are given by an exponential family,

$$\varphi_e(\mathbf{x}, \mathbf{y}_e, \mathbf{w}) = \exp\left(\mathbf{w}_e^T \phi_e(\mathbf{x}, \mathbf{y})\right),$$

where $\mathbf{w}_e$ is the vector of the appropriate block entries for that hyperedge. This choice gives us a log-linear model

$$\log P(\mathbf{y}|\mathbf{x}, \mathbf{w}) = \mathbf{w}^T \phi(\mathbf{x}, \mathbf{y}) - \log Z(\mathbf{x}, \mathbf{w}). \tag{6.1}$$

6.2.1 Max-Margin Learning

Typically in learning probabilistic models one aims to learn maximum likelihood parameters, which in the exponential CRF amounts to solving

$$\operatorname*{argmax}_{\mathbf{w}} \log\left(\prod_{i=1}^{m} P(\mathbf{y}_i|\mathbf{x}_i, \mathbf{w})\right) = \operatorname*{argmax}_{\mathbf{w}} \sum_{i=1}^{m} \left[\mathbf{w}^T \phi(\mathbf{x}_i, \mathbf{y}_i) - \log Z(\mathbf{x}_i, \mathbf{w})\right].$$

This estimation problem is hampered by the need to compute the logarithm of the partition function Z. For a general graph this problem is hard to solve. Approximation methods for its computation are the subject of active research (cf. Wainwright et al. 2003). Also, in the absence of regularization the max-likelihood model is likely to suffer from overfitting.

An alternative formulation (cf. Altun et al. 2003b; Taskar et al. 2004b), inspired by SVMs, is to estimate parameters that in some sense maximize the ratio

$$\frac{P(\mathbf{y}_i|\mathbf{x}_i, \mathbf{w})}{P(\mathbf{y}|\mathbf{x}_i, \mathbf{w})}$$

between the probability of the correct labeling $\mathbf{y}_i$ and the closest competing incorrect labeling $\mathbf{y}$. With the exponential family, the problem translates to the problem of maximizing the minimum linear margin

$$\mathbf{w}^T \phi(\mathbf{x}_i, \mathbf{y}_i) - \mathbf{w}^T \phi(\mathbf{x}_i, \mathbf{y})$$

in the log-space.

In classical SVM learning the required margin between an example $(\mathbf{x}, y)$ and an (incorrect) pseudoexample $(x, -y)$ is taken to be constant. In structured classification, it is proposed to grade the required margin based on the (structured) loss $\ell(\mathbf{y}, \mathbf{y}_i)$, so that the margin requirement is a nondecreasing function $\gamma(\mathbf{y}, \mathbf{y}_i)$ of the loss of corresponding pseudoexamples. We consider the detailed loss functions and the margin scaling below.

Using the canonical hyperplane representation (cf. Cristianini and Shawe-Taylor 2000) the problem can be exactly stated as the following minimization problem:

$$\underset{\mathbf{w}}{\text{minimize}} \ \frac{1}{2}||\mathbf{w}||^2$$
$$\text{s.t. } \mathbf{w}^T \Delta\phi(\mathbf{x}_i, \mathbf{y}) \geq \gamma(\mathbf{y}_i, \mathbf{y}), \text{ for all } i \text{ and } \mathbf{y}, \tag{6.2}$$

where $\Delta\phi(\mathbf{x}_i, \mathbf{y}) = \phi(\mathbf{x}_i, \mathbf{y}_i) - \phi(\mathbf{x}_i, \mathbf{y})$ and $\gamma(\mathbf{y}_i, \mathbf{y})$ is the margin required from the pseudoexample $(\mathbf{x}_i, \mathbf{y})$. Note that in the problem (6.2) the need to compute the log-partition function has been avoided. Also, margin-maximization provides resistance against overfitting.

As with SVMs we are not usually able to find a model satisfying margin constraints exactly, and so it is necessary to add slack variables ξ_i to allow examples to deviate from the margin boundary. Altogether this results in the following optimization problem:

$$\underset{\mathbf{w}}{\text{minimize}} \ \frac{1}{2}||\mathbf{w}||^2 + C\sum_{i=1}^{m} \xi_i$$
$$\text{s.t. } \mathbf{w}^T \Delta\phi(\mathbf{x}_i, \mathbf{y}) \geq \gamma(\mathbf{y}_i, \mathbf{y}) - \xi_i, \text{ for all } i \text{ and } \mathbf{y}. \tag{6.3}$$

For many feature representations such as, for example, strings, images, or graphs, the problem can be very high-dimensional, making it advisable to seek a dual representation:

$$\underset{\alpha \geq 0}{\text{maximize}} \ \alpha^T \gamma - \frac{1}{2}\alpha^T K \alpha, \text{ s.t. } \sum_{\mathbf{y}} \alpha(i, \mathbf{y}) \leq C, \forall i, \mathbf{y}, \tag{6.4}$$

where $K = \Delta\Phi^T \Delta\Phi$ is the *joint* kernel matrix for *pseudoexamples* $(\mathbf{x}_i, \mathbf{y})$ and $\gamma = (\gamma(\mathbf{y}_i, \mathbf{y}))_{i,\mathbf{y}}$ encodes the margin requirements for each $(\mathbf{x}_i, \mathbf{y})$.

This approach makes it possible to avoid working with explicit feature vectors. However, in the dual problem there are exponentially many dual variables $\alpha(i, \mathbf{y})$, one for each pseudoexample. There are a few main routes by which the exponential complexity can be circumvented:

- Dual working set methods where the constraint set is grown incrementally by adding the worst margin violator,

$$\underset{i, \mathbf{y}}{\operatorname{argmin}} \, \mathbf{w}^T \Delta \phi(\mathbf{x}_i, \mathbf{y}) - \gamma(\mathbf{y}_i, \mathbf{y}),$$

to the dual problem. One can guarantee an approximate solution with a polynomial number of support vectors using this approach (Altun et al., 2003b; Tsochantaridis et al., 2004).

- Primal methods where the solution of the above inference problem is integrated into the primal optimization problem, hence avoiding the need to write down the exponential-sized constraint set (Taskar et al., 2004a).

- Marginal dual methods, in which the problem is translated to a polynomially sized form by considering the marginals of the dual variables (Taskar et al., 2004b; Bartlett et al., 2004).

The methodology presented in this chapter belongs to the third category.

6.2.2 Loss Functions

We assume that associated with the set $\mathcal{Y}$ is a loss function $\ell : \mathcal{Y} \times \mathcal{Y} \mapsto \mathbb{R}_+$ that associates for each pair $\mathbf{y}, \mathbf{y}' \in \mathcal{Y}$ a nonnegative loss $\ell(\mathbf{y}, \mathbf{y}')$. There are many ways to define loss functions for a multilabel classification setting, and it will depend on the application which loss function is the most suitable. Nonetheless a few general guidelines can be set. The loss function should obviously fulfill some basic conditions: $\ell(\mathbf{y}, \mathbf{y}') = 0$ if and only if $\mathbf{y} = \mathbf{y}'$, $\ell(\mathbf{y}, \mathbf{y}')$ is maximal when $y_j \neq y'_j$ for every $1 \leq j \leq k$, and ℓ should be monotonically nondecreasing with respect to inclusion of the sets of incorrect microlabels. These conditions are, for example, satisfied by the *zero-one* loss

$$\ell_{0/1}(\mathbf{y}, \mathbf{y}') = [\mathbf{y} \neq \mathbf{y}'].$$

For structured classification, another useful property is that the loss decomposes so that it can be expressed as a combination of the losses of the hyperedges. This is beneficial for algorithmic efficiency and it is not a significant restriction: the need to express the loss of some set of variables $g \subset V$ implies a statistical dependency between those variables. If this dependency is not preempted by the dependencies of the hyperedges that intersect with g, then g really should be a hyperedge in H. We therefore restrict ourselves to losses that are defined as weighted combinations of hyperedge losses:

$$\ell(\mathbf{y}, \mathbf{y}') = \sum_{e \in E} \ell_e(\mathbf{y}_e, \mathbf{y}'_e).$$

The simplest way of defining a loss of this type is to take $\ell_e(\mathbf{y}_e, \mathbf{y}'_e) = [\mathbf{y}_e \neq \mathbf{y}'_e]$, in which case the overall loss is the number of incorrectly predicted hyperedges. If all

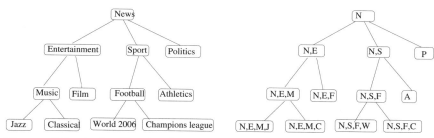

Figure 6.2 A classification hierarchy represented as a tree (*left*) and a hypergraph consisting of partial paths of the tree as hyperedges (*right*).

singleton hyperedges $\{v\}, v \in V$ are in E, defining $\ell_e(\mathbf{y}_e, \mathbf{y}'_e) = 0$ for all nonsingleton hyperedges ($|e| > 1$) gives us the Hamming loss:

$$\ell_\Delta(\mathbf{y}, \mathbf{y}') = \sum_{\{v\} \in E} [y_v \neq y'_v],$$

which penalizes the errors made in vertices individually, but does not take into account the structure implied by the nonsingleton hyperedges; this is also referred to as the microlabel loss.

Example 1 *For particular structures, one can define more elaborate losses. For example, for hierarchical classification (cf. figure 6.2), predicting the parent micro-label correctly is typically more important than predicting the child correctly, as the child may deal with some detailed concept that the user may not be interested in; for example whether a document was about* CHAMPIONS LEAGUE *football or not may not be relevant to a person who is interested in* FOOTBALL *in general. Also, from the learner's point of view, if the parent class has already been predicted incorrectly, we don't want to penalize the mistake in the child. Loss functions with these kinds of properties can be defined in more than one way. If one represents the classification hierarchy as a set of nodes and directed edges $i \mapsto j$, one may define an edge loss*

$$\ell_{\tilde{H}}(\mathbf{y}, \mathbf{y}') = \sum_{e=\{i \mapsto j\} \in E} c_e[y_j \neq y'_j \ \& \ y_i = y'_i],$$

that penalizes a mistake in a child only if the label of the parent was correct. If, on the other hand, the hierarchy is represented as a hypertree with the hyperedges given by the partial paths $p = (v_1, \ldots, v_k)$ where v_i is the parent of v_{i+1}, and v_k is either a leaf or an internal node, one can define a path *loss*

$$\ell_H(\mathbf{y}, \mathbf{y}') = \sum_{p=(v_1, \ldots, v_k) \in E} c_p[y_k \neq y'_k \ \& \ (y_h = y'_h \forall h \in anc(k))],$$

where $anc(j)$ denotes the set of ancestors h of node j.

6.2.3   Scaling the Margin Requirement

As discussed above it is useful to enforce larger margins for pseudoexamples with high loss and vice versa. A natural way to incorporate this is to define the required margin to be a function $\gamma(y_i, y)$ that is monotonically increasing with respect to the loss. Examples of margin scaling include:

- Linear scaling (Taskar et al., 2004a,b): $\gamma(\mathbf{y}_i, \mathbf{y}) = \ell(\mathbf{y}_i, \mathbf{y})$. The benefit of linear scaling is that any decomposability properties of the loss function are translated to the margin requirement. The potential drawback is the fact that some capacity of the learning machine is wasted in tuning the margins of high-loss pseudoexamples; to some degree the classification problem is turned into an ordinal regression problem.

- Inverse scaling (Tsochantaridis et al., 2004): $\gamma(\mathbf{y}_i, \mathbf{y}) - \xi_i = 1 - \xi_i/\ell(\mathbf{y}_i, \mathbf{y})$. Here the slack is downscaled so high-loss examples receive smaller slacks. Inverse scaling is strictly concave with respect to the loss, which makes the margin requirement loss sensitive in the low-loss regime but less sensitive in the high-loss regime. However, the margin requirement is in general not decomposable even if the loss function ℓ is.

Avoiding the tradeoff between retaining decomposability and the apparent waste of capacity in enforcing high margins in the high-loss regime seems difficult. In this chapter, we follow the first approach, as we prefer to retain the possibility of decomposing the learning problem, hence making it possible to tackle larger structures and training sets.

6.2.4   Feature Representation

In a learning problem, there are two general types of features that can be distinguished:

Global features are given by the feature map $\phi^x : \mathcal{X} \mapsto \mathcal{F}_x$. They are not tied to a particular vertex or hyperedge but represent the structured object as a whole. For example, the bag-of-words of a document is not tied to a single class of documents in a hierarchy, but a given word can relate to different classes with different importance.

Local features, are given by a feature map $\phi^x_e : \mathcal{X} \mapsto \mathcal{F}_{xe}$ tied to a particular vertex or hyperedge of the structure. For example, for sequence annotation based on a hidden Markov model each position in the sequence is tied to a set of attributes, e.g. the type and biochemical properties of the nucleotide or amino acid, location-specific sequence homology, and so on.

When the features are used in structured classification on a hypergraph H, the features need to be associated with the labelings of the hypergraph. This is done via constructing a joint feature map $\phi : \mathcal{X} \times \mathcal{Y} \mapsto \mathcal{F}_{xy}$. There are important design choices to be made in how the hypergraph structure should be reflected in the feature representation.

Orthogonal feature representation is defined as

$$\phi(\mathbf{x}, \mathbf{y}) = (\phi_e(\mathbf{x}, \mathbf{y}_e))_{e \in E} \,,$$

so that there is a block for each hyperedge, that in turn is divided into blocks for specific hyperedge-labeling pairs $(e, \mathbf{u}_e)$, i.e. $\phi_e(\mathbf{x}, \mathbf{y}_e) = (\phi_e^{\mathbf{u}_e}(\mathbf{x}, \mathbf{y}_e))_{\mathbf{u}_e \in \mathcal{Y}_e}$.

The map ϕ_e^u should both incorporate the x-features relevant to the hyperedge and encode the dependency on the labeling of the hyperedge. A simple choice is to define

$$\phi_e^{\mathbf{u}_e}(\mathbf{x}, \mathbf{y}_e) = [\mathbf{u}_e = \mathbf{y}_e]\, (\phi^x(\mathbf{x}), \phi_e^x(\mathbf{x}))^T$$

that incorporates both the global and local features if the hyperedge is labeled $\mathbf{y}_e = \mathbf{u}_e$, and a zero vector otherwise. Intuitively, the features are turned "on" only for the particular labeling of the hyperedge that is consistent with $\mathbf{y}$.

Note that in this representation, global features get weighted in a context-dependent manner: some features may be more important in labeling one hyperedge than another. Thus, the global features will be "localized" by the learning algorithm. The size of the feature vectors grows linearly in the number of hyperedges, which requires careful implementation if solving the primal optimization problem (6.3) rather than the dual.

The kernel induced by the above feature map decomposes as

$$K(\mathbf{x}, \mathbf{y}; \mathbf{x}', \mathbf{y}') = \sum_{e \in E} \phi_e(\mathbf{x}, \mathbf{y}_e)^T \phi_e(\mathbf{x}', \mathbf{y}_e') = \sum_{e \in E} K_e(\mathbf{x}, \mathbf{y}_e; \mathbf{x}', \mathbf{y}_e'), \qquad (6.5)$$

which means that there is no crosstalk between the hyperedges:

$$\phi_e(\mathbf{x}, \mathbf{y}_e)^T \phi_{e'}(\mathbf{x}, y_{e'}) = 0$$

if $e \neq e'$, hence the name "orthogonal". The number of terms in the sum when calculating the kernel obviously scales linearly in the number of hyperedges.

Additive feature representation is defined as

$$\phi(\mathbf{x}, \mathbf{y}) = \sum_{e \in E} \sum_{u \in \mathcal{Y}_e} [\mathbf{y}_e = u]\, (\phi^x(\mathbf{x}), \phi_e^x(\mathbf{x}))^T \,;$$

thus the features of the hyperedges are added together.

This feature representation differs from the orthogonal one in a few important respects. First, the dimension of the feature vector is independent of the size of the hypergraph; thus optimization in the primal representation (6.3) is more feasible for large structures. Second, as there are no hyperedge-specific feature weights, the existence of local features is mandatory in this approach; otherwise the hypergraph structure is not reflected in the computed output. Third, the kernel

$$K(\mathbf{x}, \mathbf{y}; \mathbf{x}', \mathbf{y}') = \left(\sum_e \phi_e(\mathbf{x}, \mathbf{y}) \right)^T \left(\sum_e \phi_e(\mathbf{x}', \mathbf{y}') \right)$$

$$= \sum_{e,e'} \phi_e(\mathbf{x}, \mathbf{y}_e)^T \phi_{e'}(\mathbf{x}, \mathbf{y}'_e) = \sum_{e,e'} K_{ee'}(\mathbf{x}, \mathbf{y}_e; \mathbf{x}', \mathbf{y}'_e)$$

induced by this representation typically has nonzero blocks $K_{ee'} \neq 0$, for $e \neq e'$, reflecting crosstalk between hyperedges. There are two consequences of this fact. First, the kernel does not exhibit the sparsity that is implied by the hypergraph, thus it creates the possibility of overfitting. Second, the complexity of the kernel will grow quadratically in the size of the hypergraph rather than linearly as is the case of orthogonal features. This is another reason why a primal optimization approach for this representation might be more justified than a dual approach.

In the sequel, we describe a method that relies on the orthogonal feature representation that will give us a dual formulation with complexity growing linearly in the number of hyperedges in H. The kernel defined by the feature vectors, denoted by

$$K^x(\mathbf{x}, \mathbf{x}') = \phi^x(\mathbf{x})^T \phi^x(\mathbf{x}')$$

is referred to as the x-kernel, while $K(\mathbf{x}, \mathbf{y}; \mathbf{x}, \mathbf{y}')$ is referred to as the *joint kernel*.

6.2.5   Marginal Dual Polytope

The feasible set of the dual problem (6.4) is a Cartesian product $\mathcal{A} = \mathcal{A}_1 \times \cdots \times \mathcal{A}_m$ of identical closed polytopes,

$$\mathcal{A}_i = \{\alpha_i \in \mathbb{R}^{|\mathcal{Y}|} \mid \alpha_i \geq 0, \|\alpha_i\|_1 \leq C\}, \tag{6.6}$$

with a vertex set $V_i = \{0, Ce_1, \ldots, Ce_{|\mathcal{Y}|}\} \subset \mathbb{R}^{|\mathcal{Y}|}$ consisting of the zero vector and the unit vectors of $\mathbb{R}^{|\mathcal{Y}|}$, scaled by C. The vertex set of $\mathcal{A}$ is the Cartesian product $V_1 \times \cdots \times V_m$.

The dimension of the set $\mathcal{A}$, $d_{\mathcal{A}} = m|\mathcal{Y}|$ is exponential in the length of the multilabel vectors. This means that optimizing directly over the the set $\mathcal{A}$ is not tractable. Fortunately, by utilizing the structure of H, the set $\mathcal{A}$ can be mapped to a set $\mathcal{M}$ of polynomial dimension, called the marginal polytope of H, where optimization becomes more tractable (cf. Taskar et al. 2004b).

Given a subset $p \subset \{1, \ldots, k\}$ of vertices, and an associated labeling y_p, the marginal of $\alpha(i, \mathbf{y})$ for the pair (p, y_p) is given by

$$\mu(i, p, y_p) = \sum_{\mathbf{u} \in \mathcal{Y}} [y_p = u_p] \alpha(i, \mathbf{u}), \tag{6.7}$$

where the sum picks up those dual variables $\alpha(i, \mathbf{u})$ that have equal value $u_p = y_p$ on the subset $p \subset \{1, \ldots, k\}$.

For the hypergraph H, the marginal dual vector containing the hyperedge marginals of the example $\mathbf{x}_i$ is given by

$$\mu_i = (\mu(i, e, \mathbf{u}_e))_{e \in E, \mathbf{u}_e \in \mathcal{Y}_e} \, .$$

The marginal vector of the whole training set is the concatenation of the single-example marginal dual vectors $\mu = (\mu_i)_{i=1}^m$. The vector has dimension $d_{\mathcal{M}} = m \sum_{e \in E} |\mathcal{Y}_e| = O(m|E| \max_e |\mathcal{Y}_e|)$. Thus the dimension is linear in the number of examples, hyperedges, and the maximum cardinality of the set of labelings of a single hyperedge.

The indicator functions in the definitions (6.7) of all relevant marginals can be collectively represented by the matrix M_H, $M_H(e, \mathbf{u}_e; \mathbf{y}) = [\mathbf{u}_e = \mathbf{y}_e]$, and the relationship between a dual vector α and the corresponding marginal vector μ is given by the linear map $M_H \alpha_i = \mu_i$ and $\mu = (M_H \alpha_i)_{i=1}^m$. The image of the set $\mathcal{A}_i$, defined by

$$\mathcal{M}_i = \{\mu_i | \, \exists \alpha_i \in \mathcal{A}_i : M_H \alpha_i = \mu_i\}$$

is called the *marginal polytope* of α_i on H.

The following properties of the set $\mathcal{M}_i$ are immediate:

Theorem 41 *Let $\mathcal{A}_i$ be the polytope of (6.6) and let $\mathcal{M}_i$ be the corresponding marginal polytope. Then*

▪ *the vertex set of $\mathcal{M}_i$ is the image of the vertex set of $\mathcal{A}_i$:*

$$V_i^\mu = \{\mu | \, \exists \alpha \in V_i^\alpha : M_{\mathcal{H}} \alpha = \mu\}.$$

▪ *As an image of a convex polytope $\mathcal{A}_i$ under the linear map M_H, $\mathcal{M}_i$ is a convex polytope.*

These properties underlie the efficient solution of the dual problem on the marginal polytope.

6.2.6 Marginal Dual Problem

The exponential size of the dual problem (6.4) can be tackled via the relationship between its feasible set $\mathcal{A} = \mathcal{A}_1 \times \cdots \times \mathcal{A}_m$ and the marginal polytopes $\mathcal{M}_i$ of each $\mathcal{A}_i$.

Given a decomposable loss function

$$\ell(\mathbf{y}_i, \mathbf{y}) = \sum_{e \in E} \ell_e(i, \mathbf{y}_e)$$

and linear margin scaling $\gamma(\mathbf{y}', \mathbf{y}) = \ell(\mathbf{y}_i, \mathbf{y})$, the linear part of the objective satisfies

$$
\sum_{i=1}^{m} \sum_{\mathbf{y} \in \mathcal{Y}} \alpha(i, \mathbf{y})\ell(i, \mathbf{y}) = \sum_{i=1}^{m} \sum_{\mathbf{y}} \alpha(i, \mathbf{y}) \sum_{e} \ell_e(i, \mathbf{y}_e)
$$
$$
= \sum_{i=1}^{m} \sum_{e \in E} \sum_{u \in \mathcal{Y}_e} \sum_{\mathbf{y}:\mathbf{y}_e = u} \alpha(i, \mathbf{y})\ell_e(i, u)
$$
$$
= \sum_{i=1}^{m} \sum_{e \in E} \sum_{u \in \mathcal{Y}_e} \mu(e, u)\ell_e(i, u)
$$
$$
= \sum_{i=1}^{m} \mu_i^T \ell_i = \mu^T \ell_H, \qquad (6.8)
$$

where $\ell_H = (\ell_i)_{i=1}^{m} = (\ell_e(i, u))_{i=1, e \in E, u \in \mathcal{Y}_e}^{m}$ is the marginal loss vector.

Given an orthogonal feature representation inducing a decomposable kernel (6.5), the quadratic part of the objective becomes

$$
\alpha K \alpha = \sum_{e} \sum_{i, i'} \sum_{\mathbf{y}, \mathbf{y}'} \alpha(i, \mathbf{y}) K_e(i, \mathbf{y}_e; i', \mathbf{y}_e') \alpha(i', \mathbf{y}')
$$
$$
= \sum_{e} \sum_{i, i'} \sum_{\mathbf{u}, \mathbf{u}'} K_e(i, \mathbf{u}; i', \mathbf{u}') \sum_{\mathbf{y}:\mathbf{y}_e = \mathbf{u}} \sum_{\mathbf{y}':\mathbf{y}_e' = \mathbf{u}'} \alpha(i, \mathbf{y})\alpha(i', \mathbf{y}')
$$
$$
= \sum_{e} \sum_{i, i'} \sum_{\mathbf{u}, \mathbf{u}'} \mu_e(i, \mathbf{u}) K_e(i, \mathbf{u}; i', \mathbf{u}') \mu_e(i, \mathbf{u}')
$$
$$
= \mu^T K_H \mu, \qquad (6.9)
$$

where $K_H = \mathrm{diag}\,(K_e, e \in E)$ is a block diagonal matrix with hyperedge-specific kernel blocks K_e.

The objective should be maximized with respect to μ while ensuring that there exist $\alpha \in \mathcal{A}$ satisfying $M\alpha = \mu$, so that the marginal dual solution represents a feasible solution of the original dual. By theorem 41 the feasible set of the marginalized problem is the marginal dual polytope, or to be exact, the Cartesian product of the marginal polytopes of single examples (which are in fact equal):

$$
\mathcal{M} = \mathcal{M}_1 \times \cdots \times \mathcal{M}_m.
$$

In summary, the marginalized optimization problem can be stated in implicit form as

$$
\max_{\mu \in \mathcal{M}} \mu^T \ell_H - \frac{1}{2}\mu^T K_H \mu. \qquad (6.10)
$$

This problem is a quadratic program (QP) with a linear number of variables in the number of training examples and in the number of hyperedges. If the cardinality of hyperedges is bounded by a constant, the number of variables is linear also in the number of microlabels.

For optimization algorithms, an explicit characterization of the feasible set is required. However, characterizing the polytope $\mathcal{M}$ in terms of linear constraints defining the faces of the polytope is in general infeasible. Singly connected graphs are an exception: for such a graph $G = (V, E)), E \subset V \times V$, the marginal polytope is exactly reproduced by the box constraints

$$\sum_{\mathbf{u}_e} \mu_e(i, \mathbf{u}_e) \leq C, \forall i, e \in E, \mu_e \geq 0 \qquad (6.11)$$

and the local consistency constraints

$$\sum_{y_k} \mu_{kj}(i, (y_k, y_j)) = \mu_j(i, y_j); \sum_{y_j} \mu_{kj}(i, (y_k, y_j)) = \mu_k(i, y_k). \qquad (6.12)$$

In this case the size of the resulting constraint set is linear in the number of vertices of the graph. Thus for small singly connected graphs they can be written down explicitly and the resulting optimization problem has linear size both in the number of examples and the size of the graph. Thus the approach can in principle be made to work, although not with off-the-shelf QP solvers (see sections 6.3 and 6.4).

For general graphs and hypergraphs the situation is more complicated (cf. Wainwright and Jordan 2003): the local consistency of edges or hyperedges is not sufficient to ensure global consistency, that is, there are marginal dual vectors μ for which there exists no $\alpha \in \mathcal{A}$ such that $M_H \alpha = \mu$. For global consistency, one needs to derive the junction tree of the hypergraph and write down the local consistency constraints of the junction tree. Consequently, the size of the constraint set is linear in the size of the junction tree, which, unfortunately, can be much more than the size of the original hypergraph. Thus in general an explicit description of the constraint set is not a tractable approach.

In the following, we derive an approach where we avoid the explicit consideration of the constraints, which in part contributes toward an efficient optimization approach.

6.3 Efficient Optimization on the Marginal Dual Polytope

Despite the polynomial number of dual variables, the marginal dual problem is still a challenging one to solve if the hypergraph is large or dense. In the following, we describe an algorithm that enables us to tackle general graph structures with reasonable computational complexity. The main ingredients are

- partial decomposition via gradient-based approaches;

- efficient optimization via the conditional gradient method;

- computation of feasible descent directions via solving an inference problem on the hypergraph.

6.3.1   Decomposition of the Learning Problem

The size of the optimization problem suggests that we should try to decompose it in some way. However, the marginalized dual problem has a property that defies full decomposition:

- The constraints decompose by the examples, i.e. we can collect all the constraints related to training example $\mathbf{x}_i$ into the linear system $A\mu_i \leq b, C\mu_i = d$. However, decomposition by the hyperedges is not possible due to the consistency constraints between hyperedges.

- The kernel decomposes by the hypergraph structure as $K_H = \operatorname{diag}(K_e, e \in E)$ but the interactions between examples (represented by a nonsparse x-kernel K^x) forbid a similar decomposition by the examples.

A partial decomposition becomes possible via gradient-based approaches. The gradient of the objective $obj(\mu) = \ell_H^T \mu - (1/2)\mu^T K_H \mu$,

$$g = \nabla[obj(\mu)] = \ell_H - K_H \mu = (\ell_i - (K_{i1}, \ldots, K_{im})\mu)_{i=1}^m = (g_i)_{i=1}^m,$$

can be consulted and updated for each example independently. Thus a general gradient-based iterative approach is possible:

1. For example, $\mathbf{x}_i$, using the gradient information g_i, find $\Delta\mu_i$ such that $\mu_i + \Delta\mu_i$ is feasible and the objective value is increased, i.e. $g_i^T \Delta\mu_i > 0$

2. If a stopping criterion is satisfied, stop, otherwise move to the next example, and repeat.

In the next section, we describe the application of a conditional gradient algorithm (c.f. Bertsekas 1999), which follows the above general template.

6.3.2   Conditional Gradient Algorithm

Let us consider optimizing the dual variables $\mu_i = (\mu_e(i, \mathbf{u}))_{e \in E, \mathbf{u} \in \mathcal{Y}_e}$ of example $\mathbf{x}_i$. We denote by $\ell_i = (\ell_e(i, \mathbf{u}_e)_{e \in E}$ the corresponding loss vector and by $K_{ij} = diag(K_{eij}, e \in E)$, where $K_{eij} = (K_e(i, \mathbf{u}; j, \mathbf{v})_{\mathbf{u}, \mathbf{v} \in \mathcal{Y}_e}$, the block of kernel values between examples i and j, on edge e (note that K_{ij} also is block diagonal like the full marginalized kernel K_H). Finally we denote by $K_{i\cdot} = (K_{ij})_{j \in \{1, \ldots, m\}}$ the columns of the kernel matrix K_H referring to example i.

Obtaining the gradient for the $\mathbf{x}_i$-subspace requires computing the corresponding part of the gradient of the objective function in (6.10), which is $g_i = \ell_i - K_{i\cdot}\mu$. However when updating μ_i only, evaluating the change in objective and updating the gradient can be done more cheaply. We have

$$\Delta g_i = -K_{ii}\Delta\mu_i$$

and

$$\Delta obj = g_i^T \Delta \mu_i - \frac{1}{2} \Delta \mu_i K_{ii} \Delta \mu_i.$$

Thus local optimization in a subspace of a single training example can be done without consulting the other training examples. On the other hand, we do not want to spend too much time in optimizing a single example: since the dual variables of the other examples are nonoptimal, so is the initial gradient g_i. Thus the optimum we would arrive at by optimizing μ_i while keeping other examples fixed would not be the global optimum of the quadratic objective. It makes more sense to optimize all examples more or less in tandem so that the full gradient approaches its optimum as quickly as possible.

In our approach, we have chosen to conduct a few optimization steps for each training example using a conditional gradient ascent (see algorithm 6.2) before moving on to the next example. The iteration limit for each example is set by using the Karush-Kuhn-Tucker(KKT) conditions as a guideline; the larger contribution to the duality gap by an example, the higher the iteration limit.

The pseudocode of our algorithm is given in algorithm 6.1. It takes as input the training data, the hypergraph H, and the loss vector $\ell_\mu = (\ell_i)_{i=1}^m$. The algorithm chooses a chunk of examples as the working set, computes the kernel for each $\mathbf{x}_i$, and makes an optimization pass over the chunk. After one pass, the gradient, slacks, and the duality gap are computed and a new chunk is picked. The process is iterated until the duality gap falls below a given threshold.

Note in particular that the joint kernel is not explicitly computed, although evaluating the gradient requires computing the product $K_H \mu$. We are able to take advantage of the special structure of the feature vectors, where the interaction between the labelings and the x-features of a hyperedge is given by a tensor product, to facilitate the computation using the x-kernel and the dual variables only.

6.3.3 Conditional Subspace Gradient Ascent

The optimization algorithm used for a single example is a variant of conditional gradient ascent (or descent) algorithms (Bertsekas, 1999). The algorithms in this family solve a constrained quadratic problem by iteratively stepping to the best feasible direction with respect to the current gradient. It exploits the fact if μ^* is an optimum solution of a maximization problem with objective function f over the feasibility domain $\mathcal{M}_i$, then it has to satisfy the first-order optimality condition, that is, the inequality

$$\nabla f(\mu_i)(\mu_i - \mu^*) \geq 0 \tag{6.13}$$

has to hold for any feasible μ_i chosen from $\mathcal{M}_i$.

The pseudocode of our variant conditional subspace gradient ascent (CSGA) is given in algorithm 6.2. The algorithm takes as input the current dual variables, gradient, constraints and the kernel block for the example $\mathbf{x}_i$, and an iteration

---

Algorithm 6.1 Maximum-margin optimization algorithm for a conditional random field on a hypergraph

---

Require: Training data $S = ((\mathbf{x}_i, \mathbf{y}_i))_{i=1}^{m}$, hyperedge set E of the hypergraph, a loss vector ℓ_H, and the feasibility domain $\mathcal{M}$.

Ensure: Dual variable vector μ and objective value $f(\mu)$.

1: Initialize $g = \ell_H$, $\xi = \ell, dg = \infty$ and $OBJ = 0$.
2: **while** $dg > dg_{min}$ & $iter < max\_iter$ **do**
3:      $[WS, Freq] = \text{UpdateWorkingSet}(\mu, g, \xi)$;
4:      Compute x-kernel values $K_{X,WS}$ with respect to the working set;
5:      **for** $i \in WS$ **do**
6:          Compute joint kernel block K_{ii} and subspace gradient g_i;
7:          $[\mu_i, \Delta obj] = \text{CSGA}(\mu_i, g_i, K_{ii}, \mathcal{M}_i, Freq_i)$;
8:      **end for**
9:      Compute gradient g, slacks ξ and duality gap dg;
10: **end while**

---

limit. It outputs new values for the dual variables μ_i and the change in objective value. As discussed above, the iteration limit is set very tight so that only a few iterations will be typically conducted.

First, we need to find a feasible μ^* which maximizes the first-order feasibility condition (6.13) at a fixed μ_i. This problem is a linear program:

$$\mu^* = \underset{\mathbf{v} \in \mathcal{M}_i}{\text{argmax}} \ g_i^T \mathbf{v}. \tag{6.14}$$

The solution gives a direction potentially increasing the value of objective function f. Then we have to choose a step length τ that gives the optimal feasible solution as a stationary point along the line segment $\mu_i(\tau) = \mu_i + \tau \Delta \mu$, $\tau \in (0, 1]$, where $\Delta \mu = \mu^* - \mu_i$, starting from the known feasible solution μ_i.

The stationary point is found by solving the equation

$$\frac{\mathbf{d}}{\mathbf{d}\tau} \left[g_i^T \mu_i(\tau) - 1/2 \mu_i(\tau)^T K_{ii} \mu_i(\tau) \right] = 0, \tag{6.15}$$

expressing the optimality condition with respect to τ. If $\tau > 1$, the stationary point is infeasible and the feasible maximum is obtained at $\tau = 1$. In our experience, the time taken to compute the stationary point was typically significantly smaller than the time taken to find μ_i^*.

6.3.4 Efficient Computation of the Feasible Ascent Direction

The main difficulty in optimizing the max-margin problem in the marginal dual form arises from the need to ensure marginal consistency: the box constraints are easy to satisfy by many algorithms, including variants of sequential margin optimization (SMO) (Platt, 1999) or simple steepest gradient search. For tree-structured graphs the constraints can be written down explicitly, as in such graphs

---

Algorithm 6.2 Conditional subspace gradient ascent optimization step

---
$\mathrm{CSGA}(\mu_i, g_i, K_{ii}, \mathcal{M}_i, maxiter_i)$

Require: Initial dual variable vector μ_i, gradient g_i, the feasible region $\mathcal{M}_i$, a joint kernel block K_{ii} for the subspace, and an iteration limit $maxiter_i$.

Ensure: New values for dual variables μ_i and change in objective Δobj.

1:    $\Delta obj = 0; iter = 0;$
2:    **while** $iter < maxiter$ **do**
3:       % find highest feasible point given g_i
4:       $\mu^* = \mathrm{argmax}_{\mathbf{v} \in \mathcal{M}_i} \ g_i^T \mathbf{v};$
5:       $\Delta\mu = \mu^* - \mu_i;$
6:       $q = g^T \Delta\mu, \ r = \Delta\mu^T K_{ii} \Delta\mu;$ % taken from the solution of (6.15)
7:       $\tau = \min(q/r, 1);$ % clip to remain feasible
8:       **if** $\tau \leq 0$ **then**
9:         **break**; % no progress, stop
10:      **else**
11:        $\mu_i = \mu_i + \tau\Delta\mu;$ % update
12:        $g_i = g_i - \tau K_{ii}\Delta\mu;$
13:        $\Delta obj = \Delta obj + \tau q - \tau^2 r/2;$
14:      **end if**
15:      $iter = iter + 1;$
16:    **end while**

---

local consistency of adjacent edges is sufficient to ensure global consistency. For general graphs, such a relation does not hold: it is easy to find examples where a locally consistent distribution can be globally inconsistent. In principle, a sufficient constraint set for a general graph can be found via construction of the junction tree of the graph and writing down consistency constraints of the hyperedges. However, this approach suffers from the fact that, for a dense graph, the junction tree and consequently the constraint set, may be very (exponentially) large. Thus, other means need to be used to ensure global consistency of the marginal dual solution.

The basis of our solution is the following relationship, which can also be seen as a consequence of (Wainwright and Jordan, 2003, theorem 4):

Lemma 42 *For any gradient g_i, there is a vertex $\alpha_i^* \in \mathcal{A}_i$ such that $\mu_i^* = M_H \alpha_i^*$ is an optimizer of (6.14).*

Proof Since $\mathcal{M}_i$ is a polyhedron and the objective is linear, it follows that among the optimal solutions of the conditional gradient (6.14) there is a vertex of $\mathcal{M}_i$. Denote this vertex by μ_i^*. Since the vertex set of $\mathcal{M}_i$ is the image of the vertex set of $\mathcal{A}_i$, μ_i^* is the image of some vertex $\alpha_i^* \in \mathcal{A}_i$. ∎

Thus, α_i^* corresponding to the conditional gradient is either the zero vector or a unit vector corresponding to some multilabel $\mathbf{y}^*$.

Lemma 43 *If $\mu_i^* \neq 0$, then for all hyperedges $e \in E$ we have $\mu_i^*(e, \mathbf{y}_e^*) = C$, and $\mu_i^*(e, u) = 0$ for all $\mathbf{y}_e^* \neq u$.*

Proof Since $M_H \alpha_i^* = \mu_i^*$ and α_i^* has a single nonzero component, $\alpha^*(i, \mathbf{y}^*) = C$, μ_i^* is the $\mathbf{y}^*$th column of M_H, multiplied by C. Thus the nonzero values of μ_i^* equal C. Let us now assume, contrary to the claim, that $\mu_i^*(e, \mathbf{u}) = \mu_i^*(e, \mathbf{u}') = C$ for some $\mathbf{u} \neq \mathbf{u}'$. But then by the definition of matrix M_H we must have $[\mathbf{y}_e^* = \mathbf{u}] = 1 = [\mathbf{y}_e^* = \mathbf{u}']$ which is a contradiction, and the claim follows. ∎

Consequently, $\mu_i^* = \mu_i(\mathbf{y}^*)$ is directly defined by the optimal labeling $\mathbf{y}^*$. The lemma also gives a recipe for constructing μ_i^* given $\mathbf{y}^*$.

We can now rewrite (6.14) in terms of the multilabels:

$$\mathbf{y}^* = \underset{\mathbf{y}}{\text{argmax}}\, g_i^T \mu_i^*(\mathbf{y}) = \underset{\mathbf{y}}{\text{argmax}} \sum_{e \in E} g_{ie}^T \mu_{ie}^*(\mathbf{y}_e) = \underset{\mathbf{y}}{\text{argmax}} \sum_{e \in E} g_{ie}(\mathbf{y}_e)C, \quad (6.16)$$

which is readily seen as an inference problem on the hypergraph H: one must find the configuration $\mathbf{y}^*$ that maximizes the sum of the hyperedge gradients $g_{ie}(\mathbf{y}_e)$.

Thus we have translated our feasible ascent direction problem into an inference problem on the hypergraph. If we can solve the inference problem (6.16) efficiently, the conditional gradient method will be very efficient.

In addition, for our purposes there is no real need to compute the exact optimum, a direction that promises ascent with high likelihood is sufficient. Hence, fast approximate inference algorithms suffice here. Some examples of available methods are the following.

identifying ascent directions

▪ For sequences and trees, inference can be implemented via dynamic programming and it has generally a linear time complexity.

▪ Hypergraphs with low tree width can be converted to their junction tree and dynamic programming can be used on the junction tree to find the maximizing configuration. The size of the junction tree depends on the tree width of the graph.

▪ Loopy belief propagation (LBP) refers to the use of the message-passing algorithm on a cyclic hypergraph. While this algorithm is not guaranteed to converge on such graphs, it has a successful track record in practical applications. For our purposes, the asymptotic convergence is not a central issue as long as the initial convergence is fast enough to find a configuration $\mathbf{y}^*$ corresponding to a descent direction.

▪ The tree reparametrization algorithm (TRP) (Wainwright et al., 2003) is based on computing a series of spanning trees of the (hyper)graph. The convergence is often faster than that of LBP. Also, in the case of TRP, the algorithm can be stopped after a few iterations once a configuration $\mathbf{y}^*$ guaranteeing descent is found.

All of the methods can be viewed as instantiations of message-passing algorithms (Wainwright and Jordan, 2003). In the next section we exemplify the optimization approach on hierarchical problems, where exact inference can be implemented by dynamic programming.

6.4   Experiments

We tested the presented learning approach on three datasets that have an associated classification hierarchy:

- Reuters Corpus Volume 1, RCV1 (Lewis et al., 2004). 2500 documents were used for training and 5000 for testing. As the label hierarchy we used the "CCAT" family of categories, which had a total of 34 nodes, organized in a tree with maximum depth 3. The tree is quite unbalanced, half of the nodes residing in depth 1.

- WIPO-alpha patent dataset (WIPO, 2001). The dataset consisted of the 1372 training and 358 testing documents comprising the D section of the hierarchy. The number of nodes in the hierarchy was 188, with maximum depth 3. Each document in this dataset belongs to exactly one leaf category, hence it contains no multiple or partial paths.

- ENZYME classification dataset. The training data consisted of 7700 protein sequences with hierarchical classification given by the Enzyme Classification (EC) system. The hierarchy consisted of 236 nodes organized into a tree of depth 3. Test data consisted of 1755 sequences.

The two first datasets were processed into bag-of-words representation with term frequencyinverse document frequency weighting (TF/IDF). No word stemming or stop-word removal was performed. For the ENZYME sequences a length-4 subsequence kernel was used. Note that in the Reuters Corpus multiple partial paths exist: it is not the case that the correct classification is simply a single path to a leaf node; for a single example multiple paths in the hierarchy may be positively labeled, and it is not necessary that a path end at a leaf node.

We compared the performance of the presented max-margin conditional random field (MMCRF)learning approach to three algorithms: SVM denotes an SVM trained for each microlabel separately, H-SVM denotes the case where the SVM for a microlabel is trained only with examples for which the ancestor labels are positive.

The SVM and H-SVM were run using the SVM-light package. After precomputation of the kernel these algorithms are as fast as one could expect, as they just involve solving an SVM for each node in the graph (with the full training set for SVM and usually a much smaller subset for H-SVM).

H-RLS is a batch version of the hierarchical least-squares algorithm described in Cesa-Bianchi et al. (2004). It essentially solves for each node i a least-squares style problem $\mathbf{w}_i = (I + S_i S_i^T + \mathbf{x}\mathbf{x}^T)^{-1} S_i \mathbf{y}_i$, where S_i is a matrix consisting of all training examples for which the parent of node i was classified as positive, $\mathbf{y}_i$ is a microlabel vector for node i of those examples, and I is the identity matrix of appropriate size. Predictions for a node i for a new example $\mathbf{x}$ is -1 if the parent of the node was classified negatively and $\text{sign}(\mathbf{w}_i^T \mathbf{x})$ otherwise.

H-RLS requires a matrix inversion for each prediction of each example, at each node along a path for which errors have not already been made. No optimization of the algorithm was made, except to use extension approaches to efficiently compute the matrix inverse (for each example an inverted matrix needs to be extended by one row/column, so a straightforward application of the Sherman-Morrison formula to efficiently update the inverse can be used).

The H-RLS and MMCRF algorithms were implemented in MATLAB. The tests were run on a high-end PC. For SVM,H-SVM, and MMCRF, the regularization parameter value $C = 1$ was used in all experiments, as in initial experiments its value did not seem to have a significant effect.

6.4.1   Obtaining Consistent Labelings

As the learning algorithms compared here all decompose the hierarchy for learning, the multilabel composed of naively combining the microlabel predictions may be inconsistent, that is, they may predict a document as part of the child but not as part of the parent. For SVM and H-SVM consistent labelings were produced by postprocessing the predicted labelings as follows: start at the root and traverse the tree in a breadth-first fashion. If the label of a node is predicted as -1, then all descendants of that node are also labeled negatively. This postprocessing

post-processing predictions

turned out to be crucial to obtain good accuracy; thus we only report results with the postprocessed labelings. Note that H-RLS performs essentially the same procedure (see above). For the max-margin CRF models, we computed by dynamic programming the consistent multilabel with maximum likelihood

$$\hat{\mathbf{y}}(x) = \underset{\mathbf{y} \in \mathcal{Y}_T}{\operatorname{argmax}} P(\mathbf{y}|x) = \underset{\mathbf{y}}{\operatorname{argmax}} \mathbf{w}^T \phi(x, \mathbf{y}),$$

where $\mathcal{Y}_T$ is the set of multilabels that correspond to unions of partial paths in T. This inference problem can be solved by the same dynamic programming algorithm as the one used for learning, with the exception that the set of multilabels considered is restricted to those consistent with the union of partial paths model.

6.4.2   Efficiency of Optimization

To give an indication of the efficiency of the MMCRF algorithm, figure 6.3 shows an example of a learning curve on the WIPO-alpha dataset. The number of marginal dual variables for this training set is just over 1 million and the marginalized kernel matrix K_H—if computed explicitly—would have approximately 5 billion entries. Note that the solutions for this optimization are not sparse: typically less than 25% of the marginal dual variables are zero. Training and test losses (ℓ_Δ) are all close to their optima within 10 minutes of starting the training, and the objective is within 2 % of the optimum in 30 minutes.

To put these results in perspective, for the WIPO dataset SVM (SVM-light) takes approximately 50 seconds per node, resulting in a total running time of about 2.5 hours. The running time of H-RLS was slower than the other methods, but this could be due to our nonoptimized implementation. It is our expectation that it would be very close to the time taken by H-SVM if coded more efficiently.

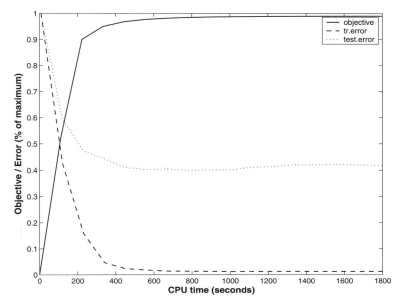

Figure 6.3 The objective function (% of optimum) and ℓ_Δ losses for MMCRF on training and test sets (WIPO-alpha).

Therefore, from a computational efficiency point of view, the methods presented in this chapter are very competitive to other methods which do not operate in the large feature/output spaces of MMCRF.

Figure 6.4 shows for WIPO-alpha the efficiency of the dynamic programming (DP) based computation of update directions as compared to solving the update directions with MATLAB's linear interior point solver LIPSOL. The DP-based updates result in an optimization an order of magnitude faster than using LIPSOL.

In addition, for DP the effect of the iteration limit for optimization speed is depicted. Setting the iteration limit too low (1) or too high (50) slows down the optimization, for different reasons. A too tight iteration limit makes the overhead in moving from one example to the other dominate the running time. A too high iteration limit makes the the algorithm spend too much time optimizing the dual variables of a single example. Unfortunately, it is not straightforward to suggest an iteration limit that would be universally the best.

6.4.3   Comparison of Predictive Accuracies of Different Algorithms.

In our final test we compare the predictive accuracy of MMCRF to other learning methods. For the MMCRF we include the results for training with ℓ_Δ and $\ell_{\tilde{H}}$ losses (see section 6.2.2 for a discussion of loss functions). For training SVM and H-SVM, these losses produce the same learned model.

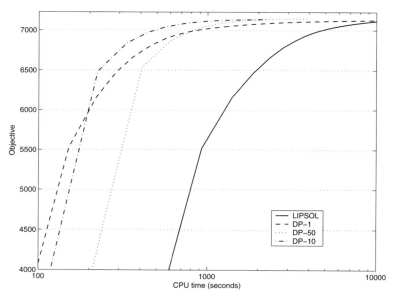

Figure 6.4 Learning curves for MMCRF using LIPSOL and dynamic programming (DP) to compute update directions (WIPO-alpha). Curves with iteration limits 1,10 and 50 are shown for DP. The LIPSOL curve is computed with iteration limit set to 1.

Table 6.1 depicts the different test losses, as well as the standard information retrieval statistics precision (P), recall (R), and F1 statistic ($F1 = 2PR/(P + R)$). Precision and recall were computed over all microlabel predictions in the test set. Flat SVM is expectedly inferior to the competing algorithms with respect to most statistics, as it cannot utilize the dependencies between the microlabels in any way. The two variants of MMCRF are the most efficient in getting the complete tree correct, as shown by the lower zero-one loss. With respect to other statistics, the structured methods are quite evenly matched overall.

6.5 Conclusion

In this chapter we have introduced a general methodology for efficient optimization of structured classification tasks in the max-margin setting. We discussed how the choice of feature representation and loss function can affect the computational burden imposed by the primal and dual formulations. We have shown that for the nonrestrictive setting where an orthogonal feature representation is used in combination with a loss function that is edge-decomposable, we can efficiently solve the optimization problem using conditional gradient methods by exploiting the block structure of the gradient. The resulting method has been tested on three datasets for which the labels are placed within a hierarchical structure. The first two of these were document classification tasks that used the standard TF/IDF

Table 6.1 Prediction losses $\ell_{0/1}$ and ℓ_Δ, precision, recall, and F1 values obtained using different learning algorithms. All figures are given as percentages. Precision and recall are computed in terms of totals of microlabel predictions in the test set

REUTERS	$\ell_{0/1}$	ℓ_Δ	P	R	F1
SVM	32.9	0.61	94.6	58.4	72.2
H-SVM	29.8	0.57	92.3	63.4	75.1
H-RLS	28.1	**0.55**	91.5	65.4	**76.3**
MMCRF-ℓ_Δ	**27.1**	0.58	91.0	64.1	75.2
MMCRF-$\ell_{\tilde{H}}$	27.9	0.59	85.4	68.3	75.9

WIPO-alpha	$\ell_{0/1}$	ℓ_Δ	P	R	F1
SVM	87.2	1.84	93.1	58.2	71.6
H-SVM	76.2	1.74	90.3	63.3	74.4
H-RLS	72.1	1.69	88.5	66.4	75.9
MMCRF-ℓ_Δ	70.9	**1.67**	90.3	65.3	75.8
MMCRF-$\ell_{\tilde{H}}$	**65.0**	1.73	84.1	70.6	**76.7**

ENZYME	$\ell_{0/1}$	ℓ_Δ	P	R	F1
SVM	99.7	1.3	99.6	41.1	58.2
H-SVM	98.5	**1.2**	98.9	41.7	58.7
H-RLS	95.6	2.0	51.9	54.7	53.3
MMCRF-ℓ_Δ	95.7	**1.2**	87.0	49.8	**63.3**
MMCRF-$\ell_{\tilde{H}}$	**85.5**	2.5	44.5	66.7	53.4

feature representation. The third dataset focused on enzyme analysis and used a string kernel as the feature mapping; this task would therefore not be practical in alternative max-margin settings where only the primal objective function is used. In all cases the approach in this chapter achieved high performance and took less computation time.

Our method can be contrasted to the structured exponentiated gradient (EG) approach presented in Bartlett et al. (2004). Both algorithms are iterative gradient-based algorithms but with significant differences. First, the update direction of the MMCRF algorithm is toward the best feasible direction while the structured EG update tends to look for sparse directions of steep ascent. Conditional gradient updates are known to work well in the early stages of optimization but less so in the final stages (Bertsekas, 1999). On the other hand, the emphasis on sparse solutions should benefit EG in the final stages of optimization as the (full) dual optimum typically is sparse. Finally, the tractable formulation of the structured EG (Bartlett et al., 2004) relies on enforcing a Gibbs distribution (with polynomial number of parameters) on the dual variables while our MMCRF does not make any additional assumptions of the distribution of the dual variables. We leave for future work study of the relative merits of these methods.

One advantage of the marginal approach used in this chapter is that there is a clear relationship between the complexity of the optimization and the representation of the output structure which is used. For the hierarchical datasets used in this chapter, the inference step can be solved exactly and efficiently using dynamic programming, thus ensuring that the computational complexity of the terms in the objective function only grow linearly with the size of the output structure. In the case of more general structures, then the inference step must either be solved by considering junction trees where possible, or by applying approximate inference methods such as loopy belief propagation. It is still an open question as to how the performance of the algorithm would be effected should a technique such as LBP be used on a more complex output structure. Given that the inference is only used to find a suitable direction across which to optimize, one could expect that exact inference is unnecessary and a good approximation is more than sufficient to guide the optimization process. In general though, this is an open question and will be the subject of future research.

Acknowledgments

This work was supported in part by the PASCAL Network of Excellence, IST-2002-506778. C. S. is supported in part by EPSRC grant no GR/S22301/01 (Development and Application of String-Type Kernels). The work by J. R. was partially funded by a Marie Curie Individual Fellowship HPMF-2002-02110 and undertaken while visiting Royal Holloway, University of London.

7   Discriminative Learning of Prediction Suffix Trees with the Perceptron Algorithm

Ofer Dekel , Shai Shalev-Shwartz , and Yoram Singer

Prediction suffix trees (PSTs) provide a popular and effective tool for tasks such as compression, classification, and language modeling. We present a large-margin perspective of PSTs for the task of sequence prediction. We generalize the notion of margin to PSTs and cast the PST learning problem as the online problem of finding a linear predictor in a Hilbert space. This view enables us to adapt the perceptron algorithm to the task of learning PSTs. The end result is an efficient algorithm that does not rely on a priori assumptions on the maximal size of the target PST. We prove a relative mistake bound, which implies that our algorithm is competitive with any fixed PST. We also prove that the depth of the PST constructed by our algorithm grows at most logarithmically with the number of mistakes made by the algorithm.

7.1   Introduction

Prediction suffix trees are elegant, effective, and well-studied models for tasks such as compression, temporal classification, and probabilistic modeling of sequences (see, for instance, Willems et al. (1995), Ron et al. (1996), Helmbold and Schapire (1997), Pereira and Singer (1999), and Buhlmann and Wyner (1999)). Different scientific communities have different names for variants of PSTs, such as context tree weighting (Willems et al., 1995) and variable-length Markov models (Ron et al., 1996; Buhlmann and Wyner, 1999). A PST observes an input stream of symbols, one symbol at a time, and attempts to predict the identity of the next symbol based on the symbols already observed. Typically, this prediction relies only on the most recent observed symbols, a suffix of the previously observed symbols which we call the *context* of the prediction. A fundamental property of PST predictors is that the exact number of previous symbols used to make each prediction depends on the specific context in which the prediction is made.

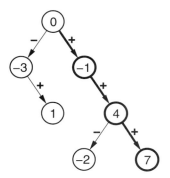

Figure 7.1 An illustration of the prediction process induced by a PST. The support of the context function is $\{-, +, +-, ++, -++, +++\}$, and the previously observed symbols are $--+++$. The relevant context is depicted in bold. The predicted value of the next symbol is $\text{sign}(2^{-1/2} \times (-1) + 2^{-1} \times 4 + 2^{-3/2} \times 7)$.

For example, say that we observe a text in the English language letter by letter, and assume that the last observed letter is a q. We know that q is always followed by the letter u, therefore we can confidently predict the next letter to be u without looking at previous letters in the stream. On the other hand, if the last observed letter is not q, we may need as many as three or four previous letters to make an accurate prediction.

Consistently underestimating the length of the suffix required to make good predictions is likely to lead to many prediction mistakes. Consistently overestimating this length will lead to poor generalization. Balancing this tradeoff is at the heart of PST learning algorithms. Techniques for learning PSTs include online Bayesian mixtures (Willems et al., 1995), tree growing based on PAC learning (Ron et al., 1996), and tree pruning based on structural risk minimization (Kearns and Mansour, 1996). All of these algorithms assume an a priori bound on the maximal suffix size which may be used to make predictions. Clearly, this poses a problem in settings where we do not have a clear a priori idea of the suffix length required to make accurate predictions. Optimally, the learning algorithm should be given the freedom to look as far back as needed to make accurate predictions. Motivated by the problem of statistical modeling of biological sequences, Bejerano and Apostolico (2000) showed that the bound on the maximal depth can be removed by devising a smart modification of Ron et al. (1996). Their modification, which can also be applied to other PST learning techniques, has time and space requirements that grow linearly with the length of the input stream. However, even this linear growth may lead to serious computational problems when modeling very long sequences.

Our approach to learning PSTs can be viewed as a balancing act between two extremes. On one hand, we do not rely on any a priori bounds on suffix length, and may "look" as far back into history as needed. On the other hand, we only use a short suffix when this is sufficient. We begin by casting the PST learning problem as a margin-based linear separation problem. Then we solve the linear separation problem with a modified version of the perceptron algorithm. We prove that our technique is competitive with any fixed PST, even one defined in hindsight. We also prove that the maximal suffix length which we use to make predictions grows logarithmically with the number of prediction mistakes. Specifically, this implies that the size of the PST constructed by our algorithm is linear in the number of mistakes it makes.

7.2 Suffix Trees for Stream Prediction

We now present the stream prediction problem more formally. A stream $\mathbf{y}$, is a (possibly infinite) sequence of symbols $y_1, y_2, \ldots$ over a finite alphabet $\mathcal{Y}$. We abbreviate the subsequence $y_i, \ldots, y_j$ by $\mathbf{y}_i^j$ and the set of all finite subsequences by $\mathcal{Y}^\star$. Our goal is to correctly predict each symbol in the stream. For simplicity, we focus on the binary prediction case, where $|\mathcal{Y}| = 2$, and for convenience we assume $\mathcal{Y} = \{-1, +1\}$ (or $\{-, +\}$ for short) as our alphabet. Our algorithms and analysis can be adapted to larger alphabets using ideas from Crammer et al. (2005).

On each time step t, we predict the symbol y_t based on a suffix of $\mathbf{y}_1^{t-1}$. We denote the hypothesis used to make this prediction by h_t. This hypothesis is confidence-rated, namely it takes the form $h_t : \mathcal{Y}^\star \to \mathbb{R}$, where the sign of $h_t(\mathbf{y}_1^{t-1})$ determines the predicted symbol and $|h_t(\mathbf{y}_1^{t-1})|$ is the confidence in this prediction. Although our notation implies that h_t is a function of the entire observed sequence $\mathbf{y}_1^{t-1}$, h_t typically ignores all but the last few symbols in $\mathbf{y}_1^{t-1}$. The hypothesis h_t is defined by a *context function* g_t, which assigns weights to different contexts. The function context functions g_t also defines a mapping from $\mathcal{Y}^\star$ into $\mathbb{R}$, and the relationship between h_t and g_t is as follows:

$$h_t(\mathbf{y}_1^{t-1}) \;\; = \;\; \sum_{i=1}^{t-1} 2^{-i/2}\, g_t\left(\mathbf{y}_{t-i}^{t-1}\right) \;\; . \tag{7.1}$$

In words, the prediction involves the application of the context function g_t to all of the suffixes of $\mathbf{y}_1^{t-1}$. In the prediction process, the contribution of each suffix $\mathbf{y}_{t-i}^{t-1}$ is multiplied by a factor which is exponentially decreasing in its length. This type of demotion of long suffixes is common to most PST-based approaches (Willems et al., 1995; Helmbold and Schapire, 1997; Pereira and Singer, 1999) and reflects the a priori assumption that statistical correlations tend to decrease as the time between events increases. Nevertheless, g_t can always compensate for this demotion by assigning proportionally large values to long sequences.

We next describe an alternative view of our prediction function as a tree. Define the *support* of a context function g as the set of sequences for which $g(\mathbf{s})$ is nonzero, $\operatorname{supp}(g) = \{\mathbf{s} \in \mathcal{Y}^\star : g(\mathbf{s}) \neq 0\}$. A set $\mathcal{T}$ of strings is said to be suffix-closed if for any $\mathbf{s} \in \mathcal{T}$, $\mathcal{T}$ also contains every suffix of $\mathbf{s}$. Let $\mathcal{T}_t$ be the smallest suffix-closed subset of $\mathcal{Y}^\star$ which contains both $\operatorname{supp}(g_t)$ and the empty string. The set $\mathcal{T}_t$ can alternatively be viewed as a rooted tree whose root is the empty sequence. Every $\mathbf{s} \in \mathcal{T}_t$ is a node in the tree, and its parent is the node which corresponds to the sequence obtained by removing the leftmost symbol from $\mathbf{s}$. From this point through the rest of the chapter we refer to $\mathcal{T}_t$ as a PST, and to the sequences in $\mathcal{T}_t$ as nodes. We denote the length of the longest sequence in $\mathcal{T}$ by $\text{depth}(\mathcal{T})$. The context function g associates a weight $g(\mathbf{s})$ with each node $\mathbf{s} \in \mathcal{T}$. Evaluating h_t using $\mathcal{T}_t$ requires following the unique path from the root which matches the current context, scaling the weight of each node in this path by $2^{-d/2}$ (where d is its depth in the tree) and summing the resulting values. More formally, (7.1) can be restated as

$$h(\mathbf{y}_1^{t-1}) = \sum_{i:\, \mathbf{y}_{t-i}^{t-1} \in \mathcal{T}} 2^{-i/2}\, g\left(\mathbf{y}_{t-i}^{t-1}\right) \quad . \tag{7.2}$$

An example of a PST with an associated prediction is illustrated in figure 7.1.

Our algorithm follows the general skeleton of an online learning algorithm. Online learning is performed in a sequence of consecutive rounds, where on round t the online algorithm predicts symbol t in the stream. Before observing any input, the PST learning algorithm starts with a default hypothesis, which is used to predict the first symbol in the stream. At the end of every round, the algorithm constructs the hypothesis which is used to make a prediction on the next round. On round t, the algorithm predicts the tth symbol in the sequence to be $\hat{y}_t = \text{sign}(h_t(\mathbf{y}_1^{t-1}))$, and then observes the correct answer y_t. Then, the algorithm may use y_t to define an updated context function g_{t+1}. Our algorithm always sets g_{t+1} such that $\text{supp}\,(g_t) \subseteq \text{supp}\,(g_{t+1})$, or in other words, $\mathcal{T}_t \subseteq \mathcal{T}_{t+1}$. Therefore, we say that our algorithm *grows* a PST. The specific procedure of adding nodes to the current PST and deriving g_{t+1} from g_t and y_t is the focus of this chapter, and will be specified later on.

margin for PST

In contrast to most previous approaches to learning PSTs, we take a decision-theoretic approach by adapting the notion of *margin* to our setting. In the context of PSTs, this approach was first proposed by Eskin (2002). We define the margin attained by the hypothesis h_t to be $y_t h_t(\mathbf{y}_1^{t-1})$. Whenever the current symbol y_t and the output of the hypothesis agree in their sign, the margin is positive. We evaluate the performance of our algorithm, or of any other fixed PST, in one of two ways. One alternative is to choose a horizon T and count the number of prediction mistakes made on the first T rounds. The second alternative uses the hinge-loss function as a margin-based proxy for the prediction error. Formally, the hinge loss attained on round t is defined to be

$$\max\left\{0, 1 - y_t h_t\left(\mathbf{y}_1^{t-1}\right)\right\} \quad . \tag{7.3}$$

Again, we choose a horizon T and sum the loss values attained on the first T rounds.

An important term which appears in our analysis is the *complexity* of a context function g. Informally, the larger the tree defined by $\text{supp}\,(g)$ and the bigger the weights assigned by g to the nodes in this tree, the harder it is to learn g. We define the complexity of a context function using its squared 2-norm, defined as

$$\|g\|^2 = \left(\sum_{\mathbf{s}\in\mathcal{Y}^\star} g^2(s) \right)^{\frac{1}{2}} . \tag{7.4}$$

We analyze our algorithms by comparing the number of prediction errors they make to the performance of an arbitrary fixed hypothesis $h^\star$, which is defined by a context function $g^\star$. We refer to $h^\star$ as our *competitor*, and note that it can even be a hypothesis chosen in hindsight, after observing the entire stream. The mistake bounds we derive grow with $\|g^\star\|$ and with the hinge loss attained by $h^\star$ on the stream. We also prove a bound on the maximal depth of $\mathcal{T}_t$ generated by our algorithm. The size of supp $(g^\star)$ does not appear in either of our bounds, hence we can compete with infinite-sized competitors $h^\star$ using only a bounded-depth PST, as long as $\|g^\star\|$ is finite.

7.3   PSTs as Separating Hyperplanes and the perceptron Algorithm

online learning for PSTs

Our goal now is to derive and analyze efficient online algorithms for PST learning. To do so, we begin by drawing an analogy between PSTs and linear margin-based predictors in a Hilbert space. We show that when casting our problem as one of linear separation, the notions of margin and of the squared 2-norm of g reduce to the familiar notions of margin and norm for linear separators.

First we define $\mathcal{H} = \{g : \mathcal{Y}^\star \to \mathbb{R} \mid \|g\| < \infty\}$, the set of all bounded-complexity context functions. For any two functions in $\mathcal{H}$, define their inner product to be

$$\langle f, g \rangle = \sum_{\mathbf{s}\in\mathcal{Y}^\star} f(\mathbf{s})g(\mathbf{s}) .$$

It is rather straightforward to show that $\mathcal{H}$, together with its inner product, satisfies the requirements of a Hilbert space. Also note that our definition of $\|g\|^2$ from (7.4) can be rewritten as $\|g\|^2 = \sqrt{\langle g, g \rangle}$. Next, we show that evaluating $h(\mathbf{s})$ is equivalent to calculating an inner product operation in $\mathcal{H}$. To do so, we define a feature map $\Phi : \mathcal{Y}^\star \to \mathcal{H}$, where

$$\Phi(\mathbf{s}) = \begin{cases} 2^{-i/2} & \text{if } \exists i \text{ s.t } \mathbf{s} = \mathbf{y}_{t\text{-}i}^{t\text{-}1} \\ 0 & \text{otherwise} \end{cases} .$$

Using this definition, we can rewrite (7.1) as

$$h(\mathbf{y}_1^{t\text{-}1}) = \langle g, \Phi(\mathbf{y}_1^{t\text{-}1}) \rangle . \tag{7.5}$$

In summary, we can view g as the normal vector of a separating hyperplane in $\mathcal{H}$: the prediction of h on $\mathbf{y}_1^{t\text{-}1}$ is $+1$ if $\Phi(\mathbf{y}_1^{t\text{-}1})$ falls in the positive half-space defined by g, and is -1 otherwise. As such, we can learn g using standard online algorithms

---

Algorithm 7.1 The unbounded-depth perceptron for PST learning

---

1:    **initialize:** $\mathcal{T}_1 = \{\epsilon\}$, $g_1(\mathbf{s}) = 0 \; \forall \mathbf{s} \in \mathcal{Y}^\star$

2:    **for** $t = 1, 2, \ldots$ **do**

3:        Calculate: $h_t\left(\mathbf{y}_1^{t\text{-}1}\right) = \sum_{i=1}^{t-1} 2^{-i/2} \, g_t\left(\mathbf{y}_{t\text{-}i}^{t\text{-}1}\right)$

4:        Predict: $\hat{y}_t = \mathrm{sign}\left(h_t\left(\mathbf{y}_1^{t\text{-}1}\right)\right)$

5:        Receive y_t

6:        **if** $(y_t h_t(\mathbf{y}_1^{t\text{-}1}) > 0)$ **then**

7:           $\mathcal{T}_{t+1} = \mathcal{T}_t$

8:           $g_{t+1} = g_t$

9:        **else**

10:           $\mathcal{T}_{t+1} = \mathcal{T}_t \cup \{\mathbf{y}_{t\text{-}i}^{t\text{-}1} : 1 \leq i \leq t-1\}$

11:           $g_{t+1}(\mathbf{s}) = \begin{cases} g_t(\mathbf{s}) + y_t \, 2^{-i/2} & \text{if } \mathbf{s} = \mathbf{y}_{t\text{-}i}^{t\text{-}1} \text{ for } 1 \leq i \leq t-1 \\ g_t(\mathbf{s}) & \text{otherwise} \end{cases}$

12:    **end for**

---

for linear separation, such as the perceptron algorithm (Agmon, 1954; Rosenblatt, 1958; Novikoff, 1962).

The perceptron, originally formulated for the task of binary classification, observes a sequence of inputs and predicts a binary outcome for each input. In our case, the input on round t is $\Phi(\mathbf{y}_1^{t\text{-}1})$ and the output is y_t. The perceptron predicts the label on round t to be $\mathrm{sign}(\langle g_t, \Phi(\mathbf{y}_1^{t\text{-}1})\rangle)$, where g_t is a member of $\mathcal{H}$ which defines the current hypothesis. In our case, g_t takes on the role of a context function. The perceptron initializes g_1 to be the zero vector in $\mathcal{H}$, which is equivalent to initializing $\mathcal{T}_1$ to be a tree with a single node (the root) with an assigned weight of zero. At the end of round t, the perceptron receives the correct label for that round, $y_t \in \{+1, -1\}$, and uses it to define g_{t+1}. If y_t was correctly predicted, then g_{t+1} is simply set to equal g_t. Otherwise, the perceptron updates its hypothesis by $g_{t+1} = g_t + y_t \Phi(\mathbf{y}_1^{t\text{-}1})$. In this case, g_{t+1} differs from g_t only on those inputs for which $\Phi(\mathbf{y}_1^{t\text{-}1})$ is nonzero, namely on every $\mathbf{y}_{t\text{-}i}^{t\text{-}1}$ for $1 \leq i \leq t-1$. For these inputs, the update takes the form $g_{t+1}(\mathbf{y}_{t\text{-}i}^{t\text{-}1}) = g_t(\mathbf{y}_{t\text{-}i}^{t\text{-}1}) + y_t \, 2^{-i/2}$. The pseudocode of the perceptron algorithm applied to the PST learning problem is given in algorithm 7.1.

drawback   We immediately point out a major drawback in this approach. The number of nonzero elements in $\Phi(\mathbf{y}_1^{t\text{-}1})$ is $t - 1$. Therefore, $|\mathrm{supp}\,(g_{t+1})| - |\mathrm{supp}\,(g_t)|$ may be on the order of t. This means that the number of new nodes added to the PST on round t may also be on the order of t. Consequently, the size of $\mathcal{T}_t$ may grow quadratically with t. For this reason we refer to the straightforward application of the perceptron algorithm to our problem as the *unbounded-depth* PST learning algorithm. Implementation tricks in Bejerano and Apostolico (2000) can reduce the space complexity of storing $\mathcal{T}_t$ to $O(t)$, but even a linearly growing memory requirement can impose serious computational problems. Let us put aside the memory growth problem for the moment, and focus on proving a mistake bound for the unbounded algorithm. In the next section, we build on the analysis below to amend this problem and devise a bounded version of our algorithm.

Theorem 44 *Let $y_1, y_2, \ldots$ be a stream of binary symbols. Let $g^\star$ be an arbitrary context function, which defines the hypothesis $h^\star$ as in (7.1). Assume that $h^\star$ attains the loss values $\ell_1^\star, \ell_2^\star, \ldots$ on the stream. Then, for any $T \geq 1$, the number of prediction mistakes made by the unbounded-depth algorithm on the first T symbols in the stream is, at most,*

a relative mistake
bound for
unbounded PSTs

$$\|g^\star\|^2 \, + \, 2 \sum_{t=1}^{T} \ell_t^\star \quad .$$

Proof Define for all $1 \leq t \leq T$,

$$\Delta_t \;=\; \|g_t - g^\star\|^2 - \|g_{t+1} - g^\star\|^2 \quad . \tag{7.6}$$

We prove the theorem by bounding $\sum_{t=1}^{T} \Delta_t$ from above and from below. First note that $\sum_t \Delta_t$ is a telescopic sum, which collapses to

$$\sum_{t=1}^{T} \Delta_t \;=\; \|g_1 - g^\star\|^2 - \|g_{T+1} - g^\star\|^2 \quad .$$

Using the facts that $\|g_{T+1} - g^\star\|^2 \geq 0$ and that $g_1 \equiv 0$, we upper-bound $\sum_t \Delta_t$ by $\|g^\star\|^2$. Next we show a lower bound on $\sum_t \Delta_t$. On rounds where the perceptron makes a correct prediction, we have that $g_{t+1} = g_t$ and $\Delta_t = 0$. On rounds on which the perceptron makes a mistake, we have that $g_{t+1} = g_t + y_t \Phi(\mathbf{y}_1^{t-1})$ and thus,

$$\begin{aligned}
\Delta_t &= \|g_t - g^\star\|^2 - \|g_{t+1} - g^\star\|^2 \\
&= \|g_t - g^\star\|^2 - \|(g_t - g^\star) + y_t \Phi(\mathbf{y}_1^{t-1})\|^2 \\
&= \|g_t - g^\star\|^2 - \left(\|g_t - g^\star\|^2 + 2 y_t \left\langle g_t - g^\star, \Phi(\mathbf{y}_1^{t-1}) \right\rangle + \|\Phi(\mathbf{y}_1^{t-1})\|^2 \right) \\
&= -2 y_t \left\langle g_t, \Phi(\mathbf{y}_1^{t-1}) \right\rangle + 2 y_t \left\langle g^\star, \Phi(\mathbf{y}_1^{t-1}) \right\rangle - \|\Phi(\mathbf{y}_1^{t-1})\|^2 \quad .
\end{aligned}$$

Using the facts that $\left\langle g_t, \Phi(\mathbf{y}_1^{t-1}) \right\rangle = h_t(\mathbf{y}_1^{t-1})$ and $\left\langle g^\star, \Phi(\mathbf{y}_1^{t-1}) \right\rangle = h^\star(\mathbf{y}_1^{t-1})$, we get

$$\Delta_t \;=\; -2 y_t h_t(\mathbf{y}_1^{t-1}) + 2 y_t h^\star(\mathbf{y}_1^{t-1}) - \|\Phi(\mathbf{y}_1^{t-1})\|^2 \quad . \tag{7.7}$$

Since we assumed that the perceptron errs on round t, we know that $y_t h_t(\mathbf{y}_1^{t-1}) \leq 0$. Additionally, the definition of $\Phi(\mathbf{y}_1^{t-1})$ implies that

$$\|\Phi(\mathbf{y}_1^{t-1})\|^2 \;=\; \sum_{i=1}^{t-1} 2^{-i} \;\leq\; 1 \quad .$$

Plugging the above inequalities back into (7.7) gives

$$\Delta_t \;\geq\; 2 y_t h^\star(\mathbf{y}_1^{t-1}) - 1 \quad . \tag{7.8}$$

The definition of the hinge loss from (7.3) implies that $\ell_t^\star \geq 1 - y_t h^\star(\mathbf{y}_1^{t-1})$ and therefore $2y_t h^\star(\mathbf{y}_1^{t-1}) \geq 2 - 2\ell_t^\star$. Overall, we have that

$$\Delta_t \geq 1 - 2\ell_t^\star \ .$$

Let M denote the number of prediction mistakes made by the algorithm on the first T symbols. Summing the above over $1 \leq t \leq T$ and using the fact that the hinge loss is nonnegative, we get

$$\sum_{t=1}^{T} \Delta_t \geq M - 2 \sum_{t=1}^{T} \ell_t^\star \ .$$

We conclude our proof by comparing this lower bound with the upper bound $\sum_t \Delta_t \leq \|g^\star\|^2$ and rearranging terms. ∎

7.4   The Self-Bounded Perceptron for PST Learning

As previously mentioned, the unbounded-depth algorithm presented in the previous section has a major drawback: its unrestricted memory requirement. We now resolve this problem by modifying the perceptron update to our needs. Our technique does not rely on a priori assumptions on the structure of the PST (e.g. maximal tree depth). The algorithm automatically determines the depth to which the PST should grow on each round, and is therefore named the *self-bounded* algorithm.

Recall that every time a prediction mistake is made, the perceptron performs the update $g_{t+1} = g_t + y_t \Phi(\mathbf{y}_1^{t-1})$. Since the nonzero elements of $\Phi(\mathbf{y}_1^{t-1})$ correspond to $\mathbf{y}_{t-i}^{t-1}$ for every $1 \leq i \leq t-1$, this update adds a path of depth $t-1$ to the current PST. To fix this problem, we introduce a new variable, d_t, and confine the new path to a maximal depth d_t before adding it. The value of d_t is determined automatically by the algorithm. Nodes in the current tree of depth greater than d_t are left untouched. In other words, the new update step takes the form

$$g_{t+1}(\mathbf{s}) = \begin{cases} g_t(\mathbf{s}) + y_t 2^{-i/2} & \text{if } \exists i \text{ s.t } \mathbf{s} = \mathbf{y}_{t-i}^{t-1} \ \wedge \ i \leq d_t \\ g_t(\mathbf{s}) & \text{otherwise.} \end{cases} \tag{7.9}$$

An analogous way of stating this update rule is obtained by defining the function $\nu_t \in \mathcal{H}$,

$$\nu_t(\mathbf{s}) = \begin{cases} -y_t 2^{-i/2} & \text{if } \exists i \text{ s.t } \mathbf{s} = \mathbf{y}_{t-i}^{t-1} \ \wedge \ i > d_t \\ 0 & \text{otherwise.} \end{cases} \tag{7.10}$$

Using the definition of ν_t, we can rewrite the update of the self-bounded perceptron from (7.9) as

$$g_{t+1} = g_t + y_t \Phi(\mathbf{y}_1^{t-1}) + \nu_t \ . \tag{7.11}$$

That is, the update of the self-bounded perceptron is obtained by first applying the standard perceptron update, and then altering the outcome of this update by ν_t. It is convenient to think of ν_t as a kind of additive noise which contaminates the updated hypothesis. Intuitively, the standard perceptron update guarantees positive progress, whereas the additive noise ν_t pushes the hypothesis slightly off its course. Our analysis in the sequel shows that the progress made by the perceptron step overshadows the damage incurred by adding the noise vector ν_t.

First note that the norm of ν_t is upper-bounded by

$$\|\nu_t\| = \left(\sum_{i=d_t+1}^{t-1} 2^{-i} \right)^{1/2} \leq 2^{-d_t/2} . \tag{7.12}$$

Therefore, the larger d_t is, the smaller the norm of the noise vector becomes. We now face a tradeoff. On one hand, we would like to keep d_t as small as possible, so that the depth of the PST will not grow significantly. On the other hand, d_t must be large enough so that the update remains similar to the original perceptron update, which we know guarantees progress. We adapt and extend ideas from Auer and Gentile (2000) to balance this tradeoff automatically on every round.

Define $\theta_t = \max\{i : \mathbf{y}_{t-i}^{t-1} \in \mathcal{T}_t\}$. In words, θ_t is the depth of the path in $\mathcal{T}_t$ which corresponds to the current context. Clearly, if $d_t \leq \theta_t$, then the update in (7.9) does not add any new nodes to the current PST. There is no point in setting $d_t < \theta_t$, since doing so would only introduce a noise vector ν_t of a larger norm while having no effect on the depth of the resulting PST. This is the algorithm's first criterion for setting d_t.

The second criterion for setting d_t ensures that the noise introduced by adding ν_t is significantly smaller than the progress due to the perceptron update. For every $1 \leq t \leq T$, let J_t be the subset of rounds $1, \ldots, t$ on which the algorithm makes a prediction mistake, and let $M_t = |J_t|$. In addition, define P_t to be

$$P_t = \sum_{i \in J_t} 2^{-d_i/2} . \tag{7.13}$$

For completeness, define $M_0 = P_0 = 0$. Referring back to (7.12), we note that P_t is an upper bound on the sum of $\|\nu_i\|$ over $i \in J_t$. The following analysis shows that P_t is proportional to the amount of damage caused on the first t rounds by adding ν_i after each perceptron update. Therefore, the algorithm must set d_t such that P_t is sufficiently small. Specifically, we show in theorem 45 that it is enough to require that

$$P_t \leq \frac{1}{2} \sqrt{M_t} . \tag{7.14}$$

If the above holds for some value of d_t, then it also holds for larger values of d_t. Therefore, we can make sure that (7.14) is satisfied for every t using the following greedy principle: whenever a prediction mistake is made, we set d_t to be the smallest value for which (7.14) holds, unless this value is less than θ_t. Note that (7.14) trivially holds for $t = 0$. Now assume that $P_{t-1} \leq \frac{1}{2} \sqrt{M_{t-1}}$. If $t \notin J_t$, then

$P_t = P_{t-1}$ and $M_t = M_{t-1}$, so clearly (7.14) is satisfied. Otherwise, $M_t = M_{t-1}+1$. Expanding the definition of P_t^2 we get

$$P_t^2 \;=\; \left(P_{t-1} + 2^{-d_t/2} \right)^2 \;=\; P_{t-1}^2 \;+\; P_{t-1}\, 2^{1-d_t/2} \;+\; 2^{-d_t} \;. \qquad (7.15)$$

Using our assumption that $P_{t-1}^2 \le \frac{1}{4} M_{t-1}$, it suffices to ensure that, $P_{t-1}\, 2^{1-d_t/2} + 2^{-d_t} \le \frac{1}{4}$. Equivalently, introducing the variable $\lambda = 2^{-d_t/2}$, we can require

$$\lambda^2 \;+\; 2 P_{t-1} \lambda \;-\; \frac{1}{4} \;\le\; 0 \;.$$

The left-hand side of this inequality is a convex parabola, which is negative between its two roots. These roots are

$$\pm \sqrt{P_{t-1}^2 + \tfrac{1}{4}} - P_{t-1} \;.$$

Additionally, by definition, we know that $\lambda > 0$. Therefore, (7.14) holds whenever

$$\lambda \;\le\; \sqrt{P_{t-1}^2 + \tfrac{1}{4}} - P_{t-1} \;.$$

Plugging in $\lambda = 2^{-d_t/2}$, the above becomes

$$d_t \;\ge\; -2\log_2 \left(\sqrt{P_{t-1}^2 + \tfrac{1}{4}} - P_{t-1} \right) \;.$$

In summary, we have shown that as long as d_t satisfies the inequality above for all t, it holds that $P_t \le \frac{1}{2}\sqrt{M_t}$ for all t. Together with our first requirement, $d_t \ge \theta_t$, we obtain the automatic update-pruning mechanism:

$$d_t \;=\; \max \left\{ \theta_t \,,\; \left\lceil -2\log_2 \left(\sqrt{P_{t-1}^2 + \tfrac{1}{4}} - P_{t-1} \right) \right\rceil \right\} \;.$$

The pseudocode of the self-bounded perceptron is given in algorithm 7.2. Our construction guarantees that $P_t \le \frac{1}{2}\sqrt{M_t}$ for all t, and it remains to show that this condition leads to a mistake bound for the self-bounded algorithm.

relative mistake
bound for
self-bounded PST

Theorem 45 *Let $y_1, y_2, \ldots$ be a stream of binary symbols. Let $g^\star$ be an arbitrary context function, which defines the hypothesis $h^\star$ as in (7.1). Assume that $h^\star$ attains the loss values $\ell_1^\star, \ell_2^\star, \ldots$ on the stream. Then, for any $T \ge 1$, the number of prediction mistakes made by the self-bounded algorithm on the first T symbols in the stream is, at most,*

$$\tfrac{3+\sqrt{5}}{2} \, \|g^\star\|^2 \;+\; 2\sum_{t=1}^{T} \ell_t^\star \;+\; \|g^\star\| \sqrt{2\sum_{t=1}^{T} \ell_t^\star} \;.$$

Proof As in the proof of theorem 44, we prove the theorem by bounding $\sum_{t=1}^{T} \Delta_t$ from above and from below, where Δ_t is defined in (7.6). The upper bound

$$\sum_t \Delta_t \le \|g^\star\|^2 \qquad (7.16)$$

is obtained in exactly the same way as in the proof of theorem 44. We thus turn to bounding $\sum_t \Delta_t$ from below. On rounds where the perceptron makes a correct prediction, we have that $g_{t+1} = g_t$ and $\Delta_t = 0$. On rounds on which the perceptron makes a mistake, we can write the update as $g_{t+1} = g_t + y_t\Phi(\mathbf{y}_1^{t\text{-}1}) + \nu_t$. Therefore,

$$
\begin{aligned}
\Delta_t &= \|g_t - g^\star\|^2 - \|g_{t+1} - g^\star\|^2 \\
&= \|g_t - g^\star\|^2 - \|(g_t - g^\star) + (y_t\Phi(\mathbf{y}_1^{t\text{-}1}) + \nu_t)\|^2 \\
&= \|g_t - g^\star\|^2 - \left(\|g_t - g^\star\|^2 + 2\left\langle g_t - g^\star, y_t\Phi(\mathbf{y}_1^{t\text{-}1}) + \nu_t\right\rangle + \|y_t\Phi(\mathbf{y}_1^{t\text{-}1}) + \nu_t\|^2\right) \\
&= -2y_t\left\langle g_t, \Phi(\mathbf{y}_1^{t\text{-}1})\right\rangle + 2y_t\left\langle g^\star, \Phi(\mathbf{y}_1^{t\text{-}1})\right\rangle - 2\left\langle g_t, \nu_t\right\rangle \\
&\quad + 2\left\langle g^\star, \nu_t\right\rangle - \|y_t\Phi(\mathbf{y}_1^{t\text{-}1}) + \nu_t\|^2 \ .
\end{aligned}
\tag{7.17}
$$

The definitions of $\Phi(\mathbf{y}_1^{t\text{-}1})$ and ν_t imply that

$$
\|y_t\Phi(\mathbf{y}_1^{t\text{-}1}) + \nu_t\|^2 = \sum_{i=1}^{d_t} 2^{-i} \leq 1 \ .
$$

The fact that $d_t \geq \theta_t$ ensures that $\langle g_t, \nu_t\rangle = 0$. In addition, as in the proof of theorem 44, we know that

$$
2(1 - \ell_t^\star) \leq -2y_t\left\langle g_t, \Phi(\mathbf{y}_1^{t\text{-}1})\right\rangle + 2y_t\left\langle g^\star, \Phi(\mathbf{y}_1^{t\text{-}1})\right\rangle \ .
$$

Finally, using the Cauchy-Schwartz inequality, we get

$$
2\left\langle g^\star, \nu_t\right\rangle \leq 2\|g^\star\|\,\|\nu_t\| \leq 2^{1-d_t/2}\|g^\star\| \ .
$$

Combining the above inequalities with (7.17) gives the lower bound,

$$
1 - 2\ell_t^\star - 2^{1-d_t/2}\|g^\star\| \leq \Delta_t \ .
$$

Summing the above over t, comparing to the upper bound in (7.16), and using the definitions of M_T and P_T, we get that

$$
M_T - 2\sum_{t=1}^{T}\ell_t^\star - 2P_T\|g^\star\| \leq \|g^\star\|^2 \ .
$$

Recalling that we have guaranteed $P_T \leq \frac{1}{2}\sqrt{M_T}$, the above becomes

$$
M_T - 2\sum_{t=1}^{T}\ell_t^\star - \sqrt{M_T}\|g^\star\| \leq \|g^\star\|^2 \ .
\tag{7.18}
$$

Substituting $\lambda = \sqrt{M_T}$ and rearranging terms, we can rewrite the above as

$$
\lambda^2 - \|g^\star\|\lambda - \left(\|g^\star\|^2 + 2\sum_{t=1}^{T}\ell_t^\star\right) \leq 0 \ .
$$

Algorithm 7.2 The self-bounded perceptron for PST learning

1:   **initialize:** $\mathcal{T}_1 = \{\epsilon\}$, $g_1(\mathbf{s}) = 0 \ \forall \mathbf{s} \in \mathcal{Y}^\star$, $P_0 = 0$

2:   **for** $t = 1, 2, \ldots$ **do**

3:      Define: $\theta_t = \max\{i \ : \ \mathbf{y}_{t\text{-}i}^{t-1} \in \mathcal{T}_t\}$

4:      Calculate: $h_t\left(\mathbf{y}_1^{t-1}\right) = \sum_{i=1}^{\theta_t} 2^{-i/2}\, g_t\left(\mathbf{y}_{t\text{-}i}^{t-1}\right)$

5:      Predict: $\hat{y}_t = \text{sign}\left(h_t\left(\mathbf{y}_1^{t-1}\right)\right)$

6:      Receive y_t

        if $(y_t h_t(\mathbf{y}_1^{t-1}) > 0)$ **then**

           Set: $P_t = P_{t-1}$, $\mathcal{T}_{t+1} = \mathcal{T}_t$, $g_{t+1} = g_t$

7:      **else**

           Set: $d_t = \max\left\{\theta_t\ ,\ \left\lceil -2\log_2\left(\sqrt{P_{t-1}^2 + \tfrac{1}{4}} - P_{t-1}\right)\right\rceil\right\}$

           Set: $P_t = P_{t-1} + 2^{-d_t/2}$

8:      $\mathcal{T}_{t+1} = \mathcal{T}_t \cup \{\mathbf{y}_{t\text{-}i}^{t-1} : 1 \le i \le d_t\}$

9:      $g_{t+1}(\mathbf{s}) = \begin{cases} g_t(\mathbf{s}) + y_t\, 2^{-i/2} & \text{if} \quad \mathbf{s} = \mathbf{y}_{t\text{-}i}^{t-1} \ \text{ for } \ 1 \le i \le d_t \\ g_t(\mathbf{s}) & \text{otherwise} \end{cases}$

10:   **end for**

The above equation is a convex parabola in λ, which is negative between its two roots. These roots are

$$\tfrac{1}{2}\left(\|g^\star\| \pm \sqrt{5\|g^\star\|^2 + 8\sum_{t=1}^T \ell_t^\star}\right).$$

Since, by definition, $\lambda \ge 0$, then (7.18) holds if and only if

$$\lambda \ \le \ \tfrac{1}{2}\left(\|g^\star\| + \sqrt{5\|g^\star\|^2 + 8\sum_{t=1}^T \ell_t^\star}\right)\ .$$

Taking the square of both sides of the above and plugging in the definition of λ gives the bound,

$$M_T \ \le \ \tfrac{1}{4}\left(\|g^\star\| + \sqrt{5\|g^\star\|^2 + 8\sum_{t=1}^T \ell_t^\star}\right)^2$$

$$= \ \tfrac{1}{4}\|g^\star\|^2 \ + \ \tfrac{1}{2}\|g^\star\|\sqrt{5\|g^\star\|^2 + 8\sum_{t=1}^T \ell_t^\star} \ + \ \tfrac{5}{4}\|g^\star\|^2 + 2\sum_{t=1}^T \ell_t^\star \ .$$

Using the the fact that $\sqrt{a^2 + b^2} \le |a| + |b|$ we get

$$M_T \ \le \ \tfrac{1}{4}\|g^\star\|^2 \ + \ \tfrac{\sqrt{5}}{2}\|g^\star\|^2 + \|g^\star\|\sqrt{2\sum_{t=1}^T \ell_t^\star} \ + \ \tfrac{5}{4}\|g^\star\|^2 + 2\sum_{t=1}^T \ell_t^\star \ ,$$

which proves the theorem.   ∎

Note that if there exists a fixed hypothesis with $\|g^\star\| < \infty$ which attains a margin of 1 on the entire input sequence, then the bound of theorem 45 reduces to a constant,

$\frac{3+\sqrt{5}}{2}\|g^\star\|$. The next theorem states that the self-bounded perceptron grows a PST whose depth grows logarithmically with the number of prediction mistakes.

logarithmic growth

Theorem 46 *Under the conditions of theorem 45, let $\mathcal{T}_1, \mathcal{T}_2, \ldots$ be the sequence of PSTs generated by the PST learning algorithm 7.2. Then, for all $T \geq 2$,*

$$\mathrm{depth}(\mathcal{T}_T) \ \leq \ \log_2(M_{T-1}) + 6.2 \ .$$

Proof   Note that $\mathrm{depth}(\mathcal{T}_T) = \max_{t \in J_T} d_t$ and recall that d_t is set to

$$\max\left\{\theta_t \ , \ \left\lceil -2\log_2\left(\sqrt{P_{t-1}^2 + \tfrac{1}{4}} - P_{t-1}\right)\right\rceil\right\} \ .$$

On rounds in J_T where $d_t = \theta_t$, the update does not increase the depth of the PST. Therefore, it suffices to show that for all $t \in J_T$,

$$\left\lceil -2\log_2\left(\sqrt{P_{t-1}^2 + \tfrac{1}{4}} - P_{t-1}\right)\right\rceil \ \leq \ \log_2(M_{T-1}) + 6.2 \ . \tag{7.19}$$

Multiplying the term inside the logarithm by $\frac{\sqrt{P_{t-1}^2 + \frac{1}{4}} + P_{t-1}}{\sqrt{P_{t-1}^2 + \frac{1}{4}} + P_{t-1}}$ enables us to rewrite the left-hand side of (7.19) as

$$\left\lceil 2\log_2\left(\sqrt{P_{t-1}^2 + \tfrac{1}{4}} + P_{t-1}\right) + 2\log_2(4) \right\rceil \ .$$

The above is upper-bounded by the expression $2\log_2\left(\sqrt{P_{t-1}^2 + \frac{1}{4}} + P_{t-1}\right) + 5$, which we denote by η. We thus need to show that $\eta \leq \log_2(M_{T-1}) + 6.2$. Using the inequality $\sqrt{a^2 + b^2} \leq |a| + |b|$, we get

$$\eta \ \leq \ 2\log_2\left(\tfrac{1}{2} + 2P_{t-1}\right) + 5 \ .$$

By construction, we have that $P_{t-1} \leq \frac{1}{2}\sqrt{M_{t-1}}$, and therefore,

$$\eta \ \leq \ 2\log_2\left(\tfrac{1}{2} + \sqrt{M_{t-1}}\right) + 5 \ .$$

Moreover, the fact that M_t is monotonic in t implies that

$$\eta \ \leq \ 2\log_2\left(\tfrac{1}{2} + \sqrt{M_{T-1}}\right) + 5 \ .$$

Since $h_1 \equiv 0$, the very first prediction of the PST always results in a mistake. Furthermore, since $T \geq 2$, we have $M_{T-1} \geq 1$. Using the inequality $\log_2(\frac{1}{2} + a) \leq \log_2(a) + 0.6$, which holds for $a > 1$, we conclude that

$$\eta \ \leq \ \log_2(M_{T-1}) + 6.2 \ .$$

■

Since a PST, $\mathcal{T}$, has at most $2^{\mathrm{depth}(\mathcal{T})}$ nodes, theorem 46 also implies that the self-bounded perceptron grows a PST whose size grows linearly with the number of prediction mistakes. The bound on tree depth given in theorem 46 becomes particularly interesting when there exists some fixed hypothesis $h^\star$ for which $\sum_t \ell_t^\star$ is finite. In that case, theorem 45 guarantees that M_T is finite, and together with theorem 46 we have a finite bound on $\mathrm{depth}(\mathcal{T}_T)$.

7.5   Conclusion

We presented an adaptation of the perceptron algorithm for learning PSTs for the task of sequence prediction. Unlike other methods for learning PSTs, our algorithm does not rely on a priori assumptions on the maximal size of the target PST. We proved that the number of prediction mistakes our algorithm makes on any sequence is comparable to the performance of any fixed PST. Moreover, our algorithm grows a PST whose depth grows at most logarithmically with the number of prediction mistakes. There are several possible extensions of the work presented in this chapter. Our algorithm can naturally be extended to other prediction problems such as multiclass categorization (see, for example, Crammer et al. (2006)). While the focus of this chapter is on the online setting, online algorithms can also serve as building blocks in the construction of well-performing batch algorithms. Online to batch conversions of the proposed algorithm are yet another important future research direction. There are various possible applications of the algorithm described in this chapter. We conclude this section with an outlook of the applicability of our sequence prediction algorithm for the task of cache management. In cache management we need to swap items between a small cache and a larger storage device. Several heuristics were proposed for cache management (e.g. removing the least recently used item). By predicting the sequence of requested items, one can maintain the contents of the cache memory in a more efficient way. Clearly, the storage requirements of the sequence prediction mechanism must be moderate. Thus, a sequence prediction algorithm which grows small PSTs might be adequate for the task of cache management.

Acknowledgments

This work was supported by the Israeli Science Foundation grant number 522-04 and by the Programme of the European Community, under the PASCAL Network of Excellence, IST-2002-506778.

8   A General Regression Framework for Learning String-to-String Mappings

Corinna Cortes, Mehryar Mohri, and Jason Weston

8.1   Introduction

The problem of learning a mapping from strings to strings arises in many areas of text and speech processing. As an example, an important component of speech recognition or speech synthesis systems is a pronunciation model, which provides the possible phonemic transcriptions of a word, or a sequence of words. An accurate pronunciation model is crucial for the overall quality of such systems. Another typical task in natural language processing is part-of-speech tagging, which consists of assigning a part-of-speech tag, e.g., *noun, verb, preposition, determiner*, to each word of a sentence. Similarly, parsing can be viewed as a string-to-string mapping where the target alphabet contains additional symbols such as parentheses to equivalently represent the tree structure.

The problem of learning string-to-string mappings may seem similar to that of regression estimation where the task consists of learning a real-valued mapping. But a key aspect of string-to-string mappings is that the target values, in this case strings, have some structure that can be exploited in learning. In particular, a similarity measure between target values can use the decomposition of the strings into their constituent symbols. More generally, since both input and output have some structure, one might wish to impose some constraints on the mappings based on prior knowledge about the task. A simple example is that of part-of-speech tagging where each tag is known to be associated with the word in the same position.

Several techniques have been described for learning string-to-string mappings, in particular maximum-margin Markov networks (M^{3}Ns) (Taskar et al., 2004b; Bartlett et al., 2004) and support vector machine learning for interdependent and structured output spaces (SVM-ISOS) (Tsochantaridis et al., 2004). These techniques treat the learning problem just outlined by learning a scoring function defined over the input-output pairs, imposing that the pair (x, y) with y matching x obtain a higher score than all other pairs (x, y'). This is done by using a binary loss function as in classification. This loss function ignores similarities between the output sequences. To correct for that effect, classification techniques such as SVM-

ISOS (Tsochantaridis et al., 2004) craft an additional term in the loss function to help account for the closeness of the outputs y and y', but the resulting loss function is different from a regression loss function.

In contrast, this chapter introduces a general framework and algorithms that treat the problem of learning string-to-string mapping as a true *regression* problem. Seeking a regression-type solution is natural since it directly exploits the similarity measures between two possible target sequences y and y' associated with an input sequence x. Such similarity measures are improperly handled by the binary losses used in previous methods.

Our framework for learning string-to-string mappings can be viewed as a conceptually cleaner generalization of kernel dependency estimation (KDE) (Weston et al., 2002, see also chapter 1, section 1.5). It decomposes the learning problem into two parts: a regression problem with a vector space image to learn a mapping from the input strings to an explicit or implicit feature space associated to the output strings, and a pre-image problem which consists of computing the output string from its feature space representation. We show that our framework can be generalized naturally to account for known constraints between the input and output sequences and that, remarkably, this generalization also leads to a closed-form solution and to an efficient iterative algorithm, which provides a clean framework for estimating the regression coefficients. The pre-image is computed from these coefficients using a simple and efficient algorithm based on classical results from graph theory. A major computational advantage of our general regression framework over the binary loss learning techniques mentioned is that it does not require an exhaustive pre-image search over the set of all output strings Y^* during training.

This chapter describes in detail our general regression framework and algorithms for string-to-string mappings and reports the results of experiments showing its effectiveness. The chapter is organized as follows. Section 8.2 presents a simple formulation of the learning problem and its decomposition into a regression problem with a vector space image and a pre-image problem. Section 8.3 presents several algorithmic solutions to the general regression problem, including the case of regression with prior constraints. Section 8.4 describes our pre-image algorithm for strings. Section 8.5 shows that several heuristic techniques can be used to substantially speed up training. Section 8.6 compares our framework and algorithm with several other algorithms proposed for learning string-to-string mapping. Section 8.7 reports the results of our experiments in several tasks.

8.2   General Formulation

This section presents a general and simple regression formulation of the problem of learning string-to-string mappings.

Let X and Y be the alphabets of the input and output strings. Assume that a training sample of size m drawn according to some distribution D is given:

$$(x_1, y_1), \ldots, (x_m, y_m) \in X^* \times Y^*. \tag{8.1}$$

The learning problem that we consider consists of finding a hypothesis $f : X^* \to Y^*$ out of a hypothesis space H that predicts accurately the label $y \in Y^*$ of a string $x \in X^*$ drawn randomly according to D. In standard regression estimation problems, labels are real-valued numbers, or more generally elements of $\mathbb{R}^N$ with $N \geq 1$. Our learning problem can be formulated in a similar way after the introduction of a feature mapping $\Phi_Y : Y^* \to F_Y = \mathbb{R}^{N_2}$. Each string $y \in Y^*$ is thus mapped to an N_2-dimensional feature vector $\Phi_Y(y) \in F_Y$.

As shown by the diagram of figure 8.1, our original learning problem is now *learning as a* decomposed into the following two problems:
two-step
approach
- *Regression problem*: The introduction of Φ_Y leads us to the problem of learning a hypothesis $g : X^* \to F_Y$ predicting accurately the feature vector $\Phi_Y(y)$ for a string $x \in X^*$ with label $y \in Y^*$, drawn randomly according to D.

- *Pre-image problem*: To predict the output string $f(x) \in Y^*$ associated to $x \in X^*$, we must determine the preimage of $g(x)$ by Φ_Y. We define $f(x)$ by

$$f(x) = \operatorname*{argmin}_{y \in Y^*} \|g(x) - \Phi_Y(y)\|^2, \tag{8.2}$$

which provides an approximate pre-image when an exact pre-image does not exist $(\Phi_Y^{-1}(g(x)) = \emptyset)$.

As with all regression problems, input strings in X^* can also be mapped to a Hilbert space F_X with $\dim(F_X) = N_1$, via a mapping $\Phi_X : X^* \to F_X$. Both mappings Φ_X and Φ_Y can be defined implicitly through the introduction of positive definite symmetric kernels K_X and K_Y such that for all $x, x' \in X^*$, $K_X(x, x') = \Phi_X(x) \cdot \Phi_X(x')$ and for all $y, y' \in Y^*$, $K_Y(y, y') = \Phi_Y(y) \cdot \Phi_Y(y')$.

This description of the problem can be viewed as a simpler formulation of the so-called kernel dependency estimation of Weston et al. (2002). In the original presentation of KDE, the first step consisted of using K_Y and kernel principal components analysis to reduce the dimension of the feature space F_Y. But that extra step is not necessary and we will not require it, thereby simplifying that framework.

In the following two sections, we examine in more detail each of the two problems just mentioned (regression and pre-image problems) and present general algorithms for both.

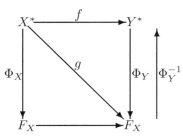

Figure 8.1 Decomposition of the string-to-string mapping learning problem into a regression problem (learning g) and a pre-image problem (computing Φ_Y^{-1} and using g to determine the string-to-string mapping f).

8.3   Regression Problems and Algorithms

This section describes general methods for regression estimation when the dimension of the image vector space is greater than one. The objective functions and algorithms presented are not specific to the problem of learning string-to-string mapping and can be used in other contexts, but they constitute a key step in learning complex string-to-string mappings.

Different regression methods can be used to learn g, including kernel ridge regression (Saunders et al., 1998), support vector regression (SVR) (Vapnik, 1995), or kernel matching pursuit (KMP) (Vincent and Bengio, 2000). SVR and KMP offer the advantage of sparsity and fast training. But a crucial advantage of kernel ridge regression in this context is, as we shall see, that it requires a single matrix inversion, independently of N_2, the number of features predicted. Thus, in the following we will consider a generalization of kernel ridge regression.

The hypothesis space we will assume is the set of all linear functions from F_X to F_Y. Thus, g is modeled as

$$\forall x \in X^*, g(x) = W(\Phi_X(x)), \tag{8.3}$$

where $W : F_X \to F_Y$ is a linear function admitting an $N_2 \times N_1$ real-valued matrix representation $\mathbf{W}$.

We start with a regression method generalizing kernel ridge regression to the case of vector space images. We will then further generalize this method to allow for the encoding of constraints between the input and output vectors.

8.3.1   Kernel Ridge Regression with Vector Space Images

For $i = 1, \ldots, m$, let $\boldsymbol{M}_{x_i} \in \mathbb{R}^{N_1 \times 1}$ denote the column matrix representing $\Phi_X(x_i)$ and $\boldsymbol{M}_{y_i} \in \mathbb{R}^{N_2 \times 1}$ the column matrix representing $\Phi_Y(y_i)$. We will denote by $\|\boldsymbol{A}\|_F^2 = \sum_{i=1}^p \sum_{j=1}^q \boldsymbol{A}_{ij}^2$ the Frobenius norm of a matrix $\boldsymbol{A} = (\boldsymbol{A}_{ij}) \in \mathbb{R}^{p \times q}$ and by $< A, B >_F = \sum_{i=1}^{p} \sum_{j=1}^{q} A_{ij} B_{ij}$ the Frobenius product of two matrices A and B in $\mathbb{R}^{p \times q}$. The following optimization problem,

$$\operatorname*{argmin}_{W \in \mathbb{R}^{N_2 \times N_1}} F(W) = \sum_{i=1}^{m} \|W M_{x_i} - M_{y_i}\|^2 + \gamma \|W\|_F^2, \tag{8.4}$$

where $\gamma \geq 0$ is a regularization scalar coefficient, generalizes ridge regression to vector space images. The solution W defines the linear hypothesis g. Let $M_X \in \mathbb{R}^{N_1 \times m}$ and $M_Y \in \mathbb{R}^{N_2 \times m}$ be the matrices defined by

$$M_X = [M_{x_1} \dots M_{x_m}] \qquad M_Y = [M_{y_1} \dots M_{y_m}]. \tag{8.5}$$

Then, the optimization problem (8.4) can be rewritten as

$$\operatorname*{argmin}_{W \in \mathbb{R}^{N_2 \times N_1}} F(W) = \|W M_X - M_Y\|_F^2 + \gamma \|W\|_F^2. \tag{8.6}$$

Proposition 47 *The solution of the optimization problem (8.6) is unique and is given by either one of the following identities:*

$$\begin{aligned} W &= M_Y M_X^\top (M_X M_X^\top + \gamma I)^{-1} \quad \text{(primal solution)} \\ W &= M_Y (K_X + \gamma I)^{-1} M_X^\top \qquad \text{(dual solution)}. \end{aligned} \tag{8.7}$$

where $K_X \in \mathbb{R}^{m \times m}$ is the Gram matrix associated to the kernel K_X: $K_{ij} = K_X(x_i, x_j)$.

Proof The function F is convex and differentiable, thus its solution is unique and given by $\nabla_W F = 0$. Its gradient is given by

$$\nabla_W F = 2 (W M_X - M_Y) M_X^\top + 2\gamma W. \tag{8.8}$$

Thus,

$$\begin{aligned} \nabla_W F = 0 \quad &\Leftrightarrow \quad 2(W M_X - M_Y) M_X^\top + 2\gamma W = 0 \\ &\Leftrightarrow \quad W(M_X M_X^\top + \gamma I) = M_Y M_X^\top \\ &\Leftrightarrow \quad W = M_Y M_X^\top (M_X M_X^\top + \gamma I)^{-1}, \end{aligned} \tag{8.9}$$

which gives the primal solution of the optimization problem. To derive the dual solution, observe that

$$M_X^\top (M_X M_X^\top + \gamma I)^{-1} = (M_X^\top M_X + \gamma I)^{-1} M_X^\top. \tag{8.10}$$

This can be derived without difficulty from a series expansion of $(M_X M_X^\top + \gamma I)^{-1}$. Since $K_X = M_X^\top M_X$,

$$W = M_Y (M_X^\top M_X + \gamma I)^{-1} M_X^\top = M_Y (K_X + \gamma I)^{-1} M_X^\top, \tag{8.11}$$

which is the second identity giving W. ∎

For both solutions, a single matrix inversion is needed. In the primal case, the complexity of that matrix inversion is in $O(N_1^3)$, or $O(N_1^{2+\alpha})$ with $\alpha < .376$, using the best known matrix inversion algorithms. When N_1, the dimension of the feature space F_X, is not large, this leads to an efficient computation of the solution. For large N_1 and relatively small m, the dual solution is more efficient since the complexity of the matrix inversion is then in $O(m^3)$, or $O(m^{2+\alpha})$.

Note that in the dual case, predictions can be made using kernel functions alone, as $\boldsymbol{W}$ does not have to be explicitly computed. For any $x \in X^*$, let $\boldsymbol{M}_x \in \mathbb{R}^{N_1 \times 1}$ denote the column matrix representing $\Phi_X(x)$. Thus, $g(x) = \boldsymbol{W}\boldsymbol{M}_x$. For any $y \in Y^*$, let $\boldsymbol{M}_y \in \mathbb{R}^{N_2 \times 1}$ denote the column matrix representing $\Phi_Y(y)$. Then, *f(x)* is determined by solving the pre-image problem:

pre-image
problem

$$f(x) = \underset{y \in Y^*}{\operatorname{argmin}} \|\boldsymbol{W}\boldsymbol{M}_x - \boldsymbol{M}_y\|^2 \tag{8.12}$$

$$= \underset{y \in Y^*}{\operatorname{argmin}} \left(\boldsymbol{M}_y^\top \boldsymbol{M}_y - 2\boldsymbol{M}_y^\top \boldsymbol{W}\boldsymbol{M}_x\right) \tag{8.13}$$

$$= \underset{y \in Y^*}{\operatorname{argmin}} \left(\boldsymbol{M}_y^\top \boldsymbol{M}_y - 2\boldsymbol{M}_y^\top \boldsymbol{M}_Y (\boldsymbol{K_X} + \gamma \boldsymbol{I})^{-1} \boldsymbol{M}_X^\top \boldsymbol{M}_x\right) \tag{8.14}$$

$$= \underset{y \in Y^*}{\operatorname{argmin}} \left(K_Y(y,y) - 2(\mathbf{K}_Y^y)^\top (\mathbf{K_X} + \gamma\mathbf{I})^{-1}\mathbf{K}_X^x\right), \tag{8.15}$$

where $\boldsymbol{K}_Y^y \in \mathbb{R}^{m \times 1}$ and $\boldsymbol{K}_X^x \in \mathbb{R}^{m \times 1}$ are the column matrices defined by

$$\boldsymbol{K}_Y^y = \begin{bmatrix} K_Y(y,y_1) \\ \dots \\ K_Y(y,y_m) \end{bmatrix} \quad \text{and} \quad \boldsymbol{K}_X^x = \begin{bmatrix} K_X(x,x_1) \\ \dots \\ K_X(x,x_m) \end{bmatrix}. \tag{8.16}$$

8.3.2   Generalization to Regression with Constraints

In many string-to-string mapping learning tasks such as those appearing in natural language processing, there are some specific constraints relating the input and output sequences. For example, in part-of-speech tagging, a tag in the output sequence must match the word in the same position in the input sequence. More generally, one may wish to exploit the constraints known about the string-to-string mapping to restrict the hypothesis space and achieve a better result.

This section shows that our regression framework can be generalized in a natural way to impose some constraints on the regression matrix $\boldsymbol{W}$. Remarkably, this generalization also leads to a closed-form solution and to an efficient iterative algorithm. Here again, the algorithm presented is not specific to string-to-string learning problems and can be used for other regression estimation problems.

incorporating
input-output
constraints via
regularization

Some natural constraints that one may wish to impose on $\boldsymbol{W}$ are linear constraints on its coefficients. To take these constraints into account, one can introduce additional terms in the objective function. For example, to impose that the coefficients with indices in some subset I_0 are null, or that two coefficients with indices in I_1 must be equal, the following terms can be added:

$$\beta_0 \sum_{(i,j)\in I_0} W_{ij}^2 + \beta_1 \sum_{(i,j,k,l)\in I_1} |W_{ij} - W_{kl}|^2, \qquad (8.17)$$

with large values assigned to the regularization factors β_0 and β_1. More generally, a finite set of linear constraints on the coefficients of $\boldsymbol{W}$ can be accounted for in the objective function by the introduction of a quadratic form defined over W_{ij}, $(i,j) \in N_2 \times N_1$.

Let $N = N_2 N_1$, and denote by $\bar{\boldsymbol{W}}$ the $N \times 1$ column matrix whose components are the coefficients of the matrix $\boldsymbol{W}$. The quadratic form representing the constraints can be written as $< \bar{\boldsymbol{W}}, \boldsymbol{R}\bar{\boldsymbol{W}} >$, where $\boldsymbol{R}$ is a positive semidefinite symmetric matrix. By Cholesky's decomposition theorem, there exists a triangular matrix $\bar{\boldsymbol{A}}$ such that $\boldsymbol{R} = \bar{\boldsymbol{A}}^\top \bar{\boldsymbol{A}}$. Denote by $\bar{\boldsymbol{A}}_i$ the transposition of the ith row of $\bar{\boldsymbol{A}}$, $\bar{\boldsymbol{A}}_i$ is an $N \times 1$ column matrix, then

$$< \bar{\boldsymbol{W}}, \boldsymbol{R}\bar{\boldsymbol{W}} >=< \bar{\boldsymbol{W}}, \bar{\boldsymbol{A}}^\top \bar{\boldsymbol{A}}\bar{\boldsymbol{W}} >= ||\bar{\boldsymbol{A}}\bar{\boldsymbol{W}}||^2 = \sum_{i=1}^{N} < \bar{\boldsymbol{A}}_i, \bar{\boldsymbol{W}} >^2 . \qquad (8.18)$$

The matrix $\bar{\boldsymbol{A}}_i$ can be associated to an $N_2 \times N_1$ matrix $\boldsymbol{A}_i$, just as $\bar{\boldsymbol{W}}$ is associated to $\boldsymbol{W}$, and $< \bar{\boldsymbol{A}}_i, \bar{\boldsymbol{W}} >^2 =< \boldsymbol{A}_i, \boldsymbol{W} >_F^2$. Thus, the quadratic form representing the linear constraints can be rewritten in terms of the Frobenius products of $\boldsymbol{W}$ with N matrices:

$$< \bar{\boldsymbol{W}}, \boldsymbol{R}\bar{\boldsymbol{W}} >= \sum_{i=1}^{N} < \boldsymbol{A}_i, \boldsymbol{W} >_F^2, \qquad (8.19)$$

with each $\boldsymbol{A}_i$, $i = 1, \ldots, N$, being an $N_2 \times N_1$ matrix. In practice, the number of matrices needed to represent the constraints may be far less than N; we will denote by C the number of constraint-matrices of the type $\boldsymbol{A}_i$ used.

Thus, the general form of the optimization problem including input-output constraints becomes

$$\operatorname*{argmin}_{\boldsymbol{W}\in\mathbb{R}^{N_2\times N_1}} F(\boldsymbol{W}) = \|\boldsymbol{W}\boldsymbol{M}_X - \boldsymbol{M}_Y\|_F^2 + \gamma\|\boldsymbol{W}\|_F^2 + \sum_{i=1}^{C} \eta_i < \boldsymbol{A}_i, \boldsymbol{W} >_F^2, \quad (8.20)$$

where $\eta_i \geq 0$, $i = 1, \ldots, C$, are regularization parameters. Since they can be factored in the matrices A_i by replacing A_i with $\sqrt{\eta_i}A_i$, in what follows we will assume without loss of generality that $\eta_1 = \ldots = \eta_C = 1$.

Proposition 48 *The solution of the optimization problem (8.20) is unique and is given by the following identity:*

$$\boldsymbol{W} = (\boldsymbol{M}_Y \boldsymbol{M}_X^\top - \sum_{i=1}^{C} a_i \, \boldsymbol{A}_i)\boldsymbol{U}^{-1}, \qquad (8.21)$$

with $U = M_X M_X^\top + \gamma I$ and

$$
\begin{bmatrix} a_1 \\ \dots \\ a_C \end{bmatrix} = \left((< A_i, A_j U^{-1} >)_{ij} + I \right)^{-1} \begin{bmatrix} < M_Y M_X^\top U^{-1}, A_1 > \\ \dots \\ < M_Y M_X^\top U^{-1}, A_C > \end{bmatrix}. \quad (8.22)
$$

Proof The new objective function F is convex and differentiable; thus, its solution is unique and given by $\nabla_W F = 0$. Its gradient is given by

$$
\nabla_W F = 2 \left(W M_X - M_Y \right) M_X^\top + 2\gamma W + 2 \sum_{i=1}^{C} < A_i, W >_F A_i. \quad (8.23)
$$

Thus,

$$
\nabla_W F = 0 \Leftrightarrow 2(W M_X - M_Y) M_X^\top + 2\gamma W + \sum_{i=1}^{C} < A_i, W >_F A_i = 0 \quad (8.24)
$$

$$
\Leftrightarrow W(M_X M_X^\top + \gamma I) = M_Y M_X^\top - \sum_{i=1}^{C} < A_i, W >_F A_i \quad (8.25)
$$

$$
\Leftrightarrow W = (M_Y M_X^\top - \sum_{i=1}^{C} < A_i, W >_F A_i)(M_X M_X^\top + \gamma I)^{-1}. \quad (8.26)
$$

To determine the solution W, we need to compute the coefficients $< A_i, W >_F$. Let $M = M_Y M_X^\top$, $a_i = < A_i, W >_F$ and $U = M_X M_X^\top + \gamma I$, then the last equation can be rewritten as

$$
W = (M - \sum_{i=1}^{C} a_i A_i) U^{-1}. \quad (8.27)
$$

Thus, for $j = 1, \dots, C$,

$$
a_j = < A_j, W >_F = < A_j, M U^{-1} >_F - \sum_{i=1}^{C} a_i < A_j, A_i U^{-1} >_F, \quad (8.28)
$$

which defines the following system of linear equations with unknowns a_j:

$$
\forall j, \, 1 \le j \le C, \quad a_j + \sum_{i=1}^{C} a_i < A_j, A_i U^{-1} >_F = < A_j, M U^{-1} >_F. \quad (8.29)
$$

Since u is symmetric, for all i, j, $1 \le i, j \le C$,

$$
< A_j, A_i U^{-1} >_F = \mathbf{tr}(A_j^\top A_i U^{-1}) = \mathbf{tr}(U^{-1} A_j^\top A_i) = < A_j U^{-1}, A_i >_F. \quad (8.30)
$$

Thus, the matrix $(< A_i, A_j U^{-1} >_F)_{ij}$ is symmetric and $(< A_i, A_j U^{-1} >_F)_{ij} + I$ is invertible. The statement of the proposition follows. ∎

Proposition 8.20 shows that, as in the constrained case, the matrix W solution of the optimization problem is unique and admits a closed-form solution. The computation of the solution requires inverting matrix $\boldsymbol{U}$, as in the unconstrained case, which can be done in time $O(N_1^3)$. But it also requires, in the general case, the inversion of matrix $(< \boldsymbol{A}_i, \boldsymbol{A}_j \boldsymbol{U}^{-1} >_F)_{ij} + \boldsymbol{I}$, which can be done in $O(C^3)$. For large C, C close to N, the space and time complexity of this matrix inversion may become prohibitive.

iterative
algorithm

Instead, one can use an iterative method for computing $\boldsymbol{W}$, using (8.31):

$$\boldsymbol{W} = (\boldsymbol{M}_Y \boldsymbol{M}_X^\top - \sum_{i=1}^{C} < \boldsymbol{A}_i, \boldsymbol{W} >_F \boldsymbol{A}_i) \boldsymbol{U}^{-1}, \tag{8.31}$$

and starting with the solution of the unconstrained solution:

$$\boldsymbol{W}_0 = \boldsymbol{M}_Y \boldsymbol{M}_X^\top \boldsymbol{U}^{-1}. \tag{8.32}$$

At iteration k, $\boldsymbol{W}_{k+1}$ is determined by interpolating its value at the previous iteration with the one given by (8.31):

$$\boldsymbol{W}_{k+1} = (1 - \alpha)\boldsymbol{W}_k + \alpha\,(\boldsymbol{M}_Y \boldsymbol{M}_X^\top - \sum_{i=1}^{C} < \boldsymbol{A}_i, \boldsymbol{W}_k >_F \boldsymbol{A}_i) \boldsymbol{U}^{-1}, \tag{8.33}$$

where $0 \le \alpha \le 1$. Let $\boldsymbol{P} \in \mathbb{R}^{(N_2 \times N_1) \times (N_2 \times N_1)}$ be the matrix such that

$$\boldsymbol{P} \boldsymbol{W} = \sum_{i=1}^{C} < \boldsymbol{A}_i, \boldsymbol{W} >_F \boldsymbol{A}_i \boldsymbol{U}^{-1}. \tag{8.34}$$

The following theorem proves the convergence of this iterative method to the correct result when α is sufficiently small with respect to a quantity depending on the largest eigenvalue of $\boldsymbol{P}$. When the matrices $\boldsymbol{A}_i$ are sparse, as in many cases encountered in practice, the convergence of this method can be very fast.

Theorem 49 *Let $\lambda_{\max}$ be the largest eigenvalue of $\boldsymbol{P}$. Then, $\lambda_{\max} \ge 0$ and for $0 < \alpha < \min\left\{ \frac{2}{\lambda_{\max}+1}, 1 \right\}$, the iterative algorithm just presented converges to the unique solution of the optimization problem (8.20).*

Proof We first show that the eigenvalues of $\boldsymbol{P}$ are all nonnegative. Let $\boldsymbol{X}$ be an eigenvector associated to an eigenvalue λ of $\boldsymbol{P}$. By definition,

$$\sum_{i=1}^{C} < \boldsymbol{A}_i, \boldsymbol{X} >_F \boldsymbol{A}_i \boldsymbol{U}^{-1} = \lambda \boldsymbol{X}. \tag{8.35}$$

Taking the dot product of each side with $\boldsymbol{X} \boldsymbol{U}$ yields

$$\sum_{i=1}^{C} < \boldsymbol{A}_i, \boldsymbol{X} >_F < \boldsymbol{A}_i \boldsymbol{U}^{-1}, \boldsymbol{X} \boldsymbol{U} >_F = \lambda < \boldsymbol{X}, \boldsymbol{X} \boldsymbol{U} >_F. \tag{8.36}$$

Since $U = M_X M_X^\top + \gamma I$, it is symmetric and positive and by Cholesky's decomposition theorem, there exists a matrix V such that $U = VV^\top$. Thus,

$$
\begin{aligned}
< X, XU >_F &=< X, XVV^\top >_F= \mathrm{tr}(X^\top XVV^\top) = \mathrm{tr}(V^\top X^\top XV) \\
&= \mathrm{tr}((XV)^\top XV) = \|XV\|_F^2,
\end{aligned}
\tag{8.37}
$$

where we used the property $\mathrm{tr}(AB) = \mathrm{tr}(BA)$, which holds for all matrices A and B. Now, using this same property and the fact that U is symmetric, for $i = 1, \dots, C$,

$$
< A_i U^{-1}, XU >_F= \mathrm{tr}(U^{-1} A_i^\top XU) = \mathrm{tr}(A_i^\top XUU^{-1}) =< A_i, X >_F .
\tag{8.38}
$$

Thus, (8.36) can be rewritten as

$$
\sum_{i=1}^{C} < A_i, X >_F^2= \lambda \|XV\|_F^2.
\tag{8.39}
$$

If $\|XV\|_F^2 = 0$, then for $i = 1, \dots, C$, $< A_i, X >_F= 0$, which implies $PX = 0 = \lambda X$ and $\lambda = 0$. Thus, if $\lambda \neq 0$, $\|XV\|_F^2 \neq 0$, and in view of (8.39),

$$
\lambda = \frac{\sum_{i=1}^{C} < A_i, X >_F^2}{\|XV\|_F^2} \geq 0.
\tag{8.40}
$$

Thus, all eigenvalues of P are nonnegative. This implies in particular that $I + P$ is invertible.

Eq. (8.31) giving W can be rewritten as

$$
W = W_0 - PW \iff W = (I + P)^{-1} W_0.
\tag{8.41}
$$

with $W_0 = M_Y M_X^\top U^{-1}$, which gives the unique solution of the optimization problem (8.20). Using the same notation, the iterative definition (8.33) can written for all $n \geq 0$ as

$$
W_{n+1} = (1 - \alpha)W_n + \alpha (W_0 - PW_n).
\tag{8.42}
$$

For $n \geq 0$, define V_{n+1} by $V_{n+1} = W_{n+1} - W_n$. Then,

$$
\forall n \geq 0, \quad V_{n+1} = -\alpha((I + P)W_n - W_0).
\tag{8.43}
$$

Thus, for all $n \geq 0$, $V_{n+1} - V_n = -\alpha(I + P)V_n$. Summing these equalities gives

$$
\forall n \geq 0, \quad V_{n+1} = [I - \alpha(I + P)]^n V_1.
\tag{8.44}
$$

Assume that $0 < \alpha < 1$. Let μ be an eigenvalue of $I - \alpha(I + P)$, then there exists $X \neq 0$ such that

$$
I - \alpha(I + P)X = \mu X \iff PX = \frac{(1 - \alpha) - \mu}{\alpha} X.
\tag{8.45}
$$

Thus, $\frac{(1-\alpha)-\mu}{\alpha}$ must be an eigenvalue of $\boldsymbol{P}$. Since the eigenvalues of $\boldsymbol{P}$ are nonnegative,

$$0 \le \frac{(1-\alpha)-\mu}{\alpha} \implies \mu \le 1 - \alpha < 1. \tag{8.46}$$

By definition of $\lambda_{\max}$,

$$\frac{(1-\alpha)-\mu}{\alpha} \le \lambda_{\max} \implies \mu \ge (1-\alpha) - \alpha\lambda_{\max} = 1 - \alpha(\lambda_{\max}+1). \tag{8.47}$$

Thus, for $\alpha < \frac{2}{\lambda_{\max}+1}$,

$$\mu \ge 1 - \alpha(\lambda_{\max}+1) > 1 - 2 = -1. \tag{8.48}$$

By (8.46) and (8.48), any eigenvalue μ of $\boldsymbol{I} - \alpha(\boldsymbol{I}+\boldsymbol{P})$ verifies $|\mu| < 1$. Thus, in view of (8.48),

$$\lim_{n\to\infty} \boldsymbol{V}_{n+1} = \lim_{n\to\infty} [\boldsymbol{I} - \alpha(\boldsymbol{I}+\boldsymbol{P})]^n \boldsymbol{V}_1 = 0. \tag{8.49}$$

By (8.43) and the continuity of $(\boldsymbol{I}+\boldsymbol{P})^{-1}$, this implies that

$$\lim_{n\to\infty} (\boldsymbol{I}+\boldsymbol{P})\boldsymbol{W}_n = \boldsymbol{W}_0 \implies \lim_{n\to\infty} \boldsymbol{W}_n = (\boldsymbol{I}+\boldsymbol{P})^{-1}\boldsymbol{W}_0, \tag{8.50}$$

which proves the convergence of the iterative algorithm to the unique solution of the optimization problem (8.20). ∎

Corollary 50 *Assume that $0 < \alpha < \min\left\{\frac{2}{\|P\|+1}, 1\right\}$, then the iterative algorithm presented converges to the unique solution of the optimization problem* (8.20).

Proof Since $\lambda_{\max} \le \|P\|$, the results follows directly theorem 49. ∎

Thus, for smaller values of α, the iterative algorithm converges to the unique solution of the optimization problem (8.20). In view of the proof of the theorem, the algorithm converges at least as fast as in

$$O(\max\{|1-\alpha|^n, |(1-\alpha) - \alpha\lambda_{\max}|^n\}) = O(|1-\alpha|^n). \tag{8.51}$$

The extra terms we introduced in the optimization function to account for known constraints on the coefficients of $\boldsymbol{W}$ (8.20), together with the existing term $\|\boldsymbol{W}\|_F^2$, can be viewed as a new and more general regularization term for $\boldsymbol{W}$. This idea can be used in other contexts. In particular, in some cases, it could be beneficial to use more general regularization terms for the weight vector in support vector machines. We leave the specific analysis of such general regularization terms to a future study.

8.4   Pre-Image Solution for Strings

8.4.1   A General Problem: Finding Pre-Images

A critical component of our general regression framework is the pre-image computation. This consists of determining the predicted output: given $z \in F_Y$, the problem consists of finding $y \in Y^*$ such that $\Phi_Y(y) = z$ (see figure 8.1). Note that this is a general problem, common to all kernel-based structured output problems, including M^3Ns (Taskar et al., 2004b) and SVM-ISOS (Tsochantaridis et al., 2004) although it is not explicitly described and discussed by the authors (see section 8.6).

Several instances of the pre-image problem have been studied in the past in cases where the pre-images are fixed-size vectors (Schölkopf and Smola, 2002). The pre-image problem is trivial when the feature mapping Φ_Y corresponds to polynomial kernels of odd degree since Φ_Y is then invertible. There also exists a fixed-point iteration approach for radial basis function (RBF) kernels. In the next section, we describe a new pre-image technique for strings that works with a rather general class of string kernels.

8.4.2 n-gram Kernels

n-gram kernels form a general family of kernels between strings, or more generally weighted automata, that measure the similarity between two strings using the counts of their common n-gram sequences. Let $|x|_u$ denote the number of occurrences of u in a string x, then the n-gram kernel k_n between two strings y_1 and y_2 in Y^*, $n \geq 1$, is defined by

$$k_n(y_1, y_2) = \sum_{|u|=n} |y_1|_u \, |y_2|_u, \tag{8.52}$$

where the sum runs over all strings u of length n. These kernels are instances of *rational kernels* and have been used successfully in a variety of difficult prediction tasks in text and speech processing (Cortes et al., 2004).

8.4.3   Pre-Image Problem for n-gram Kernels

The pre-image problem for n-gram kernels can be formulated as follows. Let Σ be the alphabet of the strings considered. Given $z = (z_1, \ldots, z_l)$, where $l = |\Sigma|^n$ and z_k is the count for an n-gram sequence u_k, find string y such that for $k = 1, \ldots, l$, $|y|_{u_k} = z_k$. Several standard problems arise in this context: the existence of y given z, its uniqueness when it exists, and the need for an efficient algorithm to determine y when it exists. We will address all these questions in the following sections.

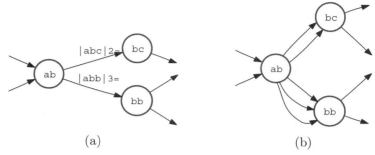

Figure 8.2 (a) The De Bruijn graph $G_{z,3}$ associated with the vector z in the case of trigrams ($n = 3$). The weight carried by the edge from vertex ab to vertex bc is the number of occurrences of the trigram abc as specified by the vector z. (b) The expanded graph $H_{z,3}$ associated with $G_{z,3}$. An edge in $G_{z,3}$ is repeated as many times as there were occurrences of the corresponding trigram.

8.4.4   Equivalent Graph-Theoretic Formulation of the Problem

De Bruijn graphs

The pre-image problem for n-gram kernels can be formulated as a graph problem by considering the *De Bruijn graph* $G_{z,n}$ associated with n and the vector z (van Lint and Wilson, 1992). $G_{z,n}$ is the graph constructed in the following way: associate a vertex to each $(n\text{-}1)$-gram sequence and add an edge from the vertex identified with $a_1 a_2 \ldots a_{n-1}$ to the vertex identified with $a_2 a_3 \ldots a_n$ weighted with the count of the n-gram $a_1 a_2 \ldots a_n$. The De Bruijn graph can be expanded by replacing each edge carrying weight c with c identical unweighted edges with the same original and destination vertices. Let $H_{z,n}$ be the resulting unweighted graph.

Euler circuit

The problem of finding the string y is then equivalent to that of finding an *Euler circuit* of $H_{z,n}$, that is, a circuit on the graph in which each edge is traversed exactly once (van Lint and Wilson, 1992). Each traversal of an edge between $a_1 a_2 \ldots a_{n-1}$ and $a_1 a_2 \ldots a_n$ corresponds to the consumption of one instance of the n-gram $a_1 a_2 \ldots a_n$. Figure 8.2 illustrates the construction of the graphs $G_{z,n}$ and $H_{z,n}$ in a special case.

8.4.5   Existence

The problem of finding an Eulerian circuit of a graph is a classical problem. Let $in\text{-}degree(q)$ denote the number of incoming edges of vertex q and $out\text{-}degree(q)$ the number of outgoing edges. The following theorem characterizes the cases where the pre-image y exists.

Theorem 51 *The vector z admits a pre-image iff for any vertex q of $H_{z,n}$, in-degree$(q) = $ out-degree(q).*

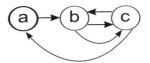

Figure 8.3 Example of a pre-image computation. The graph is associated with the vector $z = (0, 1, 0, 0, 0, 2, 1, 1, 0)$ whose coordinates indicate the counts of the bigrams $aa, ab, ac, ba, bb, bc, ca, cb, cc$. The graph verifies the conditions of theorem 51, thus it admits an Eulerian circuit, which in this case corresponds to the pre-image $y = bcbca$ if we start from the vertex a which can serve here as both the start and end symbol.

Proof The proof is a direct consequence of the graph formulation of the problem and a classical result related to the problem of Euler (1741) and Wilson (1979). ■

8.4.6 Compact Algorithm

There exists a linear-time algorithm for determining an Eulerian circuit of a graph verifying the conditions of theorem 51 (Wilson, 1979). Here, we give a simple, compact, and recursive algorithm that produces the same result as that algorithm with the same linear complexity:

$$O(|H_{z,n}|) = O(\sum_{i=1}^{l} z_i) = O(|y|). \tag{8.53}$$

Note that the complexity of the algorithm is optimal since writing the output sequence y takes the same time ($O(|y|)$). The following is the pseudocode of our algorithm.

```
EULER(q)
  1  path ← ε
  2  for  each unmarked edge e leaving q do
  3       MARK(e)
  4       path ← e EULER(dest(e)) path
  5  return path
```

A call to the function EULER with argument q returns a path corresponding to an Eulerian circuit from q. Line 1 initializes the path to the empty path. Then, each time through the loop of lines 2-4, a new outgoing edge of q is examined. If it has not been previously marked (line 3), then *path* is set to the concatenation of the edge e with the path returned by a call to EULER with the destination vertex of e and the old value of *path*.

While this is a very simple algorithm for generating an Eulerian circuit, the proof of its correctness is in fact not as trivial as that of the standard Euler algorithm. However, its compact form makes it easy to modify and analyze the effect of the modifications.

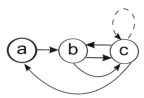

Figure 8.4   Case of nonunique pre-images. Both *bcbcca* and *bccbca* are possible pre-images. Our EULER algorithm can produce both solutions, depending on the order in which outgoing edges of the vertex *c* are examined. The graph differs from that of figure 8.3 only by the self-loop at the vertex identified with *c*.

8.4.7   Uniqueness

In general, when it exists, the pre-image sequence is not unique. Figure 8.4 gives a simple example of a graph with two distinct Eulerian circuits and distinct pre-image sequences. A recent result of Kontorovich (2004) gives a characterization of the set of strings that are unique pre-images. Let Φ_n be the feature mapping corresponding to n-gram sequences, that is, $\Phi_n(y)$ is the vector whose components are the counts of the n-grams appearing in y.

Theorem 52 (Kontorovich (2004)) *The set of strings y such that $\Phi(y)$ admits a unique pre-image is a regular language.*

In all cases, our algorithm can generate all possible pre-images starting from a given $(n\text{-}1)$-gram. Indeed, different pre-images simply correspond to different orders of examining outgoing edges. In practice, for a given vector z, the number of outgoing edges at each vertex is small (often 1, rarely 2). Thus, the extra cost of generating all possible pre-images is very limited.

8.4.8   Generalized Algorithm

The algorithm we presented can be used to generate efficiently all possible pre-images corresponding to a vector z when it admits a pre-image. However, due to regression errors, the vector z might not admit a pre-image. Also, as a result of regression, the components of z may be noninteger.

One solution to this problem is to round the components to obtain integer counts. As we shall see, incrementing or decrementing a component by one only leads to the local insertion or deletion of one symbol.

To deal with regression errors and the fact that y might not admit a pre-image, we can simply use the same algorithm. To allow for cases where the graph is not connected, the function EULER is called at each vertex q whose outgoing edges are not all marked. The resulting path is the concatenation of the paths returned by different calls to this function.

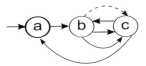

Figure 8.5 Illustration of the application of the generalized algorithm to the case of a graph that does not admit the Euler property. The graph differs from that of figure 8.3 by just one edge (*dashed*). The possible pre-images returned by the algorithm are *bccbca* and *bcbcca*.

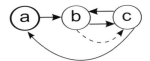

Figure 8.6 Further illustration of the application of the generalized algorithm to the case of a graph that does not admit the Euler property. The graph differs from that of figure 8.3 by just one edge (*dashed*). The pre-image returned by the algorithm is *bcba*.

The algorithm is guaranteed to return a string y whose length is $|y| = \sum_{i=1}^{l} z_i$ since each edge of the graph $H_{z,n}$ is visited exactly once. Clearly, the result is a pre-image when z admits one. But how different is the output string y from the original pre-image when we modify the count of one of the components of z by one, either by increasing or decreasing it? Figures 8.3 and 8.4 can serve to illustrate that in a special case since the graph of figure 8.4 differs from that of figure 8.3 by just one edge, which corresponds to the existence or not of the bigram cc.[1] The possible pre-images output by the algorithm given the presence of the bigram cc only differ from the pre-image in the absence of the bigram cc by one letter, c. Their edit-distance is one. Furthermore, the additional symbol c cannot appear at any position in the string; its insertion is only *locally* possible.

Figure 8.5 illustrates another case where the graph differs from that of figure 8.3 by one edge corresponding to the bigram bc. As in the case just discussed, the potential pre-images can only contain one additional symbol, c, which is inserted locally.

Figure 8.6 illustrates yet another case where the graph differs from that of figure 8.3 by one edge missing which corresponds to the bigram bc. The graph does not have the Euler property. Yet, our algorithm can be applied and outputs the pre-image $bcba$.

Thus, in summary, the algorithm we presented provides a simple and efficient solution to the pre-image problem for strings for the family of n-gram kernels. It also has the nice property that changing a coordinate in feature space has minimal impact on the actual pre-image found.

---

1. We can impose the same start and stop symbol, a, for all sequences.

<table>
<tr><td>using a priori
knowledge</td><td>One can use additional information to further enhance the accuracy of the pre-image algorithm. For example, if a large number of sequences over the target alphabet are available, we can create a statistical model such as an n-gram model based on those sequences. When the algorithm generates several pre-images, we can use that statistical model to rank these different pre-images by exploiting output symbol correlations. In the case of n-gram models, this can be done in linear time in the sum of the lengths of the pre-image sequences output by the algorithm.</td></tr>
</table>

8.5 Speeding up Training

This section examines two techniques for speeding up training when using our general regression framework.

8.5.1 Incomplete Cholesky Decomposition

One solution is to apply incomplete Cholesky decomposition to the kernel matrix $\boldsymbol{K}_X \in \mathbb{R}^{m \times m}$ (Bach and Jordan, 2002). This consists of finding a matrix $\boldsymbol{L} \in \mathbb{R}^{m \times n}$, with $n \ll m$, such that

$$\boldsymbol{K}_X = \boldsymbol{L}\boldsymbol{L}^\top. \tag{8.54}$$

Matrix $\boldsymbol{L}$ can be found in time $O(mn^2)$ using an incomplete Cholesky decomposition which takes $O(mn^2)$ operations (see e.g., Bach and Jordan, 2002) for the use of this technique in the context of kernel independent component analysis). To invert $\boldsymbol{K}_X + \gamma \boldsymbol{I}$ one can use the so-called inversion lemma or Woodbury formula:

$$(\boldsymbol{A} + \boldsymbol{B}\boldsymbol{C})^{-1} = \boldsymbol{A}^{-1} - \boldsymbol{A}^{-1}\boldsymbol{B}(\boldsymbol{I} + \boldsymbol{C}\boldsymbol{A}^{-1}\boldsymbol{B})^{-1}\boldsymbol{C}\boldsymbol{A}^{-1}, \tag{8.55}$$

which here leads to

$$(\gamma\boldsymbol{I} + \boldsymbol{L}\boldsymbol{L}^\top)^{-1} = \frac{1}{\gamma}[\boldsymbol{I} - \boldsymbol{L}\,(\gamma\boldsymbol{I} + \boldsymbol{L}^\top\boldsymbol{L})^{-1}\,\boldsymbol{L}^\top]. \tag{8.56}$$

Since $(\gamma\boldsymbol{I} + \boldsymbol{L}^\top\boldsymbol{L}) \in \mathbb{R}^{n \times n}$, the cost of the matrix inversion in the dual computation is reduced from $O(m^3)$ to $O(n^3)$. This method can thus be quite effective at reducing the computational cost. Our experiments (section 8.7.4) have shown, however, that the simple greedy technique described in the next section is often far more effective.

8.5.2 Greedy Technique

<table>
<tr><td>overcoming
nonsparsity</td><td>This consists, as with kernel matching pursuit (Vincent and Bengio, 2000), of defining a subset $n \ll m$ of kernel functions in an incremental fashion. This subset is</td></tr>
</table>

then used to define the expansion. Consider the case of a finite-dimensional output space:

$$g(x) = (\sum_{i \in S} \alpha_{i1} K_X(x_i, x), \ldots, \sum_{i \in S} \alpha_{iN_2} K_X(x_i, x)), \tag{8.57}$$

where S is the set of indices of the kernel functions used in the expansion, initialized to $\emptyset$. The algorithm then consists of repeating the following steps so long as $|S| < n$:

1. Determine the training point x_j with the largest residual:

$$j = \underset{i \in \{1, \ldots, m\} \setminus S}{\operatorname{argmax}} ||\Phi_Y(y_i) - g(x_i)||^2; \tag{8.58}$$

2. Add x_j to the set of "support vectors" and update α:

$$\begin{aligned} & S \leftarrow S \cup \{x_j\}; \\ & \alpha \leftarrow \underset{\hat{\alpha}}{\operatorname{argmin}} \sum_{i=1}^{m} ||\Phi_Y(y_i) - g(x_i)||^2. \end{aligned} \tag{8.59}$$

The matrix inversion required in step 2 is done with $\alpha = \mathbf{K}_S^{-1} \mathbf{K}_{S,*} Y$ where $\mathbf{K}_S$ is the kernel matrix between input examples indexed by S only, and $\mathbf{K}_{S,*}$ is the kernel matrix between S and all other examples.

In practice, this can be computed incrementally via rank one updates (Smola and Bartlett, 2001), which results in a running time complexity of $O(nm^2 N_2)$ as with KMP (Vincent and Bengio, 2000) (but there, $N_2 = 1$). A further linear speedup is possible by restricting the subset of the data points in step 1. Note that this approach differs from KMP in that we select basis functions that approximate all the output dimensions at once, resulting in faster evaluation times. The union of the support vectors over all output dimensions is indeed smaller.

One could also apply this procedure to the iterative regression algorithm incorporating constraints of section 8.3.2. One would need to add a "support vector" greedily as above, run several iterations of the update rule given in (8.27), and then repeat n times.

8.6 Comparison with Other Algorithms

This section compares our regression framework for learning string-to-string mappings with other algorithms described in the literature for the same task. It describes the objective function optimized by these other algorithms, which can all be viewed as classification-based, and points out important differences in the computational complexity of these algorithms.

8.6.1 Problem Formulation

relation to other work

Other existing algorithms for learning a string-to-string mapping (Collins and

Duffy, 2002; Tsochantaridis et al., 2004; Taskar et al., 2004b) formulate the problem as that of learning a function $f : X \times Y \to \mathbb{R}$ defined over the pairs of input-output strings, such that the output $\hat{y}(x)$ associated to the input x is given by

$$\hat{y}(x) = \underset{y \in Y}{\operatorname{argmax}} f(x, y). \tag{8.60}$$

The hypothesis space considered is typically that of linear functions. Pairs of input-output strings are mapped to a feature space F via a mapping $\Phi_{XY} : X \times Y \to F$. Thus, the function f learned is defined as

$$\forall (x, y) \in X \times Y, \quad f(x, y) = w \cdot \Phi_{XY}(x, y), \tag{8.61}$$

where $w \in F$. Thus, a joint embedding Φ_{XY} is used, unlike the separate embeddings Φ_X and Φ_Y adopted in our framework. The learning problem can be decomposed into the following two problems, as in our case:

- learning the weight vector w to determine the linear function f, which is similar to our problem of determining W;

- given x, computing $\hat{y}(x)$ following (8.60), which is also a pre-image problem. Indeed, let g_x be the function defined by $g_x(y) = f(x, y)$, then

$$\hat{y}(x) = \underset{y \in Y}{\operatorname{argmax}} g_x(y). \tag{8.62}$$

When the joint embedding Φ_{XY} can be decomposed as

$$\Phi_{XY}(x, y) = \Phi_X(x) \otimes \Phi_Y(y), \tag{8.63}$$

where $\otimes$ indicates the tensor product of the vectors, the hypothesis functions sought coincide with those assumed in our regression framework. In both cases, the problem then consists of learning a matrix $\boldsymbol{W}$ between the same two spaces as in our approach. The only difference lies in the choice of the loss function.

Other joint embeddings Φ_{XY} may help encode conveniently some prior knowledge about the relationship between input and output sequences (see Weston et al. (2004) and chapter 4 of this book for an empirical analysis of the benefits of joint feature spaces). For example, with

$$\langle \Phi_{XY}(x, y), \Phi_{XY}(x', y') \rangle = \langle \Phi_X(x) \otimes \Phi_Y(y), \boldsymbol{R} \left(\Phi_X(x') \otimes \Phi_Y(y') \right) \rangle \tag{8.64}$$

the matrix $\boldsymbol{R}$ can be used to favor some terms of $\boldsymbol{W}$. In our method, such relationships can also be accounted for by imposing some constraints on the matrix $\boldsymbol{W}$ and solving the generalized regression problem with constraints described in section 8.3.2.

The weight vector w in previous techniques is learned using the kernel perceptron algorithm (Collins and Duffy, 2002), or a large-margin maximization algorithm (Tsochantaridis et al., 2004; Taskar et al., 2004b). These techniques treat the learning problem outlined above by imposing that the pair (x, y) with y matching

x obtain a higher score than all other pairs (x, y'). This is done by using a binary loss function as in classification which ignores the similarities between the output sequences. To correct for that effect, classification techniques such as SVM-ISOS (Tsochantaridis et al., 2004) modify the binary loss function to impose the following condition for $i = 1, \ldots, m$ and any $y \in Y - \{y_i\}$:

existing approaches mimic regression setting

$$f(x_i, y_i) > f(x_i, y) + L(y_i, y), \tag{8.65}$$

where L is a loss function based on the output strings. This makes the loss function similar, though not equivalent, to the objective function of a regression problem. To further point out this similarity, consider the case of the joint embedding (8.63). The inequality can then be rewritten as

$$\Phi_Y(y_i)^\top \boldsymbol{W} \Phi_X(x_i) - \Phi_Y(y)^\top \boldsymbol{W} \Phi_X(x_i) \geq L(y_i, y). \tag{8.66}$$

In our general regression framework, using (8.4), a solution with zero empirical error, i.e., $\boldsymbol{W}\Phi_X(x_i) = \Phi_Y(y_i)$ for $i = 1, \ldots, m$, verifies the following equality:

$$||\boldsymbol{W}\Phi_X(x_i) - \Phi_Y(y)||^2 = ||\boldsymbol{W}\Phi_X(x_i) - \Phi_Y(y_i)||^2 + L(y_i, y), \tag{8.67}$$

where $L(y_i, y) = ||\Phi_Y(y_i) - \Phi_Y(y)||^2$. Assuming that the outputs are normalized, i.e., $||\Phi_Y(y)|| = 1$ for all y, this equation is equivalent to

$$\Phi_Y(y_i)^\top \boldsymbol{W} \Phi_X(x_i) - \Phi_Y(y)^\top \boldsymbol{W} \Phi_X(x_i) = \frac{1}{2} L(y_i, y), \tag{8.68}$$

which is similar to the zero-one loss constraint of (8.66) with the inequality replaced with an equality here.

We argue that in structured output prediction problems, it is often natural to introduce a similarity measure capturing the closeness of the outputs. In view of that, minimizing the corresponding distance is fundamentally a regression problem.

8.6.2   Computational Cost

The computational cost of other techniques for learning string-to-string mapping significantly differs from that of our general regression framework.

In the case of other techniques, a pre-image computation is required at every iteration during training, and the algorithms can be shown to converge in polynomial time if the pre-image computation itself can be computed in polynomial time. In our case, pre-image calculations are needed only at testing time, and do not affect training time. Since the pre-image computation may be often very costly, this can represent a substantial difference in practice.

The complexity of our Euler circuit string pre-image algorithm is linear in the length of the pre-image string y it generates. It imposes no restriction on the type of regression technique used, nor does it constrain the choice of the features over the input X.

The computation of the pre-image in several of the other techniques consists of applying the Viterbi algorithm, possibly combined with a heuristic pruning, to a dynamically expanded graph representing the set of possible candidate pre-images. The complexity of the algorithm is then $O(|y||G|)$ where y is the string for which a pre-image is sought and G the graph expanded. The practicality of such pre-image computations often relies on some rather restrictive constraints on the type of features used, which may impact the quality of the prediction. As an example, in the experiments described by Taskar et al. (2004b), a Markovian assumption is made about the output sequences, and furthermore the dependency between the input and output symbols is strongly restricted: y_i, the output symbol at position i, depends only on x_i, the symbol at the same position in the input.

The two approaches differ significantly in terms of the number of variables to estimate in the dual case. With the kernel perceptron algorithm (Collins and Duffy, 2002) and the large-margin maximization algorithms of Tsochantaridis et al. (2004) and Taskar et al. (2004b), the number of variables to estimate is at most $m|Y|$, where $|Y|$, the number of possible labels, could be potentially very large. On the positive side, this problem is partially alleviated thanks to the sparsity of the solution. Note that the speed of training is also proportional to the number of nonzero coefficients.

In the case of our general regression framework with no constraints, the number of dual variables is m^2, and is therefore independent of the number of output labels. On the negative side, the solution is in general not sparse. The greedy incremental technique described in section 8.5 helps overcome this problem, however.

8.7   Experiments

8.7.1   Description of the Dataset

To test the effectiveness of our algorithms, we used exactly the same dataset as the one used in the experiments reported by Taskar et al. (2004b) with the same specific crossvalidation process and the same folds: the data are partitioned into ten folds, and ten times one fold is used for training, and the remaining nine are used for testing.

The dataset, including the partitioning, is available for download from `http://ai.stanford.edu/~btaskar/ocr/`. It is a subset of the handwritten words collected by Rob Kassel at the MIT Spoken Language Systems Group for an optical character recognition (OCR) task. It contains 6877 word instances with a total of 52,152 characters. The first character of each word has been removed to keep only lowercase characters. (This decision was not made by us. We simply kept the dataset unchanged to make the experiments comparable.) The image of each character has been rasterized and normalized into a $16 \times 8 = 128$ binary-pixel representation.

The general handwriting recognition problem associated with this dataset is to determine a word y given the sequence of pixel-based images of its handwritten segmented characters $x = x_1 \cdots x_k$. We report our experimental results in this task with two different settings.

8.7.2 Perfect Segmentation

Our first experimental setting matches exactly that of Taskar et al. (2004b), where a perfect image segmentation is given with a one-to-one mapping of images to characters. Image segment x_i corresponds exactly to one word character, the character, y_i, of y in position i.

To exploit these conditions in learning, we will use the general regression framework with constraints described in section 8.3.2. The input and output feature mappings Φ_X and Φ_Y are defined as follows.

Let v_i, $i = 1, \ldots, N_1$, denote all the image segments in our training set and let k_X be a positive definite symmetric kernel defined over such image segments. We denote by l the maximum length of a sequence of images in the training sample.

The feature vector $\Phi_X(x)$ associated to an input sequence of images $x = x_1 \cdots x_q$, $q \leq l$, is defined by

$$\Phi_X(x) = [k'_X(v_1, x_{p(v_1)}), \ldots, k'_X(v_{N_1}, x_{p(v_{N_1})})]^\top, \tag{8.69}$$

where for $i = 1, \ldots, N_1$, $k'_X(v_i, x_{p(v_i)}) = k_X(v_i, x_{p(v_i)})$ if $p(v_i) \leq q$, $k'_X(v_i, x_{p(v_i)}) = 0$ otherwise. Thus, we use a so-called empirical kernel map to embed the input strings in the feature space F_X of dimension N_1.

The feature vector $\Phi_Y(y)$ associated to the output string $y = y_1 \cdots y_q$, $q \leq l$, is a $26l$-dimensional vector defined by

$$\Phi_Y(y) = [\phi_Y(y_1), \ldots, \phi_Y(y_q), 0, \ldots, 0]^\top, \tag{8.70}$$

where $\phi_Y(y_i)$, $1 \leq i \leq q$, is a 26-dimensional vector whose components are all zero except from the entry of index y_i, which is equal to one. With this feature mapping, the pre-image problem is straightforward since each position can be treated separately. For each position i, $1 \leq i \leq l$, the alphabet symbol with the largest weight is selected.

Given the embeddings Φ_X and Φ_Y, the matrix $\mathbf{W}$ learned by our algorithm is in $\mathbb{R}^{N_2 \times N_1}$, with $N_1 \approx 5000$ and $N_2 = 26l$. Since the problem setting is very restricted, we can impose some constraints on $\boldsymbol{W}$. For a given position i, $1 \leq i \leq l$, we can assume that input features corresponding to other positions, that is, input features v_j for which $p(v_j) \neq i$, are (somewhat) irrelevant for predicting the character in position i. This translates into imposing that the coefficients of $\boldsymbol{W}$ corresponding to such pairs be small. For each position i, there are $26(N_1 - |\{v_j : p(v_j) = i\}|)$ such constraints, resulting in a total of

$$C = \sum_{i=1}^{l} 26(N_1 - |\{v_j : p(v_j) = i\}|) = 26N_1(l - 1) \tag{8.71}$$

Table 8.1 Experimental results with the perfect segmentation setting. The M³N and SVM results are read from the graph in Taskar et al. (2004b)

Technique	Accuracy	
REG-constraints $\eta = 0$	84.1%	$\pm .8\%$
REG-constraints $\eta = 1$	88.5%	$\pm .9\%$
REG	79.5%	$\pm .4\%$
REG-Viterbi ($n = 2$)	86.1%	$\pm .7\%$
REG-Viterbi ($n = 3$)	98.2%	$\pm .3\%$
SVMs (cubic kernel)	80.9%	$\pm .5\%$
M³Ns (cubic kernel)	87.0%	$\pm .4\%$

constraints. These constraints can be easily encoded following the scheme outlined in section 8.3.2. To impose a constraint on the coefficient $\boldsymbol{W}_{rs}$ of $\boldsymbol{W}$, it suffices to introduce a matrix $\boldsymbol{A}$ whose entries are all zero except from the coefficient of row index r and column index s, which is set to one. Thus, $< \boldsymbol{W}, \boldsymbol{A} >= \boldsymbol{W}_{rs}$. To impose all C constraints, C matrices $\boldsymbol{A}_i$, $i = 1, \ldots, C$, of this type can be defined. In our experiments, we used the same regularization parameter η for all of these constraints.

In our experiments, we used the efficient iterative method outlined in section 8.3.2 to compute $\boldsymbol{W}$. However, it is not hard to see that in this case, thanks to the simplicity of the constraint matrices $\boldsymbol{A}_i$, $i = 1, \ldots, C$, the resulting matrix $(< \boldsymbol{A}_i, \boldsymbol{A}_j \boldsymbol{U}^{-1} >_F)_{ij} + \boldsymbol{I}$ can be given a simple block structure that makes it easier to invert. Indeed, it can be decomposed into l blocks in $\mathbb{R}^{N_1 \times N_1}$ that can be inverted independently. Thus, the overall complexity of matrix inversion, which dominates the cost of the algorithm, is only $O(lN_1^3)$ here.

Table 8.1 reports the results of our experiments using a polynomial kernel of third degree for k_X, and the best empirical value for the ridge regression coefficient γ which was $\gamma = 0.01$. The accuracy is measured as the percentage of the total number of word characters correctly predicted. REG refers to our general regression technique, REG-constraints to our general regression with constraints. The results obtained with the regularization parameter η set to 1 are compared to those with no constraint, i.e., $\eta = 0$. When $\eta = 1$, the constraints are active and we observe a significant improvement of the generalization performance.

For comparison, we also trained a single predictor over all images of our training sample, regardless of their positions. This resulted in a regression problem with a 26-dimensional output space, and $m \approx 5000$ examples in each training set. This effectively corresponds to a hard weight-sharing of the coefficients corresponding to different positions within matrix $\boldsymbol{W}$, as described in section 8.3.2. The first 26 lines of $\boldsymbol{W}$ are repeated $(l - 1)$ times. That predictor can be applied independently to each image segment x_i of a sequence $x = x_1 \cdots x_q$. Here too, we used a polynomial kernel of third degree and $\gamma = 0.01$ for the ridge regression parameter. We also experimented with the use of an n-gram statistical model based on the words of the training data to help discriminate between different word sequence hypotheses, as mentioned in section 8.4.8.

Table 8.1 reports the results of our experiments within this setting. REG refers to the hard weight-sharing regression without using a statistical language model and is directly comparable to the results obtained using support vector machines (SVMs). REG-Viterbi with $n = 2$ or $n = 3$ corresponds to the results obtained within this setting using different n-gram order statistical language models. In this case, we used the Viterbi algorithm to compute the pre-image solution, as in M^3Ns. The result shows that coupling a simple predictor with a more sophisticated pre-image algorithm can significantly improve the performance. The high accuracy achieved in this setting can be viewed as reflecting the simplicity of this task. The dataset contains only 55 unique words, and the same words appear in both the training and the test set.

We also compared all these results with the best result reported by Taskar et al. (2004b) for the same problem and dataset. The experiment allowed us to compare these results with those obtained using M^3Ns. But we are interested in more complex string-to-string prediction problems where restrictive prior knowledge such as a one-to-one mapping is not available. Our second set of experiments corresponds to a more realistic and challenging setting.

8.7.3   String-to-String Prediction

Our method generalizes indeed to the much harder and more realistic problem where the input and output strings may be of different length and where no prior segmentation or one-to-one mapping is given. For this setting, we directly estimate the counts of all the n-grams of the output sequence from one set of input features and use our pre-image algorithm to predict the output sequence.

In our experiment, we chose the following polynomial kernel K_X between two image sequences:

$$K_X(x_1, x_2) = \sum_{x_{1,i}, x_{2,j}} \left(1 + x_{1,i} \, x_{2,j}\right)^d, \qquad (8.72)$$

where the sum runs over all n-grams $x_{1,i}$ and $x_{2,j}$ of input sequences x_1 and x_2. The n-gram order and the degree d are both parameters of the kernel. For the kernel K_Y we used n-gram kernels.

As a result of the regression, the output values, that is, the estimated counts of the individual n-grams in an output string are nonintegers and need to be discretized for the Euler circuit computation (see section 8.4.8). The output words are in general short, so we did not anticipate counts higher than one. Thus, for each output feature, we determined just one threshold above which we set the count to one. Otherwise, we set the count to zero. These thresholds were determined by examining each feature at a time and imposing that averaged over all the strings in the training set, the correct count of the n-gram be predicted.

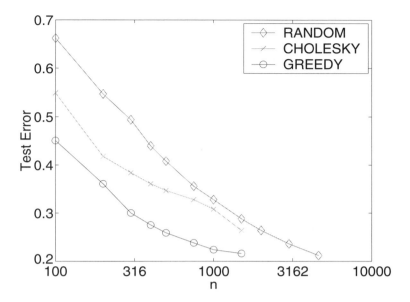

Figure 8.7 Comparison of random subsampling of n points from the OCR dataset, incomplete Cholesky decomposition after n iterations, and greedy incremental learning with n basis functions. The main bottleneck, for all of these algorithms is the matrix inversion where the size of the matrix is $n \times n$, we therefore plot test error against n. The furthest right point is the test error rate of training on the full training set of $n = 4617$ examples.

Note that, as a consequence of this thresholding, the predicted strings do not always have the same length as the target strings. Extra and missing characters are counted as errors in our evaluation of the accuracy.

We obtained the best results using unigrams and second-degree polynomials in the input space and bigrams in the output space. For this setting, we obtained an accuracy of 65.3 ± 2.3.

A significant higher accuracy can be obtained by combining the predicted integer counts from several different input and output kernel regressors, and computing an Euler circuit using only the n-grams predicted by the majority of the regressors. Combining five such regressors, we obtained a test accuracy of 75.6 ± 1.5.

A performance degradation for this setting was naturally expected, but we view it as relatively minor given the increased difficulty of the task. Furthermore, our results can be improved by combining a statistical model with our pre-image algorithm.

8.7.4 Faster Training

As pointed out in section 8.5, faster training is needed when the size of the training data increases significantly. This section compares the greedy incremental technique described in that section with the partial Cholesky decomposition technique and the baseline of randomly subsampling n points from the data, which of course also results in reduced complexity, giving only an $n \times n$ matrix to invert. The different techniques are compared in the perfect segmentation setting on the first fold of the data. The results should be indicative of the performance gain in other folds.

In both partial Cholesky decomposition and greedy incremental learning, n iterations are run and then an $n \times n$ matrix is inverted, which may be viewed as the bottleneck. Thus, to determine the learning speed we plot the test error for the regressions problem vs. n. The results are shown in figure 8.7. The greedy learning technique leads to a considerable reduction in the number of kernel computations required and the matrix inversion size for the same error rate as the full dataset. Furthermore, in greedy incremental learning we are left with only n kernels to compute for a given test point, independently of the number of outputs. These reasons combined make the greedy incremental method an attractive approximation technique for our regression framework.

8.8   Conclusion

We presented a general regression framework for learning string-to-string mappings and illustrated its use in several experiments. Several paths remained to be explored to further extend the applicability of this framework.

The pre-image algorithm for strings that we described is general and can be used in other contexts. But the problem of pre-image algorithms for strings may have other efficient solutions that need to be examined.

Efficiency of training is another key aspect of all string-to-string mapping algorithms. We presented several heuristics and approximations that can be used to substantially speed up training in practice. Other techniques could be studied to further increase speed and extend the application of our framework to very large tasks without sacrificing accuracy.

Much of the framework and algorithms presented can be used in a similar way for other prediction problems with structured outputs. A new pre-image algorithm needs to be introduced, however, for other learning problems with structured outputs.

9 Learning as Search Optimization

Hal Daumé III and Daniel Marcu

Mappings to structured output spaces (strings, trees, partitions, etc.) are typically learned using extensions of classification algorithms to simple graphical structures (e.g., linear chains) in which search and parameter estimation can be performed exactly. Unfortunately, in many complex problems, exact search and parameter estimation are both intractable. Instead of learning exact models and searching via heuristic means, we embrace the search framework and treat the structured output problem as being *defined* by search. We present a framework for learning as search optimization (section 9.3), and two parameter updates with convergence theorems and bounds (section 9.3.4). We present an empirical evaluation both on standard sequence labeling tasks (sections 9.4.1 and 9.4.2) as well as a significantly more complicated task from natural language processing: entity detection and tracking (section 9.4.4). Empirical evidence shows that our integrated approach to learning and search can outperform exact models at small computational cost.

9.1 Introduction

Many general techniques for learning with structured outputs are computationally demanding, are ill-suited for dealing with large datasets, and employ parameter optimization for an intractable search (decoding/pre-image) problem. In some instances, such as syntactic parsing, efficient task-specific decoding algorithms have been developed, but, unfortunately, these are rarely applicable outside of one specific task.

Rather than separating the learning problem from the search problem, we propose to consider these two aspects in an integrated manner. By doing so, we learn model parameters appropriate for the search procedure, avoiding the need to heuristically combine an a priori unrelated learning technique and search algorithm. After phrasing the learning problem in terms of search, we present two online parameter update methods: a simple perceptron-style update and an approximate large-margin update. We apply our model to two simple tasks: a simple syntactic chunking task for which exact search *is* possible (to allow for comparison to exact learning and decoding methods) and a joint tagging/chunking task for which exact search is intractable. Finally, we apply our model to a complex natural language processing task for which exact search is highly intractable.

9.2   Previous Work

Most work on the structured outputs problem extends standard classifiers to linear chains. Among these are maximum entropy Markov models and conditional random fields (McCallum et al., 2000; Lafferty et al., 2001); case-factor diagrams (McAllester et al., 2004); sequential Gaussian process models (Altun et al., 2004b); support vector machines for structured outputs (Tsochantaridis et al., 2005) and max-margin Markov models (Taskar et al., 2004b); and kernel dependency estimation models (Weston et al., 2002). These models learn distributions or weights on simple graphs (typically linear chains). Probabilistic models are typically optimized by gradient descent on the log-likelihood, which requires computable expectations of features across the structure (Lafferty et al., 2001). Margin-based techniques are typically optimized by solving a quadratic program (QP) whose constraints specify that the best structure must be weighted higher than all other structures (Taskar et al., 2004b). Markov (i.e., locality) assumptions can reduce the exponentially many constraints to a polynomial, but training remains computationally expensive.

At the heart of all these algorithms, batch or online, likelihood- or margin-based, is the computation:

$$\hat{y} = \arg\max_{y \in \mathcal{Y}} f(x, y; w) \tag{9.1}$$

This seemingly innocuous argmax statement is necessary in *all* models, and "simply" computes the structure $\hat{y}$ from the set of all possible structures $\mathcal{Y}$ that maximizes some function f on an input x, parameterized by a weight vector w. This computation is typically left unspecified, since it is "problem specific."

Unfortunately, this argmax computation is, in real problems with complex structure, intractable. Compounding this issue is that this best guess $\hat{y}$ is only one ingredient to the learning algorithms: likelihood-based models require feature expectations and the margin-based methods require either a k-best list of ys (McDonald et al., 2004) or a marginal distribution across the graphical structure. One alternative that alleviates some of these issues is to use a perceptron algorithm, where *only* the argmax is required (Collins, 2002), but performance can be adversely affected by the fact that even the argmax cannot be computed exactly; see McCallum and Wellner (2004) for an example.

Algorithm 9.1 The generic search algorithm

Algorithm Search(*problem, initial, enqueue*)
nodes ← MakeQueue(MakeNode(*problem,initial*))
while *nodes* is not empty **do**
  node ← RemoveFront(*nodes*)
  if GoalTest(*node*) **then return** *node*
  next ← Operators(*node*)
  nodes ← *enqueue*(*problem, nodes, next*)
end while
return failure

9.3 Search Optimization

learning as search optimization

We present the learning as search optimization (LaSO) framework for predicting structured outputs. The idea is to delve into (9.1) to first reduce the requirement that an algorithm needs to compute an argmax, and also to produce generic algorithms that can be applied to problems that are significantly more complex that the standard sequence labeling tasks that the majority of prior work has focused on.

9.3.1 Search

The generic search problem is covered in great depth in any introductory AI book. Its importance stems from the intractability of computing the "best" solution to many problems; instead, one must search for a "good" solution. Most AI texts contain a definition of the search problem and a general search algorithm; we work here with that from Russell and Norvig (1995). A search problem is a structure containing four fields: STATES (the world of exploration), OPERATORS (transitions in the world), GOAL TEST (a subset of states), and PATH COST (computes the cost of a path).

One defines a general search algorithm given a search problem, an initial state, and a "queuing function." The search algorithm will either fail (if it cannot find a goal state) or will return a path. Such an algorithm (algorithm 9.1) operates by cycling through a queue, taking the first element off, testing it as a goal, and expanding it according to operators if otherwise. Each node stores the path taken to get there and the cost of this path. The *enqueue* function places the expanded nodes, *next*, onto the queue according to some variable ordering that can yield depth-first, breadth-first, greedy, beam, hill-climbing, and A* search (among others). Since most search techniques can be described in this framework, we will treat it as fixed.

9.3.2 Search Parameterization

Given the search framework described, for a given task the search problem will be fixed, the initial state will be fixed, and the generic search algorithm will be fixed. The only place left, therefore, for parameterization is in the *enqueue* function, whose job it is to essentially rank hypotheses on a queue. The goal of learning, therefore, is to produce an *enqueue* function that places good hypotheses high on the queue and bad hypotheses low on the queue. In the case of optimal search, this means that we will find the optimal solution quickly; in the case of approximate search (with which we are most interested), this is the difference between finding a good solution or not.

In our model, we will assume that the enqueue function is based on two components: a path component g and a heuristic component h, and that the score of a node will be given by $g + h$. This formulation includes A* search when h is an admissible heuristic, heuristic search when h is inadmissible, best-first search when h is identically zero, and any variety of beam search when a queue is cut off at a particular point at each iteration. We will assume h is given and that g is a linear function of features of the input x and the path to and including the current node, n: $g = \langle \mathbf{w}, \mathbf{\Phi}(x, n) \rangle$, where $\mathbf{\Phi}(\cdot, \cdot)$ is the vector of features.[1]

9.3.3 Learning the Search Parameters

The supervised learning problem in this search-based framework is to take a search problem, a heuristic function, and training data with the goal of producing a good weight vector $\mathbf{w}$ for the path function g. As in standard structured output learning, we will assume that our training data consist of N-many pairs $(x^{(n)}, y^{(n)}) \in \mathcal{X} \times \mathcal{Y}$ that tell us for a given input $x^{(n)}$ what is the correct structured output $y^{(n)}$. We will make one more important *monotonicity assumption*: for any given node $n \in \mathcal{S}$ and an output $y \in \mathcal{Y}$, we can tell whether n can or cannot lead to y. In the case that n can lead to y, we refer to n as "y-good."

adapting *enqueue* via online learning

The learning problem can thus be formulated as follows: we wish to find a weight vector $\mathbf{w}$ such that (1) the first goal state dequeued is y-good and (2) the queue always contains at least one y-good state. In this framework, we explore an online learning scenario, where learning is tightly entwined with the search procedure. From a pragmatic perspective, this makes sense: it is useless to the model to learn parameters for cases that it will never actually encounter. We propose a learning algorithm of the form shown in algorithm 9.2. In this algorithm, we write *siblings* (*node*, y) to denote the set of y-good siblings of this node. This can be calculated recursively by backtracing to the first y-good ancestor and then tracing forward through only y-good nodes to the same search depth as n (in tasks where there is a

---

1. All algorithms described in this chapter can be kernelized, though we do not explore this option here.

Algorithm 9.2 The generic search/learning algorithm

Algorithm Learn(*problem*, *initial*, *enqueue*, **w**, *x*, *y*)
nodes ← MakeQueue(MakeNode(*problem*,*initial*))
while *nodes* is not empty **do**
   node ← RemoveFront(*nodes*)
   if none of *nodes* ∪ {*node*} is *y*-good **or** GoalTest(*node*) and *node* is not *y*-good
   then
     sibs ← *siblings*(*node*, *y*)
     w ← *update*(**w**, *x*, *sibs*, {*node*} ∪ *nodes*)
     nodes ← MakeQueue(*sibs*)
   else
     if GoalTest(*node*) **then return w**
     next ← Operators(*node*)
     nodes ← *enqueue*(*problem*, *nodes*, *next*, **w**)
   end if
end while

---

unique *y*-good search path—which is common—the sibling of a node is simply the appropriate initial segment of this path).

There are two changes to the search algorithm to facilitate learning (comparing algorithm 9.1 and algorithm 9.2). The first change is that whenever we make an error (a non *y*-good goal node is dequeued or none of the queue is *y*-good), we
rollback on error   update the weight vector **w**. Secondly, when an error is made, instead of continuing along this bad search path, we instead clear the queue and insert all the *correct* moves we could have made.

Note that this algorithm cannot fail (in the sense that it will always find a goal state). Aiming at a contradiction, suppose it were to fail; this would mean that *nodes* would have become empty. Since "Operators" will never return an empty set, this means that *sibs* must have been empty. But since a node that is inserted into the queue is either itself *y*-good or has a *y*-good ancestor, the queue could never have become empty.[2]

9.3.4 Parameter Updates

We propose two methods for updating the model parameters; both function in an online manner. To facilitate discussion, it will be useful to define a particular notion of *margin* that we will use for the remainder of this chapter. The following notation will be useful: for each example *x*, for each positive integer *j*, let S_{xj} be the set of all search nodes node that are reachable after executing *j* steps of search for the

---

2. There may be a complication with cyclic search spaces – in this case, both algorithms need to be augmented with some memory to avoid such loops, as is standard.

example x. Note that the value of S_{xj} will be dependent on the search algorithm used. For example, for greedy search, S_{xj} will be the set of all nodes that are j steps away from the starting node.

search margin   We now define a search margin. We say that a weight vector $\mathbf{w}$ obtains a margin γ on a training set D if: for each $(x, y) \in D$, for each positive integer j, there exists a y-good node $g \in S_{xj}$ such that $\langle \mathbf{w}, \Phi(x, g) \rangle - \langle \mathbf{w}, \Phi(x, n) \rangle > \gamma$ for all y-bad $n \in S_{xj}$. In words, a weight vector attains a margin of γ if after some number of search steps at a fixed beam, it is always possible to pick out a y-good node from the beam with a margin of γ. We similarly define a dataset to be linearly separable if there exists a weight vector that attains a positive margin on the training set.

9.3.4.1 Perceptron Updates

A simple perceptron-style update rule (Rosenblatt, 1958), given $(\mathbf{w}, x, sibs, nodes)$:

$$\mathbf{w} \leftarrow \mathbf{w} + \Delta \tag{9.2}$$

$$\Delta = \sum_{n \in sibs} \frac{\Phi(x, n)}{|sibs|} - \sum_{n \in nodes} \frac{\Phi(x, n)}{|nodes|} \tag{9.3}$$

When an update is made, the feature vector for the incorrect decisions are subtracted off, and the feature vectors for all possible correct decisions are added. Whenever $|sibs| = |nodes| = 1$, this looks exactly like the standard perceptron update. When there is only one sibling but many nodes, this resembles the gradient of the log-likelihood for conditional models using stochastic updates. In that work, different "weighting" schemes are proposed, including, for instance, one that weights the nodes in the sums proportional to the loss suffered; such schemes are also possible in our framework. We do not explore such options here. Based on this update, we can prove the following theorem, which depends on the assumption of a positive real R such that $\forall (x, y) \in D$ it holds that $\|\Phi(x, g) - \Phi(x, n)\| \leq R$, for all j and all $n \in S_{xj}$ and y-good $g \in S_{xj}$.

mistake bound   **Theorem 53** *For any training sequence that is separable by a margin of size γ*
for LaSO   *using a weight vector with unit norm, using the perceptron update rule the number of errors made during training is bounded above by R^2/γ^2.*

Proof   The proof mirrors the proof of the standard perceptron convergence theorem (Rosenblatt, 1958).

Let $\mathbf{w}^{(k)}$ denote the weight vector before the kth update; so that $\mathbf{w}^{(1)}$ is the zero vector. Suppose the kth update is made on example (x, y) with a current beam B that does not contain a y-good node. Note that since the start node is always y-good, B must have been the result of at least one step of enqueuing.

The parent node of the beam B must have been y-good; let S denote the set of all y-good children of this parent node. Then, by definition of the perceptron updates, we have

$$\left\|\mathbf{w}^{(k+1)}\right\|^2 = \left\|\mathbf{w}^{(k)} + \Delta\right\|^2 = \left\|\mathbf{w}^{(k)}\right\|^2 + 2\left\langle\mathbf{w}^{(k)}, \Delta\right\rangle + ||\Delta||^2$$
$$\leq \left\|\mathbf{w}^{(k)}\right\|^2 + 0 + R^2$$

The first equality is by definition, and the second is by algebra. The inequality is due to two observations. First, each node in B must outweigh each node in S, implying that the average score of each node in B outweighs the average score of each node in S. Second, that $||\Delta||$ is bounded by R (by assumption). By induction, we see that $\left\|\mathbf{w}^{(k+1)}\right\|^2 \leq kR^2$.

Next, let $\mathbf{u}$ be a weight vector that obtains a margin of γ on the training set; we obtain a lower bound on $\left\langle\mathbf{u}, \mathbf{w}^{(k+1)}\right\rangle$.

$$\left\langle\mathbf{u}, \mathbf{w}^{(k+1)}\right\rangle = \left\langle\mathbf{u}, \mathbf{w}^{(k)}\right\rangle + \langle\mathbf{u}, \Delta\rangle \geq \left\langle\mathbf{u}, \mathbf{w}^{(k)}\right\rangle + \gamma$$

Here, the fact that $\langle\mathbf{u}, \Delta\rangle \geq \gamma$ follows from the definition of margin and the fact that the elements that enter into Δ form a subset of S_{xj} for some $j > 0$, and the fact that $||\mathbf{u}|| \leq q$. By induction, $\left\langle\mathbf{u}, \mathbf{w}^{(k+1)}\right\rangle \geq k\gamma$.

Putting the two results together, we get $\sqrt{k}R \geq \left\|\mathbf{w}^{(k+1)}\right\| \geq \left\langle\mathbf{u}, \mathbf{w}^{(k+1)}\right\rangle \geq k\gamma$, which, after algebra, leads us to conclude that $k \leq (R/\gamma)^2$. ∎

link to classical
AI problems

It is worth commenting that subsequent to the initial publication of the LaSO technique, Xu and Fern (2006) have shown that it can be modified slightly to be applicable to a host of AI planning problems. Of particular interest is an extension they show to the above theorem. Namely, under a slightly stronger definition of margin, they obtain a bound that depends explicitly on the size of the beam. Moreover, their bound holds even when there is not a "dominant" path that holds across the training set. Their bound reduces to ours under the same assumptions, but provides an interesting perspective on the search problem: larger beams imply more computation, but actually give rise to tighter convergence bounds (for an equivalent margin size).

9.3.4.2 *Approximate Large-Margin Updates*

One disadvantage of the perceptron algorithm is that it only updates the weights when errors are made. This can lead to a brittle estimate of the parameters, in which the "good" states are weighted only minimally better than the "bad" states. We would like to enforce a large margin between the good states and bad states, but would like to do so without adding significant computational complexity to the problem. In the case of binary classification, Gentile (2001) has presented an online, approximate large-margin algorithm that trains similarly to a perceptron called ALMA. The primary difference (aside from a step size on the weight updates) is that updates are made if either (a) the algorithm makes a mistake or (b) *the algorithm is close to making a mistake.* Here, we adapt this algorithm to structured outputs in our framework.

Our algorithm, like ALMA, has four parameters: α, B, C, p. α determines the degree of approximation required: for $\alpha = 1$, the algorithm seeks the true maximal margin solution; for $\alpha < 1$, it seeks one within α of the maximal. B and C can be seen as tuning parameters, but a default setting of $B = 1/\alpha$ and $C = \sqrt{2}$ is reasonable (see theorem 54 below). We measure the instance vectors with norm p and the weight vector with its dual value q (where $1/p + 1/q = 1$). We use $p = q = 2$, but large p produces sparser solutions, since the weight norm will approach ℓ_1. The ALMA-inspired update is

$$\mathbf{w} \leftarrow proj\big(\mathbf{w} + Ck^{-1/2}\ proj(\Delta)\big). \tag{9.4}$$

Here, k is the "generation" number of the weight vector (initially 1 and incremented at every update) and $proj(\mathbf{u})$ is the projection of $\mathbf{u}$ into the l_2 unit sphere: $\mathbf{u}/\max\{1, \|\mathbf{u}\|_2\}$. One final change to the algorithm is to downweight the score of all y-good nodes by $(1 - \alpha)Bk^{-1/2}$. Thus, a good node will only survive if it is good by a large margin. This setup gives rise to a bound on the number of updates made using the large-margin updates.

Theorem 54 *For any training sequence that is separable by a margin of size γ using a unit-norm weight vector using the approximate large-margin update rule with parameters $\alpha, B = \sqrt{8}/\alpha, C = \sqrt{2}$, the number of errors made during training is bounded above by $\frac{2}{\gamma^2}\left(\frac{2}{\alpha} - 1\right)^2 + \frac{8}{\alpha} - 4$.*

Proof (sketch) The proof largely follows theorem 3 of Gentile (2001) and is too lengthy to include in full. There are two primary differences between the proof of our statement and the proof of the binary classification counterpart. The first difference is analogous to the change in the perceptron proof (see theorem 53) and requires that we derive the inequality $\langle \mathbf{u}, \Delta \rangle \leq \gamma$ when $\mathbf{u}$ is a unit weight vector with unit norm.

The second aspect of the original ALMA proof that needs to be modified has to do with bounding the normalization factor when projecting $\mathbf{w}$ back into the unit sphere. In order to obtain the stated result, suppose that $\mathbf{u}$ obtains a margin of γ and is of unit length. As in the ALMA result, denote the normalization factor after update k by N_k. We obtain

$$N_{k+1}^2 \leq \left\|\mathbf{w}^{(k)} + \eta_k\Delta\right\|^2 \leq \left\|\mathbf{w}^{(k)}\right\|^2 + \eta_k^2 + 2\eta_k\left\langle \mathbf{w}^{(k)}, \Delta \right\rangle$$
$$\leq 1 + \eta_k^2 + 2(1 - \alpha)\eta_k\gamma.$$

Here, the first inequality is by definition, the second is by algebra and the fact that Δ has unit norm. The last inequality is by definition of the margin. This can be verified by the fact that $\left\langle \mathbf{w}, \sum_{n \in sibs} \mathbf{\Phi}(x, n)/|sibs| - \sum_{n \in nodes} \mathbf{\Phi}(x, n)/|nodes| \right\rangle \leq$

$\langle \mathbf{w}, \max_{n \in sibs} \mathbf{\Phi}(x,n) - \min_{n \in nodes} \mathbf{\Phi}(x,n) \rangle \leq \gamma$, due to the definition of the margin. Therefore, N_k is bounded by $1 + (8/\alpha - 6)/k$. To bound number of updates m by $\gamma m \leq (4/\alpha - 2)\sqrt{4/\alpha - 3 + m/2}$. Algebra completes the proof.   ∎

This theorem gives rise to the following easy corollary, analogous to the perceptron case.

Corollary 55 *Suppose for a given* α, B *and* C *are such that* $C^2 + 2(1-\alpha)BC = 1$; *letting* $\rho = (C\gamma)^{-2}$, *the number of corrections made is bounded above by*

$$\min_{\mathbf{w},\gamma} \frac{1}{\gamma} D_{\mathbf{w},\gamma} + \frac{\rho^2}{2} + \rho \left[\frac{\rho^2}{4} + \frac{1}{\gamma} D_{\mathbf{w},\gamma} + 1 \right]^{1/2}. \tag{9.5}$$

9.4   Experiments

In this section, we describe the results of experiments from related natural language processing tasks of varying difficulty.

9.4.1   Syntactic Chunking

The syntactic chunking problem is a sequence segmentation and labeling problem; for example:

> [Great American]$_{\text{NP}}$ [said]$_{\text{VP}}$ [it]$_{\text{NP}}$ [increased]$_{\text{VP}}$ [its loan-loss reserves]$_{\text{NP}}$ [by]$_{\text{PP}}$ [\$ 93 million]$_{\text{NP}}$ [after]$_{\text{PP}}$ [reviewing]$_{\text{VP}}$ [its loan portfolio]$_{\text{NP}}$, [raising]$_{\text{VP}}$ [its total loan and real estate reserves]$_{\text{NP}}$ [to]$_{\text{PP}}$ [\$ 217 million]$_{\text{NP}}$.

Typical approaches to this problem recast it as a sequence labeling task and then solve it using any of the standard sequence labeling models; see Sha and Pereira (2003) for a prototypical example using conditional random fields (CRFs). The reduction to sequence labeling is typically done through the "BIO" encoding, where the beginning of an X phrase is tagged B-X, the nonbeginning (inside) of an X phrase is tagged I-X, and any word not in a phrase is tagged O (outside). More recently, Sarawagi and Cohen (2005) have described a straightforward extension to the CRF (called a semi-CRF) in which the segmentation and labeling are done directly.

experimental setup   We explore similar models in the context of syntactic chunking, where entire chunks are hypothesized, and no reduction to word-based labels is made. We use the same set of features across all models, separated into "base features" and "metafeatures." The base features apply to words individually, while metafeatures apply to entire chunks. The base features we use are: the chunk length, the word (original, lowercase, stemmed, and original-stem), the case pattern of the word, the first and last 1, 2, and 3 characters, and the part of speech and its first character. We additionally consider membership features for lists of names, locations, abbreviations, stop words, etc. The metafeatures we use are, for any base feature b, b at position i (for any subposition of the chunk), b before/after the chunk, the entire b-sequence in the chunk, and any 2- or 3-gram tuple of bs in the chunk. We use a first-order Markov assumption (chunk label only depends on the most recent previous label) and all features are placed on labels, not on transitions. In this task, the argmax computation from (9.1) *is* tractable; moreover, through a minor adaptation of the standard hidden Markov model (HMM) forward and backward algorithms, we can compute feature expectations, which enable us to do training in a likelihood-based fashion.

Our search space is structured so that each state is the segmentation and labeling of an initial segment of the input string, and an operation extends a state by an entire labeled chunk (of any number of words). For instance, on the example shown at the beginning of this section, the initial hypothesis would be empty; the first correct child would be to hypothesize a chunk of length 2 with the tag NP. The next correct hypothesis would be a chunk of length 1 with tag VP. This process would continue until the end of the sentence is reached. For beam search, we execute search as described, but after every expansion we only retain the b best hypotheses to continue on to the next round.

Our models for this problem are denoted LaSO-perc and LaSO-alma. We vary the beam size over $\{1, 5, 25, \infty\}$, where ∞ denotes full, exact Viterbi search and forward-backward updates similar to those used in the semi-CRF. This points out an important issue in our framework: if the graphical structure of the problem *is* amenable to exact search and exact updates, then the framework can accommodate this. In this case, for example, when using exact search, updates are only made at the end of decoding when the highest ranking output is incorrect (after adjusting the weights down for LaSO-alma); but, other than this exception, the sum over the bad nodes in the updates is computed over the entire search lattice and strongly resemble and are almost identical to those used in the conditional likelihood models for the gradient of the log normalization constant. We always use averaged weights.

We report results on the CoNLL 2000 dataset, which includes 8936 training sentences ($212k$ words) and 2012 test sentences ($47k$ words). We compare our proposed models against several baselines. The first baseline is denoted ZDJ02 and is state of the art for this task (Zhang et al., 2002). The second baseline is the likelihood-trained model, denoted SemiCRF. The third baseline is the standard structured perceptron algorithm, denoted Perceptron. We use 10% of the training data to tune model parameters. For the SemiCRF, this is the prior variance; for the online algorithms, this is the number of iterations to run (for ALMA, $\alpha = 0.9$; changing α in the range $[0.5, 1]$ does not affect the score by more than ± 0.1 in all cases).

The results, in terms of training time, test decoding time, precision, recall and F-score are shown in table 9.1. As we can see, the SemiCRF is by far the most computationally expensive algorithm, more than twice as slow to train than even the LaSO-perc algorithm with infinite beam. The Perceptron has

Table 9.1 Results on syntactic chunking task; columns are training and testing time (h:m), and precision/recall/F-score on test data

	Train	Test	Pre	Rec	F
ZDJ02	-	-	94.3	94.0	94.1
SEMICRF	53:56	:31	92.3	92.1	92.2
PERCEPTRON	18:05	:22	93.4	93.5	93.4
LaSO-PERC (Beam 1)	:55	:01	92.5	92.3	92.4
LaSO-PERC (Beam 5)	1:49	:04	93.7	92.6	93.1
LaSO-PERC (Beam 25)	6:32	:11	94.2	94.1	94.1
LaSO-PERC (Beam ∞)	21:43	:24	94.3	94.1	94.2
LaSO-ALMA (Beam 1)	:51	:01	93.6	92.5	93.0
LaSO-ALMA (Beam 5)	2:04	:04	93.8	94.4	94.3
LaSO-ALMA (Beam 25)	5:59	:10	93.9	94.6	94.4
LaSO-ALMA (Beam ∞)	20:12	:25	94.0	94.8	94.4

roughly comparable training time to the exactly trained LaSO algorithms (slightly faster since it only updates for the best solution), but its performance falls short. Moreover, decoding time for the SEMICRF takes a half-hour for the 2000 test sentences, while the greedy decoding takes only 52 seconds. It is interesting to note that at the larger beam sizes, the large-margin algorithm is actually faster than the perceptron algorithm.

In terms of the quality of the output, the SEMICRF falls short of the previous reported results (92.2 vs. 94.1 F-score). Our simplest model, LaSO-PERC (beam 1) already outperforms the SEMICRF with an F-score of 92.4; the large-margin variant achieves 93.0. Increasing the beam past 5 does not seem to help with large-margin updates, where performance only increases from 94.3 to 94.4 going from a beam of 5 to an infinite beam (at the cost of an extra 18 hours of training time).

9.4.2 Joint Tagging and Chunking

In section 9.4.1, we described an approach to chunking based on search without reduction. This assumed that part of speech tagging had been performed as a preprocessing step. In this section, we discuss models in which part-of-speech tagging and chunking are performed jointly. This task has previously been used as a benchmark for factorized CRFs (Sutton et al., 2004). In that work, the authors discuss many approximate inference methods to deal with the fact that inference in such joint models is intractable.

For this task, we *do* use the BIO encoding of the chunks so that a more direct comparison to the factorized CRFs would be possible. We use the same features as the last section, together with the regular expressions given by Sutton et al.

Table 9.2 Results on joint tagging/chunking task; columns are time to train (h:m), tag accuracy, chunk accuracy, joint accuracy, and chunk F-score

	Train	Test	Tag	Chunk	Joint	F
SUTTON	-	-	98.9	97.4	96.5	93.9
LaSO-PERC (Beam 1)	1:29	:01	98.9	95.5	94.7	93.1
LaSO-PERC (Beam 5)	3:24	:04	98.9	95.8	95.1	93.5
LaSO-PERC (Beam 10)	4:47	:09	98.9	95.9	95.1	93.5
LaSO-PERC (Beam 25)	4:59	:16	98.9	95.9	95.1	93.7
LaSO-PERC (Beam 50)	5:53	:30	98.9	95.8	94.9	93.4
LaSO-ALMA (Beam 1)	:41	:01	99.0	96.5	95.8	93.9
LaSO-ALMA (Beam 5)	1:43	:03	99.0	96.8	96.1	94.2
LaSO-ALMA (Beam 10)	2:21	:07	99.1	97.3	96.4	94.4
LaSO-ALMA (Beam 25)	3:38	:20	99.1	97.4	96.6	94.3
LaSO-ALMA (Beam 50)	3:15	:23	99.1	97.4	96.6	94.4

(2004) (so that our feature set and their feature set are nearly identical). We do, however, omit their final feature, which is active whenever the part of speech at position i matches the most common part of speech assigned by Brill's tagger to the word at position i in a very large corpus of tagged data. This feature is somewhat unrealistic: the CoNLL dataset is a small subset of the Penn Treebank, but the Brill tagger is trained on all of the Treebank. By using this feature, we are, in effect, able to leverage the rest of the Treebank for part of speech tagging. Using just their features without the Brill feature, our performance is quite poor, so we added the lists described in the previous section.

In this problem, states in our search space are again initial taggings of sentences (both part-of-speech tags and chunk tags), but the operators simply hypothesize the part-of-speech and chunk tag for the single next word, with the obvious constraint that an I-X tag cannot follow anything but a B-X or I-X tag.

The results are shown in table 9.2. The models are compared against SUTTON, the factorized CRF with tree reparameterization. We do not report on infinite beams, since such a calculation is intractable. We report training time,[3] testing time, tag accuracy, chunk accuracy, joint accuracy, and F-score for chunking. In this table, we can see that the large-margin algorithms are much faster to train than the perceptron (they require fewer iterations to converge – typically two or three compared to seven or eight). In terms of chunking F-score, none of the perceptron-style algorithms is able to outperform the SUTTON model, but our LaSO-ALMA

---

3. Sutton et al. report a training time of 13.6 hours on 5% of the data (400 sentences); it is unclear from their description how this scales. The scores reported from their model are, however, based on training on the full dataset.

algorithms easily outperform it. With a beam of only 1, we achieve the same F-score (93.9) and with a beam of 10 we get an F-score of 94.4. Comparing table 9.1 and table 9.2, we see that, in general, we can do a better job chunking with the large-margin algorithm when we do part of speech tagging simultaneously.

To verify theorem 54 experimentally, we have run the same experiments using a 1000-sentence ($25k$ word) subset of the training data (so that a positive margin could be found) with a beam of 5. On these data, LaSO-ALMA made $15,932$ corrections. The empirical margin at convergence was 0.01299; according to theorem 54, the number of updates should have been $\leq 17,724$, which is borne out experimentally.

9.4.3 Effect of Beam Size

Clearly, from the results presented in the preceding sections, the beam size plays an important role in the modeling. In many problems, particularly with generative models, training is done exactly, but decoding is done using an inexact search. In this chapter, we have suggested that learning and decoding should be done in the *same* search framework, and in this section we briefly support this suggestion with empirical evidence. For these experiments, we use the joint tagging/chunking model from section 9.4.2 and experiment by independently varying the beam size for *training* and the beam size for *decoding*. We show these results in table 9.3, where the training beam size runs vertically and the decoding beam size runs horizontally; the numbers we report are the chunk F-score.

In these results, we can see that the diagonal (same training beam size as testing beam size) is heavy, indicating that training and testing with the same beam size is useful. This difference is particularly strong when one of the sizes is 1 (i.e., pure greedy search is used). When training with a beam of 1, decoding with a beam of 5 drops the F-score from 93.9 (which is respectable) to 90.5 (which is poor). Similarly, when a beam of 1 is used for decoding, training with a beam of 5 drops performance from 93.9 to 92.8. The differences are less pronounced with beams ≥ 10, but the trend is still evident. We believe (without proof) that when the beam size is large enough that the loss incurred due to search errors is at most the loss incurred due to modeling errors, then using a different beam for training and testing is acceptable. However, when some amount of the loss is due to search errors, then a large part of the learning procedure is aimed at learning how to *avoid* search errors, not necessarily modeling the data. It is in these cases that it is important that the beam sizes match.

9.4.4 Entity Detection and Tracking - EDT

In many natural language applications, such as automatic document summarization, machine translation, question answering, and information retrieval, it is advantageous to preprocess text documents to identify references to entities. An *entity*, loosely defined, is a person, location, organization, or geopolitical entity (GPE) that

Table 9.3 Effect of beam size on performance; columns are for constant decoding beam; rows are for constant training beam. Numbers are chunk F-score on the joint task

	1	**5**	**10**	**25**	**50**
1	**93.9**	92.8	91.9	91.3	90.9
5	90.5	**94.3**	**94.4**	94.1	94.1
10	89.6	**94.3**	**94.4**	94.2	94.2
25	88.7	94.2	**94.5**	**94.3**	94.3
50	88.4	94.2	**94.4**	94.2	**94.4**

exists in the real world. Being able to identify references to real-world entities of these types is an important and difficult natural language processing problem. It involves finding text spans that correspond to an entity, identifying what *type of entity* it is (person, location, etc.), identifying what *type of mention* it is (name, nominal, pronoun, etc.) and finally identifying which *other* mentions in the document it corefers with. The difficulty lies in the fact that there are often many ambiguous ways to refer to the same entity. For example, consider the two sentences below:

$\underline{\text{Bill Clinton}}_{\text{PER}-1}^{\text{NAM}}$ gave a speech today to $\underline{\text{the Senate}}_{\text{ORG}-2}^{\text{NAM}}$. $\underline{\text{The President}}_{\text{PER}-1}^{\text{NOM}}$ outlined $\underline{\text{his}}_{\text{PER}-1}^{\text{PRO}}$ plan for budget reform to $\underline{\text{them}}_{\text{ORG}-2}^{\text{PRO}}$.

There are five entity *mentions* in these two sentences, each of which is underlined (the corresponding mention type and entity type appear as superscripts and subscripts, respectively, with coreference chains marked in the subscripts), but only two *entities*: { Bill Clinton, The president, his } and { the Senate, them }. The *mention detection* task is to identify the entity mentions and their types, without regard for the underlying entity sets, while *coreference resolution* groups a given mentions into sets.

Current state-of-the-art solutions to this problem split it into two parts: mention detection and coreference (Soon et al., 2001; Ng and Cardie, 2002; Florian et al., 2004). First, a model is run that attempts to identify each mention in a text and assign it a type (person, organization, etc.). Then, one holds these mentions fixed and attempts to identify which ones refer to the same entity. This is typically accomplished through some form of clustering, with clustering weights often tuned through some local learning procedure. This pipelining scheme has the significant drawback that the mention detection module cannot take advantage of information from the coreference module. Moreover, within the coreference task, performing learning and clustering as separate tasks makes learning rather ad hoc. In this section, we build a model that solves the mention detection and coreference problems in a simultaneous, joint manner. By doing so, we are able to obtain an empirically superior system as well as integrate a large collection of features that one cannot consider in the standard pipelined approach.

The LaSO framework essentially requires us to specify two components: the search space (and corresponding operations) and the features. These two are inherently tied, since the features rely on the search space, but for the time being we will ignore the issue of the feature functions and focus on the search.

9.4.4.1   Search Space

We structure search in a left-to-right decoding framework: a hypothesis is a complete identification of the initial segment of a document. For instance, on a document with N words, a hypothesis that ends at position $0 < n < N$ is essentially what you would get if you took the full structured output and chopped it off at word n. In the example given in section 9.4.4, one hypothesis might correspond to "<u>Bill Clinton</u> gave a" (which would be a y-good hypothesis), or to "<u>Bill</u> Clinton <u>gave a</u>" (which would not be a y-good hypothesis).

A hypothesis is expanded through the application of the search operations. In our case, the search procedure first chooses the number of words it is going to consume (for instance, to form the mention "Bill Clinton," it would need to consume two words). Then, it decides on an entity type and a mention type (or it opts to call this chunk not an entity (NAE), corresponding to nonunderlined words). Finally, assuming it did not choose to form an NAE, it decides on which of the foregoing coreference chains this entity belongs to, or none (if it is the first mention of a new entity). All these decisions are made simultaneously, and the given hypothesis is then scored.

9.4.4.2   An Example

For concreteness, consider again the text given in the introduction. Suppose that we are at the word "them" and the hypothesis we are expanding is correct. That is, we have correctly identified "Bill Clinton" with entity type "person" and mention type "name"; that we have identified "the Senate" with entity type "organization" and mention type "name"; and that we have identified both "The President" and "his" as entities with entity type "person" and mention types "nominal" and "pronoun," respectively, and that "The President" points back to the chain ⟨Bill Clinton⟩ and that "his" points back to the chain ⟨Bill Clinton, The President⟩.

At this point of search, we have two choices for length: one or two (because there are only two words left: "them" and a period). A first hypothesis would be that the word "them" is NAE; a second hypothesis would be that "them" is a named person and is a new entity; a third hypothesis would be that "them" is a named person and is coreferent with the "Bill Clinton" chain; a fourth hypothesis would be that "them" is a pronominal organization and is a new entity; next, "them" could be a pronominal organization that is coreferent with "the Senate"; and so on. Similar choices would be considered for the string "them ." when two words are selected.

9.4.4.3   Linkage Type

One significant issue that arises in the context of assigning a hypothesis to a coreference chain is how to compute features over that chain. As we will discuss in section 9.4.4.4, the majority of our coreference-specific features are over *pairs* of chunks: the proposed new mention and an antecedent. However, since in general a proposed mention can have well more than one antecedent, we are left with a decision about how to combine this information.

The first, most obvious solution is to essentially do nothing: simply compute the features over all pairs and add them up as usual. This method, however, intuitively has the potential for overcounting the effects of large chains. To compensate for this, one might advocate the use of an *average link* computation, where the score for a coreference chain is computed by averaging over its elements. One might also consider a *max link* or *min link* scenario, where one of the extrema is chosen as the value. Other research has suggested that a simple *last link*, where a mention is simply matched against the most recent mention in a chain might be appropriate, while *first link* might also be appropriate because the first mention of an entity tends to carry the most information.

In addition to these standard linkages, we also consider an *intelligent link* scenario, where the method of computing the link structure depends on the *mention type*. The intelligent link is computed as follows, based on the mention type of the current mention, m:

If m =NAM then: match *first* on NAM elements in the chain; if there are none, match against the *last* NOM element; otherwise, use *max link*.

If m =NOM then: match against the *max* NOM in the chain; otherwise, match against the most *last* NAM; otherwise, use *max link*.

If m =PRO then: use *average link* across all PRO or NAM; if there are none, use *max link*.

The construction of this methodology is guided by intuition (for instance, matching names against names is easy, and the first name tends to be the most complete) and subsequently tuned by experimentation on the development data. One might consider *learning* the best link method, and this may result in better performance, but we do not explore this option in this work. The initial results we present will be based on using intelligent link, but we will also compare the different linkage types explicitly.

9.4.4.4   Feature Functions

All the features we consider are of the form *base feature* × *decision feature*, where base features are functions of the input and decisions are functions of the hypothesis. For instance, a base feature might be something like "the current chunk contains the word 'Clinton' " and a decision feature might be something like "the current chunk is a named person."

Base features. For pedagogical purposes and to facilitate model comparisons, we have separated the base features into 11 classes: lexical, syntactic, pattern-based, count-based, semantic, knowledge-based, class-based, list-based, inference-based, string match features, and history-based features. We will deal with each of these in turn. Finally, we will discuss how these base features are combined into *meta features* that are actually used for prediction.

The class of *lexical features* contains simply computable features of single words. This includes chunk length, words, prefixes and suffixes, stems, etc. The class of *syntactic features* is based on running the LaSO-based part-of-speech tagger and syntactic chunker on the data. We have included a large number of *pattern-based features* surrounding the current word, built largely as regular expressions for identifying pluralization, pleonasticity, and possessiveness. Several *count-based features* apply only to the coreference task and attempt to capture regularities in the size and distribution of coreference chains. These include the total number of entities detected thus far, the total number of mentions, the entity-to-mention ratio, the entity-to-word ratio, the mention-to-word ratio, the size of the hypothesized entity chain, etc. We include a number of *semantic features* drawn from WordNet (Fellbaum, 1998), including synsets and hypernyms both of the current word and previous and next verbs and nouns.

We use a number of *knowledge-based features* that account for the fact that many name to nominal coreference chains are best understood in terms of background knowledge (for instance, that "George W. Bush" is the "President"); we have attempted to take advantage of recent techniques from large scale data mining to extract lists of such pairs (Fleischman et al., 2003; Ravichandran et al., 2005). Additionally, we use *class-based* features based on clustering (Ravichandran et al., 2005) and collocation (Dunning, 1993) calculations. We use standard *list-based features* calculated based on about 40 lists of names, places, and organizations. These combine with *inference-based features* that attempt to infer number and gender based on local context. For the coreference task, we use standard *string match features*: string match, substring match, string overlap, pronoun match, and normalized edit distance. We also attempt to match acronyms by looking at initial letters from the words in long chunks. Finally, we use a set of *history-based features* (Sutton and McCallum, 2004). For instance, if at the beginning of the document we tagged the word "Arafat" as a person's name (perhaps because it followed "Mr." or "Palestinian leader"), and later in the document we again see the word "Arafat," we should be more likely to call this a person's name, again.

Decision features. Our decision features are divided into three classes: simple, coreference, and boundary features. The simple decision features include: is this chunk tagged as an entity; what is its entity type; what is its entity subtype; what is its mention type; what is its entity type/mention type pair. The coreference decision features include: is this entity the start of a chain or continuing an existing chain; what is the entity type of this started (or continued) chain; what is the entity subtype of this started (or continued) chain; what is the mention type of this started chain; what is the mention type of this continued chain; and the mention type of the most recent antecedent. The boundary decision features include: the second- and third-order Markov features over entity type, entity subtype, and mention type; features appearing at the previous (and next) words within a window of three; the words that appear and the previous and next mention boundaries, specified also by entity type, entity subtype, and mention type.

9.4.4.5   Experimental Results

Data. We use the official 2004 ACE training and test set for evaluation purposes; however, we exclude from the training set the Fisher conversations data, since this is very different from the other datasets and there are no Fisher data in the 2004 test set. This amounts to 392 training documents, consisting of $8.1k$ sentences and $160k$ words. There are a total of $24k$ mentions in the data corresponding to $10k$ entities (note that the data are not annotated for cross-document coreference, so instances of "Bill Clinton" appearing in two different documents are counted as two different entities). Roughly half of the entities are people, a fifth are organizations, a fifth are GPEs, and the remaining are mostly locations or facilities. The test data are 192 documents, $3.5k$ sentences, and $64k$ words, with $10k$ mentions to $4.5k$ entities. In all cases, we use a beam of 16 for training and test, and ignore features that occur fewer than five times in the training data.

Evaluation metrics. There are many evaluation metrics possible for these data. We will use as our primary measure of quality the ACE metric. This is computed, roughly, by first matching system mentions with reference mentions, then using those to match system entities with reference entities. There are costs, once this matching is complete, for type errors, false alarms, and misses, which are combined together to give an ACE score, ranging from 0 to 100, with 100 being perfect (we use v.10 of the ACE evaluation script).

Results. The results on the full EDT task are shown in figure 9.1, again compared against the four top-performing systems in the ACE 2004 evaluation workshop. We compare two versions of our system: the jointly trained system and a pipelined version. The pipelined version is the simple concatenation of our stand-alone mention detection model and our coreference module, described in the previous two chapters. As we can see from these results, our EDT model performs comparably to the third-best ACE 2004 system when run in a pipelined fashion, but on par with the first- and second-best systems when run jointly (again, Sys1 annotated extra data). This shows that the joint decoding framework is useful in the EDT task.

Joint vs. pipelined. We compare the performance of the joint system with the pipelined system. For the pipelined system, to build the mention detection module, we use the same technique as for the full system, but simply do not include in the hypotheses the coreference chain information (essentially treating each mention as if it were in its own chain). For the stand-alone coreference system, we assume that the correct mentions and types are always given, and simply

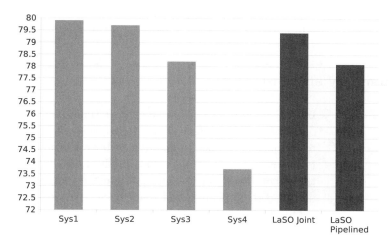

Figure 9.1 ACE scores on the full EDT task for the four best-performing systems at ACE 2004, our LaSO-based joint system, and a pipelined version of our system.

hypothesize the chain (though still in a left-to-right manner). Run as such, the joint model achieves an ACE score of 79.4 and the pipelined model achieves an ACE score of 78.1, a reasonably substantial improvement for performing both tasks simultaneously. We have also computed the performance of these two systems, ignoring the coreference scores (this is done by considering each mention to be its own entity and recomputing the ACE score). In this case, the joint model, ignoring its coreference output, achieves an ACE score of 85.6 and the pipelined model achieves a score of 85.3. The joint model does marginally better, but it is unlikely to be statistically significant. In the 2004 ACE evaluation, the best three performing systems achieved scores of 79.9, 79.7, and 78.2; it is unlikely that our system is significantly worse than these.

One subtle difficulty with the joint model has to do with the online nature of the learning algorithm: at the beginning of training, the model is guessing randomly at what words are entities and what words are not entities. Because of the large number of initial errors made in this part of the task, the weights learned by the coreference model are initially very noisy. We experimented with two methods for compensating for this effect. The first was to give the mention identification model as "head start": it was run for one full pass through the training data, ignoring the coreference aspect and the following iterations were then trained jointly. The second method was to only update the coreference weights when the mention was identified correctly. On development data, the second was more efficient and outperformed the first by a 0.6 ACE score, so we use this for the experiments reported in this section.

Linkage types. As stated in the previous section, the coreference-only task with intelligent link achieves an ACE score of 89.1. The next best score is with min link (88.7) followed by average link with a score of 88.1. There is then a rather large drop with max link to 86.2, followed by another drop for last link to 83.5, and first link performs the poorest, scoring 81.5.

9.5   Summary and Discussion

In this chapter, we have suggested that one view the learning with structured outputs problem as a search optimization problem and that the same search technique should be applied during both learning and decoding. We have presented two parameter update schemes in the LaSO framework, one perceptron-style and the other based on an approximate large-margin scheme, both of which can be modified to work in kernel space or with alternative norms (but not both).

Our framework most closely resembles that used by the incremental parser of Collins and Roark (2004). There are, however, several differences between the two methodologies. Their model builds on standard perceptron-style updates (Collins, 2002) in which a full pass of decoding is done before any updates are made, and thus does not fit into the search optimization framework we have outlined. Collins and Roark found experimentally that stopping the parsing early whenever the correct solution falls out of the beam results in drastically improved performance. However, they had little theoretical justification for doing so. These "early updates," however, do strongly resemble our update strategy, with the difference that when Collins and Roark make an error, they stop decoding the current input and move on to the next; on the other hand, when our model makes an error, it continues from the correct solution(s). This choice is justified both theoretically and experimentally. On the tasks reported in this chapter, we observe the same phenomenon: early updates are better than no early updates, and the search optimization framework is better than early updates. For instance, in the joint tagging/chunking task from section 9.4.2, using a beam of 10, we achieved an F-score of 94.4 in our framework; using only early updates, this drops to 93.1; and using standard perceptron updates, it drops to 92.5. Using the incremental perceptron framework on the EDT task results in abysmal scores. This happens because each output requires roughly one thousand decisions, and by not restarting at failure modes throws out too much data.

Our work also bears a resemblance to training *local classifiers* and combining them together with global inference (Punyakanok and Roth, 2000). The primary difference is that when learning local classifiers, one must assume to have access to all possible decisions and must rank them according to some loss function. Alternatively, in our model, one only needs to consider alternatives that are in the queue at any given time, which gives us direct access to those aspects of the search problem that are easily confused. This, in turn, resembles the online large-margin algorithms proposed by McDonald et al. (2004), which suffer from the problem that the argmax must be computed exactly. Finally, one can also consider our framework in the context of game theory, where it resembles the iterated gradient ascent technique described by Kearns et al. (2000) and the closely related marginal best-response framework (Zinkevich et al., 2005).

We believe that LaSO provides a powerful framework to learn to predict structured outputs. It enables one to build highly effective models of complex tasks efficiently, without worrying about how to normalize a probability distribution, compute expectations, or estimate marginals. It necessarily suffers against probabilistic models in that the output of the classifier will not be a probability; however, in problems with exponential search spaces, normalizing a distribution is quite impractical. In this sense, it compares favorably with the energy-based models proposed by, for example, LeCun and Huang (2005), which also avoid probabilistic normalization, but still require the exact computation of the argmax. We have applied the model to two comparatively trivial tasks: chunking and joint tagging/chunking. Since LaSO is not limited to problems with clean graphical structures, we believe that this framework will be appropriate for many other complex structured learning problems.

Acknowledgments

We thank Alan Fern, Michael Collins, Andrew McCallum, Charles Sutton, Thomas Dietterich, Fernando Pereira, and Ryan McDonald for enlightening discussions, as well as the anonymous reviewers on previous versions of this work, all of whom gave very helpful comments. This work was supported by DARPA-ITO grant NN66001-00-1-9814 and NSF grant IIS-0326276.

10 Energy-Based Models

*Yann LeCun, Sumit Chopra, Raia Hadsell, Marc'Aurelio Ranzato, and
Fu Jie Huang*

Energy-based models (EBMs) capture dependencies between variables by associating a scalar energy to each configuration of the variables. Inference consists in clamping the value of observed variables and finding configurations of the remaining variables that minimize the energy. Learning consists in finding an energy function in which observed configurations of the variables are given lower energies than unobserved ones. The EBM approach provides a common theoretical framework for many learning models, including traditional discriminative and generative approaches, as well as graph-transformer networks, conditional random fields (CRFs), maximum-margin Markov networks (M^3Ns), and several manifold learning methods.

Probabilistic models must be properly normalized, which sometimes requires evaluation of intractable integrals over the space of all possible variable configurations. Since EBMs have no reqpuirement for proper normalization, this problem is naturally circumvented. EBMs can be viewed as a form of nonprobabilistic factor graphs that provide considerably more flexibility in the design of architecture and the training criterion than probabilistic approaches.

10.1 Introduction

The main purpose of statistical modeling and machine learning is to encode dependencies between variables. By capturing those dependencies, a model can be used to answer questions about the values of unknown variables given the values of known variables.

Energy-based models capture dependencies by associating a scalar *energy* (a measure of compatibility) to each configuration of the variables. *Inference*, i.e., making a prediction or decision, consists in setting the value of observed variables and finding values of the remaining variables that minimize the energy. *Learning* consists in finding an energy function that associates low energies to correct values of the remaining variables, and higher energies to incorrect values. A *loss functional*, minimized during learning, is used to measure the quality of the available energy functions. Within this common inference/learning framework, the wide choice of energy functions and loss functionals allows for the design of many types of statistical models, both probabilistic and nonprobabilistic.

Energy-based learning provides a unified framework for many probabilistic and nonprobabilistic approaches to learning, particularly for nonprobabilistic training of graphical models and other structured models. Energy-based learning can be seen as an alternative to probabilistic estimation for prediction, classification, or decision-making tasks. Because there is no requirement for proper normalization, energy-based approaches avoid the problems associated with estimating the normalization constant in probabilistic models. Furthermore, the absence of the normalization condition allows for much more flexibility in the design of learning machines. Most probabilistic models can be viewed as special types of EBMs in which the energy function satisfies certain normalizability conditions, and in which the loss function, optimized by learning, has a particular form.

chapter overview | This chapter presents a tutorial on EBMs, with an emphasis on their use for structured output problems and sequence labeling problems. Section 10.1 introduces EBMs and describes deterministic inference through energy minimization. Section 10.2 introduces energy-based learning and the concept of the loss function. A number of standard and nonstandard loss functions are described, including the perceptron loss, several margin-based losses, and the negative log-likelihood (NLL) loss. The NLL loss can be used to train a model to produce conditional probability estimates. Section 10.3 shows how simple regression and classification models can be formulated in the EBM framework. Section 10.4 concerns models that contain latent variables. Section 10.5 analyzes the various loss functions in detail and gives sufficient conditions that a loss function must satisfy so that its minimization will cause the model to approach the desired behavior. A list of "good" and "bad" loss functions is given. Section 10.6 introduces the concept of nonprobabilistic factor graphs and informally discusses efficient inference algorithms. Section 10.7 focuses on sequence labeling and structured output models. Linear models such as M^3Ns and CRFs are reformulated in the EBM framework. The literature on discriminative learning for speech and handwriting recognition, going back to the late 80's and early 90's, is reviewed. This includes globally trained systems that integrate nonlinear discriminant functions, such as neural networks, and sequence alignment methods, such as dynamic time warping and hidden Markov models (HMMs). Hierarchical models such as the graph transformer network architecture are also reviewed. Finally, the differences, commonalities, and relative advantages of energy-based approaches, probabilistic approaches, and sampling-based approximate methods such as contrastive divergence are discussed in section 10.8.

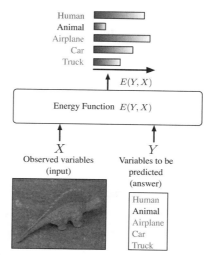

Figure 10.1   A model measures the compatibility between observed variables X and variables to be predicted Y using an *energy function $E(Y, X)$*. For example, X could be the pixels of an image, and Y a discrete label describing the object in the image. Given X, the model produces the answer Y that minimizes the energy E.

10.1.1   Energy-Based Inference

Let us consider a model with two sets of variables, X and Y, as represented in figure 10.1. Variable X could be a vector containing the pixels from an image of an object. Variable Y could be a discrete variable that represents the possible category of the object. For example, Y could take six possible values: animal, human figure, airplane, truck, car, and "none of the above." The model is viewed as an *energy function* which measures the "goodness" (or badness) of each possible configuration of X and Y. The output number can be interpreted as the degree of *compatibility* between the values of X and Y. In the following, we use the convention that small energy values correspond to highly compatible configurations of the variables, while large energy values correspond to highly incompatible configurations of the variables. Functions of this type are given different names in different technical communities; they may be called contrast functions, value functions, or NLL functions. In the following, we will use the term *energy function* and denote it $E(Y, X)$. A distinction should be made between the energy function, which is minimized by the inference process, and the loss functional (introduced in section 10.2), which is minimized by the learning process.

energy $E(X, Y)$ as compatibility mesure

In the most common use of a model, the input X is given (observed from the world), and the model produces the answer Y that is most compatible with the observed X. More precisely, the model must produce the value Y^*, chosen from a set $\mathcal{Y}$, for which $E(Y, X)$ is the smallest:

prediction as
energy
minimization

$$Y^* = \operatorname{argmin}_{Y \in \mathcal{Y}} E(Y, X). \tag{10.1}$$

When the size of the set $\mathcal{Y}$ is small, we can simply compute $E(Y, X)$ for all possible values of $Y \in \mathcal{Y}$ and pick the smallest.

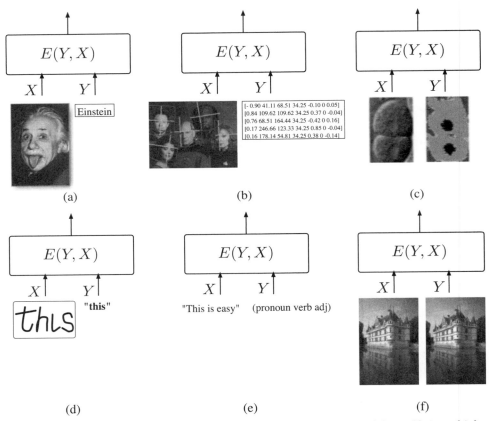

Figure 10.2   Several applications of EBMs: (a) **face recognition:** Y is a high-cardinality discrete variable; (b) **face detection and pose estimation:** Y is a collection of vectors with location and pose of each possible face; (c) **image segmentation:** Y is an image in which each pixel is a discrete label; (d-e) **handwriting recognition and sequence labeling:** Y is a sequence of symbols from a highly structured but potentially infinite set (the set of English sentences). The situation is similar for many applications in natural language processing and computational biology; (f) **image restoration:** Y is a high-dimensional continuous variable (an image).

In general, however, picking the best Y may not be simple. Figure 10.2 depicts several situations in which $\mathcal{Y}$ may be too large to make an exhaustive search practical. In figure 10.2(a), the model is used to recognize a face. In this case, the set $\mathcal{Y}$ is discrete and finite, but its cardinality may be tens of thousands (Chopra et al., 2005). In figure 10.2(b), the model is used to find the faces in an image and estimate their poses. The set $\mathcal{Y}$ contains a binary variable for each location indicating whether a face is present at that location, and a set of continuous variables representing the size and orientation of the face (Osadchy et al., 2005). In figure 10.2(c), the model is used to segment a biological image: each pixel must be classified into one of five categories (cell nucleus, nuclear membrane, cytoplasm, cell membrane, external medium). In this case, $\mathcal{Y}$ contains all the *consistent* label images, i.e. the ones for which the nuclear membranes are encircling the nuclei, the nuclei and cytoplasm are inside the cells walls, etc. The set is discrete, but intractably large. More importantly, members of the set must satisfy complicated consistency constraints (Ning et al., 2005). In figure 10.2(d), the model is used to recognize a handwritten sentence. Here $\mathcal{Y}$ contains all possible sentences of the English language, which is a discrete but infinite set of sequences of symbols (LeCun et al., 1998a). In figure 10.2(f), the model is used to restore an image (by cleaning the noise, enhancing the resolution, or removing scratches). The set $\mathcal{Y}$ contains all possible images (all possible pixel combinations). It is a continuous and high-dimensional set.

For each of the above situations, a specific strategy, called the *inference procedure*, must be employed to find the Y that minimizes $E(Y, X)$. In many real situations, the inference procedure will produce an approximate result, which may or may not be the global minimum of $E(Y, X)$ for a given X. In fact, there may be situations where $E(Y, X)$ has several equivalent minima. The best inference procedure to use often depends on the internal structure of the model. For example, if $\mathcal{Y}$ is continuous and $E(Y, X)$ is smooth and well-behaved with respect to Y, one may use a gradient-based optimization algorithm. If Y is a collection of discrete variables and the energy function can be expressed as a *factor graph*, i.e. a sum of energy functions (factors) that depend on different subsets of variables, efficient inference procedures for factor graphs can be used (see section 10.6) (Kschischang et al., 2001; MacKay, 2003). A popular example of such a procedure is the *max-sum* algorithm. When each element of $\mathcal{Y}$ can be represented as a path in a weighted directed acyclic graph, then the energy for a particular Y is the sum of values on the edges and nodes along a particular path. In this case, the best Y can be found efficiently using dynamic programming (e.g. with the Viterbi algorithm or A^*). This situation often occurs in sequence labeling problems such as speech recognition, handwriting recognition, natural language processing, and biological sequence analysis (e.g. gene finding, protein folding prediction, etc.). Different situations may call for the use of other optimization procedures, including continuous optimization methods such as linear programming, quadratic programming, nonlinear optimization methods, or discrete optimization methods such as simulated annealing, graph cuts, or graph matching. In many cases, exact optimization is impractical, and one must resort to approximate methods, including methods that use surrogate energy functions (such as variational methods).

10.1.2   What Questions Can a Model Answer?

In the preceding discussion, we have implied that the question to be answered by the model is What is the Y that is most compatible with this X?, a situation that occurs in *prediction, classification,* or *decision-making* tasks. However, a model may be used to answer questions of several types:

potential
applications

1. *Prediction, classification, and decision-making*: Which value of Y is most compatible with this X? This situation occurs when the model is used to make hard decisions or to produce an action. For example, if the model is used to drive a robot and avoid obstacles, it must produce a single best decision such as "steer left," "steer right," or "go straight."

2. *Ranking*: Is Y_1 or Y_2 more compatible with this X? This is a more complex task than classification because the system must be trained to produce a complete ranking of all the answers, instead of merely producing the best one. This situation occurs in many data-mining applications where the model is used to select multiple samples that best satisfy a given criterion.

3. *Detection*: Is this value of Y compatible with X? Typically, detection tasks, such as detecting faces in images, are performed by comparing the energy of a *face* label with a threshold. Since the threshold is generally unknown when the system is built, the system must be trained to produce energy values that increase as the image looks less like a face.

4. *Conditional density estimation*: What is the conditional probability distribution over $\mathcal{Y}$ given X? This case occurs when the output of the system is not used directly to produce actions, but is given to a human decision maker or is fed to the input of another, separately built system.

We often think of X as a high-dimensional variable (e.g. an image) and Y as a discrete variable (e.g. a label), but the converse case is also common. This occurs when the model is used for such applications as image restoration, computer graphics, speech and language production, etc. The most complex case is when both X and Y are high-dimensional.

10.1.3   Decision Making vs. Probabilistic Modeling

For decision-making tasks, such as steering a robot, it is merely necessary that the system give the lowest energy to the correct answer. The energies of other answers are irrelevant, as long as they are larger. However, the output of a system must sometimes be combined with that of another system, or fed to the input of another system (or to a human decision maker). Because energies are uncalibrated (i.e. measured in arbitrary units), combining two, separately trained energy-based

calibration of energies

models is not straightforward: there is no a priori guarantee that their energy scales are commensurate. Calibrating energies so as to permit such combinations can be done in a number of ways. However, the only *consistent* way involves turning the collection of energies for all possible outputs into a normalized probability distribution. The simplest and most common method for turning a collection of arbitrary energies into a collection of numbers between 0 and 1 whose sum (or integral) is 1 is through the *Gibbs distribution*:

$$P(Y|X) = \frac{e^{-\beta E(Y,X)}}{\int_{y \in \mathcal{Y}} e^{-\beta E(y,X)}}, \tag{10.2}$$

where β is an arbitrary positive constant akin to an inverse temperature, and the denominator is called the *partition function* (by analogy with similar concepts in statistical physics). The choice of the Gibbs distribution may seem arbitrary, but other probability distributions can be obtained (or approximated) through a suitable redefinition of the energy function. Whether the numbers obtained this way are good probability estimates does not depend on how energies are turned into probabilities, but on how $E(Y, X)$ is estimated from data.

restrictions of probabilistic modeling

It should be noted that the above transformation of energies into probabilities is only possible if the integral $\int_{y \in \mathcal{Y}} e^{-\beta E(y,X)}$ converges. This somewhat restricts the energy functions and domains $\mathcal{Y}$ that can be used. More importantly, there are many practical situations where computing the partition function is intractable (e.g. when $\mathcal{Y}$ has high cardinality), or outright impossible (e.g. when $\mathcal{Y}$ is a high-dimensional variable and the integral has no analytical solution). Hence probabilistic modeling comes with a high price, and should be avoided when the application does not require it.

10.2 Energy-Based Training: Architecture and Loss Function

Training an EBM consists in finding an energy function that produces the best Y for any X. The search for the best energy function is performed within a family of energy functions $\mathcal{E}$ indexed by a parameter W

$$\mathcal{E} = \{E(W, Y, X) : \ W \in \mathcal{W}\}. \tag{10.3}$$

The *architecture* of the EBM is the internal structure of the parameterized energy function $E(W, Y, X)$. At this point, we put no particular restriction on the nature of X, Y, W, and $\mathcal{E}$. When X and Y are real vectors, $\mathcal{E}$ could be as simple as a linear combination of basis functions (as in the case of kernel methods), or a set of neural net architectures and weight values. Section 10.3 gives examples of simple architectures for common applications to classification and regression. When X and Y are variable-size images, sequences of symbols or vectors, or more complex structured objects, $\mathcal{E}$ may represent a considerably richer class of functions. Sections 10.4, 10.6, and 10.7 discuss several examples of such architectures. One advantage of the energy-based approach is that it puts very few restrictions on the nature of $\mathcal{E}$.

To train the model for prediction, classification, or decision making, we are given a set of training samples $\mathcal{S} = \{(X^i, Y^i) : i = 1 \ldots P\}$, where X^i is the input for the ith training sample, and Y^i is the corresponding desired answer. In order to find the best energy function in the family $\mathcal{E}$, we need a way to assess the quality of any particular energy function, based solely on two elements: the training set, and our prior knowledge about the task. This quality measure is called the *loss functional* (i.e. a function of function) and denoted $\mathcal{L}(E, \mathcal{S})$. For simplicity, we often denote it $\mathcal{L}(W, \mathcal{S})$ and simply call it the *loss function*. The learning problem is simply to find the W that minimizes the loss:

$$W^* = \min_{W \in \mathcal{W}} \mathcal{L}(W, \mathcal{S}). \tag{10.4}$$

For most cases, the loss functional is defined as follows:

$$\mathcal{L}(E, \mathcal{S}) = \frac{1}{P} \sum_{i=1}^{P} L(Y^i, E(W, \mathcal{Y}, X^i)) + R(W). \tag{10.5}$$

It is an average taken over the training set of a *per-sample loss functional*, denoted $L(Y^i, E(W, \mathcal{Y}, X^i))$, which depends on the desired answer Y^i and on the energies obtained by keeping the input sample fixed and varying the answer Y. Thus, for each sample, we evaluate a "slice" of the energy surface. The term $R(W)$ is the *regularizer*, and can be used to embed our prior knowledge about which energy functions in our family are preferable to others (in the absence of training data). With this definition, the loss is invariant under permutations of the training samples and under multiple repetitions of the training set.

Naturally, the ultimate purpose of learning is to produce a model that will give good answers for new input samples that are not seen during training. We can rely on general results from statistical learning theory which guarantee that, under simple interchangeability conditions on the samples and general conditions on the family of energy functions (finite VC dimension), the deviation between the value of the loss after minimization on the training set, and the loss on a large, separate set of test samples is bounded by a quantity that converges to zero as the size of training set increases (Vapnik, 1995).

10.2.1 Designing a Loss Functional

Intuitively, the per-sample loss functional should be designed in such a way that it assigns a low loss to *well-behaved* energy functions: energy functions that give the lowest energy to the correct answer and higher energy to all other (incorrect) answers. Conversely, energy functions that do not assign the lowest energy to the correct answers would have a high loss. Characterizing the appropriateness of loss functions (the ones that select the best energy functions) is further discussed in following sections.

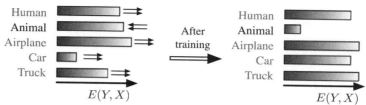

Figure 10.3 How training affects the energies of the possible answers in the discrete case: the energy of the correct answer is decreased, and the energies of incorrect answers are increased, particularly if they are lower than that of the correct answer.

main intuition

Considering only the task of training a model to answer questions of type 1 (prediction, classification, and decision making), the main intuition of the energy-based approach is as follows. Training an EBM consists in shaping the energy function, so that for any given X, the inference algorithm will produce the desired value for Y. Since the inference algorithm selects the Y with the lowest energy, the learning procedure must shape the energy surface so that the desired value of Y has lower energy than all other (undesired) values. Figures 10.3 and 10.4 show examples of energy as a function of Y for a given input sample X^i in cases where Y is a discrete variable and a continuous scalar variable. We note three types of answers:

- Y^i: the correct answer.

- Y^{*i}: the answer produced by the model, i.e. the answer with the lowest energy.

- $\bar{Y}^i$: the *most offending incorrect answer*, i.e. the answer that has the lowest energy among all the incorrect answers. To define this answer in the continuous case, we can simply view all answers within a distance ϵ of Y^i as correct, and all answers beyond that distance as incorrect.

With a properly designed loss function, the learning process should have the effect of "pushing down" on $E(W, Y^i, X^i)$, and "pulling up" on the incorrect energies,

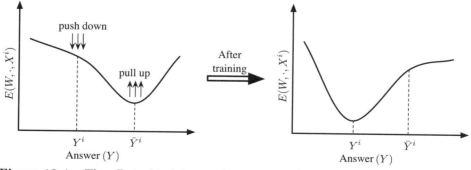

Figure 10.4 The effect of training on the energy surface as a function of the answer Y in the continuous case. After training, the energy of the correct answer Y^i is lower than that of incorrect answers.

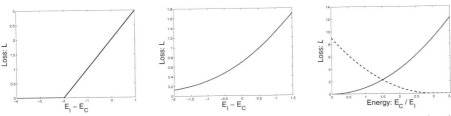

Figure 10.5 The hinge loss (*left*) and log loss (*center*) penalize $E(W, Y^i, X^i) - E(W, \bar{Y}^i, X^i)$ linearly and logarithmically, respectively. The square-square loss (*right*) separately penalizes large values of $E(W, Y^i, X^i)$ (*solid line*) and small values of $E(W, \bar{Y}^i, X^i)$ (*dashed line*) quadratically.

particularly on $E(W, \bar{Y}^i, X^i)$. Different loss functions do this in different ways. Section 10.5 gives sufficient conditions that the loss function must satisfy in order to be guaranteed to shape the energy surface correctly. We show that some widely used loss functions do not satisfy the conditions, while others do.

To summarize: given a training set $\mathcal{S}$, building and training an EBM involves designing four components:

components of EBMs

1. *The architecture*: the internal structure of $E(W, Y, X)$.

2. *The inference algorithm*: the method for finding a value of Y that minimizes $E(W, Y, X)$ for any given X.

3. *The loss function*: $\mathcal{L}(W, \mathcal{S})$ measures the quality of an energy function using the training set.

4. *The learning algorithm*: the method for finding a W that minimizes the loss functional over the family of energy functions $\mathcal{E}$, given the training set.

Properly designing the architecture and the loss function is critical. Any prior knowledge we may have about the task at hand is embedded into the architecture and into the loss function (particularly the regularizer). Unfortunately, not all combinations of architectures and loss functions are allowed. With some combinations, minimizing the loss will not make the model produce the best answers. Choosing the combinations of architecture and loss functions that can learn effectively and efficiently is critical to the energy-based approach, and thus is a central theme of this tutorial.

10.2.2   Examples of Loss Functions

We now describe a number of standard loss functions that have been proposed and used in the machine learning literature. We shall discuss them and classify them as "good" or "bad" in an energy-based setting. For the time being, we set aside the regularization term, and concentrate on the data-dependent part of the loss function.

10.2.2.1 *Energy Loss*

The simplest and the most straightforward of all the loss functions is the energy loss. For a training sample (X^i, Y^i), the per-sample loss is defined simply as

$$L_{energy}(Y^i, E(W, \mathcal{Y}, X^i)) = E(W, Y^i, X^i). \tag{10.6}$$

This loss function, although very popular for things like regression and neural network training, cannot be used to train most architectures: while this loss will push down on the energy of the desired answer, it will not pull up on any other energy. With some architectures, this can lead to a *collapsed solution* in which the energy is constant and equal to zero. The energy loss will only work with architectures that are designed in such a way that pushing down on $E(W, Y^i, X^i)$ will automatically make the energies of the other answers larger. A simple example of such an architecture is $E(W, Y^i, X^i) = ||Y^i - G(W, X^i)||^2$, which corresponds to regression with mean-squared error with G being the regression function.

standard loss
functions do not
pull up

10.2.2.2 *Generalized Perceptron Loss*

The generalized perceptron loss for a training sample (X^i, Y^i) is defined as

$$L_{perceptron}(Y^i, E(W, \mathcal{Y}, X^i)) = E(W, Y^i, X^i) - \min_{Y \in \mathcal{Y}} E(W, Y, X^i). \tag{10.7}$$

This loss is always positive, since the second term is a lower bound on the first term. Minimizing this loss has the effect of pushing down on $E(W, Y^i, X^i)$, while pulling up on the energy of the answer produced by the model.

While the perceptron loss has been widely used in many settings, including for models with structured outputs such as handwriting recognition (LeCun et al., 1998a) and parts-of-speech tagging (Collins, 2002), it has a major deficiency: there is no mechanism for creating an energy gap between the correct answer and the incorrect ones. Hence, as with the energy loss, the perceptron loss may produce flat (or almost flat) energy surfaces if the architecture allows it. Consequently, a meaningful, uncollapsed result is only guaranteed with this loss if a model is used that cannot produce a flat energy surface. For other models, one cannot guarantee anything.

10.2.2.3 *Generalized Margin Losses*

Several loss functions can be described as *margin* losses; the hinge loss, log loss, LVQ2 loss, minimum classification error loss, square-square loss, and square-exponential loss all use some form of margin to create an energy gap between the correct answer and the incorrect answers. Before discussing the generalized margin loss we give the following definitions.

Definition 56 *Let Y be a discrete variable. Then for a training sample (X^i, Y^i), the **most offending incorrect answer** $\bar{Y}^i$ is the answer that has the lowest energy among all answers that are incorrect:*

$$\bar{Y}^i = \text{argmin}_{Y \in \mathcal{Y} \text{ and } Y \neq Y^i} E(W, Y, X^i). \tag{10.8}$$

If Y is a continuous variable, then the definition of the most offending incorrect answer can be defined in a number of ways. The simplest definition is as follows.

Definition 57 *Let Y be a continuous variable. Then for a training sample (X^i, Y^i), the **most offending incorrect answer** $\bar{Y}^i$ is the answer that has the lowest energy among all answers that are at least ϵ away from the correct answer:*

$$\bar{Y}^i = \text{argmin}_{Y \in \mathcal{Y}, \|Y - Y^i\| > \epsilon} E(W, Y, X^i). \tag{10.9}$$

The generalized margin loss is a more robust version of the generalized perceptron loss. It directly uses the energy of the most offending incorrect answer in the contrastive term:

$$L_{\text{margin}}(W, Y^i, X^i) = Q_m \left(E(W, Y^i, X^i), E(W, \bar{Y}^i, X^i) \right). \tag{10.10}$$

Here m is a positive parameter called the *margin* and $Q_m(e)$ is a convex function whose gradient has a positive dot product with the vector $[1, -1]$ in the region where $E(W, Y^i, X^i) + m > E(W, \bar{Y}^i, X^i)$. In other words, the loss surface is slanted toward low values of $E(W, Y^i, X^i)$ and high values of $E(W, \bar{Y}^i, X^i)$ wherever $E(W, Y^i, X^i)$ is not smaller than $E(W, \bar{Y}^i, X^i)$ by at least m. Some special cases of the generalized margin loss are given below:

generalized margin losses

Hinge loss: A particularly popular example of generalized margin loss is the *hinge loss*, which is used in combination with linearly parameterized energies and a quadratic regularizer in support vector machines (Vapnik, 1995), support vector Markov models (Altun and Hofmann, 2003), and M³Ns (Taskar et al., 2004b):

$$L_{\text{hinge}}(W, Y^i, X^i) = \max \left(0, m + E(W, Y^i, X^i) - E(W, \bar{Y}^i, X^i) \right), \tag{10.11}$$

where m is the positive margin. The shape of this loss function is given in figure 10.5. The difference between the energies of the correct answer and the most offending incorrect answer is penalized linearly when larger than $-m$. The hinge loss only depends on energy differences, hence individual energies are not constrained to take any particular value.

Log loss: A common variation of the hinge loss is the *log loss*, which can be seen as a "soft" version of the hinge loss with an infinite margin (see figure 10.5, center):

$$L_{\text{log}}(W, Y^i, X^i) = \log \left(1 + e^{E(W, Y^i, X^i) - E(W, \bar{Y}^i, X^i)} \right). \tag{10.12}$$

LVQ2 loss: One of the very first proposals for discriminatively training sequence labeling systems (particularly speech recognition systems) is a version of Kohonen's LVQ2 loss. This loss has been advocated by Driancourt and Bottou since the early

90's (Driancourt and Bottou, 1991; Driancourt and Gallinari, 1992a,b; Driancourt, 1994; McDermott, 1997; McDermott and Katagiri, 1992):

$$L_{\text{lvq2}}(W, Y^i, X^i) = \min\left(1, \max\left(0, \frac{E(W, Y^i, X^i) - E(W, \bar{Y}^i, X^i)}{\delta E(W, \bar{Y}^i, X^i)}\right)\right), \quad (10.13)$$

where δ is a positive parameter. LVQ2 is a zero-margin loss, but it has the peculiarity of saturating the ratio between $E(W, Y^i, X^i)$ and $E(W, \bar{Y}^i, X^i)$ to $1 + \delta$. This mitigates the effect of outliers by making them contribute a nominal cost M to the total loss. This loss function is a continuous approximation of the number of classification errors. Unlike generalized margin losses, the LVQ2 loss is nonconvex in $E(W, Y^i, X^i)$ and $E(W, \bar{Y}^i, X^i)$.

MCE loss: The MCE (minimum classification error) loss was originally proposed by Juang et al. in the context of discriminative training for speech recognition systems (Juang et al., 1997). The motivation was to build a loss function that also approximately counts the number of classification errors, while being smooth and differentiable. The number of classification errors can be written as

$$\theta\left(E(W, Y^i, X^i) - E(W, \bar{Y}^i, X^i)\right), \quad (10.14)$$

where θ is the step function (equal to zero for negative arguments, and 1 for positive arguments). However, this function is not differentiable, and therefore very difficult to optimize. The MCE loss "softens" it with a sigmoid:

$$L_{\text{mce}}(W, Y^i, X^i) = \sigma\left(E(W, Y^i, X^i) - E(W, \bar{Y}^i, X^i)\right), \quad (10.15)$$

where σ is the logistic function $\sigma(x) = (1 + e^{-x})^{-1}$. As with the LVQ2 loss, the saturation ensures that mistakes contribute a nominal cost to the overall loss. Although the MCE loss does not have an explicit margin, it does create a gap between $E(W, Y^i, X^i)$ and $E(W, \bar{Y}^i, X^i)$. The MCE loss is nonconvex.

Square-square loss: Unlike the hinge loss, the square-square loss treats the energy of the correct answer and the most offending answer separately (LeCun and Huang, 2005; Hadsell et al., 2006):

$$L_{\text{sq−sq}}(W, Y^i, X^i) = E(W, Y^i, X^i)^2 + \left(\max(0, m - E(W, \bar{Y}^i, X^i))\right)^2. \quad (10.16)$$

Large values of $E(W, Y^i, X^i)$ and small values of $E(W, \bar{Y}^i, X^i)$ below the margin m are both penalized quadratically (see figure 10.5). Unlike the margin loss, the square-square loss "pins down" the correct answer energy at zero and "pins down" the incorrect answer energies above m. Therefore, it is only suitable for energy functions that are bounded below by zero, notably in architectures whose output module measures some sort of distance.

Square-exponential (LeCun and Huang, 2005; Chopra et al., 2005; Osadchy et al., 2005): The *square-exponential* loss is similar to the *square-square* loss. It only differs in the contrastive term: instead of a quadratic term it has the exponential of the negative energy of the most offending incorrect answer:

$$L_{\text{sq-exp}}(W, Y^i, X^i) = E(W, Y^i, X^i)^2 + \gamma e^{-E(W, \bar{Y}^i, X^i)}, \qquad (10.17)$$

where γ is a positive constant. Unlike the square-square loss, this loss has an infinite margin and pushes the energy of the incorrect answers to infinity with exponentially decreasing force.

Negative log-likelihood loss: The motivation for the NLL loss comes from probabilistic modeling. It is defined as

$$L_{\text{nll}}(W, Y^i, X^i) = E(W, Y^i, X^i) + \mathcal{F}_\beta(W, \mathcal{Y}, X^i). \qquad (10.18)$$

Where $\mathcal{F}$ is the *free energy* of the ensemble $\{E(W, y, X^i), y \in \mathcal{Y}\}$:

$$\mathcal{F}_\beta(W, \mathcal{Y}, X^i) = \frac{1}{\beta} \log \left(\int_{y \in \mathcal{Y}} \exp\left(-\beta E(W, y, X^i)\right) \right), \qquad (10.19)$$

where β is a positive constant akin to an inverse temperature. This loss can only be used if the exponential of the negative energy is integrable over $\mathcal{Y}$, which may not be the case for some choices of energy function or $\mathcal{Y}$.

The form of the NLL loss stems from a probabilistic formulation of the learning problem in terms of the maximum conditional probability principle. Given the training set $\mathcal{S}$, we must find the value of the parameter that maximizes the conditional probability of all the answers given all the inputs in the training set. Assuming that the samples are independent, and denoting by $P(Y^i|X^i, W)$ the conditional probability of Y^i given X^i that is produced by our model with parameter W, the conditional probability of the training set under the model is a simple product over samples:

$$P(Y^1, \ldots, Y^P | X^1, \ldots, X^P, W) = \prod_{i=1}^{P} P(Y^i | X^i, W). \qquad (10.20)$$

Applying the maximum likelihood estimation principle, we seek the value of W that maximizes the above product, or the one that minimizes the negative log of the above product:

$$-\log \prod_{i=1}^{P} P(Y^i | X^i, W) = \sum_{i=1}^{P} -\log P(Y^i | X^i, W). \qquad (10.21)$$

Using the Gibbs distribution (10.2), we get

$$-\log \prod_{i=1}^{P} P(Y^i | X^i, W) = \sum_{i=1}^{P} \beta E(W, Y^i, X^i) + \log \int_{y \in \mathcal{Y}} e^{-\beta E(W, y, X^i)}. \qquad (10.22)$$

The final form of the NLL loss is obtained by dividing the above expression by P and β (which has no effect on the position of the minimum):

$$\mathcal{L}_{\mathrm{nll}}(W, \mathcal{S}) = \frac{1}{P} \sum_{i=1}^{P} \left(E(W, Y^i, X^i) + \frac{1}{\beta} \log \int_{y \in \mathcal{Y}} e^{-\beta E(W, y, X^i)} \right). \quad (10.23)$$

While many of the previous loss functions involved only $E(W, \bar{Y}^i, X^i)$ in their contrastive term, the NLL loss combines all the energies for all values of Y in its contrastive term $\mathcal{F}_\beta(W, \mathcal{Y}, X^i)$. This term can be interpreted as the Helmholtz free energy (log partition function) of the ensemble of systems with energies $E(W, Y, X^i)$, $Y \in \mathcal{Y}$. This contrastive term causes the energies of all the answers to be pulled up. The energy of the correct answer is also pulled up, but not as hard as it is pushed down by the first term. This can be seen in the expression of the gradient for a single sample:

$$\frac{\partial L_{\mathrm{nll}}(W, Y^i, X^i)}{\partial W} = \frac{\partial E(W, Y^i, X^i)}{\partial W} - \int_{Y \in \mathcal{Y}} \frac{\partial E(W, Y, X^i)}{\partial W} P(Y | X^i, W), \quad (10.24)$$

where $P(Y|X^i, W)$ is obtained through the Gibbs distribution:

$$P(Y|X^i, W) = \frac{e^{-\beta E(W, Y, X^i)}}{\int_{y \in \mathcal{Y}} e^{-\beta E(W, y, X^i)}}. \quad (10.25)$$

Hence, the contrastive term pulls up on the energy of each answer with a force proportional to the likelihood of that answer under the model. Unfortunately, there are many interesting models for which computing the integral over $\mathcal{Y}$ is intractable. Evaluating this integral is a major topic of research. Considerable efforts have been devoted to approximation methods, including clever organization of the calculations, Monte-Carlo sampling methods, and variational methods. While these methods have been devised as approximate ways of minimizing the NLL loss, they can be viewed in the energy-based framework as different strategies for choosing the Ys whose energies will be pulled up.

Interestingly, the NLL loss reduces to the generalized perceptron loss when $\beta \to \infty$ (zero temperature), and reduces to the log loss (10.12) when $\mathcal{Y}$ has two elements (e.g. binary classification).

The NLL loss has been used extensively by many authors under various names. In the neural network classification literature, it is known as the *cross-entropy loss* (Solla et al., 1988). It was also used by Bengio et al. to train an energy-based language model (Bengio et al., 2003). It has been widely used under the name *maximum mutual information estimation* for discriminatively training speech recognition systems since the late 80's, including HMMs with mixtures of Gaussians (Bahl et al., 1986), and HMM-neural net hybrids (Bengio et al., 1990, 1992; Haffner, 1993; Bengio, 1996). It has also been used extensively for global discriminative training of handwriting recognition systems that integrate neural nets and HMMs under the names *maximum mutual information* (Bengio et al., 1993; LeCun and Bengio, 1994; Bengio et al., 1995; LeCun et al., 1997; Bottou et al., 1997) and *discrim-*

inative forward training (LeCun et al., 1998a). Finally, it is the loss function of choice for training other probabilistic discriminative sequence labeling models such as input/output HMM (Bengio and Frasconi, 1996), CRFs (Lafferty et al., 2001), and discriminative random fields (Kumar and Hebert, 2004).

Minimum empirical error loss: Some authors have argued that the NLL loss puts too much emphasis on mistakes: (10.20) is a product whose value is dominated by its smallest term. Hence, Ljolje et al. (1990) proposed the *minimum empirical error (MEE) loss*, which combines the conditional probabilities of the samples additively instead of multiplicatively:

$$L_{\mathrm{mee}}(W, Y^i, X^i) = 1 - P(Y^i | X^i, W). \tag{10.26}$$

Substituting (10.2) we get

$$L_{\mathrm{mee}}(W, Y^i, X^i) = 1 - \frac{e^{-\beta E(W, Y^i, X^i)}}{\int_{y \in \mathcal{Y}} e^{-\beta E(W, y, X^i)}}. \tag{10.27}$$

As with the MCE loss and the LVQ2 loss, the MEE loss saturates the contribution of any single error. This makes the system more robust to label noise and outliers, which is of particular importance to applications such as speech recognition, but it makes the loss nonconvex. As with the NLL loss, MEE requires evaluating the partition function.

10.3   Simple Architectures

To substantiate the ideas presented thus far, this section demonstrates how simple models of classification and regression can be formulated as EBMs. This sets the stage for the discussion of good and bad loss functions, as well as for the discussion of advanced architectures for structured prediction.

10.3.1   Regression

Figure 10.6(a) shows a simple architecture for regression or function approximation. The energy function is the squared error between the output of a regression function $G_W(X)$ and the variable to be predicted Y, which may be a scalar or a vector:

$$E(W, Y, X) = \frac{1}{2} \|G_W(X) - Y\|^2. \tag{10.28}$$

The inference problem is trivial: the value of Y that minimizes E is equal to $G_W(X)$. The minimum energy is always equal to zero. When used with this architecture, the energy loss, perceptron loss, and NLL loss are all equivalent because the contrastive

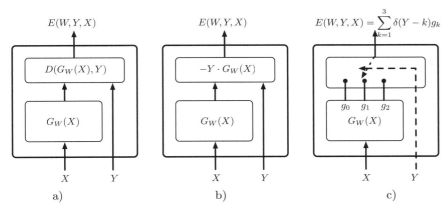

Figure 10.6   Simple learning models viewed as EBMs: **(a) a regressor:** The energy is the discrepancy between the output of the regression function $G_W(X)$ and the answer Y. The best inference is simply $Y^* = G_W(X)$; **(b) a simple two-class classifier:** The set of possible answers is $\{-1, +1\}$. The best inference is $Y^* = \text{sign}(G_W(X))$; **(c) a multiclass classifier:** The discriminant function produces one value for each of the three categories. The answer, which can take three values, controls the position of a "switch," which connects one output of the discriminant function to the energy function. The best inference is the index of the smallest output component of $G_W(X)$.

term of the perceptron loss is zero, and that of the NLL loss is constant (it is a Gaussian integral with a constant variance):

$$\mathcal{L}_{\text{energy}}(W, \mathcal{S}) = \frac{1}{P} \sum_{i=1}^{P} E(W, Y^i, X^i) = \frac{1}{2P} \sum_{i=1}^{P} ||G_W(X^i) - Y^i||^2. \quad (10.29)$$

This corresponds to standard regression with mean-squared error.

A popular form of regression occurs when G is a linear function of the parameters:

$$G_W(X) = \sum_{k=1}^{N} w_k \phi_k(X) = W^T \Phi(X). \quad (10.30)$$

The $\phi_k(X)$ are a set of N *features*, and w_k are the components of an N-dimensional parameter vector W. For concision, we use the vector notation $W^T \Phi(X)$, where W^T denotes the transpose of W, and $\Phi(X)$ denotes the vector formed by each $\phi_k(X)$. With this linear parameterization, training with the energy loss reduces to an easily solvable least-squares minimization problem, which is convex:

$$W^* = \text{argmin}_W \left[\frac{1}{2P} \sum_{i=1}^{P} ||W^T \Phi(X^i) - Y^i||^2 \right]. \quad (10.31)$$

In simple models, the feature functions are handcrafted by the designer, or separately trained from unlabeled data. In the dual form of kernel methods, they are defined as $\phi_k(X) = K(X, X^k)$, $k = 1 \ldots P$, where K is the kernel function. In more complex models such as multilayer neural networks and others, the ϕ's may themselves be parameterized and subject to learning, in which case the regression function is no longer a linear function of the parameters and hence the loss function may not be convex in the parameters.

10.3.2   Two-Class Classifier

Figure 10.6(b) shows a simple two-class classifier architecture. The variable to be predicted is binary: $\mathcal{Y} = \{-1, +1\}$. The energy function can be defined as

$$E(W, Y, X) = -YG_W(X), \tag{10.32}$$

where $G_W(X)$ is a scalar-valued *discriminant function* parameterized by W. Inference is trivial:

$$Y^* = \operatorname{argmin}_{Y \in \{-1,1\}} -YG_W(X) = \operatorname{sign}(G_W(X)). \tag{10.33}$$

Learning can be done using a number of different loss functions, which include the perceptron loss, hinge loss, and NLL loss. Substituting (10.32) and (10.33) into the perceptron loss (10.7), we get

$$\mathcal{L}_{\text{perceptron}}(W, \mathcal{S}) = \frac{1}{P} \sum_{i=1}^{P} \left(\operatorname{sign}(G_W(X^i)) - Y^i \right) G_W(X^i). \tag{10.34}$$

The stochastic gradient descent update rule to minimize this loss is

$$W \leftarrow W + \eta \left(Y^i - \operatorname{sign}(G_W(X^i)) \right) \frac{\partial G_W(X^i)}{\partial W}, \tag{10.35}$$

where η is a positive step size. If we choose $G_W(X)$ in the family of linear models, the energy function becomes $E(W, Y, X) = -YW^T\Phi(X)$, the perceptron loss becomes

$$\mathcal{L}_{\text{perceptron}}(W, \mathcal{S}) = \frac{1}{P} \sum_{i=1}^{P} \left(\operatorname{sign}(W^T\Phi(X^i)) - Y^i \right) W^T\Phi(X^i), \tag{10.36}$$

and the stochastic gradient descent update rule becomes the familiar perceptron learning rule: $W \leftarrow W + \eta \left(Y^i - \operatorname{sign}(W^T\Phi(X^i)) \right) \Phi(X^i)$.

The hinge loss (10.11) with the two-class classifier energy (10.32) yields

$$\mathcal{L}_{\text{hinge}}(W, \mathcal{S}) = \frac{1}{P} \sum_{i=1}^{P} \max(0, m + 2Y^iG_W(X^i)). \tag{10.37}$$

Using this loss with $G_W(X) = W^TX$ and a regularizer of the form $||W||^2$ gives the familiar linear support vector machine.

The NLL loss (10.23) with (10.32) yields

$$\mathcal{L}_{\text{nll}}(W, \mathcal{S}) = \frac{1}{P} \sum_{i=1}^{P} \left[-Y^iG_W(X^i) + \log\left(e^{Y^iG_W(X^i)} + e^{-Y^iG_W(X^i)} \right) \right]. \tag{10.38}$$

Using the fact that $\mathcal{Y} = \{-1, +1\}$, we obtain

$$\mathcal{L}_{\text{nll}}(W, \mathcal{S}) = \frac{1}{P} \sum_{i=1}^{P} \log \left(1 + e^{-2Y^i G_W(X^i)} \right), \tag{10.39}$$

which is equivalent to the log loss (10.12). Using a linear model as described above, the loss function becomes

$$\mathcal{L}_{\text{nll}}(W, \mathcal{S}) = \frac{1}{P} \sum_{i=1}^{P} \log \left(1 + e^{-2Y^i W^T \Phi(X^i)} \right). \tag{10.40}$$

This particular combination of architecture and loss is the familiar *logistic regression* method.

10.3.3 Multiclass Classifier

Figure 10.6(c) shows an example of architecture for multiclass classification for three classes. A discriminant function $G_W(X)$ produces an output vector $[g_1, g_2, \ldots, g_C]$ with one component for each of the C categories. Each component g_j can be interpreted as a "penalty" for assigning X to the jth category. A discrete switch module selects which of the components is connected to the output energy. The position of the switch is controlled by the discrete variable $Y \in \{1, 2, \ldots, C\}$, which is interpreted as the category. The output energy is equal to $E(W, Y, X) = \sum_{j=1}^{C} \delta(Y - j) g_j$, where $\delta(Y - j)$ is the Kronecker delta function: $\delta(u) = 1$ for $u = 0$; $\delta(u) = 0$ otherwise. Inference consists in setting Y to the index of the smallest component of $G_W(X)$.

The perceptron loss, hinge loss, and NLL loss can be directly translated to the multiclass case.

10.3.4 Implicit Regression

The architectures described in the previous section are simple functions of Y with a single minimum within the set $\mathcal{Y}$. However, there are tasks for which multiple answers are equally good. Examples include robot navigation, where turning left or right may get around an obstacle equally well, or a language model in which the sentence segment "the cat ate the" can be followed equally well by "mouse" or "bird."

More generally, the dependency between X and Y sometimes cannot be expressed as a function that maps X to Y (e.g., consider the constraint $X^2 + Y^2 = 1$). In this case, which we call *implicit regression*, we model the constraint that X and Y must satisfy and design the energy function such that it measures the violation of the constraint. Both X and Y can be passed through functions, and the energy is a function of their outputs. A simple example is

$$E(W, Y, X) = \frac{1}{2} \| G_X(W_X, X) - G_Y(W_Y, Y) \|^2. \tag{10.41}$$

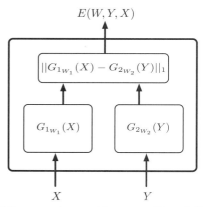

$$E(W, Y, X)$$

$$||G_{1_{W_1}}(X) - G_{2_{W_2}}(Y)||_1$$

$$G_{1_{W_1}}(X) \qquad G_{2_{W_2}}(Y)$$

$$X \qquad Y$$

Figure 10.7   The implicit regression architecture. X and Y are passed through two functions $G_{1_{W_1}}$ and $G_{2_{W_2}}$. This architecture allows multiple values of Y to have low energies for a given X.

Siamese
architectures

For some problems, the function G_X must be different from the function G_Y. In other cases, G_X and G_Y must be instances of the same function G. An interesting example is the *Siamese* architecture (Bromley et al., 1993): variables X_1 and X_2 are passed through two instances of a function G_W as shown in figure 10.7. A binary label Y determines the constraint on $G_W(X_1)$ and $G_W(X_2)$: if $Y = 0$, $G_W(X_1)$ and $G_W(X_2)$ should be equal, and if $Y = 1$, $G_W(X_1)$ and $G_W(X_2)$ should be different. In this way, the regression on X_1 and X_2 is implicitly learned through the constraint Y rather than explicitly learned through supervision. Siamese architectures are used to learn similarity metrics with labeled examples. When two input samples X_1 and X_2 are known to be similar (e.g. two pictures of the same person), $Y = 0$; when they are different, $Y = 1$.

Siamese architectures were originally designed for signature verification (Bromley et al., 1993). More recently they have been used with the square-exponential loss (10.17) to learn a similarity metric with application to face recognition (Chopra et al., 2005). They have also been used with the square-square loss (10.16) for unsupervised learning of manifolds (Hadsell et al., 2006).

In other applications, a single nonlinear function combines X and Y. An example of such architecture is the trainable language model of Bengio et al (Bengio et al., 2003). Under this model, the input X is a sequence of several successive words in a text, and the answer Y is the the next word in the text. Since many different words can follow a particular word sequence, the architecture must allow multiple values of Y to have low energy. The authors used a multilayer neural net as the function $G(W, X, Y)$, and chose to train it with the NLL loss. Because of the high cardinality of $\mathcal{Y}$ (equal to the size of the English dictionary), they had to use approximations (importance sampling) and had to train the system on a cluster machine.

The current section often referred to architectures in which the energy was linear or quadratic in W, and the loss function was convex in W, but it is important to keep in mind that much of the discussion applies equally well to more complex architectures, as we will see later.

10.4   Latent Variable Architectures

Energy minimization is a convenient way to represent the general process of reasoning and inference. In the usual scenario, the energy is minimized with respect to the variables to be predicted Y, given the observed variables X. During training, the correct value of Y is given for each training sample. However there are numerous applications where it is convenient to use energy functions that depend on a set of hidden variables Z whose correct value is never (or rarely) given to us, even during training. For example, we could imagine training the face detection system depicted in figure 10.2(b) with data for which the scale and pose information of the faces is not available. For these architectures, the inference process for a given set of variables X and Y involves minimizing over these unseen variables Z:

$$E(Y, X) = \min_{Z \in \mathcal{Z}} E(Z, Y, X). \tag{10.42}$$

latent/missing
variables

Such hidden variables are called *latent variables*, by analogy with a similar concept in probabilistic modeling. The fact that the evaluation of $E(Y, X)$ involves a minimization over Z does not significantly impact the approach described so far, but the use of latent variables is so ubiquitous that it deserves special treatment.

In particular, some insight can be gained by viewing the inference process in the presence of latent variables as a simultaneous minimization over Y and Z:

$$Y^* = \mathrm{argmin}_{Y \in \mathcal{Y}, Z \in \mathcal{Z}} E(Z, Y, X). \tag{10.43}$$

Latent variables can be viewed as intermediate results on the way to finding the best output Y. At this point, one could argue that there is no conceptual difference between the Z and Y variables: Z could simply be folded into Y. The distinction arises during training: we are given the correct value of Y for a number of training samples, but we are never given the correct value of Z.

Latent variables are very useful in situations where a hidden characteristic of the process being modeled can be inferred from observations, but cannot be predicted directly. One such example is in recognition problems. For example, in face recognition the gender of a person or the orientation of the face could be a latent variable. Knowing these values would make the recognition task much easier. Likewise in invariant object recognition the pose parameters of the object (location, orientation, scale) or the illumination could be latent variables. They play a crucial role in problems where segmentation of the sequential data must be performed simultaneously with the recognition task. A good example is speech recognition, in which the segmentation of sentences into words and words into phonemes must take place simultaneously with recognition, yet the correct segmentation into phonemes is rarely available during training. Similarly, in handwriting recognition, the segmentation of words into characters should take place simultaneously with the recognition. The use of latent variables in face recognition is discussed in this section, and section 10.7.3 describes a latent variable architecture for handwriting recognition.

10.4.1   An Example of Latent Variable Architecture

To illustrate the concept of latent variables, we consider the task of face detection, beginning with the simple problem of determining whether a face is present or not in a small image. Imagine that we are provided with a face-detecting function $G_{\text{face}}(X)$ which takes a small image window as input and produces a scalar output.

energy-based face detection... It outputs a small value when a human face fills the input image, and a large value if no face is present (or if only a piece of a face or a tiny face is present). An energy-based face detector built around this function is shown in figure 10.8(a). The variable Y controls the position of a binary switch (1 = "face", 0 = "nonface"). The output energy is equal to $G_{\text{face}}(X)$ when $Y = 1$, and to a fixed threshold value T when $Y = 0$:

$$E(Y, X) = Y G_{\text{face}}(X) + (1 - Y)T.$$

The value of Y that minimizes this energy function is 1 (face) if $G_{\text{face}}(X) < T$ and 0 (nonface) otherwise.

..and localization   Let us now consider the more complex task of *detecting and locating* a single face in a large image. We can apply our $G_{\text{face}}(X)$ function to multiple windows in the large image, compute which window produces the lowest value of $G_{\text{face}}(X)$, and detect a face at that location if the value is lower than T. This process is implemented by the energy-based architecture shown in figure 10.8(b). The latent "location" variable Z selects which of the K copies of the G_{face} function is routed to the output energy. The energy function can be written as

$$E(Z, Y, X) = Y \left[\sum_{k=1}^{K} \delta(Z - k) G_{\text{face}}(X_k) \right] + (1 - Y)T, \tag{10.44}$$

where the X_k's are the image windows. Locating the best-scoring location in the image consists in minimizing the energy with respect to Y and Z. The resulting value of Y will indicate whether a face was found, and the resulting value of Z will indicate the location.

10.4.2   Probabilistic Latent Variables

When the best value of the latent variable for a given X and Y is ambiguous, one may consider combining the contributions of the various possible values by marginalizing over the latent variables instead of minimizing with respect to those variables.

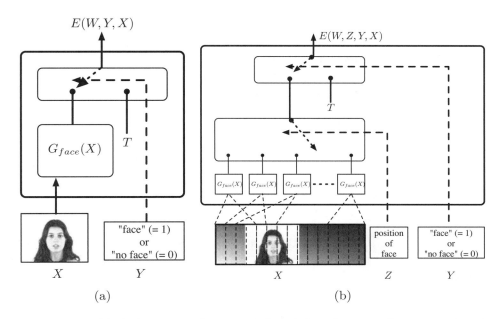

Figure 10.8 (a) Architecture of an energy-based face detector. Given an image, it outputs a small value when the image is filled with a human face, and a high value equal to the threshold T when there is no face in the image. (b) Architecture of an energy-based face detector that simultaneously locates and detects a face in an input image by using the location of the face as a latent variable.

When latent variables are present, the joint conditional distribution over Y and Z given by the Gibbs distribution is

$$P(Z, Y|X) = \frac{e^{-\beta E(Z,Y,X)}}{\int_{y \in \mathcal{Y},\, z \in \mathcal{Z}} e^{-\beta E(y,z,X)}}. \tag{10.45}$$

Marginalizing over Z gives

$$P(Y|X) = \frac{\int_{z \in \mathcal{Z}} e^{-\beta E(Z,Y,X)}}{\int_{y \in \mathcal{Y},\, z \in \mathcal{Z}} e^{-\beta E(y,z,X)}}. \tag{10.46}$$

Finding the best Y after marginalizing over Z reduces to

$$Y^* = \mathrm{argmin}_{Y \in \mathcal{Y}} -\frac{1}{\beta} \log \int_{z \in \mathcal{Z}} e^{-\beta E(z,Y,X)}. \tag{10.47}$$

This is actually a conventional energy-based inference in which the energy function has merely been redefined from $E(Z, Y, X)$ to $\mathcal{F}(\mathcal{Z}) = -\frac{1}{\beta} \log \int_{z \in \mathcal{Z}} e^{-\beta E(z,Y,X)}$, which is the *free energy* of the ensemble $\{E(z, Y, X),\, z \in \mathcal{Z}\}$. The above inference formula by marginalization reduces to the previous inference formula by minimization when $\beta \to \infty$ (zero temperature).

10.5   Analysis of Loss Functions for Energy-Based Models

This section discusses the conditions that a loss function must satisfy so that its minimization will result in a model that produces the correct answers. To give an intuition of the problem, we first describe simple experiments in which certain combinations of architectures and loss functions are used to learn a simple dataset, with varying results. A more formal treatment follows in section 10.5.2.

10.5.1   "Good" and "Bad" Loss Functions

Consider the problem of learning a function that computes the square of a number: $Y = f(X)$, where $f(X) = X^2$. Though this is a trivial problem for a learning machine, it is useful for demonstrating the issues involved in the design of an energy function and loss function that work together. For the following experiments, we use a training set of 200 samples (X^i, Y^i) where $Y^i = X^{i^2}$, randomly sampled with a uniform distribution between -1 and $+1$.

interplay of loss and energy

First, we use the architecture shown in figure 10.9(a). The input X is passed through a parametric function G_W, which produces a scalar output. The output is compared with the desired answer using the absolute value of the difference ($L1$ norm):

$$E(W, Y, X) = ||G_W(X) - Y||_1. \tag{10.48}$$

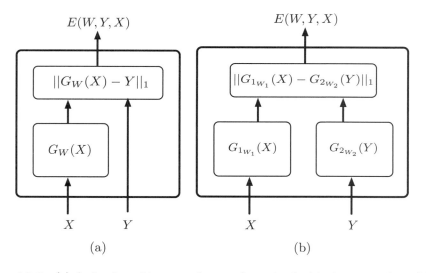

Figure 10.9   (a) A simple architecture that can be trained with the *energy* loss. (b) An implicit regression architecture where X and Y are passed through functions $G_{1_{W_1}}$ and $G_{2_{W_2}}$ respectively. Training this architecture with the energy loss causes a collapse (a flat energy surface). A loss function with a contrastive term corrects the problem.

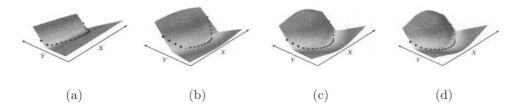

(a)   (b)   (c)   (d)

Figure 10.10   The shape of the energy surface at four intervals while training the system in figure 10.9(a) with stochastic gradient descent to minimize the *energy loss*. The *X*-axis is the input, and the *Y*-axis the output. The energy surface is shown (a) at the start of training, (b) after 10 epochs through the training set, (c) after 25 epochs, and (d) after 39 epochs. The energy surface has attained the desired shape where the energy around training samples (*dark spheres*) is low and energy at all other points is high.

Any reasonable parameterized family of functions could be used for G_W. For these experiments, we chose a two-layer neural network with 1 input unit, 20 hidden units (with sigmoids), and 1 output unit. Figure 10.10(a) shows the initial shape of the energy function in the space of the variables X and Y, using a set of random initial parameters W. The dark spheres mark the location of a few training samples.

First, the simple architecture is trained with the energy loss (10.6):

$$\mathcal{L}_{\text{energy}}(W, \mathcal{S}) = \frac{1}{P} \sum_{i=1}^{P} E(W, Y^i, X^i) = \frac{1}{P} \sum_{i=1}^{P} ||G_W(X) - Y||_1. \qquad (10.49)$$

This corresponds to a classical form of robust regression. The learning process can be viewed as pulling down on the energy surface at the location of the training samples (the spheres in figure 10.10), without considering the rest of the points on the energy surface. The energy surface as a function of Y for any X has the shape of a V with fixed slopes. By changing the function $G_W(X)$, the apex of that V can move around for different X^i. The loss is minimized by placing the apex of the V at the position $Y = X^2$ for any value of X, and this has the effect of making the energies of all other answers larger, because the V has a single minimum. Figure 10.10 shows the shape of the energy surface at fixed intervals during training with simple stochastic gradient descent. The energy surface takes the proper shape after a few iterations through the training set. Using more sophisticated loss functions such as the NLL loss or the perceptron loss would produce exactly the same result as the energy loss because, with this simple architecture, their contrastive term is constant.

Consider a slightly more complicated architecture, shown in figure 10.9(b), to learn the same dataset. In this architecture X is passed through function $G_{1_{W_1}}$ and Y is passed through function $G_{2_{W_2}}$. For the experiment, both functions were two-layer neural networks with 1 input unit, 10 hidden units, and 10 output units. The energy is the L_1 norm of the difference between their 10-dimensional outputs:

$$E(W, X, Y) = ||G_{1_{W_1}}(X) - G_{2_{W_2}}(Y)||_1, \qquad (10.50)$$

where $W = [W_1 W_2]$. Training this architecture with the energy loss results in a *collapse* of the energy surface. Figure 10.11 shows the shape of the energy surface during training; the energy surface becomes essentially flat. What has happened? The shape of the energy as a function of Y for a given X is no longer fixed. With the energy loss, there is no mechanism to prevent G_1 and G_2 from ignoring their inputs and producing identical output values. This results in the collapsed solution: the energy surface is flat and equal to zero everywhere.

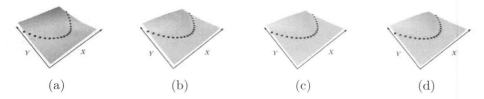

| (a) | (b) | (c) | (d) |

Figure 10.11   The shape of the energy surface at four intervals while training the system in figure 10.9(b) using the energy loss. Along the X-axis is the input variable and along the Y-axis is the answer. The shape of the surface (a) at the start of the training, (b) after three epochs through the training set, (c) after six epochs, and (d) after nine epochs. Clearly the energy is collapsing to a flat surface.

Now consider the same architecture, but trained with the *square-square* loss:

$$L(W, Y^i, X^i) = E(W, Y^i, X^i)^2 - \big(max(0, m - E(W, \bar{Y}^i, X^i))\big)^2. \qquad (10.51)$$

Here m is a positive margin, and $\bar{Y}^i$ is the most offending incorrect answer. The second term in the loss explicitly prevents the collapse of the energy by pushing up on points whose energy threatens to go below that of the desired answer. Figure 10.12 shows the shape of the energy function during training; the surface successfully attains the desired shape.

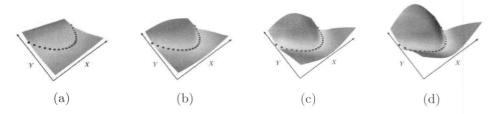

| (a) | (b) | (c) | (d) |

Figure 10.12   The shape of the energy surface at four intervals while training the system in figure 10.9(b) using *square-square* loss. Along the X-axis is the variable X and along the Y-axis is the variable Y. The shape of the surface at (a) the start of the training, (b) after 15 epochs over the training set, (c) after 25 epochs, and (d) after 34 epochs. The energy surface has attained the desired shape: the energies around the training samples are low and energies at all other points are high.

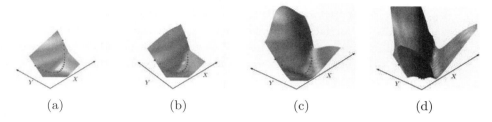

$$\text{(a)} \qquad\qquad \text{(b)} \qquad\qquad \text{(c)} \qquad\qquad \text{(d)}$$

Figure 10.13 The shape of the energy surface at four intervals while training the system in figure 10.9(b) using the negative log-likelihood loss. Along the X-axis is the input variable and along the Y-axis is the answer. The shape of the surface at (a) the start of training, (b) after 3 epochs over the training set, (c) after 6 epochs, and (d) after 11 epochs. The energy surface has quickly attained the desired shape.

Another loss function that works well with this architecture is the *negative log-likelihood* loss:

$$L(W, Y^i, X^i) = E(W, Y^i, X^i) + \frac{1}{\beta} \log \left(\int_{y \in \mathcal{Y}} e^{-\beta E(W, y, X^i)} \right). \tag{10.52}$$

The first term pulls down on the energy of the desired answer, while the second term pushes up on all answers, particularly those that have the lowest energy. Note that the energy corresponding to the desired answer also appears in the second term. The shape of the energy function at various intervals using the NLL loss is shown in figure 10.13. The learning is much faster than the square-square loss. The minimum is deeper because, unlike with the square-square loss, the energies of the incorrect answers are pushed up to infinity (although with a decreasing force). However, each iteration of the NLL loss involves considerably more work because pushing up every incorrect answer is computationally expensive when no analytical expression for the derivative of the second term exists. In this experiment, a simple sampling method was used: the integral is approximated by a sum of 20 points regularly spaced between -1 and +1 in the Y direction. Each learning iteration thus requires computing the gradient of the energy at 20 locations, versus 2 locations in the case of the square-square loss. However, the cost of locating the most offending incorrect answer must be taken into account for the square-square loss.

An important aspect of the NLL loss is that it is invariant to global shifts of energy values, and only depends on differences between the energies of the Ys for a given X. Hence, the desired answer may have different energies for different X's, and may not be zero. This has an important consequence: *the quality of an answer cannot be measured by the energy of that answer without considering the energies of all other answers.*

In this section we have seen the results of training four combinations of architectures and loss functions. In the first case we used a simple architecture along with a simple energy loss, which was satisfactory. The constraints in the architecture of the system automatically lead to the increase in energy of undesired answers while

decreasing the energies of the desired answers. In the second case, a more complicated architecture was used with the simple energy loss and the machine collapsed
for lack of a contrastive term in the loss. In the third and the fourth cases the
same architecture was used as in the second case but with loss functions containing
explicit contrastive terms. In these cases the machine performed as expected and
did not collapse.

10.5.2   Sufficient Conditions for Good Loss Functions

In the previous section we offered some intuitions about which loss functions are
good and which ones are bad with the help of illustrative experiments. In this section
a more formal treatment of the topic is given. First, a set of sufficient conditions
are stated. The energy function and the loss function must satisfy these conditions
in order to be guaranteed to work in an energy-based setting. Then we discuss the
quality of the loss functions introduced previously from the point of view of these
conditions.

10.5.3   Conditions on the Energy

Generally in energy-based learning, the inference method chooses the answer with
minimum energy. Thus the condition for the correct inference on a sample (X^i, Y^i)
is as follows.

Condition 58 *For sample (X^i, Y^i), the machine will give the correct answer for
X^i if*

$$E(W, Y^i, X^i) < E(X, Y, X^i), \forall Y \in \mathcal{Y} \text{ and } Y \neq Y^i. \quad (10.53)$$

In other words, the inference algorithm will give the correct answer if the energy of
the desired answer Y^i is less than the energies of all the other answers Y.

   To ensure that the correct answer is robustly stable, we may choose to impose
that its energy be lower than energies of incorrect answers by a positive margin
m. If $\bar{Y}^i$ denotes the most offending incorrect answer, then the condition for the
answer to be correct by a margin m is as follows.

Condition 59 *For a variable Y and sample (X^i, Y^i) and positive margin m, the
inference algorithm will give the correct answer for X^i if*

$$E(W, Y^i, X^i) < E(W, \bar{Y}^i, X^i) - m. \quad (10.54)$$

10.5.4   Sufficient Conditions on the Loss Functional

If the system is to produce the correct answers, the loss functional should be
designed in such a way that minimizing it will cause $E(W, Y^i, X^i)$ to be lower
than $E(W, \bar{Y}^i, X^i)$ by some margin m. Since only the relative values of those two

energies matter, we only need to consider the shape of a slice of the loss functional in the two-dimensional space of those two energies. For example, in the case where $\mathcal{Y}$ is the set of integers from 1 to k, the loss functional can be written as

$$L(W, Y^i, X^i) = L(Y^i, E(W, 1, X^i), \ldots, E(W, k, X^i)). \qquad (10.55)$$

The projection of this loss in the space of $E(W, Y^i, X^i)$ and $E(W, \bar{Y}^i, X^i)$ can be viewed as a function Q parameterized by the other $k - 2$ energies:

$$L(W, Y^i, X^i) = Q_{[E_y]}(E(W, Y^i, X^i), E(W, \bar{Y}^i, X^i)), \qquad (10.56)$$

where the parameter $[E_y]$ contains the vector of energies for all values of Y except Y^i and $\bar{Y}^i$.

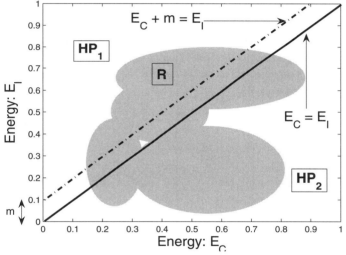

Figure 10.14   Figure showing the various regions in the plane of the two energies E_C and E_I. E_C are the (correct answer) energies associated with (X^i, Y^i), and E_I are the (incorrect answer) energies associated with $(X^i, \bar{Y}^i)$.

We assume the existence of at least one set of parameters W for which condition 59 is satisfied for a single training sample (X^i, Y^i). Clearly, if such a W does not exist, there cannot exist any loss function whose minimization would lead to condition 59. For the purpose of notational simplicity let us denote the energy $E(W, Y^i, X^i)$ associated with the training sample (X^i, Y^i) by E_C (as in "correct energy") and $E(W, \bar{Y}^i, X^i)$ by E_I (as in "incorrect energy"). Consider the plane formed by E_C and E_I. As an illustration, figure 10.17(a) shows a three-dimensional plot of the *square-square* loss function in which the abscissa is E_C and the ordinate is E_I. The third axis gives the value of the loss for the corresponding values of E_C and E_I. In general, the loss function is a family of 2D surfaces in this 3D space, where each surface corresponds to one particular configuration of all the energies except E_C and E_I. The solid red line in the figure corresponds to the points in the 2D plane for which $E_C = E_I$. The dashed blue line correspond to the margin line $E_C + m = E_I$. Let the two half-planes $E_C + m < E_I$ and $E_C + m \geq E_I$ be denoted by HP_1 and HP_2 respectively.

Let R be the *feasible region*, defined as the set of values (E_C, E_I) corresponding to all possible values of $W \in \mathcal{W}$. This region may be nonconvex, discontinuous, open, or one-dimensional and could lie anywhere in the plane. It is shown shaded in figure 10.14. As a consequence of our assumption that a solution exists which satisfies condition 59, R must intersect the half-plane HP_1.

Let two points (e_1, e_2) and (e_1', e_2') belong to the feasible region R, such that $(e_1, e_2) \in HP_1$ (that is, $e_1 + m < e_2$) and $(e_1', e_2') \in HP_2$ (that is, $e_1' + m \geq e_2'$). We are now ready to present the sufficient conditions on the loss function.

Condition 60 *Let (X^i, Y^i) be the ith training example and m be a positive margin. Minimizing the loss function L will satisfy conditions 2 or 3 if there exists at least one point (e_1, e_2) with $e_1 + m < e_2$ such that for all points (e_1', e_2') with $e_1' + m \geq e_2'$, we have*

$$Q_{[E_y]}(e_1, e_2) < Q_{[E_y]}(e_1', e_2'), \tag{10.57}$$

where $Q_{[E_y]}$ is given by

$$L(W, Y^i, X^i) = Q_{[E_y]}(E(W, Y^i, X^i), E(W, \bar{Y}^i, X^i)). \tag{10.58}$$

In other words, the surface of the loss function in the space of E_C and E_I should be such that there exists at least one point in the part of the feasible region R intersecting the half-plane HP_1 such that the value of the loss function at this point is less than its value at all other points in the part of R intersecting the half-plane HP_2.

Note that this is only a sufficient condition and not a necessary condition. There may be loss functions that do not satisfy this condition but whose minimization still satisfies condition 59.

10.5.5   Which Loss Functions Are Good or Bad

Table 10.1 lists several loss functions, together with the value of the margin with which they satisfy condition 60. The energy loss is marked "none" because it does not satisfy condition 60 for a general architecture. The perceptron loss and the LVQ2 loss satisfy it with a margin of zero. All others satisfy condition 60 with a strictly positive value of the margin.

Table 10.1   A list of loss functions, together with the margin which allows them to satisfy condition 60. A margin > 0 indicates that the loss satisfies the condition for any strictly positive margin, and "none" indicates that the loss does not satisfy the condition

Loss (equation #)	Formula	Margin
energy loss (10.6)	$E(W, Y^i, X^i)$	none
perceptron (10.7)	$E(W, Y^i, X^i) - \min_{Y \in \mathcal{Y}} E(W, Y, X^i)$	0
hinge (10.11)	$\max\left(0, m + E(W, Y^i, X^i) - E(W, \bar{Y}^i, X^i)\right)$	m
log (10.12)	$\log\left(1 + e^{E(W, Y^i, X^i) - E(W, \bar{Y}^i, X^i)}\right)$	> 0
LVQ2 (10.13)	$\min\left(M, \max(0, E(W, Y^i, X^i) - E(W, \bar{Y}^i, X^i))\right)$	0
MCE (10.15)	$\left(1 + e^{-\left(E(W, Y^i, X^i) - E(W, \bar{Y}^i, X^i)\right)}\right)^{-1}$	> 0
square-square (10.16)	$E(W, Y^i, X^i)^2 - \left(\max(0, m - E(W, \bar{Y}^i, X^i))\right)^2$	m
square-exp (10.17)	$E(W, Y^i, X^i)^2 + \beta e^{-E(W, \bar{Y}^i, X^i)}$	> 0
NLL/MMI (10.23)	$E(W, Y^i, X^i) + \frac{1}{\beta} \log \int_{y \in \mathcal{Y}} e^{-\beta E(W, y, X^i)}$	> 0
MEE (10.27)	$1 - e^{-\beta E(W, Y^i, X^i)} / \int_{y \in \mathcal{Y}} e^{-\beta E(W, y, X^i)}$	> 0

10.5.5.1   *Energy Loss*

The energy loss is a bad loss function in general, but there are certain forms of energies for which it is a good loss function. For example, consider an energy function of the form

$$E(W, Y^i, X^i) = \sum_{k=1}^{K} \delta(Y^i - k) \|U^k - G_W(X^i)\|^2. \tag{10.59}$$

This energy passes the output of the function G_W through K radial basis functions (one corresponding to each class) whose centers are the vectors U^k. If the centers U^k are fixed and distinct, then the energy loss satisfies condition 60 and hence is a good loss function.

To see this, consider the two-class classification case (the reasoning for $K > 2$ follows along the same lines). The architecture of the system is shown in figure 10.15.

Let $d = \|U^1 - U^2\|^2$, $d_1 = \|U^1 - G_W(X^i)\|^2$, and $d_2 = \|U^2 - G_W(X^i)\|^2$. Since U^1 and U^2 are fixed and distinct, there is a strictly positive lower bound on $d_1 + d_2$ for all G_W. Being only a two-class problem, E_C and E_I correspond directly to the energies of the two classes. In the (E_C, E_I) plane no part of the loss function exists where $E_C + E_I \leq d$. The region where the loss function is defined is shaded in figure 10.16(a). The exact shape of the loss function is shown in figure 10.16(b).

$$E(W,Y,X) = \sum_{k=1}^{2} \delta(Y-k) \cdot ||U^k - G_W(X)||^2$$

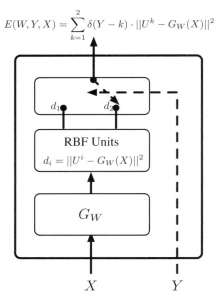

Figure 10.15   The architecture of a system where two RBF units with centers U^1 and U^2 are placed on top of the machine G_W, to produce distances d_1 and d_2.

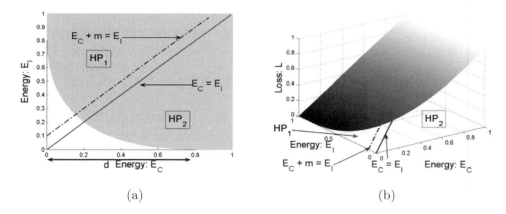

(a)   (b)

Figure 10.16   (a) When using the radial basis function(RBF) architecture with fixed and distinct RBF centers, only the shaded region of the (E_C, E_I) plane is allowed. The nonshaded region is unattainable because the energies of the two outputs cannot be small at the same time. The minimum of the energy loss is at the intersection of the shaded region and the vertical axis. (b) The 3D plot of the energy loss when using the RBF architecture with fixed and distinct centers. Lighter shades indicate higher loss values and darker shades indicate lower values.

One can see from the figure that as long as $d \geq m$, the loss function satisfies condition 60. We conclude that this is a good loss function.

However, when the RBF centers U^1 and U^2 are not fixed and are allowed to be learned, then there is no guarantee that $d_1 + d_2 \geq d$. Then the RBF centers could become equal and the energy could become zero for all inputs, resulting in a collapsed energy surface. Such a situation can be avoided by having a contrastive term in the loss function.

10.5.5.2   Generalized Perceptron Loss

The generalized perceptron loss has a margin of zero. Therefore, it could lead to a collapsed energy surface and is not generally suitable for training energy-based models. However, the absence of a margin is not always fatal (LeCun et al., 1998a; Collins, 2002). First, the set of collapsed solutions is a small piece of the parameter space. Second, although nothing prevents the system from reaching the collapsed solutions, nothing drives the system toward them either. Thus the probability of hitting a collapsed solution is quite small.

10.5.5.3   Generalized Margin Loss

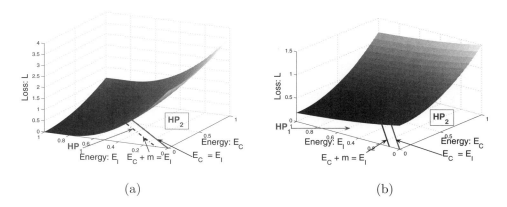

(a)   (b)

Figure 10.17 (a) The *square-square* loss in the space of energies E_C and E_I. The value of the loss monotonically decreases as we move from HP_2 into HP_1, indicating that it satisfies condition 60. (b) The *square-exponential* loss in the space of energies E_C and E_I. The value of the loss monotonically decreases as we move from HP_2 into HP_1, indicating that it satisfies condition 60.

We now consider the *square-square* and *square-exponential* losses. For the two-class case, the shape of the surface of the losses in the space of E_C and E_I is shown in figure 10.17. One can clearly see that there exists at least one point (e_1, e_2) in HP_1 such that

$$Q_{[E_y]}(e_1, e_2) < Q_{[E_y]}(e_1', e_2') \tag{10.60}$$

for all points (e_1', e_2') in HP_2. These loss functions satisfy condition 60.

10.5.5.4 *Negative Log-Likelihood Loss*

It is not obvious that the NLL loss satisfies condition 60. The proof follows.

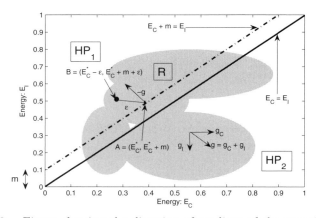

Figure 10.18   Figure showing the direction of gradient of the negative log-likelihood loss in the feasible region R in the space defined by the two energies E_C and E_I.

For any fixed parameter W and a sample (X^i, Y^i) consider the gradient of the loss with respect to the energy E_C of the correct answer Y^i and the energy E_I of the most offending incorrect answer $\bar{Y}^i$. We have

$$g_C = \frac{\partial L(W, Y^i, X^i)}{\partial E_C} = 1 - \frac{e^{-E(W, Y^i, X^i)}}{\sum_{Y \in \mathcal{Y}} e^{-E(W, Y, X^i)}}, \tag{10.61}$$

and

$$g_I = \frac{\partial L(W, Y^i, X^i)}{\partial E_I} = -\frac{e^{-E(W, \bar{Y}^i, X^i)}}{\sum_{Y \in \mathcal{Y}} e^{-E(W, Y, X^i)}}. \tag{10.62}$$

Clearly, for any value of the energies, $g_C > 0$ and $g_I < 0$. The overall direction of the gradient at any point in the space of E_C and E_I is shown in figure 10.18. One can conclude that when going from HP_2 to HP_1, the loss decreases monotonically.

Now we need to show that there exists at least one point in HP_1 at which the loss is less than at all the points in HP_2. Let $A = (E_C^*, E_C^* + m)$ be a point on the margin line for which the loss is minimum. E_C^* is the value of the correct energy at this point. That is,

$$E_C^* = \text{argmin}\{Q_{[E_y]}(E_C, E_C + m)\}. \tag{10.63}$$

Since from the above discussion, the negative of the gradient of the loss $Q_{[E_y]}$ at all points (and in particular on the margin line) is in the direction which is inside HP_1, by monotonicity of the loss we can conclude that

$$Q_{[E_y]}(E_C^*, E_C^* + m) \le Q_{[E_y]}(E_C, E_I), \tag{10.64}$$

where $E_C + m > E_I$.

Consider a point B at a distance ϵ away from the point $(E_C^*, E_C^* + m)$, and inside HP_1 (see figure 10.18). That is the point

$$(E_C^* - \epsilon, E_C^* + m + \epsilon). \tag{10.65}$$

Using the first-order Taylor's expansion on the value of the loss at this point, we get

$$\begin{aligned}
Q_{[E_y]}&(E_C^* - \epsilon, E_C^* + m + \epsilon) \\
&= Q_{[E_y]}(E_C^*, E_C^* + m) - \epsilon \frac{\partial Q_{[E_y]}}{\partial E_C} + \epsilon \frac{\partial Q_{[E_y]}}{\partial E_I} + O(\epsilon^2) \\
&= Q_{[E_y]}(E_C^*, E_C^* + m) + \epsilon \left[\frac{\partial Q_{[E_y]}}{\partial E_C} + \frac{\partial Q_{[E_y]}}{\partial E_I} \right] \begin{bmatrix} -1 \\ 1 \end{bmatrix} + O(\epsilon^2). \tag{10.66}
\end{aligned}$$

From the previous discussion the second term on the right-hand side is negative. So for sufficiently small ϵ we have

$$Q_{[E_y]}(E_C^* - \epsilon, E_C^* + m + \epsilon) < Q_{[E_y]}(E_C^*, E_C^* + m). \tag{10.67}$$

Thus we conclude that there exists at least one point in HP_1 at which the loss is less than at all points in HP_2.

Note that the energy of the most offending incorrect answer E_I is bounded above by the value of the energy of the next most offending incorrect answer. Thus we only need to consider a finite range of E_I's and the point B cannot be at infinity.

10.6 Efficient Inference: Nonprobabilistic Factor Graphs

This section addresses the important issue of efficient energy-based inference. Sequence labeling problems and other learning problem with structured outputs can often be modeled using energy functions whose structure can be exploited for efficient inference algorithms.

Learning and inference with EBMs involves a minimization of the energy over the set of answers $\mathcal{Y}$ and latent variables $\mathcal{Z}$. When the cardinality of $\mathcal{Y} \times \mathcal{Z}$ is large, this

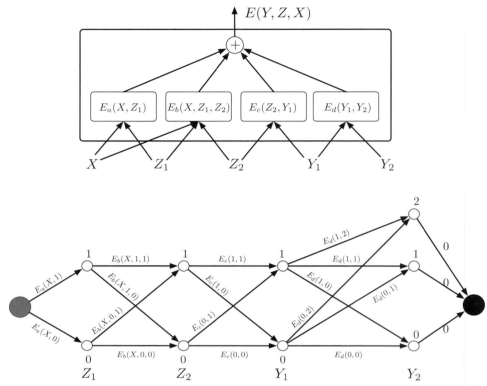

Figure 10.19   *Top:* A log domain factor graph. The energy is a sum of factors that take different subsets of variables as inputs. *Bottom:* Each possible configuration of Z and Y can be represented by a path in a trellis. Here Z_1, Z_2, and Y_1 are binary variables, while Y_2 is ternary.

minimization can become intractable. One approach to the problem is to exploit the structure of the energy function in order to perform the minimization efficiently. One case where the structure can be exploited occurs when the energy can be expressed as a sum of individual functions (called factors) that each depend on different subsets of the variables in $\mathcal{Y}$ and $\mathcal{Z}$. These dependencies are best expressed in the form of a *factor graph* (Kschischang et al., 2001; MacKay, 2003). Factor graphs are a general form of graphical models, or belief networks.

Graphical models are normally used to represent probability distributions over variables by directly encoding the dependency relationships between variables. At first glance, it is difficult to dissociate graphical models from probabilistic modeling (witness their original name: "Bayesian networks"). However, factor graphs can be studied outside the context of probabilistic modeling, and EBM learning applies to them.

A simple example of a factor graph is shown in figure 10.19 (top). The energy function is the sum of four factors:

$$E(Y, Z, X) = E_a(X, Z_1) + E_b(X, Z_1, Z_2) + E_c(Z_2, Y_1) + E_d(Y_1, Y_2), \qquad (10.68)$$

where $Y = [Y_1, Y_2]$ are the output variables and $Z = [Z_1, Z_2]$ are the latent variables. Each factor can be seen as representing soft constraints between the values of its input variables. The inference problem consists in finding

$$(\bar{Y}, \bar{Z}) = \mathrm{argmin}_{y \in \mathcal{Y},\, z \in \mathcal{Z}} \left(E_a(X, z_1) + E_b(X, z_1, z_2) + E_c(z_2, y_1) + E_d(y_1, y_2) \right). \qquad (10.69)$$

encoding of output dependencies

This factor graph represents a *structured output* problem, because the factor E_d encodes dependencies between $Y1$ and $Y2$ (perhaps by forbidding certain combinations of values).

Let's assume that Z_1, Z_2, and Y_1 are discrete binary variables, and Y_2 is a ternary variable. The cardinality of the domain of X is immaterial since X is always observed. The number of possible configurations of Z and Y given X is $2 \times 2 \times 2 \times 3 = 24$. A naive minimization algorithm through exhaustive search would evaluate the entire energy function 24 times (96 single-factor evaluations). However, we notice that for a given X, E_a only has two possible input configurations: $Z_1 = 0$ and $Z_1 = 1$. Similarly, E_b and E_c only have four possible input configurations, and E_d has six. Hence, there is no need for more than $2+4+4+6 = 16$ single-factor evaluations. The set of possible configurations can be represented by a graph (a trellis) as shown in figure 10.19 (bottom). The nodes in each column represent the possible values of a single variable. Each edge is weighted by the output energy of the factor for the corresponding values of its input variables. With this representation, a single path from the start node to the end node represents one possible configuration of all the variables. The sum of the weights along a path is equal to the total energy for the corresponding configuration. Hence, the inference problem can be reduced to searching for the shortest path in this graph. This can be performed using a dynamic programming method such as the Viterbi algorithm, or the A* algorithm. The cost is proportional to the number of edges (16), which is exponentially smaller than the number of paths in general. To compute $E(Y, X) = \min_{z \in \mathcal{Z}} E(Y, z, X)$, we follow the same procedure, but we restrict the graph to the subset of arcs that are compatible with the prescribed value of Y.

The above procedure is sometimes called the *min-sum algorithm*, and it is the log domain version of the traditional max-product for graphical models. The procedure can easily be generalized to factor graphs where the factors take more than two variables as inputs, and to factor graphs that have a tree structure instead of a chain structure. However, it only applies to factor graphs that are bipartite trees (with no loops). When loops are present in the graph, the min-sum algorithm may give an approximate solution when iterated, or may not converge at all. In this case, a descent algorithm such as simulated annealing could be used.

As mentioned in section 10.4, variables can be handled through minimization or through marginalization. The computation is identical to the one required for computing the contrastive term of the NLL loss (the log partition function), hence we will make no distinctions. The contrastive term in the NLL loss function is

$$-\frac{1}{\beta} \log \int_{Y \in \mathcal{Y}, \, z \in \mathcal{Z}} e^{-\beta E(Z, Y, X)}, \tag{10.70}$$

or simply

$$-\frac{1}{\beta} \log \int_{Y \in \mathcal{Y}} e^{-\beta E(Y, X)}, \tag{10.71}$$

when no latent variables are present.

At first, this seems intractable, but the computation can be factorized just as with the min-sum algorithm. The result is the so-called *forward algorithm* in the log domain. Values are propagated forward, starting at the start node on the left, and following the arrows in the trellis. Each node k computes a quantity α_k:

$$\alpha_k = -\frac{1}{\beta} \log \sum_j e^{-\beta(E_{kj} + \alpha_j)}, \tag{10.72}$$

where E_{jk} is the energy attached to the edge linking node j to node k. The final α at the end node is the quantity in (10.70). The procedure reduces to the min-sum algorithm for large values of β.

In a more complex factor graph with factors that take more than two variables as input, or that have a tree structure, this procedure generalizes to a nonprobabilistic form of belief propagation in the log domain. For loopy graphs, the procedure can be iterated, and may lead to an approximate value for (10.70), if it converges at all (Yedidia et al., 2005).

The above procedures are an essential component for constructing models with structures and/or sequential output.

10.6.1   EBMs vs. Internally Normalized Models

It is important to note that at no point in the above discussion did we need to manipulate normalized probability distributions. The only quantities that are manipulated are energies. This is in contrast with HMMs and traditional Bayesian nets. In HMMs, the outgoing transition probabilities of a node must sum to 1, and the emission probabilities must be properly normalized. This ensures that the overall distribution over sequences is normalized. Similarly, in directed Bayesian nets, the rows of the conditional probability tables are normalized.

late normalization EBMs manipulate energies, so no normalization is necessary. When energies are transformed into probabilities, the normalization over Y occurs as the very last step in the process. This idea of *late normalization* solves several problems associated with the internal normalization of HMMs and Bayesian nets. The first problem

label-bias problem is the so-called *label-bias problem*, first pointed out by Bottou (1991): transitions leaving a given state compete with each other, but not with other transitions in the model. Hence, paths whose states have few outgoing transitions tend to have higher probability than paths whose states have many outgoing transitions. This seems like an artificial constraint. To circumvent this problem, a late normalization scheme was first proposed by Denker and Burges (1995) in the context of handwriting and speech recognition. Another flavor of the label-bias problem is the *missing probability mass problem* discussed by LeCun et al. (1998a). They also make use of a late normalization scheme to solve this problem. Normalized models distribute the probability mass among all the answers that are explicitly modeled by the system. To cope with "junk" or other unforeseen and unmodeled inputs, designers must often add a so-called *background model* that takes some probability mass away from the set of explicitlymodeled answers. This could be construed as a thinly disguised way of removing the normalization constraint. To put it another way, since *every explicit normalization is another opportunity for mishandling unforeseen events*, one should strive to minimize the number of explicit normalizations in a model. A recent demonstration of successful handling of the label-bias problem through normalization removal is the comparison between maximum entropy Markov models by McCallum et al. (2000), and conditional random fields by Lafferty et al. (2001).

comparing probabilities The second problem is controlling the relative importance of probability distributions of different natures. In HMMs, emission probabilities are often Gaussian mixtures in high-dimensional spaces (typically 10 to 100), while transition probabilities are discrete probabilities over a few transitions. The dynamic range of the former is considerably larger than that of the latter. Hence transition probabilities count for almost nothing in the overall likelihood. Practitioners often raise the transition probabilities to some power in order to increase their influence. This trick is difficult to justify in a probabilistic framework because it breaks the normalization. In the energy-based framework, there is no need to make excuses for breaking the rules. Arbitrary coefficients can be applied to any subset of energies in the model. The normalization can always be performed at the end.

normalization and discriminant training The third problem concerns discriminative learning. Discriminative training often uses iterative gradient-based methods to optimize the loss. It is often complicated, expensive, and inefficient to perform a normalization step after each parameter update by the gradient method. The EBM approach eliminates the problem (LeCun et al., 1998a). More importantly, the very reason for internally normalizing HMMs and Bayesian nets is somewhat contradictory with the idea of training them discriminatively. The normalization is only necessary for generative models.

10.7   EBMs for Sequence Labeling and Structured Outputs

The problem of classifying or labeling sequences of symbols or sequences of vectors has long been a topic of great interest in several technical communities. The earliest and most notable example is speech recognition. Discriminative learning methods were proposed to train HMM-based speech recognition systems in the late 80's (Bahl et al., 1986; Ljolje et al., 1990). These methods for HMMs brought about a considerable improvement in the accuracy of speech recognition systems, and remains an active topic of research to this day.

With the appearance of multilayer neural network training procedures, several groups proposed combining neural networks and time alignment methods for speech recognition. The time alignment was implemented either through elastic template matching (dynamic time warping) with a set of reference words, or using an HMM. One of the main challenges was to design an integrated training method for simultaneously training the neural network and the time alignment module. In the early 90's, several authors proposed such methods for combining neural nets and dynamic time warping (Driancourt and Bottou, 1991; Driancourt et al., 1991; Driancourt and Gallinari, 1992a,b; Driancourt, 1994), and for neural net and HMM combinations (Bengio et al., 1990; Bourlard and Morgan, 1990; Bottou, 1991; Haffner et al., 1991; Haffner and Waibel, 1991; Bengio et al., 1992; Haffner and Waibel, 1992; Haffner, 1993; Driancourt, 1994; Morgan and Bourlard, 1995; Konig et al., 1996). Extensive lists of references on the topic are available in McDermott (1997) and Bengio (1996). Most approaches used one-dimensional convolutional networks (*time-delay neural networks, TDNNs*) to build robustness to variations of pitch, voice timbre, and speed of speech. Earlier models combined discriminative classifiers with time alignment, but without integrated sequence-level training (Sakoe et al., 1988; McDermott and Katagiri, 1992; Franzini et al., 1990).

time-delay neural networks

Applying similar ideas to handwriting recognition proved more challenging, because the 2D nature of the signal made the segmentation problem considerably more complicated. This task required the integration of image segmentation heuristics in order to generate segmentation hypotheses. To classify the segments with robustness to geometric distortions, 2D convolutional nets were used (Bengio et al., 1993; LeCun and Bengio, 1994; Bengio et al., 1995). A general formulation of integrated learning of segmentation and recognition with late normalization resulted in the *graph transformer network* architecture (LeCun et al., 1997, 1998a).

Detailed descriptions of several sequence labeling models in the framework of EBMs are presented in the next three sections.

10.7.1 Linear Structured Models: CRF, SVMM, and M³Ns

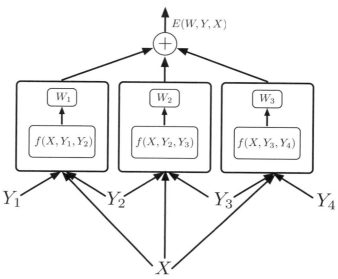

Figure 10.20   A log domain factor graph for linear structured models, which include conditional random fields, support vector Markov models, and maximum-margin Markov networks.

Outside of the discriminative training tradition in speech and handwriting recognition, graphical models have traditionally been seen as probabilistic generative models, and trained as such. However, in recent years, a resurgence of interest for discriminative training has emerged, largely motivated by sequence labeling problems in natural language processing, notably conditional random fields (Lafferty et al., 2001), perceptron-like models (Collins, 2002), support vector Markov models (SVMMs) (Altun et al., 2003a), and M³Ns (Taskar et al., 2004b).

These models can be easily described in an EBM setting. The energy function in these models is assumed to be a linear function of the parameters W:

$$E(W, Y, X) = W^T F(X, Y), \qquad (10.73)$$

where $F(X, Y)$ is a vector of feature functions that depend on X and Y. The answer Y is a sequence of l individual labels $(Y_1, \ldots, Y_l)$, often interpreted as a temporal sequence. The dependencies between individual labels in the sequence is captured by a factor graph, such as the one represented in figure 10.20. Each factor is a linear function of the trainable parameters. It depends on the input X and on a pair of individual labels (Y_m, Y_n). In general, each factor could depend on more than two individual labels, but we will limit the discussion to pairwise factors to simplify the notation:

$$E(W, Y, X) = \sum_{(m,n)\in\mathcal{F}} W_{mn}^T f_{mn}(X, Y_m, Y_n). \tag{10.74}$$

Here $\mathcal{F}$ denotes the set of factors (the set of pairs of individual labels that have a direct interdependency), W_{mn} is the parameter vector for factor (m, n), and $f_{mn}(X, Y_m, Y_n)$ is a (fixed) feature vector. The global parameter vector W is the concatenation of all the W_{mn}. It is sometimes assumed that all the factors encode the same kind of interaction between input and label pairs: the model is then called a homogeneous field. The factors share the same parameter vector and features, and the energy can be simplified as

$$E(W, Y, X) = \sum_{(m,n)\in\mathcal{F}} W^T f(X, Y_m, Y_n). \tag{10.75}$$

The linear parameterization of the energy ensures that the corresponding probability distribution over W is in the exponential family:

$$P(W|Y, X) = \frac{e^{-W^T F(X,Y)}}{\int_{w'\in\mathcal{W}} e^{-w^T F(X,Y)}}. \tag{10.76}$$

This model is called the *linear structured model*.

We now describe various versions of linear structured models that use different loss functions. Sections 10.7.2 and 10.7.3 will describe nonlinear and hierarchical models.

10.7.1.1 *Perceptron Loss*

The simplest way to train the linear structured model is with the perceptron loss. LeCun et al. (1998a) proposed its use for general, nonlinear energy functions in sequence labeling (particularly handwriting recognition), calling it *discriminative Viterbi training*. More recently, Collins (2000, 2002) has advocated its use for linear structured models in the context of natural language processing:

$$\mathcal{L}_{\text{perceptron}}(W) = \frac{1}{P} \sum_{i=1}^{P} E(W, Y^i, X^i) - E(W, Y^{*i}, X^i), \tag{10.77}$$

where $Y^{*i} = \text{argmin}_{y\in\mathcal{Y}} E(W, y, X^i)$ is the answer produced by the system. The linear property gives a particularly simple expression for the loss:

$$\mathcal{L}_{\text{perceptron}}(W) = \frac{1}{P} \sum_{i=1}^{P} W^T \left(F(X^i, Y^i) - F(X^i, Y^{*i}) \right). \tag{10.78}$$

Optimizing this loss with stochastic gradient descent leads to a simple form of the perceptron learning rule:

$$W \leftarrow W - \eta \left(F(X^i, Y^i) - F(X^i, Y^{*i}) \right). \tag{10.79}$$

As stated before, the main problem with the perceptron loss is the absence of margin, although this problem is not fatal when the energy is a linear function of the parameters, as in Collin's model. The lack of a margin, which theoretically may lead to stability problems, was overlooked in LeCun et al. (1998a).

10.7.1.2 Margin Loss: Max-Margin Markov Networks

The main idea behind margin-based Markov networks (Altun et al., 2003a; Altun and Hofmann, 2003; Taskar et al., 2004b) is to use a margin loss to train the linearly parameterized factor graph of figure 10.20 with the energy function of (10.73). The loss function is the simple hinge loss with an L_2 regularizer:

$$\mathcal{L}_{\text{hinge}}(W) = \frac{1}{P} \sum_{i=1}^{P} \max(0, m + E(W, Y^i, X^i) - E(W, \bar{Y}^i, X^i)) + \gamma ||W||^2. \tag{10.80}$$

Because the energy is linear in W, the loss becomes particularly simple:

$$\mathcal{L}_{\text{hinge}}(W) = \frac{1}{P} \sum_{i=1}^{P} \max \left(0, m + W^T \Delta F(X^i, Y^i) \right) + \gamma ||W||^2, \tag{10.81}$$

where $\Delta F(X^i, Y^i) = F(X^i, Y^i) - F(X^i, \bar{Y}^i)$. This loss function can be optimized with a variety of techniques. The simplest method is stochastic gradient descent. However, the hinge loss and linear parameterization allow for the use of a dual formulation as in the case of conventional support vector machines. The question of which optimization method is most suitable is not settled. As with neural net training, it is not clear whether second order methods bring a significant speed improvement over well-tuned stochastic gradient methods. To our knowledge, no systematic experimental study of this issue has been published.

Altun et al. (2003a) have studied several versions of this model that use other loss functions, such as the exponential margin loss proposed by Collins (2000):

$$\mathcal{L}_{\text{hinge}}(W) = \frac{1}{P} \sum_{i=1}^{P} \exp(E(W, Y^i, X^i) - E(W, \bar{Y}^i, X^i)) + \gamma ||W||^2. \tag{10.82}$$

This loss function tends to push the energies $E(W, Y^i, X^i)$ and $E(W, \bar{Y}^i, X^i)$ as far apart as possible, an effect which is moderated only by regularization.

10.7.1.3   Negative Log-Likelihood Loss: Conditional Random Fields

Conditional random fields (Lafferty et al., 2001) use the NLL loss function to train a linear structured model:

$$\mathcal{L}_{\text{nll}}(W) = \frac{1}{P} \sum_{i=1}^{P} E(W, Y^i, X^i) + \frac{1}{\beta} \log \sum_{y \in \mathcal{Y}} e^{-\beta E(W, y, X^i)}. \tag{10.83}$$

The linear form of the energy (10.75) gives the following expression:

$$\mathcal{L}_{\text{nll}}(W) = \frac{1}{P} \sum_{i=1}^{P} W^T F(X^i, Y^i) + \frac{1}{\beta} \log \sum_{y \in \mathcal{Y}} e^{-\beta W^T F(X^i, y)}. \tag{10.84}$$

Following (10.24), the derivative of this loss with respect to W is

$$\frac{\partial \mathcal{L}_{\text{nll}}(W)}{\partial W} = \frac{1}{P} \sum_{i=1}^{P} F(X^i, Y^i) - \sum_{y \in \mathcal{Y}} F(X^i, y) P(y|X^i, W), \tag{10.85}$$

where

$$P(y|X^i, W) = \frac{e^{-\beta W^T F(X^i, y)}}{\sum_{y' \in \mathcal{Y}} e^{-\beta W^T F(X^i, y')}}. \tag{10.86}$$

The problem with this loss function is the need to sum over all possible label combinations, as there are an exponentially large number of such combinations (2^l for a sequence of l binary labels). However, one of the efficient inference algorithms mentioned in section 10.6 can be used.

One of the alleged advantages of CRFs is that the loss function is convex with respect to W. However, the convexity of the loss function, while mathematically satisfying, does not seem to be a significant practical advantage. Although the original optimization algorithm for CRF was based on iterative scaling, recent work indicates that stochastic gradient methods may be more efficient (Vishwanathan et al., 2006).

10.7.2   Nonlinear Graph-Based EBMs

The discriminative learning methods for graphical models developed in the speech and handwriting communities in the 90's allowed for nonlinear parameterizations of the factors, mainly mixtures of Gaussians and multilayer neural nets. Nonlinear factors allow the modeling of highly complex dependencies between inputs and labels (such as mapping the pixels of a handwritten word to the corresponding invariance   character labels). One particularly important aspect is the use of architectures that are invariant (or robust) to irrelevant transformations of the inputs, such as time dilation or pitch variation in speech, and geometric variations in handwriting. This is best handled by hierarchical, multilayer architectures that can learn low-level features and higher-level representations in an integrated fashion. Most authors have used one-dimensional convolutional nets (TDNNs) for speech and pen-based handwriting (Bengio et al., 1990; Bottou, 1991; Haffner et al., 1991; Haffner and Waibel, 1991; Driancourt and Bottou, 1991; Driancourt et al., 1991; Driancourt and Gallinari, 1992a,b; Bengio et al., 1992; Haffner and Waibel, 1992; Haffner, 1993; Driancourt, 1994; Bengio, 1996), and 2D convolutional nets for image-based handwriting (Bengio et al., 1993; LeCun and Bengio, 1994; Bengio et al., 1995; LeCun et al., 1997, 1998a).

nonconvexity vs. convexity

To some observers, the recent interest in the linear structured model looks like somewhat of a throwback to the past, and a regression on the complexity scale. One apparent advantage of linearly parameterized energies is that they make the perceptron loss, hinge loss, and NLL loss convex. It is often argued that convex loss functions are inherently better because they allow the use of efficient optimization algorithms with guaranteed convergence to the global minimum. However, several authors have recently argued that convex loss functions are no guarantee of good performance, and that nonconvex losses may in fact be easier to optimize than convex ones in practice, even in the absence of theoretical guarantees (Huang and LeCun, 2006; Collobert et al., 2006).

efficiency

Furthermore, it has been argued that convex loss functions can be efficiently optimized using sophisticated second-order optimization methods. However, it is a well-known but often overlooked fact that a carefully tuned stochastic gradient descent method is often considerably faster in practice than even the most sophisticated second-order optimization methods (which appear better on paper). This is because stochastic gradients can take advantage of the redundancy between the samples by updating the parameters on the basis of a single sample, whereas "batch" optimization methods waste considerable resources to compute exact descent directions, often nullifying the theoretical speed advantage (Becker and LeCun, 1989; LeCun et al., 1998a,b; Bottou, 2004; Bottou and LeCun, 2004; Vishwanathan et al., 2006).

Figure 10.21 shows an example of speech recognition system that integrates a TDNN and word matching using dynamic time warping (DTW). The raw speech signal is first transformed into a sequence of acoustic vectors (typically 10 to 50 spectral or cepstral coefficients, every 10 ms). The acoustic vector sequence is fed to a TDNN that transforms it into a sequence of high-level features. Temporal subsampling in the TDNN can be used to reduce the temporal resolution of the feature vectors (Bottou, 1991). The sequence of feature vectors is then compared to word templates. In order to reduce the sensitivity of the matching to variations in speed of pronunciation, DTW aligns the feature sequence with the template sequences. Intuitively, DTW consists in finding the best "elastic" warping that maps a sequence of vectors (or symbols) to another. The solution can be found efficiently with dynamic programming (e.g. the Viterbi algorithm or the A* algorithm).

DTW can be reduced to a search for the shortest path in a directed acyclic graph in which the cost of each node is the mismatch between two items in the two input sequences. Hence, the overall system can be seen as a latent variable EBM in which $\mathcal{Y}$ is the set of words in the lexicon, and $\mathcal{Z}$ represents the set of templates

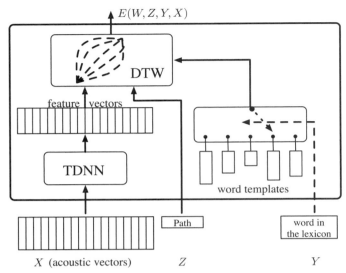

Figure 10.21   Figure showing the architecture of a speech recognition system using latent variables. An acoustic signal is passed through a time-delay neural network (TDNN) to produce a high level feature vector. The feature vector is then compared to the word templates. Dynamic time warping (DTW) aligns the feature vector with the word templates so as to reduce the sensitivity of the matching to variations in pronunciation.

earlier work

for each word, and the set of paths for each alignment graph. The earliest proposal for integrated training of neural nets and time alignment is by Driancourt and Bottou (1991), who proposed using the LVQ2 loss (10.13) to train this system. It is a simple matter to backpropagate gradients through the DTW module and further backpropagate gradients into the TDNN in order to update the weights. Similarly, gradients can be backpropagated to the word templates in order to update them as well. Excellent results were obtained for isolated word recognition, despite the zero margin of the LVQ2 loss. A similar scheme was later used by McDermott (1997).

neural network and HMM combinations

A slightly more general method consists in combining neural networks (e.g. TDNN) with HMMs instead of DTW. Several authors proposed integrated training procedures for such combinations during the 90's. The first proposals were by Bengio et al. (1992); Bengio (1996), who used the NLL/MMI loss optimized with stochastic gradient descent; and Bottou (1991), who proposed various loss functions. A similar method was subsequently proposed by Haffner et al. in his multistate TDNN model (Haffner and Waibel, 1992; Haffner, 1993). Similar training methods were devised for handwriting recognition. Bengio and LeCun described a neural net/HMM hybrid with global training using the NLL/MMI loss optimized with stochastic gradient descent (Bengio et al., 1993; LeCun and Bengio, 1994). Shortly thereafter, Konig et al. proposed the REMAP method, which applies the expectation maximization algorithm to the HMM in order to produce target outputs for a neural net-based acoustic model (Konig et al., 1996).

The basic architecture of neural net/HMM hybrid systems is similar to the one in figure 10.21, except that the word (or language) models are probabilistic finite-state machines instead of sequences. The emission probabilities at each node are generally simple Gaussians operating on the output vector sequences produced by the neural net. The only challenge is to compute the gradient of the loss with respect to the neural net outputs by backpropagating gradients through the HMM trellis. Since the procedure is very similar to the one used in graph transformer networks, we refer to the next section for a description.

It should be noted that many authors had previously proposed methods that combined a separately trained discriminative classifier and an alignment method for speech and handwriting, but they did not use integrated training methods.

10.7.3   Hierarchical Graph-Based EBMs: Graph Transformer Networks

Sections 10.7.2 and 10.7.1 discussed models in which inference and learning involved marginalizing or minimizing over all configurations of variables of a dynamic factor graph. These operations are performed efficiently by building a trellis in which each path corresponds to a particular configuration of those variables. Section 10.7.2 concentrated on models where the factors are nonlinear functions of the parameters, while section 10.7.1 focused on simpler models where the factors are linearly parameterized. The present section discusses a class of models called *graph transformer networks* (GTNs) (LeCun et al., 1998a). GTNs are designed for

"procedural" representation

situations where the sequential structure is so complicated that the corresponding dynamical factor graph cannot be explicitly represented, but must be represented *procedurally*. For example, the factor graph that must be built on the fly in order to recognize an entire handwritten sentence in English is extremely large. The corresponding trellis contains a path for every grammatically correct transcription of the sentence, for every possible segmentation of the sentence into characters. Generating this trellis (or its associated factor graph) in its entirety is impractical, hence the trellis must be represented procedurally. Instead of representing the factor graph, the GTN approach views the trellis as the main data structure being manipulated by the machine. A GTN can be seen as a multilayer architecture in which the states are trellises, just as a neural net is a multilayer architecture in

graph-to-graph mapping

which the states are fixed-size vectors. A GTN can be viewed as a network of modules, called *graph transformers*, that take one or more graphs as input and produce another graph as output. The operation of most modules can be expressed as the composition of the input graph with another graph, called a transducer, associated with the module (Mohri, 1997). The objects attached to the edges of the input graphs, which can be numbers, labels, images, sequences, or any other entity, are fed to trainable functions whose outputs are attached to the edge of the output graphs. The resulting architecture can be seen as a *compositional hierarchy* in which low-level features and parts are combined into higher-level objects through graph composition.

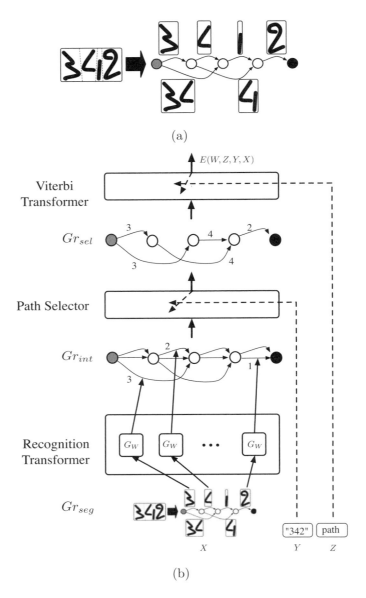

(a)

(b)

Figure 10.22   The architecture of a *graph transformer network* for handwritten word recognition. (a) The segmentation graph Gr_{seg} is generated from the input image. (b) The hierarchical multimodular architecture takes a set of graphs and outputs another set of graphs.

For speech recognition, acoustic vectors are assembled into phones, phones into triphones, triphones into words, and words into sentences. Similarly, in handwriting recognition, ink segments are assembled into characters, characters into words, and words into sentences.

GTN application   Figure 10.22 shows an example of GTN architecture for simultaneously segmenting and recognizing handwritten words (LeCun et al., 1998a). The first step involves
oversegmenting the image and generating a segmentation graph out of it (see figure 10.22(a)). The segmentation graph Gr_{seg} is a directed acyclic graph (DAG) in
which each path from the start node to the end node represents a particular way
of segmenting the input image into character candidates. Each internal node is associated with a candidate cut produced by the segmentation. Every arc between a
source and a destination node is associated with the part of the image that lies between the two cuts. Hence every piece of ink appears once and only once along each
path. The next stage passes the segmentation graph Gr_{seg} through the recognition
transformer which produces the interpretation graph Gr_{int} with the same number
of nodes as Gr_{seg}. The recognition transformer contains as many identical copies
of the discriminant functions $G_W(X)$ as there are arcs in the interpretation graph
(this number changes for every new input). Each copy of G_W takes the image associated with one arc in the segmentation graph and produces several arcs between
the corresponding nodes in the interpretation graph. Each output arc is labeled by
a character category, and weighted by the energy of assigning the image to that
category. Hence, each path in the interpretation graph represents one possible interpretation of the input for one possible segmentation, with the sum of the weights
along the path representing the combined energy of that interpretation. The interpretation graph is then passed through a path selector module that selects only
those paths from the interpretation graph that have the same sequence of labels as
given by Y (the answer). The output of this module is another graph called Gr_{sel}.
Finally, a so-called Viterbi transformer selects a single path in Gr_{sel} indexed by
the latent variable Z. Each value of Z corresponds to a different path in Gr_{sel}, and
can be interpreted as a particular segmentation of the input. The output energy
is obtained either by minimizing or by marginalizing over Z. Minimizing over Z is
achieved by running a shortest-path algorithm on the Gr_{sel} (e.g., the Viterbi algorithm, hence the name Viterbi transformer). The output energy is then the sum
of the arc energies along the shortest path. Marginalizing over Z is achieved by
running the forward algorithm on Gr_{sel}, as indicated in section 10.6, (10.72). The
path selector and Viterbi transformer can be seen as particular types of "switch"
modules that select paths in their input graph.

          In the handwriting recognition systems described in LeCun et al. (1998a), the dis-
criminant function $G_W(X)$ was a 2D convolutional network. This class of function is
designed to learn low-level features and high-level representations in an integrated
manner, and is therefore highly nonlinear in W. Hence the loss function is not
convex in W. The optimization method proposed is a refined version of stochastic
gradient descent.

          In LeCun et al. (1998a), two primary methods for training GTNs are proposed:
discriminative Viterbi training, which is equivalent to using the generalized perceptron loss (10.7), and *discriminative forward training*, which is equivalent to using
the NLL loss (10.23). Any of the good losses in table 10.1 could also be used.

Training by minimizing the perceptron loss with stochastic gradient descent is performed by applying the following update rule:

$$W \leftarrow W - \eta \left(\frac{\partial E(W, Y^i, X^i)}{\partial W} - \frac{\partial E(W, Y^{*i}, X^i)}{\partial W} \right). \tag{10.87}$$

backpropagation through graphs

How can the gradients of $E(W, Y^i, X^i)$ and $E(W, Y^i, X^i)$ be computed? The answer is simply to backpropagate gradients through the entire structure, all the way back to the discriminant functions $G_W(X)$. The overall energy can be written in the following form:

$$E(W, Y, X) = \sum_{kl} \delta_{kl}(Y) G_{kl}(W, X), \tag{10.88}$$

where the sum runs over all arcs in Gr_{int}, $G_{kl}(W, X)$ is the lth component of the k copy of the discriminant function, and $\delta_{kl}(Y)$ is a binary value equal to 1 if the arc containing $G_{kl}(W, X)$ is present in the final graph, and 0 otherwise. Hence, the gradient is simply

$$\frac{\partial E(W, Y, X)}{\partial W} = \sum_{kl} \delta_{kl}(Y) \frac{\partial G_{kl}(W, X)}{\partial W}. \tag{10.89}$$

One must simply keep track of the $\delta_{kl}(Y)$.

In section 10.5 we concluded that the generalized perceptron loss is not a good loss function. While the zero margin may limit the robustness of the solution, the perceptron loss seems appropriate as a way to refine a system that was pretrained on segmented characters as suggested in LeCun et al. (1998a). Nevertheless, the GTN-based bank check reading system described in LeCun et al. (1998a) that was deployed commercially was trained with the NLL loss.

The second method for training GTNs uses the NLL loss function, with a marginalization over Z using the forward algorithm of (10.72) over Gr_{sel}, instead of a minimization.

Training by minimizing the NLL loss with stochastic gradient descent is performed by applying the following update rule:

$$W \leftarrow W - \eta \left(\frac{\partial \mathcal{F}_z(W, Y^i, X^i)}{\partial W} - \frac{\partial \mathcal{F}_{y,z}(W, X^i)}{\partial W} \right), \tag{10.90}$$

where

$$\mathcal{F}_z(W, Y^i, X^i) = -\frac{1}{\beta} \log \sum_{z \in \mathcal{Z}} e^{-\beta E(W, Y^i, z, X^i)} \tag{10.91}$$

is the free energy obtained by marginalizing over Z, keeping X^i and Y^i fixed, and

$$\mathcal{F}_{y,z}(W, X^i) = -\frac{1}{\beta} \log \sum_{y \in \mathcal{Y}, \, z \in \mathcal{Z}} e^{-\beta E(W, y, z, X^i)} \tag{10.92}$$

is the free energy obtained by marginalizing over Y and Z, keeping X^i fixed. Computing those gradients is slightly more complicated than in the minimization case. By chain rule the gradients can be expressed as

$$\frac{\partial \mathcal{F}_{y,z}(W, X^i)}{\partial W} = \sum_{kl} \frac{\partial \mathcal{F}_{y,z}(W, X^i)}{\partial G_{kl}} \frac{\partial G_{kl}(W, X)}{\partial W}, \qquad (10.93)$$

where the sum runs over all edges in the interpretation graph. The first factor is the derivative of the quantity obtained through the forward algorithm (10.72) with respect to one particular edge in the interpretation graph. These quantities can be computed by backpropagating gradients through the trellis, viewed as a feed-forward network with node functions given by (10.72). We refer to LeCun et al. (1998a) for details.

Contrary to the claim in Lafferty et al. (2001), the GTN system trained with the NLL loss as described in LeCun et al. (1998a) does assign a well-defined probability distribution over possible label sequences. The probability of a particular interpretation is given by (10.45):

$$P(Y|X) = \frac{\int_{z\in\mathcal{Z}} e^{-\beta E(Z,Y,X)}}{\int_{y\in\mathcal{Y},\, z\in\mathcal{Z}} e^{-\beta E(y,z,X)}}. \qquad (10.94)$$

It would seem natural to train GTNs with one of the generalized margin losses. To our knowledge, this has never been done.

10.8 Conclusion

There are still outstanding questions to be answered about energy-based and probabilistic models. This section offers a relatively philosophical discussion of these questions, including an energy-based discussion of approximate methods for inference and learning. Finally, a summary of the main ideas of this chapter is given.

10.8.1 EBMs and Probabilistic Models

In section 10.1.3, the transformation of energies to probabilities through the Gibbs distribution was introduced:

$$P(Y|X, W) = \frac{e^{-\beta E(W,Y,X)}}{\int_{y\in\mathcal{Y}} e^{-\beta E(W,y,X)}}. \qquad (10.95)$$

Any probability distribution over $\mathcal{Y}$ can be approximated arbitrarily closely by a distribution of that form. With finite energy values, distributions where the probability of some Y is exactly zero can only be approximated. Estimating the parameters of a probabilistic model can be performed in a number of different ways, including maximum likelihood estimation with Bayes inversion, maximum conditional likelihood estimation, and (when possible) Bayesian averaging (possibly with variational approximations). Maximizing the conditional likelihood of the training samples is equivalent to minimizing what we called the NLL loss.

Hence, at a high level, discriminative probabilistic models can be seen as a special case of EBMs in which

- the energy is such that the integral $\int_{y \in \mathcal{Y}} e^{-\beta E(W, y, X)}$ (partition function) converges;
- the model is trained by minimizing the NLL loss.

disadvantages of
probabilistic
models

An important question concerns the relative advantages and disadvantages of probabilistic models vs. energy-based models. Probabilistic models have two major disadvantages. First, the normalization requirement limits the choice of energy functions we can use. For example, there is no reason to believe that the model in figure 10.7 is normalizable over Y. In fact, if the function $G_{W_2}(Y)$ is upper-bounded, the integral $\int_{-\infty}^{+\infty} e^{-\beta E(W, y, X)} dy$ does not converge. A common fix is to include an additive term $R_y(Y)$ to the energy, interpreted as a log prior on Y, whose negative exponential is integrable. Second, computing the contrastive term in the NLL loss function (or its gradient with respect to W) may be very complicated, expensive, or even intractable. The various types of models can be divided into five rough categories of increasing complexity:

categorization of
probabilistic
models

- **Trivial**: When $\mathcal{Y}$ is discrete with a small cardinality, the partition function is a sum with a small number of terms that can be computed simply. Another trivial case is when the partition function does not depend on W, and hence can be ignored for the purpose of learning. For example, this is the case when the energy is a quadratic form in Y with a fixed matrix. These are cases where the energy loss can be used without fear of collapse.

- **Analytical**: When the partition function and its derivative can be computed analytically. For example, when the energy is a quadratic form in Y in which the matrix depends on trainable parameters, the partition function is a Gaussian integral (with variable covariance matrix) and its derivative is an expectation under a Gaussian distribution, both of which have closed-form expressions.

- **Computable**: When the partition function is a sum over an exponential number of terms, but the computation can be factorized in such a way as to make it tractable. The most notable case of this is when the partition function is a sum over configurations of output variables and latent variables of a tree-type graphical model. In this case, belief propagation can be used to compute the partition function. When the graphical model is a simple chain graph (as in the case of HMMs), the set of configurations can be represented by the paths of a weighted trellis. Running the forward algorithm through this trellis yields the partition function. A simple backpropagation-like procedure can be used to compute its gradient (e.g., see LeCun et al. (1998a) and references therein).

- **Approachable**: When the partition function cannot be computed exactly, but can be approximated reasonably well using various methods. One notable example is when the partition function is a sum over configurations of a loopy graphical model. The sum cannot be computed exactly, but loopy belief propagation or other variational methods may yield a suitable approximation. With those approximations, the energies of the various answers will still be pulled up, although not as systematically and with the same force as if using the full partition function. In a sense, variational methods could be interpreted in the context of EBM as a way to choose a subset of energies to pull up.

■ **Intractable**: When the partition function is truly intractable with no satisfactory variational approximation. In this case, one is reduced to using *sampling methods*. A sampling method is a policy for choosing suitable candidate answers whose energy will be pulled up. The probabilistic approach to this is to sample answers according to their probability under the model, and to pull up their energy. On average, each answer will be pulled up by the appropriate amount according to the partition function.

In this context, using an energy-based loss function other than the NLL can be seen as a sampling method with a particular policy for picking the answers whose energy will be pulled up. For example, the hinge loss systematically chooses the most offending incorrect answer as the one whose energy should be pulled up. In the end, using such strategies will produce energy surfaces with which differences of energies cannot be interpreted as likelihood ratios (the same is true with variational methods). We should emphasize again that this is inconsequential if the model is to be used for prediction, classification, or decision making.

Variational approximation methods can be interpreted in the EBM framework as a particular choice of contrastive term for the loss function. A common approach is to view variational methods and energy-based loss functions as approximations to the probabilistic method. What we propose here is to view the probabilistic approach as a special case of a much larger family of energy-based methods. Energy-based methods are equally well justified as probabilistic methods. They are merely designed for training models to answer a different kind of question than probabilistic models.

An important open question is whether the variational methods that are commonly used (e.g., mean field approximations with popular architectures) actually satisfy condition 60 (see section 10.5.2).

10.8.2   Efficiency in Learning

The most important question that affects the efficiency of learning is: How many energies of incorrect answers must be explicitly pulled up before the energy surface takes the right shape?. Energy-based loss functions that pull up the most offending incorrect answer only pull up on a single energy at each learning iteration. By contrast, the NLL loss pulls up on all incorrect answers at each iteration, including those that are unlikely to produce a lower energy than the correct answer. Hence, unless the NLL computation can be done at very low cost (as in the case of "trivial" and "analytical" models), the energy-based approach is bound to be more efficient.

An important open question is whether alternative loss functions exist whose contrastive term and its derivative are considerably simpler to compute than that of the NLL loss, while preserving the nice property that they pull up a large volume of incorrect answers whose energies are "threateningly low." Perhaps, a figure of merit for architectures and loss functions could be defined which would compare the amount of computation required to evaluate the loss and its derivative relative to the volume of incorrect answers whose energy is pulled up as a result.

For models in the "intractable" category, each individual energy that needs to be pulled up or pushed down requires an evaluation of the energy and of its gradient (if a gradient-based optimization method is used). Hence, finding parameterizations of the energy surface that will cause the energy surface to take the right shape with the minimum amount of pushing or pulling is of crucial importance. If $\mathcal{Y}$ is high-dimensional, and the energy surface is infinitely malleable, then the energy surface will have to be pulled up in many places to make it take a suitable shape. Conversely, more "rigid" energy surfaces may take a suitable shape with less pulling, but are less likely to approach the correct shape. There seems to be a bias-variance dilemma similar to the one that influences the generalization performance.

10.8.3   Learning with Approximate Inference

Very often, the inference algorithm can only give us an approximate answer, or is not guaranteed to give us the global minimum of the energy. Can energy-based learning work in this case? The theory for this does not yet exist, but a few intuitions may shed light on the issue.

There may be certain answers in $\mathcal{Y}$ that our inference algorithm never finds, perhaps because they reside in faraway regions of the space that the algorithm can never reach. Our model may give low energy to wrong answers in these regions, but since the inference algorithm cannot find them, they will never appear in the contrastive term, and their energies will never be pulled up. Fortunately, since those answers are not found by the inference algorithm, we do not need to worry about their energies.

It is an interesting advantage of energy-based learning that only the incorrect answers whose energies are pulled up actually matter. This is in contrast with probabilistic loss functions (e.g. NLL) in which the contrastive term must pull up the energy of every single answer, including the ones that our inference algorithm will never find, which can be wasteful.

10.8.4   Approximate Contrastive Samples, Contrastive Divergence

Loss functions differ in how the contrastive sample is selected, and how hard its energy is pulled up. One interesting suggestion is to pull up on answers that are always near the correct answer, so as to make the correct answer a local minimum, but not necessarily a global one. This idea is the basis of the *contrastive divergence algorithm* proposed by Hinton (2002) and Teh et al. (2003). Contrastive divergence learning can be seen as an approximation of NLL learning with two shortcuts. First, the contrastive term in (10.24) is approximated by drawing samples from the distribution $P(Y|X^i, W)$ using a Markov chain Monte Carlo method (MCMC). Second, the samples are picked by starting the Markov chain at the desired answer, and by running only a few steps of the chain. This produces a sample $\tilde{Y}^i$ that is near the desired answer. Then, a simple gradient update of the parameters is performed:

$$W \leftarrow W - \eta \left(\frac{\partial E(W, Y^i, X^i)}{\partial W} - \frac{\partial E(W, \tilde{Y}^i, X^i)}{\partial W} \right). \qquad (10.96)$$

Since the contrastive sample is always near the desired answer, one can hope that the desired answer will become a local minimum of the energy. Running MCMC for just a few steps limits computational expense. However, there is no guarantee that all incorrect answers with low energy will be pulled up.

10.8.5   Summary

This tutorial was written to introduce and explicate the following major ideas:

- Many existing learning models can be be expressed simply in the framework of energy-based learning.

- Among the many loss functions proposed in the literature, some are good (with a nonzero margin), and some can be bad.

- Probabilistic learning is a special case of energy-based learning where the loss function is the NLL, a.k.a. the maximum mutual information criterion.

- Optimizing the loss function with stochastic gradient methods is often more efficient than black box convex optimization methods.

- Stochastic gradient methods can be applied to any loss function including non-convex ones. Local minima are rarely a problem in practice because of the high dimensionality of the space.

- Support vector Markov models, M^3Ns, and conditional random fields are all sequence modeling systems that use linearly parameterized energy factors. Sequence modeling systems with nonlinear parameterization for speech and handwriting recognition have been a very active research area since the early 90's.

- Graph transformer networks are hierarchical sequence modeling systems in which the objects that are manipulated are trellises containing all the alternative interpretations at a given level. Global training can be performed using stochastic gradient by using a form of backpropagation algorithm to compute the gradients of the loss with respect to all the parameters in the system.

Acknowledgments

The authors thank Geoffrey Hinton, Leon Bottou, Yoshua Bengio, Sebastian Seung, and Brendan Frey for helpful discussions.

11   Generalization Bounds and Consistency for Structured Labeling

David McAllester

This chapter gives generalization bounds for structured output learning. We show that generalization bounds justify the use of Hamming distance in training algorithms independent of the choice of the loss function used to define generalization error. In particular, even when generalization error is measured by 0-1 loss the generalization bounds involve a Hamming distance. A natural training algorithm is to simply minimize the generalization bound over the concept parameters. Minimizing the generalization bound is consistent — as the amount of training data increases the performance of the algorithm approaches the minimal generalization error achievable over the parameter settings. Unfortunately, the generalization bound is not convex in concept parameters. We consider several different ways to make the generalization bound convex all of which are equivalent to classical hinge loss in the case of binary classification but none of which are consistent.

11.1   Introduction

Structured output classification can be viewed as a kind of decoding. We assume a probability distribution on pairs $\langle x, y \rangle$ where x is observable and y is latent. A decoder is a machine for predicting y given only x. In communication channels, as in structured labeling, one typically deals with cases where y is a structured signal.

In this chapter we will be concerned only with a kind of linear decoding. We assume a fixed mapping Φ from pairs to feature vectors, i.e., for any pair $\langle x, y \rangle$ we have $\Phi(x, y) \in \Re^d$. We will consider decoders of the following form where $w \in \Re^d$ is a weight vector.

$$f_w(x) = \underset{y}{\operatorname{argmax}} \ \Phi(x, y) \cdot w \tag{11.1}$$

learning objective   The ultimate objective is to set the parameters w so as to minimize the expectation of $d(y, f_w(x))$ where d is a measure of distortion.

$$w^* = \operatorname*{argmin}_{w} \mathrm{E}_{\langle x, y\rangle \sim D} \left[d(y, f_w(x)) \right] \tag{11.2}$$

A popular alternative to (11.2) is logistic regression. In logistic regression the weight vector w is used to represent a probability distribution $P(y|x, w)$ defined as follows:

$$P(y|x, w) = \frac{1}{Z(x, w)} \exp(\Phi(x, y) \cdot w), \tag{11.3}$$

$$Z(x, w) = \sum_{\hat{y}} \exp(\Phi(x, \hat{y}) \cdot w). \tag{11.4}$$

Models of this form include Markov random fields (MRFs), probabilistic context-free grammars (PCFGs), hidden Markov models (HMMs), conditional random fields (CRFs) (Lafferty et al., 2001), dynamic Bayes nets (Kanazawa et al., 1995), and probabilistic relational models (PRMs) (Getoor et al., 2001). In logistic regression the goal is to minimize expected log loss.

$$w^* = \operatorname*{argmin}_{w} \mathrm{E}_{\langle x, y\rangle \sim D} \left[\log \frac{1}{P(y|x, w)} \right] \tag{11.5}$$

A significant advantage of logistic regression is that (11.5) is convex in w while (11.2) is not. However, the objective in (11.2) seems a more accurate reflection of the actual quantity of interest. The main question addressed in this chapter is how **main question** one should select the parameter vector w so as to approximate (11.2) given only a finite sample of training data drawn from D.

For binary classification, the case with $y \in \{-1, 1\}$, support vector machines (SVMs) provide a popular approach to optimizing (11.2). But for the general case of structured decoding there are several different generalizations of binary SVMs. Here we give generalization bounds designed to provide insight into these alternatives.

Generalization bounds were given by Collins for 0-1 distortion Collins (2004) and a bound has been given by Taskar et al. (2004b) for the case of Hamming distance distortion. The use of Hamming distance produces a much tighter bound and seems to support the idea that Hamming distortion has advantages in practice. Here we show that the improvements in the generalization analysis achieved by Taskar et al. can be achieved for an arbitrary bounded distortion, including 0-1 distortion. Interestingly, Hamming distance still appears in the analysis, but not as a consequence **convexity and** of the choice of distortion. We also consider issues of asymptotic consistency. With **consistency** more than two possible signals, SVM algorithms are not consistent — they fail to **tradeoff** converge on the optimal decoder even in the limit of infinite training data. However, the training algorithm that sets w by minimizing the (nonconvex) generalization bound is consistent. This gives a tradeoff between convexity and consistency in decoding with structured signals.

11.2 PAC-Bayesian Generalization Bounds

string-to-tree
mapping

In the decoding problem considered here, the goal is to learn a mapping $f : \mathcal{X} \to \mathcal{Y}$ where $\mathcal{X}$ is a set of observable "codes" and $\mathcal{Y}$ is a set of latent (unobserved) "signals." Here we follow the approach given in Bartlett et al. (2004) based on "parts." In addition to the sets $\mathcal{X}$ and $\mathcal{Y}$ we assume a set $\mathcal{P}$ of parts. In parsing we have that x is a string and y is a parse tree with yield x — the decoder takes as input a string and produces as output a parse tree. Furthermore, we have given a stochastic (or weighted) grammar G and each "part" is just a production of G. Each pair $\langle x, y \rangle$ of a string x and parse tree y is associated with a set of parts — the productions of G that appear in the parse tree y. Note that a given parse tree can use the same production more than once. Also note that for parsing with a finite grammar the set of parts is finite even though the spaces $\mathcal{X}$ and $\mathcal{Y}$ are infinite.

assumptions

In general we assume sets $\mathcal{X}$, $\mathcal{Y}$, and $\mathcal{P}$ and we assume a function c such that for $x \in \mathcal{X}$, $y \in \mathcal{Y}$, and $p \in \mathcal{P}$ we have that $c(p, \langle x, y \rangle)$ is a nonnegative integer — $c(p, \langle x, y \rangle)$ gives the number of times that the part p appears in the pair $\langle x, y \rangle$. Furthermore, we assume a distribution on D on $\mathcal{X} \times \mathcal{Y}$ such that for any $x \in \mathcal{X}$ we have that the conditional distribution $P(y|x)$ has a countable support (a feasible set) which we denote by $\mathcal{Y}(x)$. We let $\mathcal{P}(x)$ denote the set of $p \in \mathcal{P}$ such that there exists $\hat{y} \in \mathcal{Y}(x)$ with $c(p, \langle x, \hat{y} \rangle) > 0$. Here we will assume that for any $x \in \mathcal{X}$ the sets $\mathcal{Y}(x)$ and $\mathcal{P}(x)$ are finite. For grammars we have that $c(p, \langle x, y \rangle)$ is the number of times the production p occurs in the parse tree y.

We consider the decoder f_w defined by (11.1) where $w, \Phi(x, y) \in \Re^{|\mathcal{P}|}$ and where $\Phi(x, y)$ is defined as follows:

$$\Phi_p(x, y) = c(p, \langle x, y \rangle). \tag{11.6}$$

In the case of grammars we have that w and $\Phi(x, y)$ are both indexed by the set of productions of the grammar. A more general form for $\Phi(x, y)$, allowing for the use of kernels, is discussed in section 11.5. For any definition of $\Phi(x, y)$ we define the margin $m(x, y, \hat{y}, w)$ as follows:

decoding margin

$$m(x, y, \hat{y}, w) = \Phi(x, y) \cdot w - \Phi(x, \hat{y}) \cdot w. \tag{11.7}$$

Intuitively, $m(x, y, \hat{y}, w)$ is the amount by which y is preferable to $\hat{y}$ under the parameter setting w.

The PAC-Bayesian theorem governs the expected distortion of a stochastic decoder. The stochastic decoder first stochastically selects an alternative parameter vector w', then returns $f_{w'}(x)$. It is possible to convert the bounds stated here for the loss of a stochastic decoder to a bound on the loss of the deterministic decoder f_w. However, this conversion seems to provides no additional insight. For any weight vector w we let $Q(w)$ be a distribution on weight vectors whose precise definition is given in section 11.6. We define the expected distortion of $Q(w)$ as follows:

$$L(Q(w), D) = \mathrm{E}_{\langle x, y \rangle \sim D, \, w' \sim Q(w)} \left[d(y, f_{w'}(x)) \right]. \tag{11.8}$$

For simplicity we assume that there exist finite values r, s, and ℓ satisfying the following conditions for all $x \in \mathcal{X}$ and $\hat{y} \in \mathcal{Y}(x)$:

$$|\mathcal{Y}(x)| \leq r \tag{11.9}$$

$$\sum_{p \in \mathcal{P}(x)} c(p, \langle x, \hat{y} \rangle) \leq s \tag{11.10}$$

$$|\mathcal{P}(x)| \leq \ell. \tag{11.11}$$

In parsing we have that finite values r, s, and ℓ exist provided that we bound the length n of the string x. In this case r is exponential in n while s is $O(n)$ and ℓ is $O(1)$ (the number of productions of the grammar). In lexicalized grammars, bounds for r, s, and ℓ can be given in terms of the length of the input string independent of the size of the lexicon.

Throughout the rest of this chapter we assume that $0 \leq d(y, \hat{y}) \leq 1$ for all $y, \hat{y} \in \mathcal{Y}(x)$ with $x \in \mathcal{X}$. We also assume a sequence $S = \langle x_1, y_1 \rangle, \ldots, \langle x_m, y_m \rangle$ of m labeled training pairs has been drawn i.i.d. from D. The following theorem is similar to that proved by Collins but generalized to handle arbitrary bounded distortion and modified so as to be consistent. More specifically, if we set w^* so as to minimize the right-hand side of (11.12), then, in the limit of infinite training data, we have that w^* minimizes generalization loss. This is discussed in more detail in section 11.4. In the theorem $I[\Phi]$ denotes the indicator function where $I[\Phi] = 1$ if Φ is true and 0 otherwise.

bound involving output complexity

Theorem 61 *With probability at least $1 - \delta$ over the draw of the training data S of m pairs we have that the following holds simultaneously for all weight vectors w.*

$$L(Q(w),\, D) \leq \frac{\mathcal{L}_1(w,\, S)}{m} + \frac{||w||^2}{m} + \sqrt{\frac{2s^2||w||^2 \ln\left(\frac{rm}{||w||^2}\right) + \ln\left(\frac{m}{\delta}\right)}{(m-1)}} \tag{11.12}$$

$$\mathcal{L}_1(w, S) = \sum_{i=1}^{m} \max_{\hat{y} \in \mathcal{Y}(x)} d(y_i,\, \hat{y}) I[m(x_i, f_w(x_i), \hat{y}, w) \leq 1] \tag{11.13}$$

Intuitively, $f_w(x_i)$ is uncertain and any value $\hat{y}$ satisfying $m(x_i, f_w(x_i), \hat{y}, w) \leq 1$ should be considered as a possible value of $f_w(x_i)$. The quantity $\mathcal{L}_1(w, S)$ is the worst-case distortion over the signals $\hat{y}$ which are considered to be possible values of $f_w(x_i)$. If all possible values of $f_w(x_i)$ are similar to y_i (as measured by the distortion function), then $\mathcal{L}_1(w, S)$ will be low. Theorem 61 should be contrasted with the following which refines the bound of Taskar et al. by handling arbitrary bounded distortion and modified so as to be consistent.

Theorem 62 *With probability at least* $1 - \delta$ *over the choice of the training data we have that the following holds simultaneously for all weight vectors* w.

$$L(Q(w),\ D) \le \frac{\mathcal{L}_H(w,\ S)}{m} + \frac{||w||^2}{m} + \sqrt{\frac{||w||^2 \ln\left(\frac{2\ell m}{||w||^2}\right) + \ln\left(\frac{m}{\delta}\right)}{2(m-1)}} \qquad (11.14)$$

$$\mathcal{L}_H(w,S) = \sum_{i=1}^{m} \max_{\hat{y} \in \mathcal{Y}(x)} d(y_i,\ \hat{y}) I[m(x_i, f_w(x_i), \hat{y}, w) \le H(x_i, f_w(x_i), \hat{y})] \quad (11.15)$$

$$H(x, y, \hat{y}) = \sum_{p \in \mathcal{P}(x)} |c(p, \langle x, \hat{y}\rangle) - c(p, \langle x, y\rangle)| \qquad (11.16)$$

Like $\mathcal{L}_1(w, S)$, the training loss $\mathcal{L}_H(w, S)$ can be viewed as the worst-case distortion on the training set over the training labels that are considered possible values of $f_w(x_i)$. However, the criterion for being considered to be a possible value for $f_w(x_i)$ involves a Hamming distance.

The proof of both theorems is given in section 11.6. The main feature of the proof of theorem 61 is a union bound over the elements of $\mathcal{Y}(x_i)$ leading to the appearance of r in the bound. The bound is also influenced by the fact that $||\Phi(x, y)||^2$ can be as large as s^2. The proof of theorem 62 replaces the union bound over $\mathcal{Y}(x)$ by a union bound over $\mathcal{P}(x)$ which is typically exponentially smaller.

At first, theorems 61 and 62 may appear incomparable. However, theorem 62 dominates theorem 61 when $\ell << r$. To establish this one must make the two margin requirements comparable. Margin requirements can be changed by rescaling the weight vector. It is well-known that in SVMs one can either work with unit norm weight vectors and bounds involving the margin, or work with unit margin and bounds involving the norm of the weight vector. To compare theorems 61 and 62 we insert $w/(2s)$ for w in theorem 61 to get the following equivalent statement.

$$L\left(Q\left(\frac{w}{2s}\right),\ D\right) \le \frac{\mathcal{L}_{2s}(w,\ S)}{m} + \frac{||w||^2}{4s^2 m} + \sqrt{\frac{||w||^2 \ln\left(\frac{4s^2 rm}{||w||^2}\right) + \ln\left(\frac{m}{\delta}\right)}{2(m-1)}} \quad (11.17)$$

$$\mathcal{L}_{2s}(w, S) = \sum_{i=1}^{m} \max_{\hat{y} \in \mathcal{Y}(x)} d(y_i,\ \hat{y}) I[m(x_i, f_w(x_i), \hat{y}, w) \le 2s] \qquad (11.18)$$

We now compare (11.17) with (11.14). We ignore the fact that the posteriors $Q(w)$ and $Q(w/2s)$ are different. Showing that the right-hand side of (11.14) dominates the right-hand side of (11.17) shows that theorem 62 can provide a better guarantee than theorem 61 even if that better guarantee is for a different classifier. We can also justify ignoring the difference between $Q(w)$ and $Q(w/2s)$ with the claim that variants of these bounds can be proved for deterministic classifiers and the deterministic classifiers f_w and $f_{w/2s}$ are the same. To compare the right-hand sides of (11.17) and (11.14) we first note that $H(x_i, f_w(x_i), \hat{y}) \le 2s$ and therefore $\mathcal{L}_H(w, S) \le \mathcal{L}_{2s}(w, S)$. Furthermore, for structured problems we have that r is exponentially larger than ℓ and hence the regularization term in (11.17) is larger than the regularization term in (11.14).

11.3   Hinge Loss

Support vector machines provide a popular alternative to logistic regression for binary classification. In this section we consider generalizations of SVMs to structured decoding. SVMs involve the optimization of hinge loss. When discussing hinge loss and its relationship to generalization bounds the following notation for the step function and the ramp function will be useful.

$$(x)^+ = I[x \geq 0]$$
$$(x)_+ = \min(0, x)$$

In the case of binary classification we have $y \in \{1, -1\}$. In this case we have that (11.1) can be written as follows:

$$f_w(x) = \operatorname*{argmax}_{y \in \{-1,1\}} \Phi(x, y) \cdot w \;=\; \texttt{sign}(\Phi(x) \cdot w) \tag{11.19}$$

where

$$\Phi(x, 1) = -\Phi(x, -1) \;=\; \frac{1}{2}\Phi(x). \tag{11.20}$$

An SVM selects w so as to minimize the following regularized hinge loss objective function where $y_i(\Phi(x) \cdot w)$ is called the margin and $(1 - m)_+$ is called the hinge loss of margin m.

$$w^* = \operatorname*{argmin}_w \sum_i \left(1 - y_i(\Phi(x_i) \cdot w)\right)_+ + \lambda ||w||^2 \tag{11.21}$$

existing SVM-based approaches

Collins (2004) considered structured SVMs using a multiclass hinge loss

$$w^* = \operatorname*{argmin}_w \sum_i \max_{\hat{y} \neq y_i} \left(1 - m(x_i, y_i, \hat{y}, w)\right)_+ + \lambda ||w||^2, \tag{11.22}$$

whereas Altun and Hofmann (2003) proposed

$$w^* = \operatorname*{argmin}_w \sum_i \max_{\hat{y}} d(y_i, \hat{y})\left(1 - m(x_i, y_i, \hat{y}, w)\right)_+ + \lambda ||w||^2, \tag{11.23}$$

in contrast to Taskar et al. (2004b) who proposed

$$w^* = \operatorname*{argmin}_w \sum_i \max_{\hat{y}} \left(H(x_i, y_i, \hat{y}) - m(x_i, y_i, \hat{y}, w)\right)_+ + \lambda ||w||^2. \tag{11.24}$$

The optimizations (11.22), (11.23), and (11.24) all reduce to (11.21) in the case of binary classification. The fact that theorem 62 dominates theorem 61 suggests that (11.24) is preferable to (11.22) or (11.23). But the precise relationship between the generalization bounds and the various notions of hinge loss is subtle. Theorems 61 and 62 directly motivate the following:

$$w^* = \operatorname*{argmin}_w \sum_i \max_{\hat{y}} d(y_i, \hat{y}) \left(1 - m(x_i, f_w(x_i), \hat{y}, w)\right)^+ + \lambda||w||^2 \qquad (11.25)$$

$$w^* = \operatorname*{argmin}_w \sum_i \max_{\hat{y}} d(y_i, \hat{y}) \left(\begin{array}{c} H(x_i, f_w(x_i), \hat{y}) \\ -m(x_i, f_w(x_i), \hat{y}, w) \end{array} \right)^+ + \lambda||w||^2 \qquad (11.26)$$

The optimization problems given by (11.25) and (11.26) are not convex in w. As a first step in approximating these by convex functions we can replace the step functions by ramps. This replacement yields the following:

$$w^* = \operatorname*{argmin}_w \sum_i \max_{\hat{y}} d(y_i, \hat{y}) \left(1 - m(x_i, f_w(x_i), \hat{y}, w)\right)_+ + \lambda||w||^2 \qquad (11.27)$$

$$w^* = \operatorname*{argmin}_w \sum_i \max_{\hat{y}} d(y_i, \hat{y}) \left(\begin{array}{c} H(x_i, f_w(x_i), \hat{y}) \\ -m(x_i, f_w(x_i), \hat{y}, w) \end{array} \right)_+ + \lambda||w||^2 \qquad (11.28)$$

But (11.27) and (11.28) are still not convex. To see this consider the case of binary classification under 0-1 distortion. Because $d(y_i, \hat{y}) = 0$ for $\hat{y} = y_i$ we need consider only the case where $\hat{y} \neq y_i$. If $f_w(x_i) = y_i$, then $(1 - m(x_i, f_w(x_i), \hat{y}, w))_+$ equals the binary hinge loss $(1 - y_i(\Phi(x) \cdot w))_+$. But if $f_w(x_i) \neq y_i$ — the case where the classical margin is less than zero — then $(1 - m(x_i, f_w(x_i), \hat{y}, w))_+ = 1$. So in the binary case $(1 - m(x_i, f_w(x_i), \hat{y}, w))_+$ is a continuous piecewise linear nonconvex function which equals the hinge loss for positive margin but equals the constant 1 for negative margin. A second step in making this convex is to replace $f_w(x_i)$ by the constant y_i. With this replacement (11.27) becomes (11.23) and (11.28) becomes the following:

$$w^* = \operatorname*{argmin}_w \sum_i \max_{\hat{y}} d(y_i, \hat{y}) \left(H(x_i, y_i, \hat{y}) - m(x_i, y_i, \hat{y}, w)\right)_+ + \lambda||w||^2. \qquad (11.29)$$

It is interesting to note that (11.29) also reduces to (11.21) in the case of binary classification. It is also interesting to note that replacing $f_w(x_i)$ by y_i in theorems 61 and 62 strictly weakens the bounds and causes them to be inconsistent.

11.4 Consistency

Consistency is an important criterion for generalization bounds. More specifically, a bound is consistent if, in the limit of infinite data, the minimum of the bound (over the parameter vector w) approaches the minimum distortion possible over the allowed parameter space. The bounds in theorems 61 and 62 are both consistent in this sense. We give a quick sketch of a proof for this in the finite-dimensional case where we have $w \in \Re^d$. We consider only theorem 61; the argument for theorem 62 is similar.

Since the unit sphere in $\Re^d$ is compact, there must exist a vector w^* on the unit sphere minimizing generalization loss.

$$w^* = \underset{w:\,||w||=1}{\mathrm{argmin}}\ \mathcal{E}(w)$$

$$\mathcal{E}(w) = \mathrm{E}_{\langle x,\,y\rangle \sim D}\left[d(y, f_w(x))\right]$$

All vectors in the same direction as w^* yield the same classification function and hence the same expected distortion. We define w_m^* to be the vector $m^{1/3}w^*$ which is in the same direction as w^* but has length $m^{1/3}$. For a sample of size m we consider the value of the generalization bound for the vector w_m^*. Note that as $m \rightarrow \infty$ we have that $||w_m|| \rightarrow \infty$ but the regularization term for w_m^* goes to zero. Furthermore, for vectors of sufficiently large norm, the only $\hat{y}$ satisfying $m(x_i, f_w(x_i), \hat{y}) < 1$ is $f_w(x_i)$. This means that for vectors of sufficiently large norm we have that $\mathcal{L}_1(w, S)/m$ is essentially equivalent to the sample average of $d(x_i, y_i, f_w(x_i))$. Putting these two observations together we get that as $m \rightarrow \infty$ we have that the generalization bound for w_m^* must approach $\mathcal{E}(w^*)$. Hence, as $m \rightarrow \infty$ the minimum of the generalization bound is at most $\mathcal{E}(w^*)$. The algorithm is guaranteed (with high probability) to perform as well as the minimum of the generalization bound.

It is well-known that the use of hinge loss in multiclass classification results in inconsistent algorithms (Lee et al., 2004). The various forms of convex hinge loss discussed in section 11.3 all fail to be consistent. It is possible to construct consistent forms of hinge loss for nonparametric, i.e., infinite feature dimension, multiclass classification (Lee et al., 2004). However, neither the convergence rates nor the practicality of these constructions has been established for the case of learning decoders.

To show inconsistency of the hinge losses considered in section 11.3, suppose that $\mathcal{X}$ contains only a single element x and that $\mathcal{Y}$ is a finite set y_1, y_2, ..., y_k, and that we are using $0 - 1$ distortion. Further assume that there is an independent weight for each y_i. In other words, $d = k$ and $\Phi_j(x, y_i)$ is 1 if $i = j$ and zero otherwise so that $\Phi(x, y_i) \cdot w = w_i$. In this case all four of the hinge loss rules, (11.22), (11.23), (11.24), and (11.29), are the same. We will work with the simplest form, (11.22). Assume that $\lambda = 0$ so that we simply want to minimize the hinge loss independent of $||w||^2$. In the limit of an infinitely large sample we have that the hinge loss term dominates the regularization term. Furthermore, suppose that for each y_i we have that the probability of the pair $\langle x, y_i \rangle$ is less than $1/2$ (note that this cannot happen in binary classification). Define the margin m_i as follows:

$$m_i = w_i - \max_{j \neq i} w_j.$$

In the limit of infinite training data we have the following:

$$w^* = \underset{w}{\mathrm{argmin}} \sum_i p_i \left(1 - m_i\right)_+ . \tag{11.30}$$

We will show that in this case the optimal value is achieved when all weights are the same so that $m_i = 0$ for all i. To see this consider any uniform vector w. Since the objective function in (11.30) is convex it suffices to show that any variation in w fails to improve the objective function. As an example of a simple variation suppose that we increase the weight of the component w_i corresponding to the choice minimizing expected distortion. As we increase w_i we increase m_i but we decrease each m_j for $j \neq i$ by the same amount. Given that $p_i < 1/2$, the net effect is an increase in the objective function. To prove that no variation from uniform improves the objective, let $\Delta \in \Re^k$ be a vector and consider $w' = w + \epsilon \Delta$. We then have the following:

$$\frac{\partial m_i}{\partial \epsilon} = \Delta_i - \max_{j \neq i} \Delta j.$$

To show that that is a nonimproving variation it suffices to show the following:

$$\sum_i p_i (\Delta_i - \max_{j \neq i} \Delta j) \leq 0.$$

But this is equivalent to the following:

$$\sum_i p_i \max_{j \neq i} \Delta_j \geq \sum_i p_i \Delta_i.$$

This can be derived as follows where i^* is argmax$_i$ Δ_i and j^* is argmax$_{j \neq i^*}$ Δ_j and the last line follows from the assumption that $p_i < 1/2$.

$$\sum_i p_i \max_{j \neq i} \Delta_j = p_{i^*} \Delta_{j^*} + \sum_{j \neq i^*} p_j \Delta_{i^*}$$

$$= p_{i^*} \Delta_{j^*} + \sum_{j \neq i^*} p_j (\Delta_j + (\Delta_{i^*} - \Delta_j))$$

$$\geq p_{i^*} \Delta_{j^*} + \left(\sum_{j \neq i^*} p_j \Delta_j \right) + (1 - p_{i^*})(\Delta_{i^*} - \Delta_{j^*})$$

$$= p_{i^*} \Delta_{i^*} + p_{i^*}(\Delta_{j^*} - \Delta_{i^*}) + \left(\sum_{j \neq i^*} p_j \Delta_j \right) + (1 - p_{i^*})(\Delta_{i^*} - \Delta_{j^*})$$

$$= \sum_i p_i \Delta_i + (\Delta_{i^*} - \Delta_{j^*})(1 - 2p_{i^*})$$

$$\geq \sum_i p_i \Delta_i$$

Now we argue for the consistency of (11.25) and (11.26). If we hold λ/n fixed and let the sample size go to infinity, then (11.25) and (11.26) become the following where $\lambda' = \lambda/n$

$$w^* = \operatorname*{argmin}_{w} \operatorname{E}_{\langle x,\, y \rangle \sim D} \left[\max_{\hat{y}} d(y, \hat{y}) \left(1 - m(x, f_w(x), \hat{y}, w) \right)^+ \right] + \lambda' ||w||^2 \qquad (11.31)$$

$$w^* = \operatorname*{argmin}_{w} \operatorname{E}_{\langle x,\, y \rangle \sim D} \left[\max_{\hat{y}} d(y, \hat{y}) \left(\begin{array}{c} H(x, f_w(x), \hat{y}) \\ -m(x, f_w(x), \hat{y}, w) \end{array} \right)^+ \right] + \lambda' ||w||^2 \quad (11.32)$$

Now we consider the limit of (11.31) and (11.32) as $\lambda' \to 0$. Intuitively this limit gives the following:

$$w^* = \operatorname*{argmin}_{w} \operatorname{E}_{\langle x,\, y \rangle \sim D} \left[\max_{\hat{y}} d(y, \hat{y}) \left(1 - m(x, f_w(x), \hat{y}, w) \right)^+ \right] \qquad (11.33)$$

$$w^* = \operatorname*{argmin}_{w} \operatorname{E}_{\langle x,\, y \rangle \sim D} \left[\max_{\hat{y}} d(y, \hat{y}) \left(H(x, f_w(x), \hat{y}) - m(x, f_w(x), \hat{y}, w) \right)^+ \right]. (11.34)$$

The optimizations (11.33) and (11.34) yield very large vectors which drive any nonzero margin to be arbitrarily large. The direction of the optimal vector for both (11.33) and (11.34) is then given by the following:

$$w^* = \operatorname*{argmin}_{w} \operatorname{E}_{\langle x,\, y \rangle \sim D} \left[d(y, f_w(x)) \right]. \qquad (11.35)$$

To convert this argument into a formal proof one needs to give an explicit schedule for λ as a function of sample size and show that this schedule corresponds to taking m to infinity holding λ' constant and then taking λ' to zero. It should suffice to consider the "schedule" obtained by optimizing λ with holdout data.

11.5 A Generalization of Theorem 62

We define two steps of increasing generality — a generalization to allow for kernels and a second generalization that generalizes the notion of part. The first generalization replaces (11.6) by the following where Ψ is a feature map on parts.

$$\Phi(x, y) = \sum_{p \in \mathcal{P}(x)} c(p, \langle x, y \rangle) \Psi(p) \qquad (11.36)$$

This generalization is important when the parts themselves contain vectorial data. For example, in speech recognition the observable state in an HMM is often taken to be an acoustic feature vector. In (11.36) we have $\Psi(p) \in \Re^d$ where we allow $d = \infty$ with the understanding that $\Re^\infty$ is the vector space of square summable infinite sequences. For the $d = \infty$ case it is usually more convenient to work in a reproducing kernel Hilbert space (RKHS) defined by a kernel K, in which case the decoder specified by weight function g is defined as follows:

$$f_g(x) = \underset{\hat{y} \in \mathcal{Y}(x)}{\operatorname{argmax}} \sum_{p \in \mathcal{P}(x)} c(p, \langle x, \hat{y} \rangle) g(p). \tag{11.37}$$

Formulation (11.37) is equivalent to (11.36) with $d = \infty$ and we will work only with (11.36).

We now generalize the notion of a part. As before we now assume sets $\mathcal{X}$ and $\mathcal{Y}$ with a distribution D on $\mathcal{X} \times \mathcal{Y}$ with the property that for all $x \in \mathcal{X}$ the marginal $P(\cdot|x)$ has a countable support $\mathcal{Y}(x)$. We also assume a feature map Φ with $\Phi(x, y) \in \Re^d$ where, as above, we allow $d = \infty$. But rather than assume parts, we assume that for each $x \in \mathcal{X}$ we are given a set of $\ell(x)$ independent vectors $B(x)$ such that for all $\hat{y} \in \mathcal{Y}(x)$ we have that $\Phi(x, \hat{y})$ is in the linear span of $B(x)$. The vectors $\Psi(p)$ in (11.36) form such a basis. We let $\Psi_i(x)$ denote the ith vector in the basis $B(x)$. We can then generalize (11.36) to the following:

$$\Phi(x, y) = \sum_{i=1}^{\ell(x)} \gamma_i(x, y) \Psi_i(x). \tag{11.38}$$

The difference between (11.36) and (11.38) is actually quite minor. In (11.38) we have that $\gamma_i(x, y)$ is any real number while in (11.36) we have that $c(p, \langle x, y \rangle)$ must be a count — a nonnegative integer. We now assume two quantities ℓ and R such that for all $x \in \mathcal{X}$ we have the following:

$$\ell(x) \le \ell \tag{11.39}$$

$$||\Psi_i(x)|| \le R. \tag{11.40}$$

We now state the generalization of theorem 62.

Theorem 63 *With probability at least $1 - \delta$ over the choice of the training data we have that the following holds simultaneously for all weight vectors w.*

$$L(Q(w),\ D) \le \frac{\mathcal{L}_H(w,\ S)}{m} + \frac{R^2 ||w||^2}{m} + \sqrt{\frac{R^2 ||w||^2 \ln\left(\frac{2\ell m}{R^2 ||w||^2}\right) + \ln\left(\frac{m}{\delta}\right)}{2(m-1)}} \tag{11.41}$$

$$\mathcal{L}_H(w, S) = \sum_{i=1}^{m} \max_{\hat{y} \in \mathcal{Y}(x)} d(y_i, \hat{y}) I[m(x_i, f_w(x_i), \hat{y}, w) \le H(x_i, f_w(x_i), \hat{y})] \tag{11.42}$$

$$H(x, y, \hat{y}) = \sum_{i=1}^{\ell(x)} |\gamma_i(x, \hat{y}) - \gamma_i(x, y)| \tag{11.43}$$

The proof of this more general theorem is a straightforward generalization of the proof of theorem 62 and is not given here.

11.6   Proofs of Theorems 61 and 62

All our proofs use the PAC-Bayesian theorem (McAllester, 2003a; Seeger, 2002; Langford and Shawe-Taylor, 2002; McAllester, 2003b).

Lemma 64 (PAC-Bayesian Theorem) *For sets $\mathcal{X}$ and $\mathcal{Y}$, any probability distribution D on $\mathcal{X} \times \mathcal{Y}$, any distortion function d on $\mathcal{Y} \times \mathcal{Y}$ with $0 \leq d(y, \hat{y}) \leq 1$, any decoder $f_w : \mathcal{X} \to \mathcal{Y}$ parameterized by parameter vector w, and any prior probability density P on the parameters w, we have that with probability at least $1 - \delta$ over the drawn of a sample $S = \langle \langle x_1, y_1 \rangle, \ldots, \langle x_m, y_m \rangle \rangle$ from distribution D that the following holds simultaneously for all densities Q on parameters:*

$$L(Q, D) \leq L(Q, S) + \sqrt{\frac{KL(Q, P) + \ln \frac{m}{\delta}}{2(m - 1)}}, \qquad (11.44)$$

where

$$L(Q, D) = \mathrm{E}_{\langle x, y \rangle \sim D, w \sim Q}\left[d(y, f_w(x))\right] \qquad (11.45)$$

$$L(Q, S) = \frac{1}{m} \sum_{i=1}^{m} \mathrm{E}_{w \sim Q}\left[d(y_i, f_w(x_i))\right]. \qquad (11.46)$$

Quadratic regularization corresponds to a Gaussian prior. We consider the $d = \infty$ case of a Gaussian process prior as the limit of the finite d case as d increases without bound. More specifically, we take the "prior" density to be a unit-variance isotropic Gaussian on weight vectors defined as follows:

$$p(w) = \frac{1}{Z} \exp\left(-\frac{||w||^2}{2}\right).$$

Theorems 61 and 62 govern the distortion of a stochastic decoder that stochastically draws w' from a distribution $Q(w)$. We now define the density $Q(w)$ as follows:

$$q(w' \mid w) = \frac{1}{Z} \exp\left(-(1/2)||(w' - \alpha w)||^2\right). \qquad (11.47)$$

Here α is a scalar multiple which will be optimized later. The distribution $Q(w)$ is a unit-variance Gaussian centered at αw. If α is very large, then the vast majority of vectors drawn from $Q(w)$ will be essentially in the same direction as w. So by tuning α we can tune the degree to which $Q(w)$ is concentrated on vectors pointing in the same direction as w. The KL divergence from Q to P can be solved analytically as follows:

$$KL\left(Q(w) \mid\mid P\right) = \frac{\alpha^2 ||w||^2}{2}. \qquad (11.48)$$

To apply the PAC-Bayesian theorem it remains only to analyze the training loss $L(Q(w), S)$. In analyzing the training loss we can consider each training point $\langle x_i, y_i \rangle$ independently.

$$L(Q, S) = \frac{1}{m} \sum_{i=1}^{m} L_i \tag{11.49}$$

$$L_i = \mathrm{E}_{w' \sim Q(w)} [d(y_i, f_{w'}(x_i))] \tag{11.50}$$

In analyzing L_i we have that $f_{w'}(x_i)$ is a random variable based on the random draw of w'. The difference between theorem 61 and theorem 62 involves a different way of analyzing the random variable $f_{w'}(x_i)$. For theorem 61 we use the following lemma.

Lemma 65 *For s and r as defined at the start of section 11.2 and α defined by*

$$\alpha = s\sqrt{8 \ln \left(\frac{rm}{||w||^2} \right)},$$

we have that with probability at least $1 - \frac{||w||^2}{m}$ over the selection of w' the following holds:

$$f_{w'}(x_i) \in \{\hat{y} : \ m(x_i, f_w(x_i), \hat{y}, w) \leq 1\}$$

Proof Let $\hat{y}_i$ abbreviate $f_w(x_i)$. We first note that by a union bound over the elements of $\mathcal{Y}(x_i)$ it suffices to show that for any given $\hat{y}$ with $m(x_i, \hat{y}_i, \hat{y}, w) \geq 1$, the probability that $f_{w'}(x_i) = \hat{y}$ is at most $||w||^2/(rm)$. Consider a fixed $\hat{y} \in \mathcal{Y}(x_i)$ with $m(x_i, \hat{y}_i, \hat{y}, w) \geq 1$. We analyze the probability that the choice of w' overcomes the margin and causes $\hat{y}$ to have a better score than $\hat{y}_i$. We first note the following for any vector $\Psi \in R^d$ with $||\Psi|| = 1$ and any $\epsilon \geq 0$.

$$\mathrm{P}_{w' \sim Q(w)} [(\alpha w - w') \cdot \Psi \geq \epsilon] \leq \exp \left(\frac{-\epsilon^2}{2} \right) \tag{11.51}$$

For $\Delta(x_i, \hat{y}_i, \hat{y}) = \Phi(x_i, \hat{y}_i) - \Phi(x_i, \hat{y})$ we then have the following:

$$m(x_i, \hat{y}_i, \hat{y}, w) = \Delta(x_i, \hat{y}_i, \hat{y}) \cdot w$$
$$||\Delta(x_i, \hat{y}_i, \hat{y})|| \leq 2s.$$

Inserting $\Delta(x_i, \hat{y}_i, \hat{y})/||\Delta(x_i, \hat{y}_i, \hat{y}||$ into (11.51) yields the following:

$$\mathrm{P}_{w' \sim Q(w)} [m(x_i, \hat{y}_i, \hat{y}, w') \leq \alpha m(x_i, \hat{y}_i, \hat{y}, w) - \epsilon ||\Delta(x_i, \hat{y}_i, \hat{y})|| \,] \leq \exp \left(\frac{-\epsilon^2}{2} \right)$$

$$\mathrm{P}_{w' \sim Q(w)} [m(x_i, \hat{y}_i, \hat{y}, w') \leq \alpha - \epsilon ||\Delta(x_i, \hat{y}_i, \hat{y})|| \,] \leq \exp \left(\frac{-\epsilon^2}{2} \right).$$

Setting ϵ equal to $\alpha/||\Delta(x_i, \hat{y}_i, \hat{y})||$ we get the following:

$$\mathrm{P}_{w' \sim Q(w)}\left[m(x_i, \hat{y}_i, \hat{y}, w') \leq 0\right] \leq \exp\left(\frac{-\alpha^2}{2||\Delta(x_i, \hat{y}_i, \hat{y})||^2}\right)$$

$$\mathrm{P}_{w' \sim Q(w)}\left[f_{w'}(x_i) = \hat{y}\right] \leq \exp\left(\frac{-\alpha^2}{2||\Delta(x_i, \hat{y}_i, \hat{y})||^2}\right)$$

$$\leq \exp\left(\frac{-\alpha^2}{8s^2}\right).$$

Setting α as in the statement of the lemma finishes the proof.   ■

Theorem 61 now follows from the PAC-Bayesian theorem, (11.48), and lemma 65. Theorem 62 follows from the PAC-Bayesian theorem, (11.48), and the following lemma which is similar in form to lemma 65.

Lemma 66 *For s and ℓ as defined at the start of section 11.2 and α defined by*

$$\alpha = \sqrt{2 \ln\left(\frac{2\ell m}{||w||^2}\right)},$$

we have that with probability at least $1 - \frac{||w||^2}{m}$ over the selection of w' the following holds.

$$f_{w'}(x_i) \in \{\hat{y} : \; m(x_i, f_w(x_i), \hat{y}, w) \leq H(x_i, f_w(x_i), \hat{y}, w)\} \tag{11.52}$$

Proof   Again let $\hat{y}_i$ denote $f_w(x_i)$. First we note that for any $p \in \mathcal{P}(x_i)$ we have the following:

$$\mathrm{P}_{w' \sim Q(w)}\left[|w'_p - \alpha w_p| \geq \epsilon\right] \leq 2\exp\left(\frac{-\epsilon^2}{2}\right). \tag{11.53}$$

Setting ϵ to α, for the above value of α, gives the following:

$$\mathrm{P}_{w' \sim Q(w)}\left[|w'_p - \alpha w_p| \geq \alpha\right] \leq \frac{||w||^2}{\ell m}. \tag{11.54}$$

Now taking a union bound over the elements of $\mathcal{P}(x_i)$ we get that with probability $1 - \frac{||w||^2}{m}$ the following holds simultaneously for all $p \in \mathcal{P}(x_i)$:

$$|w'_p - \alpha w_p| \leq \alpha. \tag{11.55}$$

Now assume that (11.55) holds for all $p \in \mathcal{P}(x_i)$. Consider $\hat{y}$ such that $m(x_i, \hat{y}_i, \hat{y}, w) > H(x_i, \hat{y}_i, \hat{y})$. Let $\Delta(x_i, \hat{y}_i, \hat{y})$ denote $\Phi(x_i, \hat{y}_i) - \Phi(x_i, \hat{y})$. We now have the following:

$$m(x_i, \hat{y}_i, \hat{y}, w') \tag{11.56}$$

$$= m(x_i, \hat{y}_i, \hat{y}, \alpha w + (w' - \alpha w)) \tag{11.57}$$

$$= \alpha m(x_i, \hat{y}_i, \hat{y}, w) - \Delta(x_i, \hat{y}_i, \hat{y}) \cdot (\alpha w - w') \tag{11.58}$$

$$> \alpha H(x_i, \hat{y}_i, \hat{y}) - \Delta(x_i, \hat{y}_i, \hat{y}) \cdot (\alpha w - w') \tag{11.59}$$

$$\geq \alpha H(x_i, \hat{y}_i, \hat{y}) - \sum_{p \in \mathcal{P}(x_i)} (c(p, \langle x_i, \hat{y}_i \rangle) - c(p, \langle x_i, \hat{y} \rangle))) |\alpha w_p - w'_p| \tag{11.60}$$

$$\geq \alpha H(x_i, \hat{y}_i, \hat{y}) - \sum_{p \in \mathcal{P}(x_i)} |c(p, \langle x_i, \hat{y}_i \rangle) - c(p, \langle x_i, \hat{y} \rangle)| \alpha \tag{11.61}$$

$$= 0. \tag{11.62}$$

Since $m(x_i, \hat{y}_i, \hat{y}, w') > 0$ we have that $f_{w'}(x_i) \neq \hat{y}$ and the lemma follows. $\blacksquare$

11.7   Conclusion

One of the goals of learning theory is to provide guidance in the construction of learning algorithms. This chapter provides consistent generalization bounds for learning decoders (structured output learning). These new bounds improve previous bounds by achieving consistency for arbitrary distortion (loss) functions. These new generalization bounds seem to provide insight into the various notions of hinge loss that have been proposed for learning decoders and suggest that nonconvex optimization may achieve superior, or at least consistent, generalization.

Acknowledgments

I thank Michael Collins, Ben Taskar, and Peter Bartlett for useful discussions regarding this chapter.

III Structured Prediction Using Probabilistic Models

12   Kernel Conditional Graphical Models

Fernando Pérez-Cruz, Zoubin Ghahramani, and Massimiliano Pontil

In this chapter we propose a modification of conditional random fields (CRFs) type algorithms that allows for solving large-scale structural classification problems. Our approach consists in upper-bounding the CRF functional in order to decompose its training into independent optimization problems per clique. Furthermore, we show that each subproblem corresponds to solving a multiclass learning task in each clique. This feature enlarges the applicability of these tools to large-scale structural learning problems. Before introducing the conditional graphical model (CGM), as we refer to this procedure, we review the family of CRF algorithms. We present the best-known methods and standard generalizations of CRFs. The objective of this introduction is to analyze from the same viewpoint the solutions proposed in the literature and to compare their different features. We conclude the chapter with a case study, in which we solve large-scale problems using CGM. We show the advantages of using CGM compared to CRF-like algorithms.

12.1   Introduction

In the last decade machine learning tools have moved from heuristic-based approaches to more theory-based ones. There has been an explosion of work on theoretical and algorithmic developments, as well as on potential applications to real-world problems. In particular, in the pattern recognition field, the appearance of the support vector machines (SVMs) (Boser et al., 1992) blossomed into research into new machine learning algorithms and they brought the kernel concept into the machine learning community (Schölkopf and Smola, 2002). Nevertheless, most real-life applications of pattern recognition cannot be readily cast as a binary (or multiclass) learning problem, because they present an inherent structure that cannot be exploited by general classification algorithms. Some of these applications, such as speech or object recognition, have developed their own research field. They use a mixture of machine learning tools and specific knowledge about each application to provide meaningful solutions to these relevant problems. However, there are still many others that can benefit from a machine learning approach, if we are capable of embedding their structure into a generic pattern recognition tool.

CRFs address this general problem as an extension of logistic regression for multiclass problems. In their seminal work, Lafferty et al. (2001) assume that the output for each sample can be expressed as a set of interdependent labels and that this dependency can be captured by an undirected graphical model. They exploit the graphical model structure to avoid the exponential growth of the complexity with the number of labels in each output. There are many different machine learning problems that can be represented by this setting (Dietterich, 2002) such as, e.g., optical character recognition, part-of-speech tagging, collective webpage classification, mobile fraud detection, or pitch accent prediction. There have been several extensions to CRFs using kernels (Altun et al., 2004a,b; Lafferty et al., 2004), Bayesian learning (Qi et al., 2005), maximum-margin solution (Altun et al., 2003b; Taskar et al., 2004b), and two-dimensional CRFs (Kumar and Hebert, 2004).

Although the use of an undirected graphical model makes these procedures tractable, they are difficult to train, needing custom-made optimization tools, and hence they cannot solve large-scale problems. In this chapter, we present (kernel) CGMs, which simplify the training phase of CRF-like algorithms to solve large-scale structural classification problems. This algorithmic proposal is based on the same principle used for solving the binary classification problem, in which the 0–1 loss is replaced by a convex upper bound to ensure the optimal solution can be easily computed. In our case, we replace the CRF-like algorithm loss by another convex loss function that decouples the training of each clique in the undirected graph. CGM optimization is solved independently per clique using any general multiclassification algorithm. CGM complexity depends on the selected multiclass learning tool, so it opens the possibility of solving large-scale problems thanks to inexpensive multiclass tools, such as SVMs.

12.1.1 Outline of the Chapter

This chapter is divided into two main sections. In the first, we review CRF-like algorithms and present them using the same notation. Studying the different approaches for solving this fascinating machine learning problem from the same perspective allows a broad comparison between these algorithms. This knowledge helps us understand which algorithm is most suitable for each structural learning problem. We have also made an effort to simplify the notation so the algorithms are readily understood. In the second part, we introduce CGMs. We first show how a simple transformation of the general CRF algorithm loss function can reduce enormously the complexity of its training procedure and then examine in detail the hinge loss case, helping us understand how the proposed procedure works. We finish the chapter with a case study, showing the advantages of CGMs for solving large-scale problems.

12.2   A Unifying Review

The objective of this section is twofold; first, to present all CRF-like algorithms in a unifying framework in order to compare them and understand their different properties; and second to introduce the proposed notation. For these algorithms notation is an issue of its own, as it can be complicated and might be difficult to follow.

setup

We address the general supervised classification problem: given a labeled training dataset $\mathcal{D} = \{(\mathbf{x}_n, \mathbf{y}_n)\}_{n=1}^{N}$, predict the label $\mathbf{y}_*$ for a new input $\mathbf{x}_*$, where $\mathbf{x}_n \in \mathcal{X}$ and the label $\mathbf{y}_n \in \mathcal{Y} = \mathcal{Y}_1 \times \mathcal{Y}_2 \times \cdots \times \mathcal{Y}_L$ in which each $\mathcal{Y}_\ell = \{1, 2, \ldots, q\}$. L might depend on each training example (L_n) and q might be different for each element in $\mathcal{Y}$ (q_ℓ), but to keep the notation simple we use a unique L for all the samples and a unique q for all the labels. This simplification is exclusively used for presentation clarity and does not limit the applicability of any of the presented procedures for the more general case. This problem can be seen as a huge multiclass learning problem with q^L possible labels, and it is general enough to contain as special cases standard multiclass classification ($L = 1$) and binary classification ($L = 1$ and $q = 2$). But we can tractably solve it, because there is some structure in $\mathcal{Y}$ that we can exploit to simplify our machine learning problem.

We start from a probabilistic model that enables us to compute the posterior probability for all the possible labelings: $p(\mathbf{y}_* | \mathbf{x}_*, \mathcal{D})$. We are interested in finding

MAP approach

the labeling with highest probability: $\max_{\mathbf{y}_*}\{p(\mathbf{y}_* | \mathbf{x}_*, \mathcal{D})\}$. From the maximum a posteriori (MAP) approach to learning models, we make the connection with regularized risk minimization, and solutions to the problem using nonprobabilistic discriminative methods, such as SVMs.

We are given a set of features ($\phi(\mathbf{x}_n, \mathbf{y}_n)$), in which we can solve the classification problem using a linear combination of these features. The *softmax* function,

$$p(\mathbf{y}_n | \mathbf{x}_n, \mathbf{w}) = \frac{\exp\left(\mathbf{w}^\top \phi(\mathbf{x}_n, \mathbf{y}_n)\right)}{\sum_{\mathbf{y}} \exp\left(\mathbf{w}^\top \phi(\mathbf{x}_n, \mathbf{y})\right)}, \tag{12.1}$$

is a standard likelihood function for linear multiclassification problems. In (12.1), we are using an exponential family model to represent the likelihood function, in which a set of features are linearly combined to construct the probability density of $\mathbf{y}_n$. The denominator is known as the partition function and it comprises the sum over all q^L possible labeling of $\mathbf{y}$ to ensure that $p(\mathbf{y}_n | \mathbf{x}_n, \mathbf{w})$ adds up to 1. In this equation we have used $\mathbf{y}$ as a compact running index to represent the sum over all possible labeling, i.e.,

$$\sum_{\mathbf{y}} \exp\left(\mathbf{w}^\top \phi(\mathbf{x}_n, \mathbf{y})\right) = \sum_{i_1=1}^{q} \sum_{i_2=1}^{q} \cdots \sum_{i_L=1}^{q} \exp\left(\mathbf{w}^\top \phi(\mathbf{x}_n, \mathbf{y})\right)$$

with $\mathbf{y} = [i_1, i_2, \ldots, i_L]^\top$.

We can compute the posterior over the weights using Bayes rule:

$$p(\mathbf{w}|\mathbf{Y}, \mathbf{X}) = \frac{p(\mathbf{Y}|\mathbf{w}, \mathbf{X})p(\mathbf{w})}{p(\mathbf{Y}|\mathbf{X})}, \tag{12.2}$$

where $\mathbf{Y} = [\mathbf{y}_1, \ldots, \mathbf{y}_N]$, $\mathbf{X} = [\mathbf{x}_1, \ldots, \mathbf{x}_N]$ and $p(\mathbf{Y}|\mathbf{w}, \mathbf{X}) = \prod_n p(\mathbf{y}_n|\mathbf{x}_n, \mathbf{w})$. The prior over $\mathbf{w}$ is usually assumed to be an independent and identical zero-mean Gaussian distribution for each component:

$$p(\mathbf{w}) = \frac{1}{\sqrt{(2\pi C)^H}} \exp\left(\frac{\|\mathbf{w}\|^2}{2C}\right), \tag{12.3}$$

where $\mathbf{w} \in \mathbb{R}^H$.

prediction   The prediction for a new data point, integrating out the weights, is

$$p(\mathbf{y}_*|\mathbf{x}_*, \mathcal{D}) = \int p(\mathbf{y}_*|\mathbf{x}_*, \mathbf{w})p(\mathbf{w}|\mathbf{Y}, \mathbf{X})d\mathbf{w}. \tag{12.4}$$

The complexity of this problem grows exponentially in L –the length of the label vector– and we need to simplify it to work with large values of q and/or L. The complexity in (12.4) depends exponentially on L in many ways. First of all, we need to solve this equation for all q^L possible labeling of $\mathbf{y}_*$. Second, the complexity of $p(\mathbf{y}_*|\mathbf{x}_*, \mathbf{w})$ depends on the partition function of (12.1), which is the sum of all q^L terms in $\mathbf{y}_*$. Finally, to compute the posterior term $p(\mathbf{w}|\mathbf{Y}, \mathbf{X})$ we need to evaluate the likelihood of the N training examples and each one needs to evaluate a sum of q^L terms. Therefore the total complexity is $O(Nq^L)$. Lafferty et al. (2001) propose the use of an undirected acyclic graph over the labels. This graph makes it possible to efficiently compute the denominator in (12.1) using a forward-backward algorithm. Lafferty et al. (2001) define conditional random fields (CRFs) as follows:

Definition 67 (Conditional Random Field) *Let $G = (V, E)$ be a graph such that $\mathbf{y}_n$ is indexed by the vertices of G, then $(\mathbf{x}_n, \mathbf{y}_n)$ is a conditional random field in case, when conditioned on $\mathbf{x}_n$, the random variables $\mathbf{y}_n = [y_{n1}, y_{n2}, \ldots, y_{nL}]^\top$ obey the Markov property with respect to the graph:*

$$p(y_{n\ell}|\mathbf{x}_n, y_{n\ell'}, \forall \ell' \neq \ell) = p(y_{n\ell}|\mathbf{x}_n, y_{n\ell'}, \forall \ell' \overset{n}{\sim} \ell), \tag{12.5}$$

where $\ell' \overset{n}{\sim} \ell$ indicates that node ℓ' is neighbor of node ℓ in the graph.

Therefore, by the fundamental theorem of random fields, the distribution of $\mathbf{y}_n$ can be simplified to

$$p(\mathbf{y}_n|\mathbf{x}_n, \mathbf{w}) \propto \exp\left(\sum_{t=1}^{T} \mathbf{w}_t^\top \boldsymbol{\phi}_t(\mathbf{x}_n, \mathbf{y}_{nt})\right), \tag{12.6}$$

where the sum over t runs over the T maximal cliques in the graph. Note that each feature depends on the tth clique, which can be used to provide a different set of features for each clique. For example, a feature can select a part of the input $\mathbf{x}_n$, which is relevant for the labels in the tth clique.

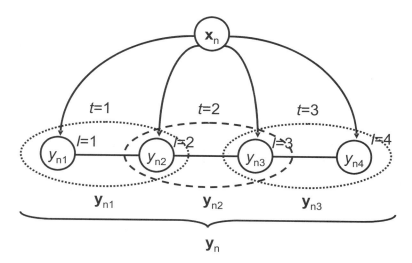

Figure 12.1 We show a chain for a four-dimensional label $\mathbf{y}_n = [y_{n1}, y_{n2}, y_{n3}, y_{n4}]^\top$. We have labeled the nodes ($y_{n\ell}$) and the cliques ($\mathbf{y}_{nt}$) from left to right, i.e. $\mathbf{y}_{n2} = [y_{n2}, y_{n3}]^\top$. Therefore boldfaced $\mathbf{y}_{n2}$ indicates the second clique and italic y_{n2} indicates the second node. We have also introduced $\mathbf{x}_n$ in the graph to indicate that the labels are conditioned on the input.

notation   Before presenting the family of CRF algorithms, let us explicitly state the notation that is being used throughout the chapter. The running indices n, ℓ, and t represent, respectively, the training samples, the nodes in the graph (the components in each $\mathbf{y}_n = [y_{n1}, y_{n2}, \ldots y_{n\ell}, \ldots, y_{nL}]^\top$), and the cliques in the graph. Therefore $y_{n\ell}$ is the ℓth entry in the nth training sample and $\mathbf{y}_{nt}$ represents the labels of the nth training sample associated with the tth clique, i.e. $\mathbf{y}_{nt} = [y_{n\ell_1}, y_{n\ell_2}, \ldots]^\top$ and its length depends on the number of variables in each clique (typically 2). We also use as running indices y_ℓ, $\mathbf{y}_t$, and $\mathbf{y}$ to denote that a sum runs, respectively, over all possible configurations in node ℓ, all possible configurations in the tth clique, and all possible labeling in the graph. Hence, for a node: $\sum_{y_\ell}(\cdot) = \sum_{i=1}^{q}(\cdot)$; for a clique with two nodes: $\sum_{\mathbf{y}_t}(\cdot) = \sum_{i_1=1}^{q}\sum_{i_2=1}^{q}(\cdot)$ with $\mathbf{y}_t = [i_1, i_2]^\top$; and for the whole graph: $\sum_{\mathbf{y}}(\cdot) = \sum_{i_1=1}^{q}\sum_{i_2=1}^{q}\cdots\sum_{i_L=1}^{q}(\cdot)$ with $\mathbf{y} = [i_1, i_2, \ldots, i_L]^\top$. The subindex in $y/\mathbf{y}$ tells us what are we summing over, the configuration of nodes (y_ℓ), cliques ($\mathbf{y}_t$), or graphs ($\mathbf{y}$). We use boldface for $\mathbf{y}$ and $\mathbf{y}_t$, as they represent a vector of labels, and italic for y_ℓ, as it represents a scalar value. Although using the index to carry extra information might be misleading at first, it greatly simplifies the notation in the chapter. For example, it allows understanding the differences between $\mathbf{y}_n$ (the output of the n training example) and $\mathbf{y}_t$ (a running index over all possible labels in the tth clique) without explicitly mentioning them. Also, we use the standard matrix notation with bold uppercase for matrices, bold lowercase for column vectors, and italic for scalars. We have depicted in figure 12.1 a simple acyclic graph over $\mathbf{y}$ to show a type of graphical model supported by CRFs and to clarify the notation. In this graph each $\mathbf{y}_n$ has four labels, $\mathbf{y}_n = [y_{n1}, y_{n2}, y_{n3}, y_{n4}]^\top$, and each clique has two labels, $\mathbf{y}_{n1} = [y_{n1}, y_{n2}]^\top$, ..., $\mathbf{y}_{n3} = [y_{n3}, y_{n4}]^\top$. We use throughout the chapter boldface for the labels of the cliques and graphs and italic for nodes.

Lafferty et al. (2001) propose to train the parameters of the CRF model by maximum likelihood (ML). We present the MAP version, because it is easier to relate to similar approaches and because we can readily obtain the ML solution MAP functional from the MAP functional by eliminating the prior term.

$$\mathbf{w}_{MAP} = \arg\max_{\mathbf{w}} p(\mathbf{w}|\mathbf{Y}, \mathbf{X}) = \arg\min_{\mathbf{w}} \left\{ -\log\left(p(\mathbf{w})\right) - \log\left(p(\mathbf{Y}|\mathbf{w}, \mathbf{X})\right) \right\}$$

$$= \arg\min_{\mathbf{w}} \left\{ \frac{1}{2} \|\mathbf{w}\|^2 + C \sum_{n=1}^{N} \left[\log\left(\sum_{\mathbf{y}} \exp\left(o(\mathbf{x}_n, \mathbf{y})\right) \right) - o(\mathbf{x}_n, \mathbf{y}_n) \right] \right\}, \tag{12.7}$$

where

$$o(\mathbf{x}_n, \mathbf{y}) = \sum_{t=1}^{T} \mathbf{w}_t^\top \boldsymbol{\phi}_t(\mathbf{x}_n, \mathbf{y}_t), \tag{12.8}$$

and the sum over $\mathbf{y}$ runs over the q^L possible labels. This sum can be efficiently computed using a forward-backward algorithm if the proposed graph for the CRF has no cycles; see Lafferty et al. (2001) for further details.

In (12.7) we readily see that the loss function compares the true output $o(\mathbf{x}_n, \mathbf{y}_n)$ with all the other outputs $\log\left(\sum_{\mathbf{y}} \exp\left(o(\mathbf{x}_n, \mathbf{y})\right)\right)$. This loss function is always nonnegative $\log\left(\sum_{\mathbf{y}} \exp\left(o(\mathbf{x}_n, \mathbf{y})\right)\right) > \log\left(\exp\left(o(\mathbf{x}_n, \mathbf{y}_n)\right)\right) = o(\mathbf{x}_n, \mathbf{y}_n)$ and it is close to zero iff $o(\mathbf{x}_n, \mathbf{y}_n) \gg o(\mathbf{x}_n, \mathbf{y}) \ \forall \mathbf{y} \neq \mathbf{y}_n$. The norm of $\mathbf{w}$ is a regularizer to avoid overfitting. This functional is convex and can be solved using different techniques (Wallach, 2002; Sha and Pereira, 2003; Dietterich et al., 2004; Vishwanathan et al., 2006; Pal et al., 2006). The inference phase can be done using a Viterbi-like algorithm over the labels in the graph.

Bayesian conditional random fields (B-CRFs) (Qi et al. (2005)) have been recently related work proposed, in which the posterior over the weight (12.2) is approximated by a Gaussian using the Power expectation propagation (EP) algorithm (Minka and Lafferty (2002)). Once the posterior has been estimated, predictions can be also made using an EP algorithm that considers an independent distribution for each label.

CRFs were initially proposed to solve the multilabel problem using a known set of features ($\boldsymbol{\phi}(\mathbf{x}_n, \mathbf{y}_n)$). Its functional in (12.7) fulfils the conditions of the representer theorem in Schölkopf and Smola (2002) (which is a generalization of the representer theorem originally proposed by Kimeldorf and Wahba (1971)). Therefore we can represent the optimal solution as a linear combination of the training examples:

$$\forall t: \quad \mathbf{w}_t = \sum_{n'=1}^{N} \sum_{\mathbf{y}_t'} \beta_{n',\mathbf{y}_t'}^t \phi_t(\mathbf{x}_{n'}, \mathbf{y}_t'). \tag{12.9}$$

If we define the kernel for each feature in each clique as $\kappa_t(\mathbf{x}_{n'}, \mathbf{y}_{n't}, \mathbf{x}_n, \mathbf{y}_{nt}) = \phi_t^\top(\mathbf{x}_{n'}, \mathbf{y}_{n't})\phi_t(\mathbf{x}_n, \mathbf{y}_{nt})$, we can obtain the MAP estimate in terms of β's by solving (12.7). In this case the output of the classifier can be written as

$$o(\mathbf{x}_n, \mathbf{y}) = \sum_{t=1}^{T} \sum_{n'=1}^{N} \sum_{\mathbf{y}_t'} \beta_{n',\mathbf{y}_t'}^t \kappa_t(\mathbf{x}_{n'}, \mathbf{y}_t', \mathbf{x}_n, \mathbf{y}_t), \tag{12.10}$$

which is the standard kernel formulation for multiclass problems. $o(\mathbf{x}_n, \mathbf{y})$ is computed as a linear combination of the kernels involving all the inputs in the training set with every possible labeling of the outputs.

The number of β grows as $N \prod_{t=1}^{T} q^{|\mathbf{y}_t|}$, where $|\mathbf{y}_t|$ indicates the number of nodes in the tth clique. For a chain (or treelike structure) the number of β is NTq^2, which is linear in the number of training samples and cliques and quadratic in the possible labelings in each node. If we had not used the graph to simplify the dependencies between the labels, the output would be $o(\mathbf{x}_n, \mathbf{y}) = \sum_{n'=1}^{N} \sum_{\mathbf{y}'} \beta_{n',\mathbf{y}'} \kappa(\mathbf{x}_{n'}, \mathbf{y}', \mathbf{x}_n, \mathbf{y})$ and the number of β's would grow as Nq^L, which increases exponentially with the length of the label vector.

Using the representer theorem and the kernel trick to solve CRFs was independently proposed by Lafferty et al. (2004) and Altun et al. (2004b). We refer to the general approach as kernel conditional random fields (K-CRFs). In both of these papers the authors propose to simplify the solution by forcing (in a smart and controlled way) that some β's should be zero at the solution. The runtime complexity to infer the label of a new input sequence does not grow with the number of training samples. Otherwise all β's are nonzero due to the applied loss function (logistic regression). Another option to get a sparse solution in terms of the β is to change the loss function by a hinge loss, which is presented in the following section.

12.2.1 Support Vector Machines

Once we have described the optimization of CRFs as the minimization in (12.7), the comparison with SVMs is straightforward, as we can substitute the logistic regression loss function by any other, such as the hinge loss used by SVMs.

multiclass SVMs and related formulations

There are two alternative formulation for multiclass SVMs (M-SMVs): Weston and Watkins (1998) and Crammer and Singer (2001). The difference lies in how they penalized the training errors. In Weston and Watkins (1998), the M-SVM penalizes any possible labeling that provides a larger output than the true labeling. Whereas in Crammer and Singer (2001), the M-SVM only penalizes the largest incorrect labeling, if it is greater than the true labeling. For this problem, in which the number of possible labelings grows exponentially, the formulation by Weston and Watkins (1998) can result in an exponential growth in the number of nonzero support vectors and therefore it is more advisable to use the formulation by Crammer and Singer (2001), although both perform similarly well for most multiclass learning problems.

The M-SVM formulation by Crammer and Singer (2001) can be represented as an unconstrained optimization problem:

$$\min_{\mathbf{w}} \left\{ \frac{1}{2} \|\mathbf{w}\|^2 + C \sum_{n=1}^{N} \left[\max_{\mathbf{y}} \left(M_{\mathbf{y}_n, \mathbf{y}} + o(\mathbf{x}_n, \mathbf{y}) - o(\mathbf{x}_n, \mathbf{y}_n) \right) \right]_+ \right\},$$

where $M_{\mathbf{y}_n, \mathbf{y}}$ is the margin that depends on the true labeling and the labeling that it is being compared against and $[u]_+ = \max(0, u)$ is the hinge loss. This functional is equivalent to (12.7) replacing the logistic regression loss function by the SVM's hinge loss.

This formulation can be expressed in the more standard constrained optimization setting, in which we need to optimize

$$\min_{\mathbf{w}, \xi_n} \left\{ \frac{1}{2} \|\mathbf{w}\|^2 + C \sum_{n=1}^{N} \xi_n \right\} \tag{12.11}$$

subject to

$$o(\mathbf{x}_n, \mathbf{y}_n) - o(\mathbf{x}_n, \mathbf{y}) \geq M_{\mathbf{y}_n, \mathbf{y}} - \xi_n \qquad \forall n, \forall \mathbf{y}, \tag{12.12}$$

where $M_{\mathbf{y}_n, \mathbf{y}_n} = 0$ to ensure that $\xi_n \geq 0$. The number of constraints grows exponentially in L (q^L) but as there is only one ξ_n per training sample there are only few active constraints for each sample, typically none or two. Thus the growth of the complexity (nonzero Lagrange multipliers) is not exponential in L. This formulation is equivalent to the hidden Markov support vector machine (HM-SVM) proposed in (Altun et al., 2003b) with small variations on how the margin is imposed and the slack variable ξ_n is penalized.

Finally, there has been an independent formulation of this solution, known as maximum-margin Markov networks (M³Ns) by Taskar et al. (2004b), in which the above formulation is simplified, not needing exponentially many Lagrange multipliers to solve it. We believe the easiest way to present M³Ns is to work from the Lagrangian of (12.11),

$$L(\mathbf{w}, \xi_n, \alpha_{n,\mathbf{y}}) = \frac{1}{2} \|\mathbf{w}\|^2 + C \sum_{n=1}^{N} \xi_n$$

$$- \sum_{n=1}^{N} \sum_{\mathbf{y}} \alpha_{n,\mathbf{y}} \left(\sum_{t=1}^{T} \mathbf{w}_t^\top \boldsymbol{\phi}_t(\mathbf{x}_n, \mathbf{y}_{nt}) - \sum_{t=1}^{T} \mathbf{w}_t^\top \boldsymbol{\phi}_t(\mathbf{x}_n, \mathbf{y}_t) \right.$$

$$\left. - \sum_{\ell=1}^{L} [1 - \delta(y_{n\ell}, y_\ell)] + \xi_n \right), \tag{12.13}$$

in which we have substituted $o(\mathbf{x}_n, \mathbf{y})$ by its definition in (12.8) and we have defined the margin per node to be the Hamming distance between the true and the possible label, as proposed by Taskar et al. (2004b). Now for each training sample and each configuration in every clique, we define

$$\beta^t_{n,\mathbf{y}_t} = \sum_{\mathbf{y} \sim \mathbf{y}_t} \alpha_{n,\mathbf{y}} \qquad \forall n, \forall t, \forall \mathbf{y}_t, \tag{12.14}$$

where the sum runs over all possible labeling of $\mathbf{y}$ with the labels in the tth clique fixed at $\mathbf{y}_t$. And for each configuration in every node, we define

$$\beta^\ell_{n,y_\ell} = \sum_{\mathbf{y} \sim y_\ell} \alpha_{n,\mathbf{y}} \qquad \forall n, \forall \ell, \forall y_\ell, \tag{12.15}$$

where the sum runs over all possible labeling of $\mathbf{y}$ with the labels in the ℓth node fixed at y_ℓ.

Thus we can rewrite the Lagrange functional (12.13) in terms of $\beta^t_{n,\mathbf{y}_t}$ and β^ℓ_{n,y_ℓ} as follows:

$$
\begin{aligned}
L(\mathbf{w}, \xi_n, \beta^t_{n,\mathbf{y}_t}, \beta^\ell_{n,y_\ell}) = {} & \frac{1}{2}\|\mathbf{w}\|^2 + C \sum_{n=1}^N \xi_n \\
& - \sum_{n=1}^N \sum_{t=1}^T \sum_{\mathbf{y}_t} \beta^t_{n,\mathbf{y}_t} \left(\mathbf{w}_t^\top \phi_t(\mathbf{x}_n, \mathbf{y}_{nt}) - \mathbf{w}_t^\top \phi_t(\mathbf{x}_n, \mathbf{y}_t) + \xi_n \right) \\
& + \sum_{n=1}^N \sum_{\ell=1}^L \sum_{y_\ell} \beta^\ell_{n,y_\ell}[1 - \delta(y_{n\ell}, y_\ell)],
\end{aligned}
\tag{12.16}
$$

in which we can see that the sum over $\mathbf{y}$ (q^L terms) has been replaced by sums over $\mathbf{y}_t$ (q^2 terms) and over y_ℓ (q terms). We have as many $\beta^t_{n,\mathbf{y}_t}$ as we did for the K-CRFs and the β^ℓ_{n,y_ℓ} are significantly fewer, reducing the exponentially many Lagrange multipliers ($\alpha_{n,\mathbf{y}}$) in (12.13).

Note that the β's are not independent of each other and when solving the Lagrange functional we have to impose an additional constraint, besides the β being positive.

$$\beta^\ell_{n,y_\ell} = \sum_{\mathbf{y}_t \sim y_\ell} \beta^t_{n,\mathbf{y}_t} \tag{12.17}$$

This constraint is necessary to ensure that the α can be recovered from the β and that we are obtaining the same solution as in the HM-SVM. This constraint must hold for all the samples, for all the nodes, for all the cliques that contain the node ℓ, and for all possible labelings in the node.

12.2.2   Summary

In this section we have presented the family of CRF algorithms. We have discussed CRF (Lafferty et al., 2001), B-CRF (Qi et al., 2005), K-CRF (Altun et al., 2004a,b;

Lafferty et al., 2004), HM-SVM (Altun et al., 2003b), and M^{3}Ns (Taskar et al., 2004b). In all these algorithms an exponentially growing structured multiclass learning problem is simplified by imposing a graphical model over the output space. This simplification allows solving the multiclassification tractably both in the needed computational power and in the training sample size. In table 12.1, we classify all these procedures according to their relevant properties. The main difference between HM-SVM and M^{3}Ns lies within the optimization procedure, as explained in the previous section (it does not show up in the table).

HM-SVM vs.
M^{3}Ns

Table 12.1   Comparisons of CFR-like algorithms

	Probabilistic output	Kernels	Loss function
CRF	No	No	Logistic regression
B-CRF	Yes	No	Logistic regression
K-CRF	No	Yes	Logistic regression
HM-SVM	No	Yes	Hinge loss
M^3Ns	No	Yes	Hinge loss

12.3   Conditional Graphical Models

The CRF-like algorithms can be represented in a general form by the following convex optimization problem:

$$\min_{\mathbf{w}} \frac{1}{2} \sum_{t=1}^{T} ||\mathbf{w}_t||^2 + C \sum_{n=1}^{N} L\left(\sum_{t=1}^{T} \mathbf{w}_t^\top \boldsymbol{\phi}_t(\mathbf{x}_n, \mathbf{y}_t) \right). \tag{12.18}$$

where $L(\cdot)$ represent the loss-function and we have replaced $\mathbf{w}$ by $\mathbf{w} = [\mathbf{w}_1, \mathbf{w}_2, \ldots, \mathbf{w}_T]^\top$. The used of a logistic regression loss function leads us to (12.7) and the use of the hinge loss to (12.11). Any other loss function gives rise to other CRF-like algorithm, i.e. LS-CRF with a quadratic loss function.

CGM main idea

In our proposal, CGMs, we upper-bound the CRF loss function to obtain an optimization functional that it is significantly easier to optimize and can be addressed using any multiclass learning tool. The idea behind CGM is identical to the one used to solve binary classification problems. In binary classification, the 0–1 loss, which is nonconvex and nondifferentiable, is replaced by a convex loss function (square loss, hinge loss, logistic regression, etc.) that upper-bounds the 0–1 loss, to ensure that the paid penalty is at least as large as the 0–1 loss. The change of the loss function allows solving a simpler optimization problem and we can concentrate on other tasks, such as defining nonlinear classifiers or obtaining the relevant features for classification.

We propose to upper-bound (12.18), using Jensen's inequality over the loss function, to build the CGM optimization functional:

$$\min_{\mathbf{w}} \sum_{t=1}^{T} \left\{ \frac{1}{2}||\mathbf{w}_t||^2 + C \sum_{n=1}^{N} L\left(\mathbf{w}_t^{\top} \phi_t(\mathbf{x}_n, \mathbf{y}_t)\right) \right\}. \tag{12.19}$$

In (12.19), we have interchanged the sum over t with the loss function $L(\cdot)$ to obtain an upper bound on (12.18), if the loss function is convex. Therefore, we are penalizing errors at least as much as we did in the original formulation.

CGM function decomposes per clique, so each $\mathbf{w}_t$ is trained independently using the features and outputs corresponding to the tth clique. This is a major advantage as we do not need to keep track of what is happening in the rest of the graph to learn the parameters of each clique. Furthermore the optimization in each clique,

$$\min_{\mathbf{w}_t} \frac{1}{2}||\mathbf{w}_t||^2 + C \sum_{n=1}^{N} L\left(\mathbf{w}_t^{\top} \phi_t(\mathbf{x}_n, \mathbf{y}_t)\right), \tag{12.20}$$

is equivalent to a regularized multiclass problem with q^2 labels.[1] We can apply any multiclassification tool to train the model in each clique without needing a custom-made procedure for defining the parameters of the model. CGM opens up the range of problems in which structured machine learning can be applied, as it has a simple training procedure and can be trained for large-scale problems. For example, if we use a standard tool such as LibSVM (Lin, 1999), we could train the CGM with up to several thousand training samples.

To infer the label of new inputs CGMs work as CRF-like algorithms do. For this phase there is no difference between both procedures and the solution provided by CGMs cannot be read independently for each clique because the outputs on the same node shared by two cliques has to be the same. To infer an output a Viterbi-like algorithm has to be run over the assumed graphical model to find the most likely output sequence, as in any CRF-like algorithm because the outputs of each clique have to agree on the labels they assign to each node. Therefore, we cannot compute the output independently for each clique, as a given node (shared among different cliques) can present a different labeling for each clique.

12.3.1 Support Vector Machines

In this section, we compare HM-SVMs and M³Ns with CGMs with hinge loss. This comparison helps us draw some useful conclusions about the validity of the

---

1. If each clique only contains two labels.

proposed algorithm and how the two approaches penalize errors in training. The HM-SVM/M³N solves the following constrained optimization problem:

$$\min_{\mathbf{w}, \xi_n} \frac{1}{2} \sum_{t=1}^{T} \|\mathbf{w}_t\|^2 + C \sum_{n=1}^{N} \xi_n, \tag{12.21}$$

subject to

$$\forall n, \forall \mathbf{y}: \quad \sum_{t=1}^{T} \mathbf{w}_t^\top \phi_t(\mathbf{x}_n, \mathbf{y}_{nt}) - \sum_{t=1}^{T} \mathbf{w}_t^\top \phi_t(\mathbf{x}_n, \mathbf{y}_t) \geq \sum_{t=1}^{T} M_{\mathbf{y}_n, \mathbf{y}_t} - \xi_n, \tag{12.22}$$

and CGM with hinge loss solves

$$\min_{\mathbf{w}, \xi_n} \sum_{t=1}^{T} \left\{ \frac{1}{2} \|\mathbf{w}_t\|^2 + C \sum_{n=1}^{N} \xi_{nt} \right\} \tag{12.23}$$

subject to

$$\forall n, \forall t, \forall \mathbf{y}_t: \quad \mathbf{w}_t^\top \phi_t(\mathbf{x}_n, \mathbf{y}_{nt}) - \mathbf{w}_t^\top \phi_t(\mathbf{x}_n, \mathbf{y}_t) \geq M_{\mathbf{y}_{nt}, \mathbf{y}_t} - \xi_{nt}. \tag{12.24}$$

Both optimization functional (12.21) and (12.23) are identical with the definition of the slacks, variables being the only difference. The main difference lies in the linear constraints that are responsible for the obtained solution for both methods.

Comparing constraints (12.24) and (12.22), we can notice the reduction in the number of constraints and therefore the needed runtime complexity during training. Initially it might seem that when using (12.24), we are multiplying the number of constraints by T, the number of cliques, as it divides (12.22) into T different constraints (one per clique). But each one of the constraints in (12.24) only needs to distinguish between $q^{|\mathbf{y}_t|}$ labels in each clique instead of the q^L different labeling of each sequence in (12.22). We end up having a significant reduction in the number of constraints[2] in our optimization formulation for CGMs in (12.23) and (12.24).

As we commented in the previous paragraph the constraint in (12.22) is the sum over all cliques of the constraint in (12.24). Thus the constraint in (12.24) is more restrictive, because it enforces the margin constraint clique by clique instead of over the whole label sequence. This is due to the modification of the loss function in (12.19), where we changed the loss in CRF-like algorithms by a convex upper bound. This constraint allows us to be more restrictive and more precise, as we only penalize the cliques that are in error. Let us illustrate these properties with two examples.

Suppose a labeling $\mathbf{y}$ fulfills the margin requirement for the nth training example, but individually one of its cliques does not. In the original M³N formulation, this labeling is not penalized and the discriminative information about the clique, which does not fulfill the margin requirement, is lost. But the formulation in (12.23) and

---

2. For a treelike structure the number of constraints drops from Nq^L to NTq^2.

(12.24) enforces the margin per clique, so it uses the information in the erroneously classified clique to build the classifier, incorporating its discriminative information into $\mathbf{w}_t$.

nature of support
vectors

The complementary example is also relevant. Suppose a labeling $\mathbf{y}$ does not fulfill the margin requirement because one of its cliques is completely flawed, although all the other cliques are correctly classified with enough margin. In M³N and the other CRF methods, this flawed clique forces the whole sequence to be a support vector and it is incorporated into the construction of the classifier of every clique, although it only presents discriminative information for one clique. In the CGM solution, this flawed clique is considered as an outlier and is incorporated into the solution of the classifier in that clique. But it does not affect the classifiers in the remaining cliques and it does not force the whole sequence to be a support vector in every clique.

In a way we can see the formulation per clique to be *more restrictive* than the formulation in (12.22), as we can learn locally in a clique from sequences that are globally correctly classified. At the same time it is *more precise*, as it only needs to learn from the cliques in which the errors occur and does not need to incorporate the whole sequence if it does not bring discriminative information for every clique in the graph.

To sum up, we started the motivation for the algorithm by arguing that solving the optimization per clique would provide a huge computational cost reduction and that we might be able to tradeoff some accuracy for getting this complexity reduction. We have finally shown that we do not only get this computational cost reduction but also a more sensible learning procedure that only incorporates those cliques that bring discriminative information for the whole sequence and not complete sequences that might only provide local discriminative information. We believe this approach can provide higher discriminative power than the previous proposed methods with a much simpler learning mechanism and with a significant reduction in computational complexity. We test these claims experimentally in the next section.

12.4 Experiments

We test the CGM with a handwritten word-recognition task. The dataset was collected by Kassel (1995) and contains around 6877 words of varying length (4 to 15 letters) written by 150 subjects. Each word is divided into 16×8 binary images for each letter and its corresponding label. Our inputs $\mathbf{x}_n$ will be a $16 \times 8L$ binary image and its corresponding label vector $\mathbf{y}_n$ will contain L elements. Thisdata set was preprocessed by Taskar et al. (2004b) to test the M³N. The dataset was divided into 10 groups for crossvalidation.

We test the CGM using the three graphical models shown in figure 12.2. The first graph contains no edges and in it we will be training a multiclass model for each letter independently. The second one is a chain, in which we have pairwise inter-

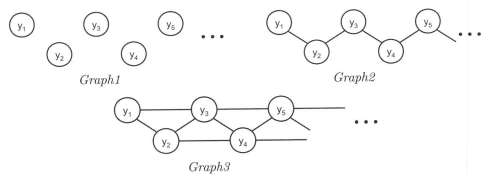

Graph1   Graph2

Graph3

Figure 12.2   We represent the three graphical models that will be used in the experiments to test the CGM.

actions between letters, and the third takes into account three-letter interactions. For this experiment, we will use the following feature vector:

$$\boldsymbol{\phi}_t(\mathbf{x}_n, \mathbf{y}_{nt}) = [\mathbf{0}, \ldots, \boldsymbol{\psi}(\mathbf{x}_{nt}), \mathbf{0}, \ldots]^\top, \qquad (12.25)$$

where $\boldsymbol{\phi}_t(\mathbf{x}_n, \mathbf{y}_{nt})$ contains $q^{|\mathbf{y}_t|}$ terms and the nonzero element is indexed by the labeling $\mathbf{y}_{nt}$. In this feature, we only consider as inputs the images of the letters in each clique. The kernel of $\boldsymbol{\phi}_t(\mathbf{x}_n, \mathbf{y}_{nt})$ is

$$\kappa_t(\mathbf{x}_{n'}, \mathbf{y}_{n't}, \mathbf{x}_n, \mathbf{y}_{nt}) = \delta(\mathbf{y}_{nt} = \mathbf{y}_{n't})k(\mathbf{x}_{nt}, \mathbf{x}_{n't}),$$

where we have defined $k(\mathbf{x}_{nt}, \mathbf{x}_{n't}) = \boldsymbol{\psi}^\top(\mathbf{x}_{nt})\boldsymbol{\psi}(\mathbf{x}_{n't}) = \exp(\|\mathbf{x}_{nt} - \mathbf{x}_{n't}\|^2/2/\sigma^2)$. To solve each one of the multiclass SVMs we have used the LibSVM code (Lin, 1999).

We have first solved this experiment using one group for training and the other nine for validation, as was done in Taskar et al. (2004b), and we have repeated it over the 10 different sets. This is not the standard crossvalidation setting. We have set $C = 5$, $M_{\mathbf{y}_{nt}, \mathbf{y}_t} = 1$, and $\sigma = \sqrt{d/16}$, where d is the dimension of $\mathbf{x}_{nt}$. We have reported the letter and word probability of error in table 12.2.

Table 12.2   We show the mean error and its standard deviation for 10-fold crossvalidation for the three graphs with one set for training and nine for validation

	Graph1	Graph2	Graph3
Word	0.795±.0012	0.369±.0013	0.195±.0009
Letter	0.271±.0009	0.125±.0011	0.058±.0005

In Taskar et al. (2004b) the authors reported an error rate of around 13% in the letter recognition task, for the same partition of the data used in this experiment. This result is directly comparable to the letter recognition for *Graph2*, as they used a chain in their experiments. The proposed CGM can be used with higher connectivity graphs, such as *Graph3*, because we can perform the training independently per clique and the error rate is reduced by over 50%.

We have also computed the crossvalidation error in the standard setting, in which nine groups are used for training and one for validation, to show that we can work with larger training sets. The mean probability of error of letter and word recognition is reported in table 12.3. For this setting *Graph3* is still better than

Table 12.3   We show the mean error and its standard deviation for 10-fold crossvalidation for the three graphs with nine set for training and one for validation

	Graph1	*Graph2*	*Graph3*
Word	0.528±.0037	0.133±.0015	0.128±.0019
Letter	0.126±.0009	0.031±.0003	0.027±.0004

Graph2, but there the difference is not as significant as it was for shorter training sequences.

The performances of *Graph2* and *Graph3* in the above experiments were significantly higher than those of *Graph1*, because they incorporate some error-correcting capabilities, as not all the transitions in the graph are allowed and the different cliques have to agree on the predicted label in the nodes they share. But if we look at the performance clique by clique (individual decisions), *Graph1* presents a lower error rate as its learning problem is much simpler. It only needs to distinguish between q labels, instead of q^2 or q^3, and the training set has the same number of entries with lower input dimension. We propose the following feature to incorporate the individual decisions in *Graph1* with the error-correcting capabilities provided by graphs with higher connectivity among their nodes. We will train *Graph2* using the following feature vector:

$$\boldsymbol{\phi}_t(\mathbf{x}_n, \mathbf{y}_{nt}) = [\mathbf{0}, \ldots, \boldsymbol{\psi}(\mathbf{x}_{nt_1}), \ldots \mid \mathbf{0}, \ldots, \boldsymbol{\psi}(\mathbf{x}_{nt_2}), \ldots]^\top,$$

which has $2q^2$ elements, twice as many entries as the feature defined in (12.25). The positions of $\boldsymbol{\psi}(\mathbf{x}_{nt_1})$ and $\boldsymbol{\psi}(\mathbf{x}_{nt_2})$ are indexed by $\mathbf{y}_{nt}$. The vectors $\mathbf{x}_{nt_1}$ and $\mathbf{x}_{nt_2}$ are, respectively, the images of the first and second letter in the tth clique.

For this feature, we can describe the weight vector as

$$\mathbf{w}_t = [\mathbf{w}_{t1} \mid \mathbf{w}_{t2}] = [\mathbf{w}_{t1_1}, \ldots, \mathbf{w}_{t1_{q^2}} \mid \mathbf{w}_{t2_1}, \ldots, \mathbf{w}_{t2_{q^2}}.]$$

In each $\mathbf{w}_{t1}$ there are q^2 terms, but in the corresponding part of the feature vector, we will only deal with the image of a letter (q different values). As the same letter can be placed in different positions by the labeling $\mathbf{y}_{nt}$, we will clamp together the $\mathbf{w}_{t1_s}$ (and $\mathbf{w}_{t2_s}$) that multiply the image of the same letter, so we can have a higher performance, as each weight vector will be trained with more training examples (all the letters in each node). But the feature vector will still keep the information about which couple of letters are allowed in each clique. The kernel for this feature will be $\kappa_t(\mathbf{x}_{n'}, \mathbf{y}_{n't}, \mathbf{x}_n, \mathbf{y}_{nt}) = \delta(\mathbf{y}_{nt} = \mathbf{y}_{n't})[k(\mathbf{x}_{nt_1}, \mathbf{x}_{n't_1}) + k(\mathbf{x}_{nt_2}, \mathbf{x}_{n't_2})]$, where $k(\cdot, \cdot)$ is defined as above.

We have computed the crossvalidation error for this feature using the previously defined sets. When a single set is used for training the mean letter recognition error and standard deviation are $0.097\pm.0006$ (for words: $0.327\pm.0012$). And when we used nine sets for training and one for validation, the performance results are $0.025\pm.0003$ (for words: $0.120\pm.0019$). We can see that these results provide lower error rates than the ones reported in tables 12.2 and 12.3 for *Graph1* and *Graph2*, because we incorporate the error-correcting capabilities of *Graph2* and the more precise performance in each individual decision. This feature vector can be also extended to *Graph3*.

12.5   Conclusions and Further Work

In this chapter, we have presented a unified framework that covers the most relevant proposals to solve the multilabel classification problem using graphical models to reduce the exponentially growing complexity with the label length. We have presented a compact notation that can be used to represent CRFs (Lafferty et al., 2001), Bayesian CRFs (Qi et al., 2005), K-CRFs (Altun et al., 2004a,b; Lafferty et al., 2004) and M^3Ns (Altun et al., 2003b; Taskar et al., 2004b). This notation is simpler than most of the notation used in those papers, and allows comparison and understanding of their similar properties. There is a different approach (Weston et al., 2002), which uses a kernel over the labels to deal with the complexity of the addressed problem. Although, we have not studied the connection of our framework with this method, as we end up using a kernel over the inputs and labels (12.10), we believe that connection can be made and it is left for further work.

In the second part of the chapter, based on the presented framework, we have proposed a new learning algorithm to solve the multilabel problem. The CGM can be solved independently per clique, which is its main difference with the algorithms proposed in the literature. Therefore the CGM is much simpler to solve, so we can use much larger training datasets and it can be applied over more complex graphs. We have also argued, and shown experimentally, that this training per clique is more precise than the training of the sequences as a whole. Because the classification of a new example is based on the individual decisions of each clique (then combined with the graph to ensure the solution is consistent), if we use all the discriminative information to train each clique we will be able to provide much more accurate answers when we predict the labels of new samples. We have left for further work the connection between the CGMs and the probabilistic approaches for solving the multilabel problem.

Acknowledgments

Fernando Pérez-Cruz is supported by the Spanish Ministry of Education postdoctoral fellowship EX2004-0698.

13   Density Estimation of Structured Outputs in Reproducing Kernel Hilbert Spaces

Yasemin Altun and Alex Smola

In this chapter we study the problem of estimating conditional probability distributions for structured output prediction tasks in reproducing kernel Hilbert spaces (RKHSs). More specifically, we prove decomposition results for undirected graphical models, give constructions for kernels, and show connections to Gaussian process classification. Finally we present efficient means of solving the optimization problem and apply this to label sequence learning. Experiments on named entity recognition and pitch accent prediction tasks demonstrate the competitiveness of our approach.

13.1   Introduction

The benefits of a framework for designing flexible and powerful input representations for machine learning problems has been demonstrated by the success of kernel-based methods in binary and multiclass classification as well as regression. However, many real-world prediction problems also involve complex output spaces, with possible dependencies between multiple output variables. Markov chain dependency structure is a prominent example of this kind and is ubiquitous in natural language processing (e.g. part-of-speech tagging, shallow parsing), speech recognition (e. g. pitch accent prediction), information retrieval (e. g. named entity recognition), and computational biology (e. g. protein secondary structure prediction). More complicated dependency structures such as hierarchies and parse trees are also commonplace.

A well-known approach for solving these problems is conditional random fields (CRFs), proposed by Lafferty et al. (2001), an extension of logistic regression that takes dependencies between random variables in a graph (e. g. neighboring labels along a chain) into account. Related approaches include Punyakanok and Roth (2000) and McCallum et al. (2000). More recently, other discriminative methods such as AdaBoost (Altun et al., 2002), perceptron learning (Collins, 2002), and support vector machines (SVMs) (Altun et al., 2003b; Taskar et al., 2004b; Tsochantaridis et al., 2004) have been extended to learning the prediction of structured objects.

In this chapter, which is an extension of our work in Altun et al. (2004a,b) and is closely related to Lafferty et al. (2004), we study the problem of estimating conditional probability distributions over structured outputs within a RKHS. Framing this as a special case of inverse problems, we show that maximizing entropy with respect to approximate moment-matching constraints in Banach spaces leads to the maximum a posteriori estimation and exponential families. The space in which the moments are defined and approximated specify a regularization of the conditional log-likelihood of the sample. When this space is ℓ_2, we have a Gaussian process over the structured input-output space. Then, one can construct and learn in RKHS and, thereby overcome the limitations of (finite-dimensional) parametric statistical models and achieve the flexibility of implicit data representations.

advantages of a probabilistic model

Our framework preserves the main strength of CRFs, namely their rigorous probabilistic semantics, which is not the case for other discriminative methods such as max-margin approaches. There are two important advantages of a probabilistic model. First, it is very intuitive to incorporate prior knowledge within a probabilistic framework. Second, in addition to predicting the best labels, one can compute posterior label probabilities and thus derive confidence scores for predictions. This is a valuable property, in particular for applications requiring a cascaded architecture of classifiers. Confidence scores can be propagated to subsequent processing stages or used to abstain on certain predictions. Another advantage over max-margin methods for structured output prediction is its consistency with infinite samples. Even though the performance of a learning method on small-sample problems does not necessarily coincide with its performance on infinite samples, asymptotic consistency analysis provides useful insights.

Performing density estimation via Gaussian processes over structured input-output spaces faces serious tractability issues, since the space of parameters, although finite, is exponential in the size of the structured object. We prove decomposition results for Markov random fields (MRFs); which allows us to obtain an optimization problem scaling polynomially with the size of the structure. This leads to the derivation of an efficient estimation algorithm, for which we provide the details for label sequence learning. We report experimental results on pitch accent prediction and named-entity recognition.

13.2   Estimating Conditional Probability Distributions over Structured Outputs

13.2.1   General Setting

In this chapter, we are interested in the prediction of structured variables. The goal is to learn a mapping $h : \mathcal{X} \to \mathcal{Y}$ from structured inputs to structured response variables, where the inputs and response variables form a dependency structure. There exists a cost function $\Delta : \mathcal{Y} \times \mathcal{Y} \to \Re$, where $\Delta(\mathbf{y}, \bar{\mathbf{y}})$ denotes the cost of predicting $\bar{\mathbf{y}}$ instead of $\mathbf{y}$. We restrict our attention to cost functions such that $\Delta(\mathbf{y}, \mathbf{y}) = 0$ and $\Delta(\mathbf{y}, \bar{\mathbf{y}}) > 0$ for $\mathbf{y} \neq \bar{\mathbf{y}}$. This function is generally the standard 0-1 classification error for multiclass classification problems. However, in the structured prediction problems, it can incorporate differences in the structure of $\mathbf{y}$ and $\bar{\mathbf{y}}$, such as Hamming loss of sequences or $1 - F_1$ score of parse trees.

Let us define $\mathcal{Z}$ as $\mathcal{X} \times \mathcal{Y}$. We assume that there is a fixed but unknown distribution P over $\mathcal{Z}$ according to which input/output pairs $(\mathbf{x}, \mathbf{y})$ are generated. If this distribution was known, the optimal predictor, i. e. the Bayes decision rule, is given by

optimal predictor

$$h_B(\mathbf{x}) = \operatorname*{argmin}_{\mathbf{y} \in \mathcal{Y}} \sum_{\mathbf{y}' \neq \mathbf{y}} p(\mathbf{y}'|\mathbf{x}) \Delta(\mathbf{y}', \mathbf{y}). \tag{13.1}$$

In the special case of 0-1 loss, this is equivalent to $h_B(\mathbf{x}) = \operatorname{argmax}_{\mathbf{y} \in \mathcal{Y}} p(\mathbf{y}|\mathbf{x})$. Then, one can reduce the (structured) prediction problem to one of estimating the conditional distribution $p(\mathbf{y}|\mathbf{x})$ and performing the argmin operation as in (13.1).

13.2.2   Maximum Entropy with Approximate Matching

In supervised learning, we are given a sample S of ℓ input-output pairs $S = \{(\mathbf{x}^1, \mathbf{y}^1), \ldots, (\mathbf{x}^\ell, \mathbf{y}^\ell)\}$. There exists a set of measurements relevant for the learning task, commonly referred as *moment* or *feature* functions, $\phi : \mathcal{Z} \to \mathcal{B}$, where $\mathcal{B}$ is a Banach space in the most general form of the problem. The goal is to find the conditional probability distribution p over $\mathcal{Y}|\mathcal{X}$ such that the expectation of the features with respect to $p(\mathbf{y}|\mathbf{x})$ for all $\mathbf{x} \in S_{\mathbf{x}}$ $(E_{\mathbf{y} \sim p}[\phi(\mathbf{x}, \mathbf{y})|\mathbf{x}])$ matches their empirical values $(\tilde{\phi})$, $E_{\mathbf{y} \sim p}[\phi(\mathbf{x}, \mathbf{y})|\mathbf{x}] = \tilde{\phi}$, Here $S_{\mathbf{x}}$ denotes the set of ℓ inputs in S, $\{\mathbf{x}^i\}$ for $i = 1, \ldots, \ell$. The empirical values of the features are generally derived from the sample by

$$\tilde{\phi} = \frac{1}{\ell} \sum_{i=1}^{\ell} \phi(\mathbf{x}^i, \mathbf{y}^i). \tag{13.2}$$

This estimation task is an instance of a more general problem, namely the *inverse problem*, where the goal is to find x satisfying $Ax = b$. Inverse problems are known to be ill-formed and are stabilized by imposing a regularity or smoothness measure, such as the entropy of the distribution (Ruderman and Bialek, 1994). Then, the estimation problem can be formulated as finding the maximum entropy distribution

p (equivalently minimizing the relative entropy of p with respect to a constant distribution q) such that it satisfies the moment-matching constraints,

$$\min_{p} \ KL(p\|q) \text{ subject to } E_{\mathbf{y} \sim p}[\phi(\mathbf{x}, \mathbf{y})|\mathbf{x}] = \tilde{\phi}.$$

In general, it is very difficult to satisfy the moment-matching constraints exactly, especially when the number of features can be very large (and possibly infinite).

For example, the solution may lie on the boundary of a feasibility region. Moreover, this can lead to severe overfitting of the data. In order to overcome this obstacle, the constraints can be relaxed to approximate matches such that the difference between the expected and the empirical values are small with respect to the norm of the space $\mathcal{B}$, denoted by $\|.\|_{\mathcal{B}}$. An adaptation of theorem 8 of Altun and Smola (2006) gives the solution of this estimation problem and establishes the duality connection between the KL divergence minimization with approximate moment-matching constraints and the *maximum a posteriori* (MAP) estimation.

Theorem 68 (Approximate KL Minimization) *Let p, q be conditional probability distributions over $\mathcal{Y}|\mathcal{X}$ and S be a sample of size ℓ. Moreover, $\phi : \mathcal{Z} \to \mathcal{B}$ is a mapping from $\mathcal{Z}$ to a Banach space $\mathcal{B}$, $\tilde{\phi} \in \mathcal{B}$ and $\mathcal{B}^*$ is the dual space of $\mathcal{B}$. Then, for any $\epsilon \geq 0$ the problem*

$$\min_{p} \ KL(p\|q) \ \text{subject to} \ \left\| E_{\mathbf{y} \sim p}[\phi(\mathbf{x}, \mathbf{y})|\mathbf{x}] - \tilde{\phi} \right\|_{\mathcal{B}} \leq \epsilon$$

has a solution of the form

$$p_{\mathbf{w}}(\mathbf{y}|\mathbf{x}) = q(\mathbf{y}|\mathbf{x}) \exp\left(\langle\phi(\mathbf{x}, \mathbf{y}), \mathbf{w}\rangle - g(\mathbf{w}; \mathbf{x})\right), \tag{13.3}$$

where $\mathbf{w} \in \mathcal{B}^*$ and g is the log-partition function guaranteeing p to be a probability distribution. Moreover, the optimal value of $\mathbf{w}$ is found as the solution of

$$\min_{\mathbf{w}} \ -\left\langle \tilde{\phi}, \mathbf{w} \right\rangle + \frac{1}{\ell} \sum_{\mathbf{x} \in S_{\mathbf{x}}} g(\mathbf{w}; \mathbf{x}) + \epsilon \|\mathbf{w}\|_{\mathcal{B}^*}. \tag{13.4}$$

Equivalently, for every feasible ϵ, there exists a $\Lambda \geq 0$ such that the minimum of $-\left\langle \tilde{\phi}, \mathbf{w} \right\rangle + \frac{1}{\ell} \sum_{\mathbf{x} \in S_{\mathbf{x}}} g(\mathbf{w}; \mathbf{x}) + \frac{\Lambda}{2} \|\mathbf{w}\|_{\mathcal{B}^*}^2$ minimizes (13.4).

Note that the well-known connection between conditional maximum entropy optimization (MaxEnt) with exact moment-matching constraints and conditional maximum likelihood estimation is a special case of theorem 68 with $\epsilon = 0$. Thus, relaxing the constraints corresponds to a regularization in the dual problem scaled by the relaxation parameter. Since the dual (13.4) is an unconstrained optimization problem (over a possibly finite domain), it is common to solve the density estimation problem by performing the optimization in the dual space.

13.2.3 Exponential Families

As we have seen in (13.3), exponential families arise from the optimization of KL divergence with respect to (approximate) moment-matching constraints. Here $\mathbf{w}$ is called the canonical or natural parameter, $\phi(\mathbf{x}, \mathbf{y})$ is the corresponding vector of sufficient statistics, and $g(\mathbf{w}; \mathbf{x})$ is the log-partition function or moment-generating function.

log-partition
function

$$g(\mathbf{w}; \mathbf{x}) := \log \sum_{\mathbf{y} \in \mathcal{Y}} \exp(\langle \phi(\mathbf{x}, \mathbf{y}), \mathbf{w} \rangle) q(\mathbf{y}|\mathbf{x}) \,. \tag{13.5}$$

The log-partition function plays an important role in estimating probability distributions. In particular, it can be used to compute the moments of the distribution; see e.g. Lauritzen (1996).

Proposition 69 $g(\mathbf{w}; \mathbf{x})$ *is a convex C^∞ function. Moreover, the derivatives of g generate the corresponding moments of ϕ*

$$\partial_{\mathbf{w}} g(\mathbf{w}; \mathbf{x}) = \mathbf{E}_{\mathbf{y}|\mathbf{x} \sim p_{\mathbf{w}}}[\phi(\mathbf{x}, \mathbf{y})] \qquad \qquad \textit{Mean} \tag{13.6a}$$
$$\partial_{\mathbf{w}}^2 g(\mathbf{w}; \mathbf{x}) = \mathrm{Cov}_{\mathbf{y}|\mathbf{x} \sim p_{\mathbf{w}}}[\phi(\mathbf{x}, \mathbf{y})] \qquad \qquad \textit{Covariance} \,. \tag{13.6b}$$

exponential
families as
universal density
estimators

It is important to use exponential families with rich sufficient statistics. One can show that if $\phi(\mathbf{z})$ for $\mathbf{z} = (\mathbf{x}, \mathbf{y}) \in \mathcal{Z}$ is powerful enough, exponential families become universal density estimators, in the sense that the set of all functions of the form $\langle \mathbf{w}, \phi(.) \rangle$ is dense in the set of all bounded continous functions defined on $C^0(\mathcal{Z})$. This is advantageous, as it can open the domain of nonparametric estimation to an area of statistics which so far was restricted to parametric distributions. In proposition 70, we show that exponential families can in fact be dense over $C^0(\mathcal{Z})$, if they are defined with respect to a universal kernel. More precisely, we restrict the Banach space $\mathcal{B}$ to be a RKHS with the kernel function k and define a linear discriminant function $F : \mathcal{Z} \to \Re$ as

$$F(.) = \langle \phi(.), \mathbf{w} \rangle \,, \tag{13.7}$$

for $F \in \mathcal{H}$ such that

$$F(\mathbf{z}) = \langle F, k(\mathbf{z}, \cdot) \rangle_{\mathcal{H}} \,, \tag{13.8}$$

where ϕ is the feature map induced by k. We can now represent p as a function of $\mathbf{w}$ and F interchangeably.

Proposition 70 (Dense Densities) *Let $\mathcal{Z}$ be a measurable set with respect to the Lebesgue measure. Moreover, let $\mathcal{H}$ be universal and $\mathcal{P}$ be the space of $C^0(\mathcal{Z})$ densities with $\|p\|_\infty < \infty$. Then the class of exponential family densities,*

$$\mathcal{P}_\mathcal{H} := \{p_F | p_F(z) : F \exp(F(z) - g(F)) \ \text{and} \ F \in \mathcal{H}\}, \tag{13.9}$$

where $g(F) := \log \int_\mathcal{Z} \exp(F(z))\, dz$,

is dense in $\mathcal{P}$. Moreover, for any $p \in \mathcal{P}$ with $\|\log p\|_\infty \le C$ and $\epsilon < 1$ we have

$$\|\log p - F\|_\infty \le \epsilon \ \text{implies} \ D(p\|p_F) \le 2\epsilon \ \text{and} \ \|p - p_F\|_\infty \le 4\epsilon e^C. \tag{13.10}$$

Proof We prove the second part first: Let $\epsilon > 0$. If $\|\log p\|_\infty \le C$, we can find some $F \in \mathcal{H}$ such that $\|F - \log p\|_\infty \le \epsilon$. By the definition of $g(F)$ it follows that

$$|g(F)| = \left| \log \sum_z \exp(F(z)) dz \right| = \left| \log p(z) \int_z \exp(F(z) - \log p(z)) dz \right| \le \epsilon. \tag{13.11}$$

Since $\log p_F = F - g(F)$ have $\|\log p - \log p_F\|_\infty \le 2\epsilon$. This immediately shows the first part of (13.10). For the second part, all we need to do is exponentiate the bound and use the fact that $\log p$ is bounded by C.

To see the general result, pick some $\delta < \epsilon/Z$ with $\epsilon < 1$, where Z is the measure of $\mathcal{Z}$. Moreover, let $p_\delta(z) := \max(p(z), \delta)$. Finally, pick F such that $\|F - \log p_\delta\| \le \epsilon$. By the same reasoning as in (13.11) it follows that $|g(F)| \le 2\epsilon$. Hence $\|p - p_F\| \le 4\epsilon \|p\|_\infty$. Since ϵ was arbitrary, this proves the claim. ∎

Note that a similar result can be obtained whenever $\mathcal{Z}$ is endowed with a measure ν, if we state our results for densities whose Radon-Nikodym derivatives with respect to ν satisfy the properties above. Moreover, similar results apply for the conditional densities, as long as $\log p(\mathbf{y}|\mathbf{x})$ is a well-behaved function of $\mathbf{x}$ and the kernel k is a universal kernel in $\mathbf{y}$ for every $\mathbf{x}$.

Many RKHS $\mathcal{H}$ are dense in $C^0(\mathcal{X})$. See Steinwart (2001) for examples and a proof. This shows that choosing a density from a suitable exponential family is not restrictive in terms of approximation quality.

13.2.4 Objective Function and Relationship to Gaussian Processes

density
estimation via
Gaussian
processes

Theorem 68 establishes that, when $\mathcal{B}$ is an RKHS, our density estimation problem is given by

$$\min_{\mathbf{w}} -\left\langle \tilde{\phi}, \mathbf{w} \right\rangle + \frac{1}{\ell} \sum_{i=1}^\ell g(\mathbf{w}; \mathbf{x}^i) + \frac{\Lambda}{2} \|\mathbf{w}\|_2^2.$$

Thus, we perform a regularized maximum likelihood estimate, where a normal distribution is assumed as a prior on $\mathbf{w}$. It follows from Williams (1999) that a normal prior on $\mathbf{w}$ corresponds to a Gaussian process on the collection of random variables $F(\mathbf{z})$ with zero mean and a covariance function k, where k is the kernel associated with RKHS $\mathcal{H}$ and F is defined as in (13.7). Using (13.2), (13.5), (13.7), and (13.8), we can rewrite the optimization as

$$F^* = \underset{F \in \mathcal{H}}{\operatorname{argmin}} \frac{1}{\ell} \sum_{i=1}^{\ell} \left(-F(\mathbf{x}^i, \mathbf{y}^i) + \log \sum_{\mathbf{y} \in \mathcal{Y}} \exp(F(\mathbf{x}^i, \mathbf{y})) \right) + \frac{\Lambda}{2} \|F\|_{\mathcal{H}}^2. \quad (13.12)$$

Equivalently, F^* maximizes

$$p(F|S) \propto p(F) \prod_i p(\mathbf{y}^i | \mathbf{x}^i; F), \quad (13.13)$$

where $p(F) \propto \exp(\frac{\Lambda}{2} \|F\|_{\mathcal{H}}^2)$. In Gaussian process classification, (13.13) is approximated by a Gaussian and F^* is the mode of the Gaussian approximating $p(F|S)$ by a second-order Taylor expansion of the log-posterior via Laplace approximation. Given F^*, one can approximate the curvature $\mathbf{C}$ at the mode and use this normal distribution $p(F|S) \approx \mathcal{N}(F^*, \mathbf{C})$ to obtain the predictive distribution of a new input $\mathbf{x}$ via

$$p(\mathbf{y}|S, \mathbf{x}) = \int p(\mathbf{y}|\mathbf{x}, F) p(F|S) dF.$$

Unfortunately, the Bayesian approach faces tractability problems with even moderate datasets during training. Exact inference for structured output prediction is intractable (Qi et al., 2005) and even the approximate inference is very expensive. Also, motivated by the maximum entropy principle, we use the MAP estimate F^* to obtain the predictive distribution $p(\mathbf{y}|S, \mathbf{x}) \approx p(\mathbf{y}|F^*(\mathbf{x}, .))$.

13.2.5   Subspace Representation

The representer theorem (Kimeldorf and Wahba, 1970) guarantees that F^*, the optimizer of (13.12), is of the form

$$F^*(\mathbf{x}, \mathbf{y}) = \sum_{i=1}^{\ell} \sum_{\bar{\mathbf{y}} \in \mathcal{Y}} \alpha_{(\mathbf{x}^i, \bar{\mathbf{y}})} k((\mathbf{x}, \mathbf{y}), (\mathbf{x}^i, \bar{\mathbf{y}})), \quad (13.14)$$

with suitably chosen coefficients α. Note that there is one $\alpha_{(i, \bar{\mathbf{y}})}$ coefficient for every training example $\mathbf{x}^i$ and its possible labeling $\bar{\mathbf{y}}$, due to the fact that F is defined over $\mathcal{X} \times \mathcal{Y}$ and the log-partition function sums over all $\bar{\mathbf{y}} \in \mathcal{Y}$ for each $\mathbf{x}^i \in S$. The feature map ϕ over $\mathcal{Z}$ is induced by the kernel function k via

$$k((\mathbf{x}, \mathbf{y}), (\bar{\mathbf{x}}, \bar{\mathbf{y}})) = \langle \phi(\mathbf{x}, \mathbf{y}), \phi(\bar{\mathbf{x}}, \bar{\mathbf{y}}) \rangle.$$

Thus, in complete analogy to Gaussian process classification and other kernel methods, we can perform the estimation and prediction by computing the inner products between sufficient statistics without the need for evaluating $\phi(\mathbf{x}, \mathbf{y})$ explicitly.

Although the application of the representer theorem reduces the optimization problem from an infinite-dimensional space ($\mathcal{H}$) to a finite-dimensional space scaling with the size of the sample and the size of $\mathcal{Y}$ ($\Re^{\ell|\mathcal{Y}|}$), this formulation suffers from scalability issues. This is because in the structured output prediction problems, $|\mathcal{Y}|$ is very large, scaling exponentially in the size of the structure. However, if there is a decomposition of the kernel into substructures, then the dimensionality can be reduced further. We now show that such a decomposition exists when $(\mathbf{x}, \mathbf{y})$ represents a Markov random field.

scalability

Let G be an undirected graph, $\mathcal{C}$ be the set of maximal cliques of G, $\mathbf{z}$ be a configuration of G, and z_c be the restriction of $\mathbf{z}$ on the clique $c \in \mathcal{C}$. The well-known theorem of Hammersley and Clifford (1971), theorem 20, states that the density over $\mathcal{Z}$ decomposes into *potential functions* defined on the maximal cliques of G. Using this theorem, it is easy to show that the Gibbs form translates into a simple decomposition of the kernel functions on MRFs.

Lemma 71 (Decomposition of Kernels on MRFs) *For positive probability density functions over an MRF Z on G, the kernel $k(\mathbf{z}, \bar{\mathbf{z}}) = \langle \phi(\mathbf{z}), \phi(\bar{\mathbf{z}}) \rangle$ satisfies*

$$k(\mathbf{z}, \bar{\mathbf{z}}) = \sum_{c \in \mathcal{C}} k(z_c, \bar{z}_c). \tag{13.15}$$

Proof We simply need to show that the sufficient statistics $\phi(z)$ satisfy a decomposition over the cliques. From theorem 68 and theorem 20, we know that $F(\mathbf{z}) = \langle \phi(\mathbf{z}), \mathbf{w} \rangle = \sum_{c \in \mathcal{C}} \psi_c(z_c; \mathbf{w})$ for all $\mathbf{z} \in \mathcal{Z}$ and any $\mathbf{w}$. Then, we can pick an orthonormal basis of $\mathbf{w}$, say e_i, and rewrite

$$\langle \phi(\mathbf{z}), e_i \rangle = \sum_{c \in \mathcal{C}} \eta_c^i(z_c)$$

for some scalar functions $\eta_c^i(z_c)$. The key point is that η_c^i depends on $\mathbf{z}$ only via its restriction on z_c. Setting $\phi_c(z_c) := (\eta_c^1(z_c), \eta_c^2(z_c), \ldots)$ allows us to compute

$$\langle \phi(\mathbf{z}), \mathbf{w} \rangle = \left\langle \phi(\mathbf{z}), \sum_i e_i \mathbf{w}_i \right\rangle = \sum_i \mathbf{w}_i \langle \phi(\mathbf{z}), e_i \rangle = \sum_{c \in \mathcal{C}} \sum_i \mathbf{w}_i \eta_c^i(z_c).$$

Rearranging terms shows that ϕ decomposes into $\phi(\mathbf{z}) = (\phi_{c_1}(z_{c_1}), \ldots, \phi_{c_n}(z_{c_n}))$. Setting

$$k(z_c, \bar{z}_c) = \langle \phi_c(z_c), \phi_c(\bar{z}_c) \rangle \tag{13.16}$$

satisfies the claim. [1]   ∎

---

1. Note that similar decomposition results can be achieved by selecting other basis functions. This might lead to interaction across different cliques. However, one can reduce such formulations to the decomposition presented in this lemma via rotating the basis functions.

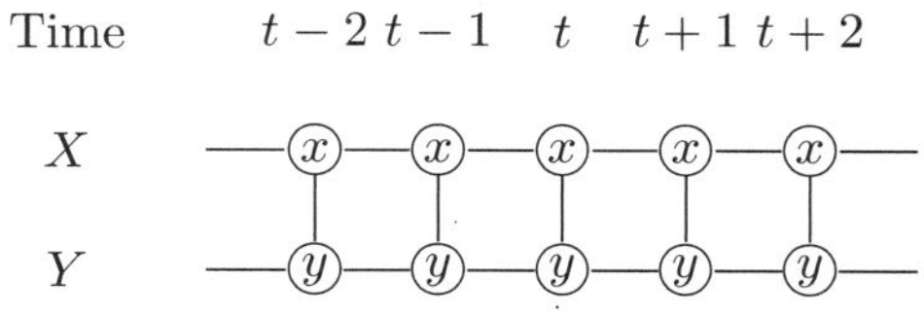

Time $t-2$ $t-1$ t $t+1$ $t+2$

X —x—x—x—x—x—

Y —y—y—y—y—y—

Figure 13.1   A time-invariant Markov chain with three types of cliques.

Many applications involve a family of graph structures such that some subsets of cliques in these graphs share the same potential function. For instance, in the case of Markov chains that are time invariant, there exist three types of cliques: $x - x$, $x - y$, and $y - y$. Figure 13.1 shows these types of cliques where each clique share the same potential function.

For such graphs, the decomposition in lemma 71 corresponds to $k(\mathbf{z}, \bar{\mathbf{z}}) = \sum_{c \in \mathcal{C}_\mathbf{z}} \sum_{\bar{c} \in \mathcal{C}_{\bar{\mathbf{z}}}} k(z_c, \bar{z}_{\bar{c}})$, where $\mathcal{C}_\mathbf{z}$ denotes the set of maximal cliques in $\mathbf{z}$ and $k(z_c, \bar{z}_{\bar{c}}) = 0$ if c and $\bar{c}$ are of different types. In order to simplify our future notation, we define $\mathcal{W}$ as the set of all possible clique configurations for all cliques defined over the set of Markov fields and $\theta^\mathbf{z}_\omega$ as the number of times the clique configuration $\omega \in \mathcal{W}$ occurs in $\mathbf{z}$. Then,

$$k(\mathbf{z}, \bar{\mathbf{z}}) = \sum_{\omega, \bar{\omega} \in \mathcal{W}} \theta^\mathbf{z}_\omega \theta^{\bar{\mathbf{z}}}_{\bar{\omega}} k(\omega, \bar{\omega}). \tag{13.17}$$

We can now use this result to decompose the linear discriminant F given by (13.8) into a linear discriminant function $f : \mathcal{W} \to \Re$ over cliques by

$$F_f(\mathbf{z}) = \sum_{\omega \in \mathcal{W}} \theta^\mathbf{z}_\omega f(\omega), \tag{13.18}$$

$$f(\omega) = \langle f, k(\omega, .) \rangle_{\mathcal{H}}. \tag{13.19}$$

This gives us a new optimization problem with a subspace representation

$$f^* = \underset{f \in \mathcal{H}}{\operatorname{argmin}} \frac{1}{\ell} \sum_{i=1}^{\ell} \left(-F_f(\mathbf{x}^i, \mathbf{y}^i) + \log \sum_{\mathbf{y} \in \mathcal{Y}} \exp(F_f(\mathbf{x}^i, \mathbf{y})) \right) + \frac{\Lambda}{2} \|f\|^2_{\mathcal{H}}, \tag{13.20}$$

$$f^*(\omega) = \sum_{\bar{\omega} \in \mathcal{W}(S_\mathbf{x})} \gamma_{\bar{\omega}} k(\omega, \bar{\omega}), \tag{13.21}$$

where $\mathcal{W}(S) \subseteq \mathcal{W}$ denotes the set of clique assignments with nonzero counts for any $(\mathbf{x}, \mathbf{y})$ for all $\mathbf{x} \in S_\mathbf{x}$ and all $\mathbf{y} \in \mathcal{Y}$. The subspace representation (13.21) holds immediately through a simple variant of the representer theorem (Lafferty et al., 2004; Altun et al., 2006) for any *local* loss function, where locality is defined as follows:

Definition 72 (Local Loss Function) *A loss $\mathcal{L}$ is local if $\mathcal{L}(\mathbf{x}, \mathbf{y}, f)$ is determined by the value of f on the set $\mathcal{W}(\{\mathbf{x}\})$, i.e., for $f, g : \mathcal{W} \to \Re$ we have that if $f(p) = g(p)$ for all $p \in \mathcal{W}(\{\mathbf{x}\})$ then $\mathcal{L}(\mathbf{x}, \mathbf{y}, f) = \mathcal{L}(\mathbf{x}, \mathbf{y}, g)$.*

improved
scalability

Note that the log-loss in (13.20) is local due to the decomposition of kernels on MRFs. This reduces the number of parameters from exponential in the size of the structure (number of vertices for MRF) to linear in the number of cliques and exponential in the number of vertices in the maximal cliques, which is generally much smaller than the total number of vertices. In this chapter, we restrict our focus to such MRFs. For instance, in the Markov chain example, let the length of the chain be m and the number of possible label assignment for each vertex be n. Then, the number of parameters is reduced from n^m to $mn + n^2$. Note that since our goal is to estimate $p(\mathbf{y}|\mathbf{x})$, which is independent of $x - x$ cliques, there are no parameters for such cliques. In general, the set of cliques for which the restriction of $(\mathbf{x}, \mathbf{y})$ is solely contained in $\mathbf{x}$ is irrelevant.

13.3   A Sparse Greedy Optimization

Using the representation of f^* over the subspaces of $\mathcal{Z}$, let us restate our optimization in terms of the subspace parameters γ. Let $\mathbf{K}$ be the matrix of kernel values of clique assignments $k(\omega, \bar{\omega})$ for all $\omega, \bar{\omega} \in \mathcal{W}(S_{\mathbf{x}})$ and $\theta^{\mathbf{z}}$ be the vector of clique counts $\theta_{\omega}^{\mathbf{z}}$ in $\mathbf{z}$ for all $\omega \in \mathcal{W}(S_{\mathbf{x}})$. Then, the linear discriminant F can be written as

$$F_{\gamma}(\mathbf{x}, \mathbf{y}) = \gamma^T \mathbf{K} \theta^{(\mathbf{x}, \mathbf{y})}$$

and the optimization problem is given by minimizing $R(\gamma; S)$ with respect to γ where

$$R(\gamma; S) = \frac{1}{\ell} \sum_{i=1}^{\ell} \left(-\gamma^T \mathbf{K} \theta^{\mathbf{x}^i, \mathbf{y}^i} + \log \sum_{\mathbf{y} \in \mathcal{Y}} \exp(\gamma^T \mathbf{K} \theta^{\mathbf{x}^i, \mathbf{y}}) \right) + \frac{\Lambda}{2} \gamma^T \mathbf{K} \gamma. \quad (13.22)$$

We now have a polynomial-size convex optimization problem, whose Jacobian and Hessian is

$$\partial_{\gamma} R = \frac{1}{\ell} \sum_{i=1}^{\ell} \left(-\mathbf{K} \theta^{(\mathbf{x}^i, \mathbf{y}^i)} + \mathbf{K} \mathbb{E}_{\mathbf{y} \sim p_{\gamma}} \left[\theta^{(\mathbf{x}^i, \mathbf{y})} | \right] \right) + \Lambda \mathbf{K} \gamma \quad (13.23a)$$

$$\partial_{\gamma}^2 R = \frac{1}{\ell} \sum_{i=1}^{\ell} \mathrm{Cov}_{\mathbf{y} \sim p_{\gamma}} [\mathbf{K} \theta^{(\mathbf{x}^i, \mathbf{y})}] + \Lambda \mathbf{K}. \quad (13.23b)$$

Note that each term of the Hessian is computed by

$$\partial^2_{\gamma_\omega,\gamma_{\bar\omega}} R = \Lambda k(\omega,\bar\omega)$$
$$+ 1/\ell \sum_{i=1}^{\ell} \sum_{\omega',\omega''} k(\omega,\omega') k(\bar\omega,\omega'') \left(\mathbf{E_y} \left[\theta^{(\mathbf{x}^i,\mathbf{y})}_{\omega'} \theta^{(\mathbf{x}^i,\mathbf{y})}_{\omega''} \right] - \mathbf{E_y} \left[\theta^{(\mathbf{x}^i,\mathbf{y})}_{\omega'} \right] \mathbf{E_y} \left[\theta^{(\mathbf{x}^i,\mathbf{y})}_{\omega''} \right] \right),$$

which involves correlation between configuration assignments of different cliques $\left(\mathbf{E_y} \left[\theta^{(\mathbf{x}^i,\mathbf{y})}_{\omega'} \theta^{(\mathbf{x}^i,\mathbf{y})}_{\omega''} \right] \right)$. Such correlations can be prohibitively expensive. For instance, in the Markov chain example, the complexity of the computation of the Hessian scales quadratically with the length of the chain. For this reason, we perform quasi-Newton optimization which simply requires first-order derivatives. The expectations can be computed using a dynamic programming algorithm in polynomial time with the size of the structure. For example, the expectations in Markov chains can be computed using the forward-backward algorithm whose complexity scales linearly in the length of the chain.

While optimization over the complete γ space is attractive for small datasets, the computation or the storage of $\mathbf{K}$ poses a serious problem when the dataset is large. Also, classification of a new observation involves evaluating the kernel function at all the cliques in $\mathcal{W}(S_\mathbf{x})$, which may be more than acceptable for many

sparse
approximation

applications. Hence, as in the case of standard Gaussian process classification, one may have to find a method for sparse solutions in terms of the γ parameters to speed up the training and prediction stages. We perform a sparse greedy subspace approximation algorithm along the lines of the method presented by Zhang (2003). In order to motivate this algorithm, we present the following lower bound on convex functions which is simply a tangent of the convex function.

Lemma 73 (Lower Bound on Convex Functions) *Let $C : \Theta \to \Re$ be a convex function on a vector space and $\theta_0 \in \Theta$. We denote by $g \in \partial_\theta C(\theta_0)$ a vector in the subdifferential of C at θ_0. Then*

$$\min_{\theta \in \Theta} C(\theta) + \|\theta\|^2 \geq C(\theta_0) + \|\theta_0\|^2 - \|\frac{g}{2} + \theta_0\|^2. \tag{13.24}$$

Proof Since C is convex, it follows that for any subdifferential $g \in \partial_\theta C(\theta_0)$ we have $C(\theta) \geq C(\theta_0) + g^\top \delta\theta$. Consequently,

$$\min_{\theta \in \Theta} C(\theta) + \|\theta\|^2 \geq \min_{\delta\theta \in \Theta} C(\theta_0) + g^\top \delta\theta + \|\theta_0 + \delta\theta\|^2. \tag{13.25}$$

The minimum is obtained for $\delta\theta = -(\frac{g}{2} + \theta_0)$, which proves the claim.   ∎

This bound provides a valuable selection and stopping criterion for the inclusion of subspaces during the greedy optimization process. Note in particular that $g + 2\theta_0$ is the gradient of the optimization problem in (13.24), hence we obtain a lower bound on the objective function in terms of the L_2 norm of the gradient. This means that optimization over a subspace spanned by a parameter is only useful if the gradient in the corresponding direction is large enough.

Algorithm 13.1 Sparse greedy subspace approximation algorithm

---

Require: Training data $(\mathbf{x}^i, \mathbf{y}^i)_{i=1:\ell}$; Maximum number of coordinates to be selected, p; Number of coordinates to be selected at each iteration, d; Threshold value for gradients, η.

1:   $\hat{\mathbf{K}} \leftarrow [], \hat{\gamma} \leftarrow []$

2:   **repeat**

3:      Pick i:

4:      (1) Pick i where $\omega = \arg\max_{\bar{\omega} \in \mathcal{W}(S_\mathbf{x})} |\partial_{\gamma_{\bar{\omega}}} R|$ and $\omega \in \mathcal{W}(\{\mathbf{x}^i\})$, or

5:      (2) Pick $i \in \{1, \dots, \ell\}$ randomly

6:      $\mathbf{v} \leftarrow \mathrm{argmax}(\mathrm{d})_{\omega \in \mathcal{W}(\{\mathbf{x}^i\})} |\partial_{\gamma_\omega} R|$ via (13.23a)

7:      Optimize R wrt $\gamma_\mathbf{v}$ via dynamic programming.

8:      Augment $\hat{\gamma} = [\hat{\gamma}; \gamma_\mathbf{v}]$.

9:      Augment $\hat{\mathbf{K}} \leftarrow [\hat{\mathbf{K}}; \mathbf{K}e_\omega]$ for all $\omega \in \mathbf{v}$

10: **until** $\partial_\gamma R < \eta$ or p coordinates selected.

Let $\hat{\gamma}$ denote the sparse linear combination of basis vectors in $\mathcal{W}(S_\mathbf{x})$ and $\hat{\mathbf{K}}$ denote the matrix of the kernel function evaluated at basis vectors in $\hat{\gamma}$ and all $\mathcal{W}(S_\mathbf{x})$. The sparse greedy subspace approximation (SGSA) algorithm (algorithm 13.1) starts with an empty matrix $\hat{\mathbf{K}}$. At each iteration, it selects a training instance $\mathbf{x}^i$ and computes the gradients of the parameters associated with clique configurations $\omega \in \mathcal{W}(\{\mathbf{x}^i\})$ to select d coordinates with the largest absolute value of the gradient vector of R over this subspace. [2] We denote those coordinates by $\mathbf{v}$. Then, R (which is defined via $\hat{\mathbf{K}}$ rather than $\mathbf{K}$ now) is optimized with respect to $\gamma_\mathbf{v}$ using a quasi-Newton method. Finally, $\hat{\gamma}$ is augmented with the selected subspaces $\hat{\gamma} = [\hat{\gamma}', \gamma_\mathbf{v}']'$ and $\hat{\mathbf{K}}$ is augmented with the columns associated with the selected subspaces, $\mathbf{K}e_\omega$ for each selected $\omega \in \mathbf{v}$. This process is repeated until the gradients vanish (i.e. they are smaller than a threshold value η) or some sparseness level is achieved (i. e. a maximum number p of coordinates are selected). Notice that the bottleneck of this method is the computation of the expectations of the clique assignments, $\mathbf{E}_\mathbf{y}\left[\theta_\omega^{(\mathbf{x},\mathbf{y})}\right]$. Therefore, once the expectations are computed, it is more efficient to include multiple coordinates rather than a single coordinate. This number, denoted by d, is a parameter of the algorithm.

We consider two alternatives for choosing the training sequence at each iteration. One method is to choose the input $\mathbf{x}$ whose set of cliques $\mathcal{W}(\{\mathbf{x}\})$ has the highest-magnitude gradients. Another option is simply to select a random input from the sample.

convergence rate

When the input pattern is selected randomly, SGSA becomes an instance of coordinate descent or the *Gauss-Seidel* method. This method is guaranteed to converge to the unique minimum asymptotically irrespective of coordinate selection sequence and the initial vector, if the optimization function is convex (Murty, 1998),

---

2. In algorithm 13.1, $\mathrm{argmax}(\mathrm{d})_x f(x)$ selects the d number of x that maximize $f(x)$.

which is the case for R. If we consider the convex sets of $\mathcal{W}(S_{\mathbf{x}})$, theorem 74 shows that this algorithm has an $O(1/k)$ convergence rate where k denotes the number of iterations.

Theorem 74 *(Zhang, 2003)* *Let M_γ be an upper bound on $R''(\gamma)$. Then, after k iterations of the algorithm, we have*

$$R(\hat{\gamma}^k; S) - R(\gamma^*; S) \leq 2M_\gamma/(k+2)$$

where γ^* is the true minimizer of $R(\gamma; S)$ and $\hat{\gamma}^k$ is the estimate at the k iteration.

Note in the above analysis, it is assumed that $\forall \omega : \gamma_\omega \geq 0$. This is obviously a special case of the SGSA algorithm. However, introducing the negative of all features functions enables us to generalize the nonnegativity constraint and therefore apply theorem 74.

One can establish better convergence rates if the best training sequence selection criterion (line 4) is not prohibitively expensive. In this case, SGSA becomes an approximation of the *Gauss-Southwell* method, which has been show to have a linear convergence rate of the form

faster
convergence rates

$$R(\hat{\gamma}^{k+1}; S) - R(\gamma^*; S) \leq \left(1 - \frac{1}{\eta}\right)^k (R(\hat{\gamma}^k; S) - R(\gamma^*; S)),$$

where $1 < \eta < \infty$ (Rätsch et al., 2002b). Here, η depends polynomially on $|\mathcal{W}(S_{\mathbf{x}})|$. It also has dependency on M_γ. In practice, we observed that the random selection yields faster (approximate) convergence in terms of computational time. Therefore, we report experiments with this selection criterion.

13.4 Experiments: Sequence Labeling

We proceed to experiments on a specific structured prediction task, namely sequence labeling, and apply our method to two problems, pitch accent prediction and named entity recognition. We consider the chain model in figure 13.1, whose clique structure comprises (y_t, y_{t+1}) and (x_t, y_t) for all positions t in the sequence. Let Σ be the set of labels for each vertex, $n = |\Sigma|$ and δ be the Kronecker delta where $\delta(a, b)$ is 1 if $a = b$, and 0 otherwise. The features corresponding to the label-input cliques $\phi(x_t, y_t)$ is given by the concatenation of vectors $(\delta(y_t, \sigma)\phi(x_t))$ for all $\sigma \in \Sigma$:

$$\phi(x_t, y_t) = (\delta(y_t, \sigma_1)\phi(x_t)^T, \ldots, \delta(y_t, \sigma_n)\phi(x_t)^T)^T. \quad (13.26)$$

This corresponds to the standard multiclass classification representation where the weight vector is given by the concatenation of the weight vector of each class $\mathbf{w} = (\mathbf{w}_1', \ldots, \mathbf{w}_n')'$. Eq. 13.26 is concatenated with a vector of 0's whose size is given by the number of features representing label-label dependencies. The features corresponding to the label-label cliques $\phi(y_t, y_{t+1})$ is given by the vector of

$(\delta(y_t, \sigma)\delta(y_{t+1}, \bar{\sigma}))$ for all $\sigma, \bar{\sigma} \in \Sigma$. This vector is concatenated to a 0 vector whose size is given by the number of features representing input-label dependencies.

Then, via (13.16) the kernel function over the cliques is

$$k((x_t, y_t), (\bar{x}_{\bar{t}}, \bar{y}_{\bar{t}})) = \delta(y_t, \bar{y}_{\bar{t}})\bar{k}(\phi(x_t), \phi(\bar{x}_{\bar{t}})),$$
$$k((y_t, y_{t+1}), (\bar{y}_{\bar{t}}, \bar{y}_{\bar{t}+1}) = \delta(y_t, \bar{y}_{\bar{t}})\delta(y_{t+1}, \bar{y}_{\bar{t}+1}),$$

and clearly the kernel value of different clique types is 0, as discussed in section 13.2.5. The exponential family represented by this kernel function gives us a semiparametric MRF. Note, when $\bar{k}$ is the linear kernel, we obtain the regularized density estimation problem of CRFs (Lafferty et al., 2001).

The major computation in algorithm 13.1 is the computation of R and $\partial_\gamma R$, which reduces to computing the expectations of clique configurations. For Markov chains, this is done by the forward-backward algorithm, using the transition and the observation matrices defined with respect to γ. The transition matrix is a $|\Sigma| \times |\Sigma|$ matrix common for all input sequences. The observation matrix of $\mathbf{x}$ is a $T \times |\Sigma|$ matrix where T is the length of $\mathbf{x}$. Let us denote the configurations of cliques of type label-input by $\mathcal{W}_{x-y} \subset \mathcal{W}(S_\mathbf{x})$ and the configurations of cliques of type label-label by $\mathcal{W}_{y-y} \subset \mathcal{W}(S_\mathbf{x})$. Furthermore for $\omega \in \mathcal{W}_{x-y}$, let ω_x and ω_y be the input and label configuration of the clique ω respectively. Then the two matrices are given by

$$T(\sigma, \bar{\sigma}) = \sum_{\omega \in \mathcal{W}_{y-y}} \delta(\omega, (\sigma, \bar{\sigma}))\gamma_\omega \tag{13.27a}$$

$$O_\mathbf{x}(t, \sigma) = \sum_{\omega \in \mathcal{W}_{x-y}} \delta(\omega_y, \sigma)\gamma_\omega \bar{k}(x_t, \omega_x). \tag{13.27b}$$

In sequence labeling, the cost function Δ is generally the Hamming loss. Then, given a new observation sequence $\mathbf{x}$, our goal is to find $\mathbf{y}^*$ via (13.1)

$$\mathbf{y}^* = \operatorname*{argmin}_{\mathbf{y}} \sum_{\mathbf{y}' \neq \mathbf{y}} p_\gamma(\mathbf{y}'|\mathbf{x}) \sum_{t=1}^{T} [\![y_t \neq y_t']\!]$$
$$= \operatorname*{argmax}_{\mathbf{y}} \sum_{t} \sum_{\mathbf{y}':y_t'=y_t} p_\gamma(\mathbf{y}'|\mathbf{x}).$$

Thus, the best label sequence is the one with the highest marginal probability at each position, which can be found by the forward-backward algorithm. Note that this is different from finding the best label sequence with respect to $p(.|\mathbf{x})$, which is given by the Viterbi algorithm.

13.4.1 Pitch Accent Prediction

Pitch accent prediction, a subtask of speech recognition, is detecting the words that are more prominent than others in an utterance. We model this problem as a sequence annotation problem, where $\Sigma = \{\pm 1\}$. We used switchboard corpus (Godfrey et al., 1992) to experimentally evaluate the described method by extracting 500

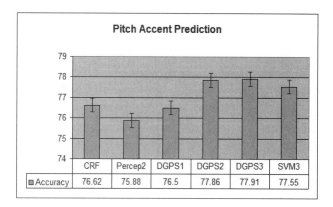

Figure 13.2   Test accuracy of pitch accent prediction task.

sentences from this corpus and running experiments using fivefold crossvalidation. Features consist of probabilistic, acoustic, and textual information from the neighborhood of the label over a window of size 5 (Gregory and Altun, 2004). We chose polynomial kernel of different degrees for kernel over the inputs.

We compared the performance of CRFs and HM-SVMs (Altun et al., 2003b) with the dense and sparse optimization of our approach according to their test accuracy on pitch accent prediction. When performing experiments on the dense optimization, we used polynomial kernels with different degrees (denoted with DGPS$\mathbf{X}$ in figure 13.2 where $\mathbf{X} \in \{1, 2, 3\}$ is the degree of the polynomial kernel). We used third-order polynomial kernel in HM-SVMs (denoted with SVM3 in figure 13.2)

As expected, CRFs and DGPS1 performed very similarly. When second-order features were incorporated implicitly using second-degree polynomial kernel (DGPS2), the performance increases. Extracting second-order features explicitly results in a 12 million-dimensional feature space, where CRFs slow down dramatically. We observed that third-order features do not provide significant improvement over DGPS2. HM-SVM3 performs slightly worse than DGPS2.

To investigate how the sparse optimization (denoted by SGPS) affects the performance, we report the test accuracy with respect to the sparseness of solution in figure 13.3 using the random training sequence selection criteria where the number of parameters selected at each iteration d is 3. [3] Sparseness is measured by the percentage of the parameters selected. The straight line is the performance of the dense optimization using second-degree polynomial kernel. Using 1% of the parameters, SGPS achieves 75% accuracy (1.48% less than the accuracy of the dense one). When 7.8% of the parameters are selected, the accuracy is 76.18%, which is not significantly different than the performance of the dense optimization (76.48%). We

---

3. The results reported here and below are obtained using a different set of features where the performance of the dense algorithm is 76.48%.

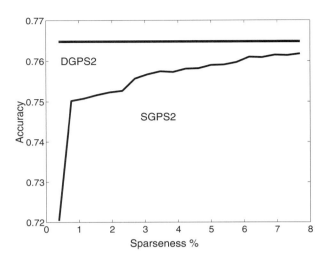

Figure 13.3   Test accuracy of pitch accent prediction w.r.t. the sparseness of GPS solution.

observed that these parameters were related to 6.2% of the observations along with 1.13 label pairs on average. Thus, during inference one needs to evaluate the kernel function only at about 6% of the observations, which reduces the inference time dramatically.

In order to experimentally verify how useful the predictive probabilities are as confidence scores, we forced the classifier to abstain from predicting a label when the probability of an individual label is lower than a threshold value. In figure 13.4, we plot precision-recall values for different thresholds. We observed that the error rate decreased 8.54%, when the classifier abstained on 14.93% of the test data. The improvement on the error rate shows the validity of the probabilities generated by the classifier.

13.4.2   Named Entity Recognition

Named entity recognition (NER), a subtask of information extraction, is finding phrases containing names in a sentence. The individual labels consist of the beginning and continuation of person, location, organization, and miscellaneous names and nonnames. We used a Spanish newswire corpus, which was provided for the special session of CoNLL 2002 on NER, to select 1000 sentences (21K words). As features, we used the word and its spelling properties from a neighborhood of size 3.

The experimental setup was similar to the pitch accent prediction task. We compared the performance of CRFs with and without the regularizer term (CRF-R, CRF respectively) with the dense and sparse optimizations of our approach methods. We set the sparseness parameter of SGPS to 25%, i.e. $p = 0.25|\mathcal{W}(S_{\mathbf{x}})||\Sigma|^2$,

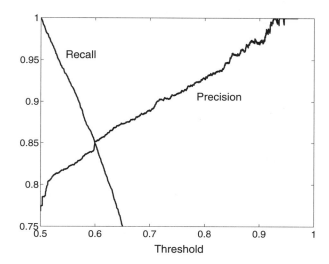

Figure 13.4 Precision-recall curves for different threshold probabilities to abstain on pitch accent prediction.

Table 13.1 Test error of named entity recognition task

	DGPS1	DGPS2	SGPS2	CRF	CRF-R
Error	4.58	4.39	4.48	4.92	4.56

where $|\Sigma| = 9$ and $\mathcal{W}(S_{\mathbf{x}}) = 21K$ on average. The results are summarized in table 13.1. Qualitatively, the behavior of the different optimization methods is comparable to the pitch accent prediction task. Second-degree polynomial DGPS achieved better performance than the other methods. SGPS with 25% sparseness achieves an accuracy that is only 0.1% below DGPS. We observed that 19% of the observations are selected along with 1.32 label pairs on average, which means that one needs to compute only one fifth of the gram matrix. Note, CRF without the regularization term corresponds to the maximum likelihood estimate, i. e. the estimation of the probability distribution such that the expectation of the features matches exactly the empirical values. The loss of accuracy in this case shows the importance of the relaxation of the moment-matching constraints.

13.5 Conclusion

We presented a method for estimation of conditional probability distributions over structured outputs within RKHSs. This approach is motivated through the well-established maximum-entropy framework. It combines the advantages of the rigorous probabilistic semantics of CRFs and overcomes the curse-of-dimensionality problem using kernels to construct and learn over RHKSs. The decomposition results for MRFs renders the problem tractable. Using this decomposition, we presented an efficient sparse approximate optimization algorithm. Empirical analysis showed that our approach is competitive with the state-of-the-art methods on sequence labeling.

Cost sensitivity is an important aspect in the structured output prediction problem. For cost functions which decompose into cliques, such as the Hamming loss in the sequence applications, we proposed estimating the conditional distribution and performing the cost-sensitive inference efficiently. Another approach is to incorporate the cost function in the optimization problem. If the cost function decomposes into the cliques, then the method presented here can be applied with minor changes. If this is not the case, the decomposition results may not hold, which may pose serious tractability problems.

Investigating the density estimation problem within the maximum-entropy framework points to new directions in terms of regularizations. In particular, defining the metric of the Banach space appropriately, one can impose different regularizations for features that possess different characteristics, such as features encoding interlabel dependencies and features encoding observation-label dependencies in sequences. This is one of the topics of our future work.

14 Gaussian Process Belief Propagation

Matthias W. Seeger

The framework of graphical models is a cornerstone of applied statistics, allowing for an intuitive graphical specification of the main features of a model, and providing a basis for general Bayesian inference computations though belief propagation (BP). In the latter, messages are passed between marginal beliefs of groups of variables. In parametric models, where all variables are of fixed finite dimension, these beliefs and messages can be represented easily in tables or parameters of exponential families, and BP techniques are widely used in this case. In this chapter, we are interested in nonparametric models, where belief representations do not have a finite dimension, but grow with the dataset size. In the presence of several dependent domain variables, each of which is represented as a nonparametric random field, we aim for a synthesis of BP and nonparametric approximate inference techniques. We highlight the difficulties in exercising this venture and suggest possible techniques for remedies. We demonstrate our program using the example of semiparametric latent factor models (Teh et al., 2005), which can be used to model conditional dependencies between multiple responses.

14.1 Introduction

Graphical models provide an intuitive way of specifying assumed conditional independence relationships between several domain variables. Moreover, they come with unified *belief propagation* algorithms[1] to compute Bayesian inference, conditioned on observed data. If the graphical model is parametric, in that the local conditional distributions are such that the marginal posterior beliefs of all unobserved variables have a representation of fixed size, independent of the number of data cases, BP

---

1. BP is a variant of the dynamic programming principle, making use of tree structure in the model. If the model graph is not a tree, variables have to be grouped in cliques until the corresponding hypergraph becomes a tree.

involves passing messages between neighboring variables in the graph, where the message representations are of fixed size, and the scaling is typically linear in the number n of data cases. The distinctive feature of parametric graphical models is the existence of a mediator variable of fixed *finite* size, such that conditioning on this variable renders the observed cases $i = 1, \ldots, n$ (together with associated latent variables) independent for different i. Because the mediator separates training from test cases, it is clear that all information from the training cases required for prediction is represented in the posterior belief for the mediator only. Mediator variables are usually called *parameters*, but our naming here is more specific.

For nonparametric models, such as Gaussian random field models, there is no mediator variable of finite size. We can propose such a variable, but it will be an infinite random object, such as a Gaussian process (GP), and for any practical inference or prediction, we need to integrate it out, which renders all variables across all cases i mutually dependent in a way which has to be represented explicitly (say, by storing the covariance matrix). We may call this problem the curse-of-dependency; it leads to the fact that a direct generalization of BP to random field models is not tractable in practice.

curse-of-dependency problem

motivation

In this chapter, we are interested in generalizing BP to Gaussian random field graphical models in a way which is efficient in practice. A general idea is to apply what we may call *bottleneck* approximations. For example, a factorization assumption means that a joint distribution is approximated by a product of marginal ones. A low rank (or sparsity) assumption means that we introduce artificial mediator variables in a data-dependent way. The concept of a mediator variable illustrates what we mean by the term "bottleneck." Dependence arises through information flowing between variables. A mediator variable creates a narrow bottleneck for this flow, separating many variables by instantiation (conditioning). A different kind of bottleneck approximation is used in section 14.4 in the context of the $m_{\boldsymbol{v}(c) \to \boldsymbol{u}}$ messages. In the *informative vector machine (IVM)* framework (Lawrence et al., 2003; Seeger, 2003) these mediators are a subset of the variables we want to represent beliefs over, and this "active" subset is selected depending on the observed data. The IVM framework has been proposed and applied to single domain variable GP models, but in this chapter we show that the representations and inference computations developed there can be used to obtain an efficient nonparametric variant of BP as well.

Our study is preliminary, in that we try to develop ideas, point out the major problems, and suggest remedies which come as bottleneck approximations. Bayesian inference in graphical models, whether parametric or nonparametric, can be intractable for a great number of reasons. Since in this chapter, we are interested in the curse-of-dependency problem only, we focus on the example of semiparametric latent factor models (Teh et al., 2005) for multioutput regression. While this is a useful nontrivial model, all variables are Gaussian, and domain variables are related linearly, with the model graph being a tree, so that many of the usual difficulties with Bayesian inference do not occur. However, we will hint at these additional problems as we go.

14.1.1   Outline of the Chapter

The structure of the chapter is as follows. In section 14.2, we point out the main differences between parametric and nonparametric graphical models, using the concepts of data and model dimension. In section 14.3, semiparametric latent factor models (SLFMs) are introduced as our working example. GP belief propagation for conditional inference in SLFMs is developed in section 14.4. Finally, we comment on how to learn hyperparameters in section 14.5. Conclusions are given in section 14.6.

notation   The notation in this chapter is as follows. Vectors $\boldsymbol{a} = (a_i)_i$ and matrices $\boldsymbol{A} = (a_{i,j})_{i,j}$ are boldface. We use subindex notation, in that $\boldsymbol{a}_I = (a_i)_{i \in I}$, "·" being the full index. For matrices, $\boldsymbol{A}_I$ is short for $\boldsymbol{A}_{I,I}$. $\boldsymbol{I}$ denotes the identity matrix. Note that $\boldsymbol{a}_I = \boldsymbol{I}_{I,\cdot}\boldsymbol{a}$. Some vectors $\boldsymbol{y}$ will have two indices: $y_{i,c}$, the index i over cases (data dimension), and c over variable components (part of model dimension), and the standard ordering (if nothing else said) is $\boldsymbol{y} = (y_{1,1}, y_{2,1}, \ldots, y_{n,1}, y_{1,2}, \ldots)^T$. We write $\boldsymbol{y}_i = (y_{i,c})_c$, $\boldsymbol{y}^{(c)} = (y_{i,c})_i$. The Kronecker product is $\boldsymbol{A} \otimes \boldsymbol{B} = (a_{i,j}\boldsymbol{B})_{i,j}$. Our subscript notation for such "double index" vectors is applied to the case index i only: $\boldsymbol{y}_I = (y_{i,c})_{i \in I, c} \in \mathbb{R}^{C|I|}$. $N(\cdot|\boldsymbol{\mu}, \boldsymbol{\Sigma})$ denotes the Gaussian distribution, where we also use an unnormalized form of the density:

$$N^U(\boldsymbol{z}|\boldsymbol{b}, \boldsymbol{B}) = \exp\left(\boldsymbol{b}^T\boldsymbol{z} - \frac{1}{2}\boldsymbol{z}^T\boldsymbol{B}\boldsymbol{z}\right).$$

14.2   Data and Model Dimension

Statistical models may be divided into *parametric* and *nonparametric* ones. If $P(\boldsymbol{z}|\boldsymbol{\theta})$ is a model for the observed variable $\boldsymbol{z}$, indexed by parameters $\boldsymbol{\theta}$, and we observe some data $\boldsymbol{z}_1, \ldots, \boldsymbol{z}_n$, a parametric model is characterized by the existence of *sufficient statistics* $\boldsymbol{\phi}(\boldsymbol{z}_1, \ldots, \boldsymbol{z}_n) \in \mathbb{R}^s$ of fixed size s, in that the likelihood of the data can be written solely in terms of the statistics: $P(\boldsymbol{z}_1, \ldots, \boldsymbol{z}_n|\boldsymbol{\theta}) = f(\boldsymbol{\phi}(\boldsymbol{z}_1, \ldots, \boldsymbol{z}_n), \boldsymbol{\theta})$. For example, if we model $\boldsymbol{z} \sim N(\cdot|\boldsymbol{\theta}, \sigma^2\boldsymbol{I})$ with known variance σ^2, where $N(\cdot|\boldsymbol{\mu}, \boldsymbol{\Sigma})$ denotes the Gaussian distribution with mean $\boldsymbol{\mu}$ and covariance matrix $\boldsymbol{\Sigma}$, then the sample mean $n^{-1}\sum_{i=1}^n \boldsymbol{z}_i$ is a sufficient statistics, so the Gaussian model is parametric.

representation
issues in
parametric
graphical models
vs ...

The existence of finite sufficient statistics has important implications in practice. Estimators of $\boldsymbol{\theta}$ or posterior beliefs for $\boldsymbol{\theta}$ can typically be represented in $O(s)$, independent of the dataset size n. If there are several domain variables, we may devise a *parametric graphical model* to describe their relationships. Here, conditional independence relationships are captured in a graphical manner, in that the variables are nodes in a graph, and roughly speaking, conditional independence is represented in terms of separation in this graph. Finally, conditional distributions between neighboring nodes are represented by parametric local models. In order to do inference on the global model, namely to compute marginal posterior beliefs of unobserved variables given data, *belief propagation* techiques can be employed, which essentially pass messages (local conditional distributions) between nodes and update the node marginals accordingly until convergence. For an introduction to parametric graphical models, see Jensen (1996), Lauritzen (1996), Pearl (1988), Jordan (1997). Note that one important factor to make this work is that messages and node marginals *can* actually be represented finitely.

...nonparametric
graphical models

The situation is different for nonparametric models, where dependencies between the cases in a dataset are represented directly, and are not mediated through some finite number of parameters $\boldsymbol{\theta}$. We can still employ a model of the form $P(\boldsymbol{z}|\boldsymbol{\theta})$, but $\boldsymbol{\theta}$ does not have a finite representation anymore. It is often easier to work with nonparametric models after the "parameters" $\boldsymbol{\theta}$ have been integrated out.[2] To this end, a prior distribution $P(\boldsymbol{\theta})$ is chosen, and the joint distribution for variables $\boldsymbol{z}_i$ of interest is obtained as $P(\boldsymbol{z}_1,\ldots,\boldsymbol{z}_n) = \int P(\boldsymbol{z}_1,\ldots,\boldsymbol{z}_n|\boldsymbol{\theta})P(\boldsymbol{\theta})\,d\boldsymbol{\theta}$. To give an example, we may associate each case $\boldsymbol{z}_i$ with a real variable u_i, then assume that the u_i are a priori jointly distributed as a Gaussian with a covariance matrix depending on parts (say $\boldsymbol{x}_i$) of the observations $\boldsymbol{z}_i$. It is useful to regard the relationship $\boldsymbol{x}_i \rightarrow u_i$ as a *random field* (or random function). Certain properties, such as the u_i changing smoothly on average w.r.t. $\boldsymbol{x}_i$, can be encoded directly into this setup, by assuming a correlation coefficient between u_i, u_j which grows with shrinking distance between $\boldsymbol{x}_i, \boldsymbol{x}_j$. In this example, a convenient $\boldsymbol{\theta}$ would be a *Gaussian process*, and the prior $P(\boldsymbol{\theta})$ would be a GP distribution. Note that we need at least countably infinitely many variables to describe a GP.

Now, suppose we have several domain variables, whose dependencies we would like to capture with a graphical model. However, we would also like to represent the individual variables by nonparametric random fields. In this chapter, we investigate the feasibility of applying the parametric BP technique to such a nonparametric graphical model. In this case, marginal beliefs and messages are random fields themselves. In simple cases, these can be represented as joint distributions over cases of interest, namely after the parameters (GPs in our case) have been integrated out. However, the representations for node marginals and messages grows superlinearly in the number n of cases, as does the cost for message propagations, and a

---

2. In fact, any practical application of nonparametric models has to work on such an integrated-out representation, because $\boldsymbol{\theta}$ cannot be represented on a machine.

straightforward BP extension along these lines would hardly be of more than academic interest. We propose to use the recently developed IVM technique for sparse approximations for single domain variable GP models (Lawrence et al., 2003), in order to represent marginal beliefs and to propagate messages. The central idea is that the BP message-passing operations can be expressed in terms of common primitives of Bayesian inference, such as combining information from multiple sources by multiplication of beliefs, or marginalization of variables, and the IVM framework provides efficient approximate solutions for these primitives.

A central problem when trying to deal with nonparametric structured graphical models, is the curse-of-dependency effect. In a parametric model, the cases z_i are independent given the parameters (mediator) $\boldsymbol{\theta}$, but in a nonparametric model, our only option is to integrate out $\boldsymbol{\theta}$, introducing dependencies between the z_i which cannot be represented by a finite mediator variable. This problem becomes worse with several domain variables.

model vs. *data* dimension

We can think of a *model dimension* (along different domain variables) and a *data dimension* (along cases z_i we are interested in). For a parametric model, the mediator separates variables along the data dimension, although they still may have some complicated dependence structure along the model dimension. Figure 14.1 illustrates the situation. We see that if the mediator $\boldsymbol{\theta}$ is conditioned upon, paths between the different replicas of the model along the data dimension are blocked, which means that these blocks are conditionally independent. BP may be run on each block independently, and the relevant messages are represented in a way which does not depend on n.

In a nonparametric model, the infinite mediator must be integrated out, which leads to all variables along model and data dimension becoming dependent in a way which has to be represented explicitly. This fact is illustrated in figure 14.2. The

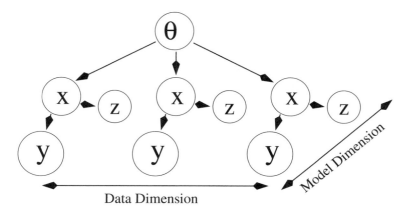

Figure 14.1   Model and data dimension for a parametric graphical model.

bidirectional edges are not part of the usual directed graphical models semantics[3]; they simply state that the replicas of x, y, z along the data dimension are all fully dependent, in that they constitute a nonparametric random field. There is no useful conditional factorization in this model, and belief representations and their manipulations are formidably expensive. Bottleneck approximations through artificial mediators are required in order to obtain practically efficient inference.

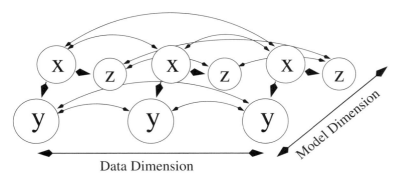

Figure 14.2   Model and data dimension for a nonparametric graphical model.

14.3   Semiparametric Latent Factor Models

In this section, we introduce the model for which we will demonstrate our GP belief propagation ideas. We are interested in predicting multiple responses $y_c \in \mathbb{R}$ $c = 1, \ldots, C$ from covariates $\boldsymbol{x} \in \mathcal{X}$, and we would like to model the responses as conditionally dependent. In statistical terminology, we would like to "share statistical strength" between the y_c; in machine learning parlance this is often referred to as "transfer of learning." Such sharing can be especially powerful if the data for the responses are partially unobserved.

co-kriging   Models related to the one proposed here are used in geostatistics and spatial prediction under the name of *co-kriging* (Cressie, 1993), where a typical problem can be described as follows. After an accidental uranium spill, a spatial map of uranium concentration is sought. We can take soil samples at selected locations and interpolate from these measurements using GP prediction. However, carbon concentration is easier to measure than uranium, and the two responses are often significantly correlated. In co-kriging, we set up a joint spatial model for several responses with the aim of improving our prediction of one of them. The model to be introduced here can be used for co-kriging, in which the nature of dependence

3. The correct way of drawing these models would be to contract the data dimension and use single nodes for x, y, z, representing the whole random fields.

between the responses is conditional, in that it depends on the covariates $\boldsymbol{x}$ (spatial location in our example).

Writing $\boldsymbol{y} = (y_c)_c$ and introducing a latent variable $\boldsymbol{v} \in \mathbb{R}^C$, our model has a factorizing likelihood $P(\boldsymbol{y}|\boldsymbol{v}) = \prod_c P(y_c|v_c)$, $P(y_c|v_c) = N(y_c|v_c, \sigma_c^2)$, i.e. the signal $\boldsymbol{v}$ is obscured by Gaussian noise, independent for each c. We intend to model the prior $P(\boldsymbol{v}|\boldsymbol{x})$ using GPs. The simplest possibility is to assume that the v_c are independent given $\boldsymbol{x}$, i.e. $P(\boldsymbol{v}|\boldsymbol{x}) = \prod_c P(v_c|\boldsymbol{x})$. In this case we can represent $P(v_c|\boldsymbol{x})$ as a *Gaussian process* with mean function 0 and covariance function $\tilde{K}^{(c)}$:

$$\mathrm{E}\left[v_c(\boldsymbol{x})v_{c'}(\boldsymbol{x}')\right] = \delta_{c,c'}\tilde{K}^{(c)}(\boldsymbol{x}, \boldsymbol{x}').$$

Details on GPs for machine learning may be found in Seeger (2004). The factorizing model will be called the *baseline model* in the sequel. The components v_c are independent a posteriori under the baseline model, so statistical strength is not shared among the different components.

On the other end of the spectrum, we can model $P(\boldsymbol{v}|\boldsymbol{x})$ as a set of dependent GPs with $C(C+1)/2$ cross-covariance functions. Tasks such as inference, hyperparameter learning, and prediction can be performed in much the same way as in a single process model, by simply extending the covariate $\boldsymbol{x}$ to $(\boldsymbol{x}, c)$. This model will be called the *naive model*. Due to the curse-of-dependency, approximate inference in the naive model scales superlinearly in Cn, which is acceptable only for rather small datasets and number of outputs C.

The *semiparametric latent factor model* (Teh et al., 2005; Seeger et al., 2004) lies in between, in that $\boldsymbol{v}|\boldsymbol{x}$ are dependent in a flexible way, yet inference and learning are more tractable than for the naive model. The key is to restrict the dependencies in a way which can be exploited in inference. We introduce a second latent variable $\boldsymbol{u} \in \mathbb{R}^P$. Here and in the following it is understood that for typical applications of our model we will have $P \ll C$. For a mixing matrix $\boldsymbol{\Phi} \in \mathbb{R}^{C,P}$ we set

$$\boldsymbol{v} = \boldsymbol{\Phi}\boldsymbol{u} + \boldsymbol{v}^{(0)}$$

where $\boldsymbol{u}$ and $\boldsymbol{v}^{(0)}$ are independent. The components $v_c^{(0)}$ have independent GP priors with mean 0 and covariance function $\tilde{K}^{(c)}$, and the components u_p have independent zero-mean GP priors with kernel $K^{(p)}$. Our model is a conditional nonparametric version of *factor analysis*. P independent factors u_p are mixed through $\boldsymbol{\Phi}$, and further independent factors $v_c^{(0)}$ are added to the result. The factors have different roles. The $v_c^{(0)}$ represent parts in the signal $\boldsymbol{v}$ which behave independently, while the u_p parameterize conditional dependencies (or correlations in this Gaussian case). The baseline model is a special case ($P = 0$), but for $P > 0$ the components v_c will be dependent a posteriori. The model combines nonparametric (processes u_p, $v_c^{(0)}$) and parametric elements (the mixing matrix $\boldsymbol{\Phi}$). Note that the definition here extends on the model of Teh et al. (2005), where they had $\boldsymbol{v}^{(0)} \equiv \boldsymbol{0}$.

cross-covariance

Note that by integrating out the $\boldsymbol{u}$ processes, we obtain induced cross-covariance functions for $\boldsymbol{x} \mapsto \boldsymbol{v}$:

$$\mathrm{E}[v_c(\boldsymbol{x})v_{c'}(\boldsymbol{x}')] = \delta_{c,c'}\tilde{K}^{(c)}(\boldsymbol{x},\boldsymbol{x}') + \sum_p \phi_{c,p}\phi_{c',p}K^{(p)}(\boldsymbol{x},\boldsymbol{x}').$$

We could therefore perform inference and prediction the naive way. However, the relationship between the domain variables $\boldsymbol{u}$ and $\boldsymbol{v}$ is structured, and in this chapter we are interested in exploiting this structure in order to obtain a more efficient method for representing the posterior $Q(\boldsymbol{v}) = P(\boldsymbol{v}|D)$ for data D, and to do predictions on unseen points. In the sequel, the posterior over $\boldsymbol{v}$ is denoted[4] by $Q(\boldsymbol{v})$.

14.4 Gaussian Process Belief Propagation

In this section, we derive GP BP for the SLFM introduced in section 14.3. As noted above, a naive approach would treat all $O(n\,C)$ variables as dependent and represent their covariance explicitly, which is not feasible in interesting practical situations. To repeat our motivation, we first make use of the tree structure of SLFM (see below) by applying BP for marginal inference, leading to a representation which is factorized along the model dimension. Dependencies along the data dimension are not structured, and additional bottleneck approximations, such as introduction of artificial mediator variables, have to be applied in order to represent and update the posterior marginals $P(v_{i,c}|D)$ efficiently. The details of these representations are formidable even in the case of SLFMs, and for simplicity we will skip over many of them. Our aim here is to point out typical problems that arise as curse-of-dependency, and to suggest general remedies. All details for the SLFM case can be found in Seeger et al. (2004).

We noted in section 14.2 that the dependencies along the data dimension are unstructured (in the sense of structure through a sparse graphical model) and have to be represented explicitly. This is a problem, because we would like to use BP techniques to exploit conditional independencies along the model dimension. This involves passing messages between node marginal beliefs, and has to be represented in a way which scales superlinearly in n. We propose to use low-rank bottleneck approximations in order to represent and work with these entities. IVM is a general framework for finding such low-rank bottlenecks in a data-dependent way, and for performing inference based on them. We will not go into details here, but merely state what will be required later on. For a single domain variable GP model ($C = 1$) with n cases $\boldsymbol{x}_i, y_i$ and latent variables $v_i \in \mathbb{R}$, the prior at the data points is $P(\boldsymbol{v}) = N(\boldsymbol{0}, \boldsymbol{K})$, where $\boldsymbol{K} = (K(\boldsymbol{x}_i, \boldsymbol{x}_j))_{i,j}$ is the covariance matrix over the input data points $\boldsymbol{x}_i$. The bottleneck variables are $\boldsymbol{v}_I = (v_i)_{i \in I}$, a part of the variables

---

4. This convention comes from *approximate* inference, where the true intractable posterior $P(\boldsymbol{v}|D)$ is approximated by a feasible $Q(\boldsymbol{v})$. We use $Q(\boldsymbol{v})$ in the same sense, because due to several bottleneck approximations, our final posterior marginals are approximate as well.

v whose posterior belief is to be represented. Here, $I \subset \{1, \ldots, n\}$ is the *active set* of size $d \ll n$. In the case of SLFMs, the likelihood $P(y_i|v_i)$ is Gaussian, but if it is not, the *expectation propagation (EP)* technique (Minka, 2001) can be used to replace them by a Gaussian function $N^U(v_i|b_i, \pi_i)$, $\pi_i \geq 0$, so the approximate posterior $Q(\boldsymbol{v})$ is Gaussian. If $P(y_i|v_i) = N(y_i|v_i, \sigma^2)$, then $\pi_i = \sigma^{-2}$, $b_i = \sigma^{-2}y_i$. The approximate IVM representation is obtained by constraining $b_i = \pi_i = 0$ for $i \notin I$. If $Q(\boldsymbol{u}) = N(\boldsymbol{h}, \boldsymbol{A})$, we see that

$$\boldsymbol{A} = \left(\boldsymbol{K}^{-1} + \boldsymbol{I}_{\cdot,I}\boldsymbol{\Pi}\boldsymbol{I}_{I,\cdot}\right)^{-1} = \boldsymbol{K} - \boldsymbol{M}\boldsymbol{M}^T, \quad \boldsymbol{h} = \boldsymbol{M}\boldsymbol{\beta},$$
$$\boldsymbol{M} = \boldsymbol{K}_{\cdot,I}\boldsymbol{\Pi}^{1/2}\boldsymbol{L}^{-T}, \quad \boldsymbol{L}\boldsymbol{L}^T = \boldsymbol{B} = \boldsymbol{I} + \boldsymbol{\Pi}^{1/2}\boldsymbol{K}_I\boldsymbol{\Pi}^{1/2}, \quad \boldsymbol{\beta} = \boldsymbol{L}^{-1}\boldsymbol{\Pi}^{-1/2}\boldsymbol{b}, \tag{14.1}$$

where $\boldsymbol{\Pi} = \text{diag}\,(\pi_i)_{i \in I}$ and $\boldsymbol{b} = (b_i)_{i \in I}$ are called *site parameters*. This representation can be derived using the Sherman-Morrison-Woodbury formula (Press et al., 1992). $\boldsymbol{L}$ is lower triangular, and $\boldsymbol{M}$ is called *stub matrix*. The IVM method convolves updates of this *IVM representation* (*i.e.* inclusions of a new i into I) with greedy selections of the best point to include next. To this end, the marginal posterior moments $\boldsymbol{h}, \boldsymbol{a} = \text{diag}\,\boldsymbol{A}$ are kept up to date at any time, and the forward selection score is based on those. Patterns are scored highly if their inclusion into I leads to a large information gain, or reduction of posterior entropy. Details about the IVM framework are given in Seeger (2003).

More generally, an IVM representation is determined by a prior $P(\boldsymbol{u}) = N(\boldsymbol{h}^{(0)}, \boldsymbol{A}^{(0)})$, an active set I (determining the bottleneck variables) of size d, and $2d$ site parameters $\boldsymbol{b}, \boldsymbol{\Pi}$, and consists of the variables $\boldsymbol{M}, \boldsymbol{\beta}, \boldsymbol{h}$, and $\boldsymbol{a}$. These are defined as in (14.1), with $\boldsymbol{K}$ being replaced by $\boldsymbol{A}^{(0)}$ and the modifications

$$\boldsymbol{\beta} = \boldsymbol{L}^{-1}\left(\boldsymbol{\Pi}^{-1/2}\boldsymbol{b} - \boldsymbol{\Pi}^{1/2}\boldsymbol{h}_I^{(0)}\right), \quad \boldsymbol{h} = \boldsymbol{h}^{(0)} + \boldsymbol{M}\boldsymbol{\beta}.$$

This general tool for representing a single Gaussian random field belief efficiently through a data-dependent bottleneck will be applied below in several contexts.

Recall the SLFM from section 14.3. $\boldsymbol{v} \in \mathbb{R}^{nC}$ are the latent variables directly associated with the responses $\boldsymbol{y}$, and $\boldsymbol{u} \in \mathbb{R}^{nP}$ are the latent variables representing conditional dependencies. What is the graphical structure in the model dimension? If we group $\boldsymbol{v}$ into $\boldsymbol{v}^{(c)} = (v_{i,c})_i$, we see that the $\boldsymbol{v}^{(c)}$ are conditionally independent given $\boldsymbol{u} \in \mathbb{R}^{nP}$. In other words, the graphical model along the model dimension is tree-structured, as shown in figure 14.3.

The BP algorithm performs inference in tree-structured graphical models[5] by designating an arbitrary root, passing messages outward from this root to the leafs, then collecting messages back to the root. This sweep has to be done at any time new evidence (observations) becomes available (and is conditioned on). In our case, all observed data are known at once, but recall that we would like to use IVM

---

5. If the graphical model is not tree-structured, BP is often used anyway, known as "loopy BP" in this case. There is no guarantee of convergence in general, and even if BP converges, the result is usually just an approximation to the true posterior marginals. Still, loopy BP often works well in practice. Loopy GP BP is not in the scope of this chapter.

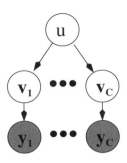

Figure 14.3 SLFM as a tree-structured graphical model.

bottlenecks for efficiency. The iterative procedure of selecting variables to become mediators one at a time, then including them into the representation, is very similar to observations becoming available in a sequential manner. We therefore employ the following "sequential" scheme. In each iteration, we select new variables to become active. As we will see, this can be interpreted as new evidence in the graphical model, and the posterior representation is updated by a BP sweep.

The local conditional distributions in a graphical model are also called potentials[6], for our purposes they are positive functions sitting on nodes joined by an edge, or on single nodes. Since $\boldsymbol{v}_i = \boldsymbol{\Phi}\boldsymbol{u}_i + \boldsymbol{v}_i^{(0)}$, the edge potentials are

$$\Psi_{u \to v}(\boldsymbol{v}^{(c)}, \boldsymbol{u}) = P(\boldsymbol{v}^{(c)} | \boldsymbol{u}) = N\left((\boldsymbol{\phi}_c^T \otimes \boldsymbol{I})\boldsymbol{u}, \tilde{\boldsymbol{K}}^{(c)}\right),$$

where $\boldsymbol{\phi}_c = \boldsymbol{\Phi}_{c,\cdot}^T$ is the cth row of $\boldsymbol{\Phi}$. The single node potentials are $\Psi_u(\boldsymbol{u}) = N(\boldsymbol{0}, \boldsymbol{K})$ with $\boldsymbol{K} = \mathrm{diag}\left(\boldsymbol{K}^{(p)}\right)_p$ and

$$\Psi_v(\boldsymbol{v}^{(c)}) = N^U\left(\boldsymbol{I}_{\cdot, I_c} \boldsymbol{b}^{(c)}, \boldsymbol{I}_{\cdot, I_c} \boldsymbol{\Pi}^{(c)} \boldsymbol{I}_{I_c, \cdot}\right),$$

where I_c, $\boldsymbol{b}^{(c)}$, $\boldsymbol{\Pi}^{(c)}$ are active set and site parameters for an IVM representation. Since we will use IVM forward selection in order to determine good active sets I_c for each marginal belief $Q(\boldsymbol{v}^{(c)})$, we see that the SLFM representation to be developed has to be able to keep the marginal posterior beliefs $Q(v_{i,c}) = N(h_{i,c}, a_{i,c})$ up to date at all times. Furthermore, by the form of Ψ_v, including a new entry into I_c can be interpreted as introducing new evidence into the model, as has been noted above. Note that this setup does not allow us to access *joint* information about Q spanning different $\boldsymbol{v}^{(c)}$ blocks (in general, BP delivers *marginal* posterior distributions only).

In the belief propagation method, nodes pass messages to their neighbors. A message can be seen as belief of a node in what the neighboring node should be, based on information the node receives from its other neighbors, *excluding* the

---

6. We are dealing with directed graphical models here. In undirected models (Markov random fields), potentials can be arbitrary positive functions.

receiver of the message.[7] Now suppose that new evidence is introduced into our SLFM-clustered graphical model, in the sense that j is included into I_c with site parameters $b_{j,c}$, $\pi_{j,c}$. This will change the message $\boldsymbol{v}^{(c)}$ sends to $\boldsymbol{u}$ which is

$$m_{\boldsymbol{v}^{(c)} \to \boldsymbol{u}}(\boldsymbol{u}) \propto \int \Psi_v(\boldsymbol{v}^{(c)}) \Psi_{u \to v}(\boldsymbol{v}^{(c)}, \boldsymbol{u}) \, d\boldsymbol{v}^{(c)}, \qquad (14.2)$$

which in turn modifies the messages $\boldsymbol{u}$ sends to $\boldsymbol{v}^{(c')}$, $c' \neq c$:

$$m_{\boldsymbol{u} \to \boldsymbol{v}^{(c')}}(\boldsymbol{v}^{(c')}) \propto \int \prod_{c'' \neq c'} m_{\boldsymbol{v}^{(c'')} \to \boldsymbol{u}}(\boldsymbol{u}) \Psi_u(\boldsymbol{u}) \Psi_{u \to v}(\boldsymbol{v}^{(c')}, \boldsymbol{u}) \, d\boldsymbol{u}. \qquad (14.3)$$

The message $m_{\boldsymbol{u} \to \boldsymbol{v}^{(c)}}$ remains the same. Finally, all marginals have to be updated:

$$Q(\boldsymbol{v}^{(c')}) \propto \Psi_v(\boldsymbol{v}^{(c')}) m_{\boldsymbol{u} \to \boldsymbol{v}^{(c')}}(\boldsymbol{v}^{(c')}),$$

$Q(\boldsymbol{v}^{(c)})$ because $\Psi_v(\boldsymbol{v}^{(c)})$ changed, and $Q(\boldsymbol{v}^{(c')})$ because $m_{\boldsymbol{u} \to \boldsymbol{v}^{(c')}}$ changed, $c' \neq c$.

In the remainder of this section, we show how this program can be executed using a sequence of IVM representations, such that after each inclusion into one of the I_c, the marginals $Q(v_{i,c})$ can be updated efficiently. The development is very technical, and some details are omitted here and given in Seeger et al. (2004). Our aim here is merely to highlight specific difficulties in the nonparametric BP extension, and these do not depend on specific details, but will rather universally appear for other models as well.

Recall our notation and the standard ordering of variables depending on double indexes (i, c) or (i, p) from section 14.1. The kernel matrices $\boldsymbol{K}$ and $\tilde{\boldsymbol{K}}^{(c)}$ are block-diagonal in the standard ordering, because the processes u_p, $v_c^{(0)}$ are all independent a priori. However, for $\boldsymbol{u}_I$ it turns out to be simpler to use the opposite ordering $\boldsymbol{u}_I = (u_{i_1,1}, u_{i_1,2}, \dots)^T$, where $I = \{i_1, i_2, \dots\}$. Let $\boldsymbol{\Psi}$ be the permutation matrix[8] such that $\boldsymbol{\Psi} \boldsymbol{u}_I$ is in standard ordering. We use the superscript $\hat{\ }$ to denote vectors and matrices in the $\boldsymbol{u}_I$ ordering, for example $\hat{\boldsymbol{K}}_I = \boldsymbol{\Psi}^T \boldsymbol{K}_I \boldsymbol{\Psi}$. Note that $\boldsymbol{\Psi}^T(\boldsymbol{\phi}_c \otimes \boldsymbol{I}) = (\boldsymbol{I} \otimes \boldsymbol{\phi}_c)$, so that $(\boldsymbol{\phi}_c \otimes \boldsymbol{I})$ in the standard ordering becomes $(\boldsymbol{I} \otimes \boldsymbol{\phi}_c)$ in the $\boldsymbol{u}_I$ ordering. We begin with the message $m_{\boldsymbol{v}^{(c)} \to \boldsymbol{u}}(\boldsymbol{u})$. We require an IVM representation $\mathcal{R}_1(c)$ (14.1) based on the prior $N(\boldsymbol{v}^{(c)}|\boldsymbol{0}, \tilde{\boldsymbol{K}}^{(c)})$ and I_c, $\boldsymbol{b}^{(c)}$, $\boldsymbol{\Pi}^{(c)}$. Let $\boldsymbol{\mu} = (\boldsymbol{\phi}_c^T \otimes \boldsymbol{I})\boldsymbol{u}$. Some algebra gives

$$m_{\boldsymbol{v}^{(c)} \to \boldsymbol{u}} \propto \exp\left(\boldsymbol{\beta}^{(1,c)T} \boldsymbol{\gamma} - \frac{1}{2} \boldsymbol{\gamma}^T \boldsymbol{\gamma} \right), \qquad (14.4)$$

$$\boldsymbol{\gamma} = \boldsymbol{L}^{(1,c)-1} \boldsymbol{\Pi}^{(c)1/2} \boldsymbol{\mu}_{I_c} = \boldsymbol{L}^{(1,c)-1} \boldsymbol{\Pi}^{(c)1/2} (\boldsymbol{\phi}_c^T \otimes \boldsymbol{I}) \boldsymbol{u}_{I_c}. \qquad (14.5)$$

---

7. Given this idea, the exact definition of messages is straightforward to derive, and consists of standard Bayesian computations involving sums (marginalization) and products. However, the fact that this intuitive procedure results in correct marginals after a single sweep is less obvious.
8. In MATLAB, $\boldsymbol{\Psi}$ is implemented by reshaping the vector into a matrix, transposing it, and reshaping back into a vector.

We do not require the stub matrix $\boldsymbol{M}^{(1,c)}$ in $\mathcal{R}_1(c)$, because this representation is not used to maintain marginal beliefs (but see $\mathcal{R}_3(c)$ below); however, we maintain $\boldsymbol{E}^{(c)} = \boldsymbol{\Pi}^{(c)1/2}\boldsymbol{L}^{(1,c)-T}$ with $\mathcal{R}_1(c)$. If $\boldsymbol{P}^{(c)} = (\boldsymbol{\phi}_c \otimes \boldsymbol{I})\boldsymbol{E}^{(c)}$, we have that $\boldsymbol{\gamma} = \boldsymbol{P}^{(c)T}\boldsymbol{u}_{I_c}$, so that $m_{\boldsymbol{v}^{(c)} \to \boldsymbol{u}}$ depends on $\boldsymbol{u}_{I_c}$ only.

At this point, we encounter a curse-of-dependency problem. Even if $m_{\boldsymbol{v}^{(c)} \to \boldsymbol{u}}$ depends on $\boldsymbol{u}_{I_c}$ only, these messages have to be combined for all $c' \neq c$ in order to form the reverse message $m_{\boldsymbol{u} \to \boldsymbol{v}^{(c)}}$. If the I_c are to be selected independently of size d_c (say), their union can be of size $\sum_c d_c$, this size governing the representation for the reverse messages. The problem is that we have bottlenecks I_c associated with the nodes $\boldsymbol{v}^{(c)}$, but by combining these we obtain an implied bottleneck for $\boldsymbol{u}$ of size $\sum_c d_c$, which is too large. This problem is especially severe in the SLFM case, because $\boldsymbol{u}$ has *all* other nodes $\boldsymbol{v}^{(c)}$ as neighbors, but similar problems will occur in other examples as well. We deal with it by imposing an explicit bottleneck I on $\boldsymbol{u}$ as well. Such "internal bottlenecks" on variables not directly related to observations have to be chosen depending on the specifics of the model. In the SLFM case the following seems sensible. We restrict all I_c to have the common prefix I of size d. Inclusions are therefore done in two phases. In the *common inclusion phase*, patterns are included into I, therefore into all I_c at the same time. In the subsequent *separate inclusion phase*, the I_c are extended independently. However, the messages $m_{\boldsymbol{v}^{(c)} \to \boldsymbol{u}}$ are always restricted to depend on $\boldsymbol{u}_I$ only. Namely,

$$m_{\boldsymbol{v}^{(c)} \to \boldsymbol{u}}(\boldsymbol{u}_I) = N^U\left(\hat{\boldsymbol{P}}^{(c)}\boldsymbol{\beta}^{(1,c)}, \hat{\boldsymbol{P}}^{(c)}\hat{\boldsymbol{P}}^{(c)T}\right), \quad \hat{\boldsymbol{P}}^{(c)} = (\boldsymbol{I} \otimes \boldsymbol{\phi}_c)\boldsymbol{E}^{(c)}_{1\ldots d,\cdot},$$

which simply drops the dependence on $\boldsymbol{u}_{I_c \setminus I}$.[9] Since the bottlenecks are the same for each $m_{\boldsymbol{v}^{(c)} \to \boldsymbol{u}}$, the implied bottleneck for $\boldsymbol{u}$ is I as well (of size $P\,d$). Again, while the generic IVM bottleneck technique of selecting mediator variables is suitable if the variables in question are closely linked to observations, we have just described a second class of bottleneck approximations for "inner messages," namely to limit the dependence of incoming messages to a common set I.

The representation $\mathcal{R}_2(c)$ is needed to form the message $m_{\boldsymbol{u} \to \boldsymbol{v}^{(c)}}$; it basically represents the distribution

$$R_c(\boldsymbol{u}) \propto P(\boldsymbol{u}) \prod_{c' \neq c} m_{\boldsymbol{v}_{c'} \to \boldsymbol{u}}(\boldsymbol{u}_I).$$

Because all $m_{\boldsymbol{v}_{c'} \to \boldsymbol{u}}$ are functions of $\boldsymbol{u}_I$ we have $R_c(\boldsymbol{u}) = R_c(\boldsymbol{u}_I)P(\boldsymbol{u} \setminus \boldsymbol{u}_I | \boldsymbol{u}_I)$, thus $\mathcal{R}_2(c)$ needs to be of size $P\,d$ only, and its size grows only during the common inclusion phase. In order to motivate the form of $\mathcal{R}_2(c)$, we need to look ahead to determine the requirements for maintaining the $Q(\boldsymbol{v}^{(c)})$ marginals. Here, $Q(\boldsymbol{v}^{(c)})$ is obtained by combining the evidence potential $\Psi_v(\boldsymbol{v}^{(c)})$ with the reverse message $m_{\boldsymbol{u} \to \boldsymbol{v}^{(c)}}$ in an IVM representation $\mathcal{R}_3(c)$ of size d_c, where now the message $m_{\boldsymbol{u} \to \boldsymbol{v}^{(c)}}$ plays the role of the prior distribution. The representations $\mathcal{R}_1(c)$, $\mathcal{R}_3(c)$ differ in

---

9. Note that $\hat{\boldsymbol{P}}^{(c)} = \boldsymbol{\Psi}^T \boldsymbol{P}^{(c)}_{1\ldots d,\cdot}$, because $\boldsymbol{u}_I$ is not in standard ordering.

their prior distributions only. Denote the message $m_{\boldsymbol{u} \to \boldsymbol{v}^{(c)}}$ by $N(\boldsymbol{v}^{(c)} | \boldsymbol{\mu}^{(c)}, \boldsymbol{\Sigma}^{(c)})$. A glance at (14.3) reveals that we have

$$\boldsymbol{\Sigma}^{(c)} = \tilde{\boldsymbol{K}}^{(c)} + (\boldsymbol{\phi}_c^T \otimes \boldsymbol{I}) \mathrm{Var}_{R_c}[\boldsymbol{u}] (\boldsymbol{\phi}_c \otimes \boldsymbol{I}). \tag{14.6}$$

Next, let $d_{\backslash c} = \sum_{c' \neq c} d_c$ and

$$\hat{\boldsymbol{P}}^{(\backslash c)} = \left(\hat{\boldsymbol{P}}^{(1)} \; \dots \; \hat{\boldsymbol{P}}^{(c-1)} \; \hat{\boldsymbol{P}}^{(c+1)} \; \dots \; \hat{\boldsymbol{P}}^{(C)} \right) \in \mathbb{R}^{Pd, d_{\backslash c}},$$

$$\hat{\boldsymbol{\beta}}^{(\backslash c)} = \left(\boldsymbol{\beta}^{(1,1)T} \; \dots \; \boldsymbol{\beta}^{(1,c-1)T} \; \boldsymbol{\beta}^{(1,c+1)T} \; \dots \; \boldsymbol{\beta}^{(1,C)T} \right)^T \in \mathbb{R}^{d_{\backslash c}}.$$

The order of the columns of $\hat{\boldsymbol{P}}^{(\backslash c)}$ is not important as long as $\hat{\boldsymbol{\beta}}^{(\backslash c)}$ follows the same ordering. These variables represent the combination $\prod_{c' \neq c} m_{\boldsymbol{v}^{(c')} \to \boldsymbol{u}}$ in the definition of $m_{\boldsymbol{u} \to \boldsymbol{v}^{(c)}}$ (see (14.3)). Some tedious algebra (Seeger et al., 2004) reveals that the following IVM-like representation $\mathcal{R}_2(c)$ is required in order to maintain $\boldsymbol{\mu}^{(c)}$, $\boldsymbol{\Sigma}^{(c)}$, the central parameters of R_c:

$$\mathcal{R}_2(c): \quad \boldsymbol{L}^{(2,c)} \boldsymbol{L}^{(2,c)T} = \boldsymbol{B}^{(2,c)} = \hat{\boldsymbol{K}}_I + \hat{\boldsymbol{K}}_I \hat{\boldsymbol{P}}^{(\backslash c)} \hat{\boldsymbol{P}}^{(\backslash c)T} \hat{\boldsymbol{K}}_I,$$

$$\boldsymbol{\beta}^{(2,c)} = \boldsymbol{L}^{(2,c)-1} \hat{\boldsymbol{K}}_I \hat{\boldsymbol{P}}^{(\backslash c)} \hat{\boldsymbol{\beta}}^{(\backslash c)}, \tag{14.7}$$

$$\boldsymbol{M}^{(2,c)} = (\boldsymbol{\phi}_c^T \otimes \boldsymbol{I}) \boldsymbol{K}_{\cdot, I} \boldsymbol{\Psi} \boldsymbol{L}^{(2,c)-T} \in \mathbb{R}^{n, Pd}.$$

This representation is of size $O(n\, P\, d)$. It is not an IVM representation in the strict sense, but is updated in a very similar manner. We now have $\boldsymbol{\mu}^{(c)} = \boldsymbol{M}^{(2,c)} \boldsymbol{\beta}^{(2,c)}$ and

$$\boldsymbol{\Sigma}^{(c)} = \tilde{\boldsymbol{K}}^{(c)} + (\boldsymbol{\phi}_c^T \otimes \boldsymbol{I}) \boldsymbol{K} (\boldsymbol{\phi}_c \otimes \boldsymbol{I}) - (\boldsymbol{\phi}_c^T \otimes \boldsymbol{I}) \boldsymbol{M}^{(4)} \boldsymbol{M}^{(4)T} (\boldsymbol{\phi}_c \otimes \boldsymbol{I}) + \boldsymbol{M}^{(2,c)} \boldsymbol{M}^{(2,c)T},$$

where

$$\mathcal{R}_4: \quad \boldsymbol{L}^{(4)} \boldsymbol{L}^{(4)T} = \boldsymbol{K}_I, \quad \boldsymbol{M}^{(4)} = \boldsymbol{K}_{\cdot, I} \boldsymbol{L}^{(4)-T} \tag{14.8}$$

is another simple representation, which is block-diagonal and therefore of size $O(n\, P\, d)$ only.

Finally, $\mathcal{R}_3(c)$ is a standard IVM representation based on the prior $N(\boldsymbol{\mu}^{(c)}, \boldsymbol{\Sigma}^{(c)})$ and with the same I_c and site parameters as $\mathcal{R}_1(c)$ (see (14.1)). As opposed to $\mathcal{R}_1(c)$, we need to maintain the stub matrix $\boldsymbol{M}^{(3,c)} \in \mathbb{R}^{n, d_c}$ here, because we want to keep the marginal moments $\boldsymbol{h}^{(c)}$, $\boldsymbol{a}^{(c)}$ of $Q(\boldsymbol{v}^{(c)})$ up to date at all times.

The size of the combined representation is $O(n\,(\sum_c d_c + d\,C\,P))$. This should be compared to $O(n \sum_c d_c)$ for the baseline method and to $O(n\, C \sum_c d_c)$ for the naive method. It is shown in Seeger et al. (2004) how to update the representation after an inclusion in the common and the separate inclusion phase (the former is more expensive). The details are tedious, but the idea is to apply a sequence of IVM updates of the corresponding IVM representations, with some intervening algebra.

The scaling behavior is enlightening,[10] in that another problem is revealed. The overall running time complexity (for both phases) is

$$O\left(n\left(PCd + \sum_c d_c\right)\sum_c d_c\right).$$

In large sample situations it makes sense to require PCd to be of the same order of magnitude as $\sum_c d_c$. In that case, the memory requirements of our method are the same as for the baseline up to a constant factor. However, it seems that modeling conditional dependencies between classes comes at a significant additional price of at least $O(n\left(\sum_c d_c\right)^2)$ as compared to $O(n\sum_c d_c^2)$ for the independent baseline. On the other hand, our method is faster than the naive implementation[11] by a factor of C. Interestingly, if the active sets I_c and site parameters $\boldsymbol{b}^{(c)}$, $\boldsymbol{\Pi}^{(c)}$ are known, then the complete representation can be computed in

$$O\left(n\left(\sum_c d_c^2 + Pd\left(CPd + \sum_c d_c\right)\right)\right),$$

which is significantly faster and actually fairly close to what the independent baseline requires. Therefore, in marked contrast to the situation for IVM applied to single process models, conditional inference *with* active set selection comes at a significantly higher cost than without.

The problem is identified easily, and points to another difference between parametric and nonparametric BP. While $\mathcal{R}_2(c)$ is of limited size Pd, for each of the $\sum_c d_c$ inclusions, $C-1$ of the representations have to be updated by rank 1 (in what amounts to an IVM update). In other words, the matrices $\hat{\boldsymbol{P}}^{(\backslash c)}\hat{\boldsymbol{P}}^{(\backslash c)T}$ are of size Pd, but are in fact updated $d_{\backslash c} > Pd$ times by rank 1. Each such update has to be worked through the whole representation in order to make sure that the marginals $\boldsymbol{h}^{(c)}$, $\boldsymbol{a}^{(c)}$ are up to date all the time, and delaying these updates does not help either. This is in marked contrast to the situation of parametric BP. In the latter case, we would essentially maintain a *single* marginal belief for $\boldsymbol{u}$ in some representation $\mathcal{R}_2$, independent of c, combining all messages $m_{\boldsymbol{v}^{(c)}\to\boldsymbol{u}}$. We would then obtain the reverse messages $m_{\boldsymbol{u}\to\boldsymbol{v}^{(c)}}$ by dividing this belief by the message $m_{\boldsymbol{v}^{(c)}\to\boldsymbol{u}}$, thus deleting its influence. Since parametric models are typically used with potentials from an exponential family, such a division operation is cheap, and the cost is *independent* of how much evidence has already been included, because evidence is accumulated in the sufficient statistics of the potentials. However, such a division cannot be done efficiently in the GP case. We need to maintain *different*

---

10. We are aware that the reader has to take these scaling figures for granted, if the details in Seeger et al. (2004) are not consulted. However, again our purpose is to describe a problem together with an intuitive explanation, whose appreciation would not be helped, or would even be obscured by challenging details.

11. The naive implementation is not feasible due to memory requirements in the first place.

representations $\mathcal{R}_2(c)$ in order to form each of the reverse messages $m_{\boldsymbol{u} \to \boldsymbol{v}^{(c)}}$, and $C - 1$ of them have to be updated *separately* after each inclusion. At this time, we do not have a satisfying remedy for this problem, but it is clearly an important point for future research.

14.4.1 Prediction

In order to predict on test data, the dominant buffers scaling as $O(n)$ are not required. We need to compute the marginals of Q on the test point which is done just as above for the training points: compute $\boldsymbol{M}^{(2,c)}$, $\boldsymbol{\Sigma}^{(c)}_{\cdot, I_c}$, $\boldsymbol{M}^{(4)}$, and $\boldsymbol{M}^{(3,c)}$ w.r.t. the test points. The cost is the same as computing the representation for the training set from scratch (with fixed active sets and site parameters), but with n replaced by the number of test points m:

$$O\left(m \left(\sum_c d_c^2 + P d \left(C P d + \sum_c d_c \right) \right) \right).$$

Again, this is fairly close to the requirements of the baseline method. Predictive distributions can be computed from the marginals using Gaussian quadrature in general (for non-Gaussian likelihoods in models different from SLFMs).

14.4.2 Selection of Points; Computing Site Parameters

Recall that if the likelihoods $P(y_{i,c}|u_{i,c})$ are not Gaussian,[12] we use EP (or assumed density filtering, ADF) projections in order to replace them by Gaussian factors $N^U(u_{i,c}|b_{i,c}, \pi_{i,c})$. This is done in much the same way as for single process models (Lawrence et al., 2003; Seeger, 2003) during the separate inclusion phase. In the common inclusion phase, a pattern i is included jointly into all I_c. The correct way of doing this would be to determine the joint marginal $Q(\boldsymbol{v}_i)$, $\boldsymbol{v}_i \in \mathbb{R}^C$ and doing the ADF projection by computing mean and covariance of $\propto Q(\boldsymbol{v}_i) \prod_c P(y_{i,c}|v_{i,c})$. This has to be done not only for patterns to be included but also in order to score an inclusion candidate, thus many times between each inclusion, requiring the joint marginals even in case of a Gaussian likelihood. We do not know a way of maintaining these joint marginals that is more efficient than using the naive method.[13] The problem is akin to joint rather than marginal inference in parametric graphical models, which also comes at substantial extra costs. Another problem is that for non-Gaussian likelihoods, we need to do C-dimensional quadrature in order to implement the ADF projection, which quickly becomes infeasible with

---

12. For SLFM, the likelihoods are Gaussian, and the site parameters are given by $b_{i,c} = \sigma_c^{-2} y_{i,c}$, $\pi_{i,c} = \sigma_c^{-2}$.

13. We suggest the use of a joint common inclusion phase in Seeger et al. (2004), which essentially amounts to running the naive method during the common inclusion phase. This requires additional approximations and is not covered here.

growing C. We settle for the approximation of doing ADF projections separately for each $v_{i,c}$, resulting in site parameters $b_{i,c}$, $\pi_{i,c}$. The updated marginal is $Q'(v_{i,c}) \propto Q(v_{i,c}) N^U(v_{i,c}|b_{i,c}, \pi_{i,c})$; its moments match the ones of $\propto Q(v_{i,c}) P(y_{i,c}|v_{i,c})$.

Next, we need an efficient way of selecting active variables (i, c) for inclusion into I_c. Information-theoretic scores (from active learning), which measure the improvement from $Q(v_{j,c})$ to $Q'(v_{j,c})$ (after inclusion), have been suggested in Lawrence et al. (2003) and Seeger (2003). For example, we may choose the information gain score $\Delta_{i,c} = -D[Q'(v_{j,c}) \| Q(v_{j,c})]$. During the separate inclusion phase, we can score a set of candidates (i', c') and pick the overall winner (i, c), which means that i is included into I_c. During the common inclusion phase, the values $\Delta_{j,c}$, $c = 1, \ldots, C$ need to be combined[14] into a score for j; suggestions include

$$\Delta_j^{avg} = C^{-1} \sum_c \Delta_{j,c}, \quad \Delta_j^{min} = \min_c \Delta_{j,c}.$$

14.5 Parameter Learning

A nonparametric model comes with parameters as well, although they are less directly related to observations than in parametric models. We refer to them as *hyperparameters* $\boldsymbol{\alpha}$. In the case of the SLFM, $\boldsymbol{\alpha}$ includes $\boldsymbol{\Phi}$ and the parameters of the $\tilde{K}^{(c)}$ and $K^{(p)}$. Note that we cannot avoid the hyperparameter learning issue[15] in this case, because $\boldsymbol{\Phi}$ has to be fitted to the data in any case. The derivations in this section are preliminary and rather serve as suggestions for future work, in that a number of approximations are proposed without experimental validation. However, once more these suggestions are derived from the single process model case, where they have proven useful.

An empirical Bayesian method for estimating $\boldsymbol{\alpha}$ is to maximize the marginal likelihood

$$P(\boldsymbol{y}|\boldsymbol{\alpha}) = \int P(\boldsymbol{y}|\boldsymbol{v}) P(\boldsymbol{v}|\boldsymbol{\alpha}) \, d\boldsymbol{v}. \tag{14.9}$$

This computation is of course intractable, but inference approximation techniques typically come with some approximation for $\log P(\boldsymbol{y}|\boldsymbol{\alpha})$. It is shown in Seeger et al. (2004) that

$$\mathcal{G} = \sum_{c=1}^{C} \left(\sum_{i=1}^{n} \mathrm{E}_Q[-\log P(y_{i,c}|v_{i,c})] + D\left[Q(\boldsymbol{v}_{I,c}) \| P(\boldsymbol{v}_{I,c})\right] \right)$$

---

14. Again, we cannot compute exactly the information gain for including j into all I_c, since this requires knowledge of the joint $Q(\boldsymbol{v}_j)$, $\boldsymbol{v}_j \in \mathbb{R}^C$.

15. Many kernel methods proposed so far "avoid" the learning issue by selecting hyperparameters by semi manual techniques such as crossvalidation. This is not possible with $\boldsymbol{\Phi}$ in general, because there are too many parameters.

is an upper bound on $-\log P(\boldsymbol{y}|\boldsymbol{\alpha})$. We can minimize $\mathcal{G}$ in order to choose $\boldsymbol{\alpha}$. If we neglect the dependence of I_c, $\boldsymbol{b}^{(c)}$, $\boldsymbol{\Pi}^{(c)}$ on $\boldsymbol{\alpha}$, we can even compute the gradient $\nabla_{\boldsymbol{\alpha}}\mathcal{G}$ efficiently. As suggested in Seeger (2003), we can use a double loop optimization scheme. In the outer loop, I_c, $\boldsymbol{b}^{(c)}$, $\boldsymbol{\Pi}^{(c)}$ are computed by conditional inference, as discussed in section 14.4. In the inner loop, $\mathcal{G}$ is minimized for fixed I_c, $\boldsymbol{b}^{(c)}$, $\boldsymbol{\Pi}^{(c)}$. These inner optimizations should be run for a few steps only.

Alternatively, EP comes with its own marginal likelihood approximation (see Seeger (2005)) which can be adopted to the case of SLFMs. First, our representation only allows access to the marginals $Q(\boldsymbol{v}^{(c)})$, so we should look for an approximation $P(\boldsymbol{y}) \approx e^{-\phi}$ with $\phi = \sum_c \phi_c$. ϕ_c is taken to be the EP marginal likelihood approximation for the "prior" $P(\boldsymbol{v}^{(c)}) = N(\boldsymbol{\mu}^{(c)}, \boldsymbol{\Sigma}^{(c)})$ and the posterior $Q(\boldsymbol{v}^{(c)})$. Following Seeger (2005), we obtain after some algebra involving $\mathcal{R}_3(c)$:

$$\phi_c = -\sum_{i=1}^n \log Z_{i,c} + \sum_{i \in I_c} \log \tilde{Z}_{i,c} + \frac{1}{2}\left(\log\left|\boldsymbol{B}^{(3,c)}\right| + \boldsymbol{b}^{(c)T}\boldsymbol{\Pi}^{(c)-1}\boldsymbol{b}^{(c)} - \boldsymbol{\beta}^{(3,c)T}\boldsymbol{\beta}^{(3,c)}\right).$$

Here, $\log Z_i = \log \mathrm{E}_{\backslash i}[P(y_{i,c}|v_{i,c})]$ and $\log \tilde{Z}_i = \log \mathrm{E}_{\backslash i}[N^U(v_{i,c}|b_{i,c}, \pi_{i,c})]$, where $Q^{\backslash i}(v_{i,c}) = Q(v_{i,c})$ for $i \notin I_c$, and $Q^{\backslash i}(v_{i,c}) \propto Q(v_{i,c})/N^U(v_{i,c}|b_{i,c}, \pi_{i,c})$ for $i \in I_c$. The criterion simplifies for the case of Gaussian noise, $P(y_{i,c}|v_{i,c}) = N(y_{i,c}|v_{i,c}, \sigma_c^2)$, since $\tilde{Z}_i = Z_i$ for $i \in I_c$ in this case:

$$\phi_c = -\sum_{i \notin I_c} \log Z_{i,c} + \frac{1}{2}\left(\log\left|\boldsymbol{B}^{(3,c)}\right| + \boldsymbol{b}^{(c)T}\boldsymbol{\Pi}^{(c)-1}\boldsymbol{b}^{(c)} - \boldsymbol{\beta}^{(3,c)T}\boldsymbol{\beta}^{(3,c)}\right).$$

The exact gradient of ϕ cannot be computed in general, because the active sets I_c and site parameters depend on $\boldsymbol{\alpha}$. However, if we assume these to be fixed, the gradient $\nabla_{\boldsymbol{\alpha}}\phi$ can be computed efficiently along the same lines as for the variational bound. We may use the same double-loop scheme in order to optimize ϕ.

14.6   Conclusions

A general marriage of parametric graphical models and nonparametric random field models, each of which is well understood and frequently used in machine learning and statistics, should prove very rewarding in that models of complicated structure can be dealt with using a more flexible nonparametric setup. However, it is not clear how this connection can be achieved in a sufficiently efficient manner in order to be of interest in practice. In this chapter, we showed where the principal problems lie and provided some ideas for tackling them. We used the example of SLFMs, for which the main difficulties of the curse of dependency arise and can be demonstrated clearly, and we suggested a number of different bottleneck approximations in order to deal with these problems. Our main proposal is to use the generic IVM framework for sparse approximations, which so far has been applied to single process models only. While the techniques we employ here already result in a significant reduction in computational complexity for the SLFM in comparison to a naive approach, additional approximation ideas will have to be developed in order to render this marriage useful to practitioners. Our work presented here is preliminary at this stage; an experimental validation of our ideas is subject to future work.

We are not aware of prior work combining Bayesian GP models with structured graphical models in an efficient manner. Friedman and Nachman (2000) suggest GP-directed graphical models, but they do not deal with reducing computational complexity in a principled manner. In fact, they propose either to use the naive approach or to assume that the posterior processes at each node are completely independent (this was called the baseline method here). Nonparametric belief propagation has been used in a very different context by Sudderth et al. (2005). They represent a belief state by a parametric mixture whose components are updated using ADF projections, but also resampled in a way related to particle filtering. Their method is somewhat more general than ours here, since they are able to represent beliefs with multiple modes,[16] but they do not deal with the curse of dependency arising through unstructured dependencies of random fields along the data dimension. It would be possible to combine their approach with ours for a structured GP model with multimodal posterior, but the complexity of such a framework would probably be formidable.

Acknowledgments

The ideas presented here originate in joint work done with Yee-Whye Teh and Michael I. Jordan. This work was supported in part by the IST Programme of the European Community, under the PASCAL Network of Excellence, IST-2002-506778. This publication only reflects the author's views.

---

16. The SLFM is a jointly Gaussian model, and the posterior $Q(v)$ (for fixed hyperparameters) is a Gaussian, so the problem of multiple modes does not arise.

References

S. Agmon. The relaxation method for linear inequalities. *Canadian Journal of Mathematics*, 6(3):382–392, 1954.

E. L. Allwein, R. E. Schapire, and Y. Singer. Reducing multiclass to binary: A unifying approach for margin classifiers. In P. Langley, editor, *Proceedings of the International Conference on Machine Learning*, pages 9 – 16, San Francisco, California, 2000. Morgan Kaufmann Publishers.

N. Alon, S. Ben-David, N. Cesa-Bianchi, and D. Haussler. Scale-sensitive dimensions, uniform convergence, and learnability. In *Proceedings of the 34rd Annual Symposium on Foundations of Computer Science*, pages 292 – 301. IEEE Computer Society Press, Los Alamitos, CA, 1993.

Y. Altun and T. Hofmann. Large margin methods for label sequence learning. In *Proceedings of 8th European Conference on Speech Communication and Technology (EuroSpeech)*, 2003.

Y. Altun and A. J. Smola. Unifying divergence minimization and statistical inference via convex duality. In *Nineteenth International Conference on Algorithmic Learning Theory (COLT'06)*, 2006.

Y. Altun, T. Hofmann, and M. Johnson. Discriminative learning for label sequences via boosting. In *Proceedings of Advances in Neural Information Processing Systems (NIPS*15)*, pages 977–984, 2002.

Y. Altun, M. Johnson, and T. Hofmann. Loss functions and optimization methods for discriminative learning of label sequences. In *Proc. EMNLP*, 2003a.

Y. Altun, I. Tsochantaridis, and T. Hofmann. Hidden Markov support vector machines. In *International Conference of Machine Learning*, 2003b.

Y. Altun, T. Hofmann, and A. J. Smola. Gaussian process classification for segmenting and annotating sequences. In *International Conference on Machine Learning, ICML*, Banff, AB, Canada, 2004a.

Y. Altun, A. J Smola, and T. Hofmann. Exponential families for conditional random fields. In *Proceedings of the 20th Annual Conference on Uncertainty in Artificial Intelligence (UAI-04)*, pages 2–9, Banff, AB, Canada, 2004b. AUAI Press.

Y. Altun, D. McAllester, and M. Belkin. Maximum margin semi-supervised learning for structured variables. In Y. Weiss, B. Schölkopf, and J. Platt, editors, *Advances in Neural Information Processing Systems 18*. MIT Press, Cambridge, MA, 2006.

N. Aronszajn. Theory of reproducing kernels. *Transactions of the American Mathematical Society*, 68:337 – 404, 1950.

P. Auer and C. Gentile. Adaptive and self-confident on-line learning algorithms. In *Proceedings of the 13th Annual Conference on Computational Learning Theory*, pages 107 – 117, San Francisco, CA, 2000. Morgan Kaufmann.

F. R. Bach and M. I. Jordan. Kernel independent component analysis. *Journal of Machine Learning Research*, 3:1–48, 2002.

L. Bahl, P. Brown, P. de Souza, and R. Mercer. Maximum mutual information estimation of hidden Markov model parameters for speech recognition. In *Proceedings of Acoustics, Speech, and Signal Processing Conference*, pages 49–52, 1986.

G. H. Bakır, J. Weston, and B. Schölkopf. Learning to find pre-images. In S. Thrun, L. Saul, and B. Schölkopf, editors, *Advances in Neural Information Processing Systems (NIPS 2003)*, Cambridge, MA, 2004. MIT Press.

D. Bamber. The area above the ordinal dominance graph and the area below the receiver operating characteristic graph. *Journal of Mathematical Psychology*, 12: 387–415, 1975.

O. Barndorff-Nielsen. *Information and Exponential Families*. Wiley, New York, 1978.

A. R. Barron. Universal approximation bounds for superpositions of a sigmoidal function. *IEEE Transactions on Information Theory*, 39(3):930 – 945, May 1993.

P. L. Bartlett and S. Mendelson. Rademacher and Gaussian complexities: Risk bounds and structural results. *Journal of Machine Learning Research*, 3:463–482, 2002.

P. L. Bartlett, P. M. Long, and Robert C. Williamson. Fat-shattering and the learnability of real-valued functions. *Journal of Computer and System Sciences*, 52(3):434 – 452, 1996.

P. L. Bartlett, O. Bousquet, and S. Mendelson. Localized Rademacher averages. In *Proceedings of the 15th Conference on Computational Learning Theory COLT'02*, pages 44–58, 2002.

P. L. Bartlett, M. Collins, B. Taskar, and D. McAllester. Exponentiated gradient algorithms for large-margin structured classification. *Neural Information Processing Systems 17*, 2004.

J. Basilico and T. Hofmann. Unifying collaborative and content-based filtering. In *International Conference on Machine Learning ICML*, 2004.

A. Becker and D. Geiger. A sufficiently fast algorithm for finding close to optimal clique trees. *Artificial Intelligence*, 125(1-2):3–17, 2001.

S. Becker and Y. LeCun. Improving the convergence of back-propagation learning with second-order methods. In D. Touretzky, G. Hinton, and T. Sejnowski, editors, *Proceedings of the 1988 Connectionist Models Summer School*, pages 29–37, San Mateo, CA, 1989. Morgan Kaufman.

G. Bejerano and A. Apostolico. Optimal amnesic probabilistic automata, or, how to learn and classify proteins in linear time and space. *Journal of Computational Biology*, 7(3/4):381–393, 2000.

S. Ben-David, N. Eiron, and P. M. Long. On the difficulty of approximately maximizing agreements. *Journal of Computer and System Sciences*, 66(3):496–514, 2003.

Y. Bengio. *Neural Networks for Speech and Sequence Recognition*. International Thompson Computer Press, London, 1996.

Y. Bengio and P. Frasconi. An input/output HMM architecture. In G. Tesauro, D Touretzky, and T. Leen, editors, *Advances in Neural Information Processing Systems*, volume 7, pages 427–434. MIT Press, Cambridge, MA, 1996.

Y. Bengio, R. Cardin, R. De Mori, and Y. Normandin. A hybrid coder for hidden Markov models using a recurrent network. In *Proceeding of ICASSP*, pages 537–540, 1990.

Y. Bengio, R. De Mori, G. Flammia, and R. Kompe. Global optimization of a neural network-hidden Markov model hybrid. *IEEE Transaction on Neural Networks*, 3(2):252–259, 1992.

Y. Bengio, Y. LeCun, and D. Henderson. Globally trained handwritten word recognizer using spatial representation, space displacement neural networks and hidden Markov models. In J. Cowan and G. Tesauro, editors, *Advances in Neural Information Processing Systems*, volume 6. Morgan Kaufmann, San Francisco, 1993.

Y. Bengio, Y. LeCun, C. Nohl, and C. Burges. Lerec: A NN/HMM hybrid for on-line handwriting recognition. *Neural Computation*, 7(6):1289–1303, 1995.

Y. Bengio, R. Ducharme, P. Vincent, and C. Jauvin. A neural probabilistic language model. *Journal of Machine Learning Research*, 3:1137–1155, 2003.

K. P. Bennett and O. L. Mangasarian. Robust linear programming discrimination of two linearly inseparable sets. *Optimization Methods and Software*, 1:23 – 34, 1992.

K. P. Bennett, A. Demiriz, and J. Shawe-Taylor. A column generation algorithm for boosting. In P. Langley, editor, *Proceedings of the International Conference on Machine Learning*, San Francisco, 2000. Morgan Kaufmann.

D. Bertsekas. *Nonlinear Programming*. Athena Scientific, Nashua, NH, 1999.

J. Besag. Spatial interaction and the statistical analysis of lattice systems (with discussion). *Journal of the Royal Statistical Society*, 36(B):192 – 326, 1974.

V. Blanz and T. Vetter. A morphable model for the synthesis of 3D faces. *SIGGRAPH'99*, pages 187–194, 1999.

K. M. Borgwardt and H.-P. Kriegel. Shortest-path kernels on graphs. In *Fifth IEEE International Conference on Data Mining (ICDM'05)*, pages 74–81, November 2005.

B. E. Boser, I. M. Guyon, and V. Vapnik. A training algorithm for optimal margin classifiers. In D. Haussler, editor, *Proceedings of the fifth Annual Workshop on Computational Learning Theory*, pages 144 – 152, New York, NY, July 1992. ACM Press.

L. Bottou. *Une approche théorique de l'apprentissage connexionniste: Applications à la reconnaissance de la parole.* PhD thesis, Université de Paris XI, 91405 Orsay cedex, France, 1991.

L. Bottou. Stochastic learning. In O. Bousquet and U. von Luxburg, editors, *Advanced Lectures on Machine Learning*, number LNAI 3176 in Lecture Notes in Artificial Intelligence, pages 146–168. Springer-Verlag, Berlin, 2004.

L. Bottou and Y. LeCun. Large-scale on-line learning. In *Advances in Neural Information Processing Systems 15*, Cambridge, MA, 2004. MIT Press.

L. Bottou, Y. LeCun, and Y. Bengio. Global training of document processing systems using graph transformer networks. In *Proc. of Computer Vision and Pattern Recognition*, pages 490–494, Puerto-Rico, 1997. IEEE Press.

S. Boucheron, O. Bousquet, and G. Lugosi. Theory of classification: A survey of some recent advances. *ESAIM: Probability and Statistics*, 9:323 – 375, 2005.

H. Bourlard and N. Morgan. A continuous speech recognition system embedding MLP into HMM. In D.S. Touretzky, editor, *Advances in Neural Information Processing Systems 2*, pages 186–193, San Francisco, 1990. Morgan Kaufmann.

S. Boyd and L. Vandenberghe. *Convex Optimization.* Cambridge University Press, Cambridge, UK, 2004.

L. Breiman. Prediction games and arcing algorithms. *Neural Computation*, 11(7): 1493 – 1518, 1999.

J. Bromley, I. Guyon, Y. LeCun, E. Sackinger, and R. Shah. Signature verification using a Siamese time delay neural network. In J. Cowan and G. Tesauro, editors, *Advances in Neural Information Processing Systems*, volume 6. Morgan Kaufmann, San Francisco, 1993.

P. Buhlmann and A. J. Wyner. Variable length Markov chains. *Annals of Statistics*, 27(2):480–513, 1999.

C. J. C. Burges. A tutorial on support vector machines for pattern recognition. *Data Mining and Knowledge Discovery*, 2(2):121 – 167, 1998.

L. Cai and T. Hofmann. Hierarchical document categorization with support vector machines. In *Proceedings of the 13th ACM Conference on Information and Knowledge Management*, pages 78–87, New York, 2004. ACM Press.

N. Cesa-Bianchi, C. Gentile, A. Tironi, and L. Zaniboni. Incremental algorithms for hierarchical classification. In *Neural Information Processing Systems*, 2004.

O. Chapelle and Z. Harchaoui. A machine learning approach to conjoint analysis. In Lawrence K. Saul, Yair Weiss, and Léon Bottou, editors, *Advances in Neural Information Processing Systems 17*, Cambridge, MA, 2005. MIT Press.

S. Chen, D. Donoho, and M. Saunders. Atomic decomposition by basis pursuit. *Siam Journal of Scientific Computing*, 20(1):33 – 61, 1999.

S. Chopra, R. Hadsell, and Y. LeCun. Learning a similarity metric discriminatively, with application to face verification. In *Proceedings of Computer Vision and Pattern Recognition Conference*, Piscataway, NJ, 2005. IEEE Press.

M. Collins. Parameter estimation for statistical parsing models: Theory and practice of distribution-free methods. In *New Developments in Parsing Technology*. Kluwer Academic, Norwell, MA, 2004.

M. Collins. Discriminative reranking for natural language parsing. In *Proceedings of International Conference on Machine Learning 2000*, 2000.

M. Collins. Discriminative training methods for hidden Markov models: Theory and experiments with perceptron algorithms. In *Proceedings of the Conference on Empirical Methods in Natural Language Processing*, 2002.

M. Collins and N. Duffy. Convolution kernels for natural language. In T. G. Dietterich, S. Becker, and Z. Ghahramani, editors, *Advances in Neural Information Processing Systems 14*, pages 625–632, Cambridge, MA, 2002. MIT Press.

M. Collins and B. Roark. Incremental parsing with the perceptron algorithm. In *Proceedings of the Conference of the Association for Computational Linguistics (ACL)*, 2004.

R. Collobert, J. Weston, and L. Bottou. Trading convexity for scalability. In *Proceedings of the 23rd International Conference on Machine Learning (ICML 2006)*. IMLS/ICML, 2006.

C. Cortes and V. Vapnik. Support-vector networks. *Machine Learning*, 20(3): 273–297, 1995.

C. Cortes, P. Haffner, and M. Mohri. Rational kernels: Theory and algorithms. *Journal of Machine Learning Research (JMLR)*, 5:1035–1062, 2004.

C. Cortes, M. Mohri, and J. Weston. A general regression technique for learning transductions. In *ICML '05: Proceedings of the 22nd International Conference on Machine Learning*, pages 153–160, New York, 2005. ACM Press. doi: http://doi.acm.org/10.1145/1102351.1102371.

R. G. Cowell, A. P. Dawid, S. L. Lauritzen, and D. J. Spiegelhalter. *Probabilistic Networks and Expert Systems*. Springer-Verlag, New York, 1999.

D. Cox and F. O'Sullivan. Asymptotic analysis of penalized likelihood and related estimators. *Annals of Statistics*, 18:1676 – 1695, 1990.

K. Crammer. *Online Learning for Complex Categorical Problems*. PhD thesis, Hebrew University of Jerusalem, 2005.

K. Crammer and Y. Singer. On the learnability and design of output codes for multiclass problems. In N. Cesa-Bianchi and S. Goldman, editors, *Proceedings of the Annual Conference on Computational Learning Theory*, pages 35 – 46, San Francisco, 2000. Morgan Kaufmann.

K. Crammer and Y. Singer. Loss bounds for online category ranking. In *Proceedings of the Annual Conference on Computational Learning Theory*, 2005.

K. Crammer and Y. Singer. On the algorithmic implementation of multiclass kernel-based vector machines. *Journal of Machine Learning Research*, 2(5):265–292, 2001.

K. Crammer, O. Dekel, J. Keshet, S. Shalev-Shwartz, and Y. Singer. Online passive aggressive algorithms. Technical report, Hebrew University of Jerusalem, 2005.

K. Crammer, O. Dekel, J. Keshet, S. Shalev-Shwartz, and Y. Singer. Online passive-aggressive algorithms. *Journal of Machine Learning Research*, 7:551–585, 2006.

N. Cressie. *Statistics for Spatial Data*. Wiley, New York, 2nd edition, 1993.

N. Cristianini and J. Shawe-Taylor. *An Introduction to Support Vector Machines*. Cambridge University Press, Cambridge, UK, 2000.

N. Cristianini, J. Shawe-Taylor, and H. Lodhi. Latent semantic kernels. In *Proceedings of the International Conference on Machine Learning*, San Francisco, 2001. Morgan Kaufmann.

N. Cristianini, J. Shawe-Taylor, A. Elisseeff, and J. Kandola. On kernel-target alignment. In T. G. Dietterich, S. Becker, and Z. Ghahramani, editors, *Advances in Neural Information Processing Systems 14*, pages 367 – 373, Cambridge, MA, 2002. MIT Press.

P. Dawid. Applications of a general propagation algorithm for probabilistic expert systems. *Statistics and Computing*, 2:25–36, 1992.

D. DeCoste and B. Schölkopf. Training invariant support vector machines. *Machine Learning*, 46(1–3):161–190, 2002. Also: Technical Report JPL-MLTR-00 - 1, Jet Propulsion Laboratory, Pasadena, CA, 2000.

M. H. DeGroot. *Optimal Statistical Decisions*. McGraw-Hill, New York, 1970.

O. Dekel, C. D. Manning, and Y. Singer. Log-linear models for label ranking. In *Advances in Neural Information Processing Systems 15*, 2003.

J. S. Denker and C. J. Burges. Image segmentation and recognition. In *The Mathematics of Induction*, Reading, MA, 1995. Addison Wesley.

T. G. Dietterich. Machine learning for sequential data: A review. In T. Caelli, editor, *In Structural, Syntactic, and Statistical Pattern Recognition; Lecture Notes in Computer Science*, volume 2396, pages 15–30. Springer-Verlag, 2002.

T. G. Dietterich, A. Ashenfelter, and Y. Bulatov. Training conditional random fields via gradient tree boosting. In *International Conference on Machine Learning*, 2004.

A. Doucet, N. de Freitas, and N. Gordon (eds). *Sequential Monte Carlo Methods in Practice*. Springer-Verlag, New York, 2001.

X. Driancourt. *Optimisation par descente de gradient stochastique de systèmes modulaires combinant réseaux de neurones et programmation dynamique. Application à la reconnaissance de la parole*. PhD thesis, Université de Paris XI, 91405 Orsay cedex, France, 1994.

X. Driancourt and L. Bottou. MLP, LVQ and DP: Comparison and cooperation. In *Proceedings of the International Joint Conference on Neural Networks*, volume 2, pages 815–819, Seattle, 1991.

X. Driancourt and P. Gallinari. A speech recognizer optimaly combining learning vector quantization, dynamic programming and multi-layer perceptron. In *Proceedings of International Conference on Acoustics, Speech, and Signal Processing*, 1992a.

X. Driancourt and P. Gallinari. Empirical risk optimisation: neural networks and dynamic programming. In *Proceedings of Neural Networks for Signal Processing (NNSP)*, 1992b.

X. Driancourt, L. Bottou, and Gallinari P. Comparison and cooperation of several classifiers. In *Proceedings of the International Conference on Artificial Neural Networks (ICANN)*, 1991.

T. Dunning. Accurate methods for the statistics of surprise and coincidence. *Computational Linguistics*, 19(1), 1993.

R. Durbin, S. Eddy, A. Krogh, and G. Mitchison. *Biological Sequence Analysis: Probabilistic Models of Proteins and Nucleic Acids*. Cambridge University Press, Cambridge, UK, 1998.

J. H. J. Einmal and D. M. Mason. Generalized quantile processes. *Annals of Statistics*, 20(2):1062 – 1078, 1992.

A. Elisseeff and J. Weston. A kernel method for multi-labeled classification. In *Advances in Neural Information Processing Systems 14*, Cambridge, MA, 2001. MIT Press.

E. Eskin. *Sparse Sequence Modeling with Applications to Computational Biology and Intrusion Detection*. PhD thesis, Columbia University, New York, 2002.

L. Euler. Solutio problematis ad geometriam situs pertinentis. *Commentarii academiae scientiarum Petropolitanae*, 8:128–140, 1741.

C. Fellbaum, editor. *Wordnet: An Electronic Lexical Database*. MIT Press, Cambridge, MA, 1998.

M. Fleischman, E. Hovy, and A. Echihabi. Offline strategies for online question answering: Answering questions before they are asked. In *Proceedings of the Conference of the Association for Computational Linguistics (ACL)*, Sapporo, Japan, July 2003.

R. Fletcher. *Practical Methods of Optimization*. Wiley, New York, 1989.

R. Florian, H. Hassan, A. Ittycheriah, H. Jing, N. Kambhatla, X. Luo, N. Nicolov, and S. Roukos. A statistical model for multilingual entity detection and tracking. In *Proceedings of the Conference of the North American Chapter of the Association for Computational Linguistics and Human Language Technology (NAACL/HLT)*, 2004.

M. Franzini, K. F. Lee, and A. Waibel. Connectionnist Viterbi training: A new hybrid method for continuous speech recognition. In *Proceedings of International Conference on Acoustics, Speech, and Signal Processing*, page 245, 1990.

N. Friedman and I. Nachman. Gaussian process networks. In C. Boutilier and M. Goldszmidt, editors, *Uncertainty in Artificial Intelligence 16*, pages 211–219, San Francisco, 2000. Morgan Kaufmann.

C. Gentile. A new approximate maximal margin classification algorithm. In T. K. Leen, T. G. Dietterich, and V. Tresp, editors, *Advances in Neural Information Processing Systems 13*, pages 500 – 506, Cambridge, MA, 2001. MIT Press.

L. Getoor, N. Friedman, D. Koller, and A. Pfeffer. Learning probabilistic relational models. In S. Dzeroski and N. Lavrac, editors, *Relational Data Mining*. Springer-Verlag, Berlin, 2001.

J. Godfrey, E. Holliman, and J. McDaniel. SWITCHBOARD: Telephone speech corpus for research and development. In *Proceedings of the International Conference on Acoustics, Speech, and Signal Processing*, pages 517–520, 1992.

M. Gregory and Y. Altun. Using conditional random fields to predict pitch accents in conversational speech. In *Proceedings of ACL'04:Forty-second Annual Meeting of the Association for Computational Linguistics*, 2004.

M. Gribskov and N. L. Robinson. Use of receiver operating characteristic (ROC) analysis to evaluate sequence matching. *Computers and Chemistry*, 20(1):25–33, 1996.

R. Hadsell, S. Chopra, and Y. LeCun. Dimensionality reduction by learning an invariant mapping. In *Proceedings of Computer Vision and Pattern Recognition Conference (CVPR'06)*. IEEE Press, 2006.

P. Haffner. Connectionist speech recognition with a global MMI algorithm. In *EUROSPEECH'93, 3rd European Conference on Speech Communication and Technology*, Berlin, September 1993.

P. Haffner and A. H. Waibel. Time-delay neural networks embedding time alignment: A performance analysis. In *EUROSPEECH'91, 2nd European Conference on Speech Communication and Technology*, Genoa, Italy, September 1991.

P. Haffner and A. H. Waibel. Multi-state time-delay neural networks for continuous speech recognition. In *Advances in Neural Information Processing Systems*, volume 4, pages 579–588, San Mateo, CA, 1992. Morgan Kaufmann.

P. Haffner, M. Franzini, and A. H. Waibel. Integrating time-alignment and neural networks for high performance continuous speech recognition. In *Proceedings of ICASSP*, pages 105–108. IEEE Press, 1991.

J. Hammersley and P. Clifford. Markov fields on finite graphs and lattices. Unpublished manuscript, 1971.

J. A. Hartigan. Estimation of a convex density contour in two dimensions. *Journal of the American Statistical Association*, 82:267 – 270, 1987.

T. Hastie, R. Tibshirani, and J. Friedman. *The Elements of Statistical Learning.* Springer-Verlag, New York, 2001.

D. Haussler. Convolutional kernels on discrete structures. Technical Report UCSC-CRL-99 - 10, Computer Science Department, University of California, Santa Cruz, 1999.

D. Heckerman. A tutorial on learning with Bayesian networks. In M. Jordan, editor, *Learning in Graphical Models.* MIT Press, Cambridge, MA, 1999.

M. Hein and O. Bousquet. Kernels, associated structures, and generalizations. Technical Report 127, Max Planck Institute for Biological Cybernetics, Tübingen, Germany, 2004.

M. Hein, O. Bousquet, and B. Schölkopf. Maximal margin classification for metric spaces. *Journal of Computer and System Sciences*, 71(3):333–359, 2005.

D. P. Helmbold and R. E. Schapire. Predicting nearly as well as the best pruning of a decision tree. *Machine Learning*, 27(1):51 – 68, 1997.

R. Herbrich. *Learning Kernel Classifiers: Theory and Algorithms.* MIT Press, Cambridge, MA, 2002.

R. Herbrich and R.C. Williamson. Algorithmic luckiness. *Journal of Machine Learning Research*, 3:175 – 212, 2002.

R. Herbrich, T. Graepel, and K. Obermayer. Large margin rank boundaries for ordinal regression. In A. J. Smola, P. L. Bartlett, B. Schölkopf, and D. Schuurmans, editors, *Advances in Large Margin Classifiers*, pages 115 – 132, Cambridge, MA, 2000. MIT Press.

R. Hettich and K. O. Kortanek. Semi-infinite programming: Theory, methods, and applications. *SIAM Review*, 35(3):380–429, 1993.

G. E. Hinton. Training products of experts by minimizing contrastive divergence. *Neural Computation*, 14:1771–1800, 2002.

T. Hofmann, I. Tsochantaridis, and Y. Altun. Learning over discrete output spaces via joint kernel functions. *Kernel Methods Workshop, Neural Processing Information Systems 15*, 2002.

J. E. Hopcroft, R. Motwani, and J. D. Ullman. *Introduction to Automata Theory, Languages, and Computation.* Addison Wesley, Reading, MA, 2nd edition, 2000.

F. J. Huang and Y. LeCun. Large-scale learning with SVM and convolutional nets for generic object categorization. In *Proceedings of Computer Vision and Pattern Recognition Conference (CVPR'06).* IEEE Press, 2006.

T. S. Jaakkola and D. Haussler. Probabilistic kernel regression models. In *Proceedings of the 1999 Conference on AI and Statistics*, 1999a.

T. S. Jaakkola and D. Haussler. Exploiting generative models in discriminative classifiers. In M. S. Kearns, S. A. Solla, and D. A. Cohn, editors, *Advances in Neural Information Processing Systems 11*, pages 487 – 493, Cambridge, MA, 1999b. MIT Press.

F. V. Jensen. *An Introduction to Bayesian Networks*. UCL Press, 1996.

F. V. Jensen and F. Jensen. Optimal junction trees. In *Proceedings of the 10th Conference on Uncertainty in Artificial Intelligence*, pages 360–366, 1994.

F. V. Jensen, S. L. Lauritzen, and K. G Olesen. Bayesian updating in causal probabilistic networks by local computations. *Computational Statistics*, 5(4): 269–282, 1990.

T. Joachims. A support vector method for multivariate performance measures. In *Proceedings of the 22nd International Conference on Machine Learning*, 2005.

T. Joachims. Text categorization with support vector machines: Learning with many relevant features. In *Proceedings of the European Conference on Machine Learning*, pages 137 – 142, Berlin, 1998. Springer-Verlag.

M. I. Jordan, editor. *Learning in Graphical Models*. Kluwer Academic, Norwell, MA, 1997.

M. I. Jordan, Z. Gharamani, T. S. Jaakkola, and L. K. Saul. An introduction to variational methods for graphical models. In M. I. Jordan, editor, *Learning in Graphical Models*, pages 105 – 162. Kluwer Academic, Norwell, MA, 1998.

M. I. Jordan, P. L. Bartlett, and J. D. McAuliffe. Convexity, classification, and risk bounds. Technical Report 638, Universicty of California, Berkeley, 2003.

B.-H. Juang, W. Chou, and C.-H. Lee. Minimum classification error rate methods for speech recognition. *IEEE Transactions on Speech and Audio Processing*, 5 (3):257–265, 1997.

J. P. Kahane. *Some Random Series of Functions*. Cambridge University Press, Cambridge, UK, 1968.

K. Kanazawa, D. Koller, and S. Russell. Stochastic simulation algorithms for dynamic probabilistic networks. In *Proceedings of the 11th Annual Conference on Uncertainty in Artificial Intelligence (UAI-95)*, pages 346–35, San Francisco, CA, 1995. Morgan Kaufmann.

J. Kandola, J. Shawe-Taylor, and N. Cristianini. On the application of diffusion kernel to text data. *NeuroCOLT Technical Report NC-TR-02-122*, 2002. URL http://www.neurocolt.com/abs/2002/abs02122.html.

W. Karush. Minima of Functions of Several Variables with Inequalities as Side Constraints. Master's thesis, Department of Mathematics, University of Chicago, 1939.

H. Kashima, K. Tsuda, and A. Inokuchi. Marginalized kernels between labeled graphs. In *Proceedings of the 20th International Conference on Machine Learning (ICML)*, pages 321–328, Washington, DC, United States, 2003.

R. Kassel. *A Comparison of Approaches to On-line Handwritten Character Recognition*. PhD thesis, MIT Spoken Language Systems Group, Cambridge, MA, 1995.

M. Kearns and Y. Mansour. A fast, bottom-up decision tree pruning algorithm with near-optimal generalization. In *Proceedings of the 14th International Conference on Machine Learning*, 1996.

M. Kearns, Y. Mansour, and S. Singh. Nash convergence of gradient dynamics in general-sum games. In *Proceedings of the Conference on Uncertainty in Artificial Intelligence (UAI)*, 2000.

A. Keller, S. Purvine, A. I. Nezvizhskii, S. Stolyar, D. R. Goodlett, and E. Kolker. Experimental protein mixture for validating tandem mass spectral analysis. *OMICS*, 6(2):207–212, 2002.

J. E. Kelley. The cutting-plane method for solving convex programs. *Journal of the Society for Industrial Applied Mathematics*, 8:703–712, 1960.

G. S. Kimeldorf and G. Wahba. A correspondence between Bayesian estimation on stochastic processes and smoothing by splines. *Annals of Mathematical Statistics*, 41:495 – 502, 1970.

G. S. Kimeldorf and G. Wahba. Some results on Tchebycheffian spline functions. *Journal of Mathematical Analysis and Applications*, 33:82 – 95, 1971.

J. Kivinen, A. J. Smola, and R. C. Williamson. Online learning with kernels. *IEEE Transactions on Signal Processing*, 52(8), Aug 2004.

V. Koltchinskii. Rademacher penalties and structural risk minimization. *IEEE Transactions on Information Theory*, 47:1902–1914, 2001.

I. R. Kondor and J. D. Lafferty. Diffusion kernels on graphs and other discrete structures. In *Proceedings of the 19th International Conference on Machine Learning (ICML-2002)*, 2002.

Y. Konig, H Bourlard, and N. Morgan. REMAP: Recursive estimation and maximization of a posteriori probabilities — application to transition-based connectionist speech recognition. In David S. Touretzky, Michael C. Mozer, and Michael E. Hasselmo, editors, *Advances in Neural Information Processing Systems*, volume 8, pages 388–394, Cambridge, MA, 1996. MIT Press.

L. Kontorovich. Uniquely decodable n-gram embeddings. *Theoretical Computer Science*, 329/1-3:271–284, 2004.

W. Krauth and M. Mézard. Learning algorithms with optimal stability in neural networks. *Journal of Physics A*, 20:745 – 752, 1987.

F. R. Kschischang, B. J. Frey, and H.-A. Loeliger. Factor graphs and the sum-product algorithm. *IEEE Transactions on Information Theory*, 47(2):498–519, 2001.

H. W. Kuhn and A. W. Tucker. Nonlinear programming. In *Proceedings of the 2nd Berkeley Symposium on Mathematical Statistics and Probabilistics*, pages 481 – 492, Berkeley, 1951. University of California Press.

S. Kumar and M. Hebert. Discriminative fields for modeling spatial dependencies in natural images. In S. Thrun, L. Saul, and B. Schölkopf, editors, *Advances in Neural Information Processing Systems 16*. MIT Press, Cambridge, MA, 2004.

J. T. Kwok and I. W. Tsang. The pre-image problem in kernel methods. *IEEE Transactions on Neural Networks*, 15(6):1517–1525, 2004.

J. Lafferty, A. McCallum, and F. Pereira. Conditional random fields: Probabilistic models for segmenting and labeling sequence data. In *Proceedings of the 18th International Conference on Machine Learning*, pages 282–289, San Francisco, 2001. Morgan Kaufmann.

J. Lafferty, X. Zhu, and Y. Liu. Kernel conditional random fields: Representation and clique selection. In *Proceedings of the 21th International Conference on Machine Learning*, pages 504–511, 2004.

J. Langford and J. Shawe-Taylor. PAC-Bayes and margins. In *Neural Information Processing Systems (NIPS)*, 2002.

S. L. Lauritzen. *Graphical Models*. Oxford University Press, Oxford, UK, 1996.

N. D. Lawrence, M. Seeger, and R. Herbrich. Fast sparse Gaussian process methods: The informative vector machine. In S. Becker, S. Thrun, and K. Obermayer, editors, *Neural Information Processing Systems 15*, pages 609–616, Cambridge, MA, 2003. MIT Press.

Y. LeCun and Y. Bengio. Word-level training of a handwritten word recognizer based on convolutional neural networks. In IAPR, editor, *Proceedings of the International Conference on Pattern Recognition*, volume 2, pages 88–92, Jerusalem, October 1994. IEEE Press.

Y. LeCun and F.-J. Huang. Loss functions for discriminative training of energy-based models. In *Proceedings of the 10th International Workshop on Artificial Intelligence and Statistics (AIStats'05)*, 2005.

Y. LeCun, L. Bottou, and Y. Bengio. Reading checks with graph transformer networks. In *International Conference on Acoustics, Speech, and Signal Processing*, volume 1, pages 151–154, Munich, 1997. IEEE Press.

Y. LeCun, L. Bottou, Y. Bengio, and P. Haffner. Gradient-based learning applied to document recognition. *Proceedings of the IEEE*, 86(11):2278–2324, 1998a.

Y. LeCun, L. Bottou, G. Orr, and K. Muller. Efficient backprop. In G. Orr and Muller K., editors, *Neural Networks: Tricks of the trade*. Springer-Verlag, 1998b.

Y. Lee, Y. Lin, and G. Wahba. Multicategory support vector machines: Theory and application to the classification of microarray data and satellite radiance data. *Journal of the American Statistical Association*, 99, 2004.

D. D. Lewis, Y. Yang, T. G. Rose, and F. Li. Rcv1: A new benchmark collection for text categorization research. *JMLR*, 5:361–397, Apr 2004.

C. J. Lin. Formulations of support vector machines: A note from an optimization point of view. Technical report, National Taiwan University, Department of Computer Science, 1999. http://www.csie.ntu.edu.tw/~cjlin/penalty.ps.gz.

A. Ljolje, Y. Ephraim, and L. R. Rabiner. Estimation of hidden Markov model parameters by minimizing empirical error rate. In *Proc. of International Conference on Acoustics, Speech, and Signal Processing*, pages 709–712, April 1990. URL `http://www.ece.ucsb.edu/Faculty/Rabiner/ece259/publications.html`.

H. Lodhi, J. Shawe-Taylor, N. Cristianini, and C. Watkins. Text classification using string kernels. Technical Report 2000 - 79, NeuroCOLT, 2000. In: T. K. Leen, T. G. Dietterich and V. Tresp (editors), *Advances in Neural Information Processing Systems 13*, Cambridge, MA, MIT Press, 2001.

D. G. Luenberger. *Linear and Nonlinear Programming*. Addison-Wesley, Reading, MA, 2nd edition, 1984. ISBN 0 - 201 - 15794 - 2.

D. J. C. MacKay. Introduction to Gaussian processes. In C. M. Bishop, editor, *Neural Networks and Machine Learning*, pages 133 – 165. Springer-Verlag, Berlin, 1998.

D. J. C. MacKay. *Information Theory, Inference, and Learning Algorithms*. Cambridge University Press, Cambridge, UK, 2003. URL `http://www.cambridge.org/0521642981`. Available from `http://www.inference.phy.cam.ac.uk/mackay/itila/`.

Y. Makovoz. Random approximants and neural networks. *Journal of Approximation Theory*, 85:98 – 109, 1996.

O. L. Mangasarian. Linear and nonlinear separation of patterns by linear programming. *Operations Research*, 13:444 – 452, 1965.

C. D. Manning and H. Schütze. *Foundations of Statistical Natural Language Processing*. MIT Press, Cambridge, MA, 1999.

D. McAllester. PAC-Bayesian stochastic model selection. *Machine Learning*, 5: 5–21, 2003a. [A short version appeared as "PAC-Bayesian Model Averaging" in COLT99].

D. McAllester. Simplified PAC-Bayesian margin bounds. In *COLT03*, 2003b.

D. McAllester, M. Collins, and F. Pereira. Case-factor diagrams for structured probabilistic modeling. In *Proceedings of the Conference on Uncertainty in Artificial Intelligence (UAI)*, 2004.

A. McCallum and B. Wellner. Conditional models of identity uncertainty with application to noun coreference. In *Advances in Neural Information Processing Systems*, 2004.

A. McCallum, D. Freitag, and F. Pereira. Maximum entropy Markov models for information extraction and segmentation. In *Proceedings of the 17th International Conference on Machine Learning*, pages 591 – 598. Morgan Kaufmann, San Francisco, 2000.

E. McDermott. *Discriminative Training for Speech Recognition*. PhD thesis, Waseda University, 1997. URL `citeseer.ifi.unizh.ch/mcdermott97discriminative.html`. [lots of references in alignment + learning].

E. McDermott and S. Katagiri. Prototype-based discriminative training for various speech units. In *Proceedings of ICASSP-92, San Francisco*, pages 417–420, 1992.

C. McDiarmid. On the method of bounded differences. In *Survey in Combinatorics*, pages 148 – 188. Cambridge University Press, Cambridge, UK, 1989.

R. McDonald, K. Crammer, and F. Pereira. Large margin online learning algorithms for scalable structured classification. In *NIPS Workshop on Learning with Structured Outputs*, 2004.

S. Mendelson. Rademacher averages and phase transitions in Glivenko-Cantelli classes. *IEEE Transactions on Information Theory*, 48(1):251–263, 2002.

S. Mendelson. A few notes on statistical learning theory. In S. Mendelson and A. J. Smola, editors, *Advanced Lectures on Machine Learning*, number 2600 in LNAI, pages 1 – 40. Springer-Verlag, 2003.

J. Mercer. Functions of positive and negative type and their connection with the theory of integral equations. *Philosophical Transactions of the Royal Society, London*, A 209:415 – 446, 1909.

C. A. Micchelli and M. Pontil. On learning vector–valued functions. *Research Note RN/03/08, Department of Computer Science, University College London*, 2003.

T. Minka. Expectation propagation for approximate Bayesian inference. In J. Breese and D. Koller, editors, *Uncertainty in Artificial Intelligence 17*, San Francisco, 2001. Morgan Kaufmann.

T. Minka and J. Lafferty. Expectation propagation for the generative aspect model. In *Conference on Uncertainty in Artificial Intelligence*, 2002.

M. Minsky and S. Papert. *Perceptrons: An Introduction to Computational Geometry*. MIT Press, Cambridge, MA, 1969.

M. Mohri. Finite-state transducers in language and speech processing. *Computational Linguistics*, 23(2):269–311, 1997.

M. Mohri, F. Pereira, and M. Riley. Weighted finite state transducers in speech recognition. *Computer Speech and Language*, 16:69–88, 2002. URL `citeseer.ist.psu.edu/article/mohri00weighted.html`.

N. Morgan and H. Bourlard. Continuous speech recognition: An introduction to the hybrid hmm/connectionist approach. *IEEE Signal Processing Magazine*, 12 (3):25–42, May 1995.

V. A. Morozov. *Methods for Solving Incorrectly Posed Problems*. Springer-Verlag, New York, 1984.

K. P. Murphy, Y. Weiss, and M. I. Jordan. Loopy belief propagation for approximate inference: An empirical study. In *Proceedings of the 15th Conference on Uncertainty in Artificial Intelligence*, 1999.

K. G. Murty. *Linear Complementarity, Linear and Nonlinear Programming*. Heldermann Verlag, 1998.

R. M. Neal. Probabilistic inference using Markov chain Monte Carlo methods. Technical Report CRG-TR-93-1, University of Toronto, 1993.

V. Ng and C. Cardie. Improving machine learning approaches to coreference resolution. In *Proceedings of the Conference of the Association for Computational Linguistics (ACL)*, 2002.

F. Ning, D. Delhomme, Y. LeCun, F. Piano, L. Bottou, and P. Barbano. Toward automatic phenotyping of developing embryos from videos. *IEEE Transactions on Image Processing*, 14(9):1360–1371, 2005. Special issue on Molecular and Cellular Bioimaging, to appear.

J. Nocedal and S. J. Wright. *Numerical Optimization*. Springer Series in Operations Research. Springer-Verlag, New York, 1999.

D. Nolan. The excess mass ellipsoid. *Journal of Multivariate Analysis*, 39:348 – 371, 1991.

A. B. J. Novikoff. On convergence proofs on perceptrons. In *Proceedings of the Symposium on the Mathematical Theory of Automata*, volume 12, pages 615 – 622. Polytechnic Institute of Brooklyn, 1962.

N. Oliver, B. Schölkopf, and A. J. Smola. Natural regularization in SVMs. In A. J. Smola, P. L. Bartlett, B. Schölkopf, and D. Schuurmans, editors, *Advances in Large Margin Classifiers*, pages 51 – 60, Cambridge, MA, 2000. MIT Press.

R. Osadchy, M. Miller, and Y. LeCun. Synergistic face detection and pose estimation with energy-based model. In *Advances in Neural Information Processing Systems (NIPS 2004)*, Cambridge, MA, 2005. MIT Press.

C. Pal, C. Sutton, and A. McCallum. Sparse forward-backward using minimum divergence beams for fast training of conditional random fields. In *International Conference on Acoustic Speech and Signal Processing*, 2006.

J. Pearl. *Probabilistic Reasoning in Intelligent Systems*. Morgan-Kaufman, San Francisco, 1988.

J. Pearl. *Causality: Models, Reasoning, and Inference*. Cambridge University Press, Cambridge, UK, 2000.

F. C. Pereira and Y. Singer. An efficient extension to mixture techniques for prediction and decision trees. *Machine Learning*, 36(3):183–199, 1999.

F. Pérez-Cruz, G. Camps, E. Soria, J. Pérez, A. R. Figueiras-Vidal, and A. Artés-Rodríguez. Multi-dimensional function approximation and regression estimation. In *International Conference on Artificial Neural Networks (ICANN) 2002*, 2002.

J. C. Platt. Fast training of support vector machines using sequential minimal optimization. In B. Schölkopf, C. J. C. Burges, and A. J. Smola, editors, *Advances in Kernel Methods - -Support Vector Learning*, pages 185 – 208, Cambridge, MA, 1999. MIT Press.

T. Poggio. On optimal nonlinear associative recall. *Biological Cybernetics*, 19:201 – 209, 1975.

W. Polonik. Minimum volume sets and generalized quantile processes. *Stochastic Processes and Their Applications*, 69:1 – 24, 1997.

W. H. Press, S. A. Teukolsky, W. T. Vetterling, and B. P. Flannery. *Numerical Recipes in C.* Cambridge University Press, Cambridge, UK, 2nd edition, 1992.

V. Punyakanok and D. Roth. The use of classifiers in sequential inference. In *Advances in Neural Information Processing Systems (NIPS)*, pages 995–1001, Cambridge, MA, 2000. MIT Press.

Y. Qi, M. Szummer, and T. P. Minka. Bayesian conditional random fields. In *Proceedings of the 10th International Workshop on Artificial Intelligence and Statistics*, 2005.

G. Rätsch. *Robust Boosting via Convex Optimization: Theory and Applications.* PhD thesis, University of Potsdam, Germany, 2001.

G. Rätsch, T. Onoda, and K. R. Müller. Soft margins for Adaboost. *Machine Learning*, 42(3):287 – 320, 2001.

G. Rätsch, S. Mika, and A. J. Smola. Adapting codes and embeddings for polychotomies. In *Neural Information Processing Systems*, volume 15, Cambridge, MA, 2002a. MIT Press.

G. Rätsch, S. Mika, and M. K. Warmuth. On the convergence of leveraging. In *Advances in Neural Information Processing Systems (NIPS)*, 2002b.

D. Ravichandran, P. Pantel, and E. Hovy. Randomized algorithms and NLP: Using locality sensitive hash functions for high speed noun clustering. In *Proceedings of the Conference of the Association for Computational Linguistics (ACL)*, 2005.

D. Ron, Y. Singer, and N. Tishby. The power of amnesia: Learning probabilistic automata with variable memory length. *Machine Learning*, 25:117 – 149, 1996.

F. Rosenblatt. The perceptron: A probabilistic model for information storage and organization in the brain. *Psychological Review*, 65(6):386 – 408, 1958.

F. Rosenblatt. *Principles of Neurodynamics: Perceptron and Theory of Brain Mechanisms.* Spartan-Books, Washington DC, 1962.

R. Rosipal and L. J. Trejo. Kernel partial least squares regression in reproducing kernel Hilbert space. *Journal of Machine Learning Research*, 2:97–203, 2002.

D. L. Ruderman and W. Bialek. Statistics of natural images: Scaling in the woods. *Physical Review Letters*, 73:814–817, 1994.

P. Ruján. A fast method for calculating the perceptron with maximal stability. *Journal de Physique I France*, 3:277 – 290, 1993.

S. Russell and P. Norvig. *Artificial Intelligence: A Modern Approach.* Prentice Hall, Upper Saddle River, NJ, 1995.

T. W. Sager. An iterative method for estimating a multivariate mode and isopleth. *Journal of the American Statistical Association*, 74(366):329 – 339, 1979.

H. Sakoe, R. Isotani, K. Yoshida, K. Iso, and T. Watanabe. Speaker-independant word recognition using dynamic programming neural networks. In *Proceedings of ICASSP-88*, pages 107–110, New York, 1988.

S. Sarawagi and W. Cohen. Semi-Markov conditional random fields for information extraction. In L. K. Saul, Y. Weiss, and L. Bottou, editors, *Advances in Neural Information Processing Systems 17*, pages 1185–1192, Cambridge, MA, 2005. MIT Press.

C. Saunders, A. Gammerman, and V. Vovk. Ridge regression learning algorithm in dual variables. In *Proceedings of the 15th International Conference on Machine Learning*, pages 515–521, San Francisco, 1998. Morgan Kaufmann.

R. Schapire, Y. Freund, P. L. Bartlett, and W. S. Lee. Boosting the margin: A new explanation for the effectiveness of voting methods. *Annals of Statistics*, 26:1651 – 1686, 1998.

B. Schölkopf. *Support Vector Learning, PhD thesis, Technische Universität Berlin*. R. Oldenbourg Verlag, Munich, 1997. http://www.kernel-machines.org.

B. Schölkopf and A. J. Smola. *Learning with Kernels*. MIT Press, Cambridge, MA, 2002.

B. Schölkopf, A. J. Smola, and K. R. Müller. Nonlinear component analysis as a kernel eigenvalue problem. *Neural Computation*, 10:1299 – 1319, 1998.

B. Schölkopf, A. J. Smola, R. C. Williamson, and P. L. Bartlett. New support vector algorithms. *Neural Computation*, 12:1207 – 1245, 2000.

B. Schölkopf, R. Herbrich, and A. J. Smola. A generalized representer theorem. In *Proceedings of the Annual Conference on Computational Learning Theory*, pages 416 – 426, 2001.

B. Schölkopf, J. Platt, J. Shawe-Taylor, A. J. Smola, and R. C. Williamson. Estimating the support of a high-dimensional distribution. *Neural Computation*, 13(7):1443–1471, 2001.

R. Schwarz and Y. L. Chow. The n-best algorithm: An efficient and exact procedure for finding the n most likely hypotheses. In *Proceedings of the IEEE International Conference on Acoustics, Speech and Signal Processing*, pages 81–84, 1990.

M. Seeger. PAC-Bayesian generalization bounds for Gaussian processes. *Journal of Machine Learning Research*, 3:233–269, 2002.

M. Seeger. *Bayesian Gaussian Process Models: PAC-Bayesian Generalisation Error Bounds and Sparse Approximations*. PhD thesis, University of Edinburgh, July 2003. See www.kyb.tuebingen.mpg.de/bs/people/seeger.

M. Seeger. Gaussian processes for machine learning. *International Journal of Neural Systems*, 14(2):69–106, 2004.

M. Seeger. Expectation propagation for exponential families. Technical report, University of California at Berkeley, 2005. See www.kyb.tuebingen.mpg.de/bs/people/seeger.

M. Seeger, M. I. Jordan, and Y.-W. Teh. Semiparametric latent factor models. Technical report, University of California, Berkeley, 2004. See www.kyb.tuebingen.mpg.de/bs/people/seeger.

F. Sha and F. Pereira. Shallow parsing with conditional random fields. In *Proceedings of Human Language Technology-NAACL*, Edmondton, AB, Canada, 2003.

A. Shapiro. On duality theory of convex semi-infinite programming. *Optimization*, 54:535 – 543, 2005.

J. Shawe-Taylor, P. L. Bartlett, R. C. Williamson, and M. Anthony. Structural risk minimization over data-dependent hierarchies. *IEEE Transactions on Information Theory*, 44(5):1926 – 1940, 1998.

Y. Shibata. On the tree representation of chordal graphs. *Journal of Graph Theory*, 12(3):421–428, 1988.

K. Shoikhet and D. Geiger. A practical algorithm for finding optimal triangulations. In *Proceedings of the National Conference on Artificial Intelligence (AAAI'97)*, pages 185–190, San Francisco, 1997. Morgan Kaufmann.

A. J. Smola. Regression Estimation with Support Vector Learning Machines. Dissertation, Technische Universität Munich, 1996.

A. J. Smola and P. L. Bartlett. Sparse greedy Gaussian process regression. *Neural Processing Information Systems 13*, pages 619–625, 2001.

A. J. Smola, P. L. Bartlett, B. Schölkopf, and D. Schuurmans, editors. *Advances in Large Margin Classifiers*. MIT Press, Cambridge, MA, 2000.

S. Solla, E. Levin, and M. Fleisher. Accelerated learning in layered neural networks. *Complex Systems*, 2(6):625–639, 1988.

W. M. Soon, H. T. Ng, and D. C. Y. Lim. A machine learning approach to coreference resolution of noun phrases. *Computational Linguistics*, 27(4):521 – 544, 2001.

I. Steinwart. On the generalization ability of support vector machines. Technical report, University of Jena, Germany, 2001.

E. Sudderth, M. Mandel, W. Freeman, and A. Willsky. Distributed occlusion reasoning for tracking with nonparametric belief propagation. In L. Saul, Y. Weiss, and L. Bottou, editors, *Neural Information Processing Systems 17*, Cambridge, MA, 2005. MIT Press.

C. Sutton and A. McCallum. Collective segmentation and labeling of distant entities in information extraction. In *International Conference on Machine Learning (ICML) workshop on Statistical Relational Learning*, 2004.

C. Sutton, K. Rohanimanesh, and A. McCallum. Dynamic conditional random fields: Factorized probabilistic models for labeling and segmenting sequence data. In *Proceedings of the International Conference on Machine Learning*, pages 783–790, 2004.

B. Taskar, V. Chatalbashev, and D. Koller. Learning associative Markov networks. In *Proceedings of 21th International Conference on Machine Learning*, pages 807–814, 2004a.

B. Taskar, C. Guestrin, and D. Koller. Max-margin Markov networks. In S. Thrun, L. Saul, and B. Schölkopf, editors, *Advances in Neural Information Processing Systems 16*. MIT Press, Cambridge, MA, 2004b.

D. M. J. Tax and R. P. W. Duin. Data domain description by support vectors. In M. Verleysen, editor, *Proceedings of European Symposium on Artificial Neural Networks (ESANN)*, pages 251 – 256, Brussels, 1999. D-Facto.

Y. W. Teh, M. Welling, S. Osindero, and G. E. Hinton. Energy-based models for sparse overcomplete representations. *Journal of Machine Learning Research*, 4: 1235–1260, 2003.

Y. W. Teh, M. Seeger, and M. I. Jordan. Semiparametric latent factor models. In Z. Ghahramani and R. Cowell, editors, *Workshop on Artificial Intelligence and Statistics 10*, 2005.

A. N. Tikhonov. The solution of ill-posed problems. *Dokolady Akademii Nauk SSSR*, 39(5), 1963.

I. Tsochantaridis, T. Hofmann, T. Joachims, and Y. Altun. Support vector machine learning for interdependent and structured output spaces. In *ICML '04: Twenty-first International Conference on Machine Learning*, pages 823–830, New York, 2004. ACM Press.

I. Tsochantaridis, T. Hofmann, T. Joachims, and Y. Altun. Large margin methods for structured and interdependent output variables. *Journal of Machine Learning Research*, 6:1453–1484, 2005.

A. B. Tsybakov. Optimal aggregation of classifiers in statistical learning. *Annals of Statistics*, 32(1):135–166, 2003.

A. B. Tsybakov. On nonparametric estimation of density level sets. *Annals of Statistics*, 25(3):948 – 969, 1997.

J. H. van Lint and R. M. Wilson. *A Course in Combinatorics*. Cambridge University Press, Cambridge, UK, 1992.

C. J. van Rijsbergen. *Information Retrieval*. Butterworths, London, 2nd edition, 1979.

V. Vapnik. *The Nature of Statistical Learning Theory*. Springer–Verlag, New York, 1995.

V. Vapnik. *Statistical Learning Theory*. Wiley, New York, 1998.

V. Vapnik and A. Y. Chervonenkis. On the uniform convergence of relative frequencies of events to their probabilities. *Theory of Probability and Its Applications*, 16(2):264 – 281, 1971.

V. Vapnik and A. Y. Chervonenkis. The necessary and sufficient conditions for consistency in the empirical risk minimization method. *Pattern Recognition and Image Analysis*, 1(3):283 – 305, 1991.

V. Vapnik and A. Lerner. Pattern recognition using generalized portrait method. *Automation and Remote Control*, 24:774 – 780, 1963.

V. Vapnik, S. Golowich, and A. J. Smola. Support vector method for function approximation, regression estimation, and signal processing. In M. C. Mozer, M. I. Jordan, and T. Petsche, editors, *Advances in Neural Information Processing Systems 9*, pages 281 – 287, Cambridge, MA, 1997. MIT Press.

J. Vert and M. Kanehisa. Graph-driven features extraction from microarray data using diffusion kernels and kernel cca. In S. Becker, S. Thrun, and K. Obermayer, editors, *Advances in Neural Information Processing Systems 15, NIPS 2002*, Cambridge, MA, 2002. MIT Press.

P. Vincent and Y. Bengio. Kernel matching pursuit. Technical Report 1179, Département d'Informatique et Recherche Opérationnelle, Université de Montréal, 2000.

S. V. N. Vishwanathan and A. J. Smola. Fast kernels for string and tree matching. In K. Tsuda, B. Schölkopf, and J. P. Vert, editors, *Kernels and Bioinformatics*, Cambridge, MA, 2004. MIT Press.

S. V. N. Vishwanathan, N. N. Schraudolph, M. W. Schmidt, and K. P. Murphy. Accelerated training of conditional random fields with stochastic gradient methods. In *Proceedings of the 23rd International Conference on Machine Learning (ICML 2006)*. IMLS/ICML, 2006.

M. J. Wainwright and M. I. Jordan. Graphical models, exponential families, and variational inference. Technical Report 649, University of California, Berkeley, Department of Statistics, September 2003.

M. J. Wainwright, T. Jaakkola, and A. Willsky. Tree-based reparameterization framework for analysis of sum-product and related algorithms. *IEEE Transactions on Information Theory*, 49:1120–1146, May 2003.

H. Wallach. Efficient Training of Conditional Random Fields. Master's thesis, Division of Informatics, University of Edinburgh, 2002.

C. Watkins. Dynamic alignment kernels. Technical report, Royal Holloway, University of London, 1999.

J. Weston and C. Watkins. Multi-class support vector machines. Technical Report CSD-TR-98-04, Department of Computer Science, Royal Holloway, University of London, Egham, UK, 1998.

J. Weston, O. Chapelle, A. Elisseeff, B. Schölkopf, and V. Vapnik. Kernel dependency estimation. In S. Becker, S. Thrun, and K. Obermayer, editors, *Advances in Neural Information Processing Systems 15*, volume 15. MIT Press, Cambridge, MA, 2002.

J. Weston, B. Schölkopf, O. Bousquet, T. Mann, and W. S. Noble. Joint kernel maps. Technical report, Max Planck Institute for Biological Cybernetics, Tübingen, Germany, 2004.

J. Weston, B. Schölkopf, and O. Bousquet. Joint kernel maps. In J. Cabestany, A. Prieto, and F. Sandoval, editors, *Proceedings of the 8th International Work-Conference on Artificial Neural Networks*, volume 3512 of *LNCS*, pages 176–191,

BerlinWhittaker90, 2005. Springer-Verlag.

J. Whittaker. *Graphical Models in Applied Multivariate Statistics*. Wiley, Chichester, UK, 1990.

F. M. J. Willems, Y. M. Shtarkov, and T. J. Tjalkens. The context tree weighting method: Basic properties. *IEEE Transactions on Information Theory*, 41(3): 653–664, 1995.

C. K. I. Williams. Prediction with Gaussian processes: From linear regression to linear prediction and beyond. In M. I. Jordan, editor, *Learning and Inference in Graphical Models*, pages 599 – 621. MIT Press, Cambridge, MA, 1999.

R. C. Williamson, A. J. Smola, and B. Schölkopf. Generalization bounds for regularization networks and support vector machines via entropy numbers of compact operators. *IEEE Transactions on Information Theory*, 47(6):2516 – 2532, 2001.

R. J. Wilson. *Introduction to Graph Theory*. Longman, 1979.

G. Winkler. *Image Analysis, Random Fields and Dynamic Monte Carlo Methods*. Springer-Verlag, Berlin, 1995.

WIPO. *World Intellectual Property Organization*. *http://www.wipo.int/classifications/en*. 2001.

L. Wolf and A. Shashua. Learning over sets using kernel principal angles (kernel machines section). *Journal of Machine Learning Research*, 4:913–931, 2003.

P. Wolfe. A duality theorem for nonlinear programming. *Quarterly of Applied Mathematics*, 19:239 – 244, 1961.

Y. Xu and A. Fern. Toward discriminative learning of planning heuristics. In *AAAI Workshop on Learning for Search*, 2006.

J. S. Yedidia, W. T. Freeman, and Y. Weiss. Constructing free-energy approximations and generalized belief propagation algorithms. *IEEE Transactions on Information Theory*, 51(7):2282–2312, July 2005.

D. H. Younger. Recognition and parsing of context-free languages in time n^3. *Information and Control*, 10:189–208, 1967.

T. Zhang. Sequential greedy approximation for certain convex optimization problems. *IEEE Transactions on Information Theory*, 49(3):682–691, 2003.

T. Zhang. Statistical behavior and consistency of classification methods based on convex risk minimization. *Annals of Statistics*, 32(1):56–85, 2004.

T. Zhang, F. Damerau, and D. Johnson. Text chunking based on a generalization of Winnow. *Journal of Machine Learning Research*, 2:615–637, 2002.

D. Zhou, D. Bousquet, T. N. Lal, J. Weston, and B. Schölkopf. Learning with local and global consistency. In S. Thrun, L. Saul, and B. Schölkopf, editors, *Advances in Neural Information Processing Systems 16*, pages 321–328. MIT Press, Cambridge, MA, USA, 2004.

A. Zien, G. Rätsch, S. Mika, B. Schölkopf, T. Lengauer, and K.-R. Müller. Engineering support vector machine kernels that recognize translation initiation sites. *Bioinformatics*, 16(9):799 – 807, 2000.

M. Zinkevich, P. Riley, M. Bowling, and A. Blum. Marginal best response, Nash equilibria, and iterated gradient ascent. In preparation, 2005.

Contributors

Yasemin Altun
Toyota Technological Institute at Chicago
Chicago, IL
altun@tti-c.org

Gökhan Bakır
Max Planck Institute for Biological Cybernetics
Tübingen, Germany
gb@tuebingen.mpg.de

Olivier Bousquet
Max Planck Institute for Biological Cybernetics
Tübingen, Germany, and
Pertinence Paris, France
o.bousquet@pertinence.com

Sumit Chopra
Courant Institute of Mathematical Sciences
New York University, New York, NY
sumit@cs.nyu.edu

Corinna Cortes
Google Research
New York, NY
corinna@google.com

Hal Daumé III
School of Computing, University of Utah
Salt Lake City, UT
me@hal3.name

Ofer Dekel
School of Computer Science and Engineering

The Hebrew University, Jerusalem, Israel
oferd@@cs.huji.ac.il

Zoubin Ghahramani
Engineering Department
Cambridge University, Cambridge, UK
zoubin@eng.cam.ac.uk

Raia Hadsell
Courant Institute of Mathematical Sciences
New York University, New York, NY
raia@cs.nyu.edu

Thomas Hofmann
Department of Computer Science
Technical University of Darmstadt, Germany, and
Google, Zurich, Switzerland
thofmann@google.com

Fu Jie Huang
Courant Institute of Mathematical Sciences
New York University, New York, NY
jhuangfu@cs.nyu.edu

Yann LeCun
Courant Institute of Mathematical Sciences
New York University, New York, NY
yann@cs.nyu.edu

Tobias Mann
Department of Genome Sciences
University of Washington, Seattle, WA
mann@gs.washington.edu

Daniel Marcu
Information Sciences Institute
University of Southern California, Marina del Rey, CA
marcu@isi.edu

David McAllester
Toyota Technological Institute at Chicago
Chicago, IL
mcallester@tti-c.org

Mehryar Mohri
Courant Institute of Mathematical Sciences

New York University, New York, NY
mohri@cims.nyu.edu

William Stafford Noble
Department of Genome Sciences
University of Washington, Seattle, WA
noble@gs.washington.edu

Fernando Pérez-Cruz
Gatsby Computational Neuroscience Unit, London, UK
and University Carlos III, Madrid, Spain
fernando@tsc.uc3m.es

Massimiliano Pontil
Department of Computer Science, UCL
London, UK
m.pontil@cs.ucl.ac.uk

Marc'Aurelio Ranzato
Courant Institute of Mathematical Sciences
New York University, New York, NY
ranzato@cs.nyu.edu

Juho Rousu
Department of Computer Science
University of Helsinki, Finland
juho.rousu@cs.helsinki.fi

Craig Saunders
Electronics and Computer Science
University of Southampton, UK
cjs@ecs.soton.ac.uk

Bernhard Schölkopf
Max Planck Institute for Biological Cybernetics
Tübingen, Germany
bs@tuebingen.mpg.de

Matthias W. Seeger
Max Planck Institute for Biological Cybernetics
Tübingen, Germany
seeger@tuebingen.mpg.de

Shai Shalev-Shwartz
School of Computer Science and Engineering

The Hebrew University, Jerusalem, Israel
shais@@cs.huji.ac.il

John Shawe-Taylor
Electronics and Computer Science
University of Southampton, UK
jst@ecs.soton.ac.uk

Yoram Singer
School of Computer Science and Engineering
The Hebrew University, Jerusalem, Israel, and
Google Inc., Mountain View, California, CA
singer@cs.huji.ac.il

Alex Smola
Statistical Machine Learning Programme
NICTA, Canberra 0200 ACT, Australia
alex.smola@nicta.com.au

Sandor Szedmak
Electronics and Computer Science
University of Southampton, UK
ss03v@ecs.soton.ac.uk

Ben Taskar
EECS Department
University of California, Berkeley, CA
taskar@cs.berkeley.edu

Ioannis Tsochantaridis
Google Inc.
Mountain View, CA
ioannis@google.com

S.V.N Vishwanathan
Statistical Machine Learning Programme
NICTA, Canberra 0200 ACT, Australia
vishy@nicta.com.au

Jason Weston
NEC Labs America
Princeton, NJ
jasonw@nec-labs.com

Index